T0396988

Pitfalls of AI Integration in Education:

Skill Obsolescence, Misuse, and Bias

Manuel B. Garcia
FEU Institute of Technology, Philippines

Joanna Rosak–Szyrocka
Częstochowa University of Technology, Poland

Aras Bozkurt
Anadolu University, Turkey

IGI Global
Scientific Publishing
Publishing Tomorrow's Research Today

Vice President of Editorial	Melissa Wagner
Director of Acquisitions	Mikaela Felty
Director of Book Development	Jocelynn Hessler
Production Manager	Mike Brehm
Cover Design	Phillip Shickler

Published in the United States of America by
IGI Global Scientific Publishing
701 East Chocolate Avenue
Hershey, PA, 17033, USA
Tel: 717-533-8845
Fax: 717-533-7115
Website: https://www.igi-global.com E-mail: cust@igi-global.com

Library of Congress Cataloging-in-Publication Data

LCCN: 2025004500 (CIP Data Pending)
ISBN13: 9798337301228
Isbn13Softcover: 9798337301235
EISBN13: 9798337301242

British Cataloguing in Publication Data
A Cataloguing in Publication record for this book is available from the British Library.

This book is for the critical thinkers, the brave educators, and the responsible innovators who refuse to accept technology at face value. It is for those who question, who challenge, and who choose to look deeper, beyond the promise of automation and efficiency, to uncover the hidden costs and unintended consequences of AI in education.

To the teachers who advocate for ethical, student-centered use of technology; to the scholars who expose bias and misuse in algorithmic systems; and to the policymakers who strive to safeguard equity in digital learning spaces—this is for you. Your vigilance, integrity, and intellectual courage are what ensure that innovation does not come at the expense of justice or humanity.

In a world increasingly driven by algorithms, may this work stand as both a warning and a call to action—a reminder that progress must be thoughtful, inclusive, and rooted in the values we hold dear. You are the stewards of a future where technology serves education, not the other way around.

Editorial Advisory Board

Table of Contents

Section 1
The Intended Consequences of AI in Education

Manuel B. Garcia, FEU Institute of Technology, Philippines
Joanna Rosak-Szyrocka, Czestochowa University of Technology, Poland
Ramazan Yılmaz, Bartın University, Turkey
Ahmed Hosny Saleh Metwally, Helwan University, Egypt
Dharel P. Acut, Cebu Technological University, Philippines
Kingsley Ofosu-Ampong, Heritage Christian University, Ghana
Fatih Erdoğdu, Zonguldak Bülent Ecevit University, Turkey
Chorng Yuan Fung, Swinburne University of Technology, Sarawak, Malaysia
Aras Bozkurt, Anadolu University, Turkey

John Paul P. Miranda, Don Honorio Ventura State University, Philippines
Maria Anna D. Cruz, Don Honorio Ventura State University, Philippines
Antonia B. Fernandez, Don Honorio Ventura State University, Philippines
Francis F. Balahadia, Laguna State Polytechnic University, Philippines
Joey S. Aviles, Angeles University Foundation, Philippines
Carisma A. Caro, Holy Angel University, Philippines
Ivan G. Liwanag, Don Honorio Ventura State University, Philippines
Elizabeth P. Gaña, Don Honorio Ventura State University, Philippines

Priyanka Bisht, Christ University, India
Jyoti Prakash Pujari, Christ University, India

Section 2
Skill Obsolescence and Educator Readiness

Section 3
Ethical, Legal, and Social Implications

Section 4
Systematic Reviews on AI Integration in Education

Detailed Table of Contents

Section 1
The Intended Consequences of AI in Education

Chapter 1

Manuel B. Garcia, FEU Institute of Technology, Philippines
Joanna Rosak-Szyrocka, Czestochowa University of Technology, Poland
Ramazan Yılmaz, Bartın University, Turkey
Ahmed Hosny Saleh Metwally, Helwan University, Egypt
Dharel P. Acut, Cebu Technological University, Philippines
Kingsley Ofosu-Ampong, Heritage Christian University, Ghana
Fatih Erdoğdu, Zonguldak Bülent Ecevit University, Turkey
Chorng Yuan Fung, Swinburne University of Technology, Sarawak, Malaysia
Aras Bozkurt, Anadolu University, Turkey

As artificial intelligence (AI) becomes increasingly integrated into educational contexts, they present new challenges to traditional assessment methods. A particularly pressing issue is academic dishonesty, which undermines learning authenticity and the credibility of educational institutions. With generative AI tools like ChatGPT making it easier for students to produce automated answers, educational assessments are at risk of measuring AI capabilities rather than students' actual knowledge. Thus, this chapter explores a range of strategies designed to adapt assessment practices in response to the influence of AI in education. These strategies offer actionable frameworks to support authentic learning and uphold academic integrity. Additionally, the chapter highlights future research directions to guide further adaptation of educational policies and practices. Given the rapid integration of AI in the education sector, this chapter provides sensible insights that reinforce the importance of integrity-focused reforms in sustaining meaningful educational outcomes in an AI-driven world.

Chapter 2

John Paul P. Miranda, Don Honorio Ventura State University, Philippines
Maria Anna D. Cruz, Don Honorio Ventura State University, Philippines
Antonia B. Fernandez, Don Honorio Ventura State University, Philippines
Francis F. Balahadia, Laguna State Polytechnic University, Philippines
Joey S. Aviles, Angeles University Foundation, Philippines
Carisma A. Caro, Holy Angel University, Philippines
Ivan G. Liwanag, Don Honorio Ventura State University, Philippines
Elizabeth P. Gaña, Don Honorio Ventura State University, Philippines

This chapter investigates the perceived erosion of critical academic skills among 745 university students due to dependency on AI tools. The survey measured six key constructs: AI Dependency (AID), Cognitive Offloading (CO), Motivational Decline (MD), Academic Skills Erosion (ASE), Academic Integrity Awareness (AIA), and External Pressures (EP), using a five-point Likert scale. Path Analysis was employed to examine the interrelationships among these constructs. The results revealed a strong positive relationship between AID and both CO and MD, which indicated that the increased reliance on AI leads to reduced cognitive engagement and diminished academic motivation. Additionally, CO and MD were positively associated with ASE, which means that students who offload cognitive tasks and experience MD are more likely to exhibit deteriorating academic skills. While AIA had a weak negative relationship with AID, EP showed a moderate positive association and highlighted the role of academic stress in driving AI reliance.

Chapter 3

Priyanka Bisht, Christ University, India
Jyoti Prakash Pujari, Christ University, India

The application of generative AI in the classroom is transforming conventional methods of literary analysis and instruction, but it also raises serious concerns and limitations. This chapter critically examines these limitations within the context of teaching 1947 Partition literature in Indian college classrooms. Using a qualitative and experimental methodology, the chapter analyzes AI-generated responses to Partition narratives, revealing ChatGPT's inability to capture the historical trauma, moral accountability, and cultural depth embedded in these texts. Findings show that AI-generated interpretations often flatten complex human experiences and reduces them to simplistic patterns or generalized tropes. The chapter argues that such algorithmic interpretations risk distorting historical memory and promoting academic irresponsibility. By exposing these flaws, the chapter contributes to current debates on AI in higher education and calls for human-led literary analysis in contexts marked by deep historical and cultural trauma.

As generative AI tools become increasingly integrated into educational practice, its use among pre-service teachers is often accompanied by hesitation and discomfort. This chapter examines the phenomenon of AI shaming among teacher education students—the stigma and reluctance to disclose AI tool use due to perceived threats to academic authenticity. Drawing on classroom insights and student reflections, it explores how social norms, institutional pressures, and identity formation shape this behavior. These experiences reveal the deep tension between embracing technological innovation and maintaining traditional standards of academic merit. The chapter highlights the implications for digital literacy, professional development, and ethical technology integration. It calls for a shift in narrative, framing AI not as a shortcut but as a tool for innovation. Actionable strategies for educators and institutions are proposed to foster open, reflective, and supportive environments for responsible AI use in teacher education.

Section 2
Skill Obsolescence and Educator Readiness

Chapter 6

This chapter examines the perspectives of classroom teachers at Science and Art Centers regarding artificial intelligence (AI). Employing a case chapter design and qualitative methodology, the research collects insights from 18 teachers during the 2023-2024 academic year through semi-structured interviews, followed by content analysis. Findings indicate that AI enhances classroom processes, reduces teacher workloads, and boosts student engagement. However, challenges such as inadequate technological infrastructure, insufficient resources, and internet connectivity issues hinder effective AI integration. Teachers also express concerns about potential ethical dilemmas associated with AI applications. The chapter underscores the necessity for comprehensive in-service training, practical guidance, and high-quality technological resources to optimize AI utilization. Furthermore, it emphasizes the importance of establishing ethical guidelines and usage protocols to address these concerns and foster a responsible approach to AI in educational settings.

Chapter 7

Elif Karamuk, Istanbul Galata University, Turkey

With the growing presence of artificial intelligence (AI) in classrooms, its influence on how students think, learn, and interact deserves close scrutiny. However, its increasing integration and accessibility raise concerns about AI dependency among students. Excessive reliance on AI may weaken essential cognitive skills, including critical thinking, problem-solving, and creativity, which are crucial for academic and professional success. Moreover, diminished human interaction with teachers and peers threatens the human aspect of education. This chapter critically examines the risks of AI over-reliance, emphasizing its long-term consequences on student development. Left unchecked, this dependency may lead to superficial learning and hinder the cultivation of independent thought. The normalization of AI-generated outputs may also blur the line between authentic learning and algorithmic convenience. It highlights the shift from AI as a supportive tool to a potential source of dependency and advocates for a more balanced, human-centered integration of technology in education.

Chapter 8

Karthik Raja Srinivasan, Universiti Malaya, Malaysia
Nur Hairani Abd Rahman, Universiti Malaya, Malaysia
Sri Devi Ravana, Universiti Malaya, Malaysia

The integration of artificial intelligence (AI) in education is altering teaching and requires educators to develop new competencies. Through a systematic review of 247 articles published between 2022 and 2024, this chapter explores three major themes, namely, AI and Teacher Competency Development, Challenges in Reskilling and Upskilling, and Strategies for Effective Reskilling. It has become evident that educators have to acquire digital literacy, data analytics skills, and AI-specific pedagogical strategies, with a corresponding need to address ethical concerns around algorithmic bias, data privacy, and equity of access. Moreover, institutional resistance, inequitable digital literacy, and especially the fast evolution of AI, which outpaces often existing training frameworks, are identified as evolving major concerns. This chapter, therefore, proposes to embed AI training into continuous professional development, enhance interdisciplinary collaborations, and adapt frameworks such as P21, TPACK, and DigCompEdu to the specific needs of AI.

    Larry C. Gantalao, Cebu Technological University, Philippines
    Jeffrey G. Dela Calzada, Cebu Technological University, Philippines
    Dennis L. Capuyan, Cebu Technological University, Philippines
    Bernabe C. Lumantas, Cebu Technological University, Philippines
    Dharel P. Acut, Cebu Technological University, Philippines
    Manuel B. Garcia, FEU Institute of Technology, Philippines

As artificial intelligence (AI) continues to transform the demands of the global workforce, technical education must evolve to meet these emerging challenges. This chapter examines the integration of AI in technical education with an emphasis on the critical need for modern infrastructure and technical expertise. It highlights the importance of investing in facilities such as AI-equipped laboratories, reliable internet, and educator training programs to foster innovation and personalized learning. Collaboration between educational institutions and industry is explored as a means to bridge the gap between academic theory and real-world applications. Additionally, the chapter advocates revising curricula to combine AI literacy with technical skills, alongside critical thinking and adaptability, to meet evolving workforce demands. It concludes with a call for educators, policymakers, and institutions to prioritize inclusive, forward-thinking strategies to modernize technical education and ensure equity in access and opportunities.

Section 3
Ethical, Legal, and Social Implications

    Sonia Martínez-Requejo, Universidad Europea de Madrid, Spain
    Sara Redondo-Duarte, Universidad Complutense de Madrid, Spain
    Eva Jiménez-García, Universidad Europea de Madrid, Spain
    Judit Ruiz-Lázaro, Universidad Nacional de Educación a Distancia, Spain

As emerging technologies, such as artificial intelligence (AI), become increasingly integrated into academic contexts, new challenges and ethical risks related to potential misuse also emerge. This chapter examines these issues from an academic perspective by analyzing how each affects both education and research. Particular attention is given to concerns such as algorithmic bias, data privacy, authorship attribution, and the erosion of critical thinking in AI-assisted learning environments. The chapter also explores the implications of unequal access to AI tools, which may exacerbate existing educational disparities. Reflection on these issues is essential for fostering an academic culture based on integrity, transparency, and respect for diversity, which are fundamental to creating a fairer and more equitable educational environment. Ultimately, the chapter urges institutions to establish clear technoethical guidelines, promote digital literacy, and engage stakeholders in open dialogue to ensure responsible and inclusive AI integration in education.

    Halil Öztürk, Special Education Department, Muğla Sıtkı Koçman University, Turkey
    Mustafa Doğuş, Anadolu University, Turkey
    Volkan Şahin, Special Education Department, Anadolu University, Turkey
    Mustafa Çakmak, Special Education Department, Anadolu University, Turkey
    İlyas Gürses, Special Education Department, Anadolu University, Turkey

Artificial intelligence (AI) is transforming special education by enabling personalized learning pathways and innovative assistive technologies. However, its growing use raises critical ethical concerns, including algorithmic bias, data privacy, and fairness. Biased algorithms can lead to misdiagnoses or inappropriate learning recommendations, while the collection of sensitive student data increases privacy risks. Many educators also lack the training to critically assess AI-generated outputs. Ensuring inclusive and transparent AI design is essential to providing equal opportunities and avoiding the reinforcement of educational disparities. Policymakers, developers, and educators must collaborate to establish clear, enforceable guidelines that protect student rights and promote ethical AI use. This chapter explores the expanding role of AI technologies in special education by advocating for a balanced approach that supports innovation while prioritizing ethical responsibility and inclusion.

    Ceren Ersoy, Gazi University, Turkey

In recent years, artificial intelligence (AI) has emerged as one of the most potent tools to promote digital transformation in education. The effective use of AI in education requires robust policy frameworks and ethical oversight mechanisms. Providing an overview of the transformative role of AI in education, this chapter discusses the prominent requirements for the ethical use of technology that supports inclusive and equitable education in education systems and offers policy recommendations that will maximize the potential of AI in creating equitable, fair, and inclusive educational environments. Special emphasis is placed on the role of interdisciplinary collaboration among stakeholders to ensure that AI systems are aligned with human-centered values and educational goals. The chapter aims to draw attention to the data-driven framework addressing the most debated issues of bias, data privacy, inclusion, risks, fair and equitable approach in education to establish an inclusive AI ecosystem in light of global standards, international policies, and evidence-based practices.

> *Jivulter C. Mangubat, Cebu Technological University, Philippines*
> *Milcah R. Mangubat, Cebu Technological University, Philippines*
> *Timoteo Bernardo L. Uy, Cebu Technological University, Philippines*
> *Dharel P. Acut, Cebu Technological University, Philippines*
> *Manuel B. Garcia, FEU Institute of Technology, Philippines*

In an era marked by rapid technological advancement, protecting the intellectual property (IP) of educational innovations has become more critical than ever. This chapter examines the intersection of educational innovation, artificial intelligence (AI), and IP protection. Patents, which safeguard the technical and functional aspects of inventions, are crucial for protecting these advancements amid rapid technological disruptions. As discussed in the chapter, several challenges are posed by AI in generating and managing IP, including the need to redefine inventorship, address skill obsolescence, and ensure equitable IP frameworks. Despite the importance of addressing these issues to foster innovation, they remain underexplored in the existing literature. Therefore, this chapter calls for a reassessment of existing legal and procedural frameworks to adapt to the evolving IP landscape and sustain the integrity of educational innovations. Overall, this chapter aims to contribute to the development of robust strategies for safeguarding educational innovations in an AI-driven era.

> *Devanshi Taneja, Christ University, India*
> *Harivarshini Prabagaren, Christ University, India*
> *Mary Rani Thomas, Christ University, India*

The integration of AI in academic and publication content generation is a recent development, significantly altering policies on citation and authorship, which were previously designed for human-generated work. While AI tools have eased administrative and academic workloads, their rapid adoption raises concerns about ethics and academic integrity. This chapter explores the role of AI as a transformative force in academia, highlighting both its benefits and potential downsides. A key concern is the potential erosion of critical thinking among researchers and scholars due to overreliance on AI, which could impact the quality of research. Despite being a game-changer for students, educators, and administrative staff, the academic community must address the ethical implications and develop new policies to ensure that AI enhances rather than undermines scholarly work. This chapter aims to foster dialogue on how academia can coexist with advancing AI innovations while maintaining research integrity and quality.

Section 4
Systematic Reviews on AI Integration in Education

Chapter 15

Asegul Hulus, University of Greenwich, Cyprus

The escalating adoption of AI in student feedback raises concerns about excessive reliance and misapplication, necessitating ethical scrutiny. This systematic review examines the patterns, consequences, and ethical implications of overdependence on AI in student feedback. Using PRISMA guidelines, 12 studies from 2020 to 2024 were analyzed with the MMAT tool and thematic analysis. Six themes emerged: "transparency and explainability," "human oversight," "fairness and bias mitigation," "data privacy," "personalization," and "continuous evaluation." These themes informed the ETHICAL-FEED framework, which integrates technofeminist perspectives to address power dynamics and gender biases in AI, fostering equity and inclusivity. The review highlights not only the pedagogical risks of unchecked AI use but also the urgent need for professional development to guide educators in ethical implementation. The framework promotes responsible AI use in education by emphasizing ethical practices, maintaining standards, and encouraging research on the intersection of technology, gender, and equity.

Chapter 16

Novrindah Alvi Hasanah, Universitas Islam Negeri Maulana Malik Ibrahim Malang,
    Indonesia
Miladina Rizka Aziza, Universitas Islam Negeri Maulana Malik Ibrahim Malang, Indonesia
Allin Junikhah, Universitas Islam Negeri Maulana Malik Ibrahim Malang, Indonesia
Yunifa Miftachul Arif, Universitas Islam Negeri Maulana Malik Ibrahim Malang, Indonesia
Manuel B. Garcia, FEU Institute of Technology, Philippines

The integration of artificial intelligence (AI) into engineering education has emerged as a transformative force, offering innovative tools to enhance teaching, learning, and administrative processes. This study presents a systematic review of the current landscape, focusing on the AI technologies application, the regulatory frameworks, and the challenges encountered in engineering education. The findings reveal how AI can improve student learning outcomes, personalize educational experiences, and automate complex processes. The review also addresses critical issues, such as ethical considerations and the imperative for regulatory compliance. Furthermore, it identifies key barriers to adoption, such as technological limitations and the preparedness of educators and students to embrace AI-powered solutions. This study provides a comprehensive understanding of the potential and limitations of AI in engineering education, offering actionable insights for educators, policymakers, and stakeholders aiming to foster effective and ethical AI integration in academic settings.

Generative artificial intelligence (GenAI) is an emerging technology that has significantly transformed the interaction between humans and machines. GenAI has the capacity to create content such as text, images, and videos, and it even uses human language. In the educational field, tools such as ChatGPT stand out for their ability to maintain coherent conversations, simulating human interactions. This study aims to offer a comprehensive and critical view of the convergence of GenAI and higher education. To this end, a systematic literature review has been carried out following the PRISMA protocol through the WoS and Dialnet databases. The analysis focuses on understanding the role of GenAI in this context, identifying both the opportunities and challenges associated with its implementation. The results of the study highlight key challenge areas, promising trends, and future prospects. Likewise, the effects of GenAI on students and teachers are analyzed, paying special attention to the ethical and social implications that accompany its integration into higher education.

The growing adoption of AI-enabled chatbots in education stems from advances in artificial intelligence, offering both opportunities and challenges. This chapter reviews 41 high-impact studies published between 2017 and 2023, examining how chatbots are used in schools, as well as their impact, benefits, and associated challenges. Chatbots have shown potential to enhance personalized learning, improve student engagement, and support administrative tasks, though these benefits vary across subjects and strategies. Despite their promise, chatbots face challenges such as technical issues, ethical risks, and inconsistent effectiveness across educational contexts. The review underscores the need for further research, particularly longitudinal studies and evaluation frameworks, to better understand chatbot integration. This chapter contributes to the discussion on AI in education, highlighting both the advantages and the complexities of its implementation, with a focus on skill obsolescence, misuse, and bias in educational practices.

Foreword

In the past few years, Artificial Intelligence (AI) has gone from being a futuristic idea to something that's a big part of our daily lives. One area where AI has made a major impact is education. It has introduced us to many exciting possibilities—like helping students learn at their own pace, making education more accessible, and making admin work easier. But at the same time, it also brings serious challenges we can't ignore. That's why this book, Pitfalls of AI Integration in Education: Skill Obsolescence, Misuse, and Bias, comes at just the right time.

This book brings together thoughts from more than sixty experts across twelve countries. These contributors come from different backgrounds and share different views, but they all care deeply about how AI is affecting education. Rather than only focusing on the good side of AI, the book asks tough questions and warns us about possible dangers—like AI making it easier to cheat, harming students' ability to think critically, spreading bias, or even making some teaching skills outdated.

This isn't just a collection of chapters—it's a guide, a warning, and an invitation to think. It doesn't say we should stop using AI in schools. Instead, it encourages us to use it carefully, fairly, and with clear values in mind. Whether you're a teacher, researcher, policymaker, school leader, or EdTech developer, there's something in this book for you.

With tools like OpenAI's ChatGPT, DALL·E, Deepseek, Perplexity, Anthorpic's Claude, Microsoft's Copilot, and Google's Gemini becoming more popular in education, it's easy to get caught up in the excitement. But this book reminds us to pause and think. Are we shaping learners who can think for themselves? Are we becoming better teachers? What kind of future are we creating?

At this important moment in education, Pitfalls of AI Integration in Education gives us a sense of direction. I truly hope this book reaches classrooms, libraries, staff rooms, and policy meetings everywhere. May it spark honest discussions and inspire real change so we can build a future in education that is fair, thoughtful, and caring.

The book is divided into four well-planned sections. It covers topics like cheating in schools, how ready teachers are to use AI, ethical concerns, and research reviews. It's meant for everyone involved in education—teachers, researchers, school leaders, and decision-makers. It doesn't give quick solutions, but instead pushes us to think deeply about how important human judgment is in a world where machines are doing more and more.

The editors and writers have done a wonderful job creating a valuable resource that is well-researched and also connected to what's really happening in schools today. The book's focus on fairness, inclusion, and global voices makes it relevant to people in many different parts of the world.

As AI continues to change how we teach and learn, this book is a much-needed guide. It's not just about pointing out problems—it's about helping us do better. It calls on schools and educators to use AI in smart and responsible ways, while holding on to the true spirit of education.

I truly appreciate Dr Manuel Garcia, Dr Joanna Rosak-Szyrocka, and Prof Dr Aras Bozkurt, the editors, for bringing together such a timely and thoughtful book. I believe it will lead to important conversations and help education systems make better choices in the times ahead.

Ramesh C. Sharma
Ambedkar University, Delhi, India

Preface

INTRODUCTION

From the dawn of civilization, the pursuit of knowledge has been tightly interwoven with the evolution of tools. In ancient Mesopotamia, cuneiform tablets marked humanity's first deliberate attempt to externalize cognition—slow, deliberate, and constrained by materiality, yet revolutionary in anchoring thought beyond the fleeting domain of speech. These early instruments of epistemic inscription laid the groundwork for what would become the architecture of formal learning. Today, the transmission of knowledge is nearly frictionless. With a few keystrokes, one can summon centuries of scholarship, simulate molecular behavior, or construct immersive, synchronous learning environments untethered from geography or time. Education has migrated from the chalk-dusted certainties of the physical classroom to the fluid architectures of cloud-native ecosystems—rich in automation, hyper-personalization, and algorithmic intervention. From blockchain-based credentialing to biometric feedback loops and adaptive learning algorithms, the very substrate of pedagogy is being reconfigured. We are no longer merely using tools to teach; we are co-constructing knowledge environments where those tools are autonomous agents in the instructional dialogue. As one might jest, the teacher is no longer the sage on the stage—nor even the guide on the side—but perhaps now, a user in the loop.

At the forefront of this transformation is artificial intelligence (AI)—a domain once confined to speculative fiction and philosophical conjecture, now embedded in the mundane infrastructure of education. From its postwar origins with thinkers like Turing and McCarthy to today's neural networks capable of producing graduate-level prose in seconds, AI has become both invisible and indispensable (Bozkurt et al., 2024; Garcia, 2024). Current systems predict attrition risk, scaffold learning paths in real time, auto-grade complex submissions, and generate assessments that adapt to learner behavior with uncanny precision. In one example, AI tutors have been deployed in low-resource contexts, providing 24/7 support at a cost inaccessible to most human-centered interventions. Affect-recognition software now gauges attention, sentiment, and confusion using facial cues and biometric signals—features that once belonged in dystopian cinema and now appear in grant proposals. And yet, beneath the dazzling veneer of algorithmic optimization, we must confront a disquieting question: Are we truly enhancing learning or merely optimizing it? Has AI brought us closer to meaningful intellectual engagement, or are we training students to interface with machines more fluently than with ideas? The tension between augmentation and automation—between intelligence amplification and instructional outsourcing—defines the stakes of this technological moment.

THE CHALLENGES AND RESEARCH GAP

It is within this increasingly automated educational landscape that critical questions begin to surface—questions often left unasked in the excitement of innovation (Xiao et al., 2025). While the benefits of AI are repeatedly documented in white papers and policy briefs, the hazards remain insufficiently scrutinized. Discussions of algorithmic opacity, digital paternalism, and the erosion of human agency are often relegated to footnotes or future work. There is a tendency, particularly within edtech circles, to adopt what we might call "solutionism"—a belief that every pedagogical challenge has a technical fix and that efficiency and personalization are the ultimate goals of education. But what becomes of critical thinking when students are guided exclusively by predictive algorithms? How do we ensure that educators remain central, rather than peripheral, to instructional decision-making? What happens when AI models trained on biased data inadvertently reinforce existing inequities? Several pressing scenarios remain underexplored in current literature. Central among these concerns are the long-term cognitive effects of AI dependence, the deskilling of educators, the devaluation of formative struggle, the automation of pedagogical authority, the normalization of surveillance, the psychological effects of machine feedback, the subtle reinforcement of stereotypes through biased models, the ecological cost of large-scale AI deployment, and the systemic inequities introduced by personalization algorithms. Issues surrounding data governance, AI-facilitated academic dishonesty, the silent rewriting of learning objectives by algorithmic logic, and the regulatory vacuum around automated decision-making are equally pressing. These are not peripheral concerns—they are central to the future of education. And yet, they remain fragmented across disciplines, understudied in scope, and underestimated in impact. This book begins where most policy papers end: with the unresolved, the inconvenient, and the structurally complex.

ABOUT THIS BOOK

The *Pitfalls of AI Integration in Education: Skill Obsolescence, Misuse, and Bias* book is a response to the research gaps and unanswered questions. It is a deliberate shift away from techno-utopianism toward a grounded, critical engagement with AI's role in shaping educational futures. While much of the prevailing discourse celebrates possibility, we have chosen to examine peril: the risk of skill atrophy when generative tools supplant creative labor, the encroachment of surveillance technologies under the guise of pedagogical support, and the entrenchment of biases within algorithmic systems that claim neutrality while operationalizing historical inequities. Our contributors span the domains of education, computer science, ethics, policy, and cognitive science, offering a multidisciplinary interrogation of the unintended, often unanticipated, consequences of AI integration in classrooms, curricula, and institutional systems. We are not alarmists but realists. We do not advocate abandoning AI, nor do we harbor nostalgia for a pre-digital past. Rather, we argue for a more discerning adoption—one anchored in pedagogical intent, procedural transparency, and an unwavering commitment to human dignity. In many ways, this book could be read as a companion to the emerging genre of speculative nonfiction—not because it forecasts distant futures, but because it interrogates the ones currently under construction, often without democratic deliberation or ethical guardrails. If history and speculative fiction alike have taught us anything, it is that technological progress, when left unchecked, tends to obscure the deeper values at stake. We invite you, therefore, to read these chapters not merely as a critique but as a provocation—to think more deeply, act more responsibly, and imagine more boldly the kinds of educational futures we truly want to build.

Written by over 70 authors from more than 20 countries, this book unfolds across 18 chapters that are distributed across four sections:

1. *The Unintended Consequences of AI in Education*
2. *Skill Obsolescence and Educator Readiness*
3. *Ethical, Legal, and Social Implications*
4. *Systematic Reviews on the Challenges of AI in Education*

Section 1: The Unintended Consequences of AI in Education

This opening section explores how AI technologies, often deployed with the promise of efficiency and personalization, can inadvertently disrupt pedagogical practices, distort learning objectives, and reshape student identity. The chapters examine overlooked impacts such as diminished critical thinking, the algorithmic misrepresentation of complex subject matter, and compromised academic integrity. Collectively, they surface the subtle yet pervasive ways AI alters educational contracts, sometimes in ways neither students nor educators fully anticipate.

Chapter 1: Rethinking Educational Assessment in the Age of Generative AI: Actionable Strategies to Mitigate Academic Dishonesty

Chapter 2: Erosion of Critical Academic Skills Due to AI Dependency Among Tertiary Students: A Path Analysis

Chapter 3: The Limits of AI in Teaching Partition Literature: A Critical Perspective on the Risks of Algorithmic Interpretation in Sensitive Historical Contexts

Chapter 4: The Emergence of Generative AI in Higher Education: Exploring the Perceived Challenges Among Teachers and Students

Chapter 5: AI Shaming among Teacher Education Students: A Reflection on Acceptance and Identity in the Age of Generative Tools

Section 2: Skill Obsolescence and Educator Readiness

The second section interrogates the shifting role of trainers, instructional designers, and educators in AI-mediated learning environments. It addresses the dual challenge of preparing teachers for AI integration while also guarding against the professional erosion that can result from automation. These chapters engage with issues such as infrastructure readiness, professional reskilling, and the hidden labor of navigating algorithmic tools—all within the broader context of preserving instructional agency and pedagogical integrity.

Chapter 6: Investigation of the Opinions of Classroom Teachers Working in Science and Art Centers on the Pitfalls of Artificial Intelligence in Education

Chapter 7: The Automation Trap: Unpacking the Consequences of Over-Reliance on AI in Education and Its Hidden Costs

Chapter 8: Reskilling and Upskilling Future Educators for the Demands of Artificial Intelligence in the Modern Era of Education

Chapter 9: Equipping the Next Generation of Technicians: Navigating School Infrastructure and Technical Knowledge in the Age of AI Integration

Section 3: Ethical, Legal, and Social Implications

The third section surfaces the normative tensions surrounding AI in education by examining how emerging technologies intersect with broader debates on transparency, equity, scholarship, privacy, inclusion, authorship, agency, rights, and justice. It expands the conversation beyond technical capability to ethical responsibility to illuminate the sociotechnical imaginaries that shape—and are shaped by—AI systems in schooling contexts.

Chapter 10: Technoethics and the Use of Artificial Intelligence in Educational Contexts: Reflections on Integrity, Transparency, and Equity

Chapter 11: Navigating the Ethical Frontier: Emerging Dilemmas at the Intersection of Special Education and Artificial Intelligence

Chapter 12: Inclusive Transformation with Artificial Intelligence: Ethical Aspects, Policies, and Strategic Approaches for Equitable Education

Chapter 13: Safeguarding Educational Innovations Amid AI Disruptions: A Reassessment of Patenting for Sustained Intellectual Property Protection

Chapter 14: AI in Academia: Balancing Integrity, Ethics, and Learning Amid Evolving Norms of Authorship and Scholarship

Section 4: Systematic Reviews on the Challenges of AI in Education

The final section consolidates the state of empirical research through systematic reviews that trace the contours of AI integration in varied educational domains. By synthesizing findings on AI misuse and overreliance, teacher feedback systems, engineering education, chatbot deployment, and broader institutional adoption, these chapters offer evidence-based insights that clarify the risks, benefits, opportunities, and regulatory uncertainties of educational AI.

Chapter 15: A Systematic Review of Educators' Overreliance and Misuse of AI in Student Feedback: Introducing the ETHICAL-FEED Framework

Chapter 16: Navigating the Use of AI in Engineering Education Through a Systematic Review of Technology, Regulations, and Challenges

Chapter 17: Challenges and Opportunities of Integrating Generative Artificial Intelligence in Higher Education: A Systematic Review

Chapter 18: A Systematic Review of the Role of AI-Enabled Chatbots in Modern Education: Benefits, Risks, and Implementation Complexity

BEYOND THE ALGORITHM: RECLAIMING THE HUMAN IN EDUCATION

What now, after reading these chapters? If this book has served its purpose, it has not only exposed the hidden costs of AI integration in education but also unsettled the reader enough to demand better. The challenge moving forward is not to reject AI outright but to reassert educational values before they are overwritten by metrics, models, and machine logic. We must ask: What kind of learning do we want to preserve, and what kind of future are we building—and for whom? The path ahead demands more than technological competence; it requires ethical imagination, policy courage, and pedagogical intentionality. It is now up to educators, researchers, designers, and decision-makers to ensure that in the age of intelligent systems, human judgment, empathy, and purpose remain at the center of learning. AI may help us teach faster or scale wider—but only we can decide what is worth teaching at all.

The next phase of inquiry must go beyond implementation frameworks and start cultivating critical literacy around AI—not just for developers and policymakers, but for students themselves (Garcia et al., 2024; Rosak-Szyrocka et al., 2024). Learners must be equipped not only to use AI tools but also to question them, resist their biases, and understand the sociotechnical systems behind the interfaces. Education must not become an onboarding program for algorithmic compliance. Instead, it should foster the kind of reflexive, interdisciplinary thinking that makes AI not just more powerful but more accountable (Bozkurt & Sharma, 2024; Garcia et al., 2025). We must prepare learners not simply to adapt to AI-driven futures but to shape them. In the end, the most urgent innovation may not be technological but philosophical: a redefinition of progress that prioritizes equity over efficiency, dignity over data, and humanity over hype. AI will continue to evolve, and with it, our systems of teaching and learning. However, whether these systems reflect democratic ideals or corporate imperatives depends on the choices we make today. Let this book be a starting point—a critical companion for anyone navigating the promises and perils of education in the algorithmic age.

Manuel B. Garcia
FEU Institute of Technology, Philippines

Joanna Rosak-Szyrocka
Czestochowa University of Technology, Poland

Aras Bozkurt
Anadolu University, Turkey

REFERENCES

Bozkurt, A., & Sharma, R. C. (2024). Trust, Credibility and Transparency in Human-AI Interaction: Why We Need Explainable and Trustworthy AI and Why We Need It Now. *Asian Journal of Distance Education*, *19*(2), 1–9. https://www.asianjde.com/ojs/index.php/AsianJDE/article/view/819

Bozkurt, A., Xiao, J., Farrow, R., Bai, J. Y. H., Nerantzi, C., Moore, S., Dron, J., Stracke, C. M., Singh, L., Crompton, H., Koutropoulos, A., Terentev, E., Pazurek, A., Nichols, M., Sidorkin, A. M., Costello, E., Watson, S., Mulligan, D., Honeychurch, S., & Asino, T. I. (2024). The Manifesto for Teaching and Learning in a Time of Generative AI: A Critical Collective Stance to Better Navigate the Future. *Open Praxis*, *16*(4), 487–513. DOI: 10.55982/openpraxis.16.4.777

Garcia, M. B. (2024). The Paradox of Artificial Creativity: Challenges and Opportunities of Generative AI Artistry. *Creativity Research Journal*, ●●●, 1–14. DOI: 10.1080/10400419.2024.2354622

Garcia, M. B., Arif, Y. M., Khlaif, Z. N., Zhu, M., de Almeida, R. P. P., de Almeida, R. S., & Masters, K. (2024). Effective Integration of Artificial Intelligence in Medical Education: Practical Tips and Actionable Insights. In *Transformative Approaches to Patient Literacy and Healthcare Innovation* (pp. 1-19). IGI Global. https://doi.org/DOI: 10.4018/979-8-3693-3661-8.ch001

Garcia, M. B., Goi, C.-L., Shively, K., Maher, D., Rosak-Szyrocka, J., Happonen, A., Bozkurt, A., & Damaševičius, R. (2025). Understanding Student Engagement in AI-Powered Online Learning Platforms: A Narrative Review of Key Theories and Models. In *Cases on Enhancing P-16 Student Engagement With Digital Technologies* (pp. 1-30). IGI Global. https://doi.org/DOI: 10.2139/ssrn.5074608

Rosak-Szyrocka, J., Żywiołek, J., Nayyar, A., & Naved, M. (2024). *The Role of Sustainability and Artificial Intelligence in Education Improvement*. CRC Press., DOI: 10.1201/9781003425779

Xiao, J., Bozkurt, A., Nichols, M., Pazurek, A., Stracke, C. M., Bai, J. Y. H., Farrow, R., Mulligan, D., Nerantzi, C., Sharma, R. C., Singh, L., Frumin, I., Swindell, A., Honeychurch, S., Bond, M., Dron, J., Moore, S., Leng, J., & Slagter van Tryon, P. J.. (2025). Venturing into the Unknown: Critical Insights into Grey Areas and Pioneering Future Directions in Educational Generative AI Research. *TechTrends*, ●●●, 1–16. DOI: 10.1007/s11528-025-01060-6

Acknowledgment

Bringing this book to life has been both a challenging and rewarding journey, and I am deeply thankful to everyone who contributed to its realization. *Pitfalls of AI Integration in Education: Skill Obsolescence, Misuse, and Bias* would not have been possible without the collaborative efforts and intellectual generosity of many individuals.

We are especially grateful to the members of the Editorial Advisory Board and our peer reviewers, whose thoughtful critiques and rigorous feedback sharpened the focus and integrity of each chapter. Their commitment to upholding scholarly excellence was essential in ensuring the quality and clarity of this publication.

To our chapter authors, we express our sincere appreciation. Their diverse perspectives, research expertise, and critical insights are the heart of this book. By confronting the complex challenges that artificial intelligence poses to education, they have contributed to a body of work that we hope will guide educators, policymakers, and researchers in navigating these evolving landscapes with caution and foresight.

We also wish to acknowledge Prof. Ramesh C. Sharma, Executive Editor of the Asian Journal of Distance Education, for his compelling foreword that grounds this book in a timely national and global context. Likewise, we thank Prof. Junhong Xiao of Open University of Shantou (China) for his eloquent afterword, which weaves together the central themes of this work and offers a forward-looking perspective on the responsible integration of AI in education.

Our appreciation also extends to IGI Global, whose support throughout the publication process has been exceptional. Collaborating with such a dedicated publisher continues to be a rewarding experience, and we are thankful for the opportunity to work together in advancing critical scholarship.

Finally, we would like to express our deepest gratitude to our families, whose understanding and encouragement sustained us through the long hours of research, editing, and revision. Their unwavering support made this endeavor possible.

To everyone who contributed to this project, whether through guidance, feedback, authorship, or moral support, we thank you. It is our sincere hope that this book sparks meaningful dialogue and inspires thoughtful action as we collectively explore the implications of AI in education.

Manuel B. Garcia
FEU Institute of Technology, Philippines

Joanna Rosak-Szyrocka
Czestochowa University of Technology, Poland

Aras Bozkurt
Anadolu University, Turkey

Section 1
The Intended Consequences of AI in Education

Chapter 1
Rethinking Educational Assessment in the Age of Generative AI:
Actionable Strategies to Mitigate Academic Dishonesty

Manuel B. Garcia
https://orcid.org/0000-0003-2615-422X
FEU Institute of Technology, Philippines

Joanna Rosak-Szyrocka
https://orcid.org/0000-0002-5548-6787
Czestochowa University of Technology, Poland

Ramazan Yılmaz
Bartın University, Turkey

Ahmed Hosny Saleh Metwally
https://orcid.org/0000-0002-9545-5870
Helwan University, Egypt

Dharel P. Acut
https://orcid.org/0000-0002-9608-1292
Cebu Technological University, Philippines

Kingsley Ofosu-Ampong
https://orcid.org/0000-0003-0561-6376
Heritage Christian University, Ghana

Fatih Erdoğdu
https://orcid.org/0000-0003-1022-8570
Zonguldak Bülent Ecevit University, Turkey

Chorng Yuan Fung
https://orcid.org/0000-0002-2007-6286
Swinburne University of Technology, Sarawak, Malaysia

Aras Bozkurt
https://orcid.org/0000-0002-4520-642X
Anadolu University, Turkey

ABSTRACT

As artificial intelligence (AI) becomes increasingly integrated into educational contexts, they present new challenges to traditional assessment methods. A particularly pressing issue is academic dishonesty, which undermines learning authenticity and the credibility of educational institutions. With generative AI tools like ChatGPT making it easier for students to produce automated answers, educational assessments are at risk of measuring AI capabilities rather than students' actual knowledge. Thus, this chapter explores a range of strategies designed to adapt assessment practices in response to the influence of AI in education. These strategies offer actionable frameworks to support authentic learning and uphold academic

DOI: 10.4018/979-8-3373-0122-8.ch001

integrity. Additionally, the chapter highlights future research directions to guide further adaptation of educational policies and practices. Given the rapid integration of AI in the education sector, this chapter provides sensible insights that reinforce the importance of integrity-focused reforms in sustaining meaningful educational outcomes in an AI-driven world.

INTRODUCTION

Educational assessment is fundamental to the learning process. It provides essential insights into both student progress and institutional effectiveness. Over time, assessment practices have evolved alongside shifts in educational theories and societal expectations. This evolution underscores the ongoing need to align them with the demands of higher education and professional fields. Traditionally, assessments have relied on structured, standardized methods such as written exams, essays, and graded assignments. These approaches often emphasize the retention of knowledge, critical thinking, and the ability to apply learned concepts in specific contexts. In classroom settings, educators have used techniques like oral questioning, quizzes, and written feedback to gauge student comprehension and progress. Final exams and cumulative projects serve as benchmarks to summarize students' overall performance. These culminating assessments prove a snapshot of their achievements at the end of a course or program. While these conventional methods have shaped the foundation of educational assessment, evolving educational landscapes and emerging challenges signal a need to explore more dynamic and flexible ways of measuring and fostering learning outcomes (e.g., Swiecki et al., 2022).

In the 21st century, advancements in information and communication technologies have significantly transformed assessment methods (See et al., 2022). Recent trends pave the way for technology-enhanced assessments like computer-based testing and online evaluations. Particularly, e-assessment has emerged as a powerful tool for aiding teachers in monitoring student progress and evaluating complex cognitive skills (Azevedo & Azevedo, 2019). Prior works underscored the benefits of e-assessment in higher education, highlighting its potential to boost student motivation, satisfaction, skill development, autonomy, and flexibility (Montenegro-Rueda et al., 2021). E-assessments are often facilitated through learning management systems, which provide a variety of assessment options, including calculation questions, essays, matching exercises, and true/false queries. In addition, online tools like self-test quizzes, discussion forums, and e-portfolios have been increasingly adopted for educational assessments (Gikandi et al., 2011). The importance of these resources was further amplified during the COVID-19 pandemic (Ofosu-Ampong et al., 2024) when platforms such as Moodle and Zoom became essential for conducting online assessments to maintain the continuity of student evaluation amidst unprecedented challenges (Montenegro-Rueda et al., 2021; Slack & Priestley, 2023).

While e-assessments offer numerous benefits (Heil & Ifenthaler, 2023), the rise of emerging technologies like artificial intelligence (AI) introduces new challenges in educational assessment (Swiecki et al., 2022). One of the most pressing concerns is the increasing use of generative AI tools, which can produce sophisticated written responses, solve complex problems, and simulate human-like interactions. These AI-powered tools, such as ChatGPT, have made it easier for students to generate content that may not accurately reflect their individual understanding or learning progress. This ease of access has heightened concerns around academic dishonesty (Gruenhagen et al., 2024), which refers to any form of cheating or misrepresentation of one's own work in an academic setting. Students may rely on AI tools to complete assessments, which undermines the authenticity of their work (Lee et al., 2024).

Educational assessment methods now face the risk of becoming avenues for misuse rather than accurate measures of student knowledge. Consequently, educators are confronted with the challenge of designing assessments that not only measure genuine skills but also discourage reliance on AI-generated content. Addressing these concerns requires a rethinking of assessment strategies to uphold academic integrity in this evolving technological landscape.

MAIN FOCUS OF THE CHAPTER

The rapid advancements in generative AI have underscored the inadequacy of conventional assessment paradigms in addressing the multifaceted demands of modern education. As AI tools become increasingly sophisticated and ubiquitous, educators are compelled to reconceptualize and reengineer assessment frameworks to ensure they remain pedagogically sound, equitable, and authentically reflective of learner competencies. This chapter argues that simply modifying existing assessment methods is not enough; instead, a fundamental rethinking is imperative to align evaluative methodologies with the transformative capabilities and ethical implications of generative AI. There is an urgent need for actionable frameworks that can be operationalized across diverse educational ecosystems—including K–12 education, tertiary institutions, and professional development environments. These frameworks must account for evolving patterns of learner engagement, emergent modalities of knowledge representation, and heightened vulnerabilities to academic misconduct enabled by AI technologies.

Consequently, the objective of this chapter is to furnish a praxis-oriented analysis of how assessment systems can be recalibrated in response to the generative AI landscape. It endeavors to offer empirically grounded insights and pedagogical strategies that educators and institutions can adopt to construct assessments that not only yield valid measures of student learning but also uphold academic integrity and cultivate higher-order cognitive skills. To ensure epistemic rigor and contextual relevance, this chapter employs a collaborative expert synthesis coupled with an integrative review of contemporary scholarship. This methodological orientation reflects both the cross-disciplinary expertise of the contributing authors and a critical engagement with current empirical and theoretical discourse. The resulting strategies are thus both theoretically robust and pedagogically responsive. Determining and proposing these actionable strategies seeks to empower institutions, educational leaders, and teachers to navigate the challenges posed by AI advancements (Acut, Gamusa, et al., 2025; Gantalao et al., 2025; Mangubat et al., 2025).

STRATEGIES IN DESIGNING ASSESSMENTS

Implement Multimodal Assessment Techniques for Holistic Learning

In the era of generative AI, diversifying assessment types is crucial to ensure the authenticity of student work and minimize opportunities for academic dishonesty. Multimodal assessments go beyond traditional written tasks by incorporating oral presentations, practical demonstrations, and portfolios. Utilizing various forms of evaluation allows educators to capture a more comprehensive picture of students' abilities and learning processes (Grapin, 2023). More importantly, it reduces the likelihood of AI-generated content misrepresenting a student's actual skills. For example, in science education, students may be required to explain the steps of a scientific experiment through oral presentations. They can also perform practical demonstrations (e.g., conducting a chemistry experiment) to showcase hands-on skills that cannot be easily fabricated by AI. Asking students to create portfolios is another example, as it allows them to compile a curated collection of their work throughout the course, demonstrating their progress, critical thinking, and reflective learning. By adopting a more varied assessment strategy, educators not only foster a more equitable learning environment but also create a system that emphasizes authentic student engagement and the application of knowledge.

Ironically, teachers can use AI to counter the challenges posed by AI-generated content in student work (Hasanah et al., 2025). Integrating AI tools into the assessment process can add a layer of objectivity and tailored feedback to multimodal assessments. These AI capabilities in areas such as speech analysis, real-time feedback, and content evaluation can help ensure the authenticity of student work while supporting more diverse and holistic assessment methods. Table 1 presents different ways AI can be effectively integrated into multimodal assessments, highlighting practical strategies that educators can employ to maintain academic integrity while adapting to the ever-evolving technological landscape in education. This comprehensive approach not only counters the misuse of AI tools by students but also enriches the learning experience, making assessments more meaningful and aligned with 21st-century skills.

Table 1. Various multimodal assessments and how to integrate AI

Assessment Type	Description	Benefits	Challenges	Examples of AI Integration
Oral Presentations	Students articulate their understanding verbally, often in front of peers or through recorded video.	Develops communication skills and real-time articulation of ideas.	Requires evaluation of subjective aspects like speaking style and confidence.	AI can analyze speech clarity and tone and provide feedback on content and presentation style.
Practical Demonstrations	Hands-on demonstration of skills, often in labs or simulations, showing the application of theoretical knowledge.	Validates real-world skills and problem-solving abilities.	It may require specific equipment or environments; evaluation criteria can be complex.	AI-based simulations can provide virtual environments for practice and give immediate feedback on performance.
Portfolios	A curated collection of a student's work over time, reflecting progress and learning.	Encourages reflection and self-assessment and showcases a range of skills.	Time-consuming to compile and evaluate; requires clear criteria.	AI can analyze portfolio content, track progress, and suggest areas for improvement.
Visual Presentations	Use of graphics, slideshows, infographics, and videos to present information.	Enhances creativity and visual communication skills.	Difficult to assess the quality of visual elements objectively.	AI can assess design aspects, clarity, and the effectiveness of visual elements used.
Interactive Activities	Engaging in tasks like quizzes, simulations, or role-playing scenarios that involve active participation.	Fosters engagement, collaboration, and practical application of knowledge.	Requires proper setup; monitoring and feedback may be challenging.	AI-based platforms can provide interactive simulations, track performance, and give real-time feedback.
Peer Evaluations	Students assess each other's work, providing feedback and constructive criticism.	Promotes critical thinking and self-reflection; develops evaluation skills.	It can be biased or inconsistent and requires guidance on effective feedback.	AI can guide students on how to give constructive feedback and assess the quality of peer evaluations.
Self-Evaluations	Students reflect on their own work and learning processes, often using rubrics or guided questions.	Enhances self-awareness and encourages lifelong learning skills.	Requires a high level of student honesty and self-assessment skills.	AI tools can provide prompts for reflection and track self-assessment trends over time.

4

Promote Higher-Order Thinking Skills Through Critical Analysis

Higher-order thinking skills are fundamental for developing modern competencies (Huang et al., 2024). Key components of these skills include critical thinking, problem-solving, creative thinking, and decision-making. However, the advent of generative AI in educational settings poses a significant risk: *students may become overly dependent on these tools*. This dependency bypasses the development and application of their higher-order thinking abilities. When students rely on AI to generate content, solve problems, or provide answers, they often neglect the deep cognitive processes involved in analyzing information, synthesizing ideas, and making complex decisions. This dependency can lead to a superficial understanding of the material and an increase in academic dishonesty, as students might submit AI-generated work that does not truly reflect their knowledge or skills (Miranda et al., 2025). Excessive reliance on AI tools can contribute to mental health issues, including what some researchers refer to as *"ChatGPT Dependency Disorder"* (Garcia, 2024a). This condition arises when students become so reliant on AI that they experience anxiety or difficulty when faced with tasks that require independent thought and problem-solving. Such dependency can ultimately undermine self-confidence, critical thinking, and creativity, which then affects both academic performance and overall mental well-being.

To counter the risk of overreliance on AI tools, it is crucial to design assessments that focus on promoting higher-order thinking. Tasks that require students to critically analyze a case study, synthesize information from multiple sources, or develop an original argument challenge them to go beyond simple knowledge recall or basic problem-solving that AI can easily replicate. For instance, instead of assigning a traditional essay, teachers can implement project-based assessments where students must address real-world problems. One practical strategy is to use a *"Design Thinking Challenge,"* where students are tasked with identifying a community issue, researching possible solutions, and creating a proposal or prototype that addresses the problem (Revano & Garcia, 2020). In this scenario, students might be asked to investigate local environmental concerns, such as plastic waste, and then propose an innovative recycling program tailored to their community's needs. This process requires them to conduct interviews, analyze data, think creatively, and present their findings through a combination of written reports, visual presentations, and oral pitches. By doing so, students are encouraged to use skills that AI cannot replicate—such as original problem-solving, empathy gained through interviews, and real-time adaptation during the presentation. Moreover, teachers can integrate reflective components where students must discuss their thought processes, challenges faced, and lessons learned.

Incorporate Human-Centered Interaction to Assess Real-Time Understanding

Assessment methods that prioritize direct human interaction have become more crucial than ever with the rise of generative AI. These methods offer students opportunities to demonstrate their knowledge and skills in real-time, without the crutch of AI tools. By integrating elements such as interviews, oral examinations, collaborative projects, role-playing activities, and Socratic seminars into the assessment process, educators can better assess students' spontaneous understanding while fostering essential communication skills that are critical in the professional world. The Media Richness Theory (Daft & Lengel, 1986) provides a relevant lens through which to view these interactions. This theory posits that communication media vary in their capacity to convey nuanced information and facilitate understanding. Richer mediums (e.g., face-to-face interactions) allow for immediate feedback, nonverbal cues, and personal engagement, making them more effective for complex communication tasks. In the context of educational assessments, interviews, oral exams, and discussions serve as 'rich' media. They facilitate a level of depth, spontaneity, and adaptability in evaluating students' skills that AI-driven assessments, which typically operate through 'leaner' media like text-based platforms, cannot easily replicate.

Generative AI tools, while capable of evaluating factual knowledge through structured methods (e.g., multiple-choice questions), struggle to assess soft skills like communication, collaboration, and critical thinking effectively (Yilmaz & Karaoglan Yilmaz, 2023). Incorporating methods like oral exams and group work into assessments not only provides real-time insight into students' abilities but also creates an environment where they must adapt their thinking dynamically in response to questions and dialogue. Interviews and oral examinations can be structured in various ways. For example, structured interviews with predetermined questions ensure consistency and fairness, while unstructured or semi-structured interviews allow for a more adaptive, conversational approach. Both formats facilitate an interactive environment where students articulate their thoughts, defend their ideas, and engage in intellectual discourse. Unlike traditional written exams, these oral formats require students to think on their feet, respond to inquiries, and explain their reasoning processes. These approaches are more effective in terms of uncovering deeper levels of understanding and critical thinking that written responses may not fully capture. Teachers can further enhance these skills by providing opportunities for students to practice and receive constructive feedback (Garcia et al., 2024). This interaction supports the development of communication skills and ensures that assessments reflect a more comprehensive evaluation of student learning, countering the limitations of AI-driven methods.

Prioritize Process-Oriented Learning Over End-Product Evaluation

The emergence of generative AI in education necessitates a paradigm shift in how we assess students' learning processes and outcomes. Traditional assessment methods, which often focus solely on the final product, may be insufficient in the context of generative AI, as they fail to capture the full scope of student development. Therefore, educators must adopt a process-oriented approach that emphasizes the learning journey rather than just the result (Garcia, 2024b). By shifting the focus to the steps, students take toward achieving their outcomes, teachers can reduce the risk of academic dishonesty facilitated by AI tools while fostering deeper engagement, critical thinking, and continuous improvement (Yilmaz & Karaoglan Yilmaz, 2023). Process-oriented assessment recognizes that learning is a dynamic and iterative process, and evaluating students' progress over time provides a more comprehensive understanding of their intellectual growth and problem-solving abilities. This approach becomes particularly crucial in the age of AI, where polished end products generated by tools like ChatGPT can obscure the learner's true depth of understanding and effort (Salinas-Navarro et al., 2024). By emphasizing research logs, draft submissions, and reflective papers, educators can create assessments that value the entire learning process, not just the final product (Preiksaitis & Rose, 2023).

Incorporating process-oriented assessments into the curriculum requires setting clear criteria for evaluating research logs, drafts, and reflective writings, along with guidelines for how these components will be weighted in the overall assessment framework (Cacho, 2024). Providing students with templates, examples, and training in metacognitive strategies and reflective writing can further enhance their ability to document their learning processes effectively. Timely feedback on research logs, drafts, and reflections is essential, as it helps guide students toward a deeper understanding rather than simply correcting errors. Organizing peer review sessions also fosters a collaborative learning environment where students give and receive feedback on their drafts and reflections, learning from one another's approaches. Generative

AI can support this process by offering automated feedback on draft submissions, which helps students identify areas for improvement before receiving instructor input. However, educators must use AI tools judiciously to enhance rather than replace authentic learning experiences. By emphasizing the learning process over the final product, process-oriented assessments not only promote academic integrity but also prepare students for lifelong learning (Salinas-Navarro et al., 2024).

Utilize Performance-Based Tasks to Demonstrate Practical Knowledge

Performance-based tasks offer an authentic approach to assessing students' real-time demonstration of skills, emphasizing the application of practical knowledge over mere theoretical understanding. In the age of generative AI, traditional assessments such as written exams are increasingly vulnerable to compromise, as students can leverage AI tools to generate content. Performance-based tasks serve as a valuable alternative, requiring active, hands-on participation that is difficult to replicate using AI. Rooted in constructivist theories, these assessments align with the principle that students learn more effectively through doing rather than passively receiving information (Anderson & Johnston, 2016). By integrating tasks like lab activities, simulations, or practical demonstrations, educators can better measure a student's ability to apply theoretical knowledge in real-world scenarios. One of the key advantages of performance-based tasks is their ability to capture a student's problem-solving process in dynamic environments (see Table 2). For instance, in lab-based assessments, students are required to apply scientific principles, conduct experiments, interpret data, and make real-time decisions based on their observations. This approach not only evaluates content knowledge but also critical thinking and adaptive learning skills (Aladini et al., 2024). Similarly, simulations in fields such as medicine or engineering place students in complex scenarios that mirror real-world challenges, demanding thoughtful navigation and decision-making (Kong et al., 2024). These tasks go beyond simply testing knowledge; they provide a window into the students' analytical and reflective abilities, which AI-generated responses cannot easily mimic (Hasanah et al., 2025).

Table 2. Types of performance-based tasks and their educational impact

Performance Task	Description	Key Skills Assessed	Example Fields of Application	Supporting Studies
Lab Activities	Hands-on experiments or tasks requiring students to apply scientific methods in real-time.	Critical thinking, problem-solving, data analysis	Science, Engineering	Gomez-del Rio and Rodriguez (2022); Kovaleva et al. (2024)
Simulations	Virtual or physical scenarios that mimic real-world processes require decision-making and adaptive learning.	Decision-making, adaptability, collaboration	Medicine, Nursing, Law	Slavinska et al. (2024); Miller et al. (2024); Petil et al. (2025)
Collaborative Group Work	Group-based tasks that require joint problem-solving and teamwork in dynamic environments.	Collaboration, communication, leadership	Business, Social Sciences, ICT	Riebe et al. (2016); Garcia (2023)

continued on following page

Table 2. Continued

Performance Task	Description	Key Skills Assessed	Example Fields of Application	Supporting Studies
Creative Problem-solving Challenges	Open-ended tasks that require innovation and creative application of knowledge.	Creativity, innovation, reflective thinking	STEM Education, Design Thinking	Valderama et al. (2022); Acut, Lobo, et al. (2025)
Portfolio Development	Compilation and presentation of students' work over time to showcase growth and achievements.	Self-assessment, reflective thinking, organizational skills	Arts, Education, Business	Ryan (2011); Doğan et al. (2024)

In the context of generative AI's increasing capabilities and features, performance-based tasks serve as a critical safeguard against academic dishonesty. While generative AI can assist students in generating written responses or solving complex problems (Acut et al., 2024), it cannot physically perform tasks or replicate real-time decision-making processes. By requiring students to actively demonstrate their skills in real time, educators ensure that assessments reflect each student's true abilities rather than the output of an AI model. The integration of performance-based assessments is, therefore, increasingly recognized as a best practice in educational settings. In science education, for example, performance assessments have been shown to enhance scientific inquiry skills and deepen students' understanding of content (Acut, 2022). Similarly, in professional fields such as nursing and law, performance-based tasks (e.g., simulations and practical exercises) effectively mirror the complexities of real-world practice and decision-making (Slavinska et al., 2024). As educators rethink assessment strategies in the age of generative AI, performance-based tasks emerge as a reliable approach to measure authentic student skills. These assessments offer a more holistic evaluation of student capabilities, better preparing them for the demands of professional environments in an AI-driven world.

Initiate Capstone Projects for Real-World Problem Solving

Capstone projects offer a comprehensive and multifaceted approach to assessing student learning (Tenhunen et al., 2023). This academic experience requires extensive research, planning, and execution over an extended period (Table 3). These projects culminate in a final presentation or defense, where students synthesize the knowledge and skills acquired throughout their academic journey (Acut, 2022). In the era of generative AI, capstone projects stand out as one of the most rigorous forms of assessment because they demand creativity, critical thinking, problem-solving, and deep subject matter expertise—skills that are not easily automated or replicated by AI systems. Unlike traditional assessments focused on memorization or short-term knowledge retention, capstone projects span several months, offering students the opportunity to explore a topic in great depth (Kim et al., 2019). This process inherently fosters higher-order thinking as students identify real-world problems, design research methodologies, collect and analyze data, and propose evidence-based solutions (Stephenson et al., 2020). The reflective nature of these projects ensures that students not only gain a deeper understanding of the subject matter but also develop the ability to apply their learning in meaningful ways.

Table 3. Comparison of capstone project types, key components, and skills assessed

Capstone Project Type	Key Components	Skills Assessed	Assessment Method	Example Fields
Research-based Project	Literature review, data collection, analysis	Critical thinking, research skills	Written reports, defense	Social Sciences, STEM
Design/Engineering Project	Prototype development, testing	Problem-solving, technical skills	Prototype, presentation	Engineering, ICT
Service-Learning Project	Community engagement, solution implementation	Collaboration, leadership	Project report, oral defense	Education, Public Health
Entrepreneurship Project	Business plan, market analysis, product development	Innovation, strategic thinking	Business proposal, pitch	Business, Economics
Artistic/Creative Project	Concept creation, artifact production	Creativity, technical expertise	Portfolio, exhibition	Fine Arts, Media Studies
Interdisciplinary Project	Integration of multiple fields, comprehensive analysis	Systems thinking, adaptability	Multi-format deliverables	Sustainability, Policy Studies
Technology Integration Project	Software/hardware development, user testing	Programming, usability design	Software demo, documentation	ICT, Education Technology

A key benefit of capstone projects is the promotion of student autonomy and self-directed learning. Since students typically choose their topics based on personal or professional interests, they are more motivated to engage deeply with the material. Landfried et al. (2023) found that capstone projects can enhance student engagement and ownership of learning, resulting in improved academic outcomes and higher satisfaction. Additionally, these projects often require collaboration with industry professionals, community partners, or interdisciplinary teams, providing students with valuable real-world experience (Badir et al., 2023). Capstone projects also help students develop key skills that are highly sought after in today's job market, including project management, research, communication, and teamwork. By guiding students through the process of project conception, development, and execution, educators help them refine these transferable skills, which are essential for success in diverse professional contexts (Darling-Hammond et al., 2019). Finally, the formal presentation or defense at the project's culmination further enhances students' ability to articulate their ideas persuasively.

From an assessment perspective, capstone projects provide educators with the opportunity to evaluate a broad range of competencies, from research proficiency to practical application. They often require the integration of multiple forms of assessment, including written reports, oral presentations, and project artifacts, offering a holistic view of student learning (Acut, 2022). The defense component adds an additional layer of rigor, as students must not only present their findings but also respond to questions and critiques, demonstrating their ability to defend their work and think critically on their feet. Previous studies have highlighted the effectiveness of capstone projects in fostering critical skills. For instance, Cheng et al. (2019) found that these projects facilitate deeper learning and the development of essential competencies such as problem-solving and independent work. Similarly, Stephenson et al. (2020) emphasized how capstone experiences integrate theoretical knowledge with practical application, preparing students for professional life. In the age of AI, where skills like creativity, adaptability, and problem-solving are increasingly valuable and less susceptible to automation, capstone projects stand out as a robust method of ensuring students are well-equipped for the future.

Facilitate Value-Based Discussions to Foster Reflective Thinking

Value-based discussions are a dialogic approach that emphasizes active listening, respect, empathy, and the exploration of the ethical, cultural, and social implications of a subject. In the context of generative AI, incorporating value-based discussions into assessments can serve as a powerful tool for preventing academic dishonesty. These discussions require students to engage with the subject matter, critically reflect on their values, and consider the broader implications of their actions, making it difficult for them to rely solely on AI-generated responses. When students are asked to reflect on ethical considerations or societal impacts, they are compelled to express their individual perspectives and reasoning. Generative AI can enhance value-based discussions by providing a starting point for exploration. For example, AI can generate prompts that urge students to analyze various ethical scenarios or cultural biases embedded in AI's outputs (Ofosu-Ampong et al., 2023; Walter, 2024). However, educators must be cautious in how they use AI in this context. The questions posed by AI should not simply reflect dominant viewpoints or specific agendas; instead, they should provoke genuine thought and debate. Teachers play a crucial role in scrutinizing these AI-generated prompts to ensure they are free of bias and encourage students to examine underlying beliefs critically (Adams, 2021). By actively engaging in these reflective discussions, students learn to articulate their thoughts, question the narratives presented to them, and make informed decisions—skills that reduce their dependence on AI for answers.

Additionally, value-based discussions can highlight the limitations of AI and the importance of human judgment. When students discuss ethical dilemmas, cultural norms, or social justice issues, they are not just responding to information; they are interpreting and negotiating meaning based on their values and experiences (Martínez-Requejo et al., 2025). This level of critical engagement is something that AI cannot authentically reproduce. As a moderator, AI can facilitate a more inclusive environment by filtering out hate speech and fostering respectful exchanges (Kiritchenko et al., 2021). However, educators must define the parameters of discourse (Bozkurt et al., 2024), ensuring that diverse perspectives are included without overly aggressive content filtering that might incorrectly categorize unconventional viewpoints as negative. By promoting transparency about AI's role in discussions and guiding students in balancing free speech with constructive communication (Xiao et al., 2025), educators can create a learning environment where students develop critical thinking skills, ethical reasoning, and a deeper understanding of complex issues—all of which make academic dishonesty less likely.

Conduct Continuous Assessments for Ongoing Learning and Feedback

Continuous assessment is an ongoing process of evaluating students' learning progress throughout a program or course. This approach employs a variety of assessment methods—such as gamified quizzes, project work, peer reviews, presentations, and assignments—rather than relying solely on final exams. By providing regular and timely feedback, continuous assessments help students improve their learning performance and outcomes while also serving as a valuable tool for combating academic dishonesty, especially in the context of AI's growing influence.

Table 4. Practical example of continuous assessment for sociology

Activity	Description
After each lecture	Short online quizzes featuring a mix of multiple-choice and open-ended questions to test students' analysis and interpretation of sociological events.
Weekly	One-page reflection essay analyzing sociological facts, motivations, and outcomes in society.
Mid-term project	Research proposal outlining a sociological effect and its significance, incorporating an appropriate methodological approach to explain or unravel new knowledge.
Class participation	Deploying robust and engaging gamification mechanisms to reward students for asking thoughtful questions and engaging in meaningful discussions.
Final project work	Research paper on a specific sociological problem in a context that requires critical analysis and synthesis of evidence to examine students' thought processes and original arguments.

The introduction of AI in education has raised concerns regarding its potential impact on the integrity of continuous assessments. However, adopting a diversified and dynamic approach can significantly reduce the likelihood of AI-generated submissions compromising academic integrity (Gruenhagen et al., 2024; Taneja et al., 2025). Teachers can combat dishonesty by incorporating creative tasks, essays, and open-ended questions that demand originality and critical thinking—tasks that AI tools cannot easily replicate. Moving beyond multiple-choice questions to assessments that emphasize application over memorization (see Table 4) helps ensure that students are evaluated on their ability to analyze, synthesize, and apply knowledge. This variety in assessment types makes it harder for students to rely solely on AI to produce responses, as the tasks require a demonstration of personal insight, reasoning, and problem-solving.

Table 5. Practical example of continuous assessment for information systems

Activity	Description
Daily coding challenge	Conduct short coding exercises to practice specific programming concepts learned in each class session.
Weekly programming assignment	Crafting code through problem-solving, focusing on the thought process behind the code, and understanding how to adapt solutions to new scenarios.
Mid-term project	Task students with designing and developing a simple mobile app that addresses societal challenges, such as waste management or climate change.
Peer code review	Facilitate collaborative learning sessions where students review each other's work, identify errors, and suggest improvements for efficiency and code readability.
Final project work	Combine multiple-choice questions on specific concepts with open-ended coding problems to assess understanding comprehensively.

The proposed continuous assessment framework for Information Systems (see Table 5) illustrates how incorporating real-world scenarios and project-based learning can diminish the impact of AI-generated content. By engaging students in problem-solving that reflects real-world complexities, educators encourage critical analysis and the application of knowledge, both of which are difficult for AI to replicate. Additionally, continuous assessments foster an environment where students receive feedback at regular intervals, allowing them to identify and address weaknesses in their understanding before being tempted to resort to dishonest means. By prioritizing ongoing engagement and the development of higher-order thinking skills, continuous assessments serve as a robust strategy to maintain academic integrity in an AI-enhanced educational landscape (Ofosu-Ampong et al., 2023; Xiao et al., 2025).

Customize Assessment Criteria to Encourage the Synthesis of Knowledge

Recalibrating assessment frameworks to prioritize epistemic synthesis and the pragmatic application of disciplinary knowledge is pivotal for cultivating higher-order cognitive engagement and robust critical thinking among learners. Conventional evaluative mechanisms tend to focus on surface-level learning—primarily rote memorization and basic factual recall (Diaz et al., 2025)—which insufficiently capture a learner's conceptual depth or capacity for transference to authentic contexts. By refocusing assessment criteria toward indicators that demand interdisciplinary reasoning, intellectual engagement, and applied problem-solving, educators can more effectively equip students with the competencies required for navigating complexity in academic inquiry.

Application-Based Assessments: These challenge students to operationalize theoretical constructs within novel and contextually relevant scenarios. In computing education, for instance, such assessments may entail the end-to-end development of functional software artifacts (see Garcia, 2025 for detailed examples). To foreground applied cognition, instructors can recalibrate their grading rubrics to include the following evaluative dimensions:

- **Operational Validity**: Does the artifact meet all functional specifications and demonstrate reliability across use cases?
- **Code Robustness and Elegance**: Is the source code optimized, syntactically coherent, and aligned with industry-standard conventions for maintainability?
- **Algorithmic Reasoning**: How effectively does the student diagnose edge cases and deploy debugging methodologies?
- **Innovative Problem Formulation**: Does the project exhibit originality in conceptualization or deploy non-traditional heuristics?

Synthesis-Based Assessments: These tasks involve the convergence of disparate conceptual frameworks to produce integrated, innovative outcomes—fostering meta-cognitive reasoning and design thinking. Within an AI-driven programming curriculum (Garcia, 2025), a synthesis-centric task might involve the architectural design and implementation of a multi-component web platform. Expert-level criteria for such assessments include:

- **Technological Integration**: To what extent does the student fluently orchestrate multiple programming paradigms, libraries, or third-party APIs?
- **Systemic Cohesion**: Is the final deliverable an architecturally coherent system with seamless interaction between components?
- **Cognitive Complexity**: Does the project incorporate advanced functionalities, such as asynchronous data flows, machine learning modules, or secure authentication systems?
- **Creative Fluency**: How distinctive is the student's approach in terms of user experience, design aesthetics, and conceptual novelty?

Implementing Customized Assessment Criteria: For rigorous implementation of these advanced assessment modalities, pedagogical strategies such as Project-Based Learning (PBL) and scenario-based case studies should be deployed. These should be scaffolded by analytically robust rubrics, which articulate clear evaluative benchmarks:

- **Conceptual Transference**: How adeptly does the learner transpose theoretical insights to resolve real-world, ill-structured problems?
- **Cross-Platform Synergy**: Does the student demonstrate sophistication in synthesizing diverse technologies to create functional and aesthetically cohesive systems?
- **Metacognitive Reflexivity**: Is the learner able to critically evaluate their development process, articulating challenges encountered and strategies for adaptive learning?
- **Collaborative Dynamics**: In team-based contexts, how does the student engage in distributed cognition, co-construction of knowledge, and equitable task allocation?

By providing well-defined criteria through rubrics, educators guide students toward deeper learning and create an environment that values originality, critical thinking, and practical application—key factors in reducing academic dishonesty.

Facilitate Peer Review Activities to Enhance Scrutiny and Understanding

Organizing peer assessment activities where students evaluate each other's work introduces an additional layer of scrutiny, contributing to a more comprehensive and equitable evaluation process. In this approach, students not only receive feedback from their instructors but also engage with their peers' perspectives, often accounting for a small portion of the overall assessment marks. This added layer enhances the credibility of the assessment, as students actively participate in the evaluation process, fostering a deeper understanding of academic standards and criteria. One of the primary benefits of peer assessment lies in its ability to develop critical thinking skills (Topping et al., 2025). By evaluating their classmates' work, students are required to thoughtfully and objectively apply evaluative criteria, analyzing and judging the quality based on established standards. This process not only cultivates an analytical mindset but also helps students identify strengths and weaknesses in their own work. The practice of scrutinizing peers' submissions allows them to gain insight into different approaches and solutions, which, in turn, enhances their own learning and ability to produce quality work. Additionally, peer assessment fosters a sense of responsibility and accountability. Knowing that their work will be reviewed by classmates often motivates students to invest more effort into producing higher-quality submissions. This sense of accountability extends to the role of evaluator, where students learn to provide fair, constructive, and respectful feedback, grasping the ethical and professional standards expected in both academic and professional settings.

To implement effective peer assessment activities, it is crucial to provide students with clear guidelines and criteria for evaluation. Utilizing rubrics and checklists ensures that the peer assessments are consistent, objective, and focused on key learning outcomes. Training sessions or workshops on how to give and receive constructive feedback can further prepare students to participate effectively in the peer review process. By organizing structured peer assessment activities, educators create a learning environment where students engage actively with the material, develop critical thinking skills, and gain a deeper understanding of the standards that underpin academic evaluation. This approach not only adds a layer of scrutiny to the assessment process but also enhances students' ability to self-assess and reflect on their learning.

FUTURE DIRECTIONS AND RESEARCH NEEDS

As generative AI continues to evolve, so too must our strategies for educational assessment. The rapid advancements in AI capabilities present both opportunities and challenges, particularly concerning academic integrity. To effectively address these challenges, future research must focus on developing innovative assessment methods, ethical guidelines, and policies that adapt to this changing technological landscape. This section outlines key areas for future research to ensure that assessments remain effective, fair, and authentic.

Exploring the Impact of Generative AI on Learning Outcomes

As generative AI becomes increasingly integrated into educational environments (Hulus, 2025; Olugbade, 2025), its influence on pedagogical processes and cognitive development warrants sustained, critical inquiry. Although preliminary investigations have documented short-term gains—such as increased accessibility and adaptive feedback—there remains a paucity of longitudinal evidence regarding its impact on core educational constructs, including epistemic engagement, durable knowledge retention, and the cultivation of higher-order cognitive faculties (Garcia et al., 2025). Moreover, the continuous interplay between learners and AI systems introduces new dynamics in metacognitive regulation and problem representation. To address these complexities, future research should pursue the following trajectories:

- Conduct studies comparing traditional and AI-integrated assessment frameworks to evaluate their efficacy in fostering deep learning and transferable competencies.
- Investigate the extent to which AI-mediated evaluations influence students' capacity for integrative thinking, adaptive reasoning, and creative problem-solving.
- Analyze shifts in students' epistemological beliefs and self-regulated learning behaviors in response to sustained interactions with generative AI tools.

Development of Ethical Guidelines for AI Use in Assessments

The integration of AI into assessment ecosystems introduces a spectrum of ethical and sociotechnical challenges that extend beyond algorithmic functionality. Critical issues such as algorithmic opacity, surveillance risk, data sovereignty, and the erosion of authorship authenticity must be addressed through normative frameworks that prioritize justice, accountability, and inclusivity. The lack of cohesive institutional protocols leaves educational stakeholders vulnerable to unintended harm and systemic inequities. Therefore, establishing a comprehensive set of ethical parameters is essential for ensuring responsible AI deployment in evaluative contexts. Future research should be oriented toward the following imperatives:

- Develop and evaluate transparent governance models to ensure responsible AI use in assessment, emphasizing student data protection and informed consent.
- Design audit mechanisms for identifying and mitigating algorithmic bias, particularly across diverse sociocultural and linguistic student populations.
- Examine the role of ethics-based policy frameworks in shaping institutional practices that promote fairness, trust, and transparency in AI-supported evaluation systems.

AI as an Assessment Tool

Despite presenting epistemological and logistical challenges, generative AI holds substantial promise as an augmentative mechanism within the assessment continuum. When integrated judiciously, AI can facilitate scalable feedback systems, automate routine evaluation tasks, and support differentiated instruction across diverse learning profiles. However, uncritical reliance on algorithmic assessment risks undermining the interpretive and relational dimensions of human evaluation. To optimize AI's role in assessment, it is essential to interrogate its pedagogical affordances while preserving the educator's epistemic authority. The following research directions are essential for realizing AI's constructive potential:

- Evaluate the pedagogical value of AI-generated feedback in supporting formative assessment and enhancing students' metacognitive awareness.
- Determine best practices for calibrating AI-human hybrid assessment models to ensure reliability, validity, and student engagement.
- Explore subject-specific implementations of AI-driven assessments that allow for personalization without compromising academic rigor or learner autonomy.

Development of Anti-Cheating Technologies

The advent of generative AI has introduced novel vectors for academic misconduct, significantly complicating the verification of student-authored work. Existing academic integrity frameworks and detection mechanisms are often ill-equipped to distinguish between authentic and algorithmically generated submissions. As such, the development of intelligent, adaptive countermeasures is imperative for sustaining trust in assessment validity. These mechanisms must be rooted in both technical rigor and ethical defensibility, capable of evolving alongside adversarial AI capabilities. Future research must address the following critical areas:

- Advance the design of AI-enabled forensics capable of identifying linguistic, syntactic, and semantic markers indicative of non-human authorship.
- Conduct empirical evaluative studies on the efficacy and limitations of existing academic integrity tools in detecting generative AI outputs.
- Facilitate interdisciplinary collaboration to co-develop context-aware anti-cheating frameworks that integrate machine learning, educational theory, and ethical oversight.

Policy and Institutional Adaptation

The increasing ubiquity of AI in pedagogical and assessment practices necessitates a systemic reconfiguration of institutional policies and governance models. Static, pre-digital frameworks are ill-suited to address the evolving nature of algorithmically mediated learning environments. Institutional stakeholders must, therefore, engage in anticipatory policymaking that foregrounds educational equity, assessment fidelity, and technological accountability. To ensure that assessment practices remain aligned with educational goals and ethical standards in an AI-augmented context, the following research avenues are proposed:

- Formulate institution-wide AI governance policies that codify principles of academic integrity, transparency, and responsible innovation in assessment.
- Investigate adaptive models of assessment that integrate AI while centering on learning outcomes, disciplinary standards, and student well-being.
- Develop strategic frameworks that align institutional assessment policies with national and international standards for ethical AI deployment in education.

CONCLUSION

In confronting the complexities introduced by advanced AI technologies, educational assessment must undergo a thoughtful transformation. The strategies outlined in this chapter offer actionable frameworks to support authentic learning and uphold academic integrity. Each of these approaches offers unique ways to assess students' deeper cognitive and practical skills, reducing the reliance on outputs that may be artificially generated. The implications of these evolving strategies reach beyond the academic world. By incorporating integrity-centered assessment practices, educators influence the cultivation of critical thinking and ethical awareness in students—skills essential for navigating an AI-driven society. Implementing these methods prepares students not only for academic success but also for responsible participation in a technology-infused world. Looking forward, commitment to these integrity-based reforms will shape the resilience of educational institutions in preserving the values of genuine scholarship. Through adaptable, ethics-focused assessment models, educators can nurture learning environments that emphasize personal accountability and true intellectual development.

REFERENCES

Acut, D. (2022). Developing SIPCaR projects utilizing modern technologies: Its impact to students' engagement, R&D skills, and learning outcomes. *LUMAT: International Journal on Math. Science and Technology Education, 10*(1), 294–318. DOI: 10.31129/LUMAT.10.1.1667

Acut, D. P., Gamusa, E. V., Pernaa, J., Yuenyong, C., Pantaleon, A. T., Espina, R. C., Sim, M. J. C., & Garcia, M. B. (2025). AI Shaming Among Teacher Education Students: A Reflection on Acceptance and Identity in the Age of Generative Tools. In *Pitfalls of AI Integration in Education: Skill Obsolescence, Misuse, and Bias.* IGI Global., DOI: 10.4018/979-8-3373-0122-8.ch005

Acut, D. P., Lobo, J. T., & Garcia, M. B. (2025). Determinants of Teachers' Intentions to Integrate Education for Sustainable Development (ESD) Into Physical Education and Health Curricula. In Garcia, M. B. (Ed.), *Global Innovations in Physical Education and Health* (pp. 439–472). IGI Global., DOI: 10.4018/979-8-3693-3952-7.ch016

Acut, D. P., Malabago, N. K., Malicoban, E. V., Galamiton, N. S., & Garcia, M. B. (2024). "ChatGPT 4.0 Ghosted Us While Conducting Literature Search:" Modeling the Chatbot's Generated Non-Existent References Using Regression Analysis. *Internet Reference Services Quarterly,* •••, 1–26. DOI: 10.1080/10875301.2024.2426793

Adams, R. (2021). Can Artificial Intelligence be Decolonized? *Interdisciplinary Science Reviews, 46*(1-2), 176–197. DOI: 10.1080/03080188.2020.1840225

Aladini, A., Bayat, S., & Abdellatif, M. S. (2024). Performance-Based Assessment in Virtual Versus Non-Virtual Classes: Impacts on Academic Resilience, Motivation, Teacher Support, and Personal Best Goals. *Asian-Pacific Journal of Second and Foreign Language Education, 9*(1), 1–27. DOI: 10.1186/s40862-023-00230-4

Anderson, A., & Johnston, B. (2016). Student Learning and Information Literacy. In A. Anderson & B. Johnston (Eds.), *From Information Literacy to Social Epistemology* (pp. 67-79). Chandos Publishing. DOI: 10.1016/B978-0-08-100545-3.00005-3

Azevedo, A., & Azevedo, J. (Eds.). (2019). *Handbook of Research on E-Assessment in Higher Education.* IGI Global., DOI: 10.4018/978-1-5225-5936-8

Badir, A., O'Neill, R., Kinzli, K.-D., Komisar, S., & Kim, J.-Y. (2023). Fostering Project-Based Learning through Industry Engagement in Capstone Design Projects. *Education Sciences, 13*(4), 1–14. DOI: 10.3390/educsci13040361

Bozkurt, A., Xiao, J., Farrow, R., Bai, J. Y. H., Nerantzi, C., Moore, S., Dron, J., Stracke, C. M., Singh, L., Crompton, H., Koutropoulos, A., Terentev, E., Pazurek, A., Nichols, M., Sidorkin, A. M., Costello, E., Watson, S., Mulligan, D., Honeychurch, S., & Asino, T. I. (2024). The Manifesto for Teaching and Learning in a Time of Generative AI: A Critical Collective Stance to Better Navigate the Future. *Open Praxis, 16*(4), 487–513. DOI: 10.55982/openpraxis.16.4.777

Cacho, R. (2024). Integrating Generative AI in University Teaching and Learning: A Model for Balanced Guidelines. *Online Learning : the Official Journal of the Online Learning Consortium, 28*(3), 1–28. DOI: 10.24059/olj.v28i3.4508

Cheng, L. T. W., Armatas, C. A., & Wang, J. W. (2019). The Impact of Diversity, Prior Academic Achievement and Goal Orientation on Learning Performance in Group Capstone Projects. *Higher Education Research & Development, 39*(5), 913–925. DOI: 10.1080/07294360.2019.1699028

Daft, R. L., & Lengel, R. H. (1986). Organizational Information Requirements, Media Richness and Structural Design. *Management Science, 32*(5), 554–571. DOI: 10.1287/mnsc.32.5.554

Darling-Hammond, L., Flook, L., Cook-Harvey, C., Barron, B., & Osher, D. (2019). Implications for Educational Practice of the Science of Learning and Development. *Applied Developmental Science, 24*(2), 97–140. DOI: 10.1080/10888691.2018.1537791

Diaz, F. C. B., Trinidad, I., Agustin, M. J., Panganiban, T. P., & Garcia, M. B. (2025). Mindfulness For Health and Well-Being: An Innovative Physical Education Course in the University of the Philippines Diliman. In *Global Innovations in Physical Education and Health.* IGI Global., DOI: 10.4018/979-8-3693-3952-7.ch006

Doğan, Y., Yıldırım, N. T., & Batdı, V. (2024). Effectiveness of Portfolio Assessment in Primary Education: A Multi-Complementary Research Approach. *Evaluation and Program Planning, 106,* 1–12. DOI: 10.1016/j.evalprogplan.2024.102461 PMID: 38925046

Gantalao, L. C., Calzada, J. G. D., Capuyan, D. L., Lumantas, B. C., Acut, D. P., & Garcia, M. B. (2025). Equipping the Next Generation of Technicians: Navigating School Infrastructure and Technical Knowledge in the Age of AI Integration. In *Pitfalls of AI Integration in Education: Skill Obsolescence, Misuse, and Bias.* IGI Global., DOI: 10.4018/979-8-3373-0122-8.ch009

Garcia, M. B. (2023). Facilitating Group Learning Using an Apprenticeship Model: Which Master is More Effective in Programming Instruction? *Journal of Educational Computing Research, 61*(6), 1207–1231. DOI: 10.1177/07356331231170382

Garcia, M. B. (2024a). Addressing the Mental Health Implications of ChatGPT Dependency: The Need for Comprehensive Policy Development. *Asian Journal of Psychiatry, 98,* 104140. Advance online publication. DOI: 10.1016/j.ajp.2024.104140 PMID: 38943840

Garcia, M. B. (2024b). The Paradox of Artificial Creativity: Challenges and Opportunities of Generative AI Artistry. *Creativity Research Journal,* ●●●, 1–14. DOI: 10.1080/10400419.2024.2354622

Garcia, M. B. (2025). Teaching and Learning Computer Programming Using ChatGPT: A Rapid Review of Literature Amid the Rise of Generative AI Technologies. *Education and Information Technologies,* ●●●, 1–25. DOI: 10.1007/s10639-025-13452-5

Garcia, M. B., Arif, Y. M., Khlaif, Z. N., Zhu, M., de Almeida, R. P. P., de Almeida, R. S., & Masters, K. (2024). Effective Integration of Artificial Intelligence in Medical Education: Practical Tips and Actionable Insights. In *Transformative Approaches to Patient Literacy and Healthcare Innovation* (pp. 1-19). IGI Global. DOI: 10.4018/979-8-3693-3661-8.ch001

Garcia, M. B., Goi, C. L., Shively, K., Maher, D., Rosak-Szyrocka, J., Happonen, A., Bozkurt, A., & Damaševičius, R. (2025). Understanding Student Engagement in AI-Powered Online Learning Platforms: A Narrative Review of Key Theories and Models. In Gierhart, A. R. (Ed.), *Cases on Enhancing P-16 Student Engagement With Digital Technologies* (pp. 1–30). IGI Global., DOI: 10.4018/979-8-3693-5633-3.ch001

Gikandi, J. W., Morrow, D., & Davis, N. E. (2011). Online Formative Assessment in Higher Education: A Review of the Literature. *Computers & Education*, *57*(4), 2333–2351. DOI: 10.1016/j.compedu.2011.06.004

Gomez-del Rio, T., & Rodriguez, J. (2022). Design and Assessment of a Project-Based Learning in a Laboratory for Integrating Knowledge and Improving Engineering Design Skills. *Education for Chemical Engineers*, *40*, 17–28. DOI: 10.1016/j.ece.2022.04.002

Grapin, S. E. (2023). Assessment of English Learners and Their Peers in the Content Areas: Expanding What "Counts" as Evidence of Content Learning. *Language Assessment Quarterly*, *20*(2), 215–234. DOI: 10.1080/15434303.2022.2147072

Gruenhagen, J. H., Sinclair, P. M., Carroll, J.-A., Baker, P. R. A., Wilson, A., & Demant, D. (2024). The Rapid Rise of Generative AI and Its Implications for Academic Integrity: Students' Perceptions and Use of Chatbots for Assistance With Assessments. *Computers and Education: Artificial Intelligence*, *7*, 1–10. DOI: 10.1016/j.caeai.2024.100273

Hasanah, N. A., Aziza, M. R., Junikhah, A., Arif, Y. M., & Garcia, M. B. (2025). Navigating the Use of AI in Engineering Education Through a Systematic Review of Technology, Regulations, and Challenges. In *Pitfalls of AI Integration in Education: Skill Obsolescence, Misuse, and Bias*. IGI Global., DOI: 10.4018/979-8-3373-0122-8.ch016

Heil, J., & Ifenthaler, D. (2023). Online Assessment in Higher Education: A Systematic Review. *Online Learning : the Official Journal of the Online Learning Consortium*, *27*(1), 187–218. DOI: 10.24059/olj.v27i1.3398

Huang, K.-L., Liu, Y., & Dong, M.-Q. (2024). Incorporating AIGC Into Design Ideation: A Study on Self-Efficacy and Learning Experience Acceptance Under Higher-Order Thinking. *Thinking Skills and Creativity*, *52*, 1–16. DOI: 10.1016/j.tsc.2024.101508

Hulus, A. (2025). A Systematic Review of Educators' Overreliance and Misuse of AI in Student Feedback: Introducing the ETHICAL-FEED Framework. In *Pitfalls of AI Integration in Education: Skill Obsolescence, Misuse, and Bias*. IGI Global., DOI: 10.4018/979-8-3373-0122-8.ch015

Kim, S. C., Covington, B., Benavente, V., & Willson, P. (2019). Capstone Projects As Experiential Evidence-Based Practice Education. *The Journal for Nurse Practitioners*, *15*(3), 51–56. DOI: 10.1016/j.nurpra.2018.12.011

Kiritchenko, S., Nejadgholi, I., & Fraser, K. C. (2021). Confronting Abusive Language Online: A Survey from the Ethical and Human Rights Perspective. *Journal of Artificial Intelligence Research*, *71*, 431–478. DOI: 10.1613/jair.1.12590

Kong, Z. Y., Omar, A. A., Lau, S. L., & Sunarso, J. (2024). Introducing Process Simulation as an Alternative to Laboratory Session in Undergraduate Chemical Engineering Thermodynamics Course: A Case Study From Sunway University Malaysia. *Digital Chemical Engineering, 12*, 1–10. DOI: 10.1016/j.dche.2024.100167

Kovaleva, Y., Happonen, A., Garcia, M. B., & Kasurinen, J. (2024). Female-Inclusive Practices for Software Engineering and Computer Science Higher Education: A Literature Review. *Proceedings of the Annual Doctoral Symposium of Computer Science 2024*. https://doi.org/https://ceur-ws.org/Vol-3776/paper08.pdf

Landfried, M., Chen, E., Savelli, L. B., Cooper, M., Price, B. N., & Emmerling, D. (2023). MPH Capstone experiences: Promising practices and lessons learned. *Frontiers in Public Health, 11*, 1–11. DOI: 10.3389/fpubh.2023.1129330 PMID: 37250082

Lee, V. R., Pope, D., Miles, S., & Zárate, R. C. (2024). Cheating in the Age of Generative AI: A High School Survey Study of Cheating Behaviors Before and After the Release of ChatGPT. *Computers and Education: Artificial Intelligence, 7*, 1–10. DOI: 10.1016/j.caeai.2024.100253

Mangubat, J. C., Mangubat, M. R., Uy, T. B. L., Acut, D. P., & Garcia, M. B. (2025). Safeguarding Educational Innovations Amid AI Disruptions: A Reassessment of Patenting for Sustained Intellectual Property Protection. In *Pitfalls of AI Integration in Education: Skill Obsolescence, Misuse, and Bias*. IGI Global., DOI: 10.4018/979-8-3373-0122-8.ch013

Martínez-Requejo, S., Redondo-Duarte, S., Jiménez-García, E., & Ruiz-Lázaro, J. (2025). Technoethics and the Use of Artificial Intelligence in Educational Contexts: Reflections on Integrity, Transparency, and Equity. In *Pitfalls of AI Integration in Education: Skill Obsolescence, Misuse, and Bias*. IGI Global., DOI: 10.4018/979-8-3373-0122-8.ch010

Miller, J. C., Fernando, E. Q., Miranda, J. P. P., Bansil, J. A., Hernandez, H. E., & Regala, A. R. (2024). Extended Reality Technologies in Physical Fitness for Health Promotion: Insights from Bibliometric Research. In *Emerging Technologies for Health Literacy and Medical Practice*. IGI Global., DOI: 10.4018/979-8-3693-1214-8.ch005

Miranda, J. P. P., Cruz, M. A. D., Fernandez, A. B., Balahadia, F. F., Aviles, J. S., Caro, C. A., Liwanag, I. G., & Gaña, E. P. (2025). Erosion of Critical Academic Skills Due to AI Dependency Among Tertiary Students: A Path Analysis. In *Pitfalls of AI Integration in Education: Skill Obsolescence, Misuse, and Bias*. IGI Global., DOI: 10.4018/979-8-3373-0122-8.ch002

Montenegro-Rueda, M., Luque-de la Rosa, A., Sarasola Sánchez-Serrano, J. L., & Fernández-Cerero, J. (2021). Assessment in Higher Education during the COVID-19 Pandemic: A Systematic Review. *Sustainability (Basel), 13*(19), 1–13. DOI: 10.3390/su131910509

Ofosu-Ampong, K., Acheampong, B., Kevor, M., & Amankwah-Sarfo, F. (2023). Acceptance of Artificial Intelligence (ChatGPT) in Education: Trust, Innovativeness and Psychological Need of Students. *Information and Knowledge Management, 13*(4), 37–47. DOI: 10.7176/IKM/13-4-03

Ofosu-Ampong, K., Agyekum, M. W., & Garcia, M. B. (2024). Long-Term Pandemic Management and the Need to Invest in Digital Transformation: A Resilience Theory Perspective. In *Transformative Approaches to Patient Literacy and Healthcare Innovation* (pp. 242-260). IGI Global. DOI: 10.4018/979-8-3693-3661-8.ch012

Olugbade, D. (2025). A Systematic Review of the Role of AI-Enabled Chatbots in Modern Education: Benefits, Risks, and Implementation Complexity. In *Pitfalls of AI Integration in Education: Skill Obsolescence, Misuse, and Bias*. IGI Global., DOI: 10.4018/979-8-3373-0122-8.ch018

Petil, E. D., Florece, M. E. A., Gomez, M. G. A., Villaruel, K. B., Fernandez, H. G. C. Q., Dela Cruz, C. M. B., & Ferrer-Rafols, R. B. (2025). Virtual Reality in Physical Education: An Innovative Approach to Optimize Physical and Mental Health. In *Global Innovations in Physical Education and Health*. IGI Global., DOI: 10.4018/979-8-3693-3952-7.ch005

Preiksaitis, C., & Rose, C. (2023). Opportunities, Challenges, and Future Directions of Generative Artificial Intelligence in Medical Education: Scoping Review. *JMIR Medical Education*, 9, 1–13. DOI: 10.2196/48785 PMID: 37862079

Revano, T. F., & Garcia, M. B. (2020). Manufacturing Design Thinkers in Higher Education Institutions: The Use of Design Thinking Curriculum in the Education Landscape. *2020 IEEE 12th International Conference on Humanoid, Nanotechnology, Information Technology, Communication and Control, Environment, and Management (HNICEM)*, 1-5. DOI: 10.1109/HNICEM51456.2020.9400034

Riebe, L., Girardi, A., & Whitsed, C. (2016). A Systematic Literature Review of Teamwork Pedagogy in Higher Education. *Small Group Research*, 47(6), 619–664. DOI: 10.1177/1046496416665221

Ryan, M. (2011). Evaluating Portfolio Use as a Tool for Assessment and Professional Development in Graduate Nursing Education. *Journal of Professional Nursing*, 27(2), 84–91. DOI: 10.1016/j.profnurs.2010.09.008 PMID: 21420040

Salinas-Navarro, D. E., Vilalta-Perdomo, E., Michel-Villarreal, R., & Montesinos, L. (2024). Using Generative Artificial Intelligence Tools to Explain and Enhance Experiential Learning for Authentic Assessment. *Education Sciences*, 14(1), 1–24. DOI: 10.3390/educsci14010083

See, B. H., Gorard, S., Lu, B., Dong, L., & Siddiqui, N. (2022). Is Technology Always Helpful?: A Critical Review of the Impact on Learning Outcomes of Education Technology in Supporting Formative Assessment in Schools. *Research Papers in Education*, 37(6), 1064–1096. DOI: 10.1080/02671522.2021.1907778

Slack, H. R., & Priestley, M. (2023). Online Learning and Assessment During the COVID-19 Pandemic: Exploring the Impact on Undergraduate Student Well-Being. *Assessment & Evaluation in Higher Education*, 48(3), 333–349. DOI: 10.1080/02602938.2022.2076804

Slavinska, A., Palkova, K., Grigoroviča, E., Edelmers, E., & Pētersons, A. (2024). Narrative Review of Legal Aspects in the Integration of Simulation-Based Education into Medical and Healthcare Curricula. *Laws*, 13(2), 1–20. DOI: 10.3390/laws13020015

Stephenson, S., Rogers, O., Ivy, C., Barron, R., & Burke, J. (2020). Designing Effective Capstone Experiences and Projects for Entry-Level Doctoral Students in Occupational Therapy: One Program's Approaches and Lessons Learned. *The Open Journal of Occupational Therapy*, 8(3), 1–12. DOI: 10.15453/2168-6408.1727 PMID: 33552752

Swiecki, Z., Khosravi, H., Chen, G., Martinez-Maldonado, R., Lodge, J. M., Milligan, S., Selwyn, N., & Gašević, D. (2022). Assessment in the Age of Artificial Intelligence. *Computers and Education: Artificial Intelligence*, 3, 1–10. DOI: 10.1016/j.caeai.2022.100075

Taneja, D., Prabagaren, H., & Thomas, M. R. (2025). AI in Academia: Balancing Integrity, Ethics, and Learning Amid Evolving Norms of Authorship and Scholarship. In *Pitfalls of AI Integration in Education: Skill Obsolescence, Misuse, and Bias*. IGI Global., DOI: 10.4018/979-8-3373-0122-8.ch014

Tenhunen, S., Männistö, T., Luukkainen, M., & Ihantola, P. (2023). A Systematic Literature Review of Capstone Courses in Software Engineering. *Information and Software Technology*, 159, 1–21. DOI: 10.1016/j.infsof.2023.107191

Topping, K. J., Gehringer, E., Khosravi, H., Gudipati, S., Jadhav, K., & Susarla, S. (2025). Enhancing Peer Assessment with Artificial Intelligence. *International Journal of Educational Technology in Higher Education*, 22(1), 1–33. DOI: 10.1186/s41239-024-00501-1

Valderama, A. M., Tuazon, J. B., & Garcia, M. B. (2022). Promoting Student Thinking and Engagement Through Question-Based and Gamified Learning. *2022 IEEE 14th International Conference on Humanoid, Nanotechnology, Information Technology, Communication and Control, Environment and Management (HNICEM)*. DOI: 10.1109/HNICEM57413.2022.10109470

Walter, Y. (2024). Embracing the Future of Artificial Intelligence in the Classroom: The Relevance of Ai Literacy, Prompt Engineering, and Critical Thinking in Modern Education. *International Journal of Educational Technology in Higher Education*, 21(1), 1–29. DOI: 10.1186/s41239-024-00448-3

Xiao, J., Bozkurt, A., Nichols, M., Pazurek, A., Stracke, C. M., Bai, J. Y. H., Farrow, R., Mulligan, D., Nerantzi, C., Sharma, R. C., Singh, L., Frumin, I., Swindell, A., Honeychurch, S., Bond, M., Dron, J., Moore, S., Leng, J., & Slagter van Tryon, P. J.. (2025). Venturing into the Unknown: Critical Insights into Grey Areas and Pioneering Future Directions in Educational Generative AI Research. *TechTrends*, •••, 1–16. DOI: 10.1007/s11528-025-01060-6

Yilmaz, R., & Karaoglan Yilmaz, F. G. (2023). The Effect of Generative Artificial Intelligence (AI)-Based Tool Use on Students' Computational Thinking Skills, Programming Self-Efficacy and Motivation. *Computers and Education: Artificial Intelligence*, 4, 1–14. DOI: 10.1016/j.caeai.2023.100147

KEY TERMS AND DEFINITIONS

Educational Assessment: The systematic process of evaluating student learning, skills, and performance through various tools and methods to measure educational outcomes.

Academic Dishonesty: The act of cheating, plagiarism, or misrepresenting one's own work in an academic setting to gain an unfair advantage.

Artificial Intelligence: A field of computer science focused on creating systems capable of performing tasks that typically require human intelligence.

Generative AI: A type of artificial intelligence that can generate new content, such as text, images, or audio, based on the data it has been trained on.

Technology-Enhanced Assessment: The use of digital tools, such as e-assessments and online platform.

Chapter 2
Erosion of Critical Academic Skills Due to AI Dependency Among Tertiary Students:
A Path Analysis

John Paul P. Miranda
https://orcid.org/0000-0003-2059-972X

Don Honorio Ventura State University, Philippines

Maria Anna D. Cruz
https://orcid.org/0009-0007-3602-1507

Don Honorio Ventura State University, Philippines

Antonia B. Fernandez
https://orcid.org/0000-0002-1322-8333

Don Honorio Ventura State University, Philippines

Francis F. Balahadia
https://orcid.org/0000-0001-6666-4975

Laguna State Polytechnic University, Philippines

Joey S. Aviles
https://orcid.org/0000-0002-7818-014X

Angeles University Foundation, Philippines

Carisma A. Caro
https://orcid.org/0009-0005-5577-6679

Holy Angel University, Philippines

Ivan G. Liwanag
https://orcid.org/0009-0005-0929-5583

Don Honorio Ventura State University, Philippines

Elizabeth P. Gaña
https://orcid.org/0009-0001-8248-4525

Don Honorio Ventura State University, Philippines

ABSTRACT

This chapter investigates the perceived erosion of critical academic skills among 745 university students due to dependency on AI tools. The survey measured six key constructs: AI Dependency (AID), Cognitive Offloading (CO), Motivational Decline (MD), Academic Skills Erosion (ASE), Academic Integrity Awareness (AIA), and External Pressures (EP), using a five-point Likert scale. Path Analysis was employed to examine the interrelationships among these constructs. The results revealed a strong positive relationship between AID and both CO and MD, which indicated that the increased reliance on AI leads to reduced cognitive engagement and diminished academic motivation. Additionally, CO and MD were positively associated with ASE, which means that students who offload cognitive tasks and

DOI: 10.4018/979-8-3373-0122-8.ch002

experience MD are more likely to exhibit deteriorating academic skills. While AIA had a weak negative relationship with AID, EP showed a moderate positive association and highlighted the role of academic stress in driving AI reliance.

INTRODUCTION

Artificial Intelligence (AI) has evolved from simple rule-based systems to sophisticated machine learning models, particularly deep learning. The widespread use of AI-driven tools such as ChatGPT, Grammarly, and Microsoft Copilot has reshaped how students approach academic work (Kelly, 2024). These tools streamline tasks like information retrieval, text generation, paraphrasing, and coding, improving accessibility and efficiency. However, growing dependency on AI raises pressing concerns about its impact on students' cognitive and academic development (Çela et al., 2024).

Despite the benefits of AI in education, its widespread adoption also presents significant challenges that warrant closer examination. AI is often portrayed as a solution to outdated pedagogical methods, but its educational applications present fundamental challenges (Hasanah et al., 2025; Izquierdo-Álvarez & Jimeno-Postigo, 2025). Rather than merely correlating AI use with skill erosion, it is necessary to investigate the ways AI might be undermining students' learning processes. Automating complex academic tasks can reduce the need for critical thinking and problem-solving, which can make students overly dependent on AI-generated solutions (Fan et al., 2024). Instead of fostering deeper engagement, AI tools may discourage students from actively processing information. Additionally, AI's increasing role in academic tasks raises concerns about whether it truly enhances learning or merely enables task completion with minimal cognitive effort (Basha, 2024).

These cognitive challenges intersect with ethical concerns surrounding AI-generated content (Acut et al., 2025), which challenges academic integrity. While AI's role in plagiarism is frequently cited, the ethical dilemmas extend beyond unauthorized content reproduction to issues of authorship, originality, and accountability (Bin-Nashwan et al., 2023; Perkins, 2023; Zhai et al., 2024). AI-generated content blurs the distinction between human and machine-produced work, challenging traditional understandings of intellectual contribution. Without clear ethical guidelines, students may, by chance, commit academic misconduct (Tang & Su, 2024). Educational institutions must address these gaps by establishing policies that emphasize transparency, fairness, and responsible AI usage (Afshan Bibi et al., 2024; Al-Zahrani, 2024).

Significantly, AI's impact on student motivation also requires further scrutiny. While some studies highlight its negative impact, such as decreased effort and engagement in problem-solving, AI can also enhance motivation by reducing frustration with difficult subjects (von Garrel & Mayer, 2024). AI tools can provide immediate support, boost confidence, and encourage students who struggle with conventional learning methods. However, easy access to AI-generated solutions can lead to disengagement, particularly when students bypass essential cognitive processes that are vital for skill acquisition. Understanding the conditions under which AI fosters motivation versus when it hinders effort is critical in evaluating its role in education (S. Huang et al., 2024).

Given these concerns, this study examines the extent to which AI dependency contributes to the erosion of critical academic skills among university students. Using path analysis, this research explores the relationship between AI dependency and key academic competencies to provide insights into how AI affects students' cognitive and academic development in higher education. By analyzing these dynamics, the study contributes to ongoing discussions about AI's role in education, particularly its benefits and potential risks.

MAIN FOCUS OF THE CHAPTER

This chapter examines the critical role of academic skills, such as critical thinking, creativity, problem-solving, self-regulation, and effective communication, in tertiary education and lifelong learning. The rapid integration of generative AI into educational practices has introduced significant changes in how students engage with learning (Gruenhagen et al., 2024; Kurtz et al., 2024). While AI tools offer benefits like enhanced efficiency and access to resources, there is growing concern that over-reliance on these tools may contribute to the erosion of essential academic skills. This issue becomes particularly evident as students increasingly depend on AI to perform cognitive tasks that traditionally require deep mental engagement and intellectual effort. Specifically, the primary concern is the phenomenon of cognitive offloading (Risko & Gilbert, 2016), where students rely on AI for information analysis, content creation, and problem-solving, potentially reducing their mental effort and limiting opportunities for critical thinking and higher-order cognitive development (Gerlich, 2025). Additionally, this dependence on AI may lead to a motivational decline, diminishing students' intrinsic motivation, persistence, and engagement in independent learning (Alasgarova & Rzayev, 2024). Over time, these cognitive and motivational shifts can contribute to the erosion of academic skills, weakening students' capacity for intellectual growth, reflective thinking, and self-regulated learning (Dergaa et al., 2024; George et al., 2024; Zhai et al., 2024). Furthermore, factors such as academic integrity awareness and external pressures play crucial roles in shaping students' AI dependency (Mustofa et al., 2025; Perkins, 2023; Ray, 2023; Zhang et al., 2024). Students with higher academic integrity awareness may be less likely to over-rely on AI, while external academic demands may increase such dependency. Despite the growing adoption of generative AI in education (Chen et al., 2025; Gruenhagen et al., 2024; Ivanov et al., 2024; Yusuf et al., 2024), there is a notable lack of empirical research exploring its long-term cognitive, motivational, and ethical implications. Existing studies predominantly focus on the technological advantages of AI, with insufficient attention given to how AI dependency interacts with these psychological and academic factors (Yan & Liu, 2024; Zhang et al., 2024).

This chapter aims to address this gap by investigating the complex pathways through which AI dependency influences cognitive offloading, motivational decline, and, ultimately, academic skills erosion among tertiary students. By examining the moderating role of academic integrity awareness and the influence of external pressures, the chapter seeks to inform educational strategies that promote responsible AI usage, support cognitive and ethical development, and safeguard the integrity of academic practices in an increasingly digitalized learning environment. This concern is deemed important in the Philippine educational context, where the rapid adoption of digital technologies in higher education has outpaced the development of comprehensive digital literacy programs. With limited access to academic integrity tools and inconsistent institutional support for AI ethics, Filipino students face unique challenges in navigating AI's role in their academic lives. Understanding these dynamics is crucial for developing culturally responsive policies and pedagogical practices that strengthen academic resilience and integrity in Philippine higher education.

Research Model and Hypotheses

As shown in Figure 1, the hypothesized path analysis model illustrates the relationships between AI Dependency, Academic Skills Erosion, and key influencing factors. In this model, AI Dependency is influenced negatively by Academic Integrity Awareness which suggests that students with higher ethical awareness are less likely to rely heavily on AI tools, while External Pressures are expected to have a positive association and indicates academic demands may increase AI reliance. AI Dependency directly affects Cognitive Offloading and Motivational Decline, where increased reliance on AI tools can lead to reduced cognitive engagement and decreased intrinsic motivation for academic tasks. Both Cognitive Offloading and Motivational Decline are hypothesized to contribute to Academic Skills Erosion which represents the decline in critical academic competencies.

Figure 1. Hypothesis path analysis model

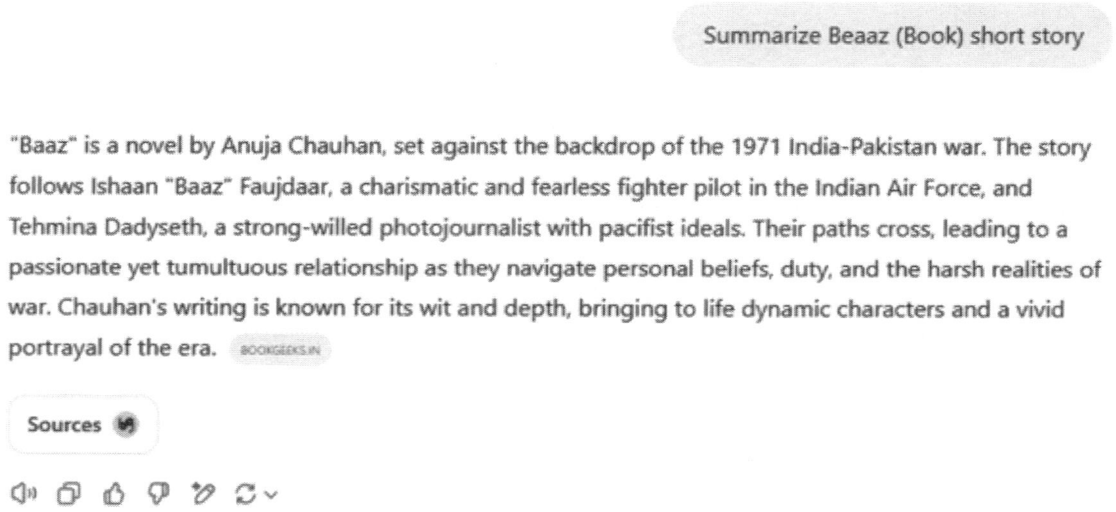

Summarize Beaaz (Book) short story

"Baaz" is a novel by Anuja Chauhan, set against the backdrop of the 1971 India-Pakistan war. The story follows Ishaan "Baaz" Faujdaar, a charismatic and fearless fighter pilot in the Indian Air Force, and Tehmina Dadyseth, a strong-willed photojournalist with pacifist ideals. Their paths cross, leading to a passionate yet tumultuous relationship as they navigate personal beliefs, duty, and the harsh realities of war. Chauhan's writing is known for its wit and depth, bringing to life dynamic characters and a vivid portrayal of the era. BOOKGEEKS.IN

Sources

Academic Integrity Awareness and AI Dependency

Academic integrity awareness, defined as students' understanding of ethical principles such as honesty, originality, and the responsible use of external resources, plays a crucial role in shaping students' academic behaviors, particularly in the context of emerging technologies like AI. It fosters a commitment to academic honesty and encouraged students to engage critically and responsibly with AI tools. Research consistently highlights that students with high academic integrity awareness demonstrate independent thinking and distinct protective factors of AI usage compared to their peers and they tend to exhibit greater autonomy and less reliance on AI for academic tasks (Chiu, 2024; Gerlich, 2025; Tamrin et al., 2024).

This suggests that academic integrity awareness does not merely coexist with AI usage behaviors but actively influences the extent to which students depend on AI. Ethical considerations, such as understanding the biases inherent in AI-generated content and recognizing the value of original thought, promote more thoughtful engagement with these tools while safeguarding students' cognitive autonomy (Nguyen et al., 2024; Zhong et al., 2024). Further empirical evidence reinforces this perspective. Perkins (Perkins, 2023) and Gustilo et al. (2024) explored how students' adherence to academic integrity principles significantly shapes their AI usage behaviors. Their studies indicated that students with higher academic integrity awareness tend to engage with AI tools more ethically and critically which can lead to reduced dependency. Similarly, Ateeq et al. (Ateeq et al., 2024) highlighted how awareness of academic integrity can mitigate the negative effects of AI dependency on students' writing skills, while Bin-Nashwan et al. (Bin-Nashwan et al., 2023) demonstrated that students with stronger ethical foundations are less likely to over-rely on AI for academic outputs. Additionally, Gruenhagen et al. (Gruenhagen et al., 2024) emphasized the rise of academic misconduct linked to AI tools which shows the critical role of integrity awareness in counteracting this trend (Birks & Clare, 2023; Hua, 2023; Rodrigues et al., 2024). These studies collectively suggest that academic integrity awareness may act as a deterrent to excessive AI dependency and may foster academic resilience and skill retention. With these, it is reasonable to propose that academic integrity awareness may also be negatively associated with AI dependency.

Hypothesis 1 (H1): Academic Integrity Awareness is negatively associated with AI Dependency

External Pressures and AI Dependency

External pressures, such as academic workload, performance expectations, and time constraints, have been consistently linked to increased reliance on AI tools in educational settings. When faced with high academic demands, deadlines, and stress of maintaining academic performance, students seek efficient strategies to manage their workload which make AI tools particularly appealing due to their ability to provide quick and accessible solutions (Zhang et al., 2024; Zhong et al., 2024). Studies suggest that these pressures not only increase the frequency of AI tool usage but also contribute to a growing dependency on such technologies (Huang et al., 2024). Moreover, academic pressures can exacerbate mental health challenges, such as stress and anxiety, which have been shown to predict higher levels of AI dependence among students (Zhai et al., 2024). Students experiencing immense workloads are more likely to offload cognitive tasks to AI which can reduce the opportunities for students to improve their critical thinking and independent problem-solving. Multifactorial analyses highlighted that situational factor, mainly workload intensity, competitive academic environments, and strict time constraints can significantly influence students' adoption of and dependence on AI technologies (Klimova & Pikhart, 2025; Shengelia et al., 2024). While some studies indicated that AI use may temporarily alleviate academic stress by improving efficiency (Shahzad et al., 2024), the long-term consequence is often an overreliance on AI and may undermine students' capacity for self-regulated learning and academic resilience. Given this body of evidence, external pressures are identified as a key driver of AI dependency as students increasingly turn to AI as a coping mechanism to manage academic demands. Thus:

Hypothesis 2 (H2): External Pressures are positively associated with AI Dependency.

AI Dependency and Cognitive Offloading

Cognitive offloading occurs when individuals shift cognitive tasks to external aids to reduce mental effort (Gerlich, 2025). Cognitive Load Theory (CLT) suggests that working memory is limited and students often like to use tools that simplify complex tasks. Traditionally, aids like handwritten notes, calculators, and search engines helped manage cognitive demands. However, AI-powered tools such as chatbots, automated problem solvers, and content generators have reshaped academic engagement by externalizing cognitive processes (Gerlich, 2025). In AI-context, cognitive offloading operates in three primary ways. First, AI can streamline cognitive tasks by providing direct answers which reduces the need for deep engagement with learning materials. Second, automation can diminish reliance on memory as students store and retrieve information digitally instead of internalizing concepts. Third, AI may encourage passive learning which provides instant solutions that discourage problem-solving, hypothesis testing, and critical thinking skills for academic growth.

Research supports the link between AI use and increased cognitive offloading. Grinschgl and Neubauer (2022) found that frequent AI interaction leads to greater reliance on external systems, reducing engagement in active learning. Dergaa et al. (2024) cautioned against AI-induced cognitive atrophy, where habitual AI use weakens problem-solving abilities. Similarly, Armitage and Gilbert (2024) observed that early exposure to AI-powered educational tools can impede independent reasoning and analytical skills, potentially hindering long-term intellectual development. The shift toward shallow cognitive processing is another key concern. Gonsalves (2024) found that AI fosters surface-level learning, where students prioritize quick answers over critical analysis. Nizamani et al. (2024) highlighted AI's role in psychological dependency, reinforcing habitual reliance on AI for intellectual tasks. Gerlich (2025) reported that increased AI use correlates with reduced internal cognitive processing, particularly in higher-order thinking tasks like content synthesis and argument evaluation. This habitual offloading has major consequences for critical thinking, independent learning, problem-solving, and analytical reasoning. AI-generated summaries reduce the need for deep reading and synthesis, weakening comprehension and original argument construction. Automated problem-solving tools eliminate trial-and-error learning, undermining resilience and self-regulation. Over time, reliance on AI may erode students' ability to engage in complex intellectual tasks without external support, limiting their capacity for independent inquiry and academic growth. Thus, this study investigates how AI dependency fosters cognitive offloading and its impact on academic skill development. Based on this framework, the following hypothesis is proposed:

Hypothesis 3 (H3): AI Dependency is positively associated with Cognitive Offloading.

AI Dependency and Motivational Decline

Motivational decline is the progressive reduction in a learner's drive to engage in academic tasks, particularly when intrinsic motivation weakens over time. According to Self-Determination Theory (SDT), intrinsic motivation is driven by the fulfillment of three core psychological needs: autonomy, competence, and relatedness (Manninen et al., 2022). When these needs are undermined, students experience lower engagement, reduced effort, and a diminished sense of self-regulation. In the context of AI-driven learning, increasing reliance on AI tools may disrupt the development of these essential competencies, leading to a decline in students' intrinsic motivation. Moreover, the psychological factors contributing to motivational decline include loss of autonomy, reduced cognitive effort, and diminished self-efficacy (Bandhu et al., 2024). Autonomy decreases when students become dependent on AI tools for decision-making, problem-solving, and content generation rather than actively engaging with learning materials. Reduced cognitive effort occurs when AI provides immediate solutions which may discourage students from engaging in deep, sustained learning (Bandhu et al., 2024). Self-efficacy weakens as students feel less capable of completing tasks independently which may lead to dependency on AI as a primary academic support rather than a supplementary tool (Zhang et al., 2024).

Empirical research highlights the negative impact of AI dependency on motivation. Chiu (2024) and Zhang et al. (2024) found that students who rely heavily on AI tools experience reduced self-regulation and motivation due to diminished cognitive engagement and lower autonomy in learning processes. Studies on ChatGPT usage among university students revealed that AI dependency correlates with decreased self-efficacy and heightened academic stress, both of which negatively affect motivation and self-regulation (Zhang et al., 2024; Zhong et al., 2024). Fan et al. (2024) found that while AI technologies like ChatGPT provide quick solutions, they promote metacognitive laziness, reducing students' willingness to engage deeply in learning and hindering the development of self-regulated learning strategies (Nguyen et al., 2024). Further research supports these concerns. Wei (2023) demonstrated that although AI-assisted instruction initially improved academic performance, it was associated with a long-term decline in motivation and the use of effective learning strategies. Expanding on this, Huang et al. (2024) found that excessive reliance on AI tools fosters psychological dependence, negatively affecting motivation and contributing to mental health challenges such as academic burnout and reduced resilience. Similarly, Sardi et al. (2025) concluded that while AI tools support academic tasks, overreliance diminishes students' intrinsic motivation to develop independent learning and self-regulation skills. This pattern is particularly pronounced among students with low academic self-efficacy, who may turn to AI as a coping mechanism to manage academic pressures which reinforces a cycle of dependency and motivational decline (Zhang et al., 2024; Zhong et al., 2024).

The evidence suggests that while AI enhances efficiency and offers immediate academic support, its overuse undermines the psychological needs that SDT identifies as essential for sustained motivation. By reducing the necessity for effortful learning, AI dependency weakens students' sense of competence, autonomy, and intrinsic motivation, potentially leading to long-term motivational decline. Based on these theoretical foundations and empirical findings, the following hypothesis is proposed:

Hypothesis 4 (H4): AI Dependency is positively associated with Motivational Decline.

Cognitive Offloading and Academic Skills Erosion

The relationship between cognitive offloading and academic skill deterioration has emerged as a critical concern in educational research. Studies demonstrated that when students increasingly delegate cognitive tasks to AI systems, they systematically reduce their mental engagement with academic challenges (Grinschgl & Neubauer, 2022). This diminished engagement manifests in measurable outcomes: students who frequently utilize AI for cognitive offloading exhibit significantly lower critical thinking abilities and decreased academic performance over time (Tamrin et al., 2024). Earlier research by George et al. (George et al., 2024) provides compelling evidence for this trend, finding that individuals exert up to 20% less effort on common daily tasks compared to counterparts eight years prior and can increase potential reliance on technology over individual cognitive ability. Their research further indicates that decreased cognitive exertion can lead to weaker neural connections over time which may result in declines in higher-order cognitive skills essential for academic performance. Multiple studies have established a direct correlation between AI-based cognitive offloading and the erosion of core academic competencies including analytical reasoning, creativity, and problem-solving skills (Gerlich, 2025; Tamrin et al., 2024). These studies collectively support the following hypothesis:

Hypothesis 5 (H5): Cognitive Offloading is positively associated with Academic Skills Erosion.

Motivational Decline and Academic Skills Erosion

Studies have also revealed a significant relationship between AI dependency and student motivation in academic settings (Chiu, 2024; Zhang et al., 2024). Studies show that students experiencing motivation decline due to AI dependency demonstrate decreased engagement with learning materials and reduced effort in skill development (Jin et al., 2023). Self-regulated learning (SRL) research provides additional support for this relationship. In SLR, it shows that students with diminished motivation exhibit markedly reduced participation in deep learning activities and may lead to deteriorating academic performance (Chiu, 2024). This is shown in ChatGPT usage studies, where researchers found that students with declining motivation increasingly resort to AI for quick solutions rather than engaging in substantive academic inquiry (Zhang et al., 2024; Zhong et al., 2024). This pattern is further supported by broader educational research, with Cohen et al. (2022) finding that students' adaptive motivation tends to decrease over time and can reduce engagement and lower academic performance, while Yusof et al. (2023) established clear links between decreased motivation, increased burnout, and deteriorating academic skills.

The impact of motivational decline on academic performance has been extensively documented across various contexts. Lopez and Tadros (2023) highlighted how educational disruptions during the COVID-19 pandemic negatively impacted student motivation and learning outcomes, while Lo et al. (2022) found that lower motivation levels were directly linked to diminished cognitive learning. Wang et al. (2024) further reinforced these findings by demonstrating that students with declining intrinsic motivation exhibited lower engagement levels which may lead to deterioration in academic skills over time. The cumulative evidence demonstrates a clear pattern: as student motivation decreases due to AI dependency, there is a corresponding erosion of essential academic skills, including critical thinking, analysis, and problem-solving capabilities. This substantial body of research, spanning both traditional educational contexts and emerging AI-influenced learning environments, provides strong support for the following hypothesis:

Hypothesis 6 (H6): Motivational Decline is positively associated with Academic Skills Erosion.

METHODOLOGY

This study utilized a quantitative research design, employing Path Analysis to investigate the inter-relationships among six key constructs: AI Dependency, Cognitive Offloading, Motivational Decline, Academic Skills Erosion, Academic Integrity Awareness, and External Pressures. Data were collected from a random sample of 745 university students through self-administered questionnaires distributed via Google Forms. The survey consisted of two sections: demographic information and 27 items measuring the constructs, all rated on a five-point Likert scale (1 = "strongly disagree" to 5 = "strongly agree").

The instrument used in this study was developed based on an extensive review of existing literature to ensure content validity and theoretical alignment. Each construct was measured using a set of items specifically designed to capture the key dimensions of the variables. AI Dependency was assessed through five items reflecting the frequency and extent of AI tool usage. Cognitive Offloading included four items measuring reliance on AI for cognitive tasks. Motivational decline were evaluated using five items focused on changes in academic motivation and self-management behaviors. Academic Skills Erosion was measured through five items addressing perceived declines in critical thinking, writing, and problem-solving skills. Academic Integrity Awareness was assessed using four items related to students' ethical considerations when using AI tools. Lastly, External Pressures were captured through three items focusing on academic stress, workload, and deadlines.

The data analysis process comprised several sequential procedures to ensure the reliability and validity of the results. All analyses, including descriptive statistics, reliability testing, and correlation analysis, were conducted in Jupyter Notebook utilizing Python libraries such as *pandas*, *numpy*, and *semopy* to summarize key data characteristics and assess initial relationships among variables. Subsequently, Path Analysis was performed within the same environment using the *semopy* library. The significance of relationships between constructs was evaluated through path coefficients, along with their corresponding standard errors, z-values, and p-values to determine statistical significance. Internal consistency reliability was assessed using both Cronbach's alpha with thresholds set at ≥ 0.70 to indicate acceptable reliability. Model fit was evaluated using multiple goodness-of-fit indices including the Chi-square statistic (χ^2), Comparative Fit Index (CFI), Tucker-Lewis Index (TLI), and Root Mean Square Error of Approximation (RMSEA). The criteria for acceptable model fit adhered to established guidelines, with CFI and TLI values ≥ 0.90 indicating good fit, Root Mean Square Error of Approximation (RMSEA) values ≤ 0.08 suggesting reasonable fit, and non-significant Chi-square values ($p > 0.05$) preferred.

Respondents

Table 1 presents the demographic characteristics of the 745 respondents who participated in the study. The average age of the participants was 20 years old (SD = 1.93). In terms of gender distribution, the majority were female (56%, n = 417), followed by male respondents (40.3%, n = 300), and a smaller proportion identified as others (3.8%, n = 28). Regarding the type of school attended, most respondents were from public institutions (56.5%, n = 421), while the remaining 43.5% (n = 324) were enrolled in private schools. The distribution across year levels showed that 3rd-year students made up the largest group (43.1%, n = 321), followed by 1st-year students (34.6%, n = 258), 2nd-year students (12.6%, n = 94), and 4th-year students (9.6%, n = 72). A significant majority of the respondents were classified as regular students (94.6%, n = 705), with only 5.4% (n = 40) identified as irregular students. When examining academic performance, more than half of the respondents rated themselves as performing good academically (58%, n = 432), while 29.3% (n = 218) reported an average performance. Excellent performers accounted for 11.8% (n = 88), whereas a very small number indicated below average (0.8%, n = 6) and poor performance (0.1%, n = 1). Regarding internet access, the majority of students reported having good connectivity (55.2%, n = 411), while others rated their access as fair (26.6%, n = 198) or excellent (10.3%, n = 77). A minority experienced poor (6%, n = 45) or very poor (1.9%, n = 14) access. In terms of proficiency in digital and online tools, most respondents considered themselves at an intermediate level (52.5%, n = 391), with others identifying as advanced (24.2%, n = 180), beginners (20.5%, n = 153), and a small portion as experts (2.8%, n = 21). When asked about their comfort level with integrating AI into their learning process, the largest proportion felt neither (50.9%, n = 397), while 41.3% (n = 308) reported being comfortable, and 3.4% (n = 25) felt very comfortable. A minority expressed discomfort, with 2.7% (n = 20) being very uncomfortable and 1.7% (n = 13) uncomfortable. Lastly, regarding the use of generative AI (GenAI) tools for academic tasks, the majority used them occasionally (36.2%, n = 270), followed by those who used them rarely (31.8%, n = 237), frequently (28.1%, n = 209), and very frequently (3.9%, n = 29).

Table 1. Demographic profile

Items	Description	N	%
Age (mean ± SD)	20.25 ± 1.925	745	100
Gender	Male	300	40.3
	Female	417	56
	Others	28	3.8
School	Public	421	56.5
	Private	324	43.5
Year level	1st year	258	34.6
	2nd year	94	12.6
	3rd year	321	43.1
	4th year	72	9.6
Academic status	Regular	705	94.6
	Irregular	40	5.4
Overall academic performance	Poor	1	0.1
	Below average	6	0.8
	Average	218	29.3
	Good	432	58
	Excellent	88	11.8
Internet access	Very poor	14	1.9
	Poor	45	6
	Fair	198	26.6
	Good	411	55.2
	Excellent	77	10.3
Proficiency in digital and online tools	Beginner	153	20.5
	Intermediate	391	52.5
	Advanced	180	24.2
	Expert	21	2.8
Comfortability of using AI into learning process	Very uncomfortable	20	2.7
	Uncomfortable	13	1.7
	Neither	397	50.9
	Comfortable	308	41.3
	Very comfortable	25	3.4
Use of GenAI tools for academic tasks	Rarely	237	31.8
	Occasionally	270	36.2
	Frequently	209	28.1
	Very frequently	29	3.9

RESULTS

Table 2 shows the descriptive statistics of the items. In terms of AI Dependency, students reported frequent use of AI tools to assist with academic assignments (M = 3.39, SD = 0.85) which indicates a high level of engagement with AI in their academic work. Moderate agreement was observed regarding the regular use of AI applications as part of their study routines (M = 3.10, SD = 0.93) and reliance on AI for researching information for assignments (M = 3.15, SD = 0.91). However, reliance on AI for completing most coursework (M = 2.81, SD = 0.99) and drafting written assignments (M = 2.79, SD = 0.98) was lower which means that while students value AI support, they maintain a preference for independent academic work. Regarding Cognitive Offloading, students showed moderate perceptions about the accuracy of AI-generated information (M = 2.81, SD = 0.96). This shows a neutral stance with some reservations about fully trusting AI outputs. The tendency to accept AI-generated answers without critical evaluation was relatively low (M = 2.60, SD = 1.00) which indicates students generally maintain a critical approach when reviewing AI-generated content. Students moderately agreed that their ability to analyze information may have diminished due to AI dependence (M = 2.74, SD = 0.96), while reliance on AI-generated solutions instead of developing their own responses was also moderate (M = 2.70, SD = 0.96) which reflect an ongoing effort by them to engage in independent problem-solving despite AI usage.

In terms of Academic Skills Erosion, students expressed neutral to moderate agreement with statements about AI's potential impact on their academic abilities. They reported mixed perceptions regarding the influence of AI on their writing skills (M = 2.72, SD = 1.00) and the ability to communicate ideas without AI assistance (M = 2.75, SD = 1.03). Concerns about reduced creative thinking due to AI reliance were slightly more pronounced (M = 2.84, SD = 0.99), alongside moderate agreement that critical evaluation skills have weakened because of AI use (M = 2.77, SD = 0.96) and challenges in generating original ideas without AI support (M = 2.79, SD = 0.97). For Motivational Decline, students reported moderate agreement that they rarely reflect on their learning process due to the quick answers provided by AI (M = 2.76, SD = 0.97) and that motivation for self-directed learning has decreased (M = 2.72, SD = 0.98), with a notable tendency towards procrastination because of AI availability (M = 2.90, SD = 0.99). In the area of Academic Integrity Awareness, students generally considered the ethical implications of using AI (M = 3.44, SD = 0.86), demonstrated strong awareness of academic dishonesty risks (M = 3.59, SD = 0.89), and expressed accountability for AI-generated content (M = 3.55, SD = 0.86). Lastly, regarding External Pressures, students moderately agreed that academic demands (M = 3.00, SD = 0.94), tight deadlines (M = 3.18, S. D = 0.91), and academic stress (M = 3.10, SD = 0.91) influence their reliance on AI tools.

Table 2. Descriptive statistics

Item		M	SD
AID1	I frequently utilize AI tools to assist with my academic assignments.	3.39	0.85
AID2	AI applications are a regular part of my study routine.	3.10	0.93
AID3	I depend on AI technologies for completing most of my coursework.	2.81	0.99
AID4	I rely on AI for researching information for my assignments.	3.15	0.91
AID5	I depend on AI to draft my written assignments.	2.79	0.99
CO1	I believe AI-generated information is always accurate.	2.81	0.96
CO2	I often accept AI-generated answers without critically evaluating them.	2.60	1.01
CO3	My ability to analyze information has diminished due to dependence on AI.	2.74	0.96
CO4	I rely on AI-generated solutions rather than developing my own.	2.70	0.96
ASE1	My writing skills have not improved because I use AI to write for me.	2.72	1.00
ASE2	I find it challenging to communicate my ideas without AI assistance.	2.75	1.03

continued on following page

Table 2. Continued

Item		M	SD
ASE3	Using AI has reduced my ability to think creatively.	2.84	1.00
ASE4	My ability to critically evaluate information has weakened due to AI use.	2.77	0.96
ASE5	I struggle to produce original ideas without the help of AI.	2.79	0.97
MD1	I rarely reflect on my learning process because AI provides quick answers.	2.76	0.97
MD2	My motivation for self-directed learning has decreased due to AI availability.	2.72	0.98
MD3	I am less persistent in challenging tasks because AI offers quick solutions.	2.86	0.94
MD4	I tend to give up easily, knowing AI can handle tough assignments.	2.72	0.99
MD5	AI tools have made me more prone to procrastination.	2.90	0.99
AIA1	I consider the ethical implications before using AI in my work	3.44	0.86
AIA2	I am aware of the potential for academic dishonesty when using AI tools.	3.59	0.89
AIA3	I reflect on whether my AI usage aligns with academic integrity standards.	3.45	0.87
AIA4	I hold myself accountable for any AI-generated content I submit.	3.55	0.86
EP1	High academic demands lead me to rely more on AI tools.	3.00	0.94
EP2	I turn to AI to cope with tight deadlines and heavy workloads.	3.18	0.91
EP3	Academic stress increases my dependence on AI for completing tasks.	3.10	0.92

Path Analysis

The reliability analysis showed strong internal consistency for all constructs. Motivational Decline (α = 0.915), Academic Skills Erosion (α = 0.911), Academic Integrity Awareness (α = 0.906), and External Pressures (α = 0.901) exhibited excellent internal consistency, while AI Dependency (α = 0.875) and Cognitive Offloading (α = 0.864) demonstrated good internal consistency. For the path analysis (Table 3), a strong positive relationship was found between AI dependency and cognitive offloading (Estimate = 1.11), supporting Hypothesis 1 (H1). This indicates that students who rely more on AI tools are more likely to offload cognitive tasks to these technologies. Similarly, AI dependency showed a strong positive association with motivational decline (Estimate = 1.21), supporting Hypothesis 2 (H2). This suggests that increased reliance on AI is linked to reduced motivational decline among students. In terms of academic skills erosion, both cognitive offloading (Estimate = 0.65) and motivational decline (Estimate = 0.51) were positively associated with the erosion of academic skills, providing support for Hypotheses 3 (H3) and 4 (H4), respectively. These results suggest that when students offload cognitive processes to AI and experience diminished motivation, their academic skills are more likely to deteriorate. The relationship between academic integrity awareness and AI dependency (Estimate = -0.06) was weak and negative which means minimal support for Hypothesis 5 (H5). This indicates that while students with higher academic integrity awareness may be slightly less dependent on AI, the effect is negligible. On the other hand, external pressures had a moderate positive association with AI dependency (Estimate = 0.52) and supported Hypothesis 6 (H6). This highlights the role of academic stress and workload demands in increasing students' reliance on AI tools. Table 3 summarizes the path coefficients which shows the strength and direction of each relationship within the model. The results emphasize the critical influence of AI dependency on cognitive and motivational processes, which in turn contribute to the erosion of academic skills. Additionally, external pressures emerged as a significant factor driving AI reliance, whereas academic integrity awareness had a limited impact.

Table 3. Path coefficients of the structural model

Dependent Variable	Independent Variable	Estimate
Cognitive Offloading	AI Dependency	1.11
Motivational Decline	AI Dependency	1.21
Academic Skills Erosion	Cognitive Offloading	0.65
Academic Skills Erosion	Motivational Decline	0.51
AI Dependency	Academic Integrity Awareness	-0.06
AI Dependency	External Pressures	0.52

Direct Effects

The relationship between AI Dependency and Cognitive Offloading shows a strong, positive, and statistically significant direct effect (SE = 0.068, $z = 16.22$, $p < 0.001$). This indicates that as students' dependency on AI increases, their tendency to offload cognitive tasks to AI tools also increases significantly and supported Hypothesis 1 (H1). Similarly, AI Dependency has a significant positive effect on Motivational Decline (SE = 0.069, $z = 17.43$, $p < 0.001$) and supported Hypothesis 2 (H2). This suggests that increased reliance on AI may contribute to reduced motivational decline among students. For Academic Skills Erosion, both Cognitive Offloading (SE = 0.050, $z = 13.03$, $p < 0.001$) and Motivational Decline (SE = 0.039, $z = 13.01$, $p < 0.001$) show significant positive effects and supported Hypotheses 3 (H3) and 4 (H4) respectively. This indicates that students who offload cognitive tasks to AI and experience motivational decline are more likely to exhibit signs of academic skills erosion. The relationship between Academic Integrity Awareness and AI Dependency is negative and statistically significant (SE = 0.025, $z = -2.29$, $p = 0.022$) and supported Hypothesis 5 (H5), though the effect size is relatively small. This suggests that students with higher academic integrity awareness are slightly less dependent on AI tools. On the other hand, External Pressures have a strong positive effect on AI Dependency (SE = 0.034, $z = 15.19$, $p < 0.001$) and supported Hypothesis 6 (H6). This implies that students experiencing higher academic stress and workload demands are more likely to rely on AI for academic tasks.

Table 4. Direct effects of the structural model

Dependent Variable	Independent Variable	Standard Error (SE)	z-value	p-value	Interpretation
Cognitive Offloading	AI Dependency	0.068	16.22	<0.001	Significant positive effect
Motivational Decline	AI Dependency	0.069	17.43	<0.001	Significant positive effect
Academic Skills Erosion	Cognitive Offloading	0.05	13.03	<0.001	Significant positive effect
Academic Skills Erosion	Motivational Decline	0.039	13.01	<0.001	Significant positive effect

continued on following page

Table 4. Continued

Dependent Variable	Independent Variable	Standard Error (SE)	z-value	p-value	Interpretation
AI Dependency	Academic Integrity Awareness	0.025	-2.29	0.022	Significant negative effect
AI Dependency	External Pressures	0.034	15.19	<0.001	Significant positive effect

Model Fit Indices

The Comparative Fit Index (CFI) was 0.92. This exceeded the recommended threshold of 0.90 which suggests a good fit between the model and the data. Similarly, the Tucker-Lewis Index (TLI) was 0.91 also indicated a good model fit. Both indices are close to the 0.95 threshold which is typically associated with excellent model fit. Additionally, the Goodness of Fit Index (GFI) and the Normed Fit Index (NFI) both yielded values of 0.90 and met the minimum criteria for good model fit. These indices collectively suggest that the hypothesized model adequately represents the observed data. The RMSEA was 0.075 which falls within the acceptable range (≤ 0.08) but slightly above the threshold for a close fit (≤ 0.06). This indicates that while the model fits reasonably well, there may be minor discrepancies between the hypothesized model and the observed data. The Adjusted Goodness of Fit Index (AGFI) was 0.89, just below the 0.90 threshold. This means that the model could benefit from slight modifications to improve parsimony. The Chi-square statistic (χ^2) was 1524.07 with a p-value of 0.0, indicating a significant difference between the model and the observed data. However, it is important to note that the chi-square test is sensitive to large sample sizes which is often resulting in significant values even when the model fit is acceptable. Finally, the Akaike Information Criterion (AIC) and the Bayesian Information Criterion (BIC), which are useful for comparing alternative models, were 113.91 and 386.10 respectively. Overall, the model demonstrates an acceptable fit to the data, with strong support from CFI, TLI, GFI, and NFI values (Table 5). While the significant chi-square and slightly elevated RMSEA suggest potential areas for improvement, the model provides a reasonable representation of the relationships among the studied constructs.

Table 5. Model fit indices

Fit Index	Value	Recommended Threshold	Interpretation
Chi-square ($\chi2$)	1524.07	p > 0.05 (desired)	Significant result suggests some model-data discrepancy
p-value	0	> 0.05 (non-significant preferred)	Indicates model differs from the data (common with large samples)
CFI (Comparative Fit Index)	0.92	≥ 0.90 (good), ≥ 0.95 (excellent)	Good fit
TLI (Tucker-Lewis Index)	0.91	≥ 0.90 (good), ≥ 0.95 (excellent)	Good fit
RMSEA (Root Mean Square Error of Approximation)	0.075	≤ 0.08 (acceptable), ≤ 0.06 (good)	Acceptable fit
GFI (Goodness of Fit Index)	0.9	≥ 0.90 (good)	Good fit
AGFI (Adjusted GFI)	0.89	≥ 0.90 (good)	Slightly below good fit threshold
NFI (Normed Fit Index)	0.9	≥ 0.90 (good)	Good fit

SOLUTIONS AND RECOMMENDATIONS

The results of this study highlighted the long-term concerns associated with AI dependency particularly in relation to cognitive skill deterioration, changes in learning processes, and implications for the professional world. The strong relationship between AI dependency and cognitive offloading, as well as motivational decline, suggests that students who heavily rely on AI tools may experience reduced intrinsic motivation and a weakening of critical academic skills (Nguyen et al., 2024). This aligns with research on the "Google effect," which demonstrates how easy access to information can reduce cognitive processing and retention (Gong & Yang, 2024; Sparrow et al., 2011). Studies also indicate that dependency on generative AI can lower learning accuracy (Al-Zahrani, 2024; Marzuki et al., 2023; Wang, 2024) and negatively impact overall academic performance (Basha, 2024; Hadi Mogavi et al., 2024; Nguyen et al., 2024). These outcomes present how AI alters learning behaviors and whether students will retain the ability to think critically and solve problems independently in professional settings.

As students increasingly depend on AI for academic tasks, they risk entering the workforce without essential problem-solving and decision-making skills. Professionals must navigate complex situations that require critical thinking, adaptability, and creativity skills that AI dependency may erode. Research suggests that students who overuse AI tools may struggle in environments where independent reasoning and analytical skills are expected (Al-Zahrani, 2024; Firth et al., 2019; Nguyen et al., 2024; Yin, 2024; Zhai et al., 2024). For example, in fields such as engineering and medicine, where troubleshooting and deep analysis are crucial, excessive AI dependency could hinder a graduate's ability to make autonomous decisions. Employers may face a workforce that is proficient in using AI tools but lacks the deeper cognitive engagement required for innovation and strategic problem-solving (Gantalao et al., 2025).

To mitigate these risks, it is essential to promote responsible AI use to enhance rather than replace cognitive engagement (Garcia, 2024). AI can foster critical thinking if integrated into active learning strategies. For example, rather than relying on AI-generated summaries, students can use AI to analyze multiple perspectives on a topic and synthesize their conclusions. Similarly, AI-powered systems can be used by students to prompt and help them explain their reasoning before presenting solutions which may help in active participation rather than passive consumption (Xiao et al., 2025). Educators can also design assignments that require students to critically evaluate AI-generated content which helps to distinguish between reliable and misleading outputs (Kamalov et al., 2023; Shahzad et al., 2024). Encouraging students to engage with AI as a collaborative tool rather than a substitute for effort can help maintain cognitive development and problem-solving abilities. In addition, supporting students in developing essential academic and professional skills, educators can implement practical strategies that balance AI use with active learning such as (1) assigning real-world problems that require critical thinking, collaboration, and creativity, (2) encourage goal-setting, reflection, and metacognitive awareness to ensure students actively engage with learning materials, (3) teach students how to use AI responsibly including evaluating the reliability of AI-generated content and recognizing its limitations, (4) establish clear guidelines on ethical AI use and reinforcing the importance of independent thought and original contributions, and (5) incorporate AI-generated content analysis in exams where students critique, refine, and justify AI outputs rather than simply using them.

Policymakers should develop comprehensive AI usage frameworks that balance the benefits of technology with the need to maintain academic rigor. While AI can support learning, institutions must take proactive measures to ensure it does not replace essential cognitive processes. By integrating critical thinking-focused AI applications, enhancing academic integrity awareness, and fostering an environment where AI is used as an assistive rather than a dominant tool, students can develop sustainable learning habits that prepare them for the evolving demands of the workforce (Ateeq et al., 2024; Rasul et al., 2024). Supporting students with time management training, mental health resources, and flexible learning options can further mitigate the negative effects of AI overreliance. Through these measures, educational institutions can help students navigate AI-driven learning while ensuring the development of crucial cognitive and professional skills.

FUTURE RESEARCH DIRECTIONS

Future research could adopt longitudinal designs to examine how AI dependency and its effects on cognitive offloading, motivational decline, and academic skills erosion evolve over time. This would provide insights into the long-term academic and cognitive outcomes associated with sustained AI use. Conducting studies across different cultural and educational contexts can help determine whether the observed relationships hold universally or are influenced by specific socio-cultural factors. Additionally, experimental studies that implement educational interventions aimed at mitigating AI dependency and enhancing academic skills could offer valuable data on effective strategies to promote critical thinking and self-directed learning. Incorporating qualitative methodologies, such as interviews or focus groups, can provide a deeper understanding of students' personal experiences, perceptions, and ethical considerations related to AI use in academic settings.

Future studies could also explore additional mediators, such as self-regulation skills, academic self-efficacy, and emotional resilience, to understand the complex mechanisms on the impact of AI dependency. Research can investigate whether the effects of AI dependency vary across different fields of study, as the reliance on AI tools may differ based on the nature of academic tasks in various disciplines. Examining the broader ethical implications of AI in education and its influence on academic integrity policies can contribute to the development of comprehensive guidelines for responsible AI integration in academic institutions. Furthermore, employing advanced statistical techniques such as SEM can offer more robust insights into the complex relationships among AI dependency, cognitive offloading, motivational decline, and academic skills erosion. This will allow for the testing of comprehensive theoretical models, including both direct and indirect effects which can enhance the understanding of causal pathways. Other advanced techniques, such as multilevel modeling or latent growth curve analysis, can also be utilized to capture the dynamic nature of these relationships over time and across different student populations.

Another growing concern in education is AI bias and its impact on critical academic skills. AI models, mainly those using machine learning algorithms, inherit biases from their training data, which can influence the information they provide to students. Biased AI-generated content can reinforce misconceptions, limit exposure to diverse perspectives, and impede the development of critical thinking and analytical reasoning. Future research should explore how AI bias affects student decision-making, problem-solving strategies, and trust in AI as an educational tool. Additionally, studies should examine methods for detecting and mitigating AI bias while fostering AI literacy among students to promote fair and equitable learning outcomes.

CONCLUSION

This study provides critical insights into the complex relationship between AI dependency and student academic performance and revealed how reliance on AI can fundamentally alter cognitive and motivational processes. The results revealed a strong link between AI dependency and cognitive offloading, accompanied by a marked decline in student motivation, both of which contribute to the deterioration of essential academic skills. While AI enhances efficiency and accessibility, its unchecked integration into education risks fostering intellectual passivity, reducing self-regulation, and diminishing students' ability to engage in higher-order thinking and problem-solving.

Notably, academic integrity awareness had little impact in curbing AI reliance, suggesting that even students who recognize ethical concerns may struggle to limit their dependence on AI tools when faced with academic pressure. External factors, such as deadlines and performance expectations, emerged as key drivers of AI dependency, creating a systemic reliance on these technologies that could have lasting implications for education. The growing normalization of AI-assisted learning raises critical ethical and structural concerns, particularly as institutions risk shifting toward automated knowledge acquisition rather than fostering deep intellectual engagement. Furthermore, these results highlighted the need for a proactive and strategic approach to AI integration in education. Rather than simply incorporating AI into learning environments, institutions must actively address its probable downsides by promoting pedagogical strategies that encourage independent thinking, analytical reasoning, and ethical AI usage. Without deliberate intervention, AI could reshape the academic landscape in ways that prioritize convenience over intellectual depth, potentially undermining the development of critical scholarship and academic resilience in the long term.

ACKNOWLEDGMENT

This research was supported by the authors' individual affiliation.

REFERENCES

Acut, D. P., Malabago, N. K., Malicoban, E. V., Galamiton, N. S., & Garcia, M. B. (2025). "ChatGPT 4.0 Ghosted Us While Conducting Literature Search:" Modeling the Chatbot's Generated Non-Existent References Using Regression Analysis. *Internet Reference Services Quarterly*, *29*(1), 27–54. Advance online publication. DOI: 10.1080/10875301.2024.2426793

Al-Zahrani, A. M. (2024). Unveiling the shadows: Beyond the hype of AI in education. *Heliyon*, *10*(9), e30696. DOI: 10.1016/j.heliyon.2024.e30696 PMID: 38737255

Alasgarova, R., & Rzayev, J. (2024). The Role of Artificial Intelligence in Shaping High School Students' Motivation. *International Journal of Technology in Education and Science*, *8*(2), 311–324. DOI: 10.46328/ijtes.553

Armitage, K. L., & Gilbert, S. J. (2024). The nature and development of cognitive offloading in children. *Child Development Perspectives, n/a*(n/a). DOI: 10.1111/cdep.12532

Ateeq, A., Alzoraiki, M., Milhem, M., & Ateeq, R. A. (2024). Artificial intelligence in education: Implications for academic integrity and the shift toward holistic assessment. *Frontiers in Education*, *9*, 1470979. https://www.frontiersin.org/journals/education/articles/10.3389/feduc.2024.1470979. DOI: 10.3389/feduc.2024.1470979

Bandhu, D., Mohan, M. M., Nittala, N. A. P., Jadhav, P., Bhadauria, A., & Saxena, K. K. (2024). Theories of motivation: A comprehensive analysis of human behavior drivers. *Acta Psychologica*, *244*, 104177. https://doi.org/https://doi.org/10.1016/j.actpsy.2024.104177. DOI: 10.1016/j.actpsy.2024.104177 PMID: 38354564

Basha, J. Y. (2024). The Negative Impacts of AI Tools on Students in Academic and Real-Life Performance. *International Journal of Social Sciences and Commerce*, *1*(3), 1–16. DOI: 10.51470/IJSSC.2024.01.03.01

Bin-Nashwan, S. A., Sadallah, M., & Bouteraa, M. (2023). Use of ChatGPT in academia: Academic integrity hangs in the balance. *Technology in Society*, *75*, 102370. https://doi.org/https://doi.org/10.1016/j.techsoc.2023.102370. DOI: 10.1016/j.techsoc.2023.102370

Birks, D., & Clare, J. (2023). Linking artificial intelligence facilitated academic misconduct to existing prevention frameworks. *International Journal for Educational Integrity*, *19*(1), 20. DOI: 10.1007/s40979-023-00142-3

Çela, E., Fonkam, M. M., & Potluri, R. M. (2024). Risks of AI-Assisted Learning on Student Critical Thinking: A Case Study of Albania. *International Journal of Risk and Contingency Management*, *12*(1), 1–19. DOI: 10.4018/IJRCM.350185

Chen, K., Tallant, A. C., & Selig, I. (2025). Exploring generative AI literacy in higher education: Student adoption, interaction, evaluation and ethical perceptions. *Information and Learning Science*, *126*(1/2), 132–148. DOI: 10.1108/ILS-10-2023-0160

Chiu, T. K. F. (2024). A classification tool to foster self-regulated learning with generative artificial intelligence by applying self-determination theory: A case of ChatGPT. *Educational Technology Research and Development*, *72*(4), 2401–2416. DOI: 10.1007/s11423-024-10366-w

Cohen, R., Katz, I., Aelterman, N., & Vansteenkiste, M. (2022). Understanding shifts in students' academic motivation across a school year: the role of teachers' motivating styles and need-based experiences. In *European Journal of Psychology of Education* (pp. 1–26). DOI: 10.1007/s10212-022-00635-8

Dergaa, I., Ben Saad, H., Glenn, J. M., Amamou, B., Ben Aissa, M., Guelmami, N., Fekih-Romdhane, F., & Chamari, K. (2024). From tools to threats: A reflection on the impact of artificial-intelligence chatbots on cognitive health. *Frontiers in Psychology*, *15*, 15. DOI: 10.3389/fpsyg.2024.1259845 PMID: 38629037

Fan, Y., Tang, L., Le, H., Shen, K., Tan, S., Zhao, Y., Shen, Y., Li, X., & Gašević, D. (2024). Beware of metacognitive laziness: Effects of generative artificial intelligence on learning motivation, processes, and performance. *British Journal of Educational Technology, n/a*(n/a). https://doi.org/https://doi.org/10.1111/bjet.13544

Firth, J., Torous, J., Stubbs, B., Firth, J. A., Steiner, G. Z., Smith, L., Alvarez-Jimenez, M., Gleeson, J., Vancampfort, D., Armitage, C. J., & Sarris, J. (2019). The "online brain": How the Internet may be changing our cognition. *World Psychiatry; Official Journal of the World Psychiatric Association (WPA)*, *18*(2), 119–129. https://doi.org/https://doi.org/10.1002/wps.20617. DOI: 10.1002/wps.20617 PMID: 31059635

Gantalao, L. C., Calzada, J. G. D., Capuyan, D. L., Lumantas, B. C., Acut, D. P., & Garcia, M. B. (2025). Equipping the Next Generation of Technicians: Navigating School Infrastructure and Technical Knowledge in the Age of AI Integration. In *Pitfalls of AI Integration in Education: Skill Obsolescence, Misuse, and Bias*. IGI Global., DOI: 10.4018/979-8-3373-0122-8.ch009

Garcia, M. B. (2024). Addressing the Mental Health Implications of ChatGPT Dependency: The Need for Comprehensive Policy Development. *Asian Journal of Psychiatry*, *98*, 104140. Advance online publication. DOI: 10.1016/j.ajp.2024.104140 PMID: 38943840

George, A. S., Baskar, T., & Srikaanth, P. B. (2024). The Erosion of Cognitive Skills in the Technological Age: How Reliance on Technology Impacts Critical Thinking, Problem-Solving, and Creativity. *Partners Universal Innovative Research Publication, 2*(3 SE-Articles), 147–163. DOI: 10.5281/zenodo.11671150

Gerlich, M. (2025). AI Tools in Society: Impacts on Cognitive Offloading and the Future of Critical Thinking. In *Societies* (Vol. 15, Issue 1). DOI: 10.3390/soc15010006

Gong, C., & Yang, Y. (2024). Google effects on memory: A meta-analytical review of the media effects of intensive Internet search behavior. *Frontiers in Public Health*, *12*, 12. DOI: 10.3389/fpubh.2024.1332030 PMID: 38304178

Gonsalves, C. (2024). Generative AI's Impact on Critical Thinking: Revisiting Bloom's Taxonomy. *Journal of Marketing Education*, *02734753241305980*, 02734753241305980. Advance online publication. DOI: 10.1177/02734753241305980

Grinschgl, S., & Neubauer, A. C. (2022). Supporting Cognition With Modern Technology: Distributed Cognition Today and in an AI-Enhanced Future. *Frontiers in Artificial Intelligence*, *5*, 5. DOI: 10.3389/frai.2022.908261 PMID: 35910191

Gruenhagen, J. H., Sinclair, P. M., Carroll, J.-A., Baker, P. R. A., Wilson, A., & Demant, D. (2024). The rapid rise of generative AI and its implications for academic integrity: Students' perceptions and use of chatbots for assistance with assessments. *Computers and Education: Artificial Intelligence, 7*, 100273. https://doi.org/https://doi.org/10.1016/j.caeai.2024.100273

Gustilo, L., Ong, E., & Lapinid, M. R. (2024). Algorithmically-driven writing and academic integrity: Exploring educators' practices, perceptions, and policies in AI era. *International Journal for Educational Integrity*, *20*(1), 3. DOI: 10.1007/s40979-024-00153-8

Hadi Mogavi, R., Deng, C., Juho Kim, J., Zhou, P., & Kwon, D. Y., Hosny Saleh Metwally, A., Tlili, A., Bassanelli, S., Bucchiarone, A., Gujar, S., Nacke, L. E., & Hui, P. (2024). ChatGPT in education: A blessing or a curse? A qualitative study exploring early adopters' utilization and perceptions. *Computers in Human Behavior: Artificial Humans, 2*(1), 100027. https://doi.org/https://doi.org/10.1016/j.chbah.2023.100027

Hasanah, N. A., Aziza, M. R., Junikhah, A., Arif, Y. M., & Garcia, M. B. (2025). Navigating the Use of AI in Engineering Education Through a Systematic Review of Technology, Regulations, and Challenges. In *Pitfalls of AI Integration in Education: Skill Obsolescence, Misuse, and Bias*. IGI Global., DOI: 10.4018/979-8-3373-0122-8.ch016

Hua, J. H. (2023). Beyond exams: Investigating AI tool impact on student attitudes, ethical awareness, and academic dishonesty in online college assessments. *International Journal of Educational Management and Development Studies*, *4*(4), 160–185. https://doi.org/https://doi.org/10.53378/353030. DOI: 10.53378/353030

Huang, J., Shi, Y., Chen, Y., Tang, L., & Zhang, Z. (2024). How social support influences learned helplessness in lung cancer patients: The chain mediation role of individual resilience and self-efficacy. *Frontiers in Psychology*, *15*, 1436495. DOI: 10.3389/fpsyg.2024.1436495 PMID: 39300997

Huang, S., Lai, X., Ke, L., Li, Y., Wang, H., Zhao, X., Dai, X., & Wang, Y. (2024). AI Technology panic-is AI Dependence Bad for Mental Health? A Cross-Lagged Panel Model and the Mediating Roles of Motivations for AI Use Among Adolescents. *Psychology Research and Behavior Management*, *17*, 1087–1102. DOI: 10.2147/PRBM.S440889 PMID: 38495087

Ivanov, S., Soliman, M., Tuomi, A., Alkathiri, N. A., & Al-Alawi, A. N. (2024). Drivers of generative AI adoption in higher education through the lens of the Theory of Planned Behaviour. *Technology in Society*, *77*, 102521. https://doi.org/https://doi.org/10.1016/j.techsoc.2024.102521. DOI: 10.1016/j.techsoc.2024.102521

Izquierdo-Álvarez, V., & Jimeno-Postigo, C. (2025). Challenges and Opportunities of Integrating Generative Artificial Intelligence in Higher Education: A Systematic Review. In *Pitfalls of AI Integration in Education: Skill Obsolescence, Misuse, and Bias*. IGI Global., DOI: 10.4018/979-8-3373-0122-8.ch017

Jin, S.-H., Im, K., Yoo, M., Roll, I., & Seo, K. (2023). Supporting students' self-regulated learning in online learning using artificial intelligence applications. *International Journal of Educational Technology in Higher Education*, *20*(1), 37. DOI: 10.1186/s41239-023-00406-5

Kamalov, F., Santandreu Calonge, D., & Gurrib, I. (2023). New Era of Artificial Intelligence in Education: Towards a Sustainable Multifaceted Revolution. In *Sustainability* (Vol. 15, Issue 16). DOI: 10.3390/su151612451

Kelly, R. (2024). [% of Students Already Use AI in Their Studies. Campus Technology.]. *Survey (London, England)*, ●●●, 86.

Klimova, B., & Pikhart, M. (2025). Exploring the effects of artificial intelligence on student and academic well-being in higher education: A mini-review. *Frontiers in Psychology*, *16*, 16. DOI: 10.3389/fpsyg.2025.1498132 PMID: 39963679

Kurtz, G., Amzalag, M., Shaked, N., Zaguri, Y., Kohen-Vacs, D., Gal, E., Zailer, G., & Barak-Medina, E. (2024). Strategies for Integrating Generative AI into Higher Education: Navigating Challenges and Leveraging Opportunities. In *Education Sciences* (Vol. 14, Issue 5). DOI: 10.3390/educsci14050503

Lo, K. W. K., Ngai, G., Chan, S. C. F., & Kwan, K. (2022). How Students' Motivation and Learning Experience Affect Their Service-Learning Outcomes: A Structural Equation Modeling Analysis. *Frontiers in Psychology*, *13*, 13. DOI: 10.3389/fpsyg.2022.825902 PMID: 35519642

Lopez, R. M., & Tadros, E. (2023). Motivational Factors for Undergraduate Students During COVID-19 Remote Learning. In *Family Journal (Alexandria, Va.)*. DOI: 10.1177/10664807231163245

Manninen, M., Dishman, R., Hwang, Y., Magrum, E., Deng, Y., & Yli-Piipari, S. (2022). Self-determination theory based instructional interventions and motivational regulations in organized physical activity: A systematic review and multivariate meta-analysis. *Psychology of Sport and Exercise*, *62*, 102248. https://doi.org/https://doi.org/10.1016/j.psychsport.2022.102248. DOI: 10.1016/j.psychsport.2022.102248

Marzuki, W., Widiati, U., Rusdin, D., Darwin, , & Indrawati, I. (2023). The impact of AI writing tools on the content and organization of students' writing: EFL teachers' perspective. *Cogent Education*, *10*(2), 2236469. DOI: 10.1080/2331186X.2023.2236469

Mustofa, R. H., Kuncoro, T. G., Atmono, D., & Hermawan, H. D. (2025). Extending the Technology Acceptance Model: The Role of Subjective Norms, Ethics, and Trust in AI Tool Adoption Among Students. Computers and Education: Artificial Intelligence, 100379.

Nguyen, T. N. T., Van Lai, N., & Nguyen, Q. T. (2024). Artificial Intelligence (AI) in Education: A Case Study on ChatGPT's Influence on Student Learning Behaviors. *Educational Process*, *13*(2), 105–121. DOI: 10.22521/edupij.2024.132.7

Perkins, M. (2023). Academic Integrity considerations of AI Large Language Models in the post-pandemic era: ChatGPT and beyond. *Journal of University Teaching & Learning Practice*, *20*(2), 6–24. DOI: 10.53761/1.20.02.07

Rasul, T., Nair, S., Kalendra, D., Balaji, M. S., Santini, F. de O., Ladeira, W. J., Rather, R. A., Yasin, N., Rodriguez, R. V., Kokkalis, P., Murad, M. W., & Hossain, M. U. (2024). Enhancing academic integrity among students in GenAI Era: A holistic framework. *International Journal of Management Education*, *22*(3), 101041. https://doi.org/https://doi.org/10.1016/j.ijme.2024.101041. DOI: 10.1016/j.ijme.2024.101041

Ray, P. P. (2023). ChatGPT: A comprehensive review on background, applications, key challenges, bias, ethics, limitations and future scope. *Internet of Things and Cyber-Physical Systems*, *3*, 121–154. https://doi.org/https://doi.org/10.1016/j.iotcps.2023.04.003. DOI: 10.1016/j.iotcps.2023.04.003

Risko, E. F., & Gilbert, S. J. (2016). Cognitive Offloading. *Trends in Cognitive Sciences*, *20*(9), 679–688. DOI: 10.1016/j.tics.2016.07.002 PMID: 27542527

Rodrigues, M., Silva, R., Borges, A. P., Franco, M., & Oliveira, C. (2024). Artificial intelligence: threat or asset to academic integrity? A bibliometric analysis. *Kybernetes, ahead-of-p*(ahead-of-print). DOI: 10.1108/K-09-2023-1666

Sardi, J., Candra, O., Yuliana, D. F., Yanto, D. T. P., & Eliza, F. (2025). How Generative AI Influences Students' Self-Regulated Learning and Critical Thinking Skills? A Systematic Review. *International Journal of Engineering Pedagogy*, *15*(1).

Shahzad, M. F., Xu, S., Lim, W. M., Yang, X., & Khan, Q. R. (2024). Artificial intelligence and social media on academic performance and mental well-being: Student perceptions of positive impact in the age of smart learning. *Heliyon*, *10*(8), e29523. DOI: 10.1016/j.heliyon.2024.e29523 PMID: 38665566

Shengelia, R., Gabisonia, L., Tsiklauri-Shengelia, Z., & Shengelia, N. (2024). Assessing AI Dependency: A Multifactorial Analysis and AIDI Index. *Proceedings of Azerbaijan High Technical Educational Institutions Journal.*

Sparrow, B., Liu, J., & Wegner, D. M. (2011). Google Effects on Memory: Cognitive Consequences of Having Information at Our Fingertips. *Science*, *333*(6043), 776–778. DOI: 10.1126/science.1207745 PMID: 21764755

Tamrin, S. I., Omar, N. F., Kamaruzaman, K. N., Zaghlol, A. K., & Aziz, M. R. A. (2024). Evaluating the Impact of AI Dependency on Cognitive Ability among Generation Z in Higher Educational Institutions: A Conceptual Framework. *Information Management and Business Review*, *16*(3), 1027–1033. DOI: 10.22610/imbr.v16i3S(I)a.4191

Tang, L., & Su, Y.-S. (2024). Ethical Implications and Principles of Using Artificial Intelligence Models in the Classroom: A Systematic Literature Review. *International Journal of Interactive Multimedia and Artificial Intelligence*, *8*(5), 25–36. DOI: 10.9781/ijimai.2024.02.010

von Garrel, J., & Mayer, J. (2024). Which features of AI-based tools are important for students? A choice-based conjoint analysis. *Computers and Education: Artificial Intelligence*, *7*, 100311. https://doi.org/https://doi.org/10.1016/j.caeai.2024.100311

Wang, C. (2024). *Exploring Students' Generative AI-Assisted Writing Processes: Perceptions and Experiences from Native and Nonnative English Speakers.* Technology, Knowledge and Learning., DOI: 10.1007/s10758-024-09744-3

Wang, X., Dai, M., & Short, K. M. (2024). One size doesn't fit all: How different types of learning motivations influence engineering undergraduate students' success outcomes. *International Journal of STEM Education, 11*(1), 41. DOI: 10.1186/s40594-024-00502-6

Wei, L. (2023). Artificial intelligence in language instruction: Impact on English learning achievement, L2 motivation, and self-regulated learning. *Frontiers in Psychology, 14,* 14. DOI: 10.3389/fpsyg.2023.1261955 PMID: 38023040

Xiao, J., Bozkurt, A., Nichols, M., Pazurek, A., Stracke, C. M., Bai, J. Y. H., Farrow, R., Mulligan, D., Nerantzi, C., Sharma, R. C., Singh, L., Frumin, I., Swindell, A., Honeychurch, S., Bond, M., Dron, J., Moore, S., Leng, J., & Slagter van Tryon, P. J.. (2025). Venturing into the Unknown: Critical Insights into Grey Areas and Pioneering Future Directions in Educational Generative AI Research. *TechTrends,* ●●●, 1–16. DOI: 10.1007/s11528-025-01060-6

Yan, Y., & Liu, H. (2024). Ethical framework for AI education based on large language models. *Education and Information Technologies.* Advance online publication. DOI: 10.1007/s10639-024-13241-6

Yin, W. J. (2024). *Will Our Educational System Keep Pace with AI? A Student's Perspective on AI and Learning.* Educause.

Yusof, R., Harith, N. H. M., Lokman, A., Abdul, M. F., Zain, B. M., & Rahmat, N. H. (2023). A Study of Perception on Students' Motivation, Burnout and Reasons for Dropout. *International Journal of Academic Research in Business & Social Sciences, 13*(7), 392–420. https://doi.org/http://dx.doi.org/10.6007/IJARBSS/v13-i7/17187. DOI: 10.6007/IJARBSS/v13-i7/17187

Yusuf, A., Pervin, N., & Román-González, M. (2024). Generative AI and the future of higher education: A threat to academic integrity or reformation? Evidence from multicultural perspectives. *International Journal of Educational Technology in Higher Education, 21*(1), 21. DOI: 10.1186/s41239-024-00453-6

Zhai, C., Wibowo, S., & Li, L. D. (2024). The effects of over-reliance on AI dialogue systems on students' cognitive abilities: A systematic review. *Smart Learning Environments, 11*(1), 28. DOI: 10.1186/s40561-024-00316-7

Zhang, S., Zhao, X., Zhou, T., & Kim, J. H. (2024). Do you have AI dependency? The roles of academic self-efficacy, academic stress, and performance expectations on problematic AI usage behavior. *International Journal of Educational Technology in Higher Education, 21*(1), 34. DOI: 10.1186/s41239-024-00467-0

Zhong, W., Luo, J., & Lyu, Y. (2024). How Do Personal Attributes Shape AI Dependency in Chinese Higher Education Context? Insights from Needs Frustration Perspective. *PLoS One, 19*(11), e0313314. https://doi.org/https://doi.org/10.1371/journal.pone.0313314. DOI: 10.1371/journal.pone.0313314 PMID: 39485818

KEY TERMS AND DEFINITIONS

AI Dependency: The extent to which students rely on AI tools for academic tasks.

Academic Skills Erosion: The decline in critical academic competencies due to external influences, such as overreliance on AI.

External Pressures: Academic demands or external factors that increase the likelihood of students relying on AI tools.

Cognitive Offloading: The reduction of cognitive effort by transferring thinking or problem-solving tasks to AI tools.

Motivational Decline: A decrease in intrinsic motivation for academic tasks as a result of heavy AI reliance.

Self-Regulation: The ability of students to manage their own learning processes, including setting goals, monitoring progress, and maintaining motivation without external assistance

Path Analysis: A statistical technique used to illustrate and analyze the directional relationships among variables in the study.

Generative AI: A type of AI that can create new content, such as text, images, or code, based on the data it has been trained on, influencing how students approach academic tasks

Cognitive Load Theory: A theory that explains how the human brain processes information, emphasizing that excessive cognitive demands can hinder learning and performance.

Self-Determination Theory: A psychological framework that focuses on human motivation, suggesting that autonomy, competence, and relatedness are key drivers of intrinsic motivation.

Chapter 3
The Limits of AI in Teaching Partition Literature:
A Critical Perspective on the Risks of Algorithmic Interpretation in Sensitive Historical Contexts

Priyanka Bisht
https://orcid.org/0000-0002-3408-0454
Christ University, India

Jyoti Prakash Pujari
https://orcid.org/0000-0003-1261-2568
Christ University, India

ABSTRACT

The application of generative AI in the classroom is transforming conventional methods of literary analysis and instruction, but it also raises serious concerns and limitations. This chapter critically examines these limitations within the context of teaching 1947 Partition literature in Indian college classrooms. Using a qualitative and experimental methodology, the chapter analyzes AI-generated responses to Partition narratives, revealing ChatGPT's inability to capture the historical trauma, moral accountability, and cultural depth embedded in these texts. Findings show that AI-generated interpretations often flatten complex human experiences and reduces them to simplistic patterns or generalized tropes. The chapter argues that such algorithmic interpretations risk distorting historical memory and promoting academic irresponsibility. By exposing these flaws, the chapter contributes to current debates on AI in higher education and calls for human-led literary analysis in contexts marked by deep historical and cultural trauma.

DOI: 10.4018/979-8-3373-0122-8.ch003

INTRODUCTION

Artificial intelligence (AI) has transformed a wide range of sectors, including digital communication, creative arts, writing, healthcare, and finance. In the last few years, AI has also significantly impacted the education sector by providing intelligent tutoring platforms, automated grading systems, and tailored learning experiences. AI-powered solutions such as the language translation models, adaptive learning software, and plagiarism detectors have revolutionized conventional teaching strategies and increased classroom accessibility and efficiency (Oyedokun, 2025; Saeed et al., 2024). The potential of AI in education to absorb vast amounts of data "...*from multiple sources for analysis and producing a text and a context that resembles human speech*" (Bisht & Pujari, 2024) is one of its primary advantages. The AI-powered tools can also evaluate students' progress, spot areas where they need more help, and offer materials that are specifically designed to improve understanding.

In the higher education as well Artificial intelligence (AI) being utilized to the maximum, to help with research, summarize difficult academic papers, and to create essay drafts. This development has prompted a lot of discussion concerning academic integrity and students' reliance on AI-produced content. As also concluded by Lahby et al., in their book *General Aspects of Applying Generative AI in Higher Education Opportunities and Challenges* (2024),

> ...*the opportunity comes with a challenge: how to encourage individuals to do original creative work in the presence of such a shortcut, how to know whether a piece of data is made by a person or a GenAI model, how much should one care about the provenance of data, and how not to accidentally destroy what remains of the planet wasting electricity at massive computational facilities (that also consume large quantities of water to cool them) in training, fine-tuning, and deploying such models.* (Lahby et al., 2024, p. vi)

It might be supposed, therefore, that there are difficulties in incorporating AI into education. Although AI is efficient and accessible, it also presents serious issues with prejudice, accuracy, ethical ramifications, and the possible decline in individual analytical abilities. Because AI-generated solutions are pattern-based as opposed to meaning-driven, they frequently fall short in understanding subtleties, subjectivity, and more difficult intellectual issues (Williamson & Prybutok, 2024).

This constraint is most noticeable in the humanities, where learning is greatly aided by comprehension, cultural context, and personal engagement (Dainys, 2024; Alshahrani & Qureshi, 2024). Hence, examining the effects of AI technologies like ChatGPT across academic disciplines is crucial, especially in literature and history classrooms, as they become increasingly common in higher education. With this framework, the chapter investigates the limitations of using ChatGPT (4o free version) in Indian college classrooms for teaching the 1947 Partition Literature.

LITERATURE REVIEW

One of the most popular educational tools among the numerous AI models currently on the market is ChatGPT. Being an advanced language model, ChatGPT can produce comprehensive descriptions, condense literary works, help with academic writing, and even offer analyses of complicated concepts (Lambert & Stevens, 2023; Bhattacharya et al., 2024; Israni, 2024; Gibson & Green, 2025). Because of this, it has become particularly well-liked by educators and pupils in colleges and universities, where there is a greater need for organized and timely information. Since many students as well as educators now use ChatGPT for assistance with assessment, feedback, writing essays, text analysis, and language translation, concerns have been raised over the model's educational effectiveness and potential effects on students' learning habits.

The issue of how to responsibly incorporate AI into education is currently a topic of discussion at universities and colleges across the globe as also pointed out in the scholarly writings of Tubella et al. (2023), Abbasi et al. (2024), Singh et al. (2024), and Xiao et al. (2025). While some institutions are actively incorporating AI-based learning into their curricula, others remain skeptical, citing risks such as plagiarism, misinformation, and over-reliance on AI-generated content (Naseer et al., 2024; Akkaş et al., 2024).

Additionally, different disciplines apply GenAI like ChatGPT in teaching in different ways. For instance, the use of AI in STEM fields, where organized responses and problem-solving are essential, has shown to be a natural fit (Yang et al., 2024; Vaidya, 2024), but its place in literature and humanities subjects is still controversial (Hu, 2023; Jerrin & G, 2024; Saroğlu, 2024). This is so because in contrast to domains like science or mathematics, where AI can produce exact results, literature necessitates interpretation, emotional nuance, and subjective involvement, elements that AI finds difficult to match.

Studying literature includes more than merely comprehending works; it also entails interacting with themes, historical settings, cultural factors, and the real-life experiences of the writers (Isro'iyah & Herminingsih, 2023). In a traditional literature classroom, students are generally urged to grow in their ability to think critically, consider existing theories, question prevailing narratives, and consider various readings of a texts before analyzing the literary work (Shobha & T.Anbu, 2023; Gillespie, 2024). On the other hand, AI relies on pattern recognition and pre-existing data to operate, frequently generating analysis, translations and answers which are devoid of depth and creativity (Manu, 2024). Additionally, by depending on AI-generated interpretations rather than honing their own analytical abilities, the teacher and the pupils avoid the process of critical engagement due to the easy access to answers.

These concerns become particularly pressing when discussing trauma literature, where analysis depends heavily on historical authenticity, ethical responsibility, and emotional depth. In Holocaust literature education, for example, scholars have examined the limitations of AI in conveying the gravity and ethical considerations of historical trauma (Chanturia & Chakhvadze, 2023). Similar to Holocaust literature, the Partition literature also deals with themes of violence, displacement, and cultural trauma (Maheswary & Lourdusamy, 2023). The 1947 Partition of India led to the forced migration of approximately 15 million people and widespread communal violence (Leaning & Bhadada, 2022). The literature on the same, serves as both a historical record and a medium for exploring personal and collective trauma.

Hence, in contrast to traditional literary analysis, which emphasizes themes, symbols, and narrative devices, the Partition literature necessitates an investigation of trauma theory, memory studies, and moral storytelling. Therefore, an ethically aware and historically educated approach is necessary when teaching the Partition literature (Haque, 2021). This raises the question that if Gen AI such as ChatGPT are integrated in teaching Partition and its literature, can it interact with such literature in a responsible and meaningful way? This chapter critically examines the same with the hypothesis that there are various pitfalls of using AI, particularly ChatGPT (4o free version), in teaching the Partition literature in Indian college classrooms.

MAIN FOCUS OF THE CHAPTER

Despite increasing research on AI in education, there remains a significant gap in studies examining ChatGPT's role in teaching the Partition literature. While scholars have explored AI's impact on Indian education, such as its use by faculty and students (Balakrishnan & Vidya, 2024), its application in medical education (Roy et al., 2024), and student engagement with AI tools (Pasupuleti & Thiyyagura, 2024), these discussions have largely overlooked literature pedagogy. Existing studies on AI in Indian literary education primarily focus on English as a Second Language (ESL) learning rather than on literary analysis. For example, Guhan and Chandramohan (2023) investigated ChatGPT's role in enhancing ESL skills, while Mahapatra (2024) explored AI's function in providing formative feedback for academic writing. Similarly, Khan (2025) examined AI-generated literature's ability to replicate human creativity, highlighting its limitations in capturing emotional depth and artistic nuance.

Given that the Partition literature, much like Holocaust literature, requires careful ethical and historical engagement, this study addresses the absence of research on ChatGPT's (4o free version) role in teaching such texts. By critically examining the theoretical, and ethical challenges ChatGPT (4o free version) presents in literary classrooms, particularly in the context of the Partition literature, this research examines, why ChatGPT (4o free version), is fundamentally inadequate for teaching Partition Literature in Indian college classrooms. Through the findings, this chapter thus, contributes to the broader discourse on AI's place in teaching literature based on history, violence and trauma. The findings will also help develop responsible strategies for integrating AI into literature pedagogy, ensuring that technological advancements enhance, rather than diminish, human intellectual and ethical engagement.

The chapter has following research questions:

1. What are the theoretical and ethical limitations of using AI, particularly ChatGPT (4o free version), in teaching the Partition literature?
2. Is there a way to minimize the drawbacks and optimize the potential advantages of integrating ChatGPT (GPT-4o free version), into the teaching of the Partition literature?

METHODOLOGY

This chapter uses a qualitative methodology to examine the drawbacks and difficulties of teaching the Partition literature in Indian college classes using ChatGPT (4o free version). In order to empirically demonstrate AI's limitations, this study performs an experimental analysis whereby ChatGPT (4o free version), is asked to translate, summarize, and analyze key Partition texts, as well as to provide historical context on the Partition of India. After that, the generated answers will undergo a critical analysis to identify any biases, inaccuracies or ethical issues. Screenshots of these answers will be provided as visual evidence, guaranteeing that the conclusions are both original and supported by empirical data.

This experiment will also be the foundation for the chapter's further discussion of ChatGPT's (4o free version) limitation in teaching the Partition literature. By employing an experimental approach, the study moves beyond abstract theoretical critiques and systematically demonstrates that ChatGPT (4o free version), actively misrepresents, depoliticizes, and simplifies complex historical and literary narratives. This methodological framework underscores the inherent unsuitability of ChatGPT (4o free version), for engaging with the Partition literature, reinforcing the argument that algorithmic processing lacks the ethical responsibility, cultural sensitivity, and analytical depth required for studying any trauma literature.

FINDINGS

ChatGPT's (4o free version) Limitations in Teaching the Partition Literature

The use of AI in literature classes presents difficult ethical and theoretical issues, which are exacerbated when discussing emotionally and historically fraught stories like the ones often published in the Partition literature. As also discussed above, the study of literature, especially books based on trauma, memory, and historical conflict, necessitates a complex engagement with human emotions, cultural settings, and ethical duties, in contrast to STEM fields where AI can offer objective solutions. AI-generated interpretations frequently fall short of capturing the richness of these stories, running the risk of simplifying or misrepresenting the experiences. Since themes of violence, displacement, and intergenerational memory are intricately woven in the Partition literature, critical engagement is required that goes beyond pattern recognition and the creation of predictive texts. The theoretical limitations of ChatGPT (4o free version), in deciphering Partition narratives are examined in this part, along with the moral ramifications of using AI to teach a subject that calls for human empathy, sensitivity, and historical understanding.

AI and the Loss of Nuance in Partition Poetry

Translation becomes essential in the context of studying the Partition texts. The Partition of India, a momentous event in the nation's history, has been represented through a multitude of texts in various languages, reflecting the country's rich linguistic diversity. From Urdu to Punjabi, Bengali, Hindi, and beyond, these texts offer unique perspectives on the trauma, displacement, and loss experienced during Partition. Translation thus becomes indispensable, allowing readers from diverse linguistic backgrounds to access and understand the emotional and historical complexities embedded in these multifaceted narratives.

In today's time, AI tools such as ChatGPT offer speed and efficiency in language translation, summarization, and textual analysis. However, their application in historically charged and emotionally complex texts exposes critical shortcomings (Sridhar 2024, Roy 2023). This is particularly evident when translating the Partition literature, where cultural, emotional, and historical nuances are central to the meaning and impact of the work.

An experimental technique was used to demonstrate these flaws. ChatGPT (4o free version) was tasked with translating and summarizing Faiz Ahmed Faiz's famous Partition poem "Subh-e-Azadi" (Ahmed, 2017), as shown in *Figure 1*.

Figure 1. Translation of the poem "Subh-e-azadi" (Ahmed, 2017) by ChatGPT

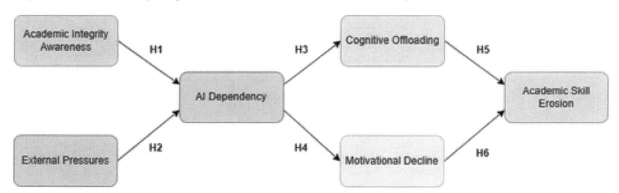

The ChatGPT (4o free version) generated translation highlights several pitfalls that significantly hinder students' and teachers' engagement with the Partition literat0ure in the classroom. These issues can be broken down into three main areas:

Loss of Poetic Nuance

Faiz's poetry is deeply metaphorical and symbolic, conveying complex emotions through rich and layered imagery. Unfortunately, ChatGPT (4o free version) struggles to capture this poetic depth, often resulting in a more literal and simplified version of the text. For example, Faiz's line "
"[1] ("This is a bright spot, this is a night of dawn."1) is a powerful metaphor reflecting the violent Partition that accompanied the light of freedom. The translation by ChatGPT (4o free version), however, loses much of this symbolic richness, presenting it as "This blemished light, this night-bitten dawn" (*ChatGPT: 4o Free Version*, 2024), particularly with the usage of the word "blemished" (*ChatGPT: 4o Free Version*, 2024) which does not convey the depth of the emotional conflict or the metaphor of the long-awaited yet unsatisfactory dawn.

The loss of poetic nuance is a critical failure because it reduces the power of the text. Faiz's work is not just about describing the Partition but also about the emotional and metaphorical layers that give it depth. By simplifying the language, ChatGPT (4o free version) diminishes the ability of students to connect with the poem's true emotional impact.

Inability to Communicate Cultural and Historical Context

The sociopolitical realities of 1947, a time of great upheaval and hardship, are strongly reflected in Faiz's poem. The poem's theme of disillusionment with independence is recognized by ChatGPT (4o free version), but it is unable to incorporate historical detail into its translation. The brutality, mass relocation, and psychological agony of the Partition that form the basis of Faiz's lyrics are not highlighted in the AI-generated output. For instance, even the title of the poem, which is widely translated as "The

Dawn of Freedom, August 1947" (Penguin Random House, 2020), is rendered by ChatGPT as "Dawn of Disillusion" (ChatGPT: 4o Free Version, 2024).

This alteration significantly shifts the meaning and tone of the poem. While Faiz's original title, "Subh-e-Azadi", conveys both the arrival of independence and the complex realities accompanying it, ChatGPT's (4o free version) translation emphasizes only disillusionment, thereby narrowing the poem's interpretive scope. This change exemplifies how AI-generated translations can impose unintended biases, shaping the reader's understanding in ways that may not fully align with the poet's nuanced critique of the Partition.

Simplifying Difficult Emotions

ChatGPT's (4o free version) translation simplifies the poetry but falls short of capturing the complex feelings of resistance, longing, and despair. The ChatGPT (4o free version), flattens Faiz's intentionally evocative and ambiguous vocabulary, making the translation less poetic and more prosaic. For example, the line "   ", translated by Penguin Random House as "It is said the journeying feet have found union with the destination" (2020), carries a layered irony. The phrase "   " ("It is said") suggests a skeptical distance from the official claims that those displaced by the Partition have successfully reached their destinations and that the painful upheaval has concluded. Faiz, however, implies the opposite that the Partition's impact is far from over, and its consequences will persist long after the initial migration.

ChatGPT's (4o free version) translation, "It is said that the union of journey and destination has happened" (ChatGPT: 4o Free Version, 2024) strips the line of this irony. The phrase "union of journey and destination" (ChatGPT: 4o Free Version, 2024) is not only incorrect but entirely misses the historical and emotional implications of forced migration. By presenting the line as a neutral or even celebratory statement, the ChatGPT's (4o free version) translation distorts the poem's meaning, failing to reflect Faiz's critique of the Partition as an ongoing and unresolved trauma.

Thus, by stripping the poem of its historical irony and emotional depth, AI-generated translations risk misrepresenting "Subh-e-Azadi". Rather than highlighting the Partition's enduring trauma, they may reinforce state narratives that frame it as a concluded event. This limitation makes ChatGPT's (4o free version) an inadequate tool for teaching the Partition literature, as it fails to equip students with the critical understanding necessary to engage with the poem's deeper meanings.

These failures have serious implications in a classroom setting. When AI-generated translations omit cultural and historical layers, students engaging with Partition poetry in English miss key aspects of its meaning. This can lead to a superficial understanding of Partition literature, reducing it to a simple narrative of independence rather than an exploration of trauma, loss, and unresolved history. Teachers must therefore emphasize critical engagement with translations, guiding students beyond ChatGPT's (4o free version) limitations to appreciate the true depth of the Partition poetry.

AI's Failure in Literary Summarization

In addition to translation, summarization is one of the most common applications of ChatGPT's (4o free version) in literature classrooms, often used by students and teachers for quick comprehension of texts (Koraishi & Karatepe, 2025). AI-generated summaries are intended to condense complex literary works into concise explanations, but in doing so, they often oversimplify themes, strip away nuance, and neglect the cultural and historical depth of a text (Sidorkin, 2024). This becomes particularly problematic when engaging with literature rooted in trauma, resistance, and political critique, such as the Partition literature.

ChatGPT's attempt to summarize Faiz Ahmed Faiz's poem "Subh-e-Azadi" (see *Figure 2*) exposes several critical flaws in AI's approach to literary analysis, demonstrating how it flattens meaning, erases historical specificity, and overlooks the poetic structure.

Figure 2. Summarization of the poem by ChatGPT

Some of the issues are as follows:

Oversimplification of Themes

ChatGPT (4o free version) reduces the poem's central idea to "deep disappointment and disillusionment with a long-awaited revolution or change" (ChatGPT: 4o Free Version, 2024). While this interpretation is broadly accurate, it lacks historical specificity and fails to recognize the poem's immediate response to the Partition of India. By removing historical and cultural context, AI-generated summaries risk distorting meaning and misleading students (Reichwein, 2023). This is not merely a technical flaw but an academic concern, as it promotes a superficial understanding of the Partition poetry rather than a nuanced engagement with its historical and emotional weight.

Erasure of Political Overtones

Faiz's poetry is deeply political, critiquing the failures of the newly independent state, the unfulfilled promises of freedom, and the social fractures that the Partition intensified. ChatGPT (4o free version), acknowledges the poet's sense of disappointment but fails to engage with the political critique embedded in the poem, a crucial omission that prevents students from understanding the poet's resistance to power structures. This reflects a broader issue with AI-generated literary analysis: by neutralizing politically charged language, ChatGPT (4o free version) depoliticizes Partition narratives and reduces their function as historical resistance. This contributes to the risk of academic irresponsibility, as AI-generated summaries fail to present the full ideological weight of the text.

Lack of Linguistic and Stylistic Analysis

A thorough literary analysis of Faiz's poetry would engage with its linguistic and stylistic elements, including rhythm, imagery, repetition, and metaphor. These elements are crucial in shaping the poem's tone, meaning, and emotional impact. However, ChatGPT (4o free version), summary strips away these features, offering a flat paraphrase rather than an interpretive analysis. This aligns with broader concerns about AI's role in literary education, by producing formulaic, pattern-based responses, AI-generated summaries discourage critical thinking and homogenize interpretation.

Hence, ChatGPT's (4o free version) assessments of the literature it analyzes are essentially inaccurate since they reduce the Partition poetry to generic sentiments of disappointment, remove political commentary, and ignore linguistic depth. This is not just a technical limitation but an ethical concern, as AI-generated literary interpretations risk promoting historical inaccuracies and diminishing the pedagogical value of the Partition Literature in academic settings.

ChatGPT's (4o free version) Blind Spot: Contemporary Partition Stories

AI-generated literary summaries and translations are heavily dependent on pre-existing datasets, which prioritize well-documented, widely studied texts over newer or less mainstream works (Laakso, 2023). This creates a significant gap in ChatGPT's (4o free version) ability to engage with contemporary Partition literature, as it tends to favor canonical authors and widely analyzed historical narratives while struggling with texts that have not yet become part of the dominant literary discourse.

For instance, when asked to summarize Saadat Hasan Manto's widely recognized short story "Toba Tek Singh" (Manto, 1955), see *Figure 3*, ChatGPT (4o free version) provided a fairly accurate summary, likely because the story is well-documented in academic and online sources. However, when prompted to summarize the 2019 short story "Beaaz (Book)" by Shivani Salil, ChatGPT (4o free version) failed to generate an accurate summary (*seeFigure 4*).

Figure 3. A summary generated by ChatGPT for "Toba Tek Singh" (Manto, 1955)

Can you summarize the poem?

This powerful poem by **Faiz Ahmed Faiz** expresses deep disappointment and disillusionment with a long-awaited revolution or change. The poet begins by describing the dawn, but instead of bringing the promised light and freedom, it is stained and weary, not the true dawn they had hoped for.

He reflects on the struggles, sacrifices, and hardships endured in the pursuit of a better future. Many hands tried to hold back the revolutionaries, and temptations along the way tested their resolve, yet they remained committed to their cause. However, even after the supposed victory, nothing has truly changed—pain and suffering persist, and the promised justice and peace remain unfulfilled.

The poem ultimately conveys a sense of unfinished struggle. The night is still heavy, and true freedom has not yet arrived. The poet urges his companions to keep moving forward, for the real destination is still far ahead.

Figure 4. Incorrect summary was produced of the short story "Beaaz (Book)"

"**Toba Tek Singh**" is a short story written by **Saadat Hasan Manto** in 1955. It is a satirical and poignant tale set during the aftermath of the **Partition of India in 1947**, focusing on the impact of the division on individuals, particularly those in a **lunatic asylum**.

Summary:

The story takes place in a mental asylum in **India** after the announcement that Hindu and Sikh lunatics from Pakistan would be transferred to India, and Muslim lunatics from India would be sent to Pakistan. The inmates, already detached from reality, struggle to comprehend the political upheaval.

The protagonist, **Bishan Singh**, a Sikh inmate, hails from a village called **Toba Tek Singh**, which has now become part of Pakistan. He is deeply disturbed by the idea of leaving his homeland but cannot grasp the concept of Partition. When the time comes for his transfer to India, he refuses to move. In the final scene, he collapses and dies in "**no man's land**" between the two borders, symbolizing the tragedy and absurdity of Partition.

Themes:

- **Partition and its impact** – The story highlights the human cost of Partition, especially for those caught in the chaos.

- **Madness vs. Sanity** – The asylum represents a microcosm of the subcontinent, where the so-called insane often make more sense than the politicians outside.

- **Loss of identity and homeland** – Bishan Singh's tragic fate reflects the pain of displacement and loss.

This powerful short story is considered one of **Manto's finest works**, offering a deep critique of political division and the suffering it brings. ↓

This discrepancy demonstrates how AI struggles with newer, non-canonical works that are not yet widely available in public databases. This also raises a critical issue for literature education, because while the Partition Literature continues to evolve with new narratives that challenge, expand, and reinterpret older perspectives, ChatGPT (4o free version) remains limited to reproducing what is already established, often excluding emerging voices and perspectives. In an academic setting, this creates a false perception that only older, widely studied works accurately represent the Partition experiences, which can lead to an incomplete and outdated understanding of the literary landscape.

The Limits of AI in Analyzing Partition Trauma

Partition trauma is a deeply complex and layered experience, often conveyed in literature through themes of displacement, fractured identities, and psychological distress. Saadat Hasan Manto's "Toba Tek Singh" (Manto, 1955) is a seminal text in the Partition literature which through the metaphor of madness and "...through their vivid portrayal of trauma and displacement, provide a rich terrain for exploring the psychological and cultural ramifications of the Partition" (Ghosh, 2025, p. 2). Hence, to assess ChatGPT's (4o free version) ability to interpret the Partition trauma, it was prompted to analyze this story.

Figure 5. ChatGPT discussing the Partition trauma in "Toba Tek Singh" (Manto, 1955)

The response produced by ChatGPT (4o free version), see *Figure 5*, offers an insightful but somewhat insufficient interpretation of the narrative. While it accurately describes the themes of displacement, identity loss, and Bhishan Singh's character, but its analysis is too general, uncritical, and devoid of a more thorough examination of trauma theory, historical nuances, and the story's satirical overtones. It describes "Toba Tek Singh" (Manto, 1955) as a story of "madness and displacement" (ChatGPT: 4o Free Version, 2024) but it doesn't examine the psychological effects of trauma on the asylum's inhabitants. It also does not acknowledge how Manto's own experiences as a witness to the violent Partition carnage and migrations, shaped his depiction of trauma, erasing the personal and historical stakes of the text.

After this, the experiment followed ChatGPT's recommendation, "Would you like me to dive deeper into specific symbols or themes in the story? Let me know!" (ChatGPT: 4o Free Version, 2024). It was expanded with the expectation that more thorough thematic and symbolic investigation would produce better outcomes. But even though the AI-generated response (see *Figure 6*) acknowledges important themes and symbols, like the asylum as a microcosm, Bhishan Singh as a symbol of displacement, and the role of absurdity in Manto's satire, it ultimately falls short of addressing these aspects critically, historically, or emotionally.

Figure 6. A deeper insight into Manto's "Toba Tek Singh" (Manto, 1955)

displaced people, and inflicted lasting psychological wounds.

Would you like me to dive deeper into specific symbols or themes in the story? Let me know!

Yes

Let's dive deeper into some of the key symbols and themes in *Toba Tek Singh* and how they reflect Partition trauma:

1. **The Asylum as a Microcosm of Chaos:**
   The mental asylum reflects the larger chaos and confusion outside its walls during Partition. The inmates' inability to comprehend the division mirrors the real-world confusion where people suddenly found their homes, communities, and identities torn apart. The idea of madness becomes a metaphor for the irrationality and senselessness of Partition itself.

2. **Bishan Singh and No Man's Land:**
   Bishan Singh's character is perhaps the most powerful symbol in the story. His refusal to leave and his ultimate death in no man's land between India and Pakistan symbolize the displacement and alienation experienced by many. His beloved village, Toba Tek Singh, remains out of his reach, representing the loss of home and identity that Partition brought.

3. **Language and Identity:**
   Throughout the story, language becomes a signifier of cultural identity and confusion. The inmates' mixed-up conversations and incomprehensible phrases reflect the breakdown of communication and understanding that Partition caused. People who once coexisted peacefully were now divided by political and religious lines, struggling to articulate their place in this new reality.

4. **Absurdity and Satire:**
   Manto uses absurdity to highlight the senselessness of Partition. The idea of exchanging lunatics between countries based on religion is an exaggerated reflection of real-life population exchanges, showing how arbitrary and cruel the division was. Through this dark humor, Manto critiques the political decisions that led to mass displacement and suffering.

5. **Loss of Belonging:**
   A recurring theme in *Toba Tek Singh* is the loss of home and belonging. Bishan Singh's attachment to his village reflects a deep-rooted connection to land and identity — a connection violently severed by Partition. His tragic end emphasizes how millions of people were left stateless, stranded between new borders that had no meaning to them.

Manto's storytelling makes the trauma of Partition deeply personal and heartbreakingly real. The madness of the asylum mirrors the madness of the world outside, and Bishan Singh's fate remains one of the most powerful literary representations of the human cost of this historical event.

Would you like me to explore any of these symbols or themes in more depth? Or maybe discuss Manto's broader commentary on Partition? Let me know!

Ask anything

+   Search   Reason

As can be seen, the ChatGPT's (4o free version), response does not address the theme that was prompted: the trauma of the Partition in the short story "Toba Tek Singh" (Manto, 1955). Instead of examining how trauma functions in the text, ChatGPT concentrates on other issues like "disillusionment" and "displacement". Considering that "Toba Tek Singh" (Manto, 1955) is one of among the most significant literary depictions of psychological trauma brought on by Partition, this omission becomes particularly apparent.

In addition to its thematic flaws, ChatGPT's (4o free version), in-depth analysis is devoid of textual evidence, as it does not cite stories or provide clear examples to back up the claims it makes. It takes close reading to conduct an effective literary analysis, where arguments are supported by particular passages, character dialogues, and narrative devices (Rejan, 2024). ChatGPT's (4o free version) response, however, is completely abstract and provides general interpretations without referencing any specific passage from the short story. Bhishan Singh's disjointed speech, for instance, and his frequent use of the absurd phrase "Upar di gur gur di annexe di bedhiyana di moong di daal" (Manto, 1955) are not examined even in the language section. These specifics are essential to comprehending how Manto depicts psychological disarray and the ridiculousness of Partition, but ChatGPT (4o free version), ignores them, turning the narrative into a paraphrased synopsis rather than a significant literary analysis.

ChatGPT's (4o free version) Oversimplified History of Partition

Students now commonly use ChatGPT and other AI tools in the classroom to get background information on historical events and to quickly summarize them (Atlas, 2023). Additionally, even educators now view AI as a means of enhancing class discussions or assisting students in understanding significant events prior to more in-depth examination (Chen et al., 2022). But even though AI-generated history can appear easily accessible, accuracy, nuance, and critical engagement are frequently sacrificed in the process (Mohamed et al., 2024). ChatGPT (4o free version) also has a tendency to flatten historical arguments, emphasize readability over depth, and leave out important viewpoints, particularly those that contradict prevailing narratives (see *Figure 7*). This begs the question of whether AI is a genuinely trustworthy teaching aid for difficult and delicate historical subjects.

Figure 7. ChatGPT discussing the background of the 1947 Partition

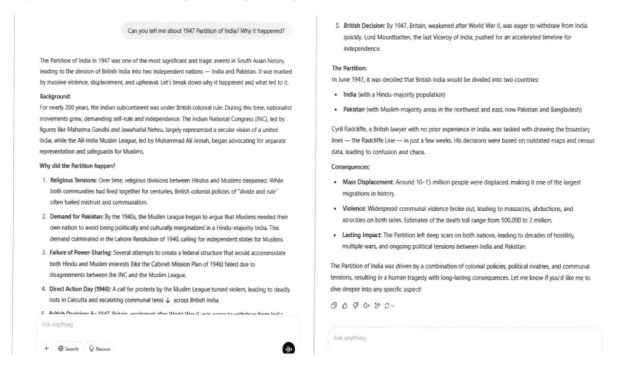

Although ChatGPT offers an organized and comprehensible account of the 1947 Partition, its answer is devoid of critical engagement with important historical arguments, references, and depth. Its failure to include citations or references to reliable sources is one of its main flaws, which makes it impossible to confirm the accuracy of its claims. The solution runs the risk of promoting a single, uncritical interpretation of history rather than capturing the complexity of Partition studies if historians and original sources are not consulted. This lack of attribution is problematic in an academic setting because historical narratives need to be supported by thorough study, a variety of viewpoints, and documented proof.

Another major problem with ChatGPT's (4o free version) explanation is that it doesn't go far enough in discussing the two-nation theory, which was essential to Pakistan's ideological stance. The response notes that the Muslim League supported the idea of a separate state, but it doesn't explain how the two-nation theory developed, how the League's internal conflicts developed, or why different political factions opposed Partition. Instead, it simplifies a highly contentious historical process into a simple communal split by presenting a cause-and-effect story.

Furthermore, ChatGPT's explanation downplays the part played by British colonial policies during Partition. Although it makes reference to Britain's hasty withdrawal from India, it does not critically analyze how colonial control exacerbated sectarian differences, the effects of Cyril Radcliffe's hurried, ignorant borderline drawing and Lord Mountbatten's hurried decision-making. The ChatGPT (4o free version) generated solution eliminates the role of colonial officials in influencing the violence and instability of 1947 by interpreting the Partition largely as a struggle between Muslims and Hindus.

Additionally, ChatGPT's (4o free version) account understates the effects of the Partition on the citizens. Although it acknowledges mass displacement and violence, it does not address the scale and nature of atrocities committed during this period. Despite a wealth of scholarship on the kidnapping and abuse of women during forced migrations, gendered violence, a crucial component of the Partition history, is entirely disregarded in its answer. Moreover, the ChatGPT's (4o free version) response lacks any survivor testimonies or oral histories, making its depiction of the Partition feel detached and impersonal, rather than reflective of lived experiences.

Last but not least, the approach ignores regional differences in how the Partition unfolded. The event is portrayed as a single, monolithic rupture rather than a highly uneven process that transpired differently in Hyderabad, Bengal, Kashmir, and Punjab. The Punjab Partition was marked by mass killings and organized militias, while Bengal saw long-term communal tensions that extended beyond 1947 (Leaning & Bhadada, 2022). ChatGPT (4o free version) provides a broad, one-size-fits-all narrative that disregards local intricacies rather than making a distinction between these regional histories.

Due to its simplicity, absence of citations, erasure of colonial policies, and exclusion of important viewpoints, ChatGPT's (4o free version) historical account is extremely untrustworthy for use in academic settings. Though convenient, AI-generated summaries deprive history of its complexity and do not equip students to critically engage with historical debates. This presents significant questions regarding the reliability of ChatGPT as a teaching aid for the Partition history.

The Consequences of AI Integration in Literature Classrooms

This chapter presents a series of experiments that demonstrate that ChatGPT (4o free version) frequently encounters a number of ethical and interpretive challenges when used to teach the Partition literature. These include the loss of lyrical depth and metaphor in translation, the simplifying of intricate historical and political criticisms, the deletion of marginalized and modern voices, the narrowing down of rich historical narratives, and the inability to meaningfully analyze emotional and difficult themes such as trauma. These discrepancies in interpretation are not coincidental; rather, they represent basic constraints in the way generative AI interprets works of literature that are concerned with trauma. Each of these mistakes is significant on its own, but taken together, they have a much more substantial impact in a classroom.

When ChatGPT generated outputs are incorporated into the classroom, either by students using them to prepare for class discussions or finish assignments, or by teachers assigning or referencing them in teaching pedagogy, they provide more than just a partial or inaccurate interpretation (Acut et al., 2025). They start to influence the way literature is perceived and read. Texts that demand in-depth thought, ethical awareness, or careful contextual reading are either reduced to simplistic interpretations or reframed as mere questions to be answered. For students, these answers are easily supplied by AI, relieving them of the process of critical engagement with the text.

This can have detrimental effects for classes on trauma literature, because the texts are majorly based on real experiences and hence, require an active involvement from the reader. For instance, in this context, a poem concerning the Partition is a site of resistance and commemoration in addition to being a historical document, a narrative about madness following the forced migration is not only symbolic; rather, it captures actual psychological anguish. Hence, the adoption of AI outputs by teachers as well as students, without engaging in critical thinking could lead to accepting simplistic, ahistorical, and unethical interpretations that detach them from the texts' fundamental meaning and intent.

Overreliance on AI extends beyond one student and reshapes the classroom by limiting the diversity of voices and ideas. Due to ChatGPT's propensity to produce uniform, generic readings of literary texts, students who depend on these outputs frequently contribute the same concepts to class discussions. In addition to flattening the range of viewpoints, this lessens the impromptu, interpretative depth that literary classes are supposed to promote (Bozkurt et al., 2024). When students bring AI generated pre-read summaries to class, they are less able to ask questions, argue, challenge, or suggest different readings. The classroom atmosphere gradually changes from one of discussion and exploration to one of silent agreement and homogenized arguments, where disagreement is uncommon, and the subtleties of interpretation are swapped out for a single, algorithm-approved interpretation.

The result of this standardization is intellectual inactivity, which is an even greater issue. When students frequently rely on AI for immediate replies, they risk neglecting the exact qualities that literary education seeks to foster- close reading, critical analysis, and reflective thought (Kim et al. 2024; Van Rensburg 2024; Gibson & Green, 2025). This not only affects their ability to engage with challenging texts like the Partition literature but also weakens their confidence in forming and defending their own interpretations. Consequently, even teachers can find it more challenging to spark stimulating discussions in the classroom if students start repeating identical AI-generated opinions instead of contributing their own.

Trauma literature such as the Partition and the Holocaust emerge from the histories of violence and rupture. They demand a discomforting engagement from the readers which arises not from the text alone, but from the traumatic realities it represents such as the forced displacement, violence, grief, injustice, and memory that resists resolution. Such literature does not offer simple conclusions but asks readers to dwell in ambiguity, to feel the contradictions of survival and loss, and to reflect on the ongoing consequences of historical trauma (Vickroy, 2015). In contrast, AI-generated responses prioritize coherence, brevity, and resolution, they are programmed to simplify, to provide closure where there should be uncertainty (Mohamed et al., 2024). When educators permit or encourage such closure in the classroom, they risk replacing critical engagement with passive acceptance, trading intellectual struggle for synthetic clarity.

CONCLUSION

The growing use of artificial intelligence in education has sparked intense debates on its possible application in literary analysis. Although AI can improve accessibility, speed up comprehension, and be used as an additional tool in literature classes, its intrinsic drawbacks raise serious questions about whether it is appropriate for interacting with highly historical, emotionally complex, and morally complex narratives like the Partition Literature.

The inability of AI to comprehend the breadth of human pain, historical trauma, and cultural nuances that characterize the Partition narratives is one of the main issues discussed in this chapter. The results of a number of experimental tests show serious shortcomings in ChatGPT's (4o free version) comprehension of the literary, ethical, and historical intricacies of the Partition stories. ChatGPT (4o free version) constantly flattens the richness, ambiguity, and emotional intensity that characterize the Partition studies, provides a shallow examination of literary themes and symbolism, skewedly selects popular narratives and gives simplistic historical explanations.

These are not minor technical limitations but structural flaws that render AI-generated outputs unfit for teaching a subject as morally and politically charged as the Partition. Lacking citation, context, and engagement with primary sources, these responses risk spreading misinformation, reinforcing hegemonic versions of history, and discouraging critical thought. Instead of fostering reflective engagement, ChatGPT offers generic, pre-formed readings that, if used uncritically, may lead students and educators alike to internalize biased or inaccurate interpretations, undermining the very goals of the Partition pedagogy.

Given these drawbacks, artificial intelligence should not be promoted as a replacement for human-led historical and literary study. Rather, archival research, victim testimonials, and critical historiography, all of which ChatGPT's (4o free version) essentially ignores, must continue to serve as the foundation for the Partition studies. However, it is crucial to place this criticism in the context of larger academic discussions. This chapter does not support the use of AI in teaching Partition literature, but it does recommend that instead of prohibiting AI completely, teachers be encouraged to understand its limitations.

In order to teach students to recognize what is lacking-historically, politically, and emotionally, the Partition texts might be presented alongside flawed AI-generated summaries. With student interpretation at the center, educators may also create tests that place a high value on reflective participation, comparative analysis, and source-based reasoning. Above all, it is important to remember that while AI may serve limited supplementary functions, it cannot substitute the role of a human educator in providing the ethical, intellectual, and affective depth essential to the study of literature and historical trauma.

REFERENCES

Abbasi, B. N., Wu, Y., & Luo, Z. (2024). Exploring the impact of artificial intelligence on curriculum development in global higher education institutions. *Education and Information Technologies*. Advance online publication. DOI: 10.1007/s10639-024-13113-z

Acut, D. P., Malabago, N. K., Malicoban, E. V., Galamiton, N. S., & Garcia, M. B. (2025). "ChatGPT 4.0 Ghosted Us While Conducting Literature Search:" Modeling the Chatbot's Generated Non-Existent References Using Regression Analysis. *Internet Reference Services Quarterly*, *29*(1), 27–54. Advance online publication. DOI: 10.1080/10875301.2024.2426793

Ahmed, F. F. (2017). Subh-e-Azadi. Penguin Random House. India. https://www.penguin.co.in/subh-e-azadi-an-anguished-evocation-of-the-pain-of-partition/

Akkaş, Ö. M., Tosun, C., & Gökçearslan, Ş. (2024). Artificial Intelligence (AI) and Cheating. In *Advances in educational technologies and instructional design book series* (pp. 182–199). DOI: 10.4018/979-8-3693-1351-0.ch009

Alshahrani, K., & Qureshi, R. J. (2024). Review the Prospects and Obstacles of AI-Enhanced Learning Environments: The Role of ChatGPT in Education. *I.J.Modern Education And Computer Science*, *16*(4), 71–86. DOI: 10.5815/ijmecs.2024.04.06

Atlas, S. (2023). *ChatGPT for Higher Education and Professional Development: A guide to Conversational AI*. DigitalCommons@URI. https://digitalcommons.uri.edu/cba_facpubs/548

Balakrishnan, S., & Vidya, B. (2024). Unveiling the role of ChatGPT in higher education: A qualitative inquiry into its implementation among teaching faculties in Chennai, India. *Multidisciplinary Science Journal*, *7*(4), 2025167. DOI: 10.31893/multiscience.2025167

Bhattacharya, P., Prasad, V. K., Verma, A., Gupta, D., Sapsomboon, A., Viriyasitavat, W., & Dhiman, G. (2024). Demystifying ChatGPT: An In-depth Survey of OpenAI's Robust Large Language Models. *Archives of Computational Methods in Engineering*, *31*(8), 4557–4600. Advance online publication. DOI: 10.1007/s11831-024-10115-5

Bisht, P., & Pujari, J. P. (2024). Past Meets the Future—ChatGPT Integrated Pedagogy to Teach the 1947 Partition in Secondary Classes. In Lahby, M., Bucchiarone, Y. M. A., & Schaeffer, S. E. (Eds.), *General Aspects of Applying Generative AI in Higher Education Opportunities and Challenges* (pp. 55–68)., DOI: 10.1007/978-3-031-65691-0_4

Bozkurt, A., Xiao, J., Farrow, R., Bai, J. Y. H., Nerantzi, C., Moore, S., Dron, J., Stracke, C. M., Singh, L., Crompton, H., Koutropoulos, A., Terentev, E., Pazurek, A., Nichols, M., Sidorkin, A. M., Costello, E., Watson, S., Mulligan, D., Honeychurch, S., & Asino, T. I. (2024). The Manifesto for Teaching and Learning in a Time of Generative AI: A Critical Collective Stance to Better Navigate the Future. *Open Praxis*, *16*(4), 487–513. DOI: 10.55982/openpraxis.16.4.777

Chanturia, N., & Chakhvadze, L. (2023). Generative Artificial Intelligence and Holocaust Education. *Baskent International Conference on Multidisciplinary Studies*. https://www.researchgate.net/publication/377078571

ChatGPT. (2024). *ChatGPT: 4o free version.* chatgpt.com. Retrieved January 1, 2025, from https://chatgpt.com/

Chen, Y., Jensen, S., Albert, L. J., Gupta, S., & Lee, T. (2022). Artificial Intelligence (AI) Student Assistants in the Classroom: Designing Chatbots to Support Student Success. *Information Systems Frontiers*, *25*(1), 161–182. DOI: 10.1007/s10796-022-10291-4

Dainys, A. (2024). Human Creativity Versus Machine Creativity: Will Humans Be Surpassed by AI? In *IntechOpen eBooks.* DOI: 10.5772/intechopen.1007369

Ghosh, S. S. (2025). Ghosts of the border: Trauma, identity, and the fragmented self in partition-era narratives of Punjab through the DSM-5 framework. *Sikh Formations*, ●●●, 1–17. DOI: 10.1080/17448727.2025.2454070

Gibson, B., & Green, C. N. (2025). Teaching Literature in the Age of AI. In *Advances in library and information science (ALIS) book series* (pp. 179–210). DOI: 10.4018/979-8-3693-3053-1.ch009

Gillespie, T. (2024). *Doing literary criticism: The Cultivation of Thinkers in the Classroom.* Taylor & Francis. DOI: 10.4324/9781003579083

Guhan, M., & Chandramohan, S. (2023). A Study on Analyzing the Role of ChatGPT in English Acquisition Among ESL Learners During English Language. *ResearchGate.* DOI: 10.13140/RG.2.2.28252.56961

Haque, S. A. (2021). *Dialogue on partition: Literature Knows No Borders.* Rowman & Littlefield. DOI: 10.5771/9781793636256

Hu, Y. (2023). Literature in the age of artificial intelligence. In *Advances in Social Science, Education and Humanities Research/Advances in social science, education and humanities research* (pp. 1781–1787). DOI: 10.2991/978-2-38476-092-3_228

Israni, R. K. (2024). The Potential Future with ChatGPT Technology and AI Tools. In *Advances in computational intelligence and robotics book series* (pp. 226–256). DOI: 10.4018/979-8-3693-6824-4.ch013

Isro'iyah, N. L., & Herminingsih, N. D. I. (2023). Teaching Culture of Others through English Literature. *International Journal of Language and Literary Studies*, *5*(2), 136–146. DOI: 10.36892/ijlls.v5i2.1248

Jerrin, N. B., & Bhuvaneswari G, . (2024). Comprehending AI's Role in Literature and Arts from a Transhumanist Perspective. *International Research Journal of Multidisciplinary Scope*, *05*(02), 846–859. DOI: 10.47857/irjms.2024.v05i02.0670

Khan, S. (2025). ChatGPT for Writing Literature and Songs: End of the Road for Poets and Songwriters? In *Lecture notes in electrical engineering* (pp. 405–414). https://doi.org/DOI: 10.1007/978-981-97-4780-1_30

Kim, J., Yu, S., Detrick, R., & Li, N. (2024). Exploring students' perspectives on Generative AI-assisted academic writing. *Education and Information Technologies.* Advance online publication. DOI: 10.1007/s10639-024-12878-7

Koraishi, O., & Karatepe, Ç. (2025). Minds vs machines: A comparative study of AI and teacher-generated summaries in ELT. *Technology in Language Teaching & Learning*, 7(1), 1796. DOI: 10.29140/tltl. v7n1.1796

Laakso, A. (2023). *Ethical challenges of large language models - a systematic literature review* (pp. 1–67) [Thesis, Helsinki University Library]. https://helda.helsinki.fi/server/api/core/bitstreams/e507d025 -8c84-4789-a043-f185fa51eb0a/content

Lahby, M., Bucchiarone, Y. M. A., & Schaeffer, S. E. (Eds.). (2024). *Preface* (pp. i–viii). General Aspects of Applying Generative AI in Higher Education Opportunities and Challenges., DOI: 10.1007/978-3-031-65691-0_4

Lambert, J., & Stevens, M. (2023). ChatGPT and Generative AI Technology: A Mixed Bag of Concerns and New Opportunities. *Computers in the Schools*, 41(4), 559–583. DOI: 10.1080/07380569.2023.2256710

Leaning, J., & Bhadada, S. (2022). *The 1947 partition of British India: Forced Migration and Its Reverberations*. SAGE Publishing India. DOI: 10.4135/9789354793127

Mahapatra, S. (2024). Impact of ChatGPT on ESL students' academic writing skills: A mixed methods intervention study. *Smart Learning Environments*, 11(1), 9. Advance online publication. DOI: 10.1186/ s40561-024-00295-9

Maheswary, B. G. U., & Lourdusamy, A. (2023). An Evaluation of the Partition Narratives: A Special Focus on Psychological Trauma. *International Journal of Philosophy and Languages (IJPL)*, 18–26. DOI: 10.47992/IJPL.2583.9934.0010

Manto, S. H. (1955). *Toba Tek Singh*. www.sacw.net. http://www.sacw.net/partition/tobateksingh.html

Manu, A. (2024). *Transcending imagination: Artificial Intelligence and the Future of Creativity*. CRC Press. DOI: 10.1201/9781003450139

Mohamed, Y. A., Mohamed, A. H. H. M., Khanan, A., Bashir, M., Adiel, M. E., & Elsadig, M. A. (2024). Navigating the Ethical Terrain of AI-Generated Text Tools: A Review. *IEEE Access : Practical Innovations, Open Solutions*, •••, 12.

Naseer, F., Khalid, M. U., Ayub, N., Rasool, A., Abbas, T., & Afzal, M. W. (2024). Automated Assessment and Feedback in Higher Education Using Generative AI. In *Advances in educational technologies and instructional design book series* (pp. 433–461). DOI: 10.4018/979-8-3693-1351-0.ch021

Oyedokun, G. E. (2025). AI and Ethics, Academic Integrity and the Future of Quality Assurance in Higher Education. *ResearchGate*. https://www.researchgate.net/publication/387999374_AI_and_Ethics _Academic_Integrity_and_the_Future_of_Quality_Assurance_in_Higher_Education

Pasupuleti, R. S., & Thiyyagura, D. (2024). An empirical evidence on the continuance and recommendation intention of ChatGPT among higher education students in India: An extended technology continuance theory. *Education and Information Technologies*, 29(14), 17965–17985. DOI: 10.1007/ s10639-024-12573-7

Reichwein, F. (2023). *Ethical and societal implications of Generative AI-Models*.

Rejan, A. (2024). Close Reading for the Twenty-First Century: Rehumanizing Literary Reading. *English Journal*, *114*(2), 59–67. DOI: 10.58680/ej2024114259

Rekhta. (n.d.). https://www.rekhta.org/nazms/subh-e-aazaadii-august-47-ye-daag-daag-ujaalaa-ye-shab -gaziida-sahar-faiz-ahmad-faiz-nazms?lang=ur

Roy, A. D., Das, D., & Mondal, H. (2024). Efficacy of ChatGPT in solving attitude, ethics, and communication case scenario used for competency-based medical education in India: A case study. *Journal of Education and Health Promotion*, *13*(1). Advance online publication. DOI: 10.4103/jehp.jehp_625_23 PMID: 38545309

Roy, D., & Putatunda, T. (2023). From Textbooks to Chatbots: Integrating AI in English literature classrooms of India. *Journal of e-Learning and Knowledge Society - SIe-L - the Italian e-Learning Association*. DOI: 10.20368/1971-8829/1135860

Saeed, S., Rana, O., & Dhanaraj, R. K. (2024). *Higher education and quality assurance practices*. IGI Global. DOI: 10.4018/979-8-3693-6765-0

Saroğlu, Ö. C. (2024). Players Retell This Story. In *Advances in human and social aspects of technology book series* (pp. 133–158). DOI: 10.4018/979-8-3693-7235-7.ch006

Shobha, J. M., & T.Anbu. (2023). *Global Trends in teaching English Language and Literature*. Alborear (OPC) Pvt. Ltd.

Sidorkin, A. M. (2024). *Embracing chatbots in higher education: The Use of Artificial Intelligence in Teaching, Administration, and Scholarship*. Taylor & Francis. DOI: 10.4324/9781032686028

Singh, A., Lakhera, G., Ojha, M., Mishra, A. K., & Nain, A. (2024). Balancing Innovation with Responsibility. In *Advances in human and social aspects of technology book series* (pp. 467–500). DOI: 10.4018/979-8-3693-4147-6.ch020

Sridhar, V. (2024). *ChatGPT and artificial Intelligence*. Academic Guru Publishing House.

Tubella, A. A., Mora-Cantallops, M., & Nieves, J. C. (2023). How to teach responsible AI in Higher Education: Challenges and opportunities. *Ethics and Information Technology*, *26*(1), 3. Advance online publication. DOI: 10.1007/s10676-023-09733-7

Vaidya, B. (2024). Harnessing AI for STEM Education in South Asia: Impact, Opportunities, and Challenges. *Journal of Development Innovations.*, *8*(2), 1–29. DOI: 10.69727/jdi.v8i2.113

Van Rensburg, J. J. (2024). Artificial human thinking: ChatGPT's capacity to be a model for critical thinking when prompted with problem-based writing activities. *Discover Education*, *3*(1), 42. Advance online publication. DOI: 10.1007/s44217-024-00113-x

Vickroy, L. (2015). Reading Trauma Narratives: The Contemporary Novel and the Psychology of Oppression. http://muse.jhu.edu/chapter/1635214

Williamson, S. M., & Prybutok, V. (2024). The Era of Artificial Intelligence Deception: Unraveling the Complexities of False Realities and Emerging Threats of Misinformation. *Information (Basel)*, *15*(6), 299. DOI: 10.3390/info15060299

Xiao, J., Bozkurt, A., Nichols, M., Pazurek, A., Stracke, C. M., Bai, J. Y. H., Farrow, R., Mulligan, D., Nerantzi, C., Sharma, R. C., Singh, L., Frumin, I., Swindell, A., Honeychurch, S., Bond, M., Dron, J., Moore, S., Leng, J., & Slagter van Tryon, P. J.. (2025). Venturing into the Unknown: Critical Insights into Grey Areas and Pioneering Future Directions in Educational Generative AI Research. *TechTrends*, ●●●, 1–16. DOI: 10.1007/s11528-025-01060-6

Yang, Y., Sun, W., Sun, D., & Salas-Pilco, S. Z. (2024). Navigating the AI-Enhanced STEM education landscape: A decade of insights, trends, and opportunities. *Research in Science & Technological Education*, ●●●, 1–25. DOI: 10.1080/02635143.2024.2370764

KEY TERMS AND DEFINITIONS

Generative AI: A type of artificial intelligence that can create new content—such as text, images, music, or code—by learning from existing data patterns and producing novel outputs that resemble human-generated work.

Partition Literature: A genre of writing that focuses on the human experiences, cultural upheaval, and political conflicts resulting from the Partition of British India in 1947, often exploring themes of displacement, identity, and historical memory.

ChatGPT: A conversational AI model developed by OpenAI that uses a large language model to generate human-like text responses, often employed for dialogue systems, tutoring, content creation, and various other natural language processing tasks.

Literary Analysis: The systematic examination of a literary text's structure, themes, characters, language, and context to interpret its deeper meanings and evaluate its artistic and cultural significance.

Historical Trauma: The collective emotional and psychological wounds experienced by a group of people due to traumatic historical events, often transmitted across generations and reflected in cultural expressions, memory, and identity.

Algorithmic Interpretation: The process by which artificial intelligence systems, particularly those using machine learning algorithms, analyze, evaluate, or generate responses based on input data—often applied in contexts like literature, art, or behavior prediction.

Cultural Depth: The richness and complexity of a society's values, traditions, symbols, and shared knowledge, often revealed through language, literature, rituals, and art, and essential for understanding nuanced human experiences.

Academic Integrity: The commitment to honesty, trust, fairness, respect, and responsibility in scholarly work, including proper citation, avoiding plagiarism, and upholding ethical standards in research and education.

ENDNOTES

[1]   "This light, smeared and spotted, this night-bitten dawn" (Penguin Random House, 2020)

Chapter 5
AI Shaming Among Teacher Education Students:
A Reflection on Acceptance and Identity in the Age of Generative Tools

Dharel P. Acut
https://orcid.org/0000-0002-9608-1292
Cebu Technological University, Philippines

Eliza V. Gamusa
Northwest Samar State University, Philippines

Johannes Pernaa
University of Helsinki, Finland

Chokchai Yuenyong
Khon Kaen University, Thailand

Anabelle T. Pantaleon
Cebu Technological University, Philippines

Raymond C. Espina
Cebu Technological University, Philippines

Mary Jane C. Sim
Cebu Technological University, Philippines

Manuel B. Garcia
https://orcid.org/0000-0003-2615-422X
FEU Institute of Technology, Philippines

ABSTRACT

As generative AI tools become increasingly integrated into educational practice, its use among pre-service teachers is often accompanied by hesitation and discomfort. This chapter examines the phenomenon of AI shaming among teacher education students—the stigma and reluctance to disclose AI tool use due to perceived threats to academic authenticity. Drawing on classroom insights and student reflections, it explores how social norms, institutional pressures, and identity formation shape this behavior. These experiences reveal the deep tension between embracing technological innovation and maintaining traditional standards of academic merit. The chapter highlights the implications for digital literacy, professional development, and ethical technology integration. It calls for a shift in narrative, framing AI not as a shortcut but as a tool for innovation. Actionable strategies for educators and institutions are proposed to foster open, reflective, and supportive environments for responsible AI use in teacher education.

DOI: 10.4018/979-8-3373-0122-8.ch005

INTRODUCTION

In recent years, the rapid development of generative AI tools like ChatGPT, DALL·E, and Bard has begun reshaping various sectors, including education (Bozkurt et al., 2024; Zawacki-Richter et al., 2019). These tools, powered by advanced machine learning algorithms, can generate coherent text, realistic images, and creative content based on user input, making them invaluable for tasks ranging from ideation to conceptualization (Adetayo, 2024; da Silva & Ulbricht, 2024; Kamalov et al., 2023). For educators and students alike, generative AI offers new ways to approach problem-solving, streamline administrative tasks, and enhance creativity in learning environments (Garcia et al., 2024; Wang et al., 2024). In the context of teacher education, where future educators are expected to develop both pedagogical adaptability and digital competence, the integration of AI tools represents a transformative yet controversial shift.

Despite the potential benefits of these AI tools, their adoption is not without controversy. Among students—particularly those preparing for teaching professions—there is an emerging socio-academic phenomenon known as AI shaming. This concept refers to the reluctance or embarrassment students feel when admitting to using AI tools, stemming from fears that their reliance on such technology may be perceived as undermining their creativity, critical thinking, or academic integrity (Acut et al., 2024; Garcia, 2024; Giray, 2024). As highlighted in recent studies, AI shaming reflects internalized stigma around perceived "inauthentic" digital labor, and is particularly prevalent among students who feel pressure to conform to traditional notions of academic rigor and authorship (E. & A., 2024). In many cases, students may view the use of AI as a form of intellectual shortcutting, leading to a sense of guilt or shame—even when AI tools are used to support legitimate learning objectives (Zhai et al., 2024).

Such stigma surrounding AI use has deeper implications beyond personal discomfort; it can shape how future educators relate to emerging technologies in their professional lives. AI shaming may deter students from fully exploring the capabilities of these tools, limiting their potential to develop essential digital literacy and technological fluency—skills that are increasingly critical for success in the 21st-century workforce (Gantalao et al., 2025; Walter, 2024). This concern is particularly urgent in teacher education programs, where students are not only learning content but also internalizing beliefs and practices they will later model in classrooms. If teacher candidates feel shame or fear regarding AI use, they may resist integrating these tools into their future pedagogical practices—thereby perpetuating outdated norms around technology avoidance or resistance (Akgun & Greenhow, 2021). This not only undermines their development as digitally competent educators but also sustains a cycle of discomfort and silence around technological integration that could otherwise enhance learning.

The concept of AI shaming intersects with broader discussions of digital identity, educational authenticity, and professional formation. Research suggests that students' attitudes toward technology are heavily influenced by their perceptions of what constitutes "real" or "legitimate" work (Wu et al., 2022). When students believe that using AI diminishes their intellectual efforts, they may experience a dissonance between their self-concept as capable learners and societal expectations for originality. As highlighted by Khlaif et al. (2022), such internal conflict can have long-term effects on how teacher candidates view their role in the classroom and their comfort level with integrating emerging technologies.

Hence, this chapter explores the lived realities, social narratives, and institutional conditions that contribute to AI shaming in teacher education. It also aims to provide a framework and practical strategies for educators and institutions to shift from a punitive culture of shame to one of responsible engagement, transparency, and digital empowerment. By addressing AI shaming head-on, we aim to shift the narrative around AI in education—from one of fear and judgment to one of critical awareness, innovation, and professional growth.

MAIN FOCUS OF THE CHAPTER

This chapter investigates the nuanced phenomenon of AI shaming in teacher education, shedding light on the complexities of integrating generative AI tools within academic and professional learning contexts (Hasanah et al., 2025). While such tools—ranging from content generators to assessment aids—hold the potential to enhance pedagogical innovation and learner autonomy, this chapter critically examines how teacher education students navigate the social stigma surrounding AI use in their academic work. Students often internalize societal and institutional expectations of originality, authenticity, and intellectual effort, which may conflict with the practical and creative affordances of AI technologies. As a result, many students conceal their AI use due to perceived threats to academic integrity, fears of being labeled as dishonest, or concerns over eroding their credibility as future educators. These tensions are particularly pronounced in programs preparing teachers to be both digitally literate and ethically grounded.

The chapter further explores broader ethical and pedagogical challenges, including risks of AI misuse, algorithmic bias, and overdependence, which may contribute to skill obsolescence and diminish core teaching competencies. It contextualizes AI shaming within the evolving discourse on academic honesty, professional identity formation, and educational equity—issues central to this volume's themes on bias, misuse, and displacement. Methodologically, this work adopts a reflective-analytical lens (Olmos-Vega et al., 2022), integrating insights from the author's teaching practice with a critical synthesis of emerging literature on AI in teacher education. The analysis draws from classroom interactions, narrative accounts, and student reflections collected through journaling activities, class forums, and guided discussions conducted from 2023 to 2024 in courses on Science, Technology, and Society (STS) and Educational Technology.

The narrative elements are informed by conceptual frameworks from educational sociology—notably Goffman's stigma theory—alongside theories of identity and discourse (Gee, 2000), and research on teacher development and professional ethics. While not empirical in the strictest sense, the chapter employs an autoethnographic orientation (Acut, 2024; Chang, 2016), supported by illustrative classroom-based cases and critical interpretation. A conceptual model is proposed to map the interrelated factors contributing to AI shaming and to offer pathways toward fostering transparency, critical digital literacy, and ethical AI integration in teacher education.

AI IN THE CONTEXT OF TEACHER EDUCATION

Current Landscape of AI Integration in Teacher Education

The integration of generative AI tools into teacher education is increasingly seen as an essential step in preparing future educators for the demands of modern classrooms. These tools offer transformative opportunities for lesson planning, resource generation, personalized learning, and formative assessment (Garcia, Rosak-Szyrocka, et al., 2025). Universities and teacher education programs around the globe have begun embedding AI-focused content into their curricula, either as part of educational technology courses or through dedicated modules on artificial intelligence and machine learning (Salas-Pilco et al., 2022). These efforts aim to ensure that teacher candidates are not only familiar with the latest technological advancements but also understand how to ethically and effectively use AI in their teaching practices (Ng et al., 2023).

Incorporating AI tools into teacher education programs has led to several pedagogical innovations. For instance, AI-based platforms like ChatGPT are being used to help teacher candidates draft lesson plans, generate classroom activities, and engage in reflective writing. Similarly, AI-driven learning management systems (LMS) are being employed to monitor student progress, analyze performance data, and suggest personalized interventions (Garcia, Goi, et al., 2025; Khan et al., 2021). These advancements allow for a more adaptive and responsive approach to teaching and learning, helping future teachers to better meet the needs of diverse learners.

However, the integration of AI into teacher education is not without challenges. Many educators express concerns about over-reliance on AI, ethical considerations related to data privacy, and the potential for AI to perpetuate bias (Kooli, 2023). These concerns are particularly relevant in teacher education programs, where future teachers must learn to navigate the balance between leveraging technology and maintaining pedagogical integrity. As a result, teacher education curricula are increasingly focused on helping students develop critical digital literacy skills, including understanding how AI works, its limitations, and how to use it in ways that enhance—not replace—human judgment in the classroom (Sperling et al., 2024).

Student Perspectives on AI Tools

Student perspectives on AI tools in teacher education are influenced by various factors, such as their prior experiences with technology, personal beliefs about AI's role in education, and the broader societal context in which they learn. Many teacher education students express ambivalence toward AI tools. On the one hand, they recognize the potential benefits, including automating routine tasks, enhancing creativity, and providing personalized learning experiences (Chan & Hu, 2023). On the other hand, concerns arise, such as fears of academic dishonesty, the perceived loss of the human element in teaching, and the potential for AI to erode their professional identities as educators (Al-Zahrani, 2024). This ambivalence is closely tied to the phenomenon of AI shaming—where students feel embarrassed or hesitant to admit using AI tools in their academic work. This reluctance often stems from societal perceptions of AI as a shortcut rather than a legitimate aid in the learning process. Educational environments, particularly in teacher education, value authenticity and originality, reinforcing these negative perceptions (Ajjawi et al., 2023). As a result, students fear being judged as less capable or dishonest if they openly use AI, which hinders their willingness to fully leverage its benefits (Zhai et al., 2024).

Studies have documented various instances of AI shaming. For example, one student admitted that AI had significantly improved the structure of their writing, yet they felt guilty as if bypassing the academic process (Ahmad et al., 2023). Similarly, in group projects, students who suggested using AI for brainstorming were met with skepticism, causing them to withdraw their ideas. This reflects how societal expectations about the "right" way to learn inhibit effective use of technology, even when it offers clear benefits (Haleem et al., 2022). These challenges reflect a broader tension between students' recognition of AI's potential and their fears of how it might impact their roles as future educators. Some students voiced concerns that relying on AI for lesson planning could reduce their creativity and autonomy (van den Berg & du Plessis, 2023). Others worried that overuse might hinder critical skill development, such as problem-solving and decision-making, essential for effective teaching (Ahmad et al., 2023). These concerns highlight a need for careful consideration of AI's role in teacher education (Lameras & Arnab, 2021). Critically, AI shaming creates barriers to productive engagement with AI tools in teacher education, suggesting a need for systemic change in how AI is perceived and discussed within academic settings. Educators play a critical role in shaping these perceptions by modeling responsible AI use (Adel et al., 2024). By reducing stigma and promoting positive engagement, they can help students integrate AI meaningfully into their learning (Bulathwela et al., 2024).

EXPERIENCES OF AI SHAMING

The phenomenon of AI shaming—where individuals feel embarrassed or hesitant to admit their use of AI tools—has become increasingly evident in educational contexts. This reluctance often stems from societal perceptions of AI as a shortcut rather than a legitimate learning aid. AI shaming is particularly prominent in educational settings, where the value of authenticity and originality is held in high regard, often leading to negative judgments about the use of AI.

Instances and Anecdotes

Across multiple classroom settings, the authors observed strikingly similar patterns of student hesitation and discomfort around the use of generative AI tools. These anecdotes highlight a recurring phenomenon: students are engaging with AI but often choose to conceal their usage due to fears of academic judgment or perceived lack of integrity.

Narrative: "Ana's Dilemma"

Ana, a third-year education major, used ChatGPT to brainstorm ideas for a microteaching lesson plan. When she shared her draft with a peer during practicum prep week, the response was dismissive: "Did you actually write this yourself or just copy-paste from AI?" Ana laughed it off, but the moment left her uneasy. In later discussions, she avoided mentioning any AI use, despite its continued support in refining her instructional strategies. Later, Ana's mentor teacher cautioned her: "Some professors frown on using AI. It can make your work look fake." Though meant as advice, the comment reinforced her anxiety. Ana began rewriting AI-assisted outputs just to hide their origin—losing valuable time and feeling increasingly disconnected from her own creative process. This narrative, based on recurring classroom patterns, underscores the internal conflict many teacher education students face: a tension between leveraging digital tools for efficiency and upholding perceived standards of "authentic" academic labor.

Classroom Reflections

In Dharel's STS class, a similar dynamic emerged. When he asked students whether they had used tools like ChatGPT for coursework, no hands were raised. Only after he shared his own experiences with AI for ideation did the atmosphere shift. Students gradually opened up, admitting to using AI for brainstorming, outlining, and revising. Their initial silence highlighted the social risks they associated with AI use—fears of being labeled lazy, dishonest, or less competent. One student shared how they relied on AI to help structure essays but never acknowledged it in class, fearing criticism. Another noted that although AI enhanced their clarity in writing, they felt guilty, as if they had bypassed the academic process entirely.

In Eliza's class, a student recounted suggesting an AI tool for brainstorming during a group project—only to have the idea dismissed as undermining their group's creativity. Another student, while using AI to summarize lessons for exam prep, chose not to disclose it to peers, worried they'd be viewed as incapable of studying independently.

Likewise, in Anabelle's classroom, a pre-service teacher admitted to using AI to draft lesson plans for her teaching practicum. Despite the resource helping her produce creative outputs, she deliberately downplayed its role during peer feedback and supervisor evaluations, fearing that openness would raise doubts about her pedagogical skills and professional readiness.

Shared Observations Across Institutions

Though these anecdotes stem from different courses and institutions, they reveal a consistent pattern: students often hide their use of AI due to internalized shame, social judgment, and institutional ambiguity. Co-authors from different educational contexts noted this trend, reinforcing the idea that AI shaming is not isolated but systemic.

These accounts, as depicted in Figure 1, demonstrate how AI use, when clouded by stigma, becomes a source of anxiety rather than empowerment. They reveal how students navigate a hidden curriculum—one where values like originality, authenticity, and individual effort are rigidly upheld, often at the expense of innovation. The implications for teacher education are profound: if future educators are to model responsible and creative use of AI in their own classrooms, they must first feel safe to explore these tools without fear of judgment.

Figure 1. Raising hands in silence: A cartoon depiction of AI shaming

Factors Contributing to AI shaming

While several studies have pointed to traditional academic expectations and institutional ambiguity as reasons for the resistance toward AI tools in education (Birks & Clare, 2023; Chen et al., 2022; Kim et al., 2024), this study offers a novel framework synthesizing classroom narratives, reflective observation, and literature. We propose a conceptual model—*The AI Shaming Framework in Teacher Education*—comprising four interrelated dimensions: Internal Conflict, Peer Judgment, Educator Influence, and Policy Silence. These elements explain how AI shaming emerges and persists in pre-service teacher education contexts.

Internal Conflict: Navigating Values vs. Efficiency

At the heart of AI shaming lies an internal tension experienced by students who recognize the utility of AI tools but simultaneously feel guilt or shame when using them. This stems from the entrenched academic valorization of originality and self-reliance, which students internalize throughout their schooling (Birks & Clare, 2023; Chen et al., 2022). Ana's composite narrative, as well as firsthand classroom observations, underscore how students feel they are compromising their academic integrity—even when AI supports learning rather than replaces effort. As a result, they either over-edit AI-generated content to remove traces of machine assistance or avoid disclosing its use altogether, leading to time-consuming processes and creative disconnection.

Peer Judgment: Social Stigma and Image Management

Students do not operate in isolation. The narratives from Dharel, Eliza, and Anabelle's classrooms show how peer interactions significantly shape perceptions of acceptable academic behavior. Comments like "Did you just copy-paste from AI?" or the outright rejection of AI in group settings reflect a performative academic culture—one in which being seen as independent and intellectually competent takes precedence. Peer influence generates fear of being perceived as lazy, deceptive, or less capable (Zhang et al., 2023), which pressures students into secrecy and self-censorship, especially in competitive learning environments.

Educator Influence: Authority Figures as Norm Enforcers

Educators play a pivotal role in shaping attitudes toward AI use. When mentors issue vague warnings (e.g., "*AI makes your work look fake*"), they may inadvertently contribute to student anxieties. As seen in Ana's story, these comments instill a sense of surveillance and moral suspicion, leading students to equate AI-assisted work with academic misconduct. In many institutions, the lack of pedagogical modeling around AI use means students do not see responsible AI use being demonstrated or encouraged. This scenario often resulted in a vacuum filled with doubt and fear (Bozkurt et al., 2024; Coman & Cardon, 2024).

Policy Silence: Ambiguity and Mistrust

Compounding the above factors is the absence of clear institutional policies or instructional scaffolds around AI usage. Many universities are still grappling with how to integrate generative AI into academic integrity policies, leaving students confused about what is acceptable (Gustilo et al., 2024; Kim et al., 2024). This policy vacuum results in students defaulting to risk-averse behaviors—avoiding or hiding

AI use altogether. In contexts like teacher education, where students are expected to uphold professional and ethical standards, this silence contributes to AI being viewed with suspicion rather than curiosity.

Conceptualizing AI shaming through this framework, as illustrated in Figure 2, allows teacher educators to move beyond reiterating known barriers to digital tool adoption. It introduces a structured lens to critically examine the layered dynamics—internal conflict, peer judgment, educator influence, and policy silence—that perpetuate stigma around AI use. This perspective not only acknowledges the emotional and social risks students face but also equips educators with a foundation to design pedagogical interventions that validate responsible AI use, foster open dialogue, and promote ethical integration in both academic and field-based contexts

Figure 2. A proposed framework for understanding AI shaming in teacher education

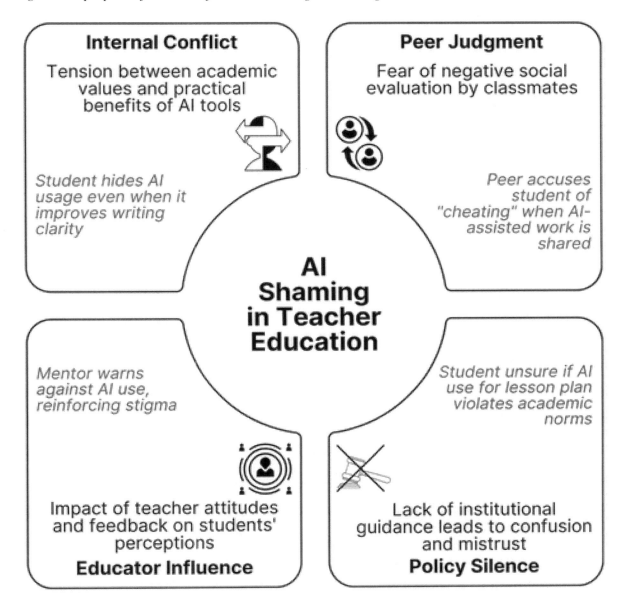

THE ROLE OF EDUCATORS

Educators play a pivotal role in shaping students' behaviors toward the use of AI. Their perceptions and approaches toward AI not only influence students' acceptance and usage of these tools but also contribute significantly to the broader culture around technology in education.

Educator Attitudes Toward AI

The attitudes that educators hold toward AI tools profoundly impact how students perceive and use these technologies in their academic work. If educators demonstrate openness and curiosity toward AI, students are more likely to feel comfortable exploring and integrating AI into their learning processes. This positive reinforcement can lead to innovative approaches in their assignments and projects. On the other hand, when educators express skepticism or dismiss the use of AI as a threat to academic integrity or authenticity, students may feel pressured to hide their AI use due to fear of judgment or negative consequences (Zhai et al., 2024). This dynamic can create a divide between students who utilize AI to enhance their learning and those who refrain from using it out of fear, leading to feelings of inadequacy or isolation among the latter.

Research shows that educator attitudes toward AI can range from enthusiasm and support to reluctance and resistance (Chan & Lee, 2023; Kaya et al., 2022). Teachers who view AI as a valuable tool for enhancing creativity and critical thinking can create an environment where students feel encouraged to experiment with these technologies (Al Darayseh, 2023). This supportive atmosphere allows students to take risks and explore AI's capabilities, ultimately fostering a sense of ownership over their learning. However, educators who focus solely on the potential pitfalls—such as concerns about AI replacing human jobs or reducing the need for traditional skills—may inadvertently reinforce the stigma around AI, contributing to AI shaming among students. Such negative perceptions can stifle students' willingness to engage with AI, potentially limiting their skill development in an increasingly digital world.

In many cases, the reluctance among educators to fully embrace AI stems from a lack of familiarity with these tools and how they can be meaningfully integrated into their curricula. Some educators worry that AI will compromise the integrity of learning by providing easy shortcuts, while others are unsure of how to assess work that has been AI-assisted (Lee et al., 2024). This lack of understanding can lead to missed opportunities for educators to utilize AI as a complementary resource in their teaching. As a result, students often sense this ambivalence and mirror it in their own attitudes toward AI, feeling uncertain about its role in their education and hesitant to use it effectively. Furthermore, the absence of institutional policies and clear ethical guidelines on AI use in education exacerbates these tensions (Nguyen et al., 2022). When educators themselves are uncertain about how to approach AI, they may pass this uncertainty onto their students, leading to inconsistent messaging about the legitimacy of AI in the classroom. Such inconsistency can foster a culture of mistrust regarding AI tools, preventing students from recognizing their potential benefits. In the absence of well-defined frameworks for AI usage, both educators and students are left grappling with how to navigate the evolving landscape of technology in education, further complicating their relationship with AI.

Table 1. Attitudes toward AI and their impact on students

Educator Attitude	Description	Impact on Students
Openness and Curiosity	Educators with this attitude actively explore AI tools and encourage critical engagement, fostering a supportive environment where students feel safe to experiment and discuss AI use. This openness reduces stigma and promotes responsible digital literacy.	Students feel empowered to experiment with AI technologies.
Skepticism and Dismissiveness	Skeptical educators often emphasize AI's risks to academic integrity, which can create fear-driven classrooms where students hide AI use or associate it with cheating. Such attitudes may reinforce AI shaming and hinder authentic technology engagement.	Students conceal their AI use due to fear of judgment.
Enthusiasm for Innovation	Teachers who embrace AI as a means of pedagogical innovation integrate it into lessons and inspire students to explore its creative and analytical potential. This enthusiasm cultivates student confidence and encourages ethical AI use.	Students engage more confidently with AI, seeing it as legitimate.
Reluctance Due to Uncertainty	Reluctant educators often lack training or clarity on AI's role in teaching, leading to inconsistent practices and mixed signals for students. This uncertainty fosters confusion, making students hesitant or unsure about legitimate AI integration.	Students mirror this uncertainty, leading to apprehension in using AI.
Institutionally Reactive	Educators adjust their AI stance based on the presence or absence of formal guidelines. In environments lacking clear policies, they may default to conservative or avoidance-based approaches.	Students experience inconsistent or overly cautious messaging about AI, leading to confusion or fear of inappropriate use.

The attitudes of educators toward AI play a crucial role in shaping students' perceptions and willingness to engage with these technologies. Fostering a culture of openness and curiosity can significantly reduce the stigma surrounding AI use, encouraging students to embrace these tools as legitimate aids in their learning journey. Moreover, implementing clear institutional policies and providing professional development on AI integration will equip educators with the necessary skills and confidence to guide their students effectively. Ultimately, creating a supportive and informed environment will empower future educators to utilize AI responsibly, enhancing their educational experiences and professional growth.

Actionable Strategies for Addressing AI Shaming

AI shaming—a phenomenon where students feel embarrassed or are judged for using AI tools—can hinder open discussions, ethical use, and digital empowerment in teacher education (Giray, 2024). To responsibly and actively promote a supportive, informed, and inclusive culture of AI use, the following six structured and actionable strategies are proposed:

1. Implement AI Literacy Workshops

Objective: To equip both pre-service teachers and educators with the foundational skills and ethical understanding necessary to use AI tools confidently and responsibly.

Description: AI literacy workshops provide structured, hands-on sessions where participants learn how to interact with AI tools, reflect on their outputs, and evaluate ethical implications.

Workshop Template:

- Session 1: Introduction to Generative AI – Understanding how tools like ChatGPT, DALL·E, and Copilot function.
- Session 2: Use Cases in Teaching and Learning – Applications in lesson planning, brainstorming, feedback generation.
- Session 3: Ethical Use and Academic Integrity – Discussing plagiarism, authorship, and transparency.
- Session 4: Practicum Task and Reflection – Engaging students with tasks that integrate AI and require critical analysis.

Example: At the University of Arizona (2025), faculty and students engaged in the *"Transforming Teaching with AI: Integrating GPT and LLMs"* workshop. This hands-on session provided a step-by-step guide to licensing, configuring, and integrating large language models (LLMs) such as ChatGPT, Gemini, and Copilot into classroom practice—at a cost-effective rate (under $50, with free student access). Participants explored the pedagogical affordances of different LLMs and gained practical skills in AI-enhanced lesson planning, feedback generation, and instructional design. Initial feedback indicated increased confidence, reduced barriers to adoption, and improved student engagement through more personalized and interactive learning experiences.

2. Integrate an AI Ethics Module into the Curriculum

Objective: To provide a formal space for students to explore philosophical, social, and professional issues surrounding AI use in education.

Description: By embedding AI ethics into education courses (e.g., Educational Technology, Foundations of Education), teacher candidates gain a deeper understanding of responsible AI use.

Sample Module Outline:

- Week 1: Introduction to AI Ethics in Education (autonomy, justice, fairness)
- Week 2: Plagiarism vs. Assistance – Gray areas of AI-generated content
- Week 3: Bias and Fairness in AI Tools
- Week 4: Institutional Policies and Writing AI Usage Disclaimers

Assessment: Case study analysis, ethical dilemmas debate, AI policy drafting

Example: In the United States, secondary Computer Science and English Language Arts teachers across urban, suburban, and semi-rural school districts piloted a project-based AI ethics curriculum to contextualize the complexities of artificial intelligence for their diverse student populations (Walsh et al., 2023). Recognizing that AI ethics is an urgent yet often overlooked topic in K–12 education, these educators adapted the curriculum to align with their students' local realities—incorporating discussions on algorithmic bias, data privacy, and the social impact of generative AI. The project featured hands-on design challenges, case study analyses, and community impact investigations, which not only deepened students' understanding of AI technologies but also fostered critical thinking, civic awareness, and interdisciplinary learning.

3. Facilitate "AI Sharing Circles"

Objective: To normalize AI use through peer dialogue, reduce stigma, and foster a reflective, non-judgmental classroom climate.

Description: AI Sharing Circles are structured, small-group conversations where students reflect on and discuss their experiences with AI. These discussions promote emotional safety, normalize diverse AI practices, and build a shared understanding of responsible use.

Protocol Format:

- Opening Round: "Share one way you've used AI this week."
- Middle Round: "What challenges or concerns have you faced?"
- Closing Round: "What support do you need to use AI more effectively?"

Facilitator's Role: Ensure psychological safety, highlight positive patterns, and connect reflections to course objectives.

Example: Prior to the 2023–2024 school year, a school district in Canada initiated a collaborative planning phase for monthly AI Sharing Circles, designed to integrate Indigenous knowledge systems with technological professional development. The Learning and Leadership Services (LLS) team, in partnership with a community Elder and the Equity team, facilitated discussions with school administrators to collect feedback and inform the design of these circles. These sessions were not standalone activities but served as complementary professional development, aligning with broader equity and instructional goals. Rooted in the Indigenous principle of Etuaptmumk (Two-Eyed Seeing), this initiative aimed to bridge Western and Indigenous ways of knowing, offering a culturally grounded approach to AI integration that fosters reflection, inclusivity, and ethical awareness in leadership and teaching practices.

4. Design Assignments that Incorporate AI Use

Objective: To reframe AI as a legitimate educational aid rather than a form of cheating or shortcut.

Description: Instructors can explicitly require or allow the use of AI tools in assignments, with follow-up reflection or comparison tasks that promote critical thinking.

Example Assignment:

- Task: Use ChatGPT to generate a draft lesson plan on ecosystems.
- Reflection: "What suggestions did you accept, reject, or modify? Why?"
- Evaluation Criteria: Clarity of AI output, alignment with curriculum, originality of final product.
- Outcome: Students learn to use AI as a partner in ideation, while developing their capacity to critique and refine AI-generated outputs.

Example: The Stanford Teaching Commons (2024) offers a comprehensive module titled "*Integrating AI into Assignments*", which guides educators through the process of embedding generative AI tools into student assessment tasks. The module emphasizes designing meaningful assessments that align with clear learning objectives and respond to student perspectives on AI use. This student-centered approach fosters responsible AI integration, critical thinking, and academic integrity, positioning AI as a tool for deeper engagement rather than shortcut learning.

5. Provide Professional Development for Educators

Objective: To build confidence and competence in facilitating AI-enhanced learning experiences.

Description: Many instructors may themselves feel uncertain about AI. Institutions must offer ongoing PD workshops focused on:

- AI literacy
- AI integration into pedagogy
- Designing AI-compatible assessments
- Addressing student fears and ethical concerns

PD Model: Blended (asynchronous modules + synchronous coaching)

Example: A study conducted at Palestine Technical University Kadoorie and Hebron University evaluated the AI literacy levels of preservice teachers and tested the impact of a professional development program grounded in the Instructional Design Framework for AI Literacy. Using a quasi-experimental pretest-posttest design, the study involved 37 undergraduate participants and utilized a validated AI literacy scale for assessment. The findings revealed that the program significantly improved AI literacy skills among preservice teachers, regardless of gender or specialization. The study recommends embedding AI tools in both pre-service and in-service teacher training and expanding research to diverse disciplines to increase generalizability and effectiveness of AI-focused professional development strategies (Younis, 2024).

6. Cultivate a Positive AI Culture in the Classroom

Objective: To establish AI as a respected and creative tool through storytelling, real-world use cases, and student empowerment.

Description: Educators can share inspiring stories of AI in education, celebrate successful student use cases, and showcase how AI is used in teaching professions.

Initiatives:

- Display posters or slides showing AI-assisted lesson plans or rubrics created by students
- Invite alumni or guest speakers who integrate AI into their teaching
- Host a "Creative AI Challenge" where students showcase ethical AI-assisted projects

Example: In discussing how educators can embrace generative AI in the classroom, Harouni, a lecturer at the Harvard Graduate School of Education, urges teachers to acknowledge and critically engage with the presence of tools like ChatGPT. He suggests that educators should guide students in learning how to use AI responsibly, ask deeper questions, and use the limitations of AI to spark creative exploration. Harouni emphasizes that when AI reveals "our failure of imagination," that's precisely when the real learning begins. He encourages the use of AI as a collaborative partner in the learning process, advocating for assignments that challenge students to rethink traditional frameworks rather than simply regurgitate information.

Table 2. Summary of actionable interventions for AI shaming

Strategy	Focus	Key Output
AI Literacy Workshops	Knowledge + Skills	AI use reflections, increased confidence
AI Ethics Curriculum Module	Values + Critical Thinking	Policy drafts, ethical debate performance
AI Sharing Circles	Emotional Safety + Dialogue	Peer support, reduced stigma
AI-Integrated Assignments	Practice + Evaluation	Critiqued outputs, reflective comparison
PD for Educators	Institutional Capacity	Teacher-designed AI-enhanced lessons
Cultivating Positive AI Culture	Identity + Belonging	Vlogs, showcases, peer-celebrated best practices

IMPLICATIONS FOR TEACHER EDUCATION

The growing presence of AI in education brings both opportunities and challenges (Garcia, 2025; Xiao et al., 2025), particularly in shaping the identities and professional trajectories of future educators. AI shaming can profoundly influence the way teacher education students perceive their role in the classroom and how they develop professionally. These implications call for a fundamental rethinking of how AI is integrated into the programs, shifting the narrative from one of shame and fear to one of empowerment and innovation.

Impacts on Student Identity and Professional Development

AI shaming can have detrimental effects on the identity formation and professional development of future educators. For many teacher education students, their training is not just about acquiring pedagogical knowledge and skills but also about forming a professional identity as an educator. When AI shaming is present, students may internalize the idea that using AI is somehow *"cheating"* or undermining their role as an authentic source of knowledge. This internal conflict can lead to self-doubt, hesitancy in adopting new technologies, and even a diminished sense of professional competence. In the context of professional development, AI shaming can create barriers to innovation and growth. Future educators who feel stigmatized for using AI may avoid these tools altogether, missing out on opportunities to enhance their teaching practices, develop new skills, and prepare for the increasingly digital classrooms of the future (Zawacki-Richter et al., 2019). As AI tools continue to evolve, educators who are not familiar with these technologies may find themselves at a disadvantage, unable to incorporate AI into their pedagogy and meet the demands of a technology-driven educational landscape (Hennessy et al., 2022).

Moreover, AI shaming can reinforce traditional, hierarchical notions of teacher authority, where educators are expected to be the sole experts in the classroom. This perception may prevent teacher education students from embracing AI as a collaborative partner in their teaching, potentially stifling creativity, curiosity, and experimentation (Zawacki-Richter et al., 2019). AI shaming can significantly disrupt the development of professional identity and self-concept among future educators. In teacher education, identity formation goes beyond acquiring instructional strategies—it encompasses evolving beliefs about what it means to be a competent, ethical, and innovative educator. When AI use is stigmatized, students may internalize feelings of guilt or inauthenticity, viewing reliance on AI as a breach of academic integrity or a threat to their legitimacy as future teachers. According to Erving Goffman's

(1963) theory of stigma, such labeling leads individuals to manage a "spoiled identity," which can result in concealment of AI use or disengagement from technology-enhanced learning environments.

Psychologically, this tension undermines students' emotional safety and their self-efficacy, a key component of Bandura's (1997) theory, which emphasizes the importance of belief in one's capabilities to organize and execute actions required to manage prospective situations. Students who are shamed for exploring AI may develop low self-confidence in their technological competencies, limiting their willingness to innovate or experiment with emerging tools. This is particularly problematic in digital learning ecosystems where adaptability is vital.

Professionally, AI shaming curbs critical opportunities for growth. Students may avoid engaging with AI tools for fear of judgment, thereby missing chances to enhance their lesson design, personalize learning, or leverage analytics for student assessment (Hennessy et al., 2022; Zawacki-Richter et al., 2019). Furthermore, shaming reinforces outdated, hierarchical models of teaching where authority is vested solely in human expertise, discouraging more collaborative, co-constructive relationships between educators and intelligent systems. Cultural contexts also shape these dynamics. In collectivist education systems, where conformity to group norms is highly valued, students may feel more pressure to suppress AI usage if institutional attitudes are negative or ambiguous (Chen & Unal, 2023; Shahzalal & Adnan, 2022). In contrast, individualist systems may afford more freedom to experiment yet can also isolate students who deviate from perceived academic norms. Without clear institutional policies or culturally responsive discourse around AI, future educators are left to navigate these tensions alone, risking confusion, professional insecurity, and disconnection from technological progress (Delello et al., 2025).

To address these challenges, teacher education programs must cultivate psychologically safe learning environments where AI use is destigmatized and critically examined (Güneyli et al., 2024). This includes integrating AI literacy into the curriculum, offering professional development grounded in digital ethics, and establishing transparent institutional policies that recognize the evolving role of AI in teaching and learning (Funa & Gabay, 2025). Only then can students fully develop into confident, reflective, and future-ready educators. In this way, AI shaming can inhibit the professional growth of future educators, limiting their ability to explore new methods of teaching and learning that leverage AI's potential. To combat these negative impacts, teacher education programs must actively work to create environments where the use of AI is normalized, supported, and recognized as a valuable part of professional development. This requires a shift in both the culture of education and the narratives that surround AI tools.

Rethinking the Narrative Around AI in Education

To mitigate the effects of AI shaming and to empower future educators, it is essential to rethink the narrative around AI in education. Instead of positioning AI as a threat to traditional teaching practices or as a tool that undermines academic integrity, the conversation must shift toward viewing AI as a means of enhancing professional capabilities and fostering innovation in the classroom (Mangubat et al., 2025; Xiao et al., 2025).

Empowering educators as AI facilitators. Teacher education programs should promote the idea that educators can serve as facilitators of AI use in the classroom. This approach reframes AI not as a replacement for teachers but as a complementary tool that can support diverse learning needs, streamline administrative tasks, and provide personalized feedback (Luckin et al., 2022). Educators should be encouraged to explore how AI can assist in lesson planning, assessment, and differentiated instruction, thereby empowering them to become AI leaders in education.

Promoting AI literacy in teacher education. Integrating AI literacy into teacher education curricula is a critical step in reducing AI shaming. Future educators must be equipped with the knowledge and skills to critically evaluate AI tools, understand their limitations, and use them ethically in their teaching (Miller et al., 2025). AI literacy also involves recognizing how AI can contribute to creative problem-solving and innovation in education, shifting the focus from fear of replacement to the potential for professional growth (Ding et al., 2024).

Fostering a growth mindset around AI. Teacher education programs should encourage a growth mindset toward AI, emphasizing that learning to work with AI is an ongoing process of professional development. Rather than seeing AI as a fixed skillset or as something that students must master immediately, educators can frame AI as an evolving tool that they can experiment with and learn from over time. This approach reduces the pressure on teacher education students to have all the answers and instead positions them as lifelong learners in a rapidly changing educational landscape (Dang & Liu, 2022; Ng et al., 2023).

Encouraging open dialogue about AI. Creating spaces for open dialogue about AI use can help dismantle the stigma and shame associated with these tools. Teacher education programs should facilitate discussions where students can share their experiences, both positive and negative, with AI. These conversations can help normalize AI use and highlight its practical benefits while also addressing any concerns about ethics, authenticity, or academic dishonesty.

Celebrating AI-driven innovation in teaching. Finally, teacher education programs should celebrate and showcase examples of AI-driven innovation in teaching. Highlighting case studies, classroom projects, or individual success stories where AI was used to enhance teaching and learning can shift the narrative from one of shame to one of possibility. By positioning AI as a tool for creative and innovative teaching, educators can inspire future teachers to experiment with AI in ways that align with their professional goals and the needs of their students (Walter, 2024).

Rethinking the narrative around AI in education is essential for addressing the phenomenon of AI shaming and for ensuring that future educators are equipped to thrive in technology-enhanced classrooms. Promoting AI as a tool for empowerment is crucial for addressing AI shaming and preparing future educators to thrive in technology-enhanced classrooms. Teacher education programs that emphasize AI's potential for enhancing creative and innovative teaching can help educators develop the confidence and skills necessary for its integration. Encouraging experimentation with AI tools, fostering open dialogue, and celebrating AI-driven success stories can shift the narrative toward possibility and growth. This approach ensures that future teachers are equipped not only to navigate AI but to use it effectively in ways that align with their professional aspirations and the diverse needs of their students.

CONCLUSION

This chapter has illuminated the complex and often underexplored phenomenon of AI shaming among teacher education students. Far from being a peripheral concern, AI shaming reflects broader anxieties about technological integration in education, professional legitimacy, and the evolving roles of teachers in AI-mediated classrooms. Student narratives revealed not just discomfort with using AI tools, but also a deeper struggle tied to identity formation, ethical uncertainty, and peer or institutional judgment. These affective dimensions demand that we go beyond mere technical training. To move forward, it is essential that teacher education programs cultivate a psychologically safe and critically reflective space where the use of generative AI is normalized, de-stigmatized, and pedagogically situated. Doing so requires not only the inclusion of AI literacy in the curriculum, but also professional development frameworks that address emotional resilience, ethical reasoning, and equity concerns surrounding AI use.

Institutions must also resist universalized approaches and instead ground interventions in local cultural contexts, recognizing that attitudes toward AI are shaped by access, norms, and pre-existing educational narratives. This is especially vital in regions where systemic constraints intersect with rapidly evolving digital expectations. Collaborative dialogue among students, educators, and policymakers is therefore crucial—not merely to manage the risks of AI, but to harness its potential responsibly and creatively. Reframing AI from a threat to a catalyst for teacher agency and innovation is key. Only then can we transform AI shaming into an opportunity for professional growth, critical consciousness, and inclusive practice in future-ready education.

REFERENCES

Acut, D. P. (2024). From Classroom Learning to Real-World Skills: An Autoethnographic Account of School Field Trips and STEM Work Immersion Program Management. *Disciplinary and Interdisciplinary Science Education Research*, 6(1), 1–13. DOI: 10.1186/s43031-024-00111-x

Acut, D. P., Malabago, N. K., Malicoban, E. V., Galamiton, N. S., & Garcia, M. B. (2024). "ChatGPT 4.0 Ghosted Us While Conducting Literature Search:" Modeling the Chatbot's Generated Non-Existent References Using Regression Analysis. *Internet Reference Services Quarterly*, ●●●, 1–26. DOI: 10.1080/10875301.2024.2426793

Adel, A., Ahsan, A., & Davison, C. (2024). ChatGPT Promises and Challenges in Education: Computational and Ethical Perspectives. *Education Sciences*, 14(8), 1–27. DOI: 10.3390/educsci14080814

Adetayo, A. J. (2024). Reimagining Learning Through AI Art: The Promise of DALL-E and MidJourney for Education and Libraries. *Library Hi Tech News*. Advance online publication. DOI: 10.1108/LHTN-01-2024-0005

Ahmad, S. F., Han, H., Alam, M. M., Rehmat, M. K., Irshad, M., Arraño-Muñoz, M., & Ariza-Montes, A. (2023). Impact of Artificial Intelligence on Human Loss in Decision Making, Laziness and Safety in Education. *Humanities & Social Sciences Communications*, 10(1), 1–14. DOI: 10.1057/s41599-023-01787-8 PMID: 37325188

Ajjawi, R., Tai, J., Dollinger, M., Dawson, P., Boud, D., & Bearman, M. (2023). From Authentic Assessment to Authenticity in Assessment: Broadening Perspectives. *Assessment &amp. Assessment & Evaluation in Higher Education*, 49(4), 499–510. DOI: 10.1080/02602938.2023.2271193

Akgun, S., & Greenhow, C. (2021). Artificial Intelligence in Education: Addressing Ethical Challenges in K-12 Settings. *AI and Ethics*, 2(3), 431–440. DOI: 10.1007/s43681-021-00096-7 PMID: 34790956

Al Darayseh, A. (2023). Acceptance of Artificial Intelligence in Teaching Science: Science Teachers' Perspective. *Computers and Education: Artificial Intelligence*, 4, 1–9. DOI: 10.1016/j.caeai.2023.100132

Al-Zahrani, A. M. (2024). Unveiling the Shadows: Beyond the Hype of AI in Education. *Heliyon*, 10(9), 1–15. DOI: 10.1016/j.heliyon.2024.e30696 PMID: 38737255

Bandura, A. (1997). *Self-Efficacy: The Exercise of Control*. https://psycnet.apa.org/record/1997-08589-000

Birks, D., & Clare, J. (2023). Linking Artificial Intelligence Facilitated Academic Misconduct to Existing Prevention Frameworks. *International Journal for Educational Integrity*, 19(1), 1–10. DOI: 10.1007/s40979-023-00142-3

Bozkurt, A., Xiao, J., Farrow, R., Bai, J. Y. H., Nerantzi, C., Moore, S., Dron, J., Stracke, C. M., Singh, L., Crompton, H., Koutropoulos, A., Terentev, E., Pazurek, A., Nichols, M., Sidorkin, A. M., Costello, E., Watson, S., Mulligan, D., Honeychurch, S., & Asino, T. I. (2024). The Manifesto for Teaching and Learning in a Time of Generative AI: A Critical Collective Stance to Better Navigate the Future. *Open Praxis*, 16(4), 487–513. DOI: 10.55982/openpraxis.16.4.777

Bulathwela, S., Pérez-Ortiz, M., Holloway, C., Cukurova, M., & Shawe-Taylor, J. (2024). Artificial Intelligence Alone Will Not Democratise Education: On Educational Inequality, Techno-Solutionism and Inclusive Tools. *Sustainability (Basel)*, *16*(2), 1–20. DOI: 10.3390/su16020781

Chan, C. K. Y., & Hu, W. (2023). Students' Voices on Generative AI: Perceptions, Benefits, and Challenges in Higher Education. *International Journal of Educational Technology in Higher Education*, *20*(1), 1–18. DOI: 10.1186/s41239-023-00411-8

Chan, C. K. Y., & Lee, K. K. W. (2023). The AI Generation Gap: Are Gen Z Students More Interested in Adopting Generative AI Such as ChatGPT in Teaching and Learning Than Their Gen X and Millennial Generation Teachers? *Smart Learning Environments*, *10*(1), 1–23. DOI: 10.1186/s40561-023-00269-3

Chang, H. (2016). *Autoethnography as Method*. Routledge., DOI: 10.4324/9781315433370

Chen, C. C., & Unal, A. F. (2023). Individualism-Collectivism: A Review of Conceptualization and Measurement. In *Oxford Research Encyclopedia of Business and Management*. Oxford University Press., DOI: 10.1093/acrefore/9780190224851.013.350

Chen, J., Lai, P., Chan, A., Man, V., & Chan, C.-H. (2022). AI-Assisted Enhancement of Student Presentation Skills: Challenges and Opportunities. *Sustainability (Basel)*, *15*(1), 1–19. DOI: 10.3390/su15010196

Coman, A. W., & Cardon, P. (2024). Perceptions of Professionalism and Authenticity in AI-Assisted Writing. *Business and Professional Communication Quarterly*, 23294906241233224. Advance online publication. DOI: 10.1177/23294906241233224

da Silva, G. S., & Ulbricht, V. R. (2024). Learning with Conversational AI: ChatGPT and Bard/Gemini in Education. *Cognition and Exploratory Learning in the Digital Age*, 101-117. DOI: 10.1007/978-3-031-66462-5_6

Dang, J., & Liu, L. (2022). A Growth Mindset About Human Minds Promotes Positive Responses to Intelligent Technology. *Cognition*, *220*, 1–14. DOI: 10.1016/j.cognition.2021.104985 PMID: 34920301

Delello, J. A., Sung, W., Mokhtari, K., Hebert, J., Bronson, A., & De Giuseppe, T. (2025). AI in the Classroom: Insights from Educators on Usage, Challenges, and Mental Health. *Education Sciences*, *15*(2), 1–27. DOI: 10.3390/educsci15020113

Ding, A.-C. E., Shi, L., Yang, H., & Choi, I. (2024). Enhancing Teacher AI Literacy and Integration Through Different Types of Cases in Teacher Professional Development. *Computers and Education Open*, *6*, 1–13. DOI: 10.1016/j.caeo.2024.100178

Benke, E., & Szoke, A. (2024). Academic Integrity in the Time of Artificial Intelligence: Exploring Student Attitudes. *Italian Journal of Sociology of Education*, *16*(2), 91–108. DOI: 10.14658/PUPJ-IJSE-2024-2-5

Funa, A. A., & Gabay, R. A. E. (2025). Policy Guidelines and Recommendations on AI Use in Teaching and Learning: A Meta-Synthesis Study. *Social Sciences & Humanities Open*, *11*, 1–13. DOI: 10.1016/j.ssaho.2024.101221

Gantalao, L. C., Calzada, J. G. D., Capuyan, D. L., Lumantas, B. C., Acut, D. P., & Garcia, M. B. (2025). Equipping the Next Generation of Technicians: Navigating School Infrastructure and Technical Knowledge in the Age of AI Integration. In *Pitfalls of AI Integration in Education: Skill Obsolescence, Misuse, and Bias*. IGI Global.

Garcia, M. B. (2024). The Paradox of Artificial Creativity: Challenges and Opportunities of Generative AI Artistry. *Creativity Research Journal*, ●●●, 1–14. DOI: 10.1080/10400419.2024.2354622

Garcia, M. B. (2025). Teaching and Learning Computer Programming Using ChatGPT: A Rapid Review of Literature Amid the Rise of Generative AI Technologies. *Education and Information Technologies*, ●●●, 1–25. DOI: 10.1007/s10639-025-13452-5

Garcia, M. B., Arif, Y. M., Khlaif, Z. N., Zhu, M., de Almeida, R. P. P., de Almeida, R. S., & Masters, K. (2024). Effective Integration of Artificial Intelligence in Medical Education: Practical Tips and Actionable Insights. In *Transformative Approaches to Patient Literacy and Healthcare Innovation* (pp. 1-19). IGI Global. DOI: 10.4018/979-8-3693-3661-8.ch001

Garcia, M. B., Goi, C.-L., Shively, K., Maher, D., Rosak-Szyrocka, J., Happonen, A., Bozkurt, A., & Damaševičius, R. (2025). Understanding Student Engagement in AI-Powered Online Learning Platforms: A Narrative Review of Key Theories and Models. In *Cases on Enhancing P-16 Student Engagement With Digital Technologies* (pp. 1-30). IGI Global. DOI: 10.2139/ssrn.5074608

Garcia, M. B., Rosak-Szyrocka, J., Yılmaz, R., Metwally, A. H. S., Acut, D. P., Ofosu-Ampong, K., Erdoğdu, F., Fung, C. Y., & Bozkurt, A. (2025). Rethinking Educational Assessment in the Age of Generative AI: Actionable Strategies to Mitigate Academic Dishonesty. In *Pitfalls of AI Integration in Education: Skill Obsolescence, Misuse, and Bias*. IGI Global.

Gee, J. P. (2000). Identity as an Analytic Lens for Research in Education. *Review of Research in Education*, 25, 99–125. DOI: 10.2307/1167322

Giray, L. (2024). AI Shaming: The Silent Stigma among Academic Writers and Researchers. *Annals of Biomedical Engineering*, 52(9), 2319–2324. DOI: 10.1007/s10439-024-03582-1 PMID: 38977530

Goffman, E. (1963). *Stigma: Notes on the Management of Spoiled Identity*. Touchstone. https://books.google.com.ph/books?id=7CNUUMKTbIoC

Güneyli, A., Burgul, N. S., Dericioğlu, S., Cenkova, N., Becan, S., Şimşek, Ş. E., & Güneralp, H. (2024). Exploring Teacher Awareness of Artificial Intelligence in Education: A Case Study from Northern Cyprus. *European Journal of Investigation in Health, Psychology and Education*, 14(8), 2358–2376. DOI: 10.3390/ejihpe14080156 PMID: 39194950

Gustilo, L., Ong, E., & Lapinid, M. R. (2024). Algorithmically-Driven Writing and Academic Integrity: Exploring Educators' Practices, Perceptions, and Policies in AI Era. *International Journal for Educational Integrity*, 20(1), 1–43. DOI: 10.1007/s40979-024-00153-8

Haleem, A., Javaid, M., Qadri, M. A., & Suman, R. (2022). Understanding the Role of Digital Technologies in Education: A Review. *Sustainable Operations and Computers*, 3, 275–285. DOI: 10.1016/j.susoc.2022.05.004

Hasanah, N. A., Aziza, M. R., Junikhah, A., Arif, Y. M., & Garcia, M. B. (2025). Navigating the Use of AI in Engineering Education Through a Systematic Review of Technology, Regulations, and Challenges. In *Pitfalls of AI Integration in Education: Skill Obsolescence, Misuse, and Bias*. IGI Global.

Hennessy, S., D'Angelo, S., McIntyre, N., Koomar, S., Kreimeia, A., Cao, L., Brugha, M., & Zubairi, A. (2022). Technology Use for Teacher Professional Development in Low- and Middle-Income Countries: A systematic review. *Computers and Education Open*, *3*, 1–32. DOI: 10.1016/j.caeo.2022.100080

Kamalov, F., Santandreu Calonge, D., & Gurrib, I. (2023). New Era of Artificial Intelligence in Education: Towards a Sustainable Multifaceted Revolution. *Sustainability (Basel)*, *15*(16), 1–27. DOI: 10.3390/su151612451

Kaya, F., Aydin, F., Schepman, A., Rodway, P., Yetişensoy, O., & Demir Kaya, M. (2022). The Roles of Personality Traits, AI Anxiety, and Demographic Factors in Attitudes toward Artificial Intelligence. *International Journal of Human-Computer Interaction*, *40*(2), 497–514. DOI: 10.1080/10447318.2022.2151730

Khan, I., Ahmad, A. R., Jabeur, N., & Mahdi, M. N. (2021). An Artificial Intelligence Approach to Monitor Student Performance and Devise Preventive Measures. *Smart Learning Environments*, *8*(1), 1–18. DOI: 10.1186/s40561-021-00161-y

Khlaif, Z. N., Sanmugam, M., Joma, A. I., Odeh, A., & Barham, K. (2022). Factors Influencing Teacher's Technostress Experienced in Using Emerging Technology: A Qualitative Study. *Technology. Knowledge and Learning*, *28*(2), 865–899. DOI: 10.1007/s10758-022-09607-9

Kim, J., Yu, S., Detrick, R., & Li, N. (2024). Exploring Students' Perspectives on Generative AI-Assisted Academic Writing. *Education and Information Technologies*, *30*(1), 1265–1300. DOI: 10.1007/s10639-024-12878-7

Kooli, C. (2023). Chatbots in Education and Research: A Critical Examination of Ethical Implications and Solutions. *Sustainability (Basel)*, *15*(7), 1–15. DOI: 10.3390/su15075614

Lameras, P., & Arnab, S. (2021). Power to the Teachers: An Exploratory Review on Artificial Intelligence in Education. *Information (Basel)*, *13*(1), 1–38. DOI: 10.3390/info13010014

Lee, D., Arnold, M., Srivastava, A., Plastow, K., Strelan, P., Ploeckl, F., Lekkas, D., & Palmer, E. (2024). The Impact of Generative AI on Higher Education Learning and Teaching: A Study of Educators' Perspectives. *Computers and Education: Artificial Intelligence*, *6*, 1–10. DOI: 10.1016/j.caeai.2024.100221

Luckin, R., Cukurova, M., Kent, C., & du Boulay, B. (2022). Empowering Educators to Be AI-Ready. *Computers and Education: Artificial Intelligence*, *3*, 1–11. DOI: 10.1016/j.caeai.2022.100076

Mangubat, J. C., Mangubat, M. R., Uy, T. B. L., Acut, D. P., & Garcia, M. B. (2025). Safeguarding Educational Innovations Amid AI Disruptions: A Reassessment of Patenting for Sustained Intellectual Property Protection. In *Pitfalls of AI Integration in Education: Skill Obsolescence, Misuse, and Bias*. IGI Global.

Miller, J. C., Miranda, J. P. P., & Tolentino, J. C. G. (2025). Artificial Intelligence in Physical Education: A Review. In *Global Innovations in Physical Education and Health*. IGI Global., DOI: 10.4018/979-8-3693-3952-7.ch002

Ng, D. T. K., Leung, J. K. L., Su, J., Ng, R. C. W., & Chu, S. K. W. (2023). Teachers' AI Digital Competencies and Twenty-First Century Skills in the Post-Pandemic World. *Educational Technology Research and Development*, *71*(1), 137–161. DOI: 10.1007/s11423-023-10203-6 PMID: 36844361

Nguyen, A., Ngo, H. N., Hong, Y., Dang, B., & Nguyen, B.-P. T. (2022). Ethical Principles for Artificial Intelligence in Education. *Education and Information Technologies*, *28*(4), 4221–4241. DOI: 10.1007/s10639-022-11316-w PMID: 36254344

Olmos-Vega, F. M., Stalmeijer, R. E., Varpio, L., & Kahlke, R. (2022). A Practical Guide to Reflexivity in Qualitative Research: AMEE Guide No. 149. *Medical Teacher*, *45*(3), 241–251. DOI: 10.1080/0142159X.2022.2057287 PMID: 35389310

Salas-Pilco, S., Xiao, K., & Hu, X. (2022). Artificial Intelligence and Learning Analytics in Teacher Education: A Systematic Review. *Education Sciences*, *12*(8), 1–18. DOI: 10.3390/educsci12080569

Shahzalal, M., & Adnan, H. M. (2022). Attitude, Self-Control, and Prosocial Norm to Predict Intention to Use Social Media Responsibly: From Scale to Model Fit towards a Modified Theory of Planned Behavior. *Sustainability (Basel)*, *14*(16), 1–38. DOI: 10.3390/su14169822

Sperling, K., Stenberg, C.-J., McGrath, C., Åkerfeldt, A., Heintz, F., & Stenliden, L. (2024). In Search of Artificial Intelligence (AI) Literacy in Teacher Education: A Scoping Review. *Computers and Education Open*, *6*, 1–13. DOI: 10.1016/j.caeo.2024.100169

Stanford Teaching Commons. (2024). Integrating AI Into Assignments. *Stanford University*. https://teachingcommons.stanford.edu/teaching-guides/artificial-intelligence-teaching-guide/integrating-ai-assignments

University of Arizona. (2025). Transforming Teaching with AI: Integrating GPT and LLMs. https://libcal.library.arizona.edu/event/14136655

van den Berg, G., & du Plessis, E. (2023). ChatGPT and Generative AI: Possibilities for Its Contribution to Lesson Planning, Critical Thinking and Openness in Teacher Education. *Education Sciences*, *13*(10), 1–12. DOI: 10.3390/educsci13100998

Walsh, B., Dalton, B., Forsyth, S., & Yeh, T. (2023). Literacy and STEM Teachers Adapt AI Ethics Curriculum. *Proceedings of the AAAI Conference on Artificial Intelligence*, *37*(13), 16048–16055. DOI: 10.1609/aaai.v37i13.26906

Walter, Y. (2024). Embracing the Future of Artificial Intelligence in the Classroom: The Relevance of AI Literacy, Prompt Engineering, and Critical Thinking in Modern Education. *International Journal of Educational Technology in Higher Education*, *21*(1), 1–29. DOI: 10.1186/s41239-024-00448-3

Wang, S., Wang, F., Zhu, Z., Wang, J., Tran, T., & Du, Z. (2024). Artificial Intelligence in Education: A Systematic Literature Review. *Expert Systems with Applications*, *252*, 1–19. DOI: 10.1016/j.eswa.2024.124167

Wu, W., Zhang, B., Li, S., & Liu, H. (2022). Exploring Factors of the Willingness to Accept AI-Assisted Learning Environments: An Empirical Investigation Based on the UTAUT Model and Perceived Risk Theory. *Frontiers in Psychology*, *13*, 1–10. DOI: 10.3389/fpsyg.2022.870777 PMID: 35814061

Xiao, J., Bozkurt, A., Nichols, M., Pazurek, A., Stracke, C. M., Bai, J. Y. H., Farrow, R., Mulligan, D., Nerantzi, C., Sharma, R. C., Singh, L., Frumin, I., Swindell, A., Honeychurch, S., Bond, M., Dron, J., Moore, S., Leng, J., & Slagter van Tryon, P. J.. (2025). Venturing into the Unknown: Critical Insights into Grey Areas and Pioneering Future Directions in Educational Generative AI Research. *TechTrends*, ●●●, 1–16. DOI: 10.1007/s11528-025-01060-6

Younis, B. (2024). Effectiveness of a Professional Development Program Based on the Instructional Design Framework for AI Literacy in Developing AI Literacy Skills Among Pre-Service Teachers. *Journal of Digital Learning in Teacher Education*, *40*(3), 142–158. DOI: 10.1080/21532974.2024.2365663

Zawacki-Richter, O., Marín, V. I., Bond, M., & Gouverneur, F. (2019). Systematic Review of Research on Artificial Intelligence Applications in Higher Education – Where Are the Educators? *International Journal of Educational Technology in Higher Education*, *16*(1), 1–27. DOI: 10.1186/s41239-019-0171-0

Zhai, C., Wibowo, S., & Li, L. D. (2024). The Effects of Over-Reliance on AI Dialogue Systems on Students' Cognitive Abilities: A Systematic Review. *Smart Learning Environments*, *11*(1), 1–37. DOI: 10.1186/s40561-024-00316-7

Zhang, Y., Wu, J., Yu, F., & Xu, L. (2023). Moral Judgments of Human vs. AI Agents in Moral Dilemmas. *Behavioral Sciences (Basel, Switzerland)*, *13*(2), 1–14. DOI: 10.3390/bs13020181 PMID: 36829410

KEY TERMS AND DEFINITIONS

AI Culture: This describes the evolving set of social norms, values, beliefs, practices, and narratives surrounding the development, acceptance, and resistance to artificial intelligence technologies, especially as they influence identity, creativity, and power dynamics in educational spaces.

AI Literacy: This refers to the ability to understand, evaluate, and use artificial intelligence technologies responsibly and ethically; it involves critical awareness of how AI systems operate, their limitations, and their implications for society, education, and decision-making.

AI Shaming: This refers to the social or academic stigma directed at individuals—particularly students or educators—who openly use artificial intelligence tools in learning environments, often rooted in misconceptions about cheating, intellectual laziness, or over-reliance on technology.

Digital Literacy: This refers to the capacity to access, evaluate, create, and communicate information using digital technologies, while navigating the ethical, cultural, and technical challenges of living in an increasingly mediated world.

Generative AI: A branch of artificial intelligence that creates original content—such as text, images, code, or audio—based on learned patterns from vast datasets, with popular tools like ChatGPT and DALL·E revolutionizing human-computer interaction in education and beyond.

Pedagogical Innovation: This refers to the design and implementation of new teaching strategies, models, or technologies that enhance student engagement, learning outcomes, and inclusivity, often involving active experimentation with digital tools and learner-centered approaches.

Professional Identity Formation: This involves the internalization of values, dispositions, roles, and responsibilities that shape how pre-service teachers see themselves as future educators, influenced by cultural, institutional, and technological forces.

Teacher Education: This encompasses the formal training, professional development, and practical experiences that prepare individuals to become competent educators, focusing on both content knowledge and pedagogical strategies responsive to contemporary educational needs.

Section 2
Skill Obsolescence and Educator Readiness

Chapter 6
Investigation of the Opinions of Classroom Teachers Working in Science and Art Centers on the Pitfalls of Artificial Intelligence in Education

Deniz Görgülü

https://orcid.org/0000-0001-5856-4069

Selçuklu Science and Art Centre, Turkey

Mete Sipahioğlu

Samsun University, Turkey

Martina Brazzolotto

Talent Education Center, Italy

ABSTRACT

This chapter examines the perspectives of classroom teachers at Science and Art Centers regarding artificial intelligence (AI). Employing a case chapter design and qualitative methodology, the research collects insights from 18 teachers during the 2023-2024 academic year through semi-structured interviews, followed by content analysis. Findings indicate that AI enhances classroom processes, reduces teacher workloads, and boosts student engagement. However, challenges such as inadequate technological infrastructure, insufficient resources, and internet connectivity issues hinder effective AI integration. Teachers also express concerns about potential ethical dilemmas associated with AI applications. The chapter underscores the necessity for comprehensive in-service training, practical guidance, and high-quality technological resources to optimize AI utilization. Furthermore, it emphasizes the importance of establishing ethical guidelines and usage protocols to address these concerns and foster a responsible approach to AI in educational settings.

DOI: 10.4018/979-8-3373-0122-8.ch006

INTRODUCTION

The integration of AI in educational settings has garnered significant attention in recent years, particularly concerning the perceptions and attitudes of teachers. As AI technologies become increasingly prevalent in classrooms, understanding how teachers view these innovations is crucial for effective implementation. Research indicates that teachers' awareness and understanding of AI directly influence their ability to integrate these technologies into their teaching practices. For instance, Ferikoğlu and Akgün (2022) found that higher levels of education correlate with increased awareness of AI among teachers, suggesting a need for ongoing professional development to enhance AI literacy. This aligns with findings from Zhang et al. (2024), who emphasized the importance of validated curricula in AI education, highlighting that teachers require evidence of student learning outcomes to adopt new educational frameworks effectively.

Moreover, the perceptions of teachers regarding AI education are shaped by their training and professional development experiences (Acut et al., 2025; Arif et al., 2025). Studies have shown that targeted professional development programs can significantly enhance teachers' self-efficacy in teaching AI concepts. For example, Kim and Kwon (2023) noted that in-service teachers who participated in AI training reported increased confidence in their pedagogical content knowledge related to AI. This is further supported by Zhang et al. (2024), who demonstrated that teacher-led AI literacy curricula could effectively engage students and improve learning outcomes, thereby reinforcing the necessity for teachers to be well-equipped with AI knowledge. To further contextualize teacher competencies in AI, incorporating internationally recognized frameworks such as the ISTE Standards for Educators (International Society for Technology in Education) and DigCompEdu (Digital Competence Framework for Educators) can provide a structured foundation (Srinivasan et al., 2025). These frameworks outline specific competencies teachers need to effectively integrate AI in classrooms, emphasizing areas like digital pedagogy, learner engagement, and the ethical use of technology. For instance, the DigCompEdu framework identifies proficiency levels that can guide professional development efforts tailored to SACs.

The role of teachers as primary stakeholders in the educational process cannot be overstated. Zulkarnain and Md Yunus (2023) highlighted that teachers' attitudes and beliefs significantly impact the integration of AI technologies in classrooms, underscoring the need to consider their perspectives when implementing AI in education. Additionally, the ethical implications of AI in education have emerged as a critical area of concern. Adams et al. (2022) discussed the new ethical obligations teachers face as AI technologies become integrated into educational practices, emphasizing the need for teachers to navigate these challenges thoughtfully.

In the Turkish education system, science and centers (SACs) serve as specialized educational institutions designed for gifted students across primary, secondary, and high school levels, allowing them to pursue their formal education concurrently. These centers are instrumental in nurturing and enhancing the talents of students recognized for their exceptional abilities in general intelligence, visual arts, and music (Özer, 2021). By offering tailored programs, SACs play a significant role in fostering the social and academic growth of gifted students, with a focus on promoting their holistic development across cognitive, affective, and social dimensions (Goksu & Yalcin, 2023).

To ensure that SACs deliver effective and efficient educational experiences, it is essential to integrate key elements such as teacher competencies (Kilic & Ozkan, 2022; Ozer & Demirbatir, 2023), educational materials (Bolat, 2020), technology integration (Kiroglu & Trust, 2024), student support services (Nacaroglu & Mutlu, 2020), and continuous professional development (Altun & Vural, 2012). Among these components, teacher competencies play a pivotal role in determining the quality of educational and training services offered to gifted students. In this context, Xiao et al. (2025) underscores the necessity for educators to equip talented students with expert-level knowledge. Similarly, Goksu and Yalcin (2023) asserted that teachers must possess both pedagogical knowledge and skills to effectively engage with gifted learners. Furthermore, Summak and Çelík-Şahín (2014) highlighted that educators working with gifted students should honor diversity, foster creativity and imagination, be attuned to students' needs, and maintain a commitment to ongoing professional growth.

Technology integration serves as a pivotal factor enhancing the quality of education in SACs. By embedding technology within educational processes, institutions can foster a more interactive and personalized learning experience (Tabier & Bakanay, 2023). The integration of technology not only facilitates the adoption of innovative pedagogical approaches but also contributes significantly to the cultivation of 21st-century skills among students (Writer & Erkoc, 2023). Moreover, technology integration enables students to collaborate independently, exchange ideas, and engage in peer learning through various tools such as online forums, collaborative documents, and educational applications (Lowther et al., 2012). Educators can leverage technological tools to tailor the teaching and learning processes to accommodate the diverse needs of students, thereby creating a differentiated learning environment that addresses individual strengths and weaknesses (Triplett, 2023). Furthermore, empirical studies indicate that teachers' proficiency in the effective use of technology correlates positively with their success in educational outcomes. Thus, it is imperative to enhance teachers' competencies in technology and support the ongoing integration of technological resources within educational contexts.

The literature has recently begun to intensively discuss developments in the field of AI in the context of technology integration in education (Alfredo et al., 2024; Bettayeb et al., 2024; Bozkurt, 2023; Bozkurt et al., 2024). These studies demonstrate that AI can organize educational content based on student preferences and needs, enabling students to benefit from education and support services beyond the classroom setting (Abbas et al., 2023; Harry & Sayudin, 2023; Nurjanah et al., 2024). At the same time, AI plays a crucial role in decision-making processes, analyzing large amounts of data to reveal student performance and identify at-risk students (Thomas, 2024). However, the digital divide and the need for teacher training are considered disadvantages in the context of AI. By providing students and teachers with necessary resources and technologies, we can increase the potential of AI in education (Shah & Shah, 2023).

The investigation into the technological competencies of educators operating within SACs is pivotal for identifying specific needs in this domain. A study conducted by Kilic and Ozkan (2022) revealed that the self-efficacy of these teachers concerning international educational technology standards is not at an adequate level. Conversely, research by Kiroglu and Trust (2024) indicated that while educators in SACs possess high competencies in utilizing Web 2.0 tools, they encounter various challenges related to technological equipment. However, there exists a notable gap in the literature regarding the perspectives of teachers in SACs on the integration of AI in educational practices.

Classroom teachers are recognized as a crucial component in the developmental trajectory of gifted students participating in support education provided by SACs. Considering that classroom teachers serve as the primary educators for these gifted learners within such specialized environments, their competencies are of paramount significance. Accordingly, this study aims to investigate the competencies of classroom teachers and assess the infrastructural status of SACs in relation to the integration of AI, drawing upon the insights and perspectives of classroom teachers employed within these centers.

In conclusion, the investigation of classroom teachers' opinions on AI is essential for understanding the broader implications of AI in education. As AI continues to evolve, it is imperative that teachers receive adequate training and support to harness its potential effectively. This chapter aims to explore these dimensions, focusing on the perceptions of classroom teachers working in SACs, thereby contributing to the ongoing discourse on AI in education.

In accordance with the research objectives, the following sub-questions were formulated to investigate the perceptions of classroom teachers employed in SACs regarding various aspects of AI:

1. What are the perceptions of classroom teachers in SACs concerning their self-efficacy related to AI?
2. How do classroom teachers in SACs perceive the role of AI in the educational landscape?
3. What changes do classroom teachers in SACs report experiencing in their professional practices and processes as a result of integrating AI?
4. What challenges do classroom teachers in SACs encounter when employing AI in their instruction?
5. What forms of support do classroom teachers in SACs deem necessary to utilize AI effectively in their teaching practices?

MAIN FOCUS OF THE CHAPTER

Despite the growing integration of Artificial Intelligence (AI) in educational settings, there remains a significant gap in understanding how classroom teachers, particularly those working in specialized environments such as Science and Art Centers (SACs), perceive and utilize AI technologies. While existing research has explored the general attitudes of teachers toward AI, there is limited focus on the specific challenges and opportunities faced by educators in SACs, who are tasked with nurturing gifted students. Furthermore, literature lacks a comprehensive examination of the infrastructural and pedagogical barriers that hinder the effective integration of AI in these specialized centers. This chapter aims to address this gap by investigating the perceptions, self-efficacy, and challenges faced by SACs teachers in adopting AI tools, as well as the support they require to effectively integrate AI into their teaching practices.

The primary objective of this chapter is to explore the perceptions of classroom teachers in SACs regarding their self-efficacy in using AI, the role of AI in education, and the changes they experience in their professional practices due to AI integration. Additionally, the study aims to identify the challenges these teachers face when employing AI in their instruction and the forms of support they deem necessary for effective AI utilization. By doing so, this research seeks to provide actionable insights into how AI can be better integrated into specialized educational settings, particularly for gifted students.

The findings of this study are significant in the context of the "Pitfalls of AI Integration in Education" as they highlight both the potential benefits and the challenges of AI adoption in SACs. While AI has the potential to enhance educational efficiency and personalize learning experiences, the study reveals that teachers often feel inadequately prepared to utilize these technologies effectively. The research underscores the need for targeted professional development programs, improved technological infrastructure, and ethical guidelines to mitigate the risks associated with AI integration. By addressing these issues, the study contributes to the broader discourse on AI in education, offering practical recommendations for policymakers, educators, and stakeholders involved in the education of gifted students.

METHOD

In this study, a case study design, a qualitative research method, was employed. Case studies serve as a valuable approach for comprehensively understanding and examining contemporary events. This type of research emphasizes the importance of gaining an in-depth understanding of an event or situation while remaining anchored within its contextual framework (Uğurlu, 2018). Accordingly, the objective of this study was to conduct a thorough examination of the perspectives of classroom teachers employed in SACs concerning artificial intelligence, a phenomenon regarded as a significant contemporary issue.

Study Group

The research employed homogeneous case sampling to establish a study group. This methodological approach is predicated on the principle of identifying a distinct subgroup from the broader population pertinent to the research inquiry. The study incorporated the perspectives of 18 educators, specifically those serving as classroom teachers within SACs during the 2023-2024 academic year. Demographic information regarding these educators is presented in Table 1.

Table 1. Demographic information about classroom teachers

Participant	Gender	Time spent as a teacher	City of assignment	Tenure at the SAC
T1	Female	21	Çorum	1
T2	Female	15	Ankara	5
T3	Female	29	İstanbul	1
T4	Female	17	Samsun	2
T5	Female	30	Ankara	2
T6	Female	22	Istanbul	15
T7	Female	14	Trabzon	3
T8	Female	19	Manisa	4
T9	Male	8	Uşak	2
T10	Female	21	İstanbul	7
T11	Male	14	Konya	3
T12	Male	16	Mersin	1
T13	Female	21	İstanbul	2
T14	Female	20	İstanbul	1
T15	Male	17	Kayseri	1
T16	Male	17	Aydın	5
T17	Male	25	Hatay	5
T18	Female	17	Muğla	7

An analysis of Table 1 reveals that the study group comprises fourteen female teachers and four male teachers. The professional seniority of the participants ranges from eight to thirty years, indicating a diverse level of experience. Furthermore, these educators are employed across various provinces in Turkey. It is also significant to note that their tenure at SACs spans from one to fifteen years.

Data Collection Tool

In the conducted study, a semi-structured interview protocol was employed to investigate the competencies of teachers and the infrastructural status of SACs concerning the integration of AI, as perceived by classroom teachers employed within these institutions. To this end, the research instrument comprised four demographic questions aimed at characterizing the study group, alongside eleven additional questions formulated to elicit the opinions of the classroom teachers regarding their experiences in SACs. These questions underwent a thorough review by academicians with expertise in educational technology, educational administration, and Turkish language and literature, leading to necessary revisions to enhance their validity and reliability. Subsequently, a pilot study was executed with a classroom teacher from a science and art center to assess the clarity and applicability of the questions. The pilot application revealed no significant issues, thereby prompting the commencement of the main data collection phase. The estimated duration for participants to respond to the questionnaire was determined to be approximately 20 minutes.

Data Collection and Analysis

In the process of determining the study group for this research, initial contact was established with classroom teachers employed at SACs, who were informed of the research objectives. A semi-structured interview form was subsequently disseminated online to those participants who expressed their willingness to engage in the study. An informed consent form was included alongside this instrument. Data collection occurred from August 22 to August 24, 2024.

The analysis of the data employed content analysis methodology. This approach facilitates the interpretation of codes and concepts deemed analogous by organizing them within thematic frameworks (Baltaci, 2019). The analytical process commenced with a thorough examination of the participants' responses, during which notes were taken, and relevant data were systematically coded. Following this, themes corresponding to these codes were developed and presented in tabular form. To enhance the validity of the research, participant perspectives were incorporated through direct quotations. Furthermore, meticulous attention was given to inter-coder agreement. The reliability of this agreement was assessed using Cohen's Kappa coefficient, which yielded a value of .82, indicating a very high level of inter-coder agreement (Bilgen & Doğan, 2017). Additionally, the validity and reliability of the research were bolstered through expert review during the data analysis phase. By adhering to these methodological rigor and validation strategies, it is evident that the validity, reliability, and transferability of the data obtained in this research are at a high level.

FINDINGS

The subsequent section provides a comprehensive discussion of the sub-problems in a systematic manner.

Opinions of Classroom Teachers in SACs on AI Self-Efficacy

In the first sub-problem of the study, the objective was to explore the question: *"What are the perceptions of classroom teachers in SACs concerning their self-efficacy related to AI?"* The codes and themes derived from the participants' responses on this matter are illustrated in Figure 1.

Figure 1. Perspectives of classroom teachers at SACs on their self-efficacy with AI

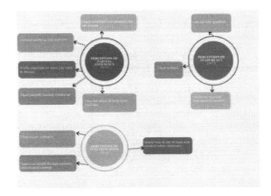

An analysis of Figure 1 reveals that a significant majority of classroom teachers employed at the science and art center perceive their proficiency in utilizing AI tools as either partially competent or insufficient. Furthermore, it is noteworthy that four teachers identify themselves as fully competent in this area. The themes related to this subject, along with pertinent insights from the teachers, are detailed below:

Partial Efficacy Perception

Within the scope of this theme, it was determined that the classroom teachers who expressed opinions had partial knowledge in using AI tools. However, it is seen that this knowledge is generally acquired through personal efforts and remains incomplete.

> T3: *"I have partially learned about AI tools. I try to learn by using them and consulting with friends, but I have many deficiencies."*
> T4: *"I have learned some of the AI tools. However, progress is being made very fast, it is difficult to keep up."*
> S15: *"I learned AI tools from YouTube."*

Inadequacy Perception

It is seen that the knowledge and experience of the classroom teachers who expressed opinions within the scope of this theme about AI are at an insufficient level. It is noteworthy that these teachers need training.

> T1: "*I am not fully competent in using AI tools.*"
> T2: "*I learned AI tools on my own, but my knowledge is not enough.*"
> T7: "*I do not think I am sufficient in this subject.*"

Perception of Full Competence

This theme highlights that classroom teachers who shared their perspectives demonstrate effective utilization of AI tools and express a sense of confidence in their proficiency in this area.

> T10: "*I have developed proficiency in utilizing AI tools through a process of continuous inquiry and exploration. My curiosity drives me to conduct research, which often leads to the discovery and experimentation with new tools. In addition, I seek guidance from knowledgeable individuals and strive to enhance my skills by participating in relevant training programs.*"
> T13: "*I consider myself sufficiently competent in the application of AI tools.*"
> T14: "*I possess a solid understanding of AI tools and actively engage in research on this topic whenever the need arises.*"

Insights on Classroom Teachers' Perspectives in SACs Regarding the Role of AI in Education

In the second sub-problem of this research, the inquiry focused on the question, "*How do classroom teachers in SACs perceive the role of AI in the educational landscape?*" The codes and themes derived from the educators' responses regarding this topic are presented in Figure 2.

Figure 2. Views of classroom teachers working in SACs on the role of AI in education

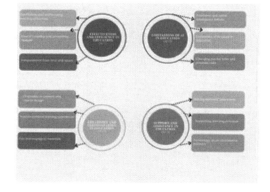

An analysis of Figure 2 reveals that the perspectives of classroom teachers employed in SACs predominantly converge around the theme of effectiveness and efficiency in education. This is followed by themes addressing the limitations of AI in educational contexts, the promotion of creativity in education, and the importance of customization. Notably, the theme of support and assistance in education emerges as having the least number of expressed opinions. The following sections will delve into the content associated with these themes and present selected opinions from educators.

Effectiveness and Efficiency in Education

The opinions of teachers within this theme pertain to the ways in which AI can enhance the effectiveness and efficiency of educational processes. It is observed that AI has the potential to increase the speed of learning and facilitate the creation and presentation of content.

> T1: *"With AI, students' learning processes become more effective and more rapid. It offers opportunities for different learning styles. However, although it contributes at the cognitive level in teaching, it is insufficient in terms of emotional and social intelligence."*
> T4: *"I believe that AI facilitates and accelerates learning. I anticipate that it will yield positive effects on education in the future."*
> T18: *"I assert that AI has a facilitating effect on research culture. It will enhance academic knowledge, yet the significance of the teacher's physical and emotional presence in the classroom must not be understated."*

Creativity and Customization in Education Theme

It was determined that the teacher opinions in this theme were related to the originality provided by AI in content and course design in education; supporting student-centered learning experiences; and the ability to provide fun and remarkable materials.

> T10: *"It is certain that AI gives the teacher a great speed. It can open new doors for you when you are blocked. But I also come across teachers who rely completely on this technology. I think this will make people lazy to think. I think it will change the teaching profession."*
> T14: *"AI gives originality in material design, lesson design, homework is done interactively. However, it can be thought that a teacher is needed to understand the inner world of children."*
> T17: *"AI makes the teacher's job easier. Although it hinders creativity, it has beneficial aspects in general."*

Support and Assistance in Education

This theme includes teachers' views on the roles of AI in facilitating tasks, supporting learning processes, and assisting teachers.

T7: "*AI can offer various opportunities to improve students' learning processes and facilitate teachers' lesson planning and assessment processes. I believe that it cannot surpass the role of the teacher in education. I think that the role of teachers in education cannot be surpassed. When used correctly, AI will provide teachers with a great assistant and development opportunity.*"

T9: "*I believe that when used correctly, AI will provide teachers with a great assistant and development opportunity. In the lesson structures I created using AI, I observed that students were more active. I observed that students were more active in the lesson structures I created using AI. AI plays a facilitative role in education.*"

T15: "*AI has a facilitative role in education. In the future, it will further empower teachers. In the future, it will further empower the teacher.*"

Limitations of AI in Education

The opinions of teachers within this theme are related to the limitations of AI in education, deficiencies in emotional and social intelligence, and potential changes and risks in the role of teachers.

T3: "*I think AI will be beneficial if used correctly in education. However, I think it will negatively affect the development of children's manual skills.*"

T8: "*AI can sometimes provide conveniences in education. Over time, it may become more supportive of the teaching profession. Maybe the teacher could take a backseat.*"

T12: "*I haven't added AI to classroom activities yet. However, I don't think it will replace a teacher.*"

Findings on Changes in Professional Tasks and Processes with AI According to Classroom Teachers Working in SACs

In the third sub-problem of the research, the inquiry "*What changes do classroom teachers in SACs report experiencing in their professional practices and processes as a result of integrating AI?*" was thoroughly examined. The codes and themes formulated from the educators' insights regarding this topic are systematically presented in Figure 3.

Figure 3. According to classroom teachers working in science and art centers, their opinions on changes in professional work and processes with artificial intelligence

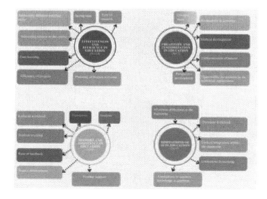

Upon examining Figure 3, it becomes evident that the perceptions of classroom teachers employed in SACs regarding the transformations in professional roles and processes attributable to AI predominantly coalesce around the theme of effectiveness and efficiency in educational practices. Subsequently, the themes of support and assistance in education, creativity and customization in instructional methodologies, as well as the limitations of AI within educational contexts are identified. The elaboration of these themes, along with select opinions expressed by the teachers, is detailed as follows:

Efficiency and Effectiveness in Education

In analyzing the perspectives of educators regarding the integration of AI in educational settings, a pronounced emphasis emerges on the time-saving advantages afforded by AI in teaching processes. Educators note AI's capacity to effectively manage various instructional tasks and its potential to enhance learning experiences. The deployment of AI facilitates educators in executing activities such as lesson planning, conducting research, and monitoring student progress more efficiently.

> T1: *"AI caters to diverse learning styles." It provides tailored learning opportunities aligned with individual student performance levels. The research process has become significantly more manageable, enabling more effective tracking of student development and providing timely feedback. Additionally, it has positively influenced my professional development by improving time management and operational efficiency."*
> T2: *"AI liberates the constraints of time and space in education, rendering it economically advantageous." As I continue to learn and adapt, I have noticed an increase in student curiosity and participation in class discussions. AI contributes to my ongoing professional development by ensuring I remain informed of the latest educational trends and practices."*
> T9: *"Through the lesson structures I have developed utilizing AI, I have observed heightened student engagement." I contend that the judicious application of technology has significantly enhanced student interest and positive attitudes toward learning. I actively incorporate AI across various facets of my teaching, from social media engagement to the creation of instructional content."*

Creativity and Customization in Education

When examining the views of teachers included in this theme, it is understood that AI contributes to the customization of lessons and creative learning experiences. Teachers can differentiate their lessons and activities according to the individual needs of students with the help of AI.

> T4: *"There are positive effects of AI in education." It provides convenience in areas such as presentations, videos, and translations. It is suitable for developing and differentiating AI methods. Ö7: "I think AI can be used to plan activities according to students' intelligence areas in differentiating classroom activities based on student characteristics."*
> T7: *"I think AI can be used to plan activities according to students' intelligence areas in differentiating classroom activities based on student characteristics." It makes the activities fun and engaging. Context: It makes the events fun and attention-grabbing."*

T10: *"AI adds excitement to the classes. Especially in creative work, it can sometimes open new doors for thinking or discussing. It contributes to my perspective. I am curious about other things and syntheses, and it helps me see them faster. I am curious about other things and syntheses; they help me see them faster."*

Support and Assistance in Education

The examination of teachers' perspectives within this theme reveals that AI alleviates and supports teachers' workloads. Specifically, AI aids teachers in various processes, including student tracking, measurement and evaluation, research, and project development.

T11: *"I use AI tools, especially in the processes of organizing, translating, and analyzing information. I carry out these tasks more quickly. It provides significant convenience in research. I can conduct research on any topic and easily access foreign sources. It has reduced my workload. With its features, I now get more work done in less time. I am producing more projects, articles, and content. AI provides a fast and interactive environment."*

T13: *"AI provides a fast and interactive environment. It accelerates activities such as preparing presentations, analyzing PDFs, interacting with chatbots, creating quizzes, developing games, and organizing events. Since I constantly adapt and teach the evolving technology in class, it hasn't made a significant change in my communication with the students. When producing projects and activities, chatbots are helpful. It facilitates my analysis of survey data. It definitely reduced my workload. AI has definitely reduced my workload."*

T16: *"AI has made content development easier. It has increased students' interest in the class. It has saved time and assisted me in completing designs that would typically take a longer duration in a shorter period."*

Limitations of AI in Education

The theme of the limitations of AI in education highlights the challenges and constraints expressed by teachers regarding its implementation. Initially, it was noted that AI can increase teachers' workload and pose integration difficulties, potentially impeding creativity.

T2: *"If it's an application I'm not familiar with, it takes me some time to learn it at first, but it becomes easier later on. At first, it increased my workload, but over time it became easier."*

T3: *"I didn't spend enough time using AI with my students."* I acknowledge that it offers functions such as effective time management and expedited process control. Initially, it augmented my workload until I became familiar with AI."*

T17: *"Although AI hinders creativity, it has its beneficial aspects. It facilitates more effective time management and has reduced my workload; however, it still presents shortcomings and remains open to further improvement."*

Findings on the Challenges Faced by Classroom Teachers Working in SACs When Using AI

In the fourth sub-problem of this research, we explored the question: *"What challenges do classroom teachers in SACs encounter when employing AI in their instruction?"* To address this inquiry, we collected and analyzed the opinions of teachers, which are subsequently organized and presented in Figure 4, illustrating the derived codes and themes.

Figure 4. Opinions of classroom teachers working in science and art centers on the difficulties they face while using artificial intelligence

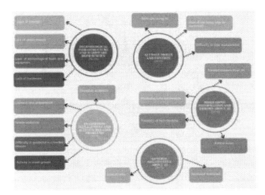

When examining Figure 4, it is observed that the opinions of classroom teachers working in SACs regarding the difficulties they encounter while using AI are mostly concentrated on the theme of technological infrastructure and equipment deficiencies. This is followed by the themes of AI usage skills and control, and the issues that arise in classroom management. The least discussed topic, however, is the general negative perceptions related to AI. The content of the themes is formed from the opinions in this scope and some of the teachers' opinions are as follows:

Technological Infrastructure and Equipment Deficiencies

It is observed that the teacher opinions included in this theme are related to the hardware and infrastructure issues encountered in the use of AI. Teachers have expressed issues such as insufficient internet, lack of smart boards, and technological equipment shortages. Practical applications of AI can mitigate some of these challenges. For instance, tools like AI-powered content creators can assist teachers in developing engaging lesson materials, while platforms such as Khan Academy's AI tutor provide personalized learning experiences tailored to individual student needs. These applications demonstrate the potential of AI to reduce teacher workload and enhance instructional quality, even in resource-constrained environments. However, successful implementation requires targeted training to ensure educators can effectively utilize these tools.

> T3: *"The absence of a smart board prevents me from using AI applications in the classroom."*
> T4: *"I face difficulties due to the lack of Turkish infrastructure in AI tools."*

T8: *"I can't benefit from AI enough due to the school's internet issue."*

AI Usage Skills and Control

It is seen that the teachers' views on this theme are related to the difficulties experienced in terms of using AI and its control. Deficiencies in usage skills, fear of not being able to control, and difficulties such as time management are among the problems expressed in this theme.

T1: *"There were times when I had trouble using AI. I have difficulties in practice because I am not fully equipped in terms of using it."*
T6: *"I am afraid of not being able to control AI."*
T14: *"Using a tool that I have not used before in the classroom causes some problems."*

Classroom Management and Activity-Related Problems

Teacher opinions included in this theme are related to classroom management and activity-related problems. Guidance difficulties due to crowded classes, discipline problems, and difficulties in the activity implementation process are some of the problems identified in this context.

T8: *"My student with screen addiction can have problems finishing the activity."*
T14: *"I cannot guide students in using AI in crowded classes. Disciplinary problems can arise there."*
T17: *"Using AI by students leads to laziness; they are ready-made."*

Misleading Information and Errors Regarding AI

Teacher opinions included in this theme address problems related to the accuracy and reliability of the information provided by AI. Difficulties such as producing incorrect or incomplete information, the necessity to verify the accuracy of information, and limited responses are among the problems expressed in this context.

T10: *"Sometimes I have to spend a lot of time to find the answer I am looking for. I also spend time verifying the resources provided by the AI."*
T13: *"AI-based chatbots make a lot of mistakes. It is necessary to check the accuracy of the information."*
T16: *"The fact that some applications are not suitable for use on smart boards creates problems in the classroom."*

General Negative Opinions About AI

Teachers' opinions on this theme pertain to the effects of AI on work processes. Problems such as increased workload, loss of time, and the unsuitability of AI for the classroom environment are included in this theme.

T5: *"My workload has increased due to AI. I have to constantly improve myself."*

T10: *"Finding the right resources after using AI can take time. Sometimes I wish I had done it myself."*

Support Required for Classroom Teachers Working in SACs to Use AI Effectively

In the fifth sub-problem of this research, we sought to address the question: *"What supports are necessary for classroom teachers operating within SACs to effectively utilize AI?"* To this end, we analyzed teacher responses to identify relevant codes and themes. The findings are summarized in Figure 5.

Figure 5. Views of classroom teachers working in SACs on the supports required for the effective use of AI

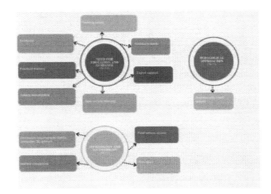

When Figure 5 is examined, it is seen that the opinions of classroom teachers working in SACs regarding the support required for them to use AI effectively are mostly gathered under the theme of need for education and guidance. This is followed by the theme of technology and accessibility. The content of the themes formed from these opinions and some of the teachers' opinions are as follows.

Need for Education and Guidance

This theme includes opinions regarding the education, guidance, and feedback that teachers need in order to use AI technologies effectively. It is understood that teachers want to learn AI technologies with applied training and expert support.

T1: *"I want to receive training and apply the training I receive effectively and give feedback."*
T3: *"I want the studies that can be done to be shared with us as seminars. In addition, we should be given applied training on AI."*
T13: *"I need the introduction of new applications related to AI."*

Technology and Accessibility

This theme includes opinions on the technological infrastructure and tools that teachers need to use AI effectively. Teachers demand that hardware deficiencies be addressed, the internet infrastructure be strengthened, and free access to applications be provided.

T2: "*I need technological support and training.*"

T4: "*Each classroom should have 2-3 computers or tablets, hardware such as 3D printers.*"

T15: "*Using paid applications is a big problem; I demand free AI applications.*"

Pedagogical Approaches

The opinion on this theme is about how AI technology should be applied in education. Accordingly, it is stated that AI should be applied in small groups.

T14: "*AI is done one-on-one with small groups in small classes. I think this approach should be adopted.*"

DISCUSSION

The initial and significant discovery of this research indicates that a substantial proportion of classroom teachers operating within SACs perceive themselves as inadequately equipped to utilize AI tools effectively. This sentiment is echoed in a variety of studies present in the existing literature (Kim & Kwon, 2023; Lin, 2023; Muttaqin, 2022; Natividad Escalona-Márquez et al., 2024; Sperling et al., 2024; Yue et al., 2024). Consequently, this perceived deficiency has led teachers to express a pronounced need for training and guidance to harness AI adeptly. This finding is corroborated by numerous studies (Brandão et al., 2024; Dan, 2022; Duque et al., 2024; Fissore et al., 2024; Nyaaba & Zhai, 2024; Uygun, 2024). Furthermore, research conducted in this domain suggests that educational content related to AI significantly enhances teachers' competencies in utilizing these tools (Kitcharoen et al., 2024; Park & Kwon, 2023).

In the examination of the intersection between AI and education, findings indicate that a significant number of classroom teachers employed in SACs perceive AI as a tool that enhances their efficiency by offering support and assistance in various professional activities. Nevertheless, it is crucial to address the potential risks associated with the integration of AI in educational settings. Specifically, teachers express concerns regarding the psycho-motor and affective development of students within AI-supported learning environments. The integration of AI into education also raises ethical concerns, particularly regarding data privacy, algorithmic biases, and the potential over-reliance on technology in decision-making processes. Teachers must be equipped to address these challenges by fostering digital literacy and critical thinking among students. Additionally, professional development programs should include ethical training, enabling educators to identify and mitigate risks associated with AI tools. Research by Adams et al. (2022) emphasizes the importance of ethical decision-making as a core competency for teachers in AI-enhanced learning environments.

The existing literature corroborates these concerns, highlighting that while AI facilitates personalized learning experiences, it may inadvertently lead to reduced engagement in physical activities or practical applications during primary and secondary education, where fundamental skills are cultivated (Aghaziarati et al., 2023; Alshehri, 2023). Furthermore, research indicates a potential regression in the development of critical skills, such as empathy and cooperation, which are essential for students' emotional and social growth in settings that leverage AI for educational purposes (Nazaretsky et al., 2022; Rütti-Joy et al., 2023). Additionally, the apprehension among educators regarding the potential marginalization of teachers in the classroom context is noteworthy. Such perspectives have been documented in the literature, with

Djajasoepena et al. (2024) emphasizing the risk of diminishing the human element of teaching due to the proliferation of AI in educational environments. Complementary findings by Butakor (2023) and Uymaz (2024) reveal that pre-service teachers harbor beliefs that AI could supplant traditional teaching roles or diminish the active participation of educators.

The study highlights significant challenges faced by educators in the integration of AI within educational settings. A primary concern identified is the inadequate technological infrastructure and resources available to teachers. Notably, this issue is particularly pronounced in institutions serving gifted students in Turkey, suggesting that current educational policies for this demographic may not adequately address the contemporary demands of a rapidly evolving educational landscape. Existing research indicates the absence of a comprehensive educational policy specifically tailored for gifted students in Turkey. Furthermore, the literature outlines a broader challenge related to technology and infrastructure in relation to AI across educational institutions (Gray, 2020; Mupaikwa, 2023; Pandya, 2024). In light of these findings, Triansyah et al. (2023) asserts that the provision of sufficient technological resources is essential for the transformative potential of AI in education to be realized effectively.

In the study, various concerns were articulated by educators regarding the management of AI within educational settings. These concerns included issues related to the potential for student laziness, readiness for learning, the risk of screen addiction, ethical dilemmas, and challenges associated with implementing AI in crowded classrooms. The literature supports these findings, revealing that teachers experience anxiety related to the control of AI technologies (Alshehri, 2023; Banerjee & Banerjee, 2023; Falebita, 2024; Gantalao et al., 2025; Hsu et al., 2023; Nja et al., 2023). Additionally, studies have indicated apprehensions about student laziness and readiness (Özbek Güven et al., 2024), screen addiction (Morales-García et al., 2024), and ethical concerns related to AI deployment in educational contexts (Akkaş et al., 2024; Ghotbi, 2024; Li et al., 2024). Furthermore, the literature suggests that the implementation of AI is not conducive to environments characterized by high student density (Bezzina & Dingli, 2024; Nasar et al., 2023; Wetzel et al., 2018).

CONCLUSION AND RECOMMENDATIONS

The findings of this research indicate that a significant number of classroom teachers employed in SACs lack adequate proficiency in AI. This scenario underscores the necessity for targeted training and guidance on AI for these educators. Furthermore, while the teachers acknowledged that AI could enhance convenience in their professional tasks and activities, they expressed notable apprehensions regarding the potential risks associated with this technology. Specifically, concerns were raised about the implications of AI on students' affective and psychomotor development. Additionally, some educators articulated the belief that AI might diminish or even supplant the traditional role of teachers. Moreover, the study identified inadequate technological infrastructure and resources as the primary barrier to the effective integration of AI within SACs. Emerging trends in AI for education point toward adaptive learning systems that personalize content delivery based on real-time data analysis. Tools like intelligent tutoring systems (ITS) and AI-powered collaborative platforms are transforming the educational landscape by enabling differentiated instruction and enhancing student engagement. Future advancements could also include AI-driven assessments that provide instantaneous feedback and predictive analytics to identify students at risk of falling behind. Incorporating these tools into SACs can address current challenges and improve educational outcomes for gifted students.

Recent findings indicate that educators have expressed significant concerns regarding the management of AI, alongside issues related to student apathy and screen addiction. In light of these concerns, several recommendations can be established:

1. Comprehensive training programs should be implemented for educators to facilitate the effective integration of AI within educational contexts.
2. To optimize the utilization of AI in science and arts centers, it is essential to enhance the technological infrastructure of these institutions.
3. 3. Strategies must be devised to address and mitigate educators' apprehensions regarding the use of AI in the classroom.
4. Further research is warranted to investigate the effects of AI on students' affective and psycho-motor development.

REFERENCES

Abbas, N., Ali, I., Manzoor, R., Hussain, T., & Hussain, M. H. A. L. i. (2023). Role of Artificial Intelligence Tools in Enhancing Students' Educational Performance at Higher Levels. *Journal of Artificial Intelligence. Machine Learning and Neural Network*, (35), 36–49. DOI: 10.55529/jaimlnn.35.36.49

Acut, D. P., Gamusa, E. V., Pernaa, J., Yuenyong, C., Pantaleon, A. T., Espina, R. C., Sim, M. J. C., & Garcia, M. B. (2025). AI Shaming Among Teacher Education Students: A Reflection on Acceptance and Identity in the Age of Generative Tools. In *Pitfalls of AI Integration in Education: Skill Obsolescence, Misuse, and Bias*. IGI Global., DOI: 10.4018/979-8-3373-0122-8.ch005

Adams, C., Pente, P., Lemermeyer, G., Turville, J., & Rockwell, G. (2022). Artificial Intelligence and Teachers' New Ethical Obligations. *International Journal of Information Ethics*, *31*(1). Advance online publication. DOI: 10.29173/irie483

Aghaziarati, A., Nejatifar, S., & Abedi, A. (2023). Artificial Intelligence in Education: Investigating Teacher Attitudes. *AI and Tech in Behavioral and Social Sciences*, *1*(1), 35–42. DOI: 10.61838/kman. aitech.1.1.6

Akkaş, Ö. M., Tosun, C., & Gökçearslan, Ş. (2024). Artificial Intelligence (AI) and Cheating. In *Advances in Educational Technologies and Instructional Design* (pp. 182-199). IGI Global. https://doi.org/DOI: 10.4018/979-8-3693-1351-0.ch009

Alfredo, R., Echeverria, V., Jin, Y., Yan, L., Swiecki, Z., Gašević, D., & Martinez-Maldonado, R. (2024). Human-Centred Learning Analytics and AI in Education: A Systematic Literature Review. *Computers and Education: Artificial Intelligence*, 6, 100215. DOI: 10.1016/j.caeai.2024.100215

Alshehri, B. (2023). Pedagogical Paradigms in the AI Era: Insights from Saudi Educators on the Long-term Implications of AI Integration in Classroom Teaching. *International Journal of Educational Sciences and Arts*, *2*(8), 159–180. DOI: 10.59992/IJESA.2023.v2n8p7

Altun, T., & Vural, S. (2012). Evaluation of the Views of Teachers and Administrators of a Science and Art Center (SAC) About Professional Development and School Improvement. *Electronic Journal of Social Sciences, 11*(42), 152-177. https://dergipark.org.tr/tr/download/article-file/70406

Arif, Y. M., Nugroho, F., Aini, Q., Fauzan, A. C., & Garcia, M. B. (2025). A Systematic Literature Review of Serious Games for Physical Education: Technologies, Implementations, and Evaluations. In *Global Innovations in Physical Education and Health*. IGI Global., DOI: 10.4018/979-8-3693-3952-7.ch001

Baltaci, A. (2019). Qualitative Research Process: How to Conduct Qualitative Research? *Ahi Evran University Journal of Social Sciences Institute*, *5*(2), 368–388. DOI: 10.31592/aeusbed.598299

Banerjee, S., & Banerjee, B. (2023). College Teachers' Anxiety Towards Artificial Intelligence: A Comparative Study. *RESEARCH REVIEW International Journal of Multidisciplinary*, *8*(5), 36–43. DOI: 10.31305/rrijm.2023.v08.n05.005

Bettayeb, A. M., Abu Talib, M., Sobhe Altayasinah, A. Z., & Dakalbab, F. (2024). Exploring the impact of ChatGPT: Conversational AI in education. *Frontiers in Education*, 9, 1379796. Advance online publication. DOI: 10.3389/feduc.2024.1379796

Bezzina, S., & Dingli, A. (2024). The Transformative Potential of Artificial Intelligence for Education. *Proceedings of the International Conference on Networked Learning, 14.* https://doi.org/DOI: 10.54337/nlc.v14i1.8077

Bilgen, Ö. B., & Doğan, N. (2017). The Comparison of Interrater Reliability Estimating Techniques [Puanlayıcılar Arası Güvenirlik Belirleme Tekniklerinin Karşılaştırılması]. *Journal of Measurement and Evaluation in Education and Psychology, 8*(1), 63–78. DOI: 10.21031/epod.294847

Bolat, H. (2020). The Metaphorical Perceptions of the Gifted and Talented Students towards Social Studies Lesson in the Science and Art Centre and in Their School. *Anemon Muş Alparslan Üniversitesi Sosyal Bilimler Dergisi, 8*(4), 1135–1144. DOI: 10.18506/anemon.647705

Bozkurt, A. (2023). ChatGPT, Generative AI and Algorithmic Paradigm Shift. *Alanyazın, 4*(1), 63–72. DOI: 10.59320/alanyazin.1283282

Bozkurt, A., Xiao, J., Farrow, R., Bai, J. Y. H., Nerantzi, C., Moore, S., Dron, J., Stracke, C. M., Singh, L., Crompton, H., Koutropoulos, A., Terentev, E., Pazurek, A., Nichols, M., Sidorkin, A. M., Costello, E., Watson, S., Mulligan, D., Honeychurch, S., & Asino, T. I. (2024). The Manifesto for Teaching and Learning in a Time of Generative AI: A Critical Collective Stance to Better Navigate the Future. *Open Praxis, 16*(4), 487–513. DOI: 10.55982/openpraxis.16.4.777

Brandão, A., Pedro, L., & Zagalo, N. (2024). Teacher Professional Development for a Future with Generative Artificial Intelligence – An Integrative Literature Review. *Digital Education Review*, (45), 151–157. DOI: 10.1344/der.2024.45.151-157

Butakor, P. K. (2023). Exploring Pre-Service Teachers' Beliefs About the Role of Artificial Intelligence in Higher Education in Ghana. *International Journal of Innovative Technologies in Social Science*, (3(39)). Advance online publication. DOI: 10.31435/rsglobal_ijitss/30092023/8057

Dan, S. (2022). Teacher Intelligence Training Based on Big Data and Artificial Intelligence. *International Journal of e-Collaboration, 18*(3), 1–11. DOI: 10.4018/IJeC.307137

Djajasoepena, R., Setiawan, I., Bhakti, M. A. C., Purnomo, A. T., Ayu, M. A., Alibasa, M. J., & Wandy, W. (2024). Utilization of Artificial Intelligence to Support the Development of Teaching and Project Modules. *Journal of Community Services: Sustainability and Empowerment, 4*(01), 7–11. DOI: 10.35806/jcsse.v4i1.440

Duque, R. C. S., Silva, J. S., Loureiro, V. J. S., Darcanchy, M., Eccard, A. F. C., Durigon, S., Placido, I. T. M., Sousa, T. S. R., Xavier, R. M. L., & Oliveira, E. A. R. (2024). Tecnologias Digitais Associadas a Ia Na Formação Docente. *Caderno Pedagógico, 21*(4), e3651. DOI: 10.54033/cadpedv21n4-053

Falebita, O. S. (2024). Assessing the Relationship Between Anxiety and the Adoption of Artificial Intelligence Tools Among Mathematics Preservice Teachers. *Interdisciplinary Journal of Education Research, 6*, 1–13. DOI: 10.38140/ijer-2024.vol6.20

Ferikoğlu, D., & Akgün, E. (2022). An Investigation of Teachers' Artificial Intelligence Awareness: A Scale Development Study. *Malaysian Online Journal of Educational Technology, 10*(3), 215–231. DOI: 10.52380/mojet.2022.10.3.407

Fissore, C., Floris, F., Conte, M. M., & Sacchet, M. (2024). Teacher Training on Artificial Intelligence in Education. *Cognition and Exploratory Learning in the Digital Age*, 227-244. https://doi.org/DOI: 10.1007/978-3-031-54207-7_13

Gantalao, L. C., Calzada, J. G. D., Capuyan, D. L., Lumantas, B. C., Acut, D. P., & Garcia, M. B. (2025). Equipping the Next Generation of Technicians: Navigating School Infrastructure and Technical Knowledge in the Age of AI Integration. In *Pitfalls of AI Integration in Education: Skill Obsolescence, Misuse, and Bias*. IGI Global., DOI: 10.4018/979-8-3373-0122-8.ch009

Ghotbi, N. (2024). Ethics of Artificial Intelligence in Academic Research and Education. *Springer International Handbooks of Education*, 1355-1366. https://doi.org/DOI: 10.1007/978-3-031-54144-5_143

Goksu, D. Y., & Yalcin, S. (2023). Effectiveness Evaluation of the Trainer Training Project Program Applied to BİLSEM Teachers Working with Specially Gifted Students. *National Education Journal*, *52*(240), 2863–2886. DOI: 10.37669/milliegitim.1184848

Gray, S. L. (2020). Artificial Intelligence in Schools: Towards a Democratic Future. *London Review of Education*, *18*(2). Advance online publication. DOI: 10.14324/LRE.18.2.02

Harry, A., & Sayudin, S. (2023). Role of AI in Education. [INJURITY]. *Interdiciplinary Journal and Hummanity*, *2*(3), 260–268. DOI: 10.58631/injurity.v2i3.52

Hsu, T.-C., Hsu, T.-P., & Lin, Y.-T. (2023). The Artificial Intelligence Learning Anxiety and Self-Efficacy of In-Service Teachers Taking AI Training Courses. *2023 International Conference on Artificial Intelligence and Education (ICAIE)*, 97-101. https://doi.org/DOI: 10.1109/ICAIE56796.2023.00034

Kilic, S., & Ozkan, T. K. (2022). A Study on the Self-Efficacy of BİLSEM Teachers in Educational Technology. *International Journal of Education Science and Technology*, *8*(3), 165–190. DOI: 10.47714/uebt.1173885

Kim, K., & Kwon, K. (2023). Exploring the AI Competencies of Elementary School Teachers in South Korea. *Computers and Education: Artificial Intelligence*, *4*, 100137. DOI: 10.1016/j.caeai.2023.100137

Kiroglu, E. S., & Trust, H. (2024). Investigation of Bilsem Teachers' Views on Web 2.0 Tools. *Bayburt Faculty of Education Journal*, *19*(41), 1803–1826. DOI: 10.35675/befdergi.1239568

Kitcharoen, P., Howimanporn, S., & Chookaew, S. (2024). Enhancing Teachers' AI Competencies through Artificial Intelligence of Things Professional Development Training. [iJIM]. *International Journal of Interactive Mobile Technologies*, *18*(02), 4–15. DOI: 10.3991/ijim.v18i02.46613

Li, Z., Dhruv, A., & Jain, V. (2024). Ethical Considerations in the Use of AI for Higher Education: A Comprehensive Guide. *2024 IEEE 18th International Conference on Semantic Computing (ICSC)*, 218-223. https://doi.org/DOI: 10.1109/ICSC59802.2024.00041

Lin, D. (2023). AI's Role in Enhancing the Construction of Regional Primary and Secondary School Teachers. *Science Insights Education Frontiers*, *15*(S1), 7. DOI: 10.15354/sief.23.s1.ab007

Lowther, D. L., Inan, F. A., Strahl, J. D., & Ross, S. M. (2012). Do One-to-One Initiatives Bridge the Way to 21st Century Knowledge and Skills? *Journal of Educational Computing Research*, *46*(1), 1–30. DOI: 10.2190/EC.46.1.a

Morales-García, W. C., Sairitupa-Sanchez, L. Z., Morales-García, S. B., & Morales-García, M. (2024). Development and validation of a scale for dependence on artificial intelligence in university students. *Frontiers in Education*, *9*, 1323898. Advance online publication. DOI: 10.3389/feduc.2024.1323898

Mupaikwa, E. (2023). The Use of Artificial Intelligence in Education. In *Advances in Library and Information Science* (pp. 26-50). IGI Global. https://doi.org/DOI: 10.4018/978-1-6684-8671-9.ch002

Muttaqin, I. (2022). Necessary to Increase Teacher Competency in Facing the Artificial Intelligence Era. *Al-Hayat: Journal of Islamic Education*, *6*(2), 549. DOI: 10.35723/ajie.v6i2.460

Nacaroglu, O., & Mutlu, F. (2020). Examination of Science and Art Center Students' Metaphorical Perceptions About the Concept of Project. *Abant İzzet Baysal University Journal of Education Faculty*, *20*(2), 992–1007. DOI: 10.17240/aibuefd.2020.-587573

Nasar, I., Uzer, Y., Aisyah, , Ridayani, , & Purwanto, M. B. (2023). Artificial Intelligence in Smart Classrooms. [AJAE]. *Asian Journal of Applied Education*, *2*(4), 547–556. DOI: 10.55927/ajae.v2i4.6038

Natividad Escalona-Márquez, L., Johanna Cedeño-Tapia, S., Alberto Camputaro, L., & Oscar Orlando Aparicio-Escalante, C. (2024). *Teachers in the Age of Artificial Intelligence: Preparation and Response to Challenges*. IntechOpen., DOI: 10.5772/intechopen.1005172

Nazaretsky, T., Ariely, M., Cukurova, M., & Alexandron, G. (2022). Teachers' Trust in AI-Powered Educational Technology and a Professional Development Program to Improve It. *British Journal of Educational Technology*, *53*(4), 914–931. DOI: 10.1111/bjet.13232

Nja, C. O., Idiege, K. J., Uwe, U. E., Meremikwu, A. N., Ekon, E. E., Erim, C. M., Ukah, J. U., Eyo, E. O., Anari, M. I., & Cornelius-Ukpepi, B. U. (2023). Adoption of Artificial Intelligence in Science Teaching: From the Vantage Point of the African Science Teachers. *Smart Learning Environments*, *10*(1), 42. Advance online publication. DOI: 10.1186/s40561-023-00261-x

Nurjanah, A., Salsabila, I. N., Azzahra, A., Rahayu, R., & Marlina, N. (2024). Artificial Intelligence (AI) Usage In Today's Teaching And Learning Process: A Review. *Syntax Idea*, *6*(3), 1517–1523. DOI: 10.46799/syntax-idea.v6i3.3126

Nyaaba, M., & Zhaı, X. (2024). Generative AI Professional Development Needs for Teacher Educators. *Journal of AI*, *8*(1), 1–13. DOI: 10.61969/jai.1385915

Özbek Güven, G., Yilmaz, Ş., & Inceoğlu, F. (2024). Determining Medical Students' Anxiety and Readiness Levels About Artificial Intelligence. *Heliyon*, *10*(4), e25894. DOI: 10.1016/j.heliyon.2024. e25894 PMID: 38384508

Özer, M. (2021). Science and Art Centers in Support of Talent Development for Gifted and Talented Students: Current Situation and Areas for Improvement. *International Journal of Society Researchers*, *17*(33), 727–749. DOI: 10.26466/opus.810856

Ozer, Z., & Demirbatir, R. E. (2023). Determining the Views of BİLSEM Art Field Teachers on STEAM Education. *Afyon Kocatepe University Journal of Social Sciences*, *25*(4), 1349–1364. DOI: 10.32709/ akusosbil.1116157

Pandya, K. T. (2024). The Role of Artificial Intelligence in Education 5.0: Opportunities and Challenges. *SDGs Studies Review, 5,* e011. DOI: 10.37497/sdgs.v5igoals.11

Park, W., & Kwon, H. (2023). Implementing Artificial Intelligence Education for Middle School Technology Education in Republic of Korea. *International Journal of Technology and Design Education, 34*(1), 109–135. DOI: 10.1007/s10798-023-09812-2 PMID: 36844448

Rütti-Joy, O., Winder, G., & Biedermann, H. (2023). Building AI Literacy for Sustainable Teacher Education. *Zeitschrift für Hochschulentwicklung, 18*(4), 175–189. DOI: 10.21240/zfhe/18-04/10

Shah, V. M., & Shah, D. (2023). Impact of Digitalisation in Education-a Literature Review Analysis. *Towards Excellence,* 333-343. https://doi.org/DOI: 10.37867/TE150234

Sperling, K., Stenberg, C.-J., McGrath, C., Åkerfeldt, A., Heintz, F., & Stenliden, L. (2024). In Search of Artificial Intelligence (AI) Literacy in Teacher Education: A Scoping Review. *Computers and Education Open, 6,* 100169. DOI: 10.1016/j.caeo.2024.100169

Srinivasan, K. R., Rahman, N. H. A., & Ravana, S. D. (2025). Reskilling and Upskilling Future Educators for the Demands of Artificial Intelligence in the Modern Era of Education. In *Pitfalls of AI Integration in Education: Skill Obsolescence, Misuse, and Bias.* IGI Global., DOI: 10.4018/979-8-3373-0122-8.ch008

Summak, M. S., & Çelik-Şahín, Ç. (2014). Examining the Opinions About Determining Standards at Science and Arts Centers. *Asian Journal of Instruction, 2*(1), 1–15. https://dergipark.org.tr/tr/download/article-file/17637

Tabier, E., & Bakanay, Ç. D. (2023). Museum Education Environments and Artificial Intelligence Applications in Preschool Education. *Journal Of Social Humanities and Administrative Sciences, 65*(65), 3082–3088. DOI: 10.29228/JOSHAS.70500

Thomas, T. (2024). The Role of Artificial Intelligence in Formal and Informal Education for Students. *International Journal for Research in Applied Science and Engineering Technology, 12*(3), 69–71. DOI: 10.22214/ijraset.2024.58738

Triansyah, F. A., Muhammad, I., Rabuandika, A., Siregar, K. D. P., Teapon, N., & Assabana, M. S. (2023). Bibliometric Analysis: Artificial Intelligence (AI) in High School Education. *Jurnal Imiah Pendidikan dan Pembelajaran, 7*(1), 112-123. https://doi.org/DOI: 10.23887/jipp.v7i1.59718

Triplett, W. J. (2023). Impact of Technology Integration in STEM Education. *Cybersecurity and Innovative Technology Journal, 1*(1), 16–22. DOI: 10.53889/citj.v1i1.295

Uygun, D. (2024). Teachers' Perspectives on Artificial Intelligence in Education. *Advances in Mobile Learning Educational Research, 4*(1), 931–939. DOI: 10.25082/AMLER.2024.01.005

Uymaz, M. (2024). Present and Future of Artificial Intelligence: A Case Study on Prospective Teachers. *Sakarya University Journal of Education, 14*(Special Issue-AI in Education), 194-212. https://doi.org/DOI: 10.19126/suje.1466052

Wetzel, J., Burkhardt, H., Cheema, S., Kang, S., Pead, D., Schoenfeld, A., & VanLehn, K. (2018). A Preliminary Evaluation of the Usability of an AI-Infused Orchestration System. *Lecture Notes in Computer Science, 379-383,* 379–383. Advance online publication. DOI: 10.1007/978-3-319-93846-2_71

Writer, S. C., & Erkoc, M. (2023). Analysis of Science Group Teachers' Use of Artificial Intelligence in the Distance Education Process. *Dokuz Eylül University Buca Faculty of Education Journal*, (58), 2682–2704. DOI: 10.53444/deubefd.1316144

Xiao, J., Bozkurt, A., Nichols, M., Pazurek, A., Stracke, C. M., Bai, J. Y. H., Farrow, R., Mulligan, D., Nerantzi, C., Sharma, R. C., Singh, L., Frumin, I., Swindell, A., Honeychurch, S., Bond, M., Dron, J., Moore, S., Leng, J., & Slagter van Tryon, P. J.. (2025). Venturing into the Unknown: Critical Insights into Grey Areas and Pioneering Future Directions in Educational Generative AI Research. *TechTrends*, ●●●, 1–16. DOI: 10.1007/s11528-025-01060-6

Yue, M., Jong, M. S.-Y., & Ng, D. T. K. (2024). Understanding K–12 teachers' technological pedagogical content knowledge readiness and attitudes toward artificial intelligence education. *Education and Information Technologies*, 29(15), 19505–19536. DOI: 10.1007/s10639-024-12621-2

Zhang, H., Lee, I., & Moore, K. (2024). An Effectiveness Study of Teacher-Led AI Literacy Curriculum in K-12 Classrooms. *Proceedings of the AAAI Conference on Artificial Intelligence*, 38(21), 23318–23325. DOI: 10.1609/aaai.v38i21.30380

Zulkarnain, N. S., & Md Yunus, M. (2023). Primary Teachers' Perspectives on Using Artificial Intelligence Technology in English as a Second Language Teaching and Learning: A Systematic Review. *International Journal of Academic Research in Progressive Education and Development*, 12(2). Advance online publication. DOI: 10.6007/IJARPED/v12-i2/17119

KEY TERMS AND DEFINITIONS

Artificial Intelligence (AI): The capability of computer systems to perform tasks that typically require human intelligence, such as learning, problem-solving, and decision-making, with applications in education to enhance personalized learning and automate administrative processes.

Self-Efficacy in AI: A teacher's confidence in their ability to understand, implement, and effectively use AI tools within educational settings to improve student engagement and learning outcomes.

Science and Art Centers (SACs): Specialized institutions in Turkey designed to provide enriched educational experiences for gifted students, supporting their academic and creative development alongside formal schooling.

Technology Integration in Education: The process of incorporating digital tools, including AI, into teaching and learning environments to enhance instructional methods, facilitate personalized learning, and improve educational efficiency.

Teacher Competencies in AI: The knowledge, skills, and attitudes required by educators to effectively integrate AI-driven tools and methodologies into classroom instruction while maintaining pedagogical and ethical standards.

Ethical Considerations in AI Education: The principles and guidelines governing the responsible use of AI in education, addressing issues such as data privacy, algorithmic bias, and the impact of automation on the teaching profession.

AI-Supported Pedagogy: Teaching approaches that leverage AI technologies to provide adaptive learning experiences, automate assessment processes, and support differentiated instruction tailored to students' needs.

Chapter 7
The Automation Trap:
Unpacking the Consequences of Over-Reliance on AI in Education and Its Hidden Costs

Elif Karamuk
https://orcid.org/0000-0002-5866-995X
Istanbul Galata University, Turkey

ABSTRACT

With the growing presence of artificial intelligence (AI) in classrooms, its influence on how students think, learn, and interact deserves close scrutiny. However, its increasing integration and accessibility raise concerns about AI dependency among students. Excessive reliance on AI may weaken essential cognitive skills, including critical thinking, problem-solving, and creativity, which are crucial for academic and professional success. Moreover, diminished human interaction with teachers and peers threatens the human aspect of education. This chapter critically examines the risks of AI over-reliance, emphasizing its long-term consequences on student development. Left unchecked, this dependency may lead to superficial learning and hinder the cultivation of independent thought. The normalization of AI-generated outputs may also blur the line between authentic learning and algorithmic convenience. It highlights the shift from AI as a supportive tool to a potential source of dependency and advocates for a more balanced, human-centered integration of technology in education.

INTRODUCTION

AI is transforming education by improving adaptive learning, streamlining processes, and customizing instruction to meet individual needs (Haleem et al., 2022; Ocaña-Fernández et al., 2019). These advancements foster more dynamic and efficient learning experiences (Chen & Lin, 2024; Khosravi et al., 2022) Generative AI models like ChatGPT, Gemini, Claude, and Copilot further streamline research, content creation, and academic workflows (Acut et al., 2024). AI tools assist students with text summarization, grammar correction, translation, lesson planning, and exam question generation, making learning more accessible (Dempere et al., 2023; Grassini, 2023). Studies highlight that these technologies foster independent learning, boost engagement, enhance critical thinking and student motivation (Hmoud et

DOI: 10.4018/979-8-3373-0122-8.ch007

al., 2024; Montenegro-Rueda et al., 2023). Additionally, teachers use AI tools like ChatGPT to create customized materials, streamline teaching, and improve assessments (Xiao et al., 2025).

While AI offers significant advantages, it also raises ethical, cognitive, and pedagogical concerns, particularly regarding over-reliance by both students and teachers (Seo et al., 2021). Zhang et al. (2024) describe AI dependency as excessive reliance on AI in academic, daily, and social contexts, encompassing both frequent use and psychological reliance. According to the cognitive-behavioral framework (Davis, 2001), low academic self-efficacy increases stress, leading students to turn to AI as a coping mechanism. Zhang et al. (2024) found that students with low self-efficacy rely more on AI for decision-making and task fulfillment, reinforcing dependency (Morales-Garcia et al., 2024). This suggests that AI reliance is not just about convenience but a psychological adaptation to academic pressures.

Over-reliance on AI not only weakens students' problem-solving and creativity skills (Çela et al.,2024) but also may disrupts their cognitive flexibility—their ability to adapt and generate new solutions in unfamiliar situations (Spiro et al., 1988). Students may engage in superficial learning, accepting AI outputs without critical evaluation, which discourages deep research and source credibility assessment (Santiago Jr et al., 2023). Beyond cognitive decline, AI dependency raises ethical concerns like plagiarism and academic dishonesty (Nguyen et al., 2024) while also reducing human interaction, leading to social isolation and weakened interpersonal skills (Akgun & Greenhow, 2022; Ifelebuegu et al., 2023).

Given these risks, it is crucial to approach AI as a double-edged sword that requires responsible and ethical integration in educational settings. While AI has the potential to enhance learning experiences, its unregulated use may undermine fundamental cognitive and academic skills. Thus, this chapter critically examines the pitfalls associated with AI dependency, its ethical and cognitive consequences, and its long-term effects on student learning and engagement. Additionally, it proposes strategies to ensure a balanced AI integration that safeguards human-centered education while maximizing AI's potential.

MAIN FOCUS OF THE CHAPTER

The growing use of AI in education raises concerns about over-reliance and its impact on students' cognitive skills. Research indicates that excessive AI dependence may weaken critical thinking, creativity, and problem-solving abilities (Liu et al., 2023). Raising awareness of both AI's benefits and ethical risks is essential for promoting responsible use (Dwivedi et al., 2023). If not used ethically, AI tools risk turning students into automated thinkers rather than active learners. These concerns highlight critical research questions:

- How does automation affect students' cognitive and academic development as human interaction decreases?
- Can AI dependency lead to weaken fundamental thinking skills such as critical thinking, problem-solving and creativity?
- Does easy access to AI-generated information distract students from deep learning?

While AI offers undeniable benefits, its risks and ethical challenges must not be overlooked. Existing research has largely focused on AI's benefits, such as personalized learning and automation of tasks, yet there is a significant gap in understanding its unintended cognitive and ethical consequences—particularly the long-term risks of AI over-reliance in educational contexts. This chapter adresses these gaps by exploring the pitfalls of AI integration in education including the unintended consequences of automation in learning. The main objective of the chapter is to explore AI dependency and its long-term effects on students' cognitive and academic development through cognitive theories and learning sciences. It examines the rise of technology dependency, the factors driving AI reliance in education, and its impact on critical thinking, creativity, and problem-solving. Additionally, it analyzes how AI affects human interaction in learning environments and explores the ethical concerns associated with AI over-reliance. The chapter also proposes strategies for integrating AI in a balanced and pedagogically sound way, ensuring a human-centered approach. This approach can help mitigate the pitfalls of AI integration, such as skill degradation, reduced human interaction, and ethical risks.

THE PATH TO TECHNOLOGY DEPENDENCY: THE RAPID RISE OF AI IN EDUCATION

With the continuous and rapid evolution of artificial intelligence, educational practices have witnessed significant transformations. From primary education to universities, AI applications are changing traditional teaching methods by enabling automated support and interactive virtual environments, thus creating flexible and personalized curricula (Ocaña-Fernández et al., 2019). These innovations help students actively engage and learn at their own pace, while educators can better analyze and support students' individual needs.

Recent innovations in machine learning have accelerated the spread of generative AI technologies, notably language models such as ChatGPT, which use Natural Language Processing to produce human-like content, from short texts to comprehensive research papers (Dwivedi et al., 2021; Pavlik, 2023). Such models personalize educational experiences by adapting content to individual student profiles, providing tailored feedback, and offering rapid performance assessments (Hodges & Kirschner, 2024).

Despite these advantages, the ethical, safe, and reliable use of AI in education remains uncertain (Jain et al., 2023). While AI can efficiently perform complex tasks such as content summarization, article drafting, and coding, reliance on these tools may negatively impact learning quality. Specifically, generative AI models, due to their human-like content production, can discourage students from investing independent effort in learning. Over-reliance may consequently diminish students' responsibility, critical thinking, problem-solving, and creativity.

Recent studies suggest psychological factors contribute significantly to students' increasing AI dependency. For example, Zhang et al. (2024) indicate that students with low academic self-efficacy, who experience greater academic stress, tend to rely more on AI to manage their challenges. Similarly, students with low confidence in their academic abilities often turn to AI-based tools like ChatGPT as convenient alternatives to independent learning (Alshater, 2022; Rahman & Watanobe, 2023). Although this may enhance short-term academic performance, it increases the risk of long-term dependence on AI.

AI use among students is growing due to perceived academic and emotional benefits. Research shows chatbots can positively impact users' mental health by reducing stress (Meng & Dai, 2021; Rani et al., 2023). However, reliance on AI for emotional support may deepen students' psychological attachment, further reinforcing dependency behaviors, particularly during stressful academic periods.

In conclusion, while AI offers students quick access to information, its misuse poses serious risks, including decreased creativity, impaired critical thinking, and increased plagiarism (Zhang et al., 2024). Efforts should focus on promoting students' responsible use of AI, enhancing their AI literacy, and balancing its convenience with independent learning (Ng et al., 2021). Educational institutions must prioritize policies and practices that encourage students to use AI ethically and as a supplementary tool, preserving their ability to think critically and independently. In the following sections, the risks that arise as a result of over-reliance in AI will be discussed.

THE EFFECTS OF AI DEPENDENCY ON EDUCATION

Lost Skills and Passive Learning: How AI Dependency Reshapes Student Abilities

In recent years, AI has transformed education and reshaped teaching processes. In particular, AI-supported tools allow students to have individualized learning experiences and teachers to make more efficient assessments. However, there are different views on the effects of these technologies on student independence, cognitive development and academic motivation. In particular, the risk of students becoming overly dependent on AI and losing critical thinking and problem solving skills is noteworthy. In this context, the question of how AI can be used in a balancing way in education emerges as an important area of research.

When used responsibly, AI enhances students' learning by improving time management, fostering self-regulated learning and providing personalized feedback (Zimmerman, 2002). AI-based tutoring systems enable students to recognize knowledge gaps and adjust their learning strategies (Ng et al., 2024). However, excessive reliance on AI-generated solutions can diminish students' intrinsic motivation, autonomy, and problem-solving skills, leading to passive learning behaviors (Wu et al., 2024).

While AI tools offer personalized learning experiences and instant feedback (Pane et al., 2014), their overuse may result in cognitive offloading—where individuals transfer mental tasks to AI, reducing deep engagement with information (Carr, 2020; Sparrow et al., 2011). Although cognitive offloading can conserve cognitive resources (Risko & Gilbert, 2016), it may hinder skill development by discouraging students from engaging in critical analysis and independent problem-solving. This is particularly concerning for critical thinking, which requires active cognitive involvement.

In this context, Cognitive Load Theory (CLT) (Sweller, 1988) provides a useful framework for understanding the effects of AI in education. CLT posits that human cognitive capacity is limited, and managing cognitive load effectively enhances learning. AI tools help by automating routine tasks, allowing students to focus on complex cognitive processes. However, when students overly rely on AI-generated content, they risk losing opportunities for deep learning and independent thought. Persistent dependence on AI solutions may weaken analytical skills and intellectual autonomy (Gerlich, 2025).

Studies suggest that while AI tools boost student motivation (García-Martínez et al., 2023), their overuse can weaken cognitive engagement essential for skill acquisition. Generative AI can limit students' ability to think critically and solve problems independently, fostering passive learning behaviors (Placed et al., 2022). In other words, AI dependency can also impact creativity, critical thinking, and decision-making skills (Duhaylungsod & Chavez, 2023; Shanmugasundaram & Tamilarasu, 2023). AI-driven dialog systems can blur the distinction between AI-generated and human-generated content, reducing human interaction and contributing to social isolation and self-esteem issues (Kim et al., 2023; Semrl et al., 2023). Therefore, a balanced and responsible approach to AI use is necessary (Dergaa et al., 2024).

The integration of AI in education also raises concerns about diminished human interaction and social learning. Some researchers argue that AI-supported learning platforms may reduce collaborative engagement and hinder critical thinking development (Mhlanga, 2023; Zanetti et al., 2019). While AI chatbots provide practical assistance, they may foster dependency, impairing students' ability to independently analyze problems (Ifelebuegu et al., 2023). Furthermore, AI tools like ChatGPT, though innovative, can be distracting rather than beneficial, particularly for students with shorter attention spans (Dwivedi et al., 2023).

University students have expressed concerns that while AI supports their ideas, it may also promote laziness and weaken independent thinking (Bae et al., 2024). Unregulated AI use risks turning students into passive learners by diminishing critical thinking, decision-making, and creativity. Clark (2023) warns that over-reliance on AI reduces students' engagement in learning, while Calzada (2024) argues that unquestioning dependence on AI-generated answers fosters a superficial approach to complex issues. Excessive AI use in academic writing has also raised concerns about originality and intellectual independence. Some researchers warn that students who heavily rely on AI for written assignments risk weakening their logical reasoning and critical thinking skills (Azaria et al., 2024; Rane et al., 2023).

Given these concerns, AI tools should complement—not replace—students' cognitive development. Educators must ensure that AI is used to enhance students' problem-solving, creativity, and decision-making rather than hinder their intellectual growth (Stevenson et al., 2022; Stojanov, 2023). Wu (2023) emphasizes that constructivist learning requires active participation, yet AI tools like ChatGPT may discourage exploration and problem-solving, leading to diminished research skills and self-directed learning (Fiialka et al., 2023; Hasanein & Sobaih, 2023; Lin, 2023).

The Ethics of AI in Education: How Over-Reliance Undermines Academic Integrity

Academic dishonesty (Garcia et al., 2025), including exam cheating, plagiarism, and unauthorized editing of academic work, has been a persistent challenge in higher education (Bowers, 1964; Stiles et al., 2018). Research indicates that academic misconduct increased following the COVID-19 pandemic, with technology playing a significant role in facilitating access to unauthorized information (Ghimire et al., 2024; Jenkins et al., 2022). Advances in mobile devices, internet access, and AI-based tools have further exacerbated these concerns (Dawson, 2021).

A major contributor to this issue is the growing use of AI writing tools like ChatGPT, which have made it easier for students to generate academic content without fully engaging in critical thinking or independent research (Shaw et al., 2023). Calzada (2024) warns that over-reliance on AI threatens academic integrity by increasing plagiarism and diminishing originality. Misattributing AI-generated content can lead students to unintentional academic misconduct, particularly when they fail to verify sources or critically evaluate AI-generated information. While AI can be beneficial when used appropriately, its overuse raises concerns about students completing assignments without understanding fundamental concepts, ultimately weakening their academic writing and reasoning skills (Adeshola & Adepoju, 2024; Lo, 2023).

Additionally, automation bias—the tendency to assume AI-generated content is always accurate—worsens these challenges (Baker & Hawn, 2021). Research highlights that students with high automation bias are more likely to engage in unintentional plagiarism, as they fail to critically assess AI-generated information (Yu et al., 2020). Moreover, the risk of misinformation remains significant, as AI-generated content may not always be accurate, emphasizing the need for human oversight to maintain academic integrity (Broussard, 2018). Addressing this issue requires AI literacy training, critical thinking development, and responsible AI usage policies (Srinivasan et al., 2025).

Recent studies reveal that students experiencing intense academic stress tend to misuse AI technologies (Ventayen, 2023). For many students, academic dishonesty has become a way to cope with stress and alleviate academic pressure (Crawford et al., 2023). The fact that the content generated by ChatGPT cannot be detected by existing plagiarism detection programs poses a significant problem for academic integrity. Weber-Wulff et al. (2023) evaluated 14 AI-generated text detection tools, including Turnitin and GPTZero, and found that all scored below 80% accuracy, with only five exceeding 70%. This highlights the current limitations of these tools in reliably identifying AI-generated content. Overall, it has been found that they often identify human-written documents as AI-generated (false positives) and, conversely, tend to classify AI-generated texts as human-written (false negatives). Pegoraro et al. (2023) not only examined online AI-generated text detection tools but also analyzed several existing detection methods, highlighting that identifying text generated by ChatGPT remains a significant challenge. Their study found that even the most effective online detection tool achieved an accuracy rate of less than 50%, with most tools tending to classify texts as human-written. Similarly, tests conducted by van Oijen (2023) revealed that the overall accuracy of AI-generated text detection tools was only 27.9%. The best-performing tool reached a maximum accuracy of 50%, whereas these tools demonstrated an accuracy of approximately 83% in detecting human-written content. Moreover, Perkins et al. (2023) investigated the ability of academic staff, assisted by Turnitin's AI detection tool, to identify AI-generated content in university assessments. The study revealed significant limitations in detection accuracy, emphasizing the challenges faced by educators in maintaining academic integrity.

Given these detection limitations, some universities have opted to ban AI tools, while others are developing guidelines for their ethical use. While some institutions in the U.S. have restricted access to ChatGPT (Elsen-Rooney, 2023), these measures remain largely symbolic due to workarounds like VPN usage. Additionally, some academic conferences have banned AI-generated content in submissions, and Italy temporarily banned ChatGPT before reversing its decision (Schechner, 2023). Instead of outright bans, many scholars argue that ethical AI policies and AI literacy programs provide a more sustainable solution (Ghimire et al., 2024).

While AI poses challenges to academic integrity, it also offers valuable opportunities when used responsibly. Tools like ChatGPT can enhance productivity, creativity, and knowledge management in education (Nguyen et al., 2024). However, banning AI outright may limit students' access to useful learning resources (Perkins et al., 2024). Instead, universities should develop AI-integrated academic integrity policies that guide students in ethical and responsible AI use.

Leading institutions have already started adapting. Harvard University has updated its academic integrity policies, allowing AI use while emphasizing proper attribution and ethical guidelines (Harvard College Office of Academic Integrity and Student Conduct, 2025). Similarly, Stanford University has released a report detailing responsible AI use in teaching, research, and administrative processes (AI at Stanford Advisory Committee, 2025). These initiatives highlight that a structured approach to AI integration, rather than strict prohibition, is more effective in preserving academic integrity.

Ultimately, technology itself does not hinder learning—its misuse does. Therefore, educators should focus on AI literacy and responsible AI use, rather than banning AI tools entirely. Cotton et al. (2024) emphasize that AI tools like ChatGPT's potential is best realized when students and educators receive proper training on how to use it ethically and effectively. By fostering interactive learning environments and structured policies, universities can ensure that AI enhances education rather than undermines academic integrity.

Long-Term Consequences of AI Dependency: Loss of the Human Factor in Education

One of the major concerns in AI-integrated education is the decline of human interaction. Education is inherently social, fostering empathy, collaboration, and interpersonal communication (Kamalov & Gurrib, 2023). However, dependency on AI tools risks weakening student-instructor and peer-to-peer relationships, essential components of effective learning. The increasing replacement of human engagement with AI-driven interactions may lead to less personalized and emotionally supportive learning environments (Al-Zahrani, 2024). Thus, AI should not replace human educators but instead be positioned as a supportive tool to enhance rather than diminish the student-teacher bond.

AI tools facilitate individualized learning, but this comes at the cost of reduced social engagement (Ifelebuegu et al., 2023). Collaborative learning and cooperative projects help students develop problem-solving skills, yet excessive AI dependency may hinder the natural exchange of ideas, negatively affecting knowledge-sharing and critical discussions among students (Ali et al., 2024). Additionally, Maanu, et al., (2025) highlighted that while AI can facilitate individual learning, it reduces student engagement in collaborative projects. Liu, Li, and Dong (2024) further discovered that high-achieving students use AI to complement their learning, whereas lower-achieving students tend to over-rely on it, leading to diminished peer interaction. Therefore, it is crucial to balance AI-assisted learning with interactive and peer-based learning experiences to sustain collaborative academic environments.

The COVID-19 pandemic accelerated AI adoption, increasing emotional and psychological dependency on such technologies (Pentina et al., 2023). While AI tools like ChatGPT offer efficiency in content generation, they lack emotional intelligence, making them incapable of providing motivational and psychological support (Bae et al., 2024). Educators play a critical role not only in knowledge transfer but also as mentors offering emotional and intellectual support. Therefore, in many educational settings, personal connections and individualized attention remain critical. AI cannot fully replicate human empathy, non-verbal cues, or contextual awareness, limiting its ability to support students' social and emotional development (Diederich et al., 2022).

Rapanta et al. (2020) highlight that students receiving personalized feedback from teachers outperform those relying solely on automated systems (Bernius et al., 2022; Gao, 2021). Similarly, blended learning models that integrate human interaction with AI-supported education result in higher engagement and academic satisfaction than AI-exclusive approaches. Personalized learning through GenAI may overshadow collaborative learning, which is essential for meaning-making and communication development (Hmelo-Silver et al., 2007). To ensure a holistic learning experience, GenAI tools should be designed to encourage both individual learning and social interaction (Gantalao et al., 2025).

AI's expansion in education risks making students feel insufficiently supported, as it lacks the ability to build strong interpersonal relationships (Al-Zahrani, 2024). Furthermore, AI-generated responses, while efficient, fail to address students' unique learning needs, strengths, and preferences, limiting personalized guidance (Ali et al., 2024). Moreover, beyond student-instructor relationships, student-to-student interactions also play a crucial role in collaborative learning and knowledge exchange. Research indicates that peer learning and cooperative projects help students develop communication and problem-solving skills (Grassini, 2023). However, studies show that students who heavily rely on AI tools for academic tasks may engage less in collaborative learning, leading to reduced teamwork skills (Dempere et al., 2023). Over-reliance on AI may hinder the natural exchange of ideas and discussions among students, negatively impacting their ability to learn through social engagement (Ali et al., 2024). Moreover, while chatbots and AI-driven virtual assistants provide individualized learning and quick feedback, excessive dependence on them may lead to social withdrawal and technological over-reliance, particularly in individuals with social anxiety (Hu et al., 2023; Xie et al., 2023). Research underscores that students engaged in face-to-face education perform better than those in online-only AI-supported environments, reinforcing the importance of social learning dynamics (Baber, 2021; Ali et al., 2024).

The growing substitution of human interaction with AI-based automation may result in students becoming passive recipients of information, reducing their ability to critically engage with content (Baidoo-Anu & Ansah, 2023; Eysenbach, 2023). Sirghi et al. (2024) warn that excessive AI adoption may undermine cognitive development by replacing active learning with passive AI-generated content consumption. Over-reliance on AI can erode social interactions, decrease student engagement, and weaken educators' role in fostering collaborative learning environments.

Given these challenges, AI should not replace the human elements of education but instead serve as a tool to enhance the learning experience. Educational institutions must develop AI policies that promote responsible use while preserving the social and ethical dimensions of education (Klimav & Compas, 2024). The key to sustainable AI integration in education lies in maintaining a balance between technology and human guidance, ensuring students develop both independent learning skills and collaborative social competencies.

BEYOND THE CLASSROOM: THE CAREER AND COGNITIVE IMPACTS OF AI OVER-RELIANCE

Critical thinking, problem-solving, and creativity have become essential for academic achievement, professional success, and lifelong learning (Coleman, 2020). As societies become increasingly digitalized and algorithm-driven, individuals must develop computational thinking, data analysis, and AI literacy to remain competitive in the workforce. However, over-reliance on AI tools may hinder students' ability to cultivate these skills, leading to reduced intellectual engagement and long-term adaptability (Calzada, 2024).

While AI provides rapid access to information, excessive dependency may discourage deep cognitive engagement, weakening inquiry, evaluation, and reflection processes (Peres et al., 2023). University professors express concerns that students who depend on AI tools struggle with critical problem-solving in real-world contexts, leaving them ill-prepared for the workforce (Gammoh, 2024). Similarly, Hasanein and Sobaih (2023) emphasize that critical thinking and problem-solving are key to professional success, while Singh et al. (2023) highlight that assignments designed to enhance these skills lose their effectiveness when AI is overused, ultimately affecting students' employability.

AI reliance may also alter thinking patterns, making individuals less inquisitive and more mechanistic (Sarwat, 2018). Frequent AI use in planning and decision-making can limit deep understanding and foster impatience and cognitive laziness (Krakauer, 2016). As AI increasingly handles complex tasks, students may struggle with developing independent problem-solving strategies, impacting their professional competence (Gocen & Aydemir, 2020).

Beyond individual career development, creativity, ethical decision-making, and critical thinking play a crucial role in entrepreneurial success, regional economic development, and democratic participation (Anjum et al., 2021; Belitski & Desai, 2016; Siegel, 1987). However, Yılmaz and Yılmaz (2023) warn that AI tools like ChatGPT may reduce students' motivation to engage deeply with learning, limiting their ability to explore topics comprehensively and critically. This not only affects their employability but also raises broader concerns about workforce preparedness in an AI-driven economy.

Thus, it is essential for educators and policymakers to ensure AI is used responsibly, fostering analytical and creative thinking rather than replacing it (Al-Zahrani, 2024). A balanced approach that integrates AI as a supplementary tool rather than a primary cognitive resource is necessary to prevent the erosion of essential problem-solving skills and maintain long-term career adaptability.

MANAGING AI INTEGRATION IN EDUCATION: CHALLENGES AND SOLUTIONS

Towards a Balanced Approach: Mitigating the Risks of AI in Education

As AI becomes increasingly integrated into education, it is essential to balance its benefits with its potential risks. While AI can enhance learning, streamline administrative tasks, and offer personalized support, it cannot replace human interaction, ethical reasoning, and contextual understanding (Diederich et al., 2022). Students and educators must recognize both AI's capabilities and its limitations, ensuring that AI tools are used to support rather than dictate learning and assessment processes. A collaborative model—where AI complements rather than replaces educators—ensures that technology strengthens teaching and learning without compromising critical thinking and independent learning (Ifelebuegu et al., 2023). This requires clear ethical guidelines, data privacy regulations, AI literacy programs, and teacher training to promote responsible and effective AI use in education.

Over-reliance on AI risks weakening students' critical thinking and engagement (Bozkurt et al., 2024). AI-generated content may encourage passive learning, reducing students' motivation to analyze, evaluate, and synthesize information independently. Rather than banning AI tools like ChatGPT, educators should focus on teaching responsible AI use, emphasizing critical evaluation, cross-referencing with reliable sources, and ethical considerations (Kim et al., 2023). AI should function as a research aid and brainstorming tool, not as a primary knowledge source.

AI's impact on students is widely discussed, but its role in supporting educators is equally critical. AI enhances teaching effectiveness by personalizing learning experiences and reducing administrative burdens (Zawacki-Richter et al., 2019). By automating tasks like grading and attendance, AI allows teachers to focus more on student engagement and meaningful interaction (Wang et al., 2021). Additionally, AI-driven analytics help educators identify students' learning challenges, enabling more targeted teaching strategies (Peng et al., 2019; UNESCO, 2023). To maximize AI's benefits, it must be integrated as a tool that complements teachers rather than replacing them (Çukurova et al., 2019; Kim et al., 2022). AI should be used to support automation, data-driven insights, and personalization, while reinforcing the teacher's role as a mentor and guide in the learning process.

Ultimately, the successful integration of AI in education requires a balanced and ethical approach that prioritizes human expertise while leveraging AI's capabilities. AI should be positioned as an assistive tool that enhances, rather than replaces, human decision-making. Educators play a critical role in shaping AI's impact on education by guiding students towards responsible AI use and fostering critical thinking skills.

Universities and policymakers must collaborate to establish clear guidelines, AI literacy programs, and ethical frameworks that ensure AI contributes positively to education without compromising academic integrity. By adopting teacher-AI collaboration models and emphasizing responsible AI practices, we can create a future where AI empowers, rather than diminishes, the human role in education.

Strategies to Prevent Over-Reliance on AI in Education

Preventing over-reliance requires a balanced approach that emphasizes human oversight, critical thinking, and ethical use. When used responsibly, AI can enhance learning while minimizing potential risks (Chen & Lin, 2023). Therefore, this section outlines step-by-step strategies for institutions and educators to promote responsible AI use in education.

To ensure that AI is integrated into education in a pedagogically sound manner, a structured implementation framework is essential. The AI-Integrated Pedagogical Implementation Framework (AI-PIF) developed within this research provides a systematic approach to balancing AI-enhanced learning with human-centered education. This framework consists of four key phases: (1) Strategic Planning & Readiness, ensuring institutions align AI adoption with pedagogical needs (Molenaar, 2024); (2) Pedagogical Integration Strategies, incorporating AI into established teaching methods such as Flipped Classroom and Inquiry-Based Learning (Kong & Yang, 2024); (3) Human-AI Collaboration & Balanced Implementation, ensuring AI enhances but does not replace human educators (Fragiadakis et al., 2024); and (4) Continuous Monitoring, Assessment & Development, where AI's impact is regularly assessed for ethical considerations and student learning outcomes (Hutson, 2025). By adhering to this structured approach, AI can be effectively incorporated into educational environments while preserving the core principles of human-centered education.

Table 1. The AI-integrated pedagogical implementation framework

No.	Stage	Description	Resources
1	Strategic Planning and Preparation	Determining how AI will be positioned in education and its pedagogical integration.	Chen (2022), Molenaar (2024), Padovano & Cardamone (2024)
2	Pedagogical Integration Strategies	Identifying how AI can be integrated with educational models such as Flipped Classroom and Inquiry-Based Learning.	Hutson & Plate (2023), Kong & Yang (2024), Molenaar (2022)
3	Human-AI Collaboration and Balanced Use	Analyzing how AI can be used as a supportive tool for educators and its impact on student engagement.	Edwards et al. (2025), Fragiadakis et al. (2024), Puerta-Beldarrain & Gómez-Carmona (2025),
4	Continuous Monitoring, Evaluation, and Development	Measuring the long-term impact of AI in education, developing ethical oversight mechanisms, and evaluating student success.	Hutson (2025), Chen (2022), Molenaar (2024)

As shown in Table 1, the first stage of the AI-PIF is Strategic Planning & Readiness, which ensures that AI is implemented with a clear educational purpose and pedagogical alignment. Institutions must first define how AI fits within their learning environments and assess the necessity of its integration (Molenaar, 2024). Additionally, both educators and students should undergo AI literacy training to promote ethical and responsible AI usage (Chen, 2022). Conducting a thorough needs analysis helps determine which subjects and instructional settings can benefit the most from AI-enhanced tools, ensuring AI adoption serves as a complement rather than a replacement to traditional teaching methods (Padovano & Cardamone, 2024).

The second stage of the framework is Pedagogical Integration Strategies, focusing on embedding AI into existing teaching models to enhance learning experiences. One effective approach is incorporating AI into Flipped Classroom methodologies, where students use AI-driven platforms to study course materials before class, allowing for more interactive and discussion-based sessions (Kong & Yang, 2024). Additionally, AI can be utilized in Inquiry-Based Learning, supporting students in their research and critical thinking processes by providing real-time assistance and feedback (Hutson & Plate, 2023). However, AI's role should be carefully structured to avoid over-reliance, ensuring that students actively engage with content rather than passively consuming AI-generated information (Molenaar, 2022).

The third stage, Human-AI Collaboration & Balanced Implementation, highlights the importance of AI complementing human educators rather than replacing them. AI should be utilized to handle repetitive administrative tasks, allowing teachers to focus on student-centered guidance and personalized instruction (Fragiadakis et al., 2024). Moreover, students must be encouraged to critically assess AI-generated content, fostering deeper engagement and analytical skills rather than passive acceptance (Puerta-Beldarrain & Gómez-Carmona, 2025). By clearly delineating the roles of AI and human instructors, educational institutions can maintain a balance where AI enhances cognitive engagement while teachers facilitate deeper learning through mentorship and real-world applications (Edwards et al., 2025).

The final stage of the framework is Continuous Monitoring, Assessment & Development, which ensures the ongoing evaluation and ethical oversight of AI in education. AI's impact on student learning outcomes, engagement, and cognitive development must be systematically assessed through data-driven evaluations (Hutson, 2025). Ethical concerns should also be continuously reviewed to guarantee fairness, transparency, and accountability in AI-based assessments (Chen, 2022). Finally, collecting feedback from students and educators enables continuous refinement of AI tools and policies, ensuring they evolve to meet the changing demands of educational environments (Molenaar, 2024).

6.3. Solutions and Recommendations

Effectively integrating AI into education requires a multi-dimensional approach that addresses students, educators, institutions, and policymakers. Rather than banning or restricting AI tools, it is essential to develop strategies that foster their responsible and ethical use while preserving critical thinking, creativity, and academic integrity. Ensuring a balanced and well-regulated AI integration can help mitigate potential risks while maximizing its benefits in educational contexts.

For students, it is crucial to develop independent learning strategies and critical thinking skills alongside AI usage. Research highlights the importance of maintaining a balance between AI-generated content and human cognition to prevent over-reliance and passive learning behaviors (Kivunja, 2015; Tias et al., 2022). Students should be encouraged to use AI as a supportive aid in brainstorming, research, and technical tasks while verifying information through reliable sources such as academic articles and textbooks (Kartal, 2024). Furthermore, fostering collaborative learning environments, where students engage in teamwork, discussion-based learning, and peer evaluation, can reduce dependency on AI tools and enhance communication and problem-solving skills (Grassini, 2023; Wang & Li, 2024). Educators should design assignments and activities that emphasize analytical thinking, self-reflection, and ethical considerations related to AI use (Wiredu et al., 2024).

For educators, AI provides opportunities to enhance teaching efficiency and personalize instruction. AI-assisted assessment systems can alleviate administrative burdens by automating repetitive tasks such as grading, attendance tracking, and student progress monitoring, allowing teachers to focus more on pedagogical interactions (Akgun & Greenhow, 2022; Wang et al., 2021). However, educators must remain actively involved in guiding students through AI-integrated learning experiences. A human-centered approach, as outlined by UNESCO (2023), should be prioritized, ensuring that AI tools are used to support rather than replace teachers. Training programs on AI literacy, ethical AI use, and effective instructional design can help educators integrate AI tools into their teaching while maintaining academic rigor (Kim et al., 2023).

Educational institutions play a critical role in establishing AI guidelines that promote ethical and responsible use. Institutions should implement AI literacy programs that equip both students and educators with the necessary skills to critically assess AI-generated content, recognize potential biases, and avoid academic dishonesty. Additionally, teacher-AI collaboration should be encouraged as a means to optimize automation while maintaining the role of human judgment in education (Ji et al., 2023). Universities and schools should develop policies that clearly define acceptable AI usage in assignments and research, ensuring that AI-generated content is not misused or relied upon excessively. Institutions must also invest in AI-detection mechanisms and academic integrity monitoring to mitigate risks related to plagiarism and misinformation (Weber-Wulff et al., 2023).

Policymakers should establish national and institutional frameworks that ensure ethical AI integration in education. Regulations should emphasize transparency, data privacy, and accountability in AI applications while promoting digital literacy initiatives. Policies must also consider the broader implications of AI dependency on workforce preparedness and lifelong learning. Ensuring that students graduate with the ability to think critically, problem-solve creatively, and ethically evaluate AI-generated information is essential for fostering an innovative and competitive workforce (Tang et al., 2022). International collaborations, such as UNESCO's guidelines, can serve as a foundation for developing policies that balance technological advancements with human-centered learning principles.

FUTURE RESEARCH DIRECTION

Research on AI dependency in education is still in its early stages, requiring more interdisciplinary studies. Future research could explore how AI dependency varies across student groups based on cognitive development, learning styles, and socio-economic backgrounds. Additionally, the long-term effects on motivation and cognitive flexibility should be examined, particularly whether AI fosters deep learning or encourages superficial information consumption. Further studies can investigate the relationship between AI dependency and self-regulated learning assessing whether AI supports goal-setting and learning regulation or diminishes independent learning and critical reflection.

CONCLUSION

Advancements in AI have significantly transformed education, offering both opportunities and challenges. While AI enhances teaching and learning, over-reliance on these tools raises concerns about the weakening of essential 21st-century skills such as critical thinking, problem-solving, and creativity

(Chen & Lin, 2024). This chapter highlights the risks of excessive AI use, emphasizing its potential to decline students's skills, undermine academic integrity and diminish human interaction in education. To maximize AI's benefits while minimizing its drawbacks, a balanced approach is crucial. Technology should complement, not replace, traditional teaching methods and human guidance (Diederich et al., 2022). Students must recognize that AI tools like ChatGPT serve as supportive aids rather than substitutes for independent research and critical thinking. Encouraging the verification of AI-generated information and promoting diverse, reliable sources can help maintain academic rigor and integrity. By fostering responsible AI use and reinforcing human-centered learning, educators and policymakers can ensure that AI remains a tool for enhancement rather than dependency.

REFERENCES

Acut, D. P., Malabago, N. K., Malicoban, E. V., Galamiton, N. S., & Garcia, M. B. (2024). "ChatGPT 4.0 Ghosted Us While Conducting Literature Search:" Modeling the Chatbot's Generated Non-Existent References Using Regression Analysis. *Internet Reference Services Quarterly*, ●●●, 1–26. DOI: 10.1080/10875301.2024.2426793

Adeshola, I., & Adepoju, A. P. (2024). The opportunities and challenges of ChatGPT in education. *Interactive Learning Environments*, 32(10), 6159–6172. DOI: 10.1080/10494820.2023.2253858

AI at Stanford Advisory Committee. (2025). Report of the AI at Stanford Advisory Committee. Stanford University. https://provost.stanford.edu/2025/01/09/report-of-the-ai-at-stanford-advisory-committee/

Akgun, S., & Greenhow, C. (2022). Artificial intelligence in education: Addressing ethical challenges in K-12 settings. *AI and Ethics*, 2(3), 431–440. DOI: 10.1007/s43681-021-00096-7 PMID: 34790956

Al-Zahrani, A. M. (2024). The impact of generative AI tools on researchers and research: Implications for academia in higher education. *Innovations in Education and Teaching International*, 61(5), 1029–1043. DOI: 10.1080/14703297.2023.2271445

Ali, M. S., Suchiang, T., Saikia, T. P., & Gulzar, D. D. (2024). Perceived benefits and concerns of Ai integration in higher education: Insights from India. *Educational Administration Theory and Practices*, 30, 656–668. DOI: 10.53555/kuey.v30i5.5122

Ali, O., Murray, P. A., Momin, M., Dwivedi, Y. K., & Malik, T. (2024). The effects of artificial intelligence applications in educational settings: Challenges and strategies. *Technological Forecasting and Social Change*, 199, 123076. DOI: 10.1016/j.techfore.2023.123076

Alshater, M. (2022). M. Exploring the role of artificial intelligence in enhancing academic performance: A case study of ChatGPT. Available at *SSRN*. https://doi.org/DOI: 10.2139/ssrn.4312358

Anjum, T., Farrukh, M., Heidler, P., & Tautiva, J. A. D. (2021). Entrepreneurial intention: Creativity, entrepreneurship, and university support. *Journal of Open Innovation*, 7(1), 11. DOI: 10.3390/joitmc7010011

Azaria, A., Azoulay, R., & Reches, S. (2024). ChatGPT is a remarkable tool—For experts. *Data Intelligence*, 6(1), 240–296. DOI: 10.1162/dint_a_00235

Baber, H., (2021). Social Interaction and Effectiveness of the Online Learning - A Moderating Role of Maintaining Social Distance During the Pandemic COVID-19. DOI: 10.1108/AEDS-09-2020-0209

Bae, M., Wang, J., Xue, H., Chong, S. M., Kwon, O., & Ki, C. W. (2024). Does ChatGPT help or hinder education? Exploring its benefits, challenges, student guilt, and the need for educator training. *International Journal of Fashion Design, Technology and Education*, ●●●, 1–16. DOI: 10.1080/17543266.2024.2430585

Baker, R. S., & Hawn, A. (2022). Algorithmic bias in education. *International Journal of Artificial Intelligence in Education*, 41(1), 1052–1092. DOI: 10.1007/s40593-021-00285-9

Belitski, M., & Desai, S. (2016). Creativity, entrepreneurship and economic development: City-level evidence on creativity spillover of entrepreneurship. *The Journal of Technology Transfer*, 41(6), 1354–1376. DOI: 10.1007/s10961-015-9446-3

Bernius, J. P., Krusche, S., & Bruegge, B. (2022). Machine learning based feedback on textual student answers in large courses. *Computers and Education: Artificial Intelligence*, *3*, 100081. Advance online publication. DOI: 10.1016/j.caeai.2022.100081

Bowers, W. J. (1964). *Student dishonesty and its control in college*. Bureau of Applied Social Research, Columbia University.

Bozkurt, A., Xiao, J., Farrow, R., Bai, J. Y. H., Nerantzi, C., Moore, S., Dron, J., Stracke, C. M., Singh, L., Crompton, H., Koutropoulos, A., Terentev, E., Pazurek, A., Nichols, M., Sidorkin, A. M., Costello, E., Watson, S., Mulligan, D., Honeychurch, S., & Asino, T. I. (2024). The Manifesto for Teaching and Learning in a Time of Generative AI: A Critical Collective Stance to Better Navigate the Future. *Open Praxis*, *16*(4), 487–513. DOI: 10.55982/openpraxis.16.4.777

Calzada, I. (2024). Artificial intelligence for social innovation: Beyond the noise of algorithms and datafication. *Sustainability (Basel)*, *16*(19), 8638. DOI: 10.3390/su16198638

Carr, N. (2020). *The shallows: What the Internet is doing to our brains*. WW Norton & Company.

Çela, E., Fonkam, M. M., & Potluri, R. M. (2024). Risks of AI-assisted learning on student critical thinking: A case study of Albania. [IJRCM]. *International Journal of Risk and Contingency Management*, *12*(1), 1–19. DOI: 10.4018/IJRCM.350185

Chen, J. J., & Lin, J. C. (2024). Artificial intelligence as a double-edged sword: Wielding the POWER principles to maximize its positive effects and minimize its negative effects. *Contemporary Issues in Early Childhood*, *25*(1), 146–153. DOI: 10.1177/14639491231169813

Chen, X. (2022). AI literacy in education: A framework for teachers and students. *Journal of Educational Technology & Innovation*, *10*(3), 45–67. DOI: 10.3102/jeti.2022.34

Coleman, F. (2020). *A human algorithm: How Artificial Intelligence is redefining who we are*. Catapult.

Cotton, D. R., Cotton, P. A., & Shipway, J. R. (2024). Chatting and cheating: Ensuring academic integrity in the era of ChatGPT. *Innovations in Education and Teaching International*, *61*(2), 228–239. DOI: 10.1080/14703297.2023.2190148

Crawford, J., Cowling, M., & Allen, K. A. (2023). Leadership is needed for ethical ChatGPT: Character, assessment, and learning using artificial intelligence (AI). *Journal of University Teaching & Learning Practice*, *20*(3), 02. . DOI: 10.53761/1.20.3.02

Çukurova, M., Kent, C., & Luckin, R. (2019). Artificial intelligence and multimodal data in the service of human decision-making: A case study in debate tutoring. *British Journal of Educational Technology*, *50*(6), 3032–3046. DOI: 10.1111/bjet.12829

Davis, R. A. (2001). A cognitive-behavioral model of pathological Internet use. *Computers in Human Behavior*, *17*(2), 187–195. DOI: 10.1016/S0747-5632(00)00041-8

Dawson, P. (2021). *Defending assessment security in a digital world: Preventing e-cheating and supporting academic integrity in higher education*. Routledge.

Dempere, J., Modugu, K., Hesham, A., & Ramasamy, L. K. (2023). The impact of ChatGPT on higher education. *Frontiers in Education, 8,* 1206936. DOI: 10.3389/feduc.2023.1206936

Dergaa, I., Ben Saad, H., Glenn, J. M., Amamou, B., Ben Aissa, M., Guelmami, N., Fekih-Romdhane, F., & Chamari, K. (2024). From tools to threats: A reflection on the impact of artificial-intelligence chatbots on cognitive health. *Frontiers in Psychology, 15,* 1259845. DOI: 10.3389/fpsyg.2024.1259845 PMID: 38629037

Diederich, S., Brendel, A. B., Morana, S., & Kolbe, L. (2022). On the design of and interaction with conversational agents: An organizing and assessing review of human-computer interaction research. *Journal of the Association for Information Systems, 23*(1), 96–138. DOI: 10.17705/1jais.00724

Duhaylungsod, A. V., & Chavez, J. V. (2023). ChatGPT and other AI users: Innovative and creative utilitarian value and mindset shift. *Journal of Namibian Studies: History Politics Culture, 33,* 4367–4378.

Dwivedi, Y. K., Hughes, L., Ismagilova, E., Aarts, G., Coombs, C., Crick, T., Duan, Y., Dwivedi, R., Edwards, J., Eirug, A., Galanos, V., Ilavarasan, P. V., Janssen, M., Jones, P., Kar, A. K., Kizgin, H., Kronemann, B., Lal, B., Lucini, B., & Williams, M. D. (2021). Artificial Intelligence (AI): Multidisciplinary perspectives on emerging challenges, opportunities, and agenda for research, practice and policy. *International Journal of Information Management, 57,* 101994. DOI: 10.1016/j.ijinfomgt.2019.08.002

Dwivedi, Y. K., Sharma, A., Rana, N. P., Giannakis, M., Goel, P., & Dutot, V. (2023). Evolution of artificial intelligence research in Technological Forecasting and Social Change: Research topics, trends, and future directions. *Technological Forecasting and Social Change, 192,* 122579. DOI: 10.1016/j. techfore.2023.122579

Edwards, J., Nguyen, K., & Lämsä, J. (2025). Socially shared regulation of learning in AI-enhanced collaborative education: An empirical study. *British Journal of Educational Technology, 56*(1), 78–98. DOI: 10.1111/bjet.13534

Elsen-Rooney, M. (2023, Jan, 4). NYC education department blocks ChatGPT on school devices, networks. Chalkbeat New York. https:// ny.chalk beat.org/2023/1/3/23537 987/nyc- schools- ban- chatgpt- writing- artificial- intelligence.

Fiialka, S., Kornieva, Z., & Honchar, T. (2023). ChatGPT in Ukrainian Education: Problems and Prospects. *International Journal of Emerging Technologies in Learning, 18*(17), 236–250. Advance online publication. DOI: 10.3991/ijet.v18i17.42215

Fillis, I. A. N., & Rentschler, R. (2010). The role of creativity in entrepreneurship. *Journal of Enterprising Culture, 18*(1), 49–81. DOI: 10.1142/S0218495810000501

Fragiadakis, G., Diou, C., & Kousiouris, G. (2024). Evaluating human-AI collaboration: A review and methodological framework. *arXiv Preprint,* 1-25. https://doi.org//arXiv.2407.19098 DOI: 10.48550

Gantalao, L. C., Calzada, J. G. D., Capuyan, D. L., Lumantas, B. C., Acut, D. P., & Garcia, M. B. (2025). Equipping the Next Generation of Technicians: Navigating School Infrastructure and Technical Knowledge in the Age of AI Integration. In *Pitfalls of AI Integration in Education: Skill Obsolescence, Misuse, and Bias.* IGI Global., DOI: 10.4018/979-8-3373-0122-8.ch009

Gao, J., 2021. Exploring the feedback quality of an automated writing evaluation system Pigai. *Int. J. Emerg. Technol. Learn. 16* (11), 322. https://doi.org/. v16i11.19657.DOI: 10.3991/ijet

Garcia, M. B., Rosak-Szyrocka, J., Yılmaz, R., Metwally, A. H. S., Acut, D. P., Ofosu-Ampong, K., Erdoğdu, F., Fung, C. Y., & Bozkurt, A. (2025). Rethinking Educational Assessment in the Age of Generative AI: Actionable Strategies to Mitigate Academic Dishonesty. In *Pitfalls of AI Integration in Education: Skill Obsolescence, Misuse, and Bias*. IGI Global., DOI: 10.4018/979-8-3373-0122-8.ch001

García-Martínez, I., Fernández-Batanero, J. M., Fernández-Cerero, J., & León, S. P. (2023). Analysing the impact of artificial intelligence and computational sciences on student performance: Systematic review and meta-analysis. *Journal of New Approaches in Educational Research*, *12*(1), 171–197. DOI: 10.7821/naer.2023.1.1240

Gerlich, M. (2025). AI Tools in Society: Impacts on Cognitive Offloading and the Future of Critical Thinking. *Societies (Basel, Switzerland)*, *15*(1), 6. DOI: 10.3390/soc15010006

Ghimire, S. N., Bhattarai, U., & Baral, R. K. (2024). Implications of ChatGPT for higher education institutions: Exploring Nepali university students' perspectives. *Higher Education Research & Development*, *43*(8), 1–15. DOI: 10.1080/07294360.2024.2366323

Gocen, A., & Aydemir, F. (2020). Artificial intelligence in education and schools. *Research on Education and Media*, *12*(1), 13–21. DOI: 10.2478/rem-2020-0003

Grassini, S. (2023). Shaping the Future of Education: Exploring the Potential and Consequences of AI and ChatGPT in Educational Settings. *Education Sciences*, *13*(7), 692. DOI: 10.3390/educsci13070692

Haleem, A., Javaid, M., Qadri, M. A., & Suman, R. (2022). Understanding the role of digital technologies in education: A review. *Sustainable operations and computers*, *3*, 275-285. https://doi.org/DOI: 10.1016/j.susoc.2022.05.004

Harvard Office of Academic Integrity and Scholarly Conduct. (2025.). Academic integrity and teaching without AI. Harvard University. https://oaisc.fas.harvard.edu/academic-integrity-and-teaching-without-ai/

Hmelo-Silver, C. E., Duncan, R. G., & Chinn, C. A. (2007). Scaffolding and achievement in problem-based and inquiry learning: A response to Kirschner, Sweller, and Clark. *Educational Psychologist*, *42*(2), 99–107. DOI: 10.1080/00461520701263368

Hmoud, M., Swaity, H., Hamad, N., Karram, O., & Daher, W. (2024). Higher Education Students' Task Motivation in the Artificial Intelligence Context: The Case of ChatGPT. *Information (Basel)*, *2024*(15), 33. DOI: 10.3390/info15010033

Hodges, C. B., & Kirschner, P. A. (2024). Innovation of instructional design and assessment in the age of generative artificial intelligence. *TechTrends*, *68*(1), 195–199. DOI: 10.1007/s11528-023-00926-x

Hutson, J., & Plate, T. (2023). Evaluating AI-driven inquiry-based learning: Challenges and best practices. *International Journal of Artificial Intelligence in Education*, *33*(2), 289–310. DOI: 10.1007/s40593-023-00312-8

Ifelebuegu, A. O., Kulume, P., & Cherukut, P. (2023). Chatbots and AI in Education (AIEd) tools: The good, the bad, and the ugly. *Journal of Applied Learning and Teaching*, 6(2). Advance online publication. DOI: 10.37074/jalt.2023.6.2.29

Jain, S., Basu, S., Ray, A., & Das, R. (2023). Impact of irritation and negative emotions on the performance of voice assistants: Netting dissatisfied customers' perspectives. *International Journal of Information Management*, 72, 102662. DOI: 10.1016/j.ijinfomgt.2023.102662

Jenkins, B. D., Golding, J. M., Le Grand, A. M., Levi, M. M., & Pals, A. M. (2023). When opportunity knocks: College students' cheating amid the COVID-19 pandemic. *Teaching of Psychology*, 50(4), 407–419. DOI: 10.1177/00986283211059067

Ji, H., Han, I., & Ko, Y. (2023). A systematic review of conversational AI in language education: Focusing on the collaboration with human teachers. *Journal of Research on Technology in Education*, 55(1), 48–63. DOI: 10.1080/15391523.2022.2142873

Kamalov, F., & Gurrib, I. (2023). A new era of Artificial Intelligence in education: A multifaceted revolution. /arXiv.2305.18303DOI: 10.48550

Kartal, G. (2024). The influence of ChatGPT on thinking skills and creativity of EFL student teachers: A narrative inquiry. *Journal of Education for Teaching*, 50(4), 1–16. DOI: 10.1080/02607476.2024.2326502

Khosravi, H., Buckingham Shum, S., Chen, G., Conati, C., Tsai, Y.-S., Kay, J., & Knight, S. (2022). Explainable artificial intelligence in education. *Computers and Education: Artificial Intelligence*, 3, 100074. DOI: 10.1016/j.caeai.2022.100074

Kim, J., Kelly, S., Colón, A. X., Spence, P. R., & Lin, X. (2024). Toward thoughtful integration of AI in education: Mitigating uncritical positivity and dependence on ChatGPT via classroom discussions. *Communication Education*, 73(4), 388–404. DOI: 10.1080/03634523.2024.2399216

Kim, J., Lee, H., & Cho, Y. H. (2022). Learning design to support student-AI collaboration: Perspectives of leading teachers for AI in education. *Education and Information Technologies*, 27(5), 6069–6104. DOI: 10.1007/s10639-021-10831-6

Kim, Y., Lee, M., Kim, D., & Lee, S. J. (2023). Towards explainable ai writing assistants for non-native english speakers. *arXiv preprint arXiv:2304.02625*.

Kivunja, C. (2015). Teaching Students to Learn and to Work Well with 21st Century Skills: Unpacking the Career and Life Skills Domain of the New Learning Paradigm. *International Journal of Higher Education*, 4(1), 1–11. DOI: 10.5430/ijhe.v4n1p1

Klimova, B., & de Campos, V. P. L. (2024). University undergraduates' perceptions on the use of ChatGPT for academic purposes: Evidence from a university in Czech Republic. *Cogent Education*, 11(1), 2373512. DOI: 10.1080/2331186X.2024.2373512

Kong, S. C., & Yang, Y. (2024). A human-centred learning and teaching framework using generative artificial intelligence for self-regulated learning development through domain knowledge learning. *IEEE Transactions on Learning Technologies*, 17(1), 110–125. DOI: 10.1109/TLT.2024.10507034

Lin, X. (2024). Exploring the role of ChatGPT as a facilitator for motivating self-directed learning among adult learners. *Adult Learning*, *35*(3), 156–166. DOI: 10.1177/10451595231184928

Liu, J., Li, S., & Dong, Q. (2024). Collaboration with generative artificial intelligence: An exploratory study based on learning analytics. *Journal of Educational Computing Research*, *62*(5), 1234–1266. DOI: 10.1177/07356331241242441

Liu, M., Ren, Y., Nyagoga, L. M., Stonier, F., Wu, Z., & Yu, L. (2023). Future of education in the era of generative artificial intelligence: Consensus among Chinese scholars on applications of ChatGPT in schools. *Future Educ. Res.*, *1*(1), 72–101. DOI: 10.1002/fer3.10

Lo, C. K. (2023). What is the impact of ChatGPT on education? A rapid review of the literature. *Education Sciences*, *13*(4), 410. DOI: 10.3390/educsci13040410

Maanu, V., Boateng, F. O., & Larbi, E. (2025). AI-assisted instructions in collaborative learning in mathematics education: A aualitative approach. *American Journal of STEM Education*, *7*, 11–36. DOI: 10.32674/68zzkz60

McPeck, J. E. (2016). *Critical thinking and education*. Routledge. DOI: 10.4324/9781315463698

Meng, J., & Dai, Y. (2021). Emotional support from AI chatbots: Should a supportive partner self-disclose or not? *Journal of Computer-Mediated Communication*, *26*(4), 207–222. DOI: 10.1093/jcmc/zmab005

Molenaar, I. (2022). Hybrid intelligence in education: Augmenting teachers with AI. *European Journal of Education*, *57*(4), 614–631. DOI: 10.1111/ejed.12527

Montenegro-Rueda, M., Fernández-Cerero, J., Fernández-Batanero, J. M., & López-Meneses, E. (2023). Impact of the implementation of ChatGPT in education: A systematic review. *Computers*, *12*(8), 153. DOI: 10.3390/computers12080153

Morales-García, W. C., Sairitupa-Sanchez, L. Z., Morales-García, S. B., & Morales-García, M. (2024). Development and validation of a scale for dependence on artificial intelligence in university students. *Frontiers in Education (9)*, 1323898). DOI: 10.3389/feduc.2024.1323898

Ng, D. T. K., Leung, J. K. L., Chu, S. K. W., & Qiao, M. S. (2021). Conceptualizing AI literacy: An exploratory review. *Computers and Education: Artificial Intelligence*, *2*, 100041. DOI: 10.1016/j.caeai.2021.100041

Ng, D. T. K., Tan, C. W., & Leung, J. K. L. (2024). Empowering student self-regulated learning and science education through ChatGPT: A pioneering pilot study. *British Journal of Educational Technology*, *55*(4), 1328–1353. DOI: 10.1111/bjet.13454

Nguyen, A., Hong, Y., Dang, B., & Huang, X. (2024). Human-AI collaboration patterns in AI-assisted academic writing. *Studies in Higher Education*, *49*(5), 847–864. DOI: 10.1080/03075079.2024.2323593

Nguyen, A., Kremantzis, M., Essien, A., Petrounias, I., & Hosseini, S. (2024). Enhancing student engagement through artificial intelligence (AI): Understanding the basics, opportunities, and challenges. *Journal of University Teaching & Learning Practice*, *21*(6), 1–13. DOI: 10.53761/caraaq92

Ocaña-Fernández, Y., Valenzuela-Fernández, L. A., & Garro-Aburto, L. L. (2019). Artificial Intelligence and Its Implications in Higher Education. *Journal of Educational Psychology-Propositos y Representaciones*, *7*(2), 553–568.

Padovano, A., & Cardamone, L. (2024). Artificial intelligence in education: A roadmap for ethical and effective implementation. *Computers & Education: Artificial Intelligence*, *5*, 100076. DOI: 10.1016/j.caeai.2024.100076

Pane, J. F., Griffin, B. A., McCaffrey, D. F., & Karam, R. (2014). Effectiveness of cognitive tutor algebra I at scale. *Educational Evaluation and Policy Analysis*, *36*(2), 127–144. DOI: 10.3102/0162373713507480

Pavlik, J. V. (2023). Collaborating with ChatGPT: Considering the implications of generative artificial intelligence for journalism and media education. *Journalism & mass communication educator*, *78*(1), 84-93. DOI: 10.1177/10776958221149577

Pegoraro, A., Kumari, K., Fereidooni, H., & Sadeghi, A. R. (2023). To ChatGPT, or not to ChatGPT: That is the question! *arXiv preprint arXiv:2304.01487.* . 2304. 01487DOI: 10. 48550/ arXiv

Peng, H., Ma, S., & Spector, J. M. (2019). Personalized adaptive learning: An emerging pedagogical approach enabled by a smart learning environment. *Smart Learning Environments*, *6*(1), 1–14. DOI: 10.1186/s40561-019-0089-y

Pentina, I., Hancock, T., & Xie, T. (2023). Exploring relationship development with social chatbots: A mixed-method study of replika. *Computers in Human Behavior*, *140*, 107600. DOI: 10.1016/j.chb.2022.107600

Peres, R., Schreier, M., Schweidel, D., & Sorescu, A. (2023). On ChatGPT and beyond: How generative artificial intelligence may affect research, teaching, and practice. *International Journal of Research in Marketing*, *40*(2), 269–275. DOI: 10.1016/j.ijresmar.2023.03.001

Perkins, M., Roe, J., Postma, D., McGaughran, J., & Hickerson, D. (2024). Detection of GPT-4 generated text in higher education: Combining academic judgement and software to identify generative AI tool misuse. *Journal of Academic Ethics*, *22*(1), 89–113. DOI: 10.1007/s10805-023-09492-6

Placed, J. A., Strader, J., Carrillo, H., Atanasov, N., Indelman, V., Carlone, L., & Castellanos, J. A. (2023). A survey on active simultaneous localization and mapping: State of the art and new frontiers. *IEEE Transactions on Robotics*, *39*(3), 1686–1705. DOI: 10.1109/TRO.2023.3248510

Puerta-Beldarrain, M., & Gómez-Carmona, D. (2025). Student engagement with AI-supported learning environments: A comparative analysis. *IEEE Transactions on Education*, *68*(1), 35–51. DOI: 10.1109/TE.2025.10857320

Rahman, M. M., & Watanobe, Y. (2023). ChatGPT for education and research: Opportunities, threats, and strategies. *Applied Sciences (Basel, Switzerland)*, *13*(9), 5783. DOI: 10.3390/app13095783

Rane, N., Shirke, S., Choudhary, S. P., & Rane, J. (2024). Artificial Intelligence in Education: A SWOT Analysis of ChatGPT and Its Impact on Academic Integrity and Research. *Journal of ELT Studies*, *1*(1), 16–35. DOI: 10.48185/jes.v1i1.1315

Rani, P. S., Rani, K. R., Daram, S. B., & Angadi, R. V. (2023). Is it feasible to reduce academic stress in Net-Zero Energy buildings? Reaction from ChatGPT. *Annals of Biomedical Engineering, 51*(12), 2654–2656. DOI: 10.1007/s10439-023-03286-y PMID: 37332007

Rapanta, C., Botturi, L., Goodyear, P., Guàrdia, L., & Koole, M. (2020). Online university teaching during and after the covid-19 crisis: Refocusing teacher presence and learning activity. *Postdigital Science and Education, 2*(3), 923–945. DOI: 10.1007/s42438-020-00155-y

Risko, E. F., & Gilbert, S. J. (2016). Cognitive offloading. *Trends in Cognitive Sciences, 20*(9), 676–688. DOI: 10.1016/j.tics.2016.07.002 PMID: 27542527

Santiago, C. S., Jr., Embang, S. I., Conlu, M. T. N., Acanto, R. B., Lausa, S. M., Ambojia, K. W. P., Laput, E. Y., Aperocho, M. D. B.,Malabag, B. A., & Balilo, B. B., Jr. (2023). Utilization of writing assistance tools in research in selected higher learning institutions in the philippines: A text mining analysis. International Journal of Learning, Teaching and Educational Research, 22(11), 259–284. . 22. 11. 14DOI: 10.26803/ijlter

Schechner, S. (2023). ChatGPT Ban Lifted in Italy After Data-Privacy Concessions. Wall Street J. https://www.wsj.com/articles/chatgpt-ban-lifted-in-italy-after-data-privacy-concessions-d03d53e7

Semrl, N., Feigl, S., Taumberger, N., Bracic, T., Fluhr, H., Blockeel, C., & Kollmann, M. (2023). AI language models in human reproduction research: Exploring ChatGPT's potential to assist academic writing. *Human Reproduction (Oxford, England), 38*(12), 2281–2288. DOI: 10.1093/humrep/dead207 PMID: 37833847

Seo, K., Tang, J., Roll, I., Fels, S., & Yoon, D. (2021). The impact of artificial intelligence on learner–instructor interaction in online learning. *International Journal of Educational Technology in Higher Education, 18*(1), 54. DOI: 10.1186/s41239-021-00292-9 PMID: 34778540

Shanmugasundaram, M., & Tamilarasu, A. (2023). The impact of digital technology, social media, and artificial intelligence on cognitive functions: A review. *Frontiers in Cognition, 2*, 1203077. DOI: 10.3389/fcogn.2023.1203077

Siegel, H. (1987). Critical thinking as an intellectual right. *Analytic Teaching, 8*(1), 19–24.

Singh, S. V., & Hiran, K. K. (2022). The impact of AI on teaching and learning in higher education technology. *Journal of Higher Education Theory and Practice, 22*(13), 135–148. DOI: 10.33423/jhetp.v22i13.5514

Sirghi, N., Voicu, M., Noja, G. G., & Gurita, O. S. (2024). Challenges of artificial intelligence on the learning process in higher education. *Amfiteatru Economic, 26*, 53–70. DOI: 10.24818/EA/2024/65/53

Sparrow, B., Liu, J., & Wegner, D. M. (2011). Google effects on memory: Cognitive consequences of having information at our fingertips. *Science, 333*(6043), 776–778. DOI: 10.1126/science.1207745 PMID: 21764755

Spiro, R., Coulson, R., Feltovich, P., & Anderson, D. (1988). Cognitive flexibility theory: Advanced knowledge acquisition in ill-structured domains. In V. Patel (Ed.), Tenth annual conference of the cognitive science society (pp. 375–383). Hillsdale, NJ: Erlbaum.

Srinivasan, K. R., Rahman, N. H. A., & Ravana, S. D. (2025). Reskilling and Upskilling Future Educators for the Demands of Artificial Intelligence in the Modern Era of Education. In *Pitfalls of AI Integration in Education: Skill Obsolescence, Misuse, and Bias*. IGI Global., DOI: 10.4018/979-8-3373-0122-8.ch008

Stiles, B. L., Wong, N. C. W., & LaBeff, E. E. (2018). College cheating thirty years later: The role of academic entitlement. *Deviant Behavior*, *39*(7), 823–834. DOI: 10.1080/01639625.2017.1335520

Stojanov, A. (2023). Learning with ChatGPT 3.5 as a more knowledgeable other: An autoethnographic study. *International Journal of Educational Technology in Higher Education*, *20*(1), 35. DOI: 10.1186/s41239-023-00404-7

Su, J., & Yang, W. (2023). A systematic review of integrating computational thinking in early childhood education. *Computers and Education Open*, *4*, 100122. DOI: 10.1016/j.caeo.2023.100122

Tang, C., Mao, S., Naumann, S. E., & Xing, Z. (2022). Improving student creativity through digital technology products: A literature review. *Thinking Skills and Creativity*, *44*, 101032. DOI: 10.1016/j.tsc.2022.101032

Tias, I. W. U., Izzatika, A., & Perdana, R. (2022). Empowerment of Critical and Creative Thinking (CCT) Skills Through Student Worksheets Based on Inquiry Social Complexity (ISC). *WSEAS Transactions on Environment and Development*, *18*, 865–872. DOI: 10.37394/232015.2022.18.81

UNESCO. (2023). Guidance for Generative AI in Education and Research https://www.unesco.org/en/articles/guidance-generative-ai-education-and-research

Van Oijen, V. (2023). AI-generated text detectors: Do they work? SURF Communities. https://communities. surf. nl/ en/ ai- in- educa tion/ artic le/ ai- gener ated- text- detec tors- do- they- work.

Ventayen, R. J. M. (2023). ChatGPT by OpenAI: Students' viewpoint on cheating using artificial intelligence-based application. *Available atSSRN* 4361548. DOI: 10.2139/ssrn.4361548

Wang, J., & Li, J. (2024). Artificial intelligence empowering public health education: Prospects and challenges. *Frontiers in Public Health*, *12*, 1389026. DOI: 10.3389/fpubh.2024.1389026 PMID: 39022411

Wang, X., Gao, Q., Lu, J., Shang, J., & Zhou, Y. (2021). The construction and practical cases of human-machine collaboration teaching mode in the era of artificial intelligence. *Journal of Distance Education*, *39*(04), 24–33.

Weber-Wulff, D., Anohina-Naumeca, A., Bjelobaba, S., Foltýnek, T., Guerrero-Dib, J., Popoola, O., Šigut, P., & Waddington, L. (2023). Testing of detection tools for AI-generated text. *International Journal for Educational Integrity*, *19*(1), 1–39. DOI: 10.1007/s40979-023-00146-z

Wiredu, J. K., Seidu Abuba, N., & Zakaria, H. (2024). Impact of generative AI in academic integrity and learning outcomes: A case study in the upper east region. *Asian Journal of Research in Computer Science*, *17*(8), 10–9734. DOI: 10.9734/ajrcos/2024/v17i7491

Wu, D., Zhang, S., Ma, Z., Yue, X. G., & Dong, R. K. (2024). Unlocking potential: Key factors shaping undergraduate self-directed learning in ai-enhanced educational environments. *Systems*, *12*(9), 332. DOI: 10.3390/systems12090332

Wu, Y. (2023). Integrating generative AI in education: How ChatGPT brings challenges for future learning and teaching. *Journal of Advanced Research in Education*, 2(4), 6–10. DOI: 10.56397/JARE.2023.07.02

Xiao, J., Bozkurt, A., Nichols, M., Pazurek, A., Stracke, C. M., Bai, J. Y. H., Farrow, R., Mulligan, D., Nerantzi, C., Sharma, R. C., Singh, L., Frumin, I., Swindell, A., Honeychurch, S., Bond, M., Dron, J., Moore, S., Leng, J., & Slagter van Tryon, P. J.. (2025). Venturing into the Unknown: Critical Insights into Grey Areas and Pioneering Future Directions in Educational Generative AI Research. *TechTrends*, ●●●, 1–16. DOI: 10.1007/s11528-025-01060-6

Yilmaz, R., & Yilmaz, F. G. K. (2023). Augmented intelligence in programming learning: Examining student views on the use of ChatGPT for programming learning. *Computers in Human Behavior: Artificial Humans*, 1(2), 100005. DOI: 10.1016/j.chbah.2023.100005

Yu, H. (2023). Reflection on Whether Chat GPT Should Be Banned by Academia from the Perspective of Education and Teaching. *Frontiers in Psychology*, 14, 1181712. DOI: 10.3389/fpsyg.2023.1181712 PMID: 37325766

Yu, R., Li, Q., Fischer, C., Doroudi, S., & Xu, D. (2020). Towards Accurate and Fair Prediction of College Success: Evaluating Different Sources of Student Data. *Proceedings of The 13th International Conference on Educational Data Mining (EDM 2020)*, 292–301

Zawacki-Richter, O., Marín, V. I., Bond, M., & Gouverneur, F. (2019). Systematic review of research on artificial intelligence applications in higher education–where are the educators? *International Journal of Educational Technology in Higher Education*, 16(1), 1–27. DOI: 10.1186/s41239-019-0171-0

Zhang, S., Zhao, X., Zhou, T., & Kim, J. H. (2024). Do you have AI dependency? The roles of academic self-efficacy, academic stress, and performance expectations on problematic AI usage behavior. *International Journal of Educational Technology in Higher Education*, 21(1), 34. DOI: 10.1186/s41239-024-00467-0

Zhu, C., Sun, M., Luo, J., Li, T., & Wang, M. (2023). How to Harness the Potential of ChatGPT in Education? *Knowledge Management & E-Learning*, 15(2), 133–152. DOI: 10.34105/j.kmel.2023.15.008

Zimmerman, B. J. (2002). Becoming a self-regulated learner: An overview. *Theory into Practice*, 41(2), 64–70. DOI: 10.1207/s15430421tip4102_2

ADDITIONAL READING

Srinivasan, K. R., Rahman, N. H. A., & Ravana, S. D. (2025). Reskilling and Upskilling Future Educators for the Demands of Artificial Intelligence in the Modern Era of Education. In *Pitfalls of AI Integration in Education: Skill Obsolescence, Misuse, and Bias*. IGI Global., DOI: 10.4018/979-8-3373-0122-8.ch008

KEY TERMS AND DEFINITIONS

Automation in Learning: The use of artificial intelligence and automation technologies in educational processes to organize and manage learning activities with reduced need for human intervention.

Artificial Intelligence: It is the development and implementation of computer systems and algorithms that mimic human-like thinking, learning, problem-solving, and decision-making abilities.

AI Dependency: It is a condition where students excessively rely on AI tools for academic tasks.

Academic Integrity: The ethical commitment to honesty, fairness, and responsibility in academic work.

Human-AI Collaboration: It is a collaboration model in which humans and artificial intelligence work together by complementing each other's abilities.

Cognitive Load Theory: A theory that explains how the human brain has a limited capacity for processing information, emphasizing the need to manage cognitive load effectively to optimize learning and problem-solving.

Cognitive Offloading: The tendency of individuals to reduce cognitive efforts such as information processing and problem-solving, to AI tools.

Self-Regulated Learning: An active and autonomous learning approach in which students consciously plan, monitor, and evaluate their own learning processes.

Automation Bias: A cognitive tendency in which individuals place excessive trust in automated systems, often accepting their outputs without critical evaluation.

Chapter 8
Reskilling and Upskilling Future Educators for the Demands of Artificial Intelligence in the Modern Era of Education

Karthik Raja Srinivasan

https://orcid.org/0009-0001-7337-9504

Universiti Malaya, Malaysia

Nur Hairani Abd Rahman

https://orcid.org/0000-0002-0046-3588

Universiti Malaya, Malaysia

Sri Devi Ravana

https://orcid.org/0000-0002-5637-9158

Universiti Malaya, Malaysia

ABSTRACT

The integration of artificial intelligence (AI) in education is altering teaching and requires educators to develop new competencies. Through a systematic review of 247 articles published between 2022 and 2024, this chapter explores three major themes, namely, AI and Teacher Competency Development, Challenges in Reskilling and Upskilling, and Strategies for Effective Reskilling. It has become evident that educators have to acquire digital literacy, data analytics skills, and AI-specific pedagogical strategies, with a corresponding need to address ethical concerns around algorithmic bias, data privacy, and equity of access. Moreover, institutional resistance, inequitable digital literacy, and especially the fast evolution of AI, which outpaces often existing training frameworks, are identified as evolving major concerns. This chapter, therefore, proposes to embed AI training into continuous professional development, enhance interdisciplinary collaborations, and adapt frameworks such as P21, TPACK, and DigCompEdu to the specific needs of AI.

DOI: 10.4018/979-8-3373-0122-8.ch008

INTRODUCTION

"Teachers are not just adopters of technology; they are critical evaluators and architects of how AI shapes the learning environment."

The integration of Artificial Intelligence (AI) within educational settings changes both the pedagogic way of teaching and learning paradigm (Yu, 2024). AI now plays an essential role in administrative functions, such as grading and managing student data, as well as in instructional tasks like personalized learning and adaptive assessments. However, as AI being included in these tasks, educators face a growing need to adapt their skills and pedagogical approaches to thrive in this evolving environment (Sperling et al., 2024; Gentile et al., 2023; Edwards et al., 2018). This chapter investigates the need for reskilling and upskilling educators in the AI era, highlighting strategies and frameworks necessary to prepare teachers for the demands of AI-enhanced education landscape.

MAIN FOCUS OF THE CHAPTER

In this new paradigm, it is expected that teachers develop digital literacy, data analysis capabilities, and innovative pedagogies designed for AI tools and systems (Novopashina et al., 2024; Riera-Negre et al., 2024). While the need for reskilling is quite evident, educators experience challenges towards effective professional development. One of the main obstacles is institutional resistance. Schools and universities are often unable to provide necessary resources such as time, finance, and expertise to support extensive AI training programs successfully. Without these resources, educators are largely on their own in learning about AI based technologies for education, which translates to uneven adoption rates and no great consistency in AI usage within the institution and another critical challenge is the issue of unequal digital literacy among teachers (Gantalao et al., 2025).

Another related challenge is the pace of AI innovation itself. The rapid evolution often outruns the possibilities of adapting educational curricula and retraining programs. Since there is continuous development of new tools and applications, professional educators have to keep up with changing requirements by insisting on lifelong learning (Delcker et al., 2024; Trevisan et al., 2024).

The main challenge is that for AI training to become mainstream within professional development, it should no longer differ from existing frameworks. That means embedding the competencies of AI in the curriculum of teacher education. Thus, the faster the ideas and tools related to AI are integrated into the teachers preparation, the faster these institutions will be better equipped with the skill set to lead in an enhanced AI classroom right from the start (Ayanwale et al., 2024; Beege et al., 2024).

This chapter aims to fill the gaps mentioned above in terms of the need for new competencies in the AI era, challenges in reskilling and upskilling educators, and strategies for effective reskilling and upskilling by critically analyzing 7 key papers related to integration of AI in education sector. These articles show three main themes (I. AI and Teacher Competency Development, II. Challenges in Reskilling and Upskilling, III. Strategies for Effective Reskilling) and these findings are most significant when considering the notion of "Pitfalls of AI Integration in Education."

LITERATURE REVIEW

While the literature underlines the ability of AI tools, this review critically evaluates the literature that focuses on the role of AI in teacher education, with a particular emphasis on development of teacher competency, reskilling challenges, and strategies for effective professional development. The challenges for teachers to build the competencies to address this shift are also taken into account.

The integration of AI in education brings along new requirements, such as digital literacy, AI literacy, and collaboration with AI-driven tools in instructional planning and assessment. According to educators there is a growing importance towards AI literacy among pre-service teachers by advocating for training programs that attend to the ethical and pedagogic nature of AI (Sperling et al., 2024; Tatar et al., 2024; Clarke & McFlynn, 2019). Similarly, Ji et al. (2023) believe that conversational AI has great potential for improving teacher-student collaboration and decreasing teachers administrative workload in language education. On the other hand, as Zhao and Yu (2024) and Gentile et al. (2023) comment, with the evolution of the teachers role in the AI ecosystem, their professional identity has to be redefined, from transmitter of knowledge to facilitator and co-learner with students. Celik et al. (2022) conducted a review spotting difficulties for scalable and context sensitive professional development models, particularly for underfunded institutions. Other challenges in creating successful and accessible teacher training courses arise in designing (Aljemely, 2024). Zhou et al. (2024) and Hurajová (2021) cites an example in which certain educators perceive AI as a threat to their professional autonomy and remain hesitant to implement AI-based teaching aids.

Table 1. Critical analysis of key articles based on common themes in AI and education

No	Title of Research Paper	Author(s)	Critical Analysis
	Theme 1: AI and Teacher Competency Development		
1	"Teacher support and student motivation to learn with Artificial Intelligence (AI)-based chatbot"	(Chiu et al., 2024)	This paper shows how AI performs an intervening role in personalized learning; however, there is a contextual role of teachers in shaping interactions through the chatbot.
2	"Leading teachers perspective on teacher-AI collaboration in education"	(Kim, 2024)	It gives an insightful outlook on the perception of teachers as co-facilitators with AI tools. However, the paper could have benefited from more empirical data to substantiate its claims about the benefits and limitations of such collaborations, especially in diverse educational contexts.
3	"Is the education system prepared for the irruption of Artificial Intelligence? A study on the perceptions of students of primary education degree from a dual perspective: Current pupils and future teachers"	(Lozano & Fontao, 2023)	This paper provides a comprehensive examination of AI but lacks actionable solution for AI preparedness. The approached perspective enriches findings where a greater sample size may have been beneficial in arriving at conclusions.
4	"The effects of pre-service early childhood teachers digital literacy and self-efficacy on their perception of AI education for young children"	(Lim, 2023)	Lim's paper explores the critical issues of digital literacy and self-efficacy that shape the attitudes of pre-service teachers toward AI in early childhood education. The findings require urgent reforms in teacher education programs to include training on AI but lack a detailed implementation roadmap.
	Theme 2: Challenges in Reskilling and Upskilling		

continued on following page

Table 1. Continued

No	Title of Research Paper	Author(s)	Critical Analysis
Theme 1: AI and Teacher Competency Development			
5	"Revolutionizing EFL special education: How ChatGPT is transforming the way teachers approach language learning"	(Alenizi et al., 2023)	This paper investigates how ChatGPT has been transforming impact on special education in English as a foreign language. It also shows ChatGPT's potential for tailored learning, therefore reducing a teacher's workload. Nonetheless, the study also notes the possible difficulties in applying it, like teachers resistance and extensive training programs, which makes the whole study of its advantages and drawbacks all-balanced.
6	"The Promises and Challenges of Artificial Intelligence for Teachers: A Systematic Review of Research"	(Celik et al., 2022)	The following paper reviews some of the opportunities and challenges of AI in education, particularly relating to teachers. It enumerates the benefits, such as personalized learning and reduction of administrative burdens, in a systematic manner while debating challenges like lack of preparedness among teachers and ethical issues. One limitation of this study is that the dependence on secondary sources is huge, with limited empirical data to validate the findings.
7	"A Multi-Level Factors Model Affecting Teachers Adoption of Artificial Intelligence in Education"	(Wu et al., 2024)	This study offers a multilevel framework to comprehend the elements affecting teacher adoption of AI by synthesizing human, institutional, and societal viewpoints in the analysis of adoption process. Nevertheless, the study's conclusions rely on self reported data, potentially introducing bias. This study is spatially constrained, complicating the generalization of findings to many educational situations.
Theme 3: Strategies for Effective Reskilling			
8	"Zone of Proximal Creativity: An Empirical Study of AI and Teacher Collaboration"	(Korucu-Kis, 2024)	This paper introduces the concept of a Zone of Proximal Creativity, illustrating how AI extends teachers creative capabilities. One of the key limitations is the small sample size, which restricts the generalization of the results.
9	"An automated virtual reality training system for teacher-student interaction: A randomized controlled trial"	(King et al., 2022)	The study provides empirical evidence for the effectiveness of VR in professional development and thus holds promise for scalable teacher training. Yet, this study does not discuss the cost and accessibility challenges of deploying VR systems in various educational settings, which is a practical implication.
10	"Artificial Intelligence (AI)-Integrated Educational Ecosystems: Opportunities and Risks"	(Lin & Chen, 2024)	This article looks into the broader ecosystem of AI integration in education, highlighting some opportunities like data-driven insights and enhanced collaboration. It further discusses some of the risks, including data privacy concerns and overdependence on AI. While this study gives a holistic view, it lacks practical recommendations on mitigating risks; hence, some gaps exists in actionable guidance for educators and policymakers.

It can be inferred that AI can help personalized learning, enhance teacher-student interaction, and make academic based administrative works easier. In the above articles the roles of teachers are also discussed, exploring what would be the role of teacher in an AI-enhanced environment, with a key focus on upskilling and adapting to technological shifts. Also, the emphasis on training, where there is a shared feeling that teachers need to be equipped with AI literacy and digital skills in order to maximize the benefits of AI tools (Shown in Table 1 critically analyses of articles from Chiu et al. (2024) to Lin and Chen (2024)).

Celik et al. (2022) systematically reviews the promises and challenges of AI for teachers, they showcase how personalized learning and administrative efficiency can be achieved through AI, while outlining challenges such as inadequate teacher training and ethical concerns. Moreover, the research lacks the ability to provide actionable solutions because of its reliance on secondary data. It identifies the problems but leaves practitioners with little evidence. Korucu-Kis (2024) innovatively explores the role of AI in enhancing creativity in teaching by introducing the concept of the Zone of Proximal Creativity. Their holistic view is selective, while failing to provide answers to the relevant challenges of dependency and data privacy; hence, their contribution in terms of policy or educational implications is limited. Shown in Table 2 are the thematic comparisons.

Table 2. Thematic comparisons

Aspect	Articles	Comparison
1. Scope of AI Integration	(Chiu et al., 2024) (Kim, 2024) (Lozano & Fontao, 2023) and (Lim, 2023)	Focus on general AI applications in education, exploring competencies, perceptions, and preparedness.
1.	(Alenizi et al., 2023) and (King et al., 2022)	Target specific applications such as ChatGPT in EFL education and virtual reality for teacher training, offering narrower yet deeper insights.
Methodology	(Chiu et al., 2024) (Kim, 2024) (Lozano & Fontao, 2023) (Lim, 2023) (Alenizi et al., 2023) and (King et al., 2022)	Rely on qualitative approaches, including teacher and student perceptions, providing exploratory insights but limited empirical data.
1.	(Lim, 2023) (Alenizi et al., 2023) and (King et al., 2022)	Include experimental or case-study methods, providing stronger empirical evidence but narrower generalizability.
Themes Addressed	(Lozano & Fontao, 2023) (Chiu et al., 2024)	Focus on systemic readiness and teacher support for AI integration.
1.	(Alenizi et al., 2023) and (King et al., 2022)	Explore innovative uses of AI tools in specific contexts, such as language learning and teacher-student interaction.
Teacher-Centered vs. Systemic	(Kim, 2024) (Lim, 2023) (Alenizi et al., 2023)	Emphasize teacher competencies, self-efficacy, and individual-level challenges.
1.	(Lozano & Fontao, 2023) (Chiu et al., 2024) (King et al., 2022)	Focus on broader systemic or structural issues, such as the readiness of educational systems and the design of training programs.

These findings represent important additions to teacher training that would fill in some gaps in AI literacy, pedagogy, and technology integration. The first is foundational AI literacy. Studies conducted by Chiu et al.(2024) and Lim (2023) indicate that teaching of digital skills and AI competencies are fundamental to teachers from navigating AI-driven tools proficiently. Training programs should include modules on understanding AI algorithms, ethical considerations, and practical applications like chatbots and adaptive learning systems. This ensures that teachers can use AI tools effectively while maintaining a critical perspective on their limitations. Last but not least, according to Lozano and Fontao (2023) have argued that training should go along with infrastructural and curriculum reforms. Training should not be limited to teachers individual skills but also consider preparing them for changes in the institutional environment in which they operate so that the introduction of AI is smooth and effective.

METHODOLOGY

Using a PRISMA framework, a systematic review of 247 articles published between 2022 and 2024, were selected by using relevant keywords such as *AI in education, teacher training, digital literacy, reskilling, pedagogical innovation, and education*. Furthermore, the selection is made in a way that it includes high-impact journals indexed to Web of Science, with a focus on applied uses of AI in education. Based on the scope of AI Integration in education (112, articles were rejected due to its reliance on evolving technology perspective rather than its application towards education), whether the article is teacher centric or systemic in general (82, articles which are more general were rejected due to its application being more systemic rather than focusing on teacher related skills), and the type of methodology used to arrive at the result was qualitatively analysed to remove articles that did not fit the overall theme of "AI in education with emphasis on competencies and skills" (46 articles, were rejected not representing the necessary skill development component). Finally, 7 articles, were selected for further analysis, which aligned with the overall theme of the book and to the chapter. The selected articles showed three core themes,

1. AI and Teacher Competency Development
2. Challenges in Reskilling and Upskilling
3. Strategies for Effective Reskilling

Based on themes, each article was further analysed for Scope of AI Integration, methodology used, key findings, limitation, and recommendation. This approach gives an in-depth analysis on how teaching tools and strategies will be effectively implemented, hence equipping educators, academic institutions and policymakers on these changing phenomena of AI adoption.

RESULTS

Based on the core themes AI and Teacher Competency Development, Challenges in Reskilling and Upskilling, and Strategies for Effective Reskilling. Selected key articles are explained.

Theme 1: AI and Teacher Competency Development

Critical Analysis of "Exploring Pre-Service Biology Teachers Intention to Teach Genetics Using an AI Intelligent Tutoring-Based System"

The research conducted by Adelana et al. (2024) examines the determinants affecting pre-service biology educators' intention to instruct genetics through AI-driven Intelligent Tutoring Systems (ITS). The study contributes to implications for teacher education programs and policymakers. Emphasis is placed on subjective norms, which means that it is important to create an atmosphere of acceptance of AI within educational institutions. Teacher may inspire this by modeling effective use of AI themselves and creating a collaborative learning environment where pre-service teachers can share experiences and challenges. The study also emphasizes the importance of comprehensive training programs which incorporate technological proficiency with pedagogical innovation (Mangubat et al., 2025). These should include practical experience with AI tools to help teachers gain confidence and competence. The study offers insights into the potential of AI tools for tackling the challenges of teaching complicated and abstract subjects.

Key Findings of the Research

- **Innovative Utilization of Artificial Intelligence in Genetics Education:** The research centers on genetics, a discipline recognized for its intellectual and abstract complexities. The authors present AI-based Intelligent Transportation Systems as a solution, emphasizing a unique method that corresponds with global trends in technology-enhanced education.

- **Theoretical Framework:** The amalgamation of the Theory of Planned Behavior (TPB) with perceived utility and gender variables constitutes a viable theoretical framework. It accurately encapsulates the interaction of attitudes, subjective norms, perceived behavioral control (PBC), and utility in influencing behavioral intention. Including gender as a dependent variable adds still another dimension and addresses the socio-cultural processes in schooling.

- **Empirical Contribution:** The study increases its credibility by presenting actual data obtained from a methodical procedure comprising pre-service teachers. Using Structural Equation Modeling (SEM improves the analysis and guarantees the quality and dependability of the results).

- **Functional Relevance:** By stressing the need of subjective norms and attitudes, the research offers realistic advice for legislators and teacher teachers. It emphasizes the importance of institutional and society support in advancing AI acceptance in resource- constrained settings like Nigeria.

The finding that perceived usefulness does not directly influence behavioral intention calls for a revision in the way AI tools are introduced to teachers, instead of insisting on utility, training programs should emphasize the transformative potential of AI in improving learning outcomes and reducing workload. The study also reveals certain limitations and avenues for additional investigation.

Limitations of the Research

- **Limited Generalization:** Since the investigation involved only pre-service biology teachers in higher education institutions, its results have minimal generalization to Nigeria. It is clear that educational and cultural contexts will differ radically from other areas, so the applicability of the findings will, hence, be a challenge to assert universally. A multi-regional, study might overcome this problem.

- **Neglect of Long-Term Implementation:** This study concentrates on the intentions of pre-service teachers, rather than their actual behaviors or long-term results. Intentions are essential; however, they may not always be implemented. Additional research is required to investigate the gradual integration of AI tools into the actual classroom by these educators.

- **Perceived Behavioral Control and Perceived Usefulness:** This study focus on pre-service teachers goals rather than on their actual practices or long-term results. Though they are quite important, intentions may not always be followed. Research on how these educators gradually include AI tools into the actual classroom is much awaited.

- **Overemphasis on Subjective Norms:** Although subjective norms significantly predict behavioral intention, the study may exaggerate their influence. This emphasis may neglect other essential issues, including institutional impediments, technological infrastructure, and resource availability, which are especially pertinent in developing nations.

- **Limited Exploration of Gender Dynamics:** While gender is a moderating variable, the analysis need to be further extended for gender based studies. Whereas female teachers are more influenced by subjective norms, the study has not probed the underlying reasons or suggested strategies to address gender-specific challenges. A more detailed analysis could enhance understanding and inform targeted interventions.

Expanding the study to include teachers from different disciplines, educational levels, and regions to enhance generalizability and identify context-specific factors are much needed. Moreover, investigating how pre-service teachers intentions evolve into actual behaviours and practices once they enter the workforce. Exploring the systemic challenges that may hinder AI adoption, such as inadequate infrastructure, funding limitations, and resistance from administrators and examining the socio-cultural factors influencing gender differences in technology adoption, providing insights for designing inclusive training programs. This would provide a clearer picture of the factors influencing long-term adoption of AI Intelligent Tutoring-Based System.

Critical Analysis of "Incorporating AI in Foreign Language Education: An Investigation into ChatGPT's Effect on Foreign Language Learners

The article by Karataş et al. (2024) investigates how AI technologies might be used in language instruction, particularly looking into ChatGPT's effects on foreign language acquisition among Turkish preparatory class students. Using a qualitative case study approach (13 preparatory students from a Turkish university) this study explores the benefits, drawbacks, and uses of ChatGPT as a learning tool.

The results highlight ChatGPT's beneficial impact on student motivation and engagement, especially due to its interactive and accessible characteristics. Students observed enhancements in writing, grammar, and vocabulary, crediting these progressions to ChatGPT's capacity for delivering immediate feedback and contextual learning experiences. The tool received acclaim for enhancing creativity, enabling pupils to craft narratives, investigate cultural subtleties, and cultivate varied linguistic skills.

Key Findings of the Research

- **Use of ChatGPT:** The study explores the advanced linguistic capabilities of ChatGPT for enhanced language learning and contributes to the new discourse on the use of AI in education, giving empirical evidence on the change it causes in language learners.
- **Positive Outcomes in Language Competencies:** The findings show increased improvement in writing, grammar, and vocabulary acquisition. For its accessibility, adaptability, and immediate feedback, ChatGPT has proven to be motivating and engaging for participants. This illustrates how AI can support the teaching of languages.
- **Methodology:** The research design is strong, using maximum variation sampling to include a diverse group of participants with varying language proficiencies (level from A2 to B2). Thematic analysis of interviews ensures that students experiences are explored in detail to capture the nuanced effects of ChatGPT on language learning.

- **Cultural and Creative Dimensions:** The possibility of creative writing and cultural exploration through ChatGPT in interactive learning activities enriches the educational experience. This aspect is particularly valuable in foreign language education, where cultural immersion is a critical component.

Notwithstanding these advantages, the study also reveals few limitations. ChatGPT demonstrated limited efficacy in enhancing speaking and listening abilities, underscoring a deficiency in its ability to promote oral communication. Students expressed apprehensions regarding excessive dependence on the tool, which may hinder their critical thinking and independent learning abilities. Additionally, instances of sporadic technical malfunctions and the potential for misuse during assignments were recognized as problems necessitating focus.

Limitations of the Research

- **Limited Sample Size:** The study's dependence on a solitary classroom of 13 kids constrains its generalizability. An expanded participant base with diverse demographics and educational situations would strengthen the validity of the findings.
- **Restricted Scope of Skill Development:** Although the study highlights advancements in writing and grammar, it concedes a limited effect on speaking and listening abilities. This underscores the necessity for supplementary tools or strategies to enhance oral communication skills.
- **Technical and Ethical Challenges:** The study recognizes problems such as intermittent technical malfunctions and the possibility of misuse during evaluations. Ethical considerations, such as academic integrity and privacy, are essential yet insufficiently examined in this environment.
- **Exclusion of Advanced AI Features:** Participants utilized the complimentary edition of ChatGPT (3.5), which may not accurately reflect the tool's functionalities in comparison to its commercial version (4.0). This constraint restricts the study's observations regarding the wider potential of AI in language instruction.
- **Excessive Dependence on Technology:** A major concern among participants was the potential dependence on ChatGPT, which could undermine critical thinking and autonomous learning. This indicates broader concerns over the use of AI and traditional educational practices.

Educators can integrate the latest AI tools, including ChatGPT, into grammar, vocabulary, and creative writing. While policymakers and educators can ensure that these AI tools complement traditional methodologies. Moreover, the training programs for teachers should provide a balanced use, integrating AI strengths while mitigating its limitations. These tools can help to tailor learning experiences and increase student engagement. However, institutions should establish clear criteria to prevent misuse and assure the ethical use of AI tools in education. This covers methods for maintaining academic integrity and protecting personal privacy.

Critical Analysis of "Integrating Artificial Intelligence in Primary Mathematics Education: Investigating Internal and External Influences on Teacher Adoption"

The article by Li (2024) explores the factors influencing the adoption of AI technologies by primary mathematics teachers in China. With a sample of 498 primary mathematics teachers, the study employs Partial Least Squares Structural Equation Modelling (PLS-SEM) to analyze data and uncover relationships among the variables, using a theoretical framework that combines the Technology Acceptance Model (TAM) and Technological Pedagogical and Content Knowledge (TPACK). The research examines the linkages between internal factors (e.g., perceived usefulness and ease of use) and external influences (e.g., parental and community involvement) on teachers' willingness to integrate AI tools into their teaching practices.

The findings indicate that internal factors, such as perceived usefulness and technological knowledge, influence teachers' attitude toward AI adoption. External factors, including parental support, contextual challenges, and community involvement, also play a critical role by shaping the ecosystem in which AI adoption occurs. The study underlines that, AI is more challenging when structural barriers in infrastructure and professional training exist. It advocates for community involvement, enhanced infrastructure, and targeted professional development initiatives to make adoption easier for all.

Findings of the Research

- The study effectively combines two theoretical models, TAM and TPACK, to examine the collective impact of perceptions of AI's usefulness, ease of use, and instructors' technological proficiency on AI adoption. This dual-framework approach offers a nuanced comprehension of the multifaceted adoption process.
- The research covers, parental and community involvement (PCI), contextual factors (CF), and educational challenges (EC) that will shed light on systemic barriers to integration. This holistic perspective surpasses from individual teacher factors to broader educational ecosystem.
- By narrowing its focus to primary mathematics, the study concentrates on a critical yet unexplored domain in which AI tools, such as intelligent tutoring systems and generative AI like ChatGPT, can provide focused assistance in addressing students' misconceptions and improving personalized learning.
- The research design utilizes Partial Least Squares Structural Equation Modelling (PLS-SEM), as a statistical method, to evaluate complex relationships among constructs. The inclusion of a large sample (498 primary mathematics teachers) ensures the findings' statistical reliability and validity.
- The findings emphasize actionable strategies, such as targeted professional development and infrastructure support, to create positive attitudes and enhance AI adoption. The study offers valuable insights for policymakers and educators aiming to integrate AI effectively.

Limitations of the Research

- **Limited Scope of Generalizability:** The research focus on primary mathematics teachers in one region of China restricts the generalizability of the findings to other regions, subjects, or educational levels.

- **Reliance on Self-Reported Data:** The reliance on self-reported questionnaires may result in biases due to social desirability or incorrect self-concepts, which could call into question the reliability of the findings.
- **Disregard of Cultural Aspects:** While the study recognizes contextual factors, it does not discuss cultural influences, such as attitudes toward technology adoption in rural versus urban settings, or differences in parental perceptions.
- **Not Sufficient Explanation of the Mediated Relationships:** Although significant indirect effects were revealed, such as the effect of PCI on AIU through CF, its in-depth examination remains scant. The examination in detail would be more rewarding for these pathways.
- **Limited Emphasis on Real Classroom Application:** While the study points out the theoretical importance of TPACK and TAM constructs, there is little demonstration of how these frameworks are translated into everyday classroom practices with AI tools.

The study identifies specialized professional development programs to equip teachers with technical competencies and pedagogical techniques using AI. Such programs of education should be designed in a way that it enhances confidence and proficiency levels in using AI tools related to adaptive learning systems and virtual tutors among educators. Moreover, according to the results, resources should be distributed equivocally, and infrastructural development should be enhanced to bring about equality in access to AI technologies, particularly in less-privileged areas, by way of educational policies. A comparison of these studies leads to the following claim "although AI has huge potential to enhance teacher competencies, its impact will depend on tailored training, contextual considerations, and systemic reforms". Adelana et al. (2024) focus on developing favorable attitudes and using social influences, whereas Karataş et al. (2024) demonstrate the practical use of some AI tools like ChatGPT. While the author Li (2024) takes a holistic approach, besides individual factors, considering both infrastructure and community-related themes under discussion.

Adelana et al. (2024) focus on pre-service teachers' behavioural intentions, drawing on TPB to examine the roles of subjective norms, attitudes, and perceived usefulness in AI adoption. The results of their work underline the fact that though attitudes and social influences significantly drive intention, perceived behavioral control and usefulness are less impactful. This agrees with the arguments by Heffernan & Heffernan (2014) that for effective adoption, AI training programs have to balance technological confidence with actionable classroom applications. However, Adelana et al.(2024) research emphasized that mere intention does not translate into real-world adoption, due to systemic and contextual challenges, a practical application need to be there.

Karataş et al. (2024) have provided a more practical lens to view the use of ChatGPT for foreign language learning. The study indicated an improvement in writing and grammar skills, thus underlining how accessible and adaptable AI tools. In order to realize the full potential of AI, education systems need to implement a comprehensive approach that embeds professional development within systemic support. To prevent over-reliance, this calls for legislators to find infrastructural inequality, create cultural readiness, and encourage responsible use of AI tools. Unless such changes are passed, AI runs the danger of being reduced to a supporting tool instead of a major contributor to significant innovation in teacher competency development.

All three studies on AI (genetics education by (Adelana et al., 2024), foreign language learning by (Karataş et al., 2024), and primary mathematics education by (Li, 2024)) provide different lenses to view AI and Teacher Competency Development, each with its transformative potential and critical gaps. Together, these studies indicate the dual need to equip teachers with AI-related skills and address systemic barriers for effective integration.

Theme 2: Challenges in Reskilling and Upskilling

Critical Analysis of "Exploring Teachers Perceptions of Artificial Intelligence as a Tool to Support their Practice in Estonian K-12 Education"

The study by Chounta et al., (2022) investigates how Estonian K-12 teachers perceive and utilize AI in their professional practice. Estonia, recognized for its digital innovation, provides a unique context for exploring the integration of AI in education. The study surveyed 140 teachers, focusing on their familiarity with AI, how can they be benefitted, its overall ethical considerations from students and institution perspective and its challenges.

The findings reveal that while many teachers acknowledge AI's potential to streamline administrative tasks and personalize learning, they lack sufficient knowledge to integrate these tools effectively. Key concerns included the effort required to learn AI systems (as for many it's a new interface system that must be learnt without the necessary computer knowledge), mistrust of AI for error-free operations, and fears about its impact on human interaction in classrooms. *Teachers saw AI as beneficial for tasks such as lesson planning, grading, and identifying students learning needs but highlighted the need for empathy and adaptability in education* are more important than technical aspects of education.

The study also aligns teachers' needs with the **Fairness, Accountability, Transparency, and Ethics (FATE)** framework, emphasizing the ethical design and deployment of AI in classrooms. The approach to fairness, transparency, and accountability in this study guarantees the findings not only become useful but also are well-founded ethically, which is an important aspect usually not taken seriously in the deployment of AI, as stated by Holstein et al. (2019). Moreover, the identification of teacher needs-such as tools for personalization and efficiency in lesson planning-adds practical relevance to the study. This approach underlines active areas where AI can help take some workload off teachers and improve educational outcomes, thus being particularly useful for policymakers and technology developers. Besides, Estonia's leading position in digital contexts provides additional contextual depth to this research.

However, this study also has some critical weaknesses that may undermine the general weight of its effect. Among the major limitations is the relatively small sample size of 140 teachers, which is only a tiny fraction of Estonia's K-12 teaching population; this might raise concerns in terms of the representativeness of the findings, and an expansion in sample size would have several advantages that allow for stronger and more generalizable results. Another weakness is the reliance upon self-reported data, as such self-assessed familiarity may not be a true reflection of the teachers' actual competencies. Research, including (Y. Zhao & Frank, 2003), shows that in some cases, self-reporting can be biased toward over or underestimation of ones abilities. Moreover, although the study recognizes some of the implementation challenges, such as the effort needed to learn the AI systems and training for teachers, it falls short of recognizing systemic issues like resource disparities and institutional support that are really needed for scalable AI adoption. Finally, the narrow focus of this study on teachers' perceptions, without extensive examination of how these perceptions are realized in classrooms. This limits the practical applicability of its findings for effective tool design.

Whereas the study addresses ethical and practical considerations effectively, the limitations as regards the scope and methodology indicate areas in which the study could be improved. For example, one could complement the ethical approach with better data collection and further focusing into implementation issues. Moreover, the implications for policy and practice that arise from this study are multilayered. Professional development is necessary in providing teachers with practical AI skills that will allow them to use AI tools efficiently in classrooms. Policymakers should make sure that participatory design techniques come first so that instructors may participate in the development process to guarantee that technology meet actual classroom demands. Particularly for underfunded institutions, infrastructure projects are important to enable fair AI inclusion in many different educational environments. Moreover, the ethical questions raised such as prejudices in AI systems and the possible decrease in human interaction showcase the need of strict rules. Building confidence among teachers and stakeholders depends on open and understandable AI systems (Heffernan & Heffernan, 2014). Through addressing these policy consequences, the research offers a road map for the responsible and efficient implementation of AI in education. Overall, the authors call for enhanced teacher training, participatory design processes, and contextualized AI tools to support educators while maintaining human centric educational values.

Critical Analysis of "What Explains Teachers Trust in AI in Education Across Six Countries?"

Viberg et al., (2024) explores the factors influencing K-12 teachers trust in AI-based educational technology (AI-EdTech) across six countries (Brazil, Israel, Japan, Norway, Sweden, and the USA). It investigates the role of AI understanding, cultural values, self-efficacy, and geographic location in shaping trust and its benefits.

Using a survey method with 508 teachers, the study employs Hofstede's cultural dimensions to assess the influence of individual cultural values such as uncertainty avoidance, masculinity, and collectivism on teachers' perceptions. The results reveal that teachers trust in AI-EdTech is strongly associated with their self-efficacy and understanding of AI, as well as cultural and geographic differences. Teachers who displayed higher self-efficacy and realistic understanding of AI reported greater perceived benefits and fewer concerns about AI-EdTech.

The study finds cultural differences, with uncertainty avoidance and long-term orientation correlating positively with trust, while masculinity correlates negatively. *Interestingly, demographic factors such as age, gender, and education level had minimal influence on trust.* These findings underscore the importance of teacher training programs to build AI literacy and address cultural and geographic variations in AI-EdTech adoption. It makes recommendations, such as culturally sensitive training programs and geographic disparities in AI readiness, that are actionable and address ethical guidelines outlined by the European Commission 2022.

Challenges in Reskilling and Upskilling Teachers in AI Integration

The studies by Chounta et al. (2022) and Viberg et al. (2024) provide comparable insights into the challenges teachers face with reskilling and upskilling for AI integration in education. While Chounta et al. (2022) focus on the perceptions of Estonian K-12 teachers whereas, Viberg et al. (2024) investigate trust in AI-EdTech across six culturally diverse countries. Both studies show significant barriers to teacher training, building trust, and systemic readiness; individual, cultural, and contextual factors are all interlinked in AI adoption.

Common Challenges

Both studies highlight how teacher training and professional development are essential for effective AI adoption. Chounta et al. (2022) determined that Estonian teachers acknowledge the potential of AI to support both administrative tasks and personalized learning but do not have the necessary knowledge and skills to do so. Similarly, Viberg et al. (2024) show how trust in AI-EdTech is highly influenced by teachers AI self-efficacy and understanding, which are often constrained by a lack of training and support. Another shared challenge is the ethical and practical skepticism of teachers regarding AI tools (Xiao et al., 2025). Across the studies, teachers were concerned with algorithmic biases, dehumanizing teaching, and the extent to which AI would be up to the challenge of various educational tasks. These fears also point toward the training programs that shall not limit to skills but also addressing ethical and practical issues of AI.

Cultural and Contextual Variations

Viberg et al. (2024) go further in exploring how cultural and geographic contexts shape teachers attitudes toward AI. Their findings show that cultural dimensions such as uncertainty avoidance and long-term orientation significantly influence trust in AI. *Teachers in societies with high uncertainty avoidance (e.g., Japan) are more inclined to see artificial intelligence as a stabilizing factor in education; those in more individualistic societies (e.g., the USA) may give autonomy first priority over AI reliance.* In contrast, Chounta et al. (2022) situate their analysis within the technologically advanced context of Estonia, where digital infrastructure is less of a barrier but where teacher skepticism remains a major hurdle. These cultural and contextual differences are important for tailoring professional development programs to specific geographic and cultural settings. While Viberg et al. (2024) advocate for culturally sensitive approaches to building trust in AI, Chounta et al. (2022) emphasize participatory design processes that involve teachers in AI development, ensuring that tools align with local educational practices and values.

Addressing the Gaps

Both studies identify systemic barriers standing in the way of teachers efforts to reskill. Viberg et al. (2024) identify a lack of infrastructure and resources in some countries as disparities in the adoption of AI, whereas Chounta et al. (2022) identify the time and effort needed by teachers to learn new AI systems as deterrent factors.

1. **Scalable Training Programs:** Policymakers need to invest in scalable professional development programs that build AI literacy and are aligned with cultural contexts (Like workshops, online courses, and peer-learning platforms that meet diverse teacher needs).
2. **Collaborative Tool Design:** Both studies stress the importance of teachers involvement in the design and implementation process of AI tools (More of a participatory approach will ensure intuitive, culturally appropriate, and pedagogically effective AI tools).

3. **Institutional Support:** schools and governments need to support infrastructural arrangements, time, and incentives for teachers in order to undertake upskilling activities. This may involve a reduction in the administrative workload, allowing them more time for professional development.

Theme 3: Strategies for Effective Reskilling

Case 1: Technological, Pedagogical, and Content Knowledge (TPACK)

The article (Towards Intelligent-TPACK An empirical study on teachers professional knowledge to ethically integrate artificial intelligence (AI)-based tools into education) by (Celik, 2023) examines the development and application of the Intelligent TPACK framework, which extends the existing TPACK model through its integration of ethical considerations about the use of AI-based tools in education. The Intelligent TPACK framework offers the teacher professional knowledge for a truly ethical and effective integration of AI into their practice. It is composed of key dimensions such as Intelligent-TK (technological knowledge), Intelligent-TPK (technological pedagogical knowledge), Intelligent-TCK (technological content knowledge), and an ethics dimension with regard to transparency, fairness, accountability, and inclusiveness.

Key Findings

Development of the Intelligent-TPACK Framework: This study extends the TPACK model to incorporate ethical knowledge, thus developing the Intelligent-TPACK. The framework addresses the need for teachers to combine technological and pedagogical skills with ethical assessments in order to use AI-based tools effectively in education.

1. **Technological Knowledge and Pedagogical Affordances:** Intelligent-TK teachers are more capable of estimating the pedagogical contributions of AI, such as personalized learning and real-time feedback. However, technological knowledge in itself is not enough but has to be intertwined with pedagogical knowledge, Intelligent-TPK, for maximum benefits to be derived from the use of AI tools.
2. **Ethical Considerations:** The study enumerates a number of ethical challenges with the integration of AI, including algorithmic bias, transparency, fairness, and accountability issues. Ethical assessments contribute positively to teachers abilities in using AI-based tools, thus promoting inclusivity and fairness in the classroom.
3. **Empirical Validation:** Using structural equation modeling, ethical assessments and pedagogical knowledge prove to be strongly enhancing teachers overall competence to integrate AI tools, whereas Intelligent-TCK also proves important in this respect.
4. **Implications for Practice:** Ethics and pedagogic considerations go alongside technical preparation in practice in training courses. Results seem to indicate that professional training within real contexts regarding the pedagogical uses of, among others, AIChatbots, Intelligent Tutoring Systems for instruction, and Automated grading systems must emphasize ethical questions.

The study highly recognizes the potential for a fundamental change in teaching and learning with AI through personalized learning experiences, adaptive feedback, and real-time monitoring tools such as dashboards and intelligent tutoring systems. Meanwhile, it points out challenges such as algorithmic bias, lack of transparency in AI systems, and limited teacher training on ethics in AI use (Martínez-Requejo et al., 2025). The empirical research was carried out on two stages, on the development and validation of the Intelligent-TPACK scale, which has been carried out first, and testing the links between its elements with structural equation modeling (SEM) afterward. For example, though TK increased the ability of teachers to understand and estimate AI tool materials in some aspects, it does need to be combined with pedagogical knowledge regarding class implementation. In this line, ethical considerations also bear substantial meaning.

The practical implications of the findings are significant but could benefit from further elaboration of ethical and pedagogical considerations about AI. The proposed framework will give a foundation for the competencies of teachers for AI-driven education, combining equity and fairness.

Case 2: DigCompEdu and P21's Framework

The study by Ng et al. (2023) *"Teachers AI digital competencies and twenty-first century skills in the post-pandemic world,"* investigates the AI digital competencies of teachers in the post-pandemic educational space, with a strong call for reskilling and upskilling of teachers. With the rapid shift to online and hybrid learning during COVID19, AI technologies have become central in education, offering personalized learning, data-driven insights and automation of administrative tasks. However, most teachers are not technically prepared to work with such AI-driven tools.

Existing frameworks, such as **DigCompEdu** (Digital Competence Framework for Educators) and **P21's Framework** (Partnership for 21st Century), needs to be inclusive of AI-specific competencies. Such adaptations thus aim at preparing educators on how to take advantage of AI for teaching, learning, and assessment.

Key Findings

1. **The Role of AI in Contemporary Education:** AI technologies have transformed pedagogy by offering instruments for individualized learning, automated evaluations, and data-informed decision-making. Nonetheless, its implementation underscores deficiencies in educators' digital skills.
2. **Adaptation of Frameworks:** This study extends the DigCompEdu and P21 frameworks by embedding AI-specific competencies. This ensures conformance with general educational goals, while considering the particular demands resulting from AI integration.
3. **Competencies:**
   a. *Technological Knowledge:* To know how to use AI-driven platforms, including intelligent tutoring systems and analytics dashboards.
   b. *Ethical Awareness:* Understanding issues related to bias, transparency challenges, and ethical dilemmas associated with AI systems.
   c. *Pedagogical Integration:* Using AI for adaptive and collaborative learning environments.
      2. **Challenges in AI Integration:** Inadequate training, scarcity of resources, and the opaque nature of AI tools are some of the challenges faced by educators.

3. It addresses problems of ethical issues, which include algorithmic prejudice, data privacy, and cannot have the issues comprehensively addressed.
4. **Professional Development Recommendations:** Training programs should emphasize ethical and technical aspects in conjunction with educational tactics.

The research represents a timely study on how AI influences education transformation, underlining the urgent need for teacher competency development. Its advantages are based on the fact that it can contribute to suggesting updates of existing frameworks, such as DigCompEdu (shown in figure 1) and P21 framework, toward the inclusion of AI-specific capabilities. These frameworks ensure systematic professional development and adaptability within diverse educational contexts.

However, by nature of relying on a conceptual analysis rather than empirical data, it loses the practical applicability. Another criticism is that the research does not adequately probe cultural diversity regarding the acceptance of AI. The ethics of AI can vary quite substantially between regions, which calls for a more nuanced discussion.

Overall, the study makes some valuable theoretical contributions to the discussion of AI in education. Future research should focus on empirical validation, cross-cultural contexts, and case studies in detail in order to illustrate the practical application of proposed frameworks. This would enhance its potential to act as a resource for educators navigating the complexities of integrating AI.

Ultimately, the study argues that preparing teachers for AI integration is essential for ensuring equitable and effective learning environments (A comparative analysis for DigCompEdu Framework, P21 Framework, and TPACK Model is show in Table 3). It provides a foundation for designing professional training programs and aligning them with updated competency frameworks to meet the demands of modern education.

Table 3. A comparative analysis for DigCompEdu Framework, P21 Framework, and TPACK Model (Celik, 2023; Ng et al., 2023)

Aspect	DigCompEdu Framework	TPACK Model	P21 Framework
Definition	A Digital Competence Framework for Educators (DigCompEdu) to develop digital competencies to effectively use technology for teaching, learning, and assessment.	A model integrating Technology, Pedagogy, and Content Knowledge (TPCK)to guide technology use in teaching.	A Partnership for 21st century (P21) framework that emphasizes 21st-century skills, combining core knowledge with critical thinking, collaboration, and digital literacy.
Year of Origin	2017	2006	2002
Purpose	To support teachers in becoming digitally competent and integrating digital tools effectively into their practice.	To provide a framework for teachers to balance technological, pedagogical, and content knowledge in education.	To prepare teachers and students with skills for the 21st century, focusing on creativity and digital competency.
Focus Areas	Digital literacy, professional engagement, digital content creation, teaching strategies, and ethical use of technology.	The interaction between content knowledge (CK), pedagogical knowledge (PK), and technological knowledge (TK).	21st-century learning skills include collaboration, communication, critical thinking, and creativity.

continued on following page

Table 3. Continued

Aspect	DigCompEdu Framework	TPACK Model	P21 Framework
Components	• Professional Engagement • Empowering Learners • Facilitating Learners • Digital Competencies • Digital Resources • Teaching and Learning • Assessment	• TK: Knowledge of technologies. • PK: Teaching strategies. • CK: Subject-specific expertise. • TPACK: Their intersection for effective teaching.	• Learning and Innovation Skills • Information, Media, and Technology Skills • Life and Career Skills
Strengths	• Provides a structured roadmap for developing digital competencies. • Addresses ethical use of technology in education.	• Focuses on integrating pedagogy with technology and content knowledge. • Flexible for various educational contexts.	• Broad focus on 21st-century skills. • Applicable across disciplines and contexts. • Includes technology and life skills.
Limitations	• Focused more on digital tools than AI-specific technologies. • Limited application to systemic barriers in under-resourced settings.	• Does not explicitly address ethical concerns or AI-specific needs. • Focuses heavily on integration without detailed examples of application.	• Generalized focus may dilute specificity for educators. • Limited focus on AI-specific or emerging technologies.
Applications in AI	• Can be adapted to include AI competencies (e.g., ethical AI use, algorithmic bias, adaptive learning systems).	• Offers a foundation for integrating AI tools into pedagogy but needs extension for addressing ethical and specific AI competencies.	• Encourages creative and critical thinking, foundational for AI literacy. • Broad applicability in AI-integrated skills development.
Use Case Examples	• Ethical AI Use in Classrooms: Training teachers to identify and mitigate bias in AI grading systems. • Real-Time Feedback: Using analytics to offer immediate insights into student progress and areas needing improvement.	• Integrated Science Learning: Teachers use AI-driven lab simulations for chemistry experiments. • Personalized Math Tutoring: AI tools recommend tailored exercises based on performance.	• Critical Thinking Workshops: Students use AI to analyze case studies and present findings collaboratively. • Simulation-Based Learning: Teachers use AI simulations for STEM lessons to replicate real-world challenges.

Figure 1. DigCompEdu Framework (Source-https://joint-research-centre.ec.europa.eu/digcompedu_en)

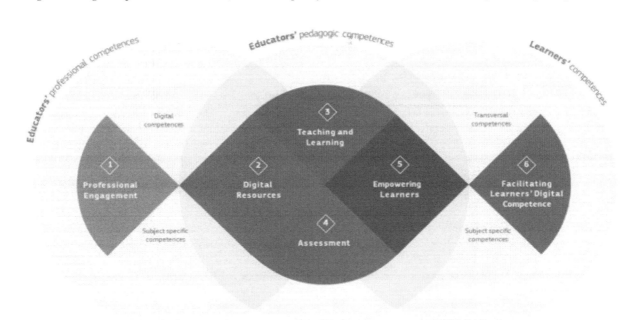

DISCUSSION

The TPACK model provides an important framework for integrating technology, pedagogy, and content knowledge into the AI based education systems. Studies from Adelana et al. (2024), Karataş et al. (2024), Ng et al.(2023), and Chounta et al. (2022) highlight the need to extend such models to include AI-specific competencies for algorithmic decision-making and ethical implications. For example, using a survey method with 508 teachers Viberg et al. (2024) explore the factors influencing K-12 teachers trust in AI-based educational technology (AI-EdTech) across six countries (Brazil, Israel, Japan, Norway, Sweden, and the USA). It investigates the role of AI understanding, cultural values, self-efficacy, and geographic location in shaping trust and its benefits.

This is moreover an added pressure to teachers who are required to move beyond basic digital literacy to develop AI literacy, enabling them to critically use AI tools and apply them ethically in diverse educational contexts. The DigCompEdu framework and P21 competencies further contribute to competency development, emphasizing digital literacy, critical thinking, and adaptability. However, these frameworks lack explicit AI integration. Ng et al. (2023) also highlighted disparities in access to AI tools and training, particularly in resource-constrained settings. Because teachers in low-income regions may lack the necessary infrastructure or institutional support needed for effective AI integration, this digital disparity can out stress educational inequalities among teachers from the same region, in addition to that inter regional disparities increases this disparity manifold. Furthermore, the fast pace of technological change can make it challenging for educators to keep up, as AI is evolving, and will evolve leading to a skills gap that hinders the adoption of AI in classrooms.

To address these challenges, studies propose multifaceted strategies for reskilling teachers. Professional development programs must prioritize hands on training with AI tools incorporating real world applications, adaptive learning platforms and intelligent tutoring systems, into teacher training (Ng et al., 2023). A special emphasis has to be given towards interdisciplinary collaboration, as recommended by Viberg et al. (2024), where teachers, technologists, and policymakers co-develop training content.

Institutional support is essential. Creating collaborative learning communities where instructors can share strategies and experiences for AI integration is recommended by (Adelana et al., 2024; Karataş et al., 2024; Celik, 2023; Ng et al., 2023; Chounta et al., 2022).

CONCLUSION

As AI transforms education, the focus must remain on empowering teachers to use these tools thoughtfully, preserving the creativity and critical thinking at the heart of learning. The integration of AI in education presents opportunities and at the same time demands a rethinking of teacher roles, competencies, and strategies for upskilling. The foundational AI Large Language Models are eroding traditional teaching mechanisms, compelling educators to reimagine their roles not just as instructors but as critical evaluators of technology ethically with pedagogical implications. Teachers' cognition towards this reflects a process of adaptation and resistance, where professional judgment and ethical considerations take center stage. This change underscores the necessity of educators as an agency in navigating the complexities of AI based technologies. Structured frameworks for developing teacher competencies considering AI technologies are found within DigCompEdu and P21, among others. However, how well they respond to the changing needs of AI as technology needs to be explored. Various studies by researchers mentioned above and recent development in terms of technology confirms that a balance between technical proficiency and ethical understanding is important in empowering teachers to make informed decisions about AI use in their classrooms. In conclusion, the integration of AI into education is a twin deterrent, bringing with it immense potential to improve teaching and learning, while simultaneously creating challenges that require careful consideration.

REFERENCES

Adelana, O., Ayanwale, M., & Sanusi, I. (2024). Exploring pre-service biology teachers intention to teach genetics using an AI intelligent tutoring—Based system. *Cogent Education*, *11*(1), 1–25. DOI: 10.1080/2331186X.2024.2310976

Alenizi, M., Mohamed, A., & Shaaban, T. (2023). Revolutionizing EFL Special Education: How ChatGPT is Transforming the Way Teachers Approach Language Learning. *Innoeduca-International Journal Of Technology And Educational Innovation*, *9*(2), 5–23. DOI: 10.24310/innoeduca.2023.v9i2.16774

Aljemely, Y. (2024). Challenges and best practices in training teachers to utilize artificial intelligence: A systematic review. *Frontiers in Education*, *9*, 1–10. DOI: 10.3389/feduc.2024.1470853

Ayanwale, M., Adelana, O., Molefi, R., Adeeko, O., & Ishola, A. (2024). Examining artificial intelligence literacy among pre-service teachers for future classrooms. *Computers and Education Open*, *6*, 1–15. DOI: 10.1016/j.caeo.2024.100179

Beege, M., Hug, C., & Nerb, J. (2024). AI in STEM education: The relationship between teacher perceptions and ChatGPT use. *Computers in Human Behavior Reports*, *16*, 1–9. DOI: 10.1016/j.chbr.2024.100494

Celik, I. (2023). Towards Intelligent-TPACK: An empirical study on teachers professional knowledge to ethically integrate artificial intelligence (AI)-based tools into education. *Computers in Human Behavior*, *138*, 107468. Advance online publication. DOI: 10.1016/j.chb.2022.107468

Celik, I., Dindar, M., Muukkonen, H., & Järvelä, S. (2022). The Promises and Challenges of Artificial Intelligence for Teachers: A Systematic Review of Research. *TechTrends*, *66*(4), 616–630. DOI: 10.1007/s11528-022-00715-y

Chiu, T., Moorhouse, B., Chai, C., & Ismailov, M. (2024). Teacher support and student motivation to learn with Artificial Intelligence (AI) based chatbot. *Interactive Learning Environments*, *32*(7), 3240–3256. DOI: 10.1080/10494820.2023.2172044

Chounta, I., Bardone, E., Raudsep, A., & Pedaste, M. (2022). Exploring Teachers Perceptions of Artificial Intelligence as a Tool to Support their Practice in Estonian K-12 Education. *International Journal of Artificial Intelligence in Education*, *32*(3), 725–755. DOI: 10.1007/s40593-021-00243-5

Clarke, L., & McFlynn, P. (2019). All Animals Learn, but Only Humans Teach: The Professional Place of Teacher Educators. *Education Sciences*, *9*(3), 192. Advance online publication. DOI: 10.3390/educsci9030192

Delcker, J., Heil, J., & Ifenthaler, D. (2024). Evidence-based development of an instrument for the assessment of teachers self-perceptions of their artificial intelligence competence. *ETR&D-Educational Technology Research And Development*, 1-19. DOI: 10.1007/s11423-024-10418-1

Edwards, C., Edwards, A., Spence, P., & Lin, X. (2018). I, teacher: Using artificial intelligence (AI) and social robots in communication and instruction. *Communication Education*, *67*(4), 473–480. DOI: 10.1080/03634523.2018.1502459

Gantalao, L. C., Calzada, J. G. D., Capuyan, D. L., Lumantas, B. C., Acut, D. P., & Garcia, M. B. (2025). Equipping the Next Generation of Technicians: Navigating School Infrastructure and Technical Knowledge in the Age of AI Integration. In *Pitfalls of AI Integration in Education: Skill Obsolescence, Misuse, and Bias*. IGI Global., DOI: 10.4018/979-8-3373-0122-8.ch009

Gentile, M., Città, G., Perna, S., & Allegra, M. (2023). Do we still need teachers? Navigating the paradigm shift of the teacher's role in the AI era. *Frontiers in Education*, 8, 1161777. Advance online publication. DOI: 10.3389/feduc.2023.1161777

Heffernan, N. T., & Heffernan, C. L. (2014). The Assessment's Ecosystem: Building a Platform that Brings Scientists and Teachers Together for Minimally Invasive Research on Human Learning and Teaching. *International Journal of Artificial Intelligence in Education*, 24(4), 470–497. DOI: 10.1007/s40593-014-0024-x

Hurajová, L. (2021). can close cooperation between ESP/CLIL experts and disciplinary teachers in higher education lead to fostering english education environment. *Journal Of Teaching English For Specific And Academic Purposes*, 9(1), 129–136. DOI: 10.22190/JTESAP2101129H

Ji, H., Han, I., & Ko, Y. (2023). A systematic review of conversational AI in language education: Focusing on the collaboration with human teachers. *Journal of Research on Technology in Education*, 55(1), 48–63. DOI: 10.1080/15391523.2022.2142873

Karataş, F., Abedi, F. Y., Ozek Gunyel, F., Karadeniz, D., & Kuzgun, Y. (2024). Incorporating AI in foreign language education: An investigation into ChatGPT's effect on foreign language learners. *Education and Information Technologies*, 29(15), 19343–19366. DOI: 10.1007/s10639-024-12574-6

Kim, J. (2024). Leading teachers perspective on teacher-AI collaboration in education. *Education and Information Technologies*, 29(7), 8693–8724. DOI: 10.1007/s10639-023-12109-5

King, S., Boyer, J., Bell, T., & Estapa, A. (2022). An Automated Virtual Reality Training System for Teacher-Student Interaction: A Randomized Controlled Trial. *JMIR Serious Games*, 10(4), e41097. Advance online publication. DOI: 10.2196/41097 PMID: 36480248

Korucu-Kis, S. (2024). Zone of proximal creativity: An empirical study on EFL teachers use of ChatGPT for enhanced practice. *Thinking Skills and Creativity*, 54, 101639. Advance online publication. DOI: 10.1016/j.tsc.2024.101639

Li, M. (2024). Integrating Artificial Intelligence in Primary Mathematics Education: Investigating Internal and External Influences on Teacher Adoption. *International Journal of Science and Mathematics Education*. Advance online publication. DOI: 10.1007/s10763-024-10515-w

Lim, E. (2023). The effects of pre-service early childhood teachers digital literacy and self-efficacy on their perception of AI education for young children. *Education and Information Technologies*, 28(10), 12969–12995. DOI: 10.1007/s10639-023-11724-6

Lin, H., & Chen, Q. (2024). Artificial intelligence (AI) -integrated educational applications and college students' creativity and academic emotions: Students and teachers perceptions and attitudes. *BMC Psychology*, 12(1), 487. Advance online publication. DOI: 10.1186/s40359-024-01979-0 PMID: 39285268

Lozano, A., & Fontao, C. (2023). Is the Education System Prepared for the Irruption of Artificial Intelligence? A Study on the Perceptions of Students of Primary Education Degree from a Dual Perspective: Current Pupils and Future Teachers. *Education Sciences*, *13*(7), 733. Advance online publication. DOI: 10.3390/educsci13070733

Mangubat, J. C., Mangubat, M. R., Uy, T. B. L., Acut, D. P., & Garcia, M. B. (2025). Safeguarding Educational Innovations Amid AI Disruptions: A Reassessment of Patenting for Sustained Intellectual Property Protection. In *Pitfalls of AI Integration in Education: Skill Obsolescence, Misuse, and Bias*. IGI Global., DOI: 10.4018/979-8-3373-0122-8.ch013

Martínez-Requejo, S., Redondo-Duarte, S., Jiménez-García, E., & Ruiz-Lázaro, J. (2025). Technoethics and the Use of Artificial Intelligence in Educational Contexts: Reflections on Integrity, Transparency, and Equity. In *Pitfalls of AI Integration in Education: Skill Obsolescence, Misuse, and Bias*. IGI Global., DOI: 10.4018/979-8-3373-0122-8.ch010

Ng, D., Leung, J., Su, J., Ng, R., & Chu, S. (2023). Teachers AI digital competencies and twenty-first century skills in the post-pandemic world. *Educational Technology Research and Development*, *71*(1), 137–161. DOI: 10.1007/s11423-023-10203-6 PMID: 36844361

Novopashina, L., Grigorieva, E., Ilyina, N., & Bidus, I. (2024). Readiness of future teachers to work at school: review of theoretical and empirical research. *Obrazovanie i nauka-. Education in Science*, *26*(2), 60–96. DOI: 10.17853/1994-5639-2024-2-60-96

Riera-Negre, L., Hidalgo-Andrade, P., Rosselló, M., & Verger, S. (2024). Exploring support strategies and training needs for teachers in navigating illness, bereavement, and death-related challenges in the classroom: A scoping review supporting teachers in classroom grief and loss. *Frontiers in Education*, *9*, 1328247. Advance online publication. DOI: 10.3389/feduc.2024.1328247

Sanusi, I., Ayanwale, M., & Chiu, T. (2024). Investigating the moderating effects of social good and confidence on teachers intention to prepare school students for artificial intelligence education. *Education and Information Technologies*, *29*(1), 273–295. DOI: 10.1007/s10639-023-12250-1

Sperling, K., Stenberg, C., Mcgrath, C., Akerfeldt, A., Heintz, F., & Stenliden, L. (2024). In search of artificial intelligence (AI) literacy in teacher education: A scoping review. *Computers and Education Open*, *6*, 100169. Advance online publication. DOI: 10.1016/j.caeo.2024.100169

Tatar, C., Jiang, S., Rosé, C., & Chao, J. (2024). Exploring Teachers Views and Confidence in the Integration of an Artificial Intelligence Curriculum into Their Classrooms: A Case Study of Curricular Co-Design Program. *International Journal of Artificial Intelligence in Education*. Advance online publication. DOI: 10.1007/s40593-024-00404-2

Trevisan, O., Christensen, R., Drossel, K., Friesen, S., Forkosh-Baruch, A., & Phillips, M. (2024). Drivers of Digital Realities for Ongoing Teacher Professional Learning. *Technology Knowledge And Learning*, *29*(4), 1851–1868. DOI: 10.1007/s10758-024-09771-0

Viberg, O., Cukurova, M., Feldman-Maggor, Y., Alexandron, G., Shirai, S., Kanemune, S., Wasson, B., Tomte, C., Spikol, D., Milrad, M., Coelho, R., & Kizilcec, R. (2024). What Explains Teachers Trust in AI in Education Across Six Countries? *International Journal of Artificial Intelligence in Education.* Advance online publication. DOI: 10.1007/s40593-024-00433-x

Wang, Y., & Wang, X. (2024). Artificial intelligence in physical education: Comprehensive review and future teacher training strategies. *Frontiers in Public Health*, *12*, 1484848. Advance online publication. DOI: 10.3389/fpubh.2024.1484848 PMID: 39583072

Wu, D., Zhang, X., Wang, K., Wu, L., & Yang, W. (2024). *A multi-level factors model affecting teachers behavioral intention in AI-enabled education ecosystem.* ETR&D-Educational Technology Research And Development., DOI: 10.1007/s11423-024-10419-0

Xiao, J., Bozkurt, A., Nichols, M., Pazurek, A., Stracke, C. M., Bai, J. Y. H., Farrow, R., Mulligan, D., Nerantzi, C., Sharma, R. C., Singh, L., Frumin, I., Swindell, A., Honeychurch, S., Bond, M., Dron, J., Moore, S., Leng, J., & Slagter van Tryon, P. J.. (2025). Venturing into the Unknown: Critical Insights into Grey Areas and Pioneering Future Directions in Educational Generative AI Research. *TechTrends*, •••, 1–16. DOI: 10.1007/s11528-025-01060-6

Yu, H. (2024). The application and challenges of ChatGPT in educational transformation: New demands for teachers roles. *Heliyon*, *10*(2), e24289. Advance online publication. DOI: 10.1016/j.heliyon.2024. e24289 PMID: 38298626

Zhang, J., & Zhang, Z. (2024). AI in teacher education: Unlocking new dimensions in teaching support, inclusive learning, and digital literacy. *Journal of Computer Assisted Learning*, *40*(4), 1871–1885. DOI: 10.1111/jcal.12988

Zhao, C., & Yu, J. (2024). Relationship between teacher's ability model and students' behavior based on emotion-behavior relevance theory and artificial intelligence technology under the background of curriculum ideological and political education. *Learning and Motivation*, *88*, 102040. Advance online publication. DOI: 10.1016/j.lmot.2024.102040

Zhao, Y., & Frank, K. A. (2003). Factors Affecting Technology Uses in Schools: An Ecological Perspective. *American Educational Research Journal*, *40*(4), 807–840. DOI: 10.3102/00028312040004807

Zhou, J., Shen, L., & Chen, W. (2024). How ChatGPT transformed teachers: The role of basic psychological needs in enhancing digital competence. *Frontiers in Psychology*, *15*, 1–9. DOI: 10.3389/fpsyg.2024.1458551 PMID: 39421844

KEY TERMS AND DEFINITIONS

Artificial Intelligence (AI): The simulation of human intelligence in machines that are programmed to think, learn, and make decisions. In education, AI is used to personalize learning, automate tasks, and support data-driven instruction.

Professional Development: Ongoing training and education that helps educators enhance their teaching skills, stay current with new technologies and pedagogical strategies, and meet professional standards.

Teacher Competency Development: The continuous process of enhancing teachers' knowledge, skills, and attitudes necessary for effective teaching, especially in response to evolving educational technologies and methodologies.

Technological Pedagogical Content Knowledge (TPACK): A framework that identifies the knowledge teachers need to effectively integrate technology into their teaching. It includes understanding the interplay between technology, pedagogy, and content knowledge.

Systematic Review: A methodical and comprehensive synthesis of existing research studies on a specific topic, following a structured protocol to identify, evaluate, and summarize findings to answer a defined research question.

Chapter 9
Equipping the Next Generation of Technicians:
Navigating School Infrastructure and Technical Knowledge in the Age of AI Integration

Larry C. Gantalao
Cebu Technological University, Philippines

Jeffrey G. Dela Calzada
Cebu Technological University, Philippines

Dennis L. Capuyan
https://orcid.org/0000-0002-7443-8959
Cebu Technological University, Philippines

Bernabe C. Lumantas
Cebu Technological University, Philippines

Dharel P. Acut
https://orcid.org/0000-0002-9608-1292
Cebu Technological University, Philippines

Manuel B. Garcia
https://orcid.org/0000-0003-2615-422X
FEU Institute of Technology, Philippines

ABSTRACT

As artificial intelligence (AI) continues to transform the demands of the global workforce, technical education must evolve to meet these emerging challenges. This chapter examines the integration of AI in technical education with an emphasis on the critical need for modern infrastructure and technical expertise. It highlights the importance of investing in facilities such as AI-equipped laboratories, reliable internet, and educator training programs to foster innovation and personalized learning. Collaboration between educational institutions and industry is explored as a means to bridge the gap between academic theory and real-world applications. Additionally, the chapter advocates revising curricula to combine AI literacy with technical skills, alongside critical thinking and adaptability, to meet evolving workforce demands. It concludes with a call for educators, policymakers, and institutions to prioritize inclusive, forward-thinking strategies to modernize technical education and ensure equity in access and opportunities.

DOI: 10.4018/979-8-3373-0122-8.ch009

INTRODUCTION

The rapid integration of artificial intelligence (AI) in various sectors has significantly transformed education, particularly in technical and vocational training programs. AI technologies are now reshaping the landscape of teaching and learning, offering unprecedented opportunities to enhance the skillsets of students (Ciavaldini-Cartaut et al., 2024; Windelband, 2023). As industries increasingly rely on AI-driven tools and systems, the demand for workers proficient in these technologies is rising. This shift necessitates that technical education institutions adapt to these changes by incorporating AI into their curricula to prepare future technicians for a highly digital and automated workforce (Rott et al., 2022). However, achieving this requires a robust framework that emphasizes both the acquisition of technical knowledge and the development of adequate school infrastructure to support AI-driven learning environments.

In technical and vocational education, technical knowledge remains at the heart of the curriculum, equipping students with the practical skills needed to thrive in fields such as engineering, manufacturing, and information technology (Cai & Kosaka, 2024). As industries evolve, the ability of future technicians to work with AI-powered systems, such as automated production lines or machine learning algorithms, becomes essential. The development of these competencies not only enhances their employability but also contributes to the overall competitiveness of the national workforce (McGrath & Yamada, 2023). Therefore, the successful integration of AI into technical education hinges on ensuring that students are equipped with relevant and up-to-date technical knowledge (Acut, Gamusa, et al., 2025; Hasanah et al., 2025). Equally important to technical knowledge is the role of school infrastructure in supporting learning. Educational institutions must provide students with access to state-of-the-art facilities, tools, and technologies to fully harness the potential of AI integration (Walter, 2024). Adequate infrastructure—including access to high-speed internet, AI-enabled labs, and advanced machinery—ensures that students can engage in hands-on, practical experiences that mirror real-world industry applications (Rintala & Nokelainen, 2019). In the absence of such infrastructure, the ability of technical institutions to effectively integrate AI into their curricula may be severely limited, thus impeding students' readiness for the AI-driven workforce.

MAIN FOCUS OF THE CHAPTER

This chapter explores how technical and vocational education can effectively address the challenges posed by AI integration, particularly in preventing skill obsolescence and ensuring infrastructure readiness. As AI transforms industries, technical programs must evolve to equip students with both foundational and emerging technological skills. The focus here is on ensuring that technical education institutions maintain essential, hands-on technical knowledge that prevents over-dependence on AI systems. A key part of this involves examining the role of school infrastructure in facilitating meaningful learning experiences. The chapter emphasizes the critical need for advanced tools, facilities, and AI-enabled environments that enable students to practice real-world applications of AI without undermining their fundamental technical capabilities. This approach helps mitigate one of the main concerns in AI education—the risk of technicians being trained on systems they do not fully understand, potentially leading to skill degradation. The scope of this chapter addresses the broader risks of how inadequate infrastructure and over-reliance on AI can exacerbate inequality in technical education. It explores the potential for AI to contribute to job displacement if educational programs fail to balance AI-centric skills with core technical competencies. Inadequate infrastructure can lead to inequities in access to AI tools, marginalizing students who lack the necessary resources to fully engage with the technology. Insights are provided into how institutions can develop a balanced curriculum that integrates AI while still emphasizing essential technical skills, contributing to the larger discourse on the responsible and equitable integration of AI into educational systems.

UNDERSTANDING SCHOOL INFRASTRUCTURE

Definition and Components of School Infrastructure

School infrastructure encompasses the physical, technological, and environmental resources necessary to support effective teaching and learning. It includes physical facilities such as classrooms, laboratories, workshops, and libraries, which provide foundational spaces for instruction (Barrett et al., 2018). These physical components are particularly vital in technical education, where hands-on practice with machinery and tools plays a significant role in developing students' skills. Technological resources, including computers, high-speed internet, and AI-enabled devices, are now integral to modern educational infrastructure. These tools enhance learning by facilitating access to digital content, enabling simulations, and fostering collaboration (Haleem et al., 2022). Equally important are learning environments designed to be flexible, inclusive, and conducive to active engagement (Garcia, Goi, et al., 2025). A well-planned environment considers factors such as lighting, acoustics, ventilation, and ergonomic furniture, which collectively influence student concentration, comfort, and participation (Latip et al., 2024).

The Impact of Infrastructure on Educational Outcomes

Infrastructure quality plays a pivotal role in shaping educational outcomes, as it directly affects students' academic performance, teachers' instructional methods, and the overall learning environment (Agyei et al., 2024). Schools equipped with modern laboratories, advanced machinery, and digital tools enable students to gain hands-on experience in their respective fields, a critical component of technical education. Studies indicate that students in such schools consistently outperform their peers in institutions lacking these resources, as access to advanced tools enhances both theoretical understanding and practical skill acquisition (Bernhard, 2018; Pandita & Kiran, 2023). Moreover, adequate infrastructure fosters an environment where students can engage more deeply with their studies, develop problem-solving abilities, and prepare for the demands of a competitive workforce (Hanaysha et al., 2023).

Teachers also benefit from high-quality infrastructure, which enables them to implement innovative teaching approaches and integrate technology into their pedagogy effectively (Akram et al., 2022). Access to resources such as smart classrooms, AI-enabled systems, and collaborative learning spaces allows educators to diversify instructional methods, making lessons more interactive and engaging (Backfisch et al., 2021). Additionally, a well-maintained physical environment promotes student safety, comfort, and accessibility, reducing distractions and minimizing absenteeism. These factors collectively contribute to improved student engagement, motivation, and academic outcomes, underscoring the importance of investing in infrastructure as a foundational element for educational success (Yangambi, 2023).

Current Challenges in School Infrastructure for Technical Education

Despite its importance, many institutions face significant challenges in providing adequate infrastructure for technical education. Resource constraints, particularly in low- and middle-income regions, lead to outdated equipment, limited access to advanced technologies, and overcrowded learning spaces (Mhlongo et al., 2023). Rapid advancements in AI and other emerging technologies exacerbate this gap, as many schools struggle to keep pace with the industry's technological requirements. Additionally, disparities in infrastructure quality between urban and rural schools further deepen educational inequities, leaving students in underserved areas at a distinct disadvantage (Sanfo, 2023). Addressing these challenges requires an approach that includes increased investment in infrastructure, strategic partnerships with industries, and policies that promote equitable access to resources. Strengthening school infrastructure ensures that all students, regardless of their socio-economic background, have the opportunity to develop the technical competencies needed for an AI-driven workforce.

THE SIGNIFICANCE OF TECHNICAL KNOWLEDGE

Definition of Technical Knowledge

Technical knowledge refers to the specialized understanding and skills necessary to perform specific tasks or solve problems within a particular field or industry. It encompasses both theoretical and practical competencies, including understanding engineering principles, expertise in operating machinery, and applying digital tools in problem-solving contexts (Banse & Grunwald, 2009). In technical education, this knowledge forms the foundation for preparing students to meet industry standards and adapt to technological advancements. Beyond mechanical or engineering disciplines, technical knowledge increasingly incorporates familiarity with emerging technologies such as AI, data analytics, and automation (Stolpe & Hallström, 2024).

Skills Required in the Modern Workforce

The modern workforce demands a harmonious integration of traditional technical skills and advanced digital literacy to navigate the complexities of an AI-driven economy. Core competencies such as troubleshooting, system analysis, and project management continue to serve as foundational pillars across technical fields. However, these must now be augmented by digital-age proficiencies like coding, data interpretation, and AI tool proficiency to remain relevant in increasingly automated industries (Autor, 2015). These skills not only enable professionals to operate cutting-edge technologies but also to analyze and optimize their functionalities, making them indispensable in sectors such as manufacturing, IT, and engineering.

Beyond technical capabilities, soft skills such as critical thinking, creativity, and adaptability have emerged as equally critical in the face of rapidly evolving technologies. These skills empower individuals to address complex, unfamiliar challenges and to integrate new innovations seamlessly into existing workflows (Poláková et al., 2023). For example, adaptability is key to embracing advancements in AI, while creativity fosters innovative problem-solving, particularly in areas where AI tools may provide unprecedented opportunities. In response to these demands, technical education must prioritize the alignment of curriculum design with these evolving skill requirements. Incorporating interdisciplinary approaches and real-world applications ensures that students are well-prepared to excel in dynamic professional environments. This strategy aligns educational practices with current industry standards while fostering adaptability to future technological advancements (Haleem et al., 2022).

Relationship between Technical Knowledge and Employability

Technical knowledge plays a pivotal role in employability, acting as a primary indicator of an individual's readiness to succeed in the competitive labor market. Employers consistently prioritize candidates who possess not only technical expertise but also the capacity to adapt to evolving technological landscapes (Montero Guerra et al., 2023). Proficiency in specialized tools, machinery, and software—coupled with hands-on experience—enhances an applicant's appeal, signaling their potential to contribute effectively from the outset. For example, industries such as manufacturing, IT, and engineering often require familiarity with advanced systems and protocols, making technical proficiency a crucial asset in securing employment (Garcia, 2022).

Beyond immediate job prospects, technical knowledge also supports long-term career growth by fostering continuous learning and adaptability (Shiri et al., 2023). In sectors where technological advancements rapidly redefine job roles, the ability to learn new skills ensures sustained relevance in the workforce. This underscores the critical role of educational institutions in aligning their programs with the dynamic needs of industry (Akhtar et al., 2024). Integrating current technologies and practical applications into curricula allows schools and training centers to bridge the gap between academic preparation and professional demands. This approach enhances employability by aligning educational experiences with industry requirements, ensuring students acquire the skills needed to succeed in competitive job markets (Cheng et al., 2021).

SCHOOL INFRASTRUCTURE AND TECHNICAL KNOWLEDGE

How Infrastructure Facilitates Technical Learning

Infrastructure serves as the backbone of effective technical education, providing the tools and environments needed to develop essential skills. Access to modern equipment and technology is critical for fostering hands-on learning experiences. For example, laboratories equipped with advanced machinery, robotics, and AI-enabled systems allow students to practice industry-relevant tasks and gain familiarity with cutting-edge tools (Elahi et al., 2023). Without access to such resources, students may face significant skill gaps that hinder their competitiveness in the workforce (see Figure 1). Collaborative learning spaces also play a pivotal role in technical education. These environments are designed to encourage teamwork, problem-solving, and innovation by integrating technology into group activities (Mangubat et al., 2025). For instance, makerspaces and innovation labs create opportunities for students to work on projects collectively, fostering interdisciplinary thinking and creativity (Soomro et al., 2023).

Examples of Effective Infrastructure Supporting Technical Education

Examples of effective infrastructure in technical education highlight the transformative impact of well-resourced facilities. Globally, institutions with specialized facilities set benchmarks for integrating practical and theoretical knowledge. For instance, Germany's dual education system seamlessly combines state-of-the-art workshops with classroom learning, giving students hands-on experience in sectors like automotive engineering, robotics, and renewable energy technologies (Delcker & Ifenthaler, 2022). Similarly, technical colleges in Singapore prioritize the integration of smart technologies, such as AI-powered manufacturing systems and Internet of Things (IoT) labs, to prepare students for careers in automation and data analytics (UNESCO, 2023b). These examples demonstrate how targeted infrastructure investments align education with industry demands, ensuring students graduate with relevant, high-level skills.

In the Philippines, innovative infrastructure initiatives are emerging to support technical education despite resource challenges. For example, the Technical Education and Skills Development Authority (TESDA) operates various technical-vocational institutions equipped with modern tools for automotive servicing, electronics, and welding. These facilities enable students to acquire National Certification (NC) credentials, boosting their employability locally and internationally (Asian Development Bank, 2021). Additionally, institutions like Cebu Technological University have established technology hubs where students can experiment with renewable energy systems, drones, and other emerging technologies.

Another noteworthy example is the partnership-driven approach to infrastructure development in the Philippines. Programs like the Dual Training System (DTS) encourage collaboration between schools and industry stakeholders to provide access to real-world facilities, such as manufacturing plants and IT centers, for on-the-job training (TESDA, 2010). Furthermore, organizations such as the Philippine Business for Social Progress (PBSP) have initiated projects to equip rural schools with computer laboratories and internet connectivity, bridging the digital divide and fostering inclusive technical education (PBSP, 2022).

These case studies underscore the importance of contextually adaptive strategies in building infrastructure for technical education. Learning from global examples and leveraging local resources and partnerships allows countries like the Philippines to address infrastructure gaps and enhance their readiness for an AI-driven workforce. This dual approach combines proven strategies from international best practices with contextually relevant solutions, ensuring that infrastructure development is both effective and sustainable.

Role of AI Tools in Enhancing Technical Knowledge

AI tools have significantly transformed technical education by offering personalized learning experiences, real-time feedback, and hands-on training through advanced simulations. These innovations bridge the gap between theoretical knowledge and practical application, making learning more efficient and engaging. Adaptive learning platforms powered by AI assess student performance, identify specific areas for improvement, and dynamically adjust instructional content to match individual learning needs (Garcia, Rosak-Szyrocka, et al., 2025; Kabudi et al., 2021). For instance, AI-driven platforms like Squirrel AI (Singh et al., 2025) and Century Tech (UNESCO, 2023a) utilized machine learning algorithms to create customized learning pathways, allowing students to focus on mastering competencies essential to their career trajectories. These platforms also track student progress, offering targeted interventions that enhance skill development and retention. Beyond personalized learning, AI-driven simulation tools play a crucial role in technical training by enabling students to practice complex tasks in a risk-free virtual environment (Elahi et al., 2023). In fields like manufacturing and engineering, AI-powered software such as Siemens' NX CAM Virtual Machine provides a highly realistic training environment where learners can refine machining techniques without using raw materials or damaging equipment (Gallagher, 2024). Similarly, AI-enhanced welding training systems, such as Soldamatic, leverage augmented reality (AR) to allow students to practice welding techniques with real-time feedback on accuracy, speed, and efficiency (Weld Australia, 2025). These tools not only improve technical skills but also reduce training costs and enhance safety.

AI's growing presence in technical industries has led to significant shifts in workforce demands. Traditional roles have become increasingly automated, leading to job displacement in certain sectors (Soori et al., 2024). However, this shift has also created new roles requiring AI proficiency, such as AI-assisted robotics technicians and predictive maintenance specialists (Rožman et al., 2023). Institutions that integrate AI into their technical curricula help bridge this gap, ensuring that students are equipped with skills relevant to evolving industry standards. Despite its benefits, AI integration in technical education is not without challenges. Some institutions struggle with infrastructure limitations, preventing them from fully leveraging AI tools. For example, underfunded schools may lack the necessary high-speed internet, computing power, or faculty training required to implement AI-driven learning (Ali et al., 2024). Additionally, AI-based assessment tools have been found to reinforce biases, disproportionately affecting students from diverse backgrounds if not carefully designed (Ferrara, 2023). Addressing these issues requires strategic investments in infrastructure and AI literacy training for educators.

Figure 1. Synergy of infrastructure, technical knowledge, and AI

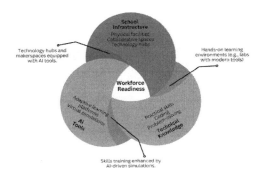

Furthermore, AI-based intelligent tutoring systems, like Carnegie Learning's MATHia and AutoTutor, support technical education by providing real-time explanations, hints, and assessments tailored to individual student needs (Gyonyoru, 2024). These systems employ natural language processing (NLP) and deep learning to simulate human-like tutoring, ensuring that learners receive immediate assistance in complex problem-solving scenarios. In healthcare-related technical fields, AI-powered virtual patients, such as those used in the Body Interact platform, allow students in medical and nursing programs to diagnose and treat patients in simulated clinical settings, improving their decision-making skills and preparedness for real-world medical challenges. As AI continues to evolve, its integration into technical education will further enhance the learning experience, equipping students with both theoretical knowledge and practical expertise. These tools ensure that learners are well-prepared to navigate and operate sophisticated technologies, ultimately making them more competent and job-ready in AI-driven industries (Ponce et al., 2024). However, for AI to be a truly transformative force, institutions must address existing challenges, invest in equitable AI implementation, and prepare students for the rapidly changing workforce. Figure 1 illustrates the synergy between school infrastructure, technical knowledge, and AI, emphasizing their collective role in equipping the next generation of technicians for the challenges and opportunities presented by AI integration in education.

CHALLENGES AND PITFALLS OF AI INTEGRATION

Potential Misuse of AI in Education

AI tools are increasingly used in education to automate processes, enhance personalized learning, and provide real-time feedback. However, their misuse can lead to unintended consequences when implemented without a thorough understanding of their limitations (Acut, Malabago, et al., 2025). A notable example is the use of AI-based grading systems, which assess student writing based on linguistic patterns rather than content depth or creativity (Malik et al., 2023). This has resulted in cases where students using innovative problem-solving approaches receive lower scores, discouraging creative thinking. Over-reliance on AI for assessments also risks deskilling educators, reducing their ability to provide qualitative evaluations that account for nuances AI may overlook. AI-driven surveillance in education presents another significant challenge. In some institutions, AI-powered monitoring systems intended to prevent cheating have sparked controversy over privacy violations and psychological stress among students (Giannakos et al., 2024). For instance, AI proctoring software has been criticized for falsely flagging students due to factors like involuntary movements, poor lighting, or connectivity issues, disproportionately affecting students with disabilities or those from low-income backgrounds. These concerns underscore the need for hybrid approaches where human oversight complements AI decision-making, ensuring fairness and accountability (Coghlan et al., 2021).

Issues of Skill Obsolescence and Degradation

The integration of AI in technical education and vocational training presents a dual challenge: while AI-driven tools enhance learning, they may also contribute to skill degradation. Automated systems now perform many routine tasks (e.g., troubleshooting machinery) that once required manual execution (Filippi et al., 2023). Without active engagement in these foundational skills, students risk becoming overly reliant on AI, which could limit their adaptability in dynamic work environments. A real-world example of this issue is evident in the automotive and manufacturing industries, where AI-powered diagnostic tools have streamlined troubleshooting processes (Malik et al., 2023). While these advancements increase efficiency, they also reduce the hands-on problem-solving experience students gain during training. If educational programs neglect fundamental skill development, future technicians may struggle when AI-driven tools fail or require human intervention for complex issues (Walter, 2024).

Beyond individual competencies, AI-driven automation raises concerns about job displacement. Historical patterns show that technological shifts have rendered certain skill sets obsolete, requiring workers to reskill continually (Zirar et al., 2023). The challenge for educational institutions is to embed adaptability and lifelong learning strategies into technical programs. This includes offering courses on AI ethics, human-AI collaboration, and emerging technologies, preparing students for evolving labor market demands (Bobitan et al., 2024).

Bias and Equity Concerns in AI-Driven Learning Environments

AI-driven educational tools rely on large datasets to analyze student performance and personalize learning experiences (Revano & Garcia, 2021). However, biases in these datasets can reinforce systemic inequalities, disproportionately disadvantaging marginalized student groups. For example, facial recognition software has been found to misidentify students from underrepresented backgrounds at higher rates due to a lack of diversity in training datasets (Chen, 2023). Similarly, AI-powered grading algorithms have been documented to unfairly penalize non-native English speakers, students from low-income schools, and learners with non-traditional educational backgrounds (Salazar et al., 2024). A major instance of AI bias occurred in the UK during the 2020 COVID-19 pandemic, when an AI-based grading algorithm disproportionately downgraded students from disadvantaged schools (Shead, 2020). The model, designed to standardize scores in the absence of traditional exams, prioritized historical school performance over individual merit, systematically favoring students from elite institutions. Public outcry forced the government to abandon the system, highlighting the risks of unchecked AI decision-making in education. Similar failures have been reported elsewhere; for instance, AI-driven admission tools used in U.S. universities may unintentionally favor specific candidate profiles due to biased data patterns in historical admissions records (Stivers, 2018).

Beyond algorithmic bias, unequal access to AI-driven tools perpetuates educational disparities. Underfunded schools often lack the necessary infrastructure—such as high-speed internet, updated hardware, and digital literacy training—limiting students' ability to fully engage with AI-enhanced learning (Kamalov et al., 2023). This digital divide is particularly stark in developing nations, where insufficient technological infrastructure has led to the failure of several AI-driven education initiatives. For example, in India, various EdTech initiatives have faced challenges due to inconsistent digital infrastructure (Kumar, 2023), while a large-scale AI-powered adaptive learning program launched in Bangladesh failed due to unreliable electricity and internet access, rendering the technology largely unusable in classrooms (Tarafdar et al., 2025). Without targeted interventions, AI-driven education risks deepening the gap between high- and low-resource institutions rather than bridging it. Industry-driven AI adoption in education presents another challenge, as commercial interests sometimes take precedence over student learning. Some EdTech companies develop proprietary AI-powered platforms that limit schools' ability to customize learning pathways or integrate alternative educational tools. In extreme cases, corporate-led AI initiatives have locked schools into expensive subscription models, forcing budget-constrained institutions to abandon AI-driven education entirely (Kamalov et al., 2023). Additionally, concerns have been raised over student data privacy, as some AI learning platforms collect extensive user data without clear regulations on how it is stored, shared, or monetized.

To address these challenges, policymakers must ensure that AI tools are built on diverse, representative datasets to minimize bias and promote fairer educational outcomes. Targeted funding should be allocated to schools in underserved communities to improve infrastructure and technological readiness. Moreover, training programs must equip educators with the skills to identify and mitigate AI biases while fostering digital literacy among students. Finally, governments and educational institutions must critically evaluate industry partnerships to ensure that AI adoption aligns with long-term educational equity goals rather than short-term commercial interests. Strengthening regulatory frameworks around AI use in schools—such as mandating transparent algorithmic audits and enforcing ethical AI guidelines—will be crucial in mitigating risks while maximizing the benefits of AI-driven learning.

Impact on School Infrastructure

The successful integration of AI in education is heavily dependent on robust school infrastructure. However, many institutions—especially in low-income regions—lack the fundamental resources necessary for AI-driven learning. Poor internet connectivity, outdated hardware, and unreliable electricity can severely limit AI's effectiveness, creating disparities in educational outcomes (Ali et al., 2024). A report from UNESCO (2024) highlights that the integration of generative artificial intelligence in education presents both opportunities and challenges in the Asia-Pacific region. However, disparities in school infrastructure significantly impact its effectiveness. Schools with limited internet access and outdated facilities struggle to implement AI-powered learning tools, leading to frequent system failures and underutilization. In contrast, well-funded institutions with high-speed internet and modern classrooms can fully leverage AI, further widening the educational divide. Addressing these infrastructure gaps is crucial to ensuring equitable access to AI-driven education across the region.

Beyond technical limitations, the financial burden of AI integration is a significant challenge. Infrastructure upgrades require substantial investments in cybersecurity, AI-compatible lab spaces, and continuous teacher training. Many schools, particularly in developing regions, struggle to secure funding for these upgrades, resulting in delayed or failed AI initiatives. In addition, experts continue to debate the role of AI in education while schools grapple with its implementation. However, despite the discussions, progress remains slow. Many of the challenges surrounding AI integration—such as high costs, security concerns, and the need for specialized IT knowledge—mirror longstanding issues in educational technology. Yet, AI introduces a new dimension to these persistent obstacles that reshape the conversation on EdTech adoption (Bozkurt et al., 2024; Xiao et al., 2025). Additionally, the financial burden of AI-powered grading systems presents a significant challenge for educators and institutions. A case involving an adjunct university professor highlights these cost implications (Kumar, 2023). After filling out the AI grading service's requested information form, the professor received a price quote that required allocating a substantial portion of their income toward grading student papers. The service demanded a valid credit card, charging a base fee in addition to per-use costs. Even if the cost could be offset through an institutional account, available funds would still fall short, and prices were likely to increase over time, with unclear cancellation policies that could incur significant fees. These financial burdens extend beyond individual users, as many educational institutions with limited budgets struggle to afford commercial AI grading services.

Addressing these challenges requires a multi-stakeholder approach involving policymakers, educators, and industry leaders. Public-private partnerships can play a crucial role in equipping schools with sustainable AI infrastructure, ensuring long-term support rather than short-term interventions. Moreover, initiatives such as open-access AI tools and low-cost digital solutions can help bridge the gap between high- and low-resource schools, ensuring that AI integration benefits all students equitably. Table 1 presents a summary of the key challenges and pitfalls associated with AI integration in education, highlighting infrastructural, technical, and ethical concerns that impact its effective implementation.

Table 1. Summary of challenges and pitfalls in AI integration in education

Challenge	Description	Examples	Proposed Solutions
Potential Misuse of AI	Misapplication of AI tools in assessment, monitoring, and prediction leading to ethical concerns and ineffective outcomes.	AI grading prioritizing linguistic patterns over creativity; Surveillance systems infringing on privacy.	Implement ethical guidelines; combine human judgment with AI outputs; train educators on responsible AI use.
Skill Obsolescence and Degradation	Over-reliance on AI reducing manual skills and rendering some competencies obsolete.	Automation replacing routine tasks like basic coding; AI reducing manual problem-solving opportunities.	Balance foundational skills with AI-based learning; embed lifelong learning and adaptability into curricula.
Bias and Equity Concerns	Algorithmic biases and unequal access to AI tools creating disparities in learning opportunities.	Biased grading algorithms disadvantaging minority groups; Digital divide excluding students in low-income regions.	Use diverse datasets; invest in digital infrastructure; develop open-access tools to bridge the digital divide.
Impact on School Infrastructure	Inadequate resources and high costs limiting effective AI implementation in schools.	Lack of internet connectivity, outdated hardware, insufficient electricity in schools, and high maintenance costs for AI-compatible tools.	Invest in infrastructure upgrades; allocate budgets for AI labs and cybersecurity; promote public-private partnerships.

STRATEGIES FOR IMPROVEMENT

Enhancing School Infrastructure for Technical Education

For AI to be effectively integrated into technical education, schools must first address infrastructure limitations that hinder the seamless adoption of AI-driven technologies. Investment in modern laboratories, AI-equipped classrooms, and reliable power supply is essential to ensure that students have access to the tools needed to develop AI literacy and technical proficiency (Kamalov et al., 2023). Additionally, high-speed internet, cloud computing capabilities, and AI-compatible software and hardware must be prioritized to support AI-powered learning environments. Schools in developing regions, particularly those in rural areas, must receive targeted funding for infrastructure upgrades to bridge the digital divide and ensure equitable access to AI-driven education (Haleem et al., 2022). However, the financial burden of upgrading school infrastructure remains a critical challenge. Many educational institutions, particularly in low-income regions, struggle to secure funding for AI-ready facilities. For example, AI deployment in the education sector across Africa faces significant hurdles, particularly due to infrastructural limitations that contribute to digital literacy gaps. The integration of AI in education also increases power consumption, further straining school budgets and making it challenging to sustain long-term implementation. Similarly, logistical issues—such as lack of maintenance personnel or inadequate training for teachers—have led to AI tools being abandoned or underutilized in some institutions. In contrast, Singapore's Ministry of

Education successfully integrated AI-driven learning tools by ensuring sustained investment in digital infrastructure, teacher training, and cybersecurity measures. Their strategic approach enabled widespread AI adoption without exacerbating educational inequalities.

Cybersecurity and data privacy measures are equally crucial. AI-powered platforms collect vast amounts of student data, and without robust security protocols, this data could be vulnerable to breaches or misuse. Institutions must implement secure cloud storage, encryption mechanisms, and strict access controls to protect sensitive student information while complying with international data protection standards (ISO/IEC 27001). However, cybersecurity implementation can be costly and requires skilled personnel, which many schools lack, further complicating AI adoption. A case from India highlights the risks of poor cybersecurity planning: an AI-powered online examination system experienced data leaks, exposing thousands of student records due to weak encryption protocols (Dayal, 2023). The success of AI integration also relies on teacher preparedness. Educators must be equipped with the skills necessary to leverage AI tools for instruction, assessment, and student engagement. Professional development programs—including workshops, AI boot camps, and partnerships with AI experts—should be prioritized to help teachers navigate AI platforms and integrate them effectively into their pedagogical practices (Chan, 2023). Without proper training, teachers may resist AI adoption due to unfamiliarity or concerns about job displacement. Some schools have reported cases where AI-powered grading and tutoring systems were abandoned after initial implementation due to low teacher confidence and lack of ongoing technical support (Kim et al., 2022). In contrast, Finland's AI in Education Initiative successfully trained teachers through national AI literacy programs, ensuring sustained adoption and pedagogical integration (Moraitis, 2025). To ensure sustainable AI integration, institutions must strategically plan investments, secure long-term funding, and provide ongoing technical and professional development support. Public-private partnerships, government subsidies, and open-access AI tools can help lower costs and facilitate broader adoption, ensuring that AI benefits all students equitably rather than exacerbating existing educational disparities.

Strengthening Collaboration Between Educational Institutions and Industry

A stronger partnership between academia and industry is crucial for aligning AI education with real-world applications. Collaborations with technology firms, research institutions, and industry leaders can provide students with access to cutting-edge AI tools, industry-relevant datasets, and internship opportunities that enhance their practical skills (Ahmed et al., 2022). For instance, partnerships between educational institutions and AI-driven companies in Japan have led to the development of AI-powered smart manufacturing training centers, equipping students with hands-on experience in robotics, automation, and machine learning applications in industrial settings. However, financial constraints and regulatory barriers often limit the scalability of such collaborations. Many educational institutions, particularly in developing regions, lack the funding necessary to establish sustained industry partnerships. In some cases, government regulations on data privacy and intellectual property rights create additional hurdles, making it difficult for schools to access proprietary AI technologies or industry datasets. For example, in the European Union, strict General Data Protection Regulation (GDPR) policies have complicated data-sharing agreements between universities and AI companies (Sartor & Lagioia, 2020).

In the Philippines, collaborations such as the University of the Philippines' Center for Intelligent Systems and industry-led AI boot camps have facilitated joint research projects and innovation hubs focused on AI development (Celdran, 2024). These initiatives bridge the gap between academic learning and workforce demands by ensuring that curricula remain up-to-date with emerging AI trends and industry needs. However, sustaining these partnerships remains a challenge, as industry stakeholders may prioritize short-term projects over long-term academic collaborations. Some universities have struggled to maintain corporate partnerships due to shifting industry interests, leading to inconsistent access to AI tools and mentorship programs. While industry collaborations have largely benefited AI education, some unintended consequences have emerged. In certain cases, commercial interests have overridden educational priorities, resulting in conflicts of interest. For example, In the United States, certain corporate-sponsored AI training programs have faced criticism for emphasizing proprietary software over open-source alternatives. Meta's Llama AI models have been labeled as "open-source," but the Open Source Initiative (OSI) argues that this characterization is misleading, as Meta restricts competitor use under its license and lacks full transparency regarding training data (Waters, 2024). Similarly, in India, collaborations between major technology companies and educational institutions have sometimes resulted in AI certification programs that predominantly focus on the company's own products. For example, TalentSprint, an EdTech firm, partners with universities to deliver certification programs in AI and other technologies (Bhattacharyya, 2021). While these programs aim to enhance employability, there is a concern that they may limit students' ability to work with diverse AI frameworks by concentrating on specific corporate technologies. These scenarios highlight the risk of industry partnerships shaping AI education in ways that primarily serve corporate agendas rather than academic and student needs.

Beyond curriculum enhancements, industry collaborations can facilitate AI resource sharing. Through public-private partnerships, educational institutions can receive access to state-of-the-art AI tools, cloud computing services, and machine learning models that would otherwise be cost-prohibitive. However, funding disparities between institutions can create inequities in access, with well-funded universities benefiting disproportionately from such partnerships while under-resourced schools remain excluded. Additionally, logistical challenges, such as aligning academic calendars with industry project timelines, can hinder the smooth execution of collaborative initiatives. To address these barriers, policymakers must create incentives for long-term industry-education partnerships, such as tax benefits for companies that invest in academic AI programs or government grants to support resource-sharing initiatives. Moreover, establishing standardized frameworks for ethical AI collaborations—including clear guidelines on data usage, intellectual property rights, and student involvement—can help build sustainable partnerships that benefit both academia and industry. Joint certification programs between universities and AI firms can further enhance students' employability (Walter, 2024).

Developing an AI-integrated Technical Education Curriculum

A revised curriculum that integrates AI literacy alongside technical skills is essential for preparing students for the demands of an AI-driven workforce. Traditional technical education programs must evolve to include AI applications in engineering, data analytics, cybersecurity, and smart manufacturing. This involves redesigning courses to incorporate AI-driven problem-solving techniques, machine learning algorithms, and automation principles (Southworth et al., 2023). For example, in technical education fields such as robotics and mechatronics, AI-powered control systems can be embedded into coursework to help students understand predictive maintenance, AI-driven automation, and real-time data analytics (Mishra et al., 2024). Similarly, in computer science and information technology, courses must emphasize AI programming languages (e.g., Python, TensorFlow), neural networks, and natural language processing to align with the increasing demand for AI-skilled professionals. Additionally, the curriculum should foster the development of critical thinking, ethical reasoning, and problem-solving skills. While AI can automate many routine tasks, human oversight remains essential in interpreting AI outputs, mitigating biases, and ensuring ethical AI deployment. Courses on AI ethics, digital literacy, and data governance should be incorporated to help students navigate the societal and ethical challenges of AI technology. Several Philippine universities have already taken steps in this direction with their Data Science and Analytics program, which balances technical AI training with discussions on AI governance and ethical implications (Cacho, 2024).

Establishing AI Literacy and Inclusivity Initiatives

To ensure that AI integration benefits all students equitably, institutions must implement AI literacy programs that cater to diverse learning needs. AI literacy encompasses not only technical skills but also critical thinking skills that help students assess AI-generated content, address ethical concerns, and prevent over-reliance on automated tools (Ali et al., 2024). Without structured AI education, students risk becoming passive consumers of AI outputs rather than active, informed users who understand its limitations. One major risk associated with rapid AI adoption in education is skill obsolescence, particularly in traditional learning domains. Studies have shown that excessive dependence on AI-powered tools for writing, computation, and problem-solving can lead to skill degradation over time. A mixed-methods study by Lee et al. (2024) in South Korea, for instance, found that English language learners (ELLs) recognized both the strengths and weaknesses of various AI-based tools, including the accessibility of translation machine learning and the error-checking capabilities of generative AI. However, interview data analysis indicated that excessive reliance on AI-based writing tools could interfere with ELLs' English writing process. These findings suggest that AI literacy initiatives must incorporate guidelines on responsible AI use to prevent skill erosion in foundational competencies.

Beyond skill obsolescence, AI misuse is another pressing concern. Unregulated AI use in education can reinforce biases, compromise academic integrity, and perpetuate misinformation. A manifesto by Bozkurt et al. (2024) on AI-assisted grading in higher education emphasized that algorithmic biases disproportionately impact students from underrepresented backgrounds, resulting in unfair assessments. Similarly, cases of AI-generated misinformation in academic research have raised concerns about students relying on AI-generated citations, some of which are fabricated or inaccurate (Acut et al., 2024). AI literacy programs must include training on ethical AI use, bias detection, and fact-checking methodologies to equip students with the skills needed to critically evaluate AI-generated outputs. AI-driven education should also incorporate adaptive learning models that personalize instruction based on student needs. AI-powered platforms like IBM Watson and Google's AI for Education can tailor learning materials to students' strengths and weaknesses, promoting inclusive and equitable access to AI-based education. However, access to such tools remains uneven, particularly in low-income regions where digital infrastructure is lacking. A report found that students in rural schools had limited engagement with AI-driven adaptive learning platforms due to poor internet connectivity and lack of teacher training, exacerbating the digital divide (Varsik & Vosberg, 2024). Schools must prioritize financial support programs, AI scholarships, and open-source AI tools to ensure that students from disadvantaged backgrounds can participate in AI-driven learning environments.

To ensure that AI literacy programs are effectively implemented, educational institutions and policymakers must develop AI literacy curricula that integrate technical knowledge with ethical considerations, digital responsibility, and critical thinking. They must also incorporate blended learning approaches that balance AI-assisted learning with traditional skill development to prevent over-reliance. Ensuring access to AI education for marginalized groups through multilingual resources, inclusive AI tools, and financial aid programs is crucial, as is mandating transparency and accountability in AI use by requiring educators to evaluate AI tools for bias, accuracy, and ethical implications. Strengthening teacher training programs will further equip educators with the knowledge and skills needed to integrate AI responsibly into the classroom. Integrating AI literacy into education systems enables institutions to cultivate a generation of learners who are not only skilled in AI but also capable of using it critically, ethically, and adaptively. Table 2 outlines strategies for enhancing AI integration in technical education, focusing on infrastructure development, curriculum adaptation, and capacity-building initiatives.

Table 2. Strategies for improving AI integration in technical education

Strategy	Key Actions	Examples and Insights
Enhancing School Infrastructure	1. Invest in modern laboratories, AI-equipped classrooms, and reliable power supply. 2. Provide high-speed internet and AI-compatible hardware/software. 3. Prioritize infrastructure upgrades in rural areas.	Addressing the digital divide in rural schools. AI-ready classrooms for hands-on learning with cutting-edge tools.
Educator Training for AI Integration	1. Organize teacher training programs for effective AI tool usage. 2. Conduct workshops, seminars, and collaborations with AI experts. 3. Encourage personalized learning through AI platforms.	Continuous professional development ensures educators stay updated. Enables automation of administrative tasks and personalized support for students.
Strengthening Education Institution-Industry Collaboration	1. Partner with technology companies and industry leaders for access to equipment and industry-relevant data. 2. Create internships, apprenticeships, and real-world project opportunities. 3. Establish joint innovation hubs.	University innovation centers focus on AI development. Align curriculum with labor market demands to enhance graduate employability.
Developing AI-Integrated Curriculum	1. Integrate AI tools, data analytics, and machine learning into technical programs. 2. Redesign courses to teach AI-enhanced problem-solving. 3. Incorporate ethics, digital literacy, and governance.	Data Science and Analytics program in several universities prepares students for data and AI-driven industries. Builds both technical and ethical competencies.
Advancing AI Literacy and Inclusion	1. Implement AI literacy programs in technical training. 2. Promote inclusive AI access through government and industry partnerships. 3. Develop ethical AI awareness programs in educational curricula.	AI learning hubs in rural areas and AI ethics workshops in technical education programs to bridge the digital divide and promote responsible AI use.

The successful integration of AI into technical education requires a multi-faceted approach that addresses infrastructure challenges, strengthens industry collaborations, modernizes curricula, and promotes inclusivity (Garcia et al., 2024). Investing in AI-ready facilities, equipping educators with AI competencies, and fostering industry-academic partnerships enable institutions to build a strong AI ecosystem that prepares students for AI-driven careers. A well-rounded curriculum—balancing technical expertise with ethical AI literacy—ensures that graduates not only excel in AI-powered workplaces but also navigate the complexities of AI governance responsibly. With proactive policy interventions, strategic investments, and continuous professional development, technical education institutions can harness the full potential of AI, fostering an innovative and ethically conscious AI-literate workforce for the future.

CONCLUSION

The integration of AI in technical education presents both opportunities and challenges, particularly in enhancing school infrastructure and technical knowledge. While AI-driven learning has the potential to revolutionize education, its successful implementation requires strategic investments in modern facilities and comprehensive educator training. Educational institutions, particularly those in resource-limited settings, must explore cost-effective solutions and industry partnerships to bridge technological gaps and ensure equitable access to AI-enhanced learning. Collaboration among academia, industry, and policymakers plays a crucial role in aligning curricula with evolving workforce demands. Integrating AI literacy and problem-solving skills into technical education ensures that students are better prepared for emerging job markets. Case studies from global and local contexts highlight the importance of adaptive policies and interdisciplinary approaches in overcoming challenges such as the digital divide, ethical concerns, and AI bias in educational content. To maximize the benefits of AI while mitigating its pitfalls, institutions should implement structured AI governance, promote ethical AI use, and adopt a balanced approach that combines human expertise with technological advancements. The transformation of technical education must be a collective effort—one that involves continuous dialogue, research, and innovation. Ensuring an inclusive and future-ready learning environment will allow AI integration to enhance, rather than disrupt, the educational landscape.

REFERENCES

Acut, D. P., Gamusa, E. V., Pernaa, J., Yuenyong, C., Pantaleon, A. T., Espina, R. C., Sim, M. J. C., & Garcia, M. B. (2025). AI Shaming Among Teacher Education Students: A Reflection on Acceptance and Identity in the Age of Generative Tools. In *Pitfalls of AI Integration in Education: Skill Obsolescence, Misuse, and Bias*. IGI Global., DOI: 10.4018/979-8-3373-0122-8.ch005

Acut, D. P., Malabago, N. K., Malicoban, E. V., Galamiton, N. S., & Garcia, M. B. (2024). "ChatGPT 4.0 Ghosted Us While Conducting Literature Search:" Modeling the Chatbot's Generated Non-Existent References Using Regression Analysis. *Internet Reference Services Quarterly*, ●●●, 1–26. DOI: 10.1080/10875301.2024.2426793

Acut, D. P., Malabago, N. K., Malicoban, E. V., Galamiton, N. S., & Garcia, M. B. (2025). "ChatGPT 4.0 Ghosted Us While Conducting Literature Search:" Modeling the Chatbot's Generated Non-Existent References Using Regression Analysis. *Internet Reference Services Quarterly*, 29(1), 27–54. Advance online publication. DOI: 10.1080/10875301.2024.2426793

Agyei, E. A., Annim, S. K., Acquah, B. Y. S., Sebu, J., & Agyei, S. K. (2024). Education Infrastructure Inequality and Academic Performance in Ghana. *Heliyon*, 10(14), 1–25. DOI: 10.1016/j.heliyon.2024. e34041 PMID: 39108894

Ahmed, F., Fattani, M. T., Ali, S. R., & Enam, R. N. (2022). Strengthening the Bridge Between Academic and the Industry Through the Academia-Industry Collaboration Plan Design Model. *Frontiers in Psychology*, 13, 1–11. DOI: 10.3389/fpsyg.2022.875940 PMID: 35734456

Akhtar, P., Moazzam, M., Ashraf, A., & Khan, M. N. (2024). The Interdisciplinary Curriculum Alignment to Enhance Graduates' Employability and Universities' Sustainability. *International Journal of Management Education*, 22(3), 1–17. DOI: 10.1016/j.ijme.2024.101037

Akram, H., Abdelrady, A. H., Al-Adwan, A. S., & Ramzan, M. (2022). Teachers' Perceptions of Technology Integration in Teaching-Learning Practices: A Systematic Review. *Frontiers in Psychology*, 13, 1–9. DOI: 10.3389/fpsyg.2022.920317 PMID: 35734463

Ali, O., Murray, P. A., Momin, M., Dwivedi, Y. K., & Malik, T. (2024). The Effects of Artificial Intelligence Applications in Educational Settings: Challenges and Strategies. *Technological Forecasting and Social Change*, 199, 1–18. DOI: 10.1016/j.techfore.2023.123076

Asian Development Bank. (2021). *Technical and Vocational Education and Training in the Philippines in the Age of Industry 4.0*. DOI: 10.22617/TCS210084

Autor, D. H. (2015). Why Are There Still So Many Jobs? The History and Future of Workplace Automation. *The Journal of Economic Perspectives*, 29(3), 3–30. DOI: 10.1257/jep.29.3.3

Backfisch, I., Lachner, A., Stürmer, K., & Scheiter, K. (2021). Variability of Teachers' Technology Integration in the Classroom: A Matter of Utility! *Computers & Education*, 166, 1–21. DOI: 10.1016/j. compedu.2021.104159

Banse, G., & Grunwald, A. (2009). *Coherence and Diversity in the Engineering Sciences*. Elsevier., DOI: 10.1016/B978-0-444-51667-1.50010-0

Barrett, P., Treves, A., Shmis, T., Ambasz, D., & Ustinova, M. (2018). *The Impact of School Infrastructure on Learning: A Synthesis of the Evidence*. World Bank., DOI: 10.1596/978-1-4648-1378-8

Bernhard, J. (2018). What Matters for Students' Learning in the Laboratory? Do Not Neglect the Role of Experimental Equipment! *Instructional Science*, *46*(6), 819–846. DOI: 10.1007/s11251-018-9469-x

Bobitan, N., Dumitrescu, D., Popa, A. F., Sahlian, D. N., & Turlea, I. C. (2024). Shaping Tomorrow: Anticipating Skills Requirements Based on the Integration of Artificial Intelligence in Business Organizations—A Foresight Analysis Using the Scenario Method. *Electronics (Basel)*, *13*(11), 1–17. DOI: 10.3390/electronics13112198

Bozkurt, A., Xiao, J., Farrow, R., Bai, J. Y. H., Nerantzi, C., Moore, S., Dron, J., Stracke, C. M., Singh, L., Crompton, H., Koutropoulos, A., Terentev, E., Pazurek, A., Nichols, M., Sidorkin, A. M., Costello, E., Watson, S., Mulligan, D., Honeychurch, S., & Asino, T. I. (2024). The Manifesto for Teaching and Learning in a Time of Generative AI: A Critical Collective Stance to Better Navigate the Future. *Open Praxis*, *16*(4), 487–513. DOI: 10.55982/openpraxis.16.4.777

Cacho, R. (2024). Integrating Generative AI in University Teaching and Learning: A Model for Balanced Guidelines. *Online Learning : the Official Journal of the Online Learning Consortium*, *28*(3), 1–28. DOI: 10.24059/olj.v28i3.4508

Cai, J., & Kosaka, M. (2024). Conceptualizing Technical and Vocational Education and Training as a Service Through Service-Dominant Logic. *SAGE Open*, *14*(2), 1–16. DOI: 10.1177/21582440241240847

Celdran, C. (2024). Establishing the Philippine AI Research Center: Pioneering AI Adoption in a Filipino Context. *CoinGeek*. https://coingeek.com/establishing-the-philippine-ai-research-center-pioneering-ai-adoption-in-a-filipino-context/

Chan, C. K. Y. (2023). A Comprehensive AI Policy Education Framework for University Teaching and Learning. *International Journal of Educational Technology in Higher Education*, *20*(1), 1–25. DOI: 10.1186/s41239-023-00408-3

Chen, Z. (2023). Ethics and Discrimination in Artificial Intelligence-Enabled Recruitment Practices. *Humanities & Social Sciences Communications*, *10*(1), 1–12. DOI: 10.1057/s41599-023-02079-x

Cheng, M., Adekola, O., Albia, J., & Cai, S. (2021). Employability in Higher Education: A Review of Key Stakeholders' Perspectives. *Higher Education Evaluation and Development*, *16*(1), 16–31. DOI: 10.1108/HEED-03-2021-0025

Ciavaldini-Cartaut, S., Métral, J.-F., Olry, P., Guidoni-Stoltz, D., & Gagneur, C.-A. (2024). Artificial Intelligence in Professional and Vocational Training. In *Palgrave Studies in Creativity and Culture* (pp. 145–155). Springer Nature Switzerland.

Coghlan, S., Miller, T., & Paterson, J. (2021). Good Proctor or "Big Brother"? Ethics of Online Exam Supervision Technologies. *Philosophy & Technology*, *34*(4), 1581–1606. DOI: 10.1007/s13347-021-00476-1 PMID: 34485025

Dayal, D. (2023). Cyber Risks in the Education Sector: Why Cybersecurity Needs to Be Top of the Class. *Digital First Magazine*. https://www.digitalfirstmagazine.com/cyber-risks-in-the-education-sector-why-cybersecurity-needs-to-be-top-of-the-class/

Delcker, J., & Ifenthaler, D. (2022). Digital Distance Learning and the Transformation of Vocational Schools From a Qualitative Perspective. *Frontiers in Education, 7*, 1–15. DOI: 10.3389/feduc.2022.908046

Elahi, M., Afolaranmi, S. O., Martinez Lastra, J. L., & Perez Garcia, J. A. (2023). A Comprehensive Literature Review of the Applications of AI Techniques Through the Lifecycle of Industrial Equipment. *Discover Artificial Intelligence, 3*(1), 1–78. DOI: 10.1007/s44163-023-00089-x

Ferrara, E. (2023). Fairness and Bias in Artificial Intelligence: A Brief Survey of Sources, Impacts, and Mitigation Strategies. *Sci, 6*(1), 1–15. DOI: 10.3390/sci6010003

Filippi, E., Bannò, M., & Trento, S. (2023). Automation Technologies and Their Impact on Employment: A Review, Synthesis and Future Research Agenda. *Technological Forecasting and Social Change, 191*, 1–21. DOI: 10.1016/j.techfore.2023.122448

Gallagher, K. (2024). Siemens NX CAM Integrates AI-Powered CAM Assist. *Siemens*. https://blogs.sw.siemens.com/nx-manufacturing/the-future-of-ai-cnc-programming-siemens-nx-cam-integrates-ai-powered-cam-assist/

Garcia, M. B. (2022). Hackathons as Extracurricular Activities: Unraveling the Motivational Orientation Behind Student Participation. *Computer Applications in Engineering Education, 30*(6), 1903–1918. DOI: 10.1002/cae.22564

Garcia, M. B., Arif, Y. M., Khlaif, Z. N., Zhu, M., de Almeida, R. P. P., de Almeida, R. S., & Masters, K. (2024). Effective Integration of Artificial Intelligence in Medical Education: Practical Tips and Actionable Insights. In *Transformative Approaches to Patient Literacy and Healthcare Innovation* (pp. 1-19). IGI Global. DOI: 10.4018/979-8-3693-3661-8.ch001

Garcia, M. B., Goi, C.-L., Shively, K., Maher, D., Rosak-Szyrocka, J., Happonen, A., Bozkurt, A., & Damašević, R. (2025). Understanding Student Engagement in AI-Powered Online Learning Platforms: A Narrative Review of Key Theories and Models. In *Cases on Enhancing P-16 Student Engagement With Digital Technologies* (pp. 1-30). IGI Global. DOI: 10.2139/ssrn.5074608

Garcia, M. B., Rosak-Szyrocka, J., Yılmaz, R., Metwally, A. H. S., Acut, D. P., Ofosu-Ampong, K., Erdoğdu, F., Fung, C. Y., & Bozkurt, A. (2025). Rethinking Educational Assessment in the Age of Generative AI: Actionable Strategies to Mitigate Academic Dishonesty. In *Pitfalls of AI Integration in Education: Skill Obsolescence, Misuse, and Bias*. IGI Global., DOI: 10.4018/979-8-3373-0122-8.ch001

Giannakos, M., Azevedo, R., Brusilovsky, P., Cukurova, M., Dimitriadis, Y., Hernandez-Leo, D., Järvelä, S., Mavrikis, M., & Rienties, B. (2024). The Promise and Challenges of Generative AI in Education. *Behaviour & Information Technology*, ●●●, 1–27. DOI: 10.1080/0144929X.2024.2394886

Gyonyoru, K. I. K. (2024). The Role of AI-Based Adaptive Learning Systems in Digital Education. *Journal of Applied Technical and Educational Sciences, 14*(2), 1–12. DOI: 10.24368/jates380

Haleem, A., Javaid, M., Qadri, M. A., & Suman, R. (2022). Understanding the Role of Digital Technologies in Education: A Review. *Sustainable Operations and Computers*, *3*, 275–285. DOI: 10.1016/j.susoc.2022.05.004

Hanaysha, J. R., Shriedeh, F. B., & In'airat, M. (2023). Impact of Classroom Environment, Teacher Competency, Information and Communication Technology Resources, and University Facilities on Student Engagement and Academic Performance. *International Journal of Information Management Data Insights*, *3*(2), 1–12. DOI: 10.1016/j.jjimei.2023.100188

Hasanah, N. A., Aziza, M. R., Junikhah, A., Arif, Y. M., & Garcia, M. B. (2025). Navigating the Use of AI in Engineering Education Through a Systematic Review of Technology, Regulations, and Challenges. In *Pitfalls of AI Integration in Education: Skill Obsolescence, Misuse, and Bias*. IGI Global., DOI: 10.4018/979-8-3373-0122-8.ch016

Kabudi, T., Pappas, I., & Olsen, D. H. (2021). Ai-Enabled Adaptive Learning Systems: A Systematic Mapping of the Literature. *Computers and Education: Artificial Intelligence*, *2*, 1–12. DOI: 10.1016/j.caeai.2021.100017

Kamalov, F., Santandreu Calonge, D., & Gurrib, I. (2023). New Era of Artificial Intelligence in Education: Towards a Sustainable Multifaceted Revolution. *Sustainability (Basel)*, *15*(16), 1–27. DOI: 10.3390/su151612451

Kim, J., Lee, H., & Cho, Y. H. (2022). Learning Design to Support Student-Ai Collaboration: Perspectives of Leading Teachers for AI in Education. *Education and Information Technologies*, *27*(5), 6069–6104. DOI: 10.1007/s10639-021-10831-6

Kumar, R. (2023). Faculty Members' Use of Artificial Intelligence to Grade Student Papers: A Case of Implications. *International Journal for Educational Integrity*, *19*(1), 1–10. DOI: 10.1007/s40979-023-00130-7

Latip, M. S. A., Latip, S. N. N. A., Tamrin, M., & Rahim, F. A. (2024). Modelling Physical Ergonomics And student Performance in Higher Education: The Mediating Effect Of student Motivation. *Journal of Applied Research in Higher Education*. Advance online publication. DOI: 10.1108/JARHE-01-2024-0052

Lee, Y.-J., Davis, R. O., & Lee, S. O. (2024). University Students' Perceptions of Artificial Intelligence-Based Tools for English Writing Courses. *Online Journal of Communication and Media Technologies*, *14*(1), 1–11. DOI: 10.30935/ojcmt/14195

Malik, A. R., Pratiwi, Y., Andajani, K., Numertayasa, I. W., Suharti, S., Darwis, A., & Marzuki, . (2023). Exploring Artificial Intelligence in Academic Essay: Higher Education Student's Perspective. *International Journal of Educational Research Open*, *5*, 1–11. DOI: 10.1016/j.ijedro.2023.100296

Mangubat, J. C., Mangubat, M. R., Uy, T. B. L., Acut, D. P., & Garcia, M. B. (2025). Safeguarding Educational Innovations Amid AI Disruptions: A Reassessment of Patenting for Sustained Intellectual Property Protection. In *Pitfalls of AI Integration in Education: Skill Obsolescence, Misuse, and Bias*. IGI Global., DOI: 10.4018/979-8-3373-0122-8.ch013

McGrath, S., & Yamada, S. (2023). Skills for Development and Vocational Education and Training: Current and Emergent Trends. *International Journal of Educational Development, 102*, 1–9. DOI: 10.1016/j.ijedudev.2023.102853

Mhlongo, S., Mbatha, K., Ramatsetse, B., & Dlamini, R. (2023). Challenges, Opportunities, and Prospects of Adopting and Using Smart Digital Technologies in Learning Environments: An Iterative Review. *Heliyon, 9*(6), 1–20. DOI: 10.1016/j.heliyon.2023.e16348 PMID: 37274691

Mishra, N., Garcia, P. S., Habal, B. G. M., & Garcia, M. B. (2024). Harnessing an AI-Driven Analytics Model to Optimize Training and Treatment in Physical Education for Sports Injury Prevention. *Proceedings of the 8th International Conference on Education and Multimedia Technology*, 309-315. DOI: 10.1145/3678726.3678740

Montero Guerra, J. M., Danvila-del-Valle, I., & Méndez-Suárez, M. (2023). The Impact of Digital Transformation on Talent Management. *Technological Forecasting and Social Change, 188*, 1–10. DOI: 10.1016/j.techfore.2022.122291

Moraitis, V. (2025). Why the Guidelines for AI in Finland's Education System Could Redefine Learning Globally. *The AI Track.* https://theaitrack.com/ai-in-finland-education-global-model/

Pandita, A., & Kiran, R. (2023). The Technology Interface and Student Engagement Are Significant Stimuli in Sustainable Student Satisfaction. *Sustainability (Basel), 15*(10), 1–21. DOI: 10.3390/su15107923

PBSP. (2022). Digital and IT equipment for Last Mile Schools. https://www.pbsp.org.ph/news/digital-and-it-equipment-for-last-mile-schools

Poláková, M., Suleimanová, J. H., Madzík, P., Copuš, L., Molnárová, I., & Polednová, J. (2023). Soft Skills and Their Importance in the Labour Market Under the Conditions of Industry 5.0. *Heliyon, 9*(8), 1–20. DOI: 10.1016/j.heliyon.2023.e18670 PMID: 37593611

Ponce, P., Anthony, B., Bradley, R., Maldonado-Romo, J., Méndez, J. I., Montesinos, L., & Molina, A. (2024). Developing a Virtual Reality and Ai-Based Framework for Advanced Digital Manufacturing and Nearshoring Opportunities in Mexico. *Scientific Reports, 14*(1), 1–24. DOI: 10.1038/s41598-024-61514-4 PMID: 38755242

Revano, T. F., & Garcia, M. B. (2021). Designing Human-Centered Learning Analytics Dashboard for Higher Education Using a Participatory Design Approach. *2021 IEEE 13th International Conference on Humanoid, Nanotechnology, Information Technology, Communication and Control, Environment, and Management (HNICEM)*, 1-5. DOI: 10.1109/HNICEM54116.2021.9731917

Rintala, H., & Nokelainen, P. (2019). Vocational Education and Learners' Experienced Workplace Curriculum. *Vocations and Learning, 13*(1), 113–130. DOI: 10.1007/s12186-019-09229-w

Rott, K. J., Lao, L., Petridou, E., & Schmidt-Hertha, B. (2022). Needs and Requirements for an Additional AI Qualification During Dual Vocational Training: Results from Studies of Apprentices and Teachers. *Computers and Education: Artificial Intelligence, 3*, 1–10. DOI: 10.1016/j.caeai.2022.100102

Rožman, M., Oreški, D., & Tominc, P. (2023). Artificial-Intelligence-Supported Reduction of Employees' Workload to Increase the Company's Performance in Today's VUCA Environment. *Sustainability (Basel)*, *15*(6), 1–21. DOI: 10.3390/su15065019

Salazar, L. R., Peeples, S. F., & Brooks, M. E. (2024). Generative AI Ethical Considerations and Discriminatory Biases on Diverse Students Within the Classroom. In *Advances in Educational Technologies and Instructional Design* (pp. 191-213). IGI Global. DOI: 10.4018/979-8-3693-0831-8.ch010

Sanfo, J.-B. M. B. (2023). Factors Explaining Rural-Urban Learning Achievement Inequalities in Primary Education in Benin, Burkina Faso, Togo, and Cameroon. *International Journal of Educational Research Open*, *4*, 1–11. DOI: 10.1016/j.ijedro.2023.100234

Sartor, G., & Lagioia, F. (2020). *The Impact of the General Data Protection Regulation (GDPR) on Artificial Intelligence*. European Parliamentary Research Service., DOI: 10.2861/293

Shead, S. (2020). How a Computer Algorithm Caused a Grading Crisis in British Schools. *CNBC*. https://www.cnbc.com/2020/08/21/computer-algorithm-caused-a-grading-crisis-in-british-schools.html

Shiri, R., El-Metwally, A., Sallinen, M., Pöyry, M., Härmä, M., & Toppinen-Tanner, S. (2023). The Role of Continuing Professional Training or Development in Maintaining Current Employment: A Systematic Review. *Health Care*, *11*(21), 1–17. DOI: 10.3390/healthcare11212900 PMID: 37958044

Singh, T. M., Reddy, C. K. K., Murthy, B. V. R., Nag, A., & Doss, S. (2025). AI and Education: Bridging the Gap to Personalized, Efficient, and Accessible Learning. In *Advances in Educational Technologies and Instructional Design* (pp. 131-160). IGI Global. DOI: 10.4018/979-8-3693-8151-9.ch005

Soomro, S. A., Casakin, H., Nanjappan, V., & Georgiev, G. V. (2023). Makerspaces Fostering Creativity: A Systematic Literature Review. *Journal of Science Education and Technology*, *32*(4), 530–548. DOI: 10.1007/s10956-023-10041-4

Soori, M., Jough, F. K. G., Dastres, R., & Arezoo, B. (2024). Robotical Automation in CNC Machine Tools: A Review. *Acta Mechanica et Automatica*, *18*(3), 434–450. DOI: 10.2478/ama-2024-0048

Southworth, J., Migliaccio, K., Glover, J., Glover, J. N., Reed, D., McCarty, C., Brendemuhl, J., & Thomas, A. (2023). Developing a Model for AI Across the Curriculum: Transforming the Higher Education Landscape via Innovation in AI Literacy. *Computers and Education: Artificial Intelligence*, *4*, 1–10. DOI: 10.1016/j.caeai.2023.100127

Stivers, S. (2018). AI and Bias in University Admissions. *ISM Insights*. https://www.ism.edu/ism-insights/ai-and-bias-in-university-admissions-3.html

Stolpe, K., & Hallström, J. (2024). Artificial Intelligence Literacy for Technology Education. *Computers and Education Open*, *6*, 1–8. DOI: 10.1016/j.caeo.2024.100159

Tarafdar, S., Afroz, S., & Ashrafuzzaman, M. (2025). Artificial Intelligence and the Future of Education in Bangladesh. In *Advances in Educational Technologies and Instructional Design* (pp. 287-320). IGI Global. DOI: 10.4018/979-8-3693-7949-3.ch011

TESDA. (2010). The Dual Training System in the Philippines. https://tesda.gov.ph/about/tesda/91

UNESCO. (2023a). CENTURY, An AI-Powered Teaching and Learning Platform. https://www.unesco.org/en/articles/century-ai-powered-teaching-and-learning-platform

UNESCO (Ed.). (2023b). *Technology in Education: A Case Study on Singapore.*, DOI: 10.54676/HOOV5879

UNESCO. (2024). How Generative AI is Reshaping Education in Asia-Pacific. https://www.unesco.org/en/articles/how-generative-ai-reshaping-education-asia-pacific

Varsik, S., & Vosberg, L. (2024). *The Potential Impact of Artificial Intelligence on Equity and Inclusion in Education.* OECD Artificial Intelligence Papers., DOI: 10.1787/15df715b-

Walter, Y. (2024). Embracing the Future of Artificial Intelligence in the Classroom: The Relevance of Ai Literacy, Prompt Engineering, and Critical Thinking in Modern Education. *International Journal of Educational Technology in Higher Education, 21*(1), 1–29. DOI: 10.1186/s41239-024-00448-3

Weld Australia. (2025). Soldamatic Augmented Reality Welding Simulators. *Weld Australia.* https://weldaustralia.com.au/welding-technology/soldamatic-augmented-reality-welding-simulators/

Windelband, L. (2023). *Artificial Intelligence and Assistance Systems for Technical Vocational Education and Training – Opportunities and Risks.* Springer International Publishing., DOI: 10.1007/978-3-031-26490-0_12

Xiao, J., Bozkurt, A., Nichols, M., Pazurek, A., Stracke, C. M., Bai, J. Y. H., Farrow, R., Mulligan, D., Nerantzi, C., Sharma, R. C., Singh, L., Frumin, I., Swindell, A., Honeychurch, S., Bond, M., Dron, J., Moore, S., Leng, J., & Slagter van Tryon, P. J.. (2025). Venturing into the Unknown: Critical Insights into Grey Areas and Pioneering Future Directions in Educational Generative AI Research. *TechTrends*, ●●●, 1–16. DOI: 10.1007/s11528-025-01060-6

Yangambi, M. (2023). Impact of School Infrastructures on Students Learning and Performance: Case of Three Public Schools in a Developing Country. *Creative Education, 14*(04), 788–809. DOI: 10.4236/ce.2023.144052

Zirar, A., Ali, S. I., & Islam, N. (2023). Worker and Workplace Artificial Intelligence (AI) Coexistence: Emerging Themes and Research Agenda. *Technovation, 124*, 1–17. DOI: 10.1016/j.technovation.2023.102747

KEY TERMS AND DEFINITIONS

AI Integration: The process of incorporating artificial intelligence into educational environments, particularly in technical education, to enhance learning, automate tasks, and improve efficiency in skill development and assessment.

Artificial Intelligence: The field of computer science that enables machines to perform tasks that typically require human intelligence, such as problem-solving, decision-making, and pattern recognition, with applications in education, automation, and workforce training.

School Infrastructure: The physical and digital resources in educational institutions, including classrooms, laboratories, internet connectivity, and AI-powered tools, which support the effective implementation of AI-driven technical education.

Technical Education: A branch of education focused on equipping students with practical and industry-specific skills in areas such as engineering, information technology, and applied sciences, preparing them for specialized careers.

Technical Knowledge: The specialized understanding and expertise required to operate, troubleshoot, and innovate within technical fields, including familiarity with AI-driven tools, programming, and machine learning applications in various industries.

Technicians: Skilled professionals who apply technical knowledge to install, maintain, and repair systems and machinery, including AI-powered technologies, ensuring their effective operation across industries.

Workforce Readiness: The preparedness of graduates and trainees to enter the labor market with the necessary technical knowledge, problem-solving skills, and adaptability to emerging AI-driven technologies in their respective fields.

Section 3
Ethical, Legal, and Social Implications

Chapter 10
Technoethics and the Use of Artificial Intelligence in Educational Contexts:
Reflections on Integrity, Transparency, and Equity

Sonia Martínez-Requejo
https://orcid.org/0000-0001-6934-2664
Universidad Europea de Madrid, Spain

Sara Redondo-Duarte
https://orcid.org/0000-0003-2012-8784
Universidad Complutense de Madrid, Spain

Eva Jiménez-García
https://orcid.org/0000-0001-6541-3517
Universidad Europea de Madrid, Spain

Judit Ruiz-Lázaro
https://orcid.org/0000-0003-2036-0428
Universidad Nacional de Educación a Distancia, Spain

ABSTRACT

As emerging technologies, such as artificial intelligence (AI), become increasingly integrated into academic contexts, new challenges and ethical risks related to potential misuse also emerge. This chapter examines these issues from an academic perspective by analyzing how each affects both education and research. Particular attention is given to concerns such as algorithmic bias, data privacy, authorship attribution, and the erosion of critical thinking in AI-assisted learning environments. The chapter also explores the implications of unequal access to AI tools, which may exacerbate existing educational disparities. Reflection on these issues is essential for fostering an academic culture based on integrity, transparency, and respect for diversity, which are fundamental to creating a fairer and more equitable educational environment. Ultimately, the chapter urges institutions to establish clear technoethical

DOI: 10.4018/979-8-3373-0122-8.ch010

guidelines, promote digital literacy, and engage stakeholders in open dialogue to ensure responsible and inclusive AI integration in education.

INTRODUCTION

The advent of emerging technologies such as artificial intelligence (hereinafter AI) has revolutionized multiple sectors, including education. These tools promise to increase the efficiency, personalization and accessibility of educational processes, but at the same time, they raise fundamental ethical concerns. These concerns include the risks associated with the misuse of AI, the possibility of algorithmic systems, and the challenges of maintaining academic integrity in an increasingly digitized environment.

These issues are not new, but their scale and impact have been magnified by the use of AI. Reflecting on the implications of these technologies is not only essential to address current problems, but also to anticipate future challenges in a constantly evolving environment (Schneider & Goddard, 2022). Building an educational culture based on ethical principles, such as transparency, fairness and equity, not only protects institutional credibility, but also fosters meaningful and sustainable learning.

Technoethics, particularly in relation to academic integrity and bias, constitutes a fundamental challenge in contemporary education, as it questions the ability of the academy to validate the learning outcomes and acquisition of competencies required for graduation. Although diverse in nature, these issues share a common denominator: they undermine the quality of learning, the fairness of assessment and the credibility of academic achievement (Cojocariu & Mares, 2021).

As emerging technologies, such as AI, become increasingly integrated into academic contexts, new challenges and ethical risks related to potential misuse also emerge. This chapter examines these issues from an academic perspective, analyzing the ways in which each affects both education and research, and proposing strategies to mitigate their adverse effects. Reflection on these issues is essential to fostering an academic culture based on integrity, transparency and respect for diversity, which are fundamental to a fairer and more equitable educational environment.

MAIN FOCUS OF THE CHAPTER

The objective of this chapter is to address the main issues raised by the emergence of AI in the educational field from a technoethical perspective as well as to offer some practical proposals that educational institutions may adopt for the ethical implementation of AI. To this end, the first section of the chapter explores the impact of AI on education from a techno-ethical perspective. Beyond merely preventing the misuse of technology, it delves into the importance of fostering a meaningful dialogue among various stakeholders. This section also examines the concept of academic integrity, its various dimensions, and its connection to technoethics. Secondly, ethical dilemmas and risks of using AI in education are discussed (bias and discrimination, privacy and data protection, lack of transparency and reliability, among others). Examples and recent research findings are provided to illustrate its impact on the educational field. Third, the chapter explores the fundamental principles that should guide the development and use of AI in education, highlighting the importance of establishing robust frameworks to ensure its responsible implementation, grounded in human values. Finally, the chapter presents practical proposals for the ethical implementation of AI in education, grounded in a holistic, pedagogical approach designed to empower all stakeholders to engage with AI in a critical and responsible manner.

BACKGROUND OF THE STUDY

The Impact of Artificial Intelligence on Education from a Techno-Ethical Perspective

Technoethics is a branch of applied ethics that focuses on the analysis and regulation of the moral implications of emerging technologies in society. According to Hamdani et al. (2024), technoethics promotes dialogue to determine the ethical use of technology, prevent misuse and establish shared principles to guide new developments. In the field of education, technoethics assumes a crucial role in providing guidance on the responsible and ethical use of advanced technologies, promoting a balanced integration between the benefits that these tools can offer and the risks they can pose if not properly managed (Garcia et al., 2024).

AI has the potential to radically transform the way learning is taught and assessed. From personalized tutoring systems to predictive analytics tools to identify students at risk of dropping out of school, AI is redefining traditional educational practices (Holmes et al., 2021). This change not only implies an improvement in the efficiency and effectiveness of learning but also opens new possibilities for tailoring education to the individual needs of each student.

In addition, the integration of AI in the classroom allows for a more student-centered approach, where educators can use analytical data to better understand how their students learn. For example, by using platforms that collect information on student performance and interactions, teachers can adjust their methodology and content, ensuring that each student receives the support they need to reach their full potential.

However, the impact of these technologies is not uniform. For example, personalization of algorithm-based learning can be highly beneficial for some students, while others may have limited access due to technological inequalities or biases in the data used to train these systems (Williamson and Eynon, 2020). This disparity can exacerbate existing gaps in the education system, creating an urgent need to develop inclusive solutions that ensure that all students benefit equally from technological advances.

This phenomenon raises important questions from a techno-ethical perspective:

- What level of autonomy should these tools have? The autonomy of AI-based tools must be carefully calibrated. While some decisions can be delegated to automated systems, it is crucial that educators maintain a central role in monitoring and interpreting the results obtained by these technologies.
- How to ensure the privacy and security of student data? Mass data collection raises serious privacy concerns. Institutions must implement robust policies to protect students' personal information and ensure that it is used only for educational and non-commercial purposes.
- Who should be held accountable for decisions made by algorithms? Ethical and legal accountability associated with automated decisions should be a priority issue. It is essential to establish clear regulatory frameworks that define responsibilities and protocols for potential errors or negative consequences arising from the use of these technologies.

The implementation of AI in education has significantly transformed - or, at the very least, challenged - the ways in which teaching and learning processes are managed and assessed. The concept of technoethics has evolved from a theoretical approach to an applied discipline that addresses practical issues. In an interconnected world, where emerging technologies impact almost every aspect of everyday life, educational institutions face a dilemma: how to maximize the benefits of these technologies while minimizing ethical and social risks.

Research has highlighted the need for an ethical approach to technology design. According to Floridi (2021), design ethics is based on the idea that technologies are not neutral; they are imbued with the values and decisions of those who create them. This principle has direct implications for education, where AI tools should be designed to reflect and promote fundamental educational values, such as equity and inclusion.

Furthermore, technoethics is not limited to preventing the misuse of technology. It also seeks to foster a dialogue between different stakeholders: developers, educators, students and policymakers. This inclusive approach allows for a broader understanding of the ethical and social implications of technologies and promotes more balanced and sustainable solutions (Luppicini et al., 2008; Grebenshchikova, 2016).

The Intersection of Technoethics and Academic Integrity

Technoethics is especially relevant in educational environments today due to the common use of digital technologies as a teaching and learning resource. In addition, with the democratization of access to large language models (LLM), the concern of teachers and regulators about the proper use of these tools by students increases, since they facilitate the almost automatic elaboration of academic works. This leads us to talk about academic integrity in order to define desirable techno ethical behaviors linked to a responsible use of AI resources.

Academic integrity is defined through a combination of honesty, trust, fairness, respect, responsibility, and courage (International Center for Academic Integrity, 2014). However, diverse perspectives exist regarding what constitutes academic integrity and how it should be promoted (Muñoz-Cantero et al., 2024; Davis, 2023). This diversity of views implies that while scholars agree on the importance of practicing academic integrity, there is no single consensus on what it is, how it should be taught, whether it can be taught, who is responsible for teaching it, and how to handle cases of misconduct (Löfström et al., 2015).

There are various perspectives on how to teach and promote academic integrity. Some scholars believe that it is the responsibility of teachers to instill these values in students, although there is no consensus on the most effective methods for doing so (Bornsztejn, 2022). A practical approach is presented by Parente and Roecklein-Canfield (2020), who outline strategies to foster academic integrity in the classroom based on best practices, such as understanding students' motivations for cheating, sharing real-life examples of unethical behavior, and identifying common strategies to mitigate cheating.

Establishing a culture of academic integrity is essential. Ilchenko (2024) suggests including educational sessions on the topic, setting clear guidelines, and promoting ethical collaboration among students. For Maslikova (2021), the development of academic integrity requires the awareness of all participants in the educational process, the articulation of key values and the implementation of values through joint scientific, educational, methodological, cultural and social acts.

Figure 1. Components of culture of academic integrity

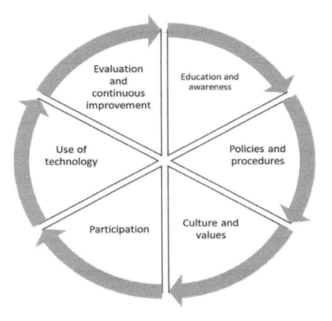

As can be seen in Figure 1, academic integrity is not an isolated concept, but the result of the interaction of different ethical dimensions and therefore a multidimensional construct. Evaluation and continuous improvement allow us to identify areas of opportunity and adjust strategies to maintain effective ethical practices. This is complemented by education and awareness-raising, which aims to build ethical awareness in students and teachers through workshops, campaigns and pedagogical activities.

Clear policies and procedures are essential to establish shared norms and manage infractions fairly, prioritizing learning over punitive punishment. Furthermore, this culture is underpinned by values that promote honesty as a fundamental principle, integrating these ideals into all educational practices. The active participation of all members of the community, from students to administrators, is crucial to building a collaborative and engaged environment.

Finally, the use of technology as a preventive and educational tool reinforces this culture, facilitating the detection of malpractice and fostering ethical digital literacy. It is only through a joint approach to these dimensions that an academic space governed by integrity can be consolidated.

ETHICAL DILEMMAS AND RISKS OF USING AI IN EDUCATION

The ethical risks posed by AI have captured the interest of governments, sparking profound discussions about the interaction between humans and technology. Thus, the European Union Parliament approved in 2023 the world's first law regulating the use of AI. Its purpose is *"to ensure that AI systems used in the EU are safe, transparent, traceable, non-discriminatory, and environmentally respectful."*

As stated in the previous section, educational institutions have among their responsibilities the task of establishing clear policies for the effective and ethical use of AI. In this context, the European Commission has also recognized the growing importance of AI in education and has developed multiple initiatives. In Spain, the Ministry of Education and Vocational Training (2021), in collaboration with other organizations, has established national policies within the Digitalization and Digital Competence Plan for the Education System to ensure the proper implementation of AI in the educational system.

In this context, many voices are calling for curriculum design to incorporate not only the professional applications of AI but also a critical exploration of its ethical, moral, and philosophical impacts on society (Shih et al., 2021). In this regard, several universities around the world have created specific guidelines for the use of AI, addressing key issues related to its ethical and responsible use.

There is growing concern in the academic field regarding the ethical implications of AI in education (Hasanah et al., 2025). While a substantial body of literature exists on the functionalities of generative AI, there remains a significant gap in understanding the perspectives and concerns of educators and students about its use (Seo et al., 2021). Sallam (2023), in a review of 60 articles on ChatGPT, identified a wide range of issues highlighted in the studies. These concerns, evident in 96.7% of the reviewed records, encompassed ethical considerations, copyright and transparency challenges, legal issues, risks of bias, plagiarism, and lack of originality. Additional concerns included inaccuracies that could lead to hallucination risks, limited knowledge, incorrect citations, cybersecurity threats, and the potential for infodemic proliferation.

A search in the Web of Science reveals the growing interest in the ethical aspects of using AI in educational contexts (see Figure 2 below). At the time of conducting the search (February 5, 2025), an increasing trend can be observed, especially during 2024, when the number of publications increased by 52.4%. The search query was the following: TITLEABS-KEY (AI* AND education* AND ethics*) AND PUBYEAR > 2015 AND PUBYEAR < 2024.

Figure 2. Papers indexed in the web of science (2020-2024) that contains the topics "AI" and "education" and "ethics".

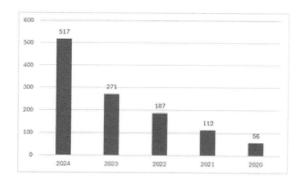

The main ethical concerns regarding the use of AI in educational settings are related to the following aspects: bias and discrimination (Kooli, 2023; Agudizel, 2023; Singer, 2021; Murphy, 2019); privacy and data protection (Seo et al., 2021; Huang, 2023); lack of transparency regarding how AI models function, which in turn affects the reliability of their responses (Murphy, 2019; Hasanein and Sobaih, 2023); misuse and abuse of AI (Loe, 2023; Wogu, 2018; Bai et al., 2023); intellectual property (Latham & Goltz, 2019, Irfan et al., 2023), and the dehumanization of the teaching-learning process (Saylam et al., 2023; Cope, 2020). These ethical risks are closely related to student learning, as the misuse of AI can impact the development of cross-curricular competencies and memory capacity, as will be discussed later.

Figure 3 summarizes the main ethical risks related to the use of AI in Education. The following sections discuss each of these aspects in detail.

Figure 3. Risks of AI in education.

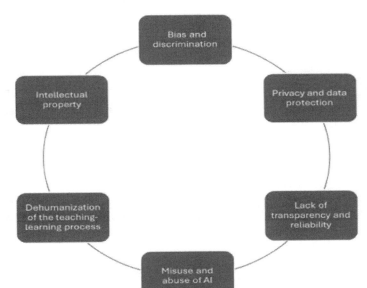

Bias and Discrimination

A key concern is that AI systems may reinforce existing biases and discrimination in research and education (Kooli, 2023; Agudizel, 2023; Singer, 2021; Murphi, 2019, Hasanein and Sobaih, 2023). Ntoutsi et al. (2020, p.4) reported different types of biases:

- Selection bias: certain individuals are more likely to be chosen for study, often manifesting as self-selection bias.
- Exclusion bias: reverse bias.
- Reporting bias: certain types of observations are more likely to be recorded, effectively creating a selection bias in the data itself.
- Detection bias: a phenomenon is more frequently observed in a specific group of subjects.

AI systems are trained on vast datasets that may contain biases related to gender, race, ethnicity, or socioeconomic status. As a result, algorithms can not only replicate but also exacerbate these inequalities and discriminatory practices (Ntoutsi et al., 2020; Li et al., 2023; Singer, 2018). This suggests that if certain student groups are overrepresented or underrepresented in the datasets used to train these systems, or if they are unfairly associated with a higher likelihood of school dropout due to structural inequalities or prevailing societal prejudices, the algorithms may perpetuate these biases (Murphy, 2019). For example, an automated assessment system trained on biased data might consistently assign lower grades to students from certain demographic groups, perpetuating discrimination and exclusion.

In the context of higher education, Li et al. (2023) highlight that, in addition to biases related to gender, sexuality, race, and religion, biases based on nationality also contribute to stereotypes and discrimination against certain students. In the case of international students and teachers, these biases can result in their marginalization and hinder their academic and social integration.

To prevent these algorithmic biases, technoethics has a key role to play. There is a need for AI developers to conduct regular audits of systems to detect and mitigate biases, thus ensuring equal opportunities for all students.

On the other hand, limited access to AI may create gaps and imbalances among students, as paid versions offer enhanced features (faster responses, more up-to-date data, or broader information). Likewise, disparities may also exist in terms of students' level of digital literacy. The role of the teacher is essential not only to prevent the development of biases but also to ensure that unequal access to AI does not advantage some students over others (Pattier & Redondo-Duarte, 2025).

Privacy and Data Protection

With the development of AI, risks of privacy violations and data breaches arise, posing serious threats to the security of students' personal information. Huang et al. (2023) highlight several risks, including privacy breaches and threats associated with data leaks, such as the unauthorized disclosure of personal information through secondary exploitation of students' private data, as well as fraud stemming from data trafficking.

Seo et al. (2021) conducted a study on the use of AI in virtual learning environments with university students. The results revealed that students appreciated the personalized support and immediate communication provided by AI. However, they also expressed concerns regarding surveillance and privacy issues related to the indiscriminate analysis of their data. Specifically, students reported feeling uncomfortable with the measurement of their unconscious behavior, such as eye tracking or facial expression analysis. In this regard, the European Union Artificial Intelligence Act (AI Act, 2023) classifies real-time and remote biometric identification systems, such as facial recognition, as presenting an unacceptable risk. This means that such technologies are subject to strict prohibitions due to the significant threats they pose to individuals' privacy and fundamental rights.

A study conducted at the University of Limerick found that students from schools focused on technology and science exhibited greater concern, indicating a more thorough understanding of the potential privacy implications (Irfan et al., 2023). On the other hand, the study conducted by Latham & Goltz (2019), through a survey at a national science festival event, found that most participants considered AI tools to be beneficial for learning, with 94% believing they could enhance their own educational experience. However, there is a significant difference between minors and adults in terms of automatic tracking by learning systems, with 63% of minors (all aged 5–10) expressing discomfort with being tracked, compared to just 8% of adults.

These studies show that AI raises significant privacy issues within the educational context, where factors such as age, and the sensitive nature of personal information are at stake. In this context, it is crucial for students to be aware of the importance of safeguarding their privacy by avoiding the sharing of personal data and, under no circumstances, disclosing confidential information, third-party data, or content protected by copyright.

Lack of Transparency and Reliability

Generative AI tools have significant limitations, as they can sometimes produce convincing yet entirely false information, which can lead to misinformation and cause confusion among students. In this regard, Lo's (2023) research highlighted several operational issues of ChatGPT concerning the reliability of information. Notably, these include the generation of incorrect or fabricated information, such as the creation of non-existent articles, along with providing complete bibliographic details, including non-functional URLs.

The study conducted by Seo et al. (2021), which involved university students enrolled in virtual degree programs, revealed that students were concerned about the potential unreliability of AI-generated responses. They feared that such inaccuracies could negatively affect their grades, potentially leading to conflicts between students and professors. Hasanein & Sobaih (2023) also highlight concerns related to reliability, the use of inaccurate or fabricated content (including false citations), and the timeliness of information, as seen with ChatGPT, whose data is currently limited to October 2023. Other issues that generative AI tools may pose is the lack of specialized knowledge in certain areas, insufficient evidence to support responses, the uncritical acceptance of all answers as accurate, and significant variations in the quality of results depending on the field of knowledge.

The complex algorithms driving these tools are often seen as opaque and difficult to grasp, emphasizing the need for both teachers and students to understand them. Burrell (2016) noted that when algorithmic systems are not easy to understand, especially in sensitive areas of education, they can lead to disbelief and resistance. Major regulatory efforts are being made in this regard. It is worth highlighting the EU Artificial Intelligence Act (AI Act, 2023), that will help ensure that certain AI systems classified as "high risk" are developed by vendors according to mandatory requirements to mitigate such risks and ensure their reliability (European Commission, 2022).

Thus, enhancing transparency regarding the operational model of AI is becoming increasingly essential in educational institutions. This is not only critical for fostering students' trust (Murphy, 2019) but also for preventing the development of environments that perpetuate dominant modes of thinking, which could ultimately hinder inclusivity (Redondo-Duarte et al., 2024).

Misuses and Abuse of AI

Another concern among educators is the use of AI to cheat on assessments and exams (Lo, 2023). If instructors are unable to identify that a student has used AI to generate responses, it may devalue the efforts of other students who completed their work honestly (Adiguzel et al., 2023). This, in turn, could exacerbate inequality within the educational system. On the other hand, AI can be used to generate similar or copied content, raising concerns about plagiarism and copyright infringement (Obaid et al., 2023).

The debate surrounding the use of generative AI has also extended to the academic and scientific fields, where a study revealed the difficulty of detecting plagiarism. In this sense, Thorp (2023) mentions a study in which abstracts were created by ChatGPT and presented to academic reviewers, who only detected 68% of these falsifications. The results of research conducted by Khalil and Er (2023, p.10) showed that: "Of the 50 essays inspected, the plagiarism-detection software considered 40 of them with a high level of originality, as evidenced by a similarity score of 20% or less".

Another key issue in the use of AI is the dependency it generates among young people. Wogu et al. (2018) highlight the dangers associated with students becoming entirely dependent on technology for their daily activities. This dependency is further compounded by the risks of using generative AIs, such as ChatGPT, which may hinder the development of essential 21st-century competencies, including critical thinking, analysis, creativity and problem-solving skills (Putra, 2023; Redondo-Duarte et al., 2024; Hasanein & Sobaih, 2023; Wogu, 2018).

An excessive reliance on these technologies could lead to a decline in intrinsic motivation for learning and a progressive deterioration of memory capabilities (Bai et al., 2023). Furthermore, AI might limit students' opportunities for exploration and discovery-based learning (Seo et al., 2021), constrain the development of social and collaborative skills, as well as hinder deeper learning (Redondo-Duarte et al., 2024). It is important to raise students' awareness of the dangers of relying solely on AI in their learning process. They should know how to use other methods to have greater control over the learning process and understand the differences in outcomes between one approach and another.

In this context, AI literacy emerges as an extension of digital or ICT literacy, yet the diverse possibilities, risks, and ethical challenges associated with AI require a distinct set of skills and critical faculties that go beyond basic technological literacy (Farrelly et al., 2023). In this sense, the development of critical thinking is particularly crucial for students, as it enables them to discern between truthful information and misinformation (Rusandi et al., 2023; Redondo-Duarte, 2023).

Intellectual Property

Closely linked to the use and misuse of AI is the issue of intellectual property. Students risk committing plagiarism if they directly use texts produced by ChatGPT, which may themselves contain exact reproductions of copyrighted materials. Thus, it is essential for educators to understand the limitations of these tools and engage students in a critical analysis of the texts they generate, evaluating their accuracy, language appropriateness, and overall quality. Additionally, students must recognize that copying or plagiarizing AI-generated responses is neither ethical nor beneficial to their learning process.

Therefore, teachers must implement strategies to raise students' awareness about plagiarism and actively work to prevent it. For example, they can establish clear guidelines for the use of GPT, along with proper citation and attribution for any GPT generated content; require students to submit drafts of their work for review before submitting the final version; asking students to present their work in class; or utilize plagiarism detection tools (Cotton et al., 2023). Teachers can also require citations and bibliographic references in students' work and verify their accuracy and relevance, as they may be incorrect or even fabricated.

Dehumanization of the Teaching-Learning Process

The use of AI in education is growing at a rapid pace, to the point that many educators are concerned that, as the use and impact of AI in education continue to expand in the future, these systems may reduce their role or even replace them.

The role of educators is likely to expand and adapt in response to the advancements brought by AI innovations in education. However, this requires diligent governance of AI development and application, with a strong focus on preserving teachers' agency and decision-making power (European Commission, 2022). In this regard, it is essential to consider the limitations of AI in the teaching-learning process. One key aspect is empathy: Can AI truly connect with students on an emotional level? While AI can monitor student performance and provide recommendations for improving learning, it cannot replace a teacher's ability to interpret students' emotions (Saylam et al., 2023; Cope et al., 2020).

Over 25 years ago, Nissenbaum & Walker (1998, p.244) raised concerns about computer-mediated instruction, stating: "Education involves imparting not only the accumulated knowledge and know-how, but also the customs, attitudes, world views, and wisdom, that constitute a human community". The dangers we face now with AI are undoubtedly different from those identified by these authors in their article, yet the situation is fundamentally the same. We are witnessing a major revolution in the teaching-learning process that impacts many stages of education, and there are significant questions that each of us must address: As teachers, do we fully understand the potential and risks of AI? Will we integrate it into our teaching, or will we pretend it doesn't exist? How will we encourage our students to use AI responsibly?

In the conclusion of their article, Nissenbaum & Walker (1998, p. 269) stated: "We know that many find the technology difficult, frustrating, distasteful, and possibly dangerous, but we hope, for society's sake, that most educators will nevertheless choose engagement". It is therefore essential for educators to engage in deep reflection on the role of education in preparing students for a constantly changing world, where interaction with AI will become a routine aspect of everyday life.

PRINCIPLES FOR THE ETHICAL USE OF AI IN EDUCATION

AI is reinventing education, personalizing instruction, identifying areas for improvement in real time, and providing new opportunities to support students and teachers. However, as highlighted in the previous section, AI presents a range of ethical challenges that necessitate a robust framework to ensure its responsible implementation, grounded in human values.

To address these concerns, it is necessary to revisit the fundamental principles that should guide both the development and use of AI in education (fairness and equity, autonomy, transparency and explainability, shared responsibility). The ethical introduction of AI in education requires that each of these principles be addressed at the same time (Ersoy, 2025; Öztürk et al., 2025), thus preventing technical innovation from leading to technical innovation from making equality less visible, respect for individuals and the sustainability of learning (Mangubat et al., 2025).

Justice and Equity

The adoption of AI in education must be founded on the principle of equity, ensuring that all students, regardless of socioeconomic background, gender, ethnicity, or ability, can benefit from its advantages. However, as discussed in the previous section, some studies have evidenced that algorithms may unintentionally maintain existing biases if they are not formulated meticulously. In this context, Crawford and Calo (2016) support their view and point out that AI systems may inadvertently discriminate by relying on historically biased data, which could exclude certain groups of students in educational settings.

To counter this issue, the application of ethics during AI development will be critical and could range from data selection to the design of models that reduce the likelihood of perpetuating inequalities (Taneja et al., 2025). According to Holmes et al. (2019), monitoring and auditing of systems are important to avoid biased algorithmic decisions. In addition, UNESCO (2023) cites the importance of implementing public policies that guarantee access to technology in order to close the digital divide from its inception in places with such gaps.

The principles of justice and equity should be reflected in AI systems providing fair opportunities for all students, regardless of their background, and preventing the reproduction of inequalities. To ensure that AI contributes positively to learning environments without exacerbating inequalities or infringing on rights, practical and actionable strategies must be implemented (Chen, 2024).

Autonomy

Respect for student autonomy is another principle underpinning the ethical use of AI in education. This requires developing technological strategies that foster students' ability to make informed decisions and develop critical thinking skills rather than replacing their judgment. This occurrence is supported by Floridi et al. (2018) in noting that AI systems should conform to human values, boosting self-determination and allowing students to learn at their own pace or according to their own interests.

However, there is a possibility that teaching will fall short of intellectual exploration and impede the development of creative or problem-solving skills (Selwyn, 2019). Therefore, AI systems must be designed to strike an appropriate balance between guiding students' direction, but at the same time enabling them to have the ability for open-ended exploration. Balance that in turn encourages independence and self-directed learning.

AI-based tools such as Canva or WriteSonic can assist students in creating their own materials, as well as AI tutors (for instance, IBM's Watson Tutor) can offer explanations and guide the students through complex subjects. However, the question here is to what extent these systems offer a representation of knowledge that is determined by the AI itself. To what extent do these AI-based systems and tools enable learners to construct their own knowledge? What pedagogical models support the design of these tools? (Pattier & Redondo-Duarte, 2025).

Transparency and Explainability

Rudin (2019) argues that creating understandable models is critical to ensure that AI decisions are not only understandable, but also equitable and fair. Dignum (2019) emphasizes that the ability to understand how AI systems make decisions can not only increase AI adoption but also improve users' digital literacy and critical thinking skills.

In the educational context, transparency in the use of AI means that those responsible explain how AI is used. By implementing methods to clarify AI decisions, education stakeholders can better understand the underlying processes and intervene when necessary. For instance, in the creation of educational materials, in the assessment of academic performance, in monitoring progress, and in the types of decisions made based on information provided by AI. Furthermore, the entire educational community should be informed about how data is collected, utilized, and protected.

From a technoethical perspective, educational institutions should implement clear policies on the appropriate use of AI-based tools, setting firm limits on when and how these technologies can be used to support - but not replace - students' academic work. In this regard, universities in Spain, such as the European University (2024) and the University of Barcelona (Franganillo et al., 2023), have published guidelines aimed at rethinking assessment methods considering the degree of AI integration in academic work. These reference documents outline different assessment scenarios depending on the permissibility of the use of AI to prevent cases of academic dishonesty.

When institutions establish clear operational parameters, it becomes significantly easier for all stakeholders, including educators and students, to demonstrate the integrity of their work. Figure 4 below shows an example of assessment scenarios using or not AI.

Figure 4. Example of assessment scenarios. Adapted from Universidad Europea (2024).

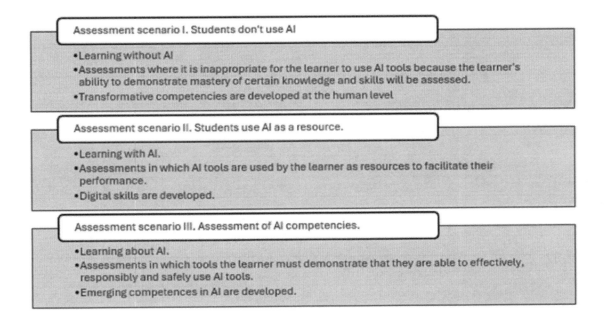

Shared Responsibility

The ethical application of AI in education cannot be done by one party alone. It requires a joint effort of developers, teachers, educational administrators and policy makers to ensure the correct use of the technology and its alignment with pedagogical purposes and ethical values. In this sense, Heidari et al. (2019) proposes an ethical governance approach that bets on a multi-stakeholder type approach in which each of the groups can play an active role in monitoring and improving the systems.

In the field of education, this implies that students should have access to flexible and transparent tools, while educators should be trained to understand their functioning and monitor their use. Within the framework of the Digital Education Action Plan (2021-2027) (European Commission, 2020), Measure 6 is entitled Ethical Guidelines on the Use of AI and Data in Teaching and Learning for Educators. These guidelines are designed to help primary and secondary school teachers understand the potential that the applications of AI and data usage can have in education and to raise awareness of the possible risks (European Commission, 2022).

Some of the key topics addressed include planning for the effective use of AI and data in schools, raising awareness and fostering engagement within the educational community, and developing emerging competencies for AI and data usage. Additionally, the document presents a series of guiding questions to encourage reflection among educational stakeholders, focusing on the following dimensions (European Commission, 2024):

- Human agency and oversight
- Transparency
- Diversity, non-discrimination, and equity
- Social and environmental well-being
- Privacy and data governance
- Technical robustness and safety
- Accountability

The measures also address common misconceptions about AI, such as: *AI is too difficult to understand, AI has no role in education, AI is not inclusive, AI systems cannot be trusted, or AI will undermine the role of the teacher.*

Thus, educational institutions will need to establish clear regulatory frameworks and specific training programs to ensure that all stakeholders understand both the risks and benefits of AI (Lazăr et al., 2024).

PRACTICAL PROPOSALS FOR ETHICAL AI IMPLEMENTATION IN EDUCATION

Once the main ethical dilemmas in the use of AI in educational contexts and the principles that should guide its ethical use have been discussed, practical proposals for its implementation are presented. Thus, this section outlines four core areas essential for achieving this goal: teacher training, evaluation of AI tools, policy and regulation development, and involving students in ethical discussions. These proposals are rooted in a holistic, pedagogical approach aimed at equipping all stakeholders to engage with AI critically and responsibly.

Teacher Training: Equipping Educators for Ethical AI Oversight

Teachers play a pivotal role in mediating the integration of AI into educational processes. Their ability to oversee, evaluate, and utilize AI tools effectively depends on comprehensive and continuous training that prioritizes ethics (Xiao et al., 2025). AI systems often function as "black boxes," making decisions based on complex algorithms that are opaque to end-users. Without proper training, educators may unknowingly implement tools that reinforce biases or compromise students' privacy. Ethical training empowers teachers to question AI outputs, as Varsik & Vosberg (2024) recognize potential ethical pitfalls, and ensure that AI aligns with pedagogical objectives and institutional values. Training should cover several critical areas, as shown in Table 1.

Table 1. Critical areas and objectives for teacher training in AI.

Critical areas	Objectives
Understanding AI fundamentals	To acquire a working knowledge of how AI operates, including its capabilities, limitations, and common biases.
Recognizing ethical issues	To identify biases in AI tools, understanding data privacy concerns, and evaluating the inclusivity of AI-driven approaches.
Developing oversight skills	To critically assess AI recommendations, cross-check them against traditional methods, and identify anomalies or inaccuracies.
Fostering a growth mindset	To consider AI as a tool to complement, rather than replace, teacher's expertise.

Institutions should offer flexible, accessible professional development opportunities through workshops, online courses, and peer learning communities. Moreover, embedding AI ethics training into teacher education programs ensures that new educators enter the profession equipped to navigate these challenges.

Evaluation of AI tools: Setting Standards for Ethical Adoption

Selecting AI tools for educational use requires rigorous evaluation to ensure they align with ethical principles and meet quality standards. Institutions must adopt a multi-dimensional framework for evaluating AI tools, considering questions such as those presented in Table 2.

Table 2. Ethical dimensions and evaluation questions for selecting AI tools.

Ethical Dimensions	Evaluation Questions
Transparency	• Does the tool provide clear information about how decisions are made? • Are the algorithms interpretable and accountable?
Bias mitigation	• Does the tool include mechanisms to detect and counteract bias in data and decision-making processes?
Privacy and security	• How does the tool safeguard student data? • Are its privacy practices compliant with local and international regulations?
Educational value	• Does the tool support diverse learning styles and needs? Does it enhance teaching and learning rather than create dependencies? (Holmes et al., 2019).

Institutions should establish committees that include educators, technologists, ethicists, and students to assess AI tools collaboratively. These committees should develop standardized evaluation protocols and provide ongoing support for monitoring the impact of adopted tools. Educational institutions can rely on third-party certifications to identify tools that meet ethical and technical standards. For example, the study of Cukurova et al. (2024) states that partnerships with organizations specializing in AI ethics can streamline the vetting process and ensure compliance with global benchmarks.

Policy and Regulation Development: Establishing Ethical Frameworks

The implementation of AI in education must be underpinned by robust policies that prioritize ethical considerations. Institutions have a responsibility to establish clear guidelines that govern AI usage. Effective AI policies should include:

- **Privacy standards**: Clear protocols for data collection, storage, and sharing to protect student and teacher privacy.
- **Transparency requirements**: Mandates for AI providers to disclose decision-making processes, biases, and limitations.
- **Accountability mechanisms**: Protocols for addressing grievances related to AI misuse or errors.
- **Inclusivity measures**: Strategies to ensure AI tools are accessible to diverse learners, including those with disabilities or from marginalized communities (UNESCO, 2023).

Developing comprehensive AI policies requires collaboration across institutional levels. Administrators, educators, students, and IT professionals should contribute to policy formulation to ensure it reflects diverse perspectives and needs. Institutions should align their policies with national regulations and international frameworks, such as UNESCO's guidelines on AI ethics in education. This alignment ensures consistency and promotes global best practices.

Involving Students in Ethical Discussions: The Critical Understanding

AI's integration into education directly affects students, making their involvement in ethical discussions crucial. Engaging students fosters critical thinking and prepares them to navigate AI's broader societal implications.

Institutions should incorporate AI ethics into curricula to help students understand: (a) how AI systems operate and influence decision-making, (b) the societal and ethical implications of AI, including issues of bias, fairness, and privacy, (c) the potential benefits and risks of AI in education and beyond.

Moreover, students should be active participants in exploring AI ethics through: (a) debates and discussions (facilitating classroom debates on real-world AI dilemmas fosters diverse perspectives and critical analysis), case studies (analyzing cases where AI has succeeded or failed ethically can provide concrete learning opportunities), (c) Project-Based Learning (students could design AI-driven projects with an ethical framework, applying their knowledge in practical ways). Involving students in discussions about AI ethics also nurtures digital citizenship. Students learn to advocate for their rights, challenge unethical practices, and contribute to shaping AI's future.

CONCLUSION

The increasing use of AI in all aspects of life highlights the need not only to understand its broad applications and benefits but also to recognize its limitations, biases, data privacy risks, and potential for misuse, such as plagiarism. While AI has immense potential to personalize learning, enhance educational efficiency, and facilitate access to knowledge, these advantages must be carefully balanced with ethical considerations such as fairness, transparency, and academic integrity (Abimbola et al., 2024). It is equally important to address the risks associated with AI, such as the perpetuation of bias, over-reliance on technology, and the dehumanization of the educational process (Putra et al., 2023; Redondo-Duarte et al., 2024).

It is therefore essential to establish policy frameworks for the ethical use of AI in education, combining a multidisciplinary approach with guidelines for ethical practices that ensure and promote student learning (Holmes et al., 2021). Such frameworks must ensure transparency of algorithms, data privacy and accountability in automated decision-making (Floridi, 2021; Rudin, 2019). This normative basis not only protects students and educators, but also reinforces trust in educational institutions, ensuring the credibility of the entire system (Chaudhry et al., 2022).

The ethical application of AI in education requires a concerted effort in multiple domains. On the one hand, teacher training empowers teachers to manage AI tools responsibly, while rigorous evaluation ensures that these tools meet ethical and educational standards (Varsik & Vosberg, 2024). On the other hand, engaging students in discussions about AI ethics is equally important. Comprehensive policies should not only structure the secure and inclusive use of AI but also involve students in ethical conversations, helping them develop critical thinking skills and preparing them to navigate a technology-driven world (Rusandi et al., 2023; Farrelly & Baker, 2023).

By implementing these practical approaches, educational institutions can ensure that AI enriches learning environments while upholding ethical principles. This involves not only developing inclusive technological tools that respect core educational values but also implementing sustainable and equitable solutions (Luppicini & Adell, 2008; UNESCO, 2023). A balanced approach that integrates AI literacy and ethical considerations is crucial to ensuring fair access and beneficial outcomes for all learners (Farrelly et al., 2023).

To achieve this, educational institutions must adopt clear policies and proactive strategies, ensuring that AI serves as a tool to support, rather than replace, core educational processes (UNESCO, 2023). This includes not only training educators in the effective and ethical use of AI, but also fostering ongoing dialogue among technology developers, educators, parents and students to create an inclusive and equitable educational environment. Ultimately, the future of education will depend not only on technological advancement, but also on our collective commitment to leveraging these tools for the common good.

REFERENCES

Abimbola, C., Eden, C., Chisom, O., & Adeniyi, I. (2024). Integrating AI in education: Opportunities, challenges, and ethical considerations. *Magna Scientia Advanced Research and Reviews, 10*(02), 006–013. https://doi.org/.DOI: 10.30574/msarr.2024.10.2.0039

Adiguzel, T., Kaya, M., & Cansu, F. (2023). Revolutionizing education with AI: Exploring the transformative potential of ChatGPT. *Contemporary Educational Technology, 15*(3), ep429. Advance online publication. DOI: 10.30935/cedtech/13152

Bai, L., Liu, X., & Su, J. (2023). ChatGPT: The cognitive effects on learning and memory. *Brain-X, 1*(3), e30. DOI: 10.1002/brx2.30

Bornsztejn, H. (2022). Do academic integrity policies within foundation studies programmes adopt an educative perspective for supporting students? *Journal of Higher Education Policy and Management, 44*(5), 428–442. DOI: 10.1080/1360080X.2022.2112272

Burrell, J. (2016). How the machine "thinks2: Understanding opacity in machine learning algorithms. *Big Data & Society, 3*(1), 1–12. DOI: 10.1177/2053951715622512

Chaudhry, M., Cukurova, M., & Luckin, R. (2022). Un marco de índice de transparencia para la IA en la educación. *ArXiv*, abs/2206.03220. https://doi.org//arXiv.2206.03220DOI: 10.48550

Chen, H. (2024). The ethical challenges of educational artificial intelligence and coping measures: A discussion in the context of the 2024 World Digital Education Conference. *Science Insights Education Frontiers, 20*(2), 3263-3281. https://doi.org/DOI: 10.15354/sief.24.re339

Cojocariu, V. M., & Mareş, G. (2022). Academic Integrity in the Technology-Driven Education Era. In: Mâ ă, L. (eds) *Ethical Use of Information Technology in Higher Education*. EAI/Springer Innovations in Communication and Computing. Springer. https://doi.org/DOI: 10.1007/978-981-16-1951-9_1

Cope, B., Kalantzis, M., & Searsmith, D. (2020). Artificial intelligence for education: Knowledge and its assessment in AI-enabled learning ecologies. *Educational Philosophy and Theory, 53*(12), 1229–1245. DOI: 10.1080/00131857.2020.1728732

Cotton, D. R., Cotton, P. A., & Shipway, J. R. (2024). Chatting and cheating: Ensuring academic integrity in the era of ChatGPT. *Innovations in Education and Teaching International, 61*(2), 228–239. DOI: 10.1080/14703297.2023.2190148

Crawford, K., & Calo, R. (2016). There is a blind spot in AI research. *Nature, 538*(7625), 311–313. DOI: 10.1038/538311a PMID: 27762391

Cukurova, M., Kralj, L., Hertz, B., & Saltidou, E. (2024). *Professional Development for Teachers in the Age of AI*. European Schoolnet Academy Thematic Seminar Report. Retrieved November 20, 2024 from: http://www.eun.org/documents/411753/11183389/EUNA-Thematic-Seminar-Report-V5.pdf/b16bf795-b147-43ac-9f58-4dd1249b5e48

Davis, A. (2023). Academic integrity in the time of contradictions. *Cogent Education, 10*(2), 2289307. Advance online publication. DOI: 10.1080/2331186X.2023.2289307

Duarte, R. Sara (2023). Oportunidades y desafíos del uso de Chat GPT en educación superior. *Aula Magna 2.0* [Blog]. https://cuedespyd.hypotheses.org/14349

Ersoy, C. (2025). Inclusive Transformation with Artificial Intelligence: Ethical Aspects, Policies, and Strategic Approaches for Equitable Education. In *Pitfalls of AI Integration in Education: Skill Obsolescence, Misuse, and Bias.* IGI Global., DOI: 10.4018/979-8-3373-0122-8.ch012

European Commission. (2020). *Digital Education Action Plan (2021-2027).* Retrieved November 25, 2024 from https://ec.europa.eu/education/education-in-the-eu/digital-education-action-plan_en

European Commission. Directorate-General for Education, Youth, Sport and Culture (2022). Ethical guidelines on the use of artificial intelligence (AI) and data in teaching and learning for educators. Publications Office of the European Union. https://data.europa.eu/doi/10.2766/153756

European Commission. (2024). Scenarios for the future of school education in the EU: A Foresight Study. Brussels: Publications Office of the European Union. Retrieved November 25, 2024 from https://www.vleva.eu/storage/1016/scenarios-for-the-future-of-school-education-in-the-NC0523475ENN.pdf

European Parliament. (2023). *Ley de IA de la UE: primera normativa sobre inteligencia artificial.* Temas. Retrieved November 25, 2024 from https://www.europarl.europa.eu/topics/es/article/20230601STO93804/ley-de-ia-de-la-ue-primera-normativa-sobre-inteligencia-artificial

Farrelly, T., & Baker, N. (2023). Generative Artificial Intelligence: Implications and Considerations for Higher Education Practice. *Education Sciences*, *13*(11), 1109. DOI: 10.3390/educsci13111109

Floridi, L. (2021). Establishing the Rules for Building Trustworthy AI. In Floridi, L. (Ed.), Philosophical Studies Series: Vol. 144. *Ethics, Governance, and Policies in Artificial Intelligence.* Springer., DOI: 10.1007/978-3-030-81907-1_4

Floridi, L., Cowls, J., Beltrametti, M., Chatila, R., Chazerand, P., Dignum, V., Luetge, C., Madelin, R., Pagallo, U., Rossi, F., Schafer, B., Valcke, P., & Vayena, E. (2018). AI4People—An ethical framework for a good AI society: Opportunities, risks, principles, and recommendations. *Minds and Machines*, *28*(4), 689–707. DOI: 10.1007/s11023-018-9482-5 PMID: 30930541

Franganillo, J., Lopezosa, C., & Salse, M. (2023). *La inteligencia artificial generativa en la docencia universitaria.* Col·lecció del CRICC. Universitat de Barcelona. http://hdl.handle.net/2445/202932

Gao, C. A., Howard, F. M., Markov, N. S., Dyer, E. C., Ramesh, S., Luo, Y., & Pearson, A. T. (2022). Comparing scientific abstracts generated by ChatGPT to original abstracts using an artificial intelligence output detector, plagiarism detector, and blinded human reviewers. npj. *Digital Medicine*, *6*, 75. DOI: 10.1038/s41746-023-00819-6 PMID: 37100871

Garcia, M. B., Garcia, P. S., Maaliw, R. R.III, Lagrazon, P. G. G., Arif, Y. M., Ofosu-Ampong, K., Yousef, A. M. F., & Vaithilingam, C. A. (2024). Technoethical Considerations for Advancing Health Literacy and Medical Practice: A Posthumanist Framework in the Age of Healthcare 5.0. In *Emerging Technologies for Health Literacy and Medical Practice.* IGI Global., DOI: 10.4018/979-8-3693-1214-8.ch001

Gold, N. E. (2021). Virginia Dignum: Responsible Artificial Intelligence: How to Develop and Use AI in a Responsible Way. *Genetic Programming and Evolvable Machines*, *22*(1), 137–139. DOI: 10.1007/s10710-020-09394-1

Grebenshchikova, E. (2016). NBIC-Convergence and Technoethics: Common Ethical Perspective. [IJT]. *International Journal of Technoethics*, *7*(1), 77–84. DOI: 10.4018/IJT.2016010106

Hamdani, A., Aulia, E., Listiana, Y., & Herlambang, Y. (2024). Moralitas di Era Digital: Tinjauan Filsafat tentang Technoethics. *Indo-MathEdu Intellectuals Journal*, *5*(1), 767–777. DOI: 10.54373/imeij.v5i1.648

Hasanah, N. A., Aziza, M. R., Junikhah, A., Arif, Y. M., & Garcia, M. B. (2025). Navigating the Use of AI in Engineering Education Through a Systematic Review of Technology, Regulations, and Challenges. In *Pitfalls of AI Integration in Education: Skill Obsolescence, Misuse, and Bias*. IGI Global., DOI: 10.4018/979-8-3373-0122-8.ch016

Hasanein, A. M., & Sobaih, A. E. E. (2023). Drivers and consequences of ChatGPT use in higher education: Key stakeholder perspectives. *European Journal of Investigation in Health, Psychology and Education*, *13*(11), 2599–2614. DOI: 10.3390/ejihpe13110181 PMID: 37998071

Heidari, H., Loi, M., Gummadi, K. P., & Krause, A. (2019). A moral framework for understanding fairness in machine learning. *Communications of the ACM*, *64*(8), 64–71. DOI: 10.1145/3419764

Holmes, W., Bialik, M., & Fadel, C. (2019). *Artificial Intelligence in Education. Promise and Implications for Teaching and Learning*. Center for Curriculum Redesign.

Holmes, W., Porayska-Pomsta, K., Holstein, K., Sutherland, E., Baker, T., Shum, S., Santos, O., Rodrigo, M., Cukurova, M., Bittencourt, I., & Koedinger, K. (2021). Ethics of AI in Education: Towards a Community-Wide Framework. *International Journal of Artificial Intelligence in Education*, *32*(3), 504–526. DOI: 10.1007/s40593-021-00239-1

Huang, L. (2023). Ethics of artificial intelligence in education: Student privacy and data protection. *Science Insights Education Frontiers*, *16*(2), 2577–2587. DOI: 10.15354/sief.23.re202

Ilchenko, O. (2024). Academic integrity as a factor of ensuring quality training of specialists in institutions of Higher Education. *The Sources of Pedagogical Skills*, (33), 100–103. DOI: 10.33989/2075-146x.2024.33.310004

International Center for Academic Integrity. (2024). The fundamental values of academic integrity. Retrieved February 19, 2025 from: https://academicintegrity.org/aws/ICAI/asset_manager/get_file/911282?ver=1

Irfan, M., Aldulaylan, F., & Alqahtani, Y. (2023). Ethics and privacy in Irish higher education: A comprehensive study of Artificial Intelligence (AI) tools implementation at University of Limerick. *Global Social Sci Rev*, *8*(2), 201–210. DOI: 10.31703/gssr.2023(VIII-II).19

Khalil, M., & Er, E. (2023, June). Will ChatGPT Get You Caught? Rethinking of Plagiarism Detection. In: *International Conference on Human-Computer Interaction* (pp. 475-487). Cham: Springer Nature Switzerland. DOI: 10.1007/978-3-031-34411-4_32

Kooli, C. (2023). Chatbots in Education and Research: A Critical Examination of Ethical Implications and Solutions. *Sustainability (Basel)*, *15*(7), 5614. DOI: 10.3390/su15075614

Latham, A., & Goltz, S. (2019). A Survey of the General Public's Views on the Ethics of Using AI in Education. In *Artificial Intelligence in Education:20th International Conference, AIED 2019,Chicago, IL, USA,June 25-29, 2019, Proceedings, Part I 20* (pp. 194-206). Springer International Publishing. https://doi.org/DOI: 10.1007/978-3-030-23204-7_17

Lazăr, A. M., Repanovici, A., Popa, D., Ionas, D. G., & Dobrescu, A. I. (2024). Ethical principles in AI use for education. *Education Sciences*, *14*(11), 1239. DOI: 10.3390/educsci14111239

Lo, C. K. (2023). What Is the Impact of ChatGPT on Education? A Rapid Review of the Literature. *Education Sciences*, *13*(4), 410. DOI: 10.3390/educsci13040410

Löfström, E., Trotman, T., Furnari, M., & Shephard, K. (2015). ¿Quién enseña integridad académica y cómo la enseña? *Educación Superior*, *69*, 435–448. DOI: 10.1007/s10734-014-9784-3

Luppicini, R., & Adell, R. (Eds.). (2008). *Handbook of research on technoethics*. IGI Global., DOI: 10.4018/978-1-60566-022-6

Mangubat, J. C., Mangubat, M. R., Uy, T. B. L., Acut, D. P., & Garcia, M. B. (2025). Safeguarding Educational Innovations Amid AI Disruptions: A Reassessment of Patenting for Sustained Intellectual Property Protection. In *Pitfalls of AI Integration in Education: Skill Obsolescence, Misuse, and Bias*. IGI Global., DOI: 10.4018/979-8-3373-0122-8.ch013

Maslikova, I. (2021). *The ways of developing a culture of education quality and academic integrity in the contemporary University*. Ukranian Cultural Studies., DOI: 10.17721/UCS.2021.2(9).12

Ministry of Education and Vocation Training. (2021). *Plan de Digitalización y Competencias Digitales del Sistema Educativo*. Spanish Government. Retrieved November 19, 2024 from https://www.educacionyfp.gob.es

Muñoz-Cantero, J., Crego, M., & Espiñeira-Bellón, E. (2024). Desarrollo de la integridad académica como oportunidad de justicia. *Revista Electrónica Interuniversitaria de Formación del Profesorado*, *27*(3), 153–169. DOI: 10.6018/reifop.615081

Murphy, R. F. (2019). *Artificial intelligence applications to support K–12 teachers and teaching*. RAND Corporation, PE-315-RC. https://doi.org/DOI: 10.7249/PE315

Nissenbaum, H., & Walker, D. (1998). Will computers dehumanize education? A grounded approach to values at risk. *Technology in Society*, *20*(3), 237–273. DOI: 10.1016/S0160-791X(98)00011-6

Ntoutsi, E., Fafalios, P., Gadiraju, U., Iosifidis, V., Nejdl, W., Vidal, M., Ruggieri, S., Turini, F., Papadopoulos, S., Krasanakis, E., Kompatsiaris, I., Kinder-Kurlanda, K., Wagner, C., Karimi, F., Fernández, M., Alani, H., Berendt, B., Kruegel, T., Heinze, C., & Staab, S. (2020). Bias in data-driven artificial intelligence systems—An introductory survey. *Wiley Interdisciplinary Reviews. Data Mining and Knowledge Discovery*, *10*(3), e1356. DOI: 10.1002/widm.1356

Obaid, O. I., Ali, A. H., & Yaseen, M. G. (2023). Impact of Chat GPT on Scientific Research: Opportunities, Risks, Limitations, and Ethical Issues. *Iraqi J. Comput. Sci. Math*, 4, 13–17. DOI: 10.52866/ijcsm.2023.04.04.002

Öztürk, H., Doğuş, M., Şahin, V., Çakmak, M., & Gürses, İ. (2025). Navigating the Ethical Frontier: Emerging Dilemmas at the Intersection of Special Education and Artificial Intelligence. In *Pitfalls of AI Integration in Education: Skill Obsolescence, Misuse, and Bias*. IGI Global., DOI: 10.4018/979-8-3373-0122-8.ch011

Parente, A., & Roecklein-Canfield, J. (2020). Strategies for fostering academic integrity in the classroom. *The FASEB Journal*, 34(S1), 1–1. DOI: 10.1096/fasebj.2020.34.s1.07239

Pattier, D., & Redondo-Duarte, S. (2025). La vida online, la inteligencia artificial y su lectura pedagógica. *Márgenes. Revista de Educación de la Universidad de Málaga*, 6(1), 28–45. DOI: 10.24310/mar.6.1.2025.20784

Piascik, P., & Brazeau, G. (2010). Promoting a Culture of Academic Integrity. *American Journal of Pharmaceutical Education*, 74(6), 1–2. DOI: 10.5688/aj7406113 PMID: 21045955

Putra, F. W., Rangka, I. B., Aminah, S., & Aditama, M. H. (2023). ChatGPT in the higher education environment: Perspectives from the theory of high order thinking skills. *Journal of Public Health (Oxford, England)*, 45(4), e840–e841. DOI: 10.1093/pubmed/fdad120 PMID: 37455540

Redondo-Duarte, S., Martínez-Requejo, S., Jiménez-García, E., & Ruiz-Lázaro, J. (2024). The potential of educational chatbots for the support and formative assessment of students. In Ibrahim, M., Aydoğmuş, M., & Tükel, Y. (Eds.), *New trends and promising directions in modern education* (pp. 113–148). Palet Yayinlari.

Redondo-Duarte, S., Ruiz-Lázaro, J., Jiménez-García, E., & Requejo, S. M. (2024). Didactic Strategies for the Use of AI in the Classroom in Higher Education. In *Integration Strategies of Generative AI in Higher Education* (pp. 23–50). IGI Global., DOI: 10.4018/979-8-3693-5518-3.ch002

Rudin, C. (2019). Stop explaining black box machine learning models for high stakes decisions and use interpretable models instead. *Nature Machine Intelligence*, 1(5), 206–215. DOI: 10.1038/s42256-019-0048-x PMID: 35603010

Rusandi, M. A., Ahman, , Saripah, I., Khairun, D. Y., & Mutmainnah, . (2023). No worries with ChatGPT: Building bridges between artificial intelligence and education with critical thinking soft skills. *Journal of Public Health (Oxford, England)*, 45(3), e602–e603. DOI: 10.1093/pubmed/fdad049 PMID: 37099761

Sallam, M. (2023). ChatGPT utility in healthcare education, research, and practice: Systematic review on the promising perspectives and valid concerns. *Health Care*, 11(6), 887. DOI: 10.3390/healthcare11060887 PMID: 36981544

Santra, P., & Majhi, D. (2023). Scholarly Communication and Machine-Generated Text: Is it Finally AI vs AI in Plagiarism Detection. *Journal of Information and Knowledge*, 60(3), 175–183. DOI: 10.17821/srels/2023/v60i3/171028

Saylam, S., Duman, N., Yildirim, Y., & Satsevich, K. (2023). Empowering education with AI: Addressing ethical concerns. *London Journal of Social Sciences*, (6), 39–48. DOI: 10.31039/ljss.2023.6.103

Selwyn, N. (2019). *Should robots replace teachers?: AI and the future of education*. John Wiley & Sons.

Seo, K., Tang, J., Roll, I., Fels, S., & Yoon, D. (2021). The impact of artificial intelligence on learner–instructor interaction in online learning. *International Journal of Educational Technology in Higher Education*, *18*(1), 1–23. DOI: 10.1186/s41239-021-00292-9 PMID: 34778540

Shih, P., Lin, C., Wu, L., & Yu, C. (2021). Learning Ethics in AI—Teaching Non-Engineering Undergraduates through Situated Learning. *Sustainability (Basel)*, *13*(7), 3718. DOI: 10.3390/su13073718

Singer, N. (2018, July 26). Amazon's facial recognition wrongly identifies 28 lawmakers, ACLU says. *The New York Times*. Retrieved February 7, 2024 from https://www.nytimes.com/2018/07/26/technology/amazon-aclu-facial-recognition-congress.html

Taneja, D., Prabagaren, H., & Thomas, M. R. (2025). AI in Academia: Balancing Integrity, Ethics, and Learning Amid Evolving Norms of Authorship and Scholarship. In *Pitfalls of AI Integration in Education: Skill Obsolescence, Misuse, and Bias*. IGI Global., DOI: 10.4018/979-8-3373-0122-8.ch014

Thorp, H. H. (2023). ChatGPT is Fun, But not an Author. *Science*, *379*(6630), 313. DOI: 10.1126/science.adg7879 PMID: 36701446

UNESCO (2023). *AI and education: Guidance for policy makers*. https://doi.org/DOI: 10.54675/PCSP7350

Universidad Europea de Madrid. (2024, July 7). Transformando la evaluación con IA. De la teoría a la práctica. Guía para el profesorado. [Unit for Innovation in Academic Programs and Learning Assessment. Vice Rectorate for Faculty and Research]. Retrieved November 29, 2024 from https://es.slideshare.net/slideshow/transformando-la-evaluacion-con-inteligencia-artificial-ccesa007-pdf/270101605

Wogu, I. A. P., Misra, S., Olu-Owolabi, E. F., Assibong, P. A., Udoh, O. D., Ogiri, S. O., & Damasevicius, R. (2018). Artificial intelligence, artificial teachers and the fate of learners in the 21st century education sector: Implications for theory and practice. *International Journal of Pure and Applied Mathematics*, *119*(16), 2245–2259. https://acadpubl.eu/hub/2018-119-16/2/232.pdf

Xiao, J., Bozkurt, A., Nichols, M., Pazurek, A., Stracke, C. M., Bai, J. Y. H., Farrow, R., Mulligan, D., Nerantzi, C., Sharma, R. C., Singh, L., Frumin, I., Swindell, A., Honeychurch, S., Bond, M., Dron, J., Moore, S., Leng, J., & Slagter van Tryon, P. J.. (2025). Venturing into the Unknown: Critical Insights into Grey Areas and Pioneering Future Directions in Educational Generative AI Research. *TechTrends*, ●●●, 1–16. DOI: 10.1007/s11528-025-01060-6

KEY TERMS AND DEFINITIONS

Academic Integrity: Set of values and principles that guarantee honesty, fairness, respect, and responsibility in the academic field. It involves avoiding plagiarism, data manipulation, and other forms of dishonesty.

AI Regulatory Framework: Set of laws and regulations designed to ensure the safe, transparent and non-discriminatory use of artificial intelligence, such as the AI law approved by the European Union in 2023.

Algorithmic Bias: Phenomenon by which AI systems can reflect or amplify existing biases in the data with which they have been trained, which can lead to discrimination based on gender, race or socioeconomic status.

Dehumanization of Learning: Risk associated with the excessive use of AI in education, where the automation of processes could replace human interaction, affecting teaching and the formation of values.

Digital Education Action Plan: European Commission strategy (2021-2027) that establishes guidelines for the ethical use of AI in education, the development of digital skills and data protection.

Ethical Technology Design: Approach that maintains that technologies are not neutral, but rather reflect the values of those who create them, so their design must prioritize principles such as equity and inclusion.

Explainability in AI: Ability of an AI system to offer clear and understandable information about how it reaches its conclusions, facilitating its supervision and regulation.

Privacy and Data Protection: Ethical and legal principle that seeks to ensure that students' personal information is protected and used only for educational purposes, avoiding its commercial exploitation or misuse.

Responsibility in AI: Principle that establishes the need to define who is responsible for decisions made by automated systems, ensuring that there are protocols to correct errors and mitigate damage.

Technoethics: Branch of applied ethics that analyzes and regulates the moral implications of emerging technologies in society. In education, it guides the responsible and ethical use of advanced technologies, balancing their benefits and risks.

Transparency in AI: Principle that requires AI systems to be understandable and verifiable in terms of their operation, decisions, and data sources to ensure their reliability and avoid bias.

Transparency Index: Model developed to continuously evaluate the level of transparency of AI applications in education, involving educators, technology experts and AI professionals.

Chapter 11
Navigating the Ethical Frontier:
Emerging Dilemmas at the Intersection of Special Education and Artificial Intelligence

Halil Öztürk
https://orcid.org/0000-0001-5646-2130
Special Education Department, Muğla Sıtkı Koçman University, Turkey

Mustafa Doğuş
https://orcid.org/0000-0001-7027-7388
Anadolu University, Turkey

Volkan Şahin
https://orcid.org/0000-0001-7930-8080
Special Education Department, Anadolu University, Turkey

Mustafa Çakmak
https://orcid.org/0000-0001-7607-3327
Special Education Department, Anadolu University, Turkey

İlyas Gürses
https://orcid.org/0000-0001-9492-4826
Special Education Department, Anadolu University, Turkey

ABSTRACT

Artificial intelligence (AI) is transforming special education by enabling personalized learning pathways and innovative assistive technologies. However, its growing use raises critical ethical concerns, including algorithmic bias, data privacy, and fairness. Biased algorithms can lead to misdiagnoses or inappropriate learning recommendations, while the collection of sensitive student data increases privacy risks. Many educators also lack the training to critically assess AI-generated outputs. Ensuring inclusive and transparent AI design is essential to providing equal opportunities and avoiding the reinforcement of educational disparities. Policymakers, developers, and educators must collaborate to establish clear, enforceable guidelines that protect student rights and promote ethical AI use. This chapter explores the expanding role of AI technologies in special education by advocating for a balanced approach that supports innovation while prioritizing ethical responsibility and inclusion.

DOI: 10.4018/979-8-3373-0122-8.ch011

INTRODUCTION

Advancements in science and technology have significantly influenced special education (SE), improving educational processes for researchers, specialists, and teachers (Hamutoglu et al., 2022; Inci & Köse, 2023). Artificial intelligence (AI) applications are among these advancements, supporting individualized education, communication, and independent living skills for individuals with special needs (Tsouktakou et al., 2024).

AI, defined as the ability of machines to analyze data, learn, and make decisions, has become an essential tool in education (Morandín-Ahuerma, 2022; Saxena et al., 2023). In SE, AI facilitates personalized learning, assessment, and communication (Holman et al., 2024; Scott et al., 2024). AI-based assessment systems analyze students' cognitive, linguistic, and social skills, assisting teachers in developing Individualized Education Programs (IEPs) (Rakap, 2024). These systems help teachers allocate more time for direct instruction while providing instant feedback to students (Goldman, 2024). Additionally, AI-powered augmentative and alternative communication (AAC) tools enhance interaction for individuals with speech impairments (Zhumazhan et al., 2024).

Despite its advantages, AI integration in SE raises ethical, pedagogical, and systemic concerns (Ersoy, 2025; Martínez-Requejo et al., 2025; Taneja et al., 2025). Since AI systems rely on large datasets, biased training data can lead to misdiagnoses, disproportionately affecting marginalized students. For example, an AI-based autism diagnostic system in the U.S. showed discrepancies in diagnosing Black students compared to White students due to biased datasets (Marino et al., 2023). Similarly, AI systems assessing neurological differences like dyslexia and ADHD may generate false positives or negatives, misguiding educators and families. Another major concern is the reduction of teacher-student interactions. AI-driven tools, while enhancing instruction, cannot replace the emotional and social guidance provided by educators. A study in Japan found that students in AI-assisted classrooms experienced a decline in social development and relationships with teachers (Walugembe et al., 2024). Students with special needs require human-centered support, and an over-reliance on AI may weaken the effectiveness of educational processes.

AI applications in SE also pose risks regarding data privacy. AI continuously analyzes students' cognitive and emotional data, and unauthorized sharing of this information raises significant ethical concerns (Howorth et al., 2024). In some countries, AI-based monitoring systems track student behavior without consent, with this data being shared with commercial entities. Protecting sensitive student information is crucial within legal and ethical frameworks.

Another issue is the accessibility of AI-assisted educational tools. Due to their high costs and technical requirements, these tools may not be equally available to all students. Schools in low-income or rural areas face challenges in adopting AI technologies, potentially exacerbating educational inequalities (Holmes et al., 2018). A study in Europe found that AI-supported tools were predominantly used by private schools and well-funded public institutions, further widening the gap in educational opportunities (Marino et al., 2023; Rakap, 2024).

Ensuring AI supports equity rather than reinforcing disparities is crucial. SE must prioritize applications that enhance well-being, promote independence, and improve quality of life (Alkan, 2024). AI should serve as a supportive tool rather than a substitute for educators. While AI facilitates efficiency in education, its risks, limitations, and potential for misguidance must be carefully considered. AI systems collect and analyze large-scale educational data to improve learning. However, this data-driven approach raises concerns about privacy violations and algorithmic bias. AI-generated assessments may exclude critical human factors, leading to inaccurate or unfair classifications (Garcia et al., 2025). For instance, a student with mild language delays may be mistakenly placed in SE, while another in need of services may be overlooked. Such errors can negatively impact students' academic and social development, creating inequalities in access to learning opportunities (Marino et al., 2023; Rakap, 2024).

The financial burden of AI is another consideration. The integration of AI in education requires robust technical infrastructure, which many institutions may lack. While wealthy institutions can invest in AI tools, schools in disadvantaged areas may struggle to implement these technologies. This disparity further exacerbates technological inequalities in SE, limiting access to personalized learning opportunities (Holmes et al., 2018). Teacher training is essential to the effective use of AI in SE. However, inadequate training may prevent educators from critically evaluating AI-based systems. While AI can reduce teacher workload, it should not entirely dictate pedagogical decisions. Teachers play a vital role in providing emotional and social support, and excessive dependence on AI may weaken meaningful student-teacher interactions (Howorth et al., 2024). Ensuring that educators adopt an informed and critical approach will contribute to the responsible and ethical implementation of AI in SE.

MAIN FOCUS OF THE CHAPTER

This chapter explores the intersection of SE and AI, focusing on the ethical implications, challenges, and opportunities presented by AI applications in SE. While AI has the potential to enhance personalized learning, improve accessibility, and support individualized educational planning, it also raises concerns related to algorithmic bias, data privacy, inclusivity, and the role of human oversight.

The chapter critically examines how AI-powered systems influence decision-making processes, student assessment, and accessibility in SE, highlighting the risks of algorithmic discrimination, data security breaches, and inequitable access to AI-driven tools. By evaluating AI's impact on learning outcomes, social interaction, and student well-being, the discussion emphasizes the necessity of transparency, accountability, and fairness in AI applications.

Furthermore, the chapter underscores the importance of ethical AI integration in SE, advocating for policies that ensure AI supports, rather than replaces, human educators. It calls for equitable AI design, safeguards against discriminatory algorithms, and inclusive digital literacy training to empower both educators and students. The discussion provides guiding principles for responsible AI use in SE, ensuring that technological advancements align with the fundamental rights and needs of students with disabilities.

ENSURING ETHICAL AI INTEGRATION IN SPECIAL EDUCATION

To integrate AI responsibly into SE, it is essential to prioritize ethical considerations such as transparency, fairness, and human oversight. AI should be used to support rather than replace educators, ensuring that students receive personalized guidance within an inclusive framework (CEC, 2023). Addressing key concerns such as algorithmic bias, privacy risks, and accessibility will help maximize AI's potential while minimizing harm.

A crucial ethical issue in AI applications is data privacy. AI-powered systems continuously analyze students' personal information to tailor learning experiences. However, the storage, security, and potential misuse of this data raise ethical concerns (Mijwil et al., 2022). Since individuals with special needs may be more vulnerable to privacy violations, ensuring secure data management is essential (Álvarez-Guerrero et al., 2024). Schools and policymakers must implement strict safeguards, including data encryption and access controls, to protect student information. Algorithmic fairness is another key issue. AI systems trained on biased datasets may reinforce discrimination rather than promote equity (Kamalov et al., 2023). AI must be designed to account for diverse learning profiles and prevent biased decision-making. Ethical guidelines should be established to ensure fairness and impartiality in AI-generated recommendations. Additionally, human oversight is essential in AI-based SE applications. Teachers and specialists must critically evaluate AI-generated assessments rather than relying solely on automated recommendations (du Boulay, 2022). AI should function as a support system, providing insights that educators can use in conjunction with their expertise.

Digital literacy training is another critical aspect. Students, teachers, and parents must be educated on digital security, privacy, and ethical AI use (Long & Magerko, 2020). Raising awareness about AI's limitations can help prevent over-reliance on automated tools and ensure responsible use in educational settings. Lastly, AI applications must be designed for inclusivity. Many current AI models are trained on datasets that do not adequately represent students with disabilities (European Commission, 2024). Future AI developments must prioritize accessibility, ensuring that AI-driven educational tools accommodate diverse learning needs.

The integration of AI in SE offers transformative possibilities for individualized instruction, assessment, and communication. However, its implementation must be approached with caution, addressing issues related to bias, privacy, accessibility, and ethical considerations. AI should enhance—not replace—educators, ensuring that students receive the necessary social and emotional support alongside academic instruction. Future AI advancements should be guided by principles of transparency, equity, and human-centered design. By safeguarding data privacy, promoting fairness in access, and maintaining teacher oversight, AI can be responsibly integrated into SE to support diverse learning needs. Policymakers, educators, and researchers must collaborate to develop comprehensive strategies that maximize AI's benefits while mitigating risks. Ethical considerations should remain at the forefront, ensuring that AI applications serve as tools for inclusion, empowerment, and improved educational outcomes for students with special needs.

ALGORITHMIC BIAS AND EQUITY

One of the most important goals of a human being is to sustain their life, and while pursuing this fundamental goal, they make decisions among certain choices to overcome the situations they encounter. When making decisions, they choose among different alternatives that arise. To explain this situation, the concepts of "decision making" or "decision taking" can be used. Although these two concepts are often used interchangeably, there are subtle differences between them. Decision making refers to the process by which individuals or groups select among certain options, whereas decision taking encompasses the act of deciding and is generally carried out in a systematic and process-oriented manner. In the decision-making process, the individual evaluates the available data and the conditions of the situation to make a choice. Therefore, decision making is more related to personal will and cognitive processes. In contrast, decision taking often involves groups, institutions, or systems playing a role. Both processes are critical in helping individuals and organizations achieve their goals.

For these critical processes to succeed, the traditional human-human collaboration in decision-making is rapidly shifting toward human-algorithm collaboration, particularly with the growing integration of AI technologies into daily life. Decision processes are evolving from a human-centric focus to algorithm and AI-supported systems (Shrestha et al., 2019). The use of algorithms in decision-making has emerged with the expectation that it will optimize processes, improve decision quality, and ultimately lead to better outcomes for all (Kasy, 2024). However, algorithmic decision-making is inherently complex, as these systems primarily rely on historical data. Consequently, machines are expected to make decisions based on patterns generated by human decisions. Historically, human decision-making has often been influenced by bias, leading to discriminatory outcomes. However, such biases are not exclusive to human decisions (Kadiresan et al., 2022). While data-driven decision-making offers speed and consistency, it can also perpetuate biases if the data itself is biased, leading to potentially flawed or unfair outcomes.

Algorithm-based systems are widely used in various domains, yet they are not immune to biases. Consider a liquid soap dispenser that operates using sensor-based algorithms. The system detects objects and motion through infrared sensors, dispensing soap when a hand is detected. However, because infrared light is absorbed more by darker surfaces, the sensors may fail to recognize hands with dark skin tones, leading to discriminatory outcomes (Jackson, 2021). Similarly, algorithm-driven decision-making in other fields can also reinforce biases. For instance, a bank's AI-powered loan system may offer higher interest rates to minority groups based on historical data (Bartlett et al., 2022). A ride-hailing app may increase prices in low-income neighborhoods with predominantly non-white populations, reinforcing economic disparities (Pandey & Caliskan, 2021). In hiring, an AI-powered resume-screening algorithm may prioritize male applicants simply because past hiring trends in the company favored men. These cases illustrate that algorithm-based decision-making, despite its promise of neutrality and efficiency, can still perpetuate biases, highlighting the need for greater oversight and fairness in AI-driven systems.

The rapid advancement of AI and machine learning has introduced powerful algorithms capable of improving lives, yet these advancements also pose the risk of significant harm (Brown et al., 2021). Machine learning algorithms are increasingly utilized to enhance or replace human decision-making, influencing individuals' lives, interests, opportunities, and rights. An algorithm is a finite sequence of step-by-step instructions designed to solve a problem or achieve a goal (Kraemer et al., 2011), used by both computers and humans to tackle various challenges. Given their widespread use, the ethical implications of algorithm-based decision-making must not be ignored, particularly regarding equitable access to rights for disadvantaged groups, such as individuals with disabilities. The presence of algorithmic bias can result in unfair or erroneous decisions, systematically disadvantaging certain groups (Peters, 2025). For instance, biased algorithms may lead to exclusionary practices that hinder accessibility and equal opportunities for people with disabilities, reinforcing societal inequalities.

Several factors contribute to algorithmic bias, which can stem from data, design, or model biases. Since machine learning systems are trained on historical data, any biases present in past decisions will be reflected in automated systems (Verma et al., 2021). Additionally, biases may be intentionally or unintentionally embedded during the algorithm development process, further influencing the model's outcomes (Akter et al., 2022). Model biases occur when machine learning models produce skewed results due to inadequate or imbalanced features. These models rely on statistical rules and principles to identify patterns within datasets. However, if they fail to accurately capture relationships between inputs and outputs, disadvantaged groups may face unintended negative consequences (Akter et al., 2022; Paulus & Kent, 2020; Rozado, 2020; Tsamados et al., 2021).

Algorithmic processes designed to automate or support decision-making can sometimes lead to outcomes that violate principles of justice and equality, disproportionately affecting certain groups in society and workplaces (Kordzadeh & Ghasemaghaei, 2022). One area where these disparities manifest is education, where algorithms are used for tasks such as predicting school dropouts, grading, admissions, and performance evaluations (Baker & Hawn, 2022; Christie et al., 2019; Milliron et al., 2014; Ramineni & Williamson, 2013; Ritter et al., 2016; Smith, 2020; Waters & Miikkulainen, 2014). In one case, an algorithm assigning exam grades based on teacher predictions unfairly awarded lower scores to public school students while favoring those in small private schools (Smith, 2020). Similarly, student performance-based algorithms may misclassify individuals with special needs, leading to misplacement or restricted educational opportunities, as tools trained on typically developing students often fail to account for learning disabilities. Beyond education, algorithmic hiring processes—including automated assessments, one-way interviews, and gamified pre-employment tests—can reinforce existing inequalities (Tilmes, 2022). Algorithms trained on past hiring data may disadvantage disabled individuals, ethnic minorities, or women. For instance, physically disabled job applicants may be unfairly screened out, while even the online application process itself can pose barriers. Slower computer usage speeds or difficulty with CAPTCHA tests could cause disabled applicants to be flagged as bots, blocking their access to job applications (Zyskowski et al., 2015). In healthcare, algorithms are increasingly shaping diagnoses, treatment recommendations, patient prioritization, and resource allocation (Coots et al., 2025). However, these systems may categorize patients with disabilities or higher healthcare costs as low-priority or high-risk, potentially limiting their access to medical services. These examples illustrate how algorithmic biases can reinforce inequalities across multiple sectors, necessitating greater transparency, oversight, and ethical safeguards.

The rapid advancement of algorithmic processes and AI technologies, coupled with the transformation of decision-making processes, suggests that these systems will become increasingly widespread, impactful, and indispensable in all aspects of societal life. These technologies influence a broad spectrum of fields—from education to healthcare, from the justice system to economic decisions—with the potential to reshape daily life for individuals and communities. If designed without bias and with inclusivity in mind, algorithms can serve as powerful tools for promoting social equality and justice. However, they also pose significant risks. Without careful oversight, algorithms could exacerbate existing inequalities or even create new forms of discrimination (Bigman et al., 2021; Ozkazanc-Pan, 2021). Additionally, a lack of transparency in algorithmic processes may erode public trust and make it more difficult for individuals to defend their rights. As such, ethical principles, transparent mechanisms, and independent oversight must be prioritized in their development and implementation (Kramer et al., 2011; Tsamados et al., 2021). The future societal impact of AI and algorithmic decision-making will depend on how these systems are designed and applied. If guided by principles of justice, equality, and transparency, algorithms can contribute to fairer and more inclusive societies. However, if left unchecked, they may deepen inequalities and perpetuate injustices. Therefore, ensuring that technology remains a tool that serves humanity must be a fundamental principle in all future developments.

To ensure that algorithms have more inclusive and fair impacts, a comprehensive approach must be established. Collaboration among scientists, software developers, policymakers, and ethicists is essential to prioritizing transparency and inclusivity at every stage, from design to implementation. Data sets that fail to adequately represent disadvantaged groups must be restructured, and algorithmic decision-making processes should be openly auditable. To anticipate societal impacts, technology companies must implement ethical oversight mechanisms, monitored by independent observers, ensuring accountability. Additionally, data protection and privacy for vulnerable groups must be a priority. By taking these measures, algorithmic risks can be minimized, and technology can serve as a tool to support social equality. This approach will ensure that technology functions as a fair and inclusive foundation, enhancing individual well-being and societal progress (Diniz et al., 2024).

PRIVACY AND DATA PROTECTION FOR VULNERABLE POPULATIONS

Data protection is crucial for ensuring social equality in the digital age. For disadvantaged groups, it is not just a technical necessity but a fundamental human right. Inequalities that make these groups vulnerable in offline environments are often mirrored and even exacerbated in digital spaces, leading to severe consequences (Bridges, 2017; Madden et al., 2017). Disadvantaged groups include individuals with disabilities, minorities, refugees, low-income individuals, those facing gender discrimination, and people marginalized due to their sexual orientation. These individuals are more vulnerable to privacy violations that can result in emotional, financial, or physical harm (McDonald & Forte, 2022). While they frequently interact with digital systems in education, healthcare, and social services, their disadvantages often expose them to greater risks. The sensitive nature of the personal data collected during their interactions with these systems increases the likelihood of discrimination, stigmatization, and other harmful outcomes (Madden et al., 2017). Among these risks, privacy violations remain a significant concern.

Privacy mechanisms are often designed with general user populations in mind, leading to assumptions that may not accommodate underserved groups, such as individuals with disabilities. These inappropriate assumptions can create barriers, making it difficult for such users to effectively utilize privacy tools, thereby increasing their vulnerability to privacy risks (Wang & Price, 2022). For example, web browsers display a lock icon to indicate a secure connection, reassuring users about their safety. However, visually impaired users may not notice this icon, or it may not be read by screen readers, limiting their ability to assess security (Wang & Price, 2022). Similarly, privacy settings that rely heavily on visual elements can be inaccessible, causing unintentional data exposure. A visually impaired individual unable to adjust social media privacy settings may accidentally share private information with the public. Likewise, a hearing-impaired person may struggle with voice-based security verifications, preventing them from accessing critical services. Individuals with cognitive disabilities may find complex interfaces difficult to navigate, leading to unintentional data disclosure. These challenges highlight how poorly designed privacy mechanisms can exclude marginalized groups and increase their risk of privacy violations, emphasizing the need for inclusive and accessible privacy solutions.

As online systems become increasingly complex, interconnected, and extensive, protecting personal privacy has become more challenging (Palen & Dourish, 2003). This shift requires individuals to adopt conscious strategies for sharing, protecting, and managing their data. However, individuals with disabilities, older adults, children, and low-income groups face greater risks due to limited access to secure technologies, inadequate information, and barriers in navigating online platforms (Chalghoumi et al., 2019; Matthews et al., 2010; Rocheleau et al., 2021). These limitations increase their vulnerability to unauthorized access, data breaches, and misuse. For instance, a visually impaired individual may rely on a screen reader to access healthcare services online. If the platform lacks accessibility standards, the screen reader may fail to read login fields correctly, leading to incorrect data entry, login failures, or the need for third-party assistance. This situation could expose sensitive personal information, such as ID numbers, health records, or passwords, to unauthorized parties. Additionally, accidentally stored or exposed data due to poor platform design may become accessible to malicious actors, compromising both privacy and trust. To prevent such risks, digital platforms must adhere to accessibility standards, such as the Web Content Accessibility Guidelines (WCAG), ensuring inclusive design and regular accessibility testing (Caldwell et al., 2008). By integrating these measures, platforms can provide secure and equitable digital experiences, particularly for users with specific accessibility needs. It can be argued that data protection policies must also be inclusive and accessible to minimize the privacy risks faced by vulnerable groups (Delaere et al., 2023). These policies should consider the specific needs of individuals with disabilities, older adults, children, and low-income groups, aiming to ensure their safer participation in the digital world (Zhuravleva et al., 2019).

INCLUSIVE AI DESIGN FOR SE

In contemporary society, AI technologies have become integral to various aspects of daily life, including education (Bozkurt et al., 2024; Xiao et al., 2025). In recent years, a wide range of AI tools has been developed, adapted, and made accessible to enhance educational practices (Huang et al., 2021). These inclusive technologies have significantly improved access to education for individuals with disabilities—who have historically been overlooked in traditional educational settings—as well as for those who face barriers to learning due to various circumstances (Avellan vd., 2020; Balachandran & Rabbiraj, 2025). AI holds immense potential in SE, particularly through its ability to provide individualized learning approaches and differentiated instructional strategies, making educational processes more accessible and effective (Kaya, 2024). The benefits of AI in SE can be broadly categorized as supporting individual differences, selecting appropriate instructional methods, and enhancing learning processes.

AI-powered personalized learning environments can play a critical role in improving students' academic performance by offering customized content tailored to their unique needs (Huang et al., 2023; Woolf, 2010). Research suggests that personalized learning approaches lead to higher retention rates, increased motivation, and enhanced performance among students with special needs (Hurwitz et al., 2020). Adaptive learning systems have the capacity to adjust to students' individual learning styles and paces, providing them with the most suitable educational materials (Kabudi et al., 2021). Moreover, AI-assisted technologies, including robotic systems and virtual reality (VR), can foster the development of social interaction skills in individuals with special needs (Huijnen et al., 2016; Scassellati et al., 2012). For instance, AI-based applications designed for individuals diagnosed with ASD contribute to the development of language and social interaction skills while also increasing student motivation (Sağdıç & Sani Bozkurt, 2020; Sağdıç et al., 2023).

The inclusive design and implementation of AI in SE not only enhance students' academic performance but also strengthen their independent living skills, social interactions, and overall integration into society (Kaya, 2024). AI-driven smart home systems, personal care applications, and accessibility solutions are being developed to support individuals with special needs in leading independent lives (Alkan, 2024). Furthermore, AI-based assistive technologies contribute to workplace success, facilitating career development for individuals with disabilities (Bozkurt et al., 2024).

Implementations of AI in SE

One of the most significant applications of AI in SE is personalized learning. AI enables the creation of individualized educational programs by adapting to students' learning speeds and styles (Kaya, 2024). This technology is particularly beneficial for students with special needs, as it continuously analyzes their performance to deliver the most appropriate instructional materials and learning experiences (Kharbat et al., 2021). AI-powered tools not only support students' academic progress but also contribute to behavioral improvements. For example, machine learning algorithms can identify students' strengths and weaknesses, allowing educators to offer tailored instructional content (Guan, 2023; Liu et al., 2020). By engaging students more actively in their learning processes, AI fosters increased academic achievement.

AI enhances the accessibility of educational materials by adapting content to meet students' individual needs. For instance, text-to-speech technologies have been developed to improve access to information for visually impaired students (Doğuş, 2024a). Similarly, AI can convert speech into text or translate it into sign language, thereby reducing communication barriers for students with hearing impairments. Speech recognition technologies enable individuals with hearing loss to engage more effectively in classroom discussions. Additionally, AI-driven applications capable of recognizing and translating sign language into spoken language are being developed (Yılmaz & Çolaklıoğlu, 2024). However, regional variations in sign languages remain a challenge to the widespread adoption of these systems (Yılmaz & Çolaklıoğlu, 2024). These advancements play a crucial role in overcoming accessibility barriers in SE, ultimately enhancing students' academic success and social integration.

AI fosters a more interactive and engaging learning experience, encouraging active student participation. Technologies such as augmented reality (AR) and virtual reality (VR) enrich learning environments by providing immersive, hands-on educational experiences (Guan, 2023). These technologies are particularly beneficial in instructional areas involving high-risk training, such as safety education, by offering realistic yet controlled learning settings (Alkan, 2024). Additionally, multisensory learning tools can be highly effective in supporting students with ASD, as they engage multiple senses to enhance retention and sustain student interest (Karami et al., 2021). By integrating AI into educational settings, students with special needs can actively participate in the learning process, fostering improvements in their academic, social, and independent living skills.

AI empowers educators by continuously monitoring and analyzing students' progress, thereby optimizing instructional strategies (Guan, 2023; Fahimirad & Kotamjani, 2018). AI-powered learning systems track student performance in real-time, identifying individual strengths and weaknesses while offering personalized learning recommendations (Kaya, 2024). These systems allow educators to monitor students' development and intervene as necessary while also providing students with customized feedback to enhance their learning experiences. Such AI-driven solutions are particularly beneficial for gifted and special needs students, as they help identify areas requiring improvement and facilitate the creation of individualized learning plans (Kaya, 2024). Consequently, AI-driven analytics tools guide educators in making data-driven decisions, improving teaching effectiveness, and fostering student success (Guan, 2023; Karsenti, 2019).

AI-based technologies provide students with a safe environment to practice various social scenarios. VR and AR applications have demonstrated significant effectiveness in enhancing social skills among individuals with ASD (Karami et al., 2021). These technologies allow students to simulate real-life interactions, such as traveling on public transportation, shopping in a store, or ordering food at a restaurant, within a controlled, low-stress environment. Additionally, AI-powered social robots and interactive simulations facilitate social engagement and communication skills, helping students build confidence and reduce anxiety in real-world social situations (Scassellati et al., 2012).

Analysis of AI Implementations for Different Special Needs Groups

While AI technologies offer promising applications for individuals with special needs, they also introduce significant risks, including biased algorithms, privacy concerns, over-reliance on automation, and potential reductions in human interaction. The following sections examine how AI applications can unintentionally reinforce inequalities and create ethical and practical challenges in SE.

AI-powered emotion recognition tools and social robots aim to support social skills development in individuals with ASD (Scassellati et al., 2012). However, these systems often fail to accommodate the unique communication styles of autistic individuals, as they are typically trained on neurotypical datasets (Arent et al., 2022). This bias can lead to inaccurate interpretations of facial expressions and social cues, reinforcing misunderstandings rather than addressing them. Additionally, excessive reliance on AI-based social training may limit natural social interactions, preventing students from developing flexible communication strategies suited to real-world settings.

AI-assisted learning platforms and AAC tools provide customized support for individuals with intellectual disabilities (Chen et al., 2020; Najjar et al., 2010). However, these systems often lack adaptability to the dynamic and evolving needs of users, leading to rigid, one-size-fits-all interventions. Moreover, decision-making algorithms used in diagnosing intellectual disabilities may rely on incomplete or biased datasets, leading to misdiagnoses (Altun et al., 2021). Over-diagnosing can result in unnecessary placement in restrictive educational settings, while under-diagnosing may deny individuals the support they require. Furthermore, AI-driven smart assistants collect vast amounts of personal data, posing privacy risks, especially when individuals may not fully understand how their information is stored or used.

AI tools for diagnosing and assisting students with dyslexia, dyscalculia, and dysgraphia offer personalized interventions (Barua et al., 2022). However, these technologies often rely on standardized assessments that do not capture the diverse learning profiles of students. Machine learning algorithms may generate inappropriate learning content if they fail to account for contextual factors such as cultural background, motivation, and emotional state (Bhushan, 2024). Additionally, AI-based handwriting analysis tools may disproportionately classify students as having learning disabilities due to motor coordination variations rather than actual cognitive impairments, leading to unnecessary labeling and stigmatization.

AI-enhanced hearing aids and speech-to-text systems improve accessibility (Yılmaz & Çolaklıoğlu, 2024). However, these technologies often struggle with complex listening environments, leading to misinterpretation of speech, particularly in group conversations or noisy settings (Coy et al., 2024). Bias in AI-driven sign language translation systems remains a major concern, as regional and cultural variations in sign language are often underrepresented in datasets (Wadhawan & Kumar, 2021). This can create inaccurate translations, reinforcing linguistic barriers instead of reducing them. Additionally, AI-powered captioning systems frequently fail to transcribe spoken content accurately, particularly for individuals with non-standard accents or speech impairments, further marginalizing these populations.

AI tools such as Seeing AI and Be My Eyes support individuals with visual impairments by describing surroundings and converting text to speech (Doğuş, 2024a). However, these systems heavily rely on external servers, making them vulnerable to data security breaches. AI-based navigation aids such as WeWalk and ARxVision use location tracking, raising ethical concerns about constant surveillance and the potential misuse of mobility data (Glidance, 2024). Furthermore, AI-driven object recognition applications may misidentify objects in complex environments, leading to potential safety risks. If these systems replace traditional mobility training, they could reduce individuals' ability to develop essential spatial awareness and navigation skills.

AI-based adaptive learning systems offer advanced learning opportunities for gifted students, yet they pose risks such as over-reliance on automation, reduced critical thinking, and potential social isolation (Kaya, 2024). AI-driven platforms tailor content to individual learning paces but may fail to encourage intellectual curiosity beyond algorithmically determined pathways, limiting creative exploration (Kuprenko, 2020; Siegle, 2023). Additionally, AI-driven assessments for identifying giftedness may reinforce biases, overlooking students from underrepresented or disadvantaged backgrounds due to training data limitations (Song & Koo, 2022). While AI presents potential benefits in SE, its ethical and practical risks must be carefully managed. Over-reliance on AI tools can diminish human interaction, increase algorithmic bias, reinforce inequalities, and compromise data privacy. To ensure that AI enhances rather than undermines educational opportunities, systems must be developed with diverse, representative datasets, incorporate human oversight, and prioritize student agency and well-being. SE professionals must critically assess AI applications to prevent automation from replacing the personalized, adaptive, and empathetic support that students with special needs require.

FUTURE ETHICAL DIRECTIONS IN AI AND SE

The rapid advancement of AI technologies presents significant opportunities in SE while also raising critical ethical concerns. AI applications designed to support the individual differences of students with special needs can enhance educational accessibility and effectiveness. Still, they also introduce ethical risks related to privacy, security, and discrimination (Yıldız, 2024). The ethical dimensions of AI in SE are primarily shaped by concerns such as data security, digital privacy, maintaining human oversight in personalized education, and ensuring algorithmic fairness (Vuran, 2020).

For AI to be implemented ethically in SE, the principles of transparency, fairness, accessibility, and human-centered design must be prioritized. While AI-powered learning systems can provide personalized educational solutions, it is crucial that their decision-making processes remain transparent and that they are subject to educator oversight (Wang, 2021). For instance, individuals with developmental disabilities may struggle with understanding emotional cues and empathy, making them vulnerable to manipulation or exploitation in AI interactions. Therefore, it is essential to educate students with special needs about digital security and to support AI-based systems with ethical monitoring mechanisms (Chadwick, 2019).

Another critical ethical issue is data privacy and security. AI applications in SE collect students' personal data to personalize learning experiences, but this process entails risks of data breaches and potential misuse (Mijwil et al., 2022). Since individuals with intellectual disabilities or ASD may unknowingly disclose personal information, strict privacy safeguards must be enforced in educational settings (Álvarez-Guerrero et al., 2024). To ensure ethical AI use, student data should be encrypted, secure storage methods should be adopted, and strict access controls should be implemented (Halamka, 2017).

Another essential ethical consideration is preserving human oversight in AI applications. AI should function as a supportive tool for teachers and educators rather than replacing them. If AI-driven assessment systems provide individualized recommendations without human intervention, their impact on educational fairness and equal opportunities must be carefully examined (du Boulay, 2022). The complete autonomy of AI systems in SE could lead to misguided recommendations or overlook individual student needs. Therefore, AI's feedback mechanisms should be reviewed and adjusted by teachers to ensure accuracy and alignment with students' actual needs (Council for Exceptional Children, [CEC], 2023).

Finally, ensuring inclusivity in SE is a fundamental component of ethical AI use. Developing AI applications that accommodate diverse learning styles and needs can promote educational equity (European Commission, 2024). However, since existing AI training datasets are primarily based on typically developing individuals, AI systems in SE. must be specifically designed to meet the needs of students with disabilities (Smith, 2015). To ensure the sustainable and ethical use of AI in SE, future developments must prioritize transparency, accountability, human oversight, data security, and equitable access. The safe and effective integration of AI as an educational tool for students with special needs depends not only on technological advancements but also on the establishment of robust ethical and social policies.

The application of AI in SE requires a careful ethical and security framework. In this regard, the following key aspects should be considered:

1. *Data Privacy and Security:* Student data must be securely stored in AI systems and protected against unauthorized access (Halamka, 2017; Kamalov et al., 2023). Transparency in data usage is essential, and explicit consent should be obtained from parents or guardians.
2. *Bias and Discrimination Prevention:* AI algorithms trained on biased datasets may produce discriminatory outcomes. Ensuring algorithmic fairness and impartiality is critical (Kamalov et al., 2023; Mazumder, 2024). AI systems should be designed to respect individual differences and avoid discriminatory behaviors that could disadvantage students with special needs.
3. *Transparency and Accountability:* AI systems should clearly explain their functioning, including the data they use and the decision-making process. Ensuring accountability in AI systems helps educators and policymakers address any potential errors or unfair decisions (Wang, 2021).
4. *Protection Against Exploitation:* AI technologies must be designed and implemented to protect students from exploitation, particularly those who may be more vulnerable due to cognitive or communication challenges (Vuran, 2020). Additional safeguards should be implemented for students at higher risk of manipulation or digital harm.
5. *Digital Literacy Training:* Students, teachers, and parents should receive education on digital security, privacy, and the ethical use of AI technologies (Long & Magerko, 2020). Raising awareness about AI-generated misinformation can help reduce over-reliance on AI-driven content.
6. *Responsible Use of AI Tools in Education:* Teachers should safeguard student rights and privacy while using AI tools, prevent over-dependence on technology, and prioritize human interaction in learning processes (Yıldız, 2024). Given that current AI systems rely on probabilistic models, the potential for misinformation must always be acknowledged. Therefore, teachers should review AI-generated content before incorporating it into educational materials (CEC, 2023).

The ethical implementation of AI in SE requires a balanced approach that promotes technological innovation while safeguarding privacy, inclusivity, and human oversight. AI has the potential to enhance learning experiences for students with special needs, but its use must be carefully regulated to prevent bias, discrimination, and privacy violations. By prioritizing transparency, accountability, and data protection, AI can be integrated into SE in a responsible and ethical manner. Future AI advancements should not only focus on technical improvements but also align with ethical guidelines and social policies, ensuring fair and inclusive educational opportunities for all learners.

REFERENCES

Afrin, M. F. N., Hoque, K. E., & Chaiti, R. D. (2024). *Emotion Recognition of Autistic Children from Facial Images Using Hybrid Model*. 1–6. https://doi.org/DOI: 10.1109/ICCCNT61001.2024.10724499

Ahmad, W., Raj, R., & Shokeen, R. (2024). Reshaping special education. *Advances in Educational Technologies and Instructional Design Book Series*, 1–44. https://doi.org/DOI: 10.4018/979-8-3693-5538-1.ch001

Ahmed, M. A., Zaidan, B. B., Zaidan, A. A., Salih, M. M., & Lakulu, M. M. B. (2018). A review on systems-based sensory gloves for sign language recognition state of the art between 2007 and 2017. *Sensors (Basel)*, *18*(7), 2208. DOI: 10.3390/s18072208 PMID: 29987266

Akter, S., Dwivedi, Y. K., Sajib, S., Biswas, K., Bandara, R. J., & Michael, K. (2022). Algorithmic bias in machine learning-based marketing models. *Journal of Business Research*, *144*, 201–216. DOI: 10.1016/j.jbusres.2022.01.083

Alıu, T. V. (2024). Artificial Intelligence in Special Education: A Literature Review. *International Journal of Advanced Networking and Applications*, *16*(2), 6360–6367. DOI: 10.35444/IJANA.2024.16208

Alkan, A. (2024). Yapay zekâ: Eğitimdeki rolü ve potansiyeli. *İnsan ve Toplum Bilimleri Araştırma Dergisi [Artificial intelligence: Its role and potential in education. Journal of Human and Social Sciences Research]*, *13*(1), 483-497.

Alkeraida, A. (2024). Teachers' Competencies in Implementing Technologies and Artificial Intelligence Applications to Teach Students with Disabilities in Inclusive Classrooms in Saudi Arabia. *Eurasian Journal of Educational Research*, *112*, 177–195. DOI: 10.14689/ejer.2024.112.10

Altun, S., Alkan, A., & Altun, H. (2021). The investigation of WISC-R profiles in children with border intelligence and intellectual disability with machine learning algorithms. *Pamukkale University Journal of Engineering Sciences*, *27*(5), 589–596. DOI: 10.5505/pajes.2020.53077

Âlvarez-Guerrero, G., Fry, D., Lu, M., & Gaitis, K. K. (2024). Online child sexual exploitation and abuse of children and adolescents with disabilities: A systematic review. *Disabilities*, *4*(2), 264–276. DOI: 10.3390/disabilities4020017

Andriichuk, N. (2017). Special Education vs Inclusive Education in the Synergy of Educational Environments. *Multidisciplinary Journal of School Education*, *6*(2 (12). https://doi.org/DOI: 10.35765/mjse.2017.0612.04

Arent, K., Brown, D. J., Kruk-Lasocka, J., Niemiec, T. L., Pasieczna, A. H., Standen, P. J., & Szczepanowski, R. (2022). The use of social robots in the diagnosis of autism in preschool children. *Applied Sciences (Basel, Switzerland)*, *12*(17), 8399. DOI: 10.3390/app12178399

Arthur-Kelly, M., & Foreman, P. (2020). *Inclusive and Special Education in Australia*. Acrefore., DOI: 10.1093/acrefore/9780190264093.013.1198

ARxVision. (t.y.). *ARxVision*. https://arx.vision

Ashraf, M. (2024). *A Systematic Review on the Potential of AI and ChatGPT for Parental Support and Child Well-Being*. https://doi.org//arxiv.2407.09492DOI: 10.48550

Askarova, S., Madiyeva, G., Mirqosimova, M., Boqiyeva, R., Nazarov, A., & Baratova, D. (2024, May). A well-designed personalized and optimized model system implementation for specific education system. *In 2024 4th International Conference on Advance Computing and Innovative Technologies in Engineering (ICACITE)* (pp. 607–611). IEEE.

Avellan, T., Sharma, S., & Turunen, M. (2020). "AI for All: Defining the What, Why, and How of Inclusive AI." *Proceedings of the 23rd International Conference on Academic Mindtrek*, 142–144. https://doi.org/DOI: 10.1145/3377290.3377317

Aydın, M., & Yurdugül, H. (2024). Developing a Curriculum Framework of Artificial Intelligence Teaching for Gifted Students. *Kastamonu Education Journal, 32*(1), 14–37. DOI: 10.24106/kefdergi.1426429

Baker, R. S., & Hawn, A. (2022). Algorithmic bias in education. *International Journal of Artificial Intelligence in Education, 32*(4), 1052–1092. DOI: 10.1007/s40593-021-00285-9

Balachandran, M., & Rabbiraj, C. (2025). Artificial intelligence: A support system in inclusive education. *International Journal of Knowledge and Learning, 18*(1), 52–64. Advance online publication. DOI: 10.1504/IJKL.2025.143069

Bandara, L. K., Nawodya, A., Amandi, K., Vihangana, K., Pandithage, D., & Gamage, N. (2024). Innovative system for early detection and intervention in developmental disorders: A multi-sensory, child-centric approach. *16th IEEE International Conference on Computational Intelligence and Communication Networks, 10*(10), 6–12. https://doi.org/DOI: 10.1109/CICN63059.2024.10847351

Bartlett, R., Morse, A., Stanton, R., & Wallace, N. (2022). Consumer-lending discrimination in the FinTech era. *Journal of Financial Economics, 143*(1), 30–56. DOI: 10.1016/j.jfineco.2021.05.047

Barua, P. D., Vicnesh, J., Gururajan, R., Oh, S. L., Palmer, E., Azizan, M. M., Kadri, N. A., & Acharya, U. R. (2022). Artificial intelligence enabled personalised assistive tools to enhance education of children with neurodevelopmental disorders—A review. *International Journal of Environmental Research and Public Health, 19*(3), 1–26. DOI: 10.3390/ijerph19031192 PMID: 35162220

Bhushan, S., Arunkumar, S., Eisa, T. A. E., Nasser, M., Singh, A. K., & Kumar, P. (2024). AI-Enhanced Dyscalculia Screening: A Survey of Methods and Applications for Children. *Diagnostics (Basel), 14*(13), 1441. DOI: 10.3390/diagnostics14131441 PMID: 39001330

Bigman, Y. E., Yam, K. C., Marciano, D., Reynolds, S. J., & Gray, K. (2021). Threat of racial and economic inequality increases preference for algorithm decision-making. *Computers in Human Behavior, 122*, 106859. DOI: 10.1016/j.chb.2021.106859

Binns, R., & Kirkham, R. (2021). How could equality and data protection law shape AI fairness for people with disabilities? [TACCESS]. *ACM Transactions on Accessible Computing, 14*(3), 1–32. DOI: 10.1145/3473673

Bozkurt, A., Xiao, J., Farrow, R., Bai, J. Y. H., Nerantzi, C., Moore, S., Dron, J., Stracke, C. M., Singh, L., Crompton, H., Koutropoulos, A., Terentev, E., Pazurek, A., Nichols, M., Sidorkin, A. M., Costello, E., Watson, S., Mulligan, D., Honeychurch, S., & Asino, T. I. (2024). The Manifesto for Teaching and Learning in a Time of Generative AI: A Critical Collective Stance to Better Navigate the Future. *Open Praxis*, *16*(4), 487–513. DOI: 10.55982/openpraxis.16.4.777

Bridges, K. M. (2017). *The poverty of privacy rights*. Stanford University Press. DOI: 10.1515/9781503602304

Brown, S., Davidovic, J., & Hasan, A. (2021). The algorithm audit: Scoring the algorithms that score us. *Big Data & Society*, *8*(1), 1–8. DOI: 10.1177/2053951720983865

Caldwell, B., Cooper, M., Reid, L. G., Vanderheiden, G., Chisholm, W., Slatin, J., & White, J. (2008). Web content accessibility guidelines (WCAG) 2.0. *WWW Consortium (W3C)*, *290*(1-34), 5-12.

Chadwick, D. D. (2019). Online risk for peoplewith intellectual disabilities. *Tizard Learning Disability Review*, *24*(4), 180–187. DOI: 10.1108/TLDR-03-2019-0008

Chen, L., Chen, P., & Lin, Z. (2020). Artificial intelligence in education: A review. *IEEE Access : Practical Innovations, Open Solutions*, *8*, 198250–198265. DOI: 10.1109/ACCESS.2020.2988510

Christie, S. T., Jarratt, D. C., Olson, L. A., & Taijala, T. T. (2019). Machine-learned school dropout early warning at scale. In *Proceedings of the 12th International Conference on Educational Data Mining* (pp. 726–731). EDM., https://files.eric.ed.gov/fulltext/ED599217.pdf

Coots, M., Linn, K. A., Goel, S., Navathe, A. S., & Parikh, R. B. (2025). Racial bias in clinical and population health algorithms: A critical review of current debates. *Annual Review of Public Health*, *46*(1), 507–523. Advance online publication. DOI: 10.1146/annurev-publhealth-071823-112058 PMID: 39626231

Council for Exceptional Children [CEC]. (2023). *Special education professional ethical principles*. https://exceptionalchildren.org/standards/ethical-principles-and-practice-standards

Diniz, E. H., Sanches, B. H., Pozzebon, M., & Luvizan, S. (2024). Do black fintechs matter? The long and winding road to develop inclusive algorithms for social justice. *Management Information Systems Quarterly*, *48*(4), 1721–1744. DOI: 10.25300/MISQ/2024/18288

Doğuş, M. (2024a). Görme yetersizliği ve yapay zekâ. A. Kaya (Ed.) *Özel eğitim ve yapay zekâ* içinde (155-186). Vize Akademik.

Doğuş, M. (2024b, Eylül). Visual Impairment and Artificial Intelligence: Where We Are and What Awaits Us in the. Future? *BILTEVT2024 International Barrier-Free Information Techonogy Congress*, Manisa, Türkiye.

Drigas, A., & Ioannidou, R. (2012). Artificial intelligence in special education: A decade review. *International Journal of Engineering Education*, *28*, 1366–1372.

du Boulay, B. (2022). Artificial intelligence in education and ethics. In *Handbook of open, distance and digital education* (pp. 1–16). Springer Nature. DOI: 10.1007/978-981-19-0351-9_6-2

Ersoy, C. (2025). Inclusive Transformation with Artificial Intelligence: Ethical Aspects, Policies, and Strategic Approaches for Equitable Education. In *Pitfalls of AI Integration in Education: Skill Obsolescence, Misuse, and Bias*. IGI Global., DOI: 10.4018/979-8-3373-0122-8.ch012

Espinoza, O. (2007). Solving the equity–equality conceptual dilemma: A new model for analysis of the educational process. *Educational Research, 49*(4), 343–363. DOI: 10.1080/00131880701717198

European Commission. (2024). *Educational support and guidance.* https://eurydice.eacea.ec.europa.eu/national-education-systems/germany/educational-support-and-guidance

Fahimirad, M., & Kotamjani, S. S. (2018). A review on application of artificial intelligence in teaching and learning in educational contexts. *International Journal of Learning and Development, 8*(4), 106–118. DOI: 10.5296/ijld.v8i4.14057

Garcia, M. B., Rosak-Szyrocka, J., Yılmaz, R., Metwally, A. H. S., Acut, D. P., Ofosu-Ampong, K., Erdoğdu, F., Fung, C. Y., & Bozkurt, A. (2025). Rethinking Educational Assessment in the Age of Generative AI: Actionable Strategies to Mitigate Academic Dishonesty. In *Pitfalls of AI Integration in Education: Skill Obsolescence, Misuse, and Bias*. IGI Global., DOI: 10.4018/979-8-3373-0122-8.ch001

Goldman, S. R., Taylor, J., Carreon, A., & Smith, S. J. (2024). Using AI to support special education teacher workload. *Journal of Special Education Technology, 39*(3), 434–447. DOI: 10.1177/01626434241257240

Guan, H. (2023). Advantages and challenges of using artificial intelligence in primary and secondary school education. *Educational Technology and Psychological Sciences, 22*. https://doi.org/. v22i. 12469DOI: 10.54097/ehss

Guz, E., Niderla, K., & Kata, G. (2024). Advancing autism therapy: Emotion analysis using rehabilitation robots and AI for children with ASD. *Journal of Modern Science, 57*(3), 340–355. DOI: 10.13166/jms/191144

Halamka, J. D. (2017). Privacy and Security. In Sheikh, A., Cresswell, K. M., Wright, A., & Bates, D. W. (Eds.), *Key advances in clinical informatics: Transforming health care through health information technology* (pp. 79–86). Academic., DOI: 10.1016/B978-0-12-809523-2.00006-6

Hamutoglu, N. B., Işbulan, O., & Kiyici, M. (2022). Major tendencies in special education within the framework of educational technology between 1960-2019. *Ankara Üniversitesi Eğitim Bilimleri Fakültesi Özel Eğitim Dergisi, 23*(4), 751–773. DOI: 10.21565/ozelegitimdergisi.835696

Heward, W. L., Alber-Morgan, S. R., & Konrad, M. (2017). *Exceptional Children: An Introduction to Special Education*. Pearson.

Holman, K., Marino, M. T., Vasquez, E., Taub, M., Hunt, J. H., & Tazi, Y. (2024). Navigating ai-powered personalized learning in special education: A guide for preservice teacher faculty. *Journal of Special Education Preparation, 4*(2), 90–95. DOI: 10.33043/5b2xqcb3

Howorth, S. K., Marino, M. T., Flanagan, S., Cuba, M. J., & Lemke, C. (2024). Integrating emerging technologies to enhance special education teacher preparation. *Journal of Research in Innovative Teaching & Learning*, (ahead-of-print). https://doi.org/DOI: 10.1108/JRIT-08-2024-0208

Huang, A. Y., Lu, O. H., & Yang, S. J. (2023). Effects of artificial Intelligence-Enabled personalized recommendations on learners' learning engagement, motivation, and outcomes in a flipped classroom. *Computers & Education*, *194*, 104684. DOI: 10.1016/j.compedu.2022.104684

Huang, J., Saleh, S., & Liu, Y. (2021). A review on artificial intelligence in education. *Academic Journal of Interdisciplinary Studies*, *10*(3), 206–217. DOI: 10.36941/ajis-2021-0077

Hurwitz, S., Perry, B., Cohen, E. D., & Skiba, R. (2020). Special education and individualized academic growth: A longitudinal assessment of outcomes for students with disabilities. *American Educational Research Journal*, *57*(2), 576–611. DOI: 10.3102/0002831219857054

Ikermane, M., & El Mouatasim, A. (2023). Digital handwriting characteristics for dysgraphia detection using artificial neural network. *Bulletin of Electrical Engineering and Informatics*, *12*(3), 1693–1699. DOI: 10.11591/eei.v12i3.4571

Inci, G., & Köse, H. (2024). The landscape of technology research in special education: A bibliometric analysis. *Journal of Special Education Technology*, *39*(1), 94–107. DOI: 10.1177/01626434231180582

Jackson, M. C. (2021). Artificial intelligence & algorithmic bias: The issues with technology reflecting history & humans. *Journal of Business & Technology Law.*, *16*, 299–316.

Jadán-Guerrero, J., Tamayo-Narvaez, K., Méndez, E., & Valenzuela, M. (2024). *Adaptive Learning Environments: Integrating Artificial Intelligence for Special Education Advances*. https://doi.org/DOI: 10.1007/978-3-031-61953-3_10

Kabudi, T., Pappas, I., & Olsen, D. H. (2021). AI-enabled adaptive learning systems: A systematic mapping of the literature. *Computers and Education: Artificial Intelligence*, *2*, 100017. DOI: 10.1016/j.caeai.2021.100017

Kadiresan, A., Baweja, Y., & Ogbanufe, O. (2022). Bias in AI-based decision-making. In *Bridging Human Intelligence and Artificial Intelligence* (pp. 275–285). Springer International Publishing. DOI: 10.1007/978-3-030-84729-6_19

Kamalov, F., Santandreu Calonge, D., & Gurrib, I. (2023). New era of artificial intelligence in education: Towards a sustainable multi-faceted revolution. *Sustainability (Basel)*, *15*(16), 12451. DOI: 10.3390/su151612451

Karami, B., Koushki, R., Arabgol, F., Rahmani, M., & Vahabie, A. H. (2021). Effectiveness of Virtual/Augmented Reality-Based Therapeutic Interventions on Individuals With Autism Spectrum Disorder: A Comprehensive Meta-Analysis. *Frontiers in Psychiatry*, *12*, 665326. DOI: 10.3389/fpsyt.2021.665326 PMID: 34248702

Karsenti, T. (2019). Acting as ethical and responsible digital citizens: The teacher's key role. *Formation et profession*, *27*(1), 112-116. https://dx.doi.org/DOI: 10.18162/fp.2019.a167

Kasy, M. (2024). Algorithmic bias and racial inequality: A critical review. *Oxford Review of Economic Policy*, *40*(3), 530–546. DOI: 10.1093/oxrep/grae031

Kauffman, J., & Hornby, G. (2020). Inclusive Vision Versus Special Education Reality. *Education Sciences*, *10*(9), 258. DOI: 10.3390/educsci10090258

Kaya, A. (Ed.). (2024). *Özel eğitim ve yapay zeka [Special education and artificial intelligence]*. Vize Akademik.

Kharbat, F. F., Alshawabkeh, A., & Woolsey, M. L. (2021). Identifying gaps in using artificial intelligence to support students with intellectual disabilities from education and health perspectives. *Aslib Journal of Information Management, 73*(1), 101–128. DOI: 10.1108/AJIM-02-2020-0054

Kim, K., & Kwon, K. (2024). Designing an Inclusive Artificial Intelligence (AI) Curriculum for Elementary Students to Address Gender Differences With Collaborative and Tangible Approaches. *Journal of Educational Computing Research, 62*(7), 1837–1864. DOI: 10.1177/07356331241271059

Kordzadeh, N., & Ghasemaghaei, M. (2022). Algorithmic bias: Review, synthesis, and future research directions. *European Journal of Information Systems, 31*(3), 388–409. DOI: 10.1080/0960085X.2021.1927212

Kosmicki, J. A., Sochat, V., Duda, M., & Wall, D. P. (2015). Searching for a minimal set of behaviors for autism detection through feature selection-based machine learning. *Translational Psychiatry, 5*(2), e514–e514. DOI: 10.1038/tp.2015.7 PMID: 25710120

Kraemer, F., Van Overveld, K., & Peterson, M. (2011). Is there an ethics of algorithms? *Ethics and Information Technology, 13*(3), 251–260. DOI: 10.1007/s10676-010-9233-7

Kuprenko, V. (2020). Artificial intelligence in education: Benefits, challenges, and use cases. https://pub.towardsai.net/artificial-intelligence-in-education-benefits-challenges-and-use-cases-db52d8921f7a

Lashley, C. (2007). Principal leadership for special education: An ethical framework. *Exceptionality, 15*(3), 177–187. DOI: 10.1080/09362830701503511

Lazar, J., Wentz, B., & Winckler, M. (2017). Information privacy and security as a human right for people with disabilities. *Disability, Human Rights, and Information Technology*, 199-211. https://doi.org/DOI: 10.9783/9780812294095-014

Lid, I. M. (2014). Universal design and disability: An interdisciplinary perspective. *Disability and Rehabilitation, 36*(16), 1344–1349. DOI: 10.3109/09638288.2014.931472 PMID: 24954388

Liu, Y., Saleh, S., Huang, J., & Syed Mohamad, S. A. (2020). Review of the application of artificial intelligence in education. *International Journal of Innovation. Creativity and Change, 12*(8), 548–562. DOI: 10.53333/IJICC2013/12850

Long, D., & Magerko, B. (2020). What is AI Literacy? Competencies and Design Considerations. *Proceedings of the 2020 CHI Conference on Human Factors in Computing Systems*, Honolulu, HI, USA. https://doi.org/DOI: 10.1145/3313831.3376727

Lorenzo, G., & Lorenzo-Lledó, A. (2024). The use of artificial intelligence for detecting the duration of autistic students' emotions in social interaction with the NAO robot: A case study. *International Journal of Information Technology : an Official Journal of Bharati Vidyapeeth's Institute of Computer Applications and Management, 16*(2), 1–7. DOI: 10.1007/s41870-023-01682-0

MacLeod, K., Causton, J. N., Radel, M., & Radel, P. (2017). Rethinking the individualized education plan process: Voices from the other side of the table. *Disability & Society, 32*(3), 381–400. DOI: 10.1080/09687599.2017.1294048

Madden, M., Gilman, M., Levy, K., & Marwick, A. (2017). Privacy, poverty, and big data: A matrix of vulnerabilities for poor Americans. *Washington University Law Review*, *95*(1), 53–125.

Mahmoudi-Dehaki, M., & Nasr-Esfahani, N. (2025). Artificial intelligence (AI) in special education: AI therapeutic pedagogy for language disorders. In *Transforming special education through artificial intelligence* (pp. 193–222). IGI Global.

Marino, M. T., Vasquez, E., Dieker, L., Basham, J., & Blackorby, J. (2023). The future of artificial intelligence in special education technology. *Journal of Special Education Technology*, *38*(3), 404–416. DOI: 10.1177/01626434231165977

Martínez-Requejo, S., Redondo-Duarte, S., Jiménez-García, E., & Ruiz-Lázaro, J. (2025). Technoethics and the Use of Artificial Intelligence in Educational Contexts: Reflections on Integrity, Transparency, and Equity. In *Pitfalls of AI Integration in Education: Skill Obsolescence, Misuse, and Bias*. IGI Global., DOI: 10.4018/979-8-3373-0122-8.ch010

Matthews, J. T., Beach, S. R., Downs, J., de Bruin, W. B., Mecca, L. P., & Schulz, . (2010). Preferences and concerns for quality of life technology among older adults and persons with disabilities: National survey results. *Technology and Disability*, *22*(1-2), 5–15. DOI: 10.3233/TAD-2010-0279

Mazumder, M. (2024, August). Significance of artificial intelligence in the realm of special education. *Artificial Intelligence in Education* (pp. 242-249). Red Unicorn.

McDonald, N., & Forte, A. (2022). Privacy and vulnerable populations. In Knijnenburg, B. P., Page, X., Wisniewski, P., Lipford, H. R., Proferes, N., & Romano, J. (Eds.), *Modern sociotechnical perspectives on privacy* (pp. 337–363). Springer. DOI: 10.1007/978-3-030-82786-1_15

Mıjwıl, M. M., Sadıkoğlu, E., Cengiz, E., & Candan, H. (2022). Siber güvenlikte yapay zekânın rolü ve önemi: Bir derleme. *Veri Bilimi*, *5*(2), 97–105.

Milliron, M. D., Malcolm, L., & Kil, D. (2014). Insight and action analytics: Three case studies to consider. *Research & Practice in Assessment*, *9*, 70–89. https://files.eric.ed.gov/fulltext/EJ1062814.pdf

Najjar, M., Courtemanche, F., Hamam, H., & Mayers, A. (2010). Deepkover-An adaptive artful intelligent assistance system for cognitively impaired people. *Applied Artificial Intelligence*, *24*(5), 381–413. DOI: 10.1080/08839514.2010.481486

Nikitina, I., & Ishchenko, T. (2024). The impact of AI on teachers: Support or replacement? *Scientific Journal of Polonia University*, *65*(4), 93–99. DOI: 10.23856/6511

Open, A. I. (2024, May 13). *Be My Eyes Accessibility with GPT-4o* [Video]. YouTube. https://www.youtube.com/watch?v=Kw- NUJ69RbwY

Orru, G., Piarulli, A., Conversano, C., & Gemignani, A. (2023). Human-like problem-solving abilities in large language models using ChatGPT. *Frontiers in Artificial Intelligence*, *6*, 1199350. DOI: 10.3389/frai.2023.1199350 PMID: 37293238

Ozkazanc-Pan, B. (2021). Diversity and future of work: Inequality abound or opportunities for all? *Management Decision*, *59*(11), 2645–2659. DOI: 10.1108/MD-02-2019-0244

Pagliara, S., Bonavolontà, G., Pia, M., Falchi, S., Zurru, A., Fenu, G., & Mura, A. (2024). The Integration of Artificial Intelligence in Inclusive Education: A Scoping Review. *Information (Basel)*, *15*(12), 774. Advance online publication. DOI: 10.3390/info15120774

Palen, L., & Dourish, P. (2003). Unpacking "privacy" for a networked world. In *Proceedings of the SIGCHI Conference on Human Factors in Computing Systems*, 129–136. SIGCHI.

Pandey, A., & Caliskan, A. (2021). Disparate impact of artificial intelligence bias in ridehailing economy's price discrimination algorithms. In *Proceedings of the 2021 AAAI/ACM Conference on AI, Ethics, and Society* (pp. 822-833). DOI: 10.1145/3461702.3462561

Panjwani-Charania, S., & Zhai, X. (2024). AI for Students with Learning Disabilities: A Systematic Review. In X. Zhai & J. Krajcik (Eds.), *Uses of Artificial Intelligence in STEM Education* (p. 0). Oxford University Press. https://doi.org/DOI: 10.1093/oso/9780198882077.003.0021

Paulus, J. K., & Kent, D. M. (2020). Predictably unequal: Understanding and addressing concerns that algorithmic clinical prediction may increase health disparities. *NPJ Digital Medicine*, *3*(1), 1–8. DOI: 10.1038/s41746-020-0304-9 PMID: 32821854

Peters, U. (2022). Algorithmic political bias in artificial intelligence systems. *Philosophy & Technology*, *35*(2), 1–25. DOI: 10.1007/s13347-022-00512-8 PMID: 35378902

Rakap, S. (2024). Navigating the role of artificial intelligence in special education: Advantages, disadvantages, and ethical considerations. *Practice*, *6*(2-3), 1–6. DOI: 10.1080/25783858.2024.2411948

Ram, B., & Verma, P. (2023). Artificial intelligence AI-based Chatbot study of ChatGPT, Google AI Bard and Baidu AI. *World Journal of Advanced Engineering Technology and Sciences*, *8*(01), 258–261. DOI: 10.30574/wjaets.2023.8.1.0045

Ramineni, C., & Williamson, D. M. (2013). Automated essay scoring: Psychometric guidelines and practices. *Assessing Writing*, *18*(1), 25–39. DOI: 10.1016/j.asw.2012.10.004

Ritter, S., Yudelson, M., Fancsali, S. E., & Berman, S. R. (2016). How mastery learning works at scale. In *Proceedings of the Third (2016) ACM Conference on Learning @ Scale* (pp. 71–79). ACM. https://doi.org/DOI: 10.1145/2876034.2876039

Rocheleau, J. N., Chalghoumi, H., Jutai, J., Farrell, S., Lachapelle, Y., & Cobigo, V. (2021). Caregivers' role in cybersecurity for aging information technology users with intellectual disabilities. *Cyberpsychology, Behavior, and Social Networking*, *24*(9), 624–629. DOI: 10.1089/cyber.2020.0572 PMID: 34182769

Rozado, D. (2020). Wide range screening of algorithmic bias in word embedding models using large sentiment lexicons reveals underreported bias types. *PLoS One*, *15*(4), e0231189. DOI: 10.1371/journal.pone.0231189 PMID: 32315320

Sağdıç, Z. A., & Sani-Bozkurt, S. (2020). Otizm spektrum bozukluğu ve yapay zekâ uygulamaları. *Açıköğretim Uygulamaları ve Araştırmaları Dergisi*, *6*(3), 92–111.

Sari, H., Tumanggor, B., & Efron, D. (2024). Improving Educational Outcomes Through Adaptive Learning Systems using AI. *International Transactions on Artificial Intelligence*, *3*(1), 21–31. DOI: 10.33050/italic.v3i1.647

Saxena, P., Saxena, V., Pandey, A., Flato, U., & Shukla, K. (2023). *Multiple aspects of artificial intelligence*. Book Saga Publications. DOI: 10.60148/muasartificialintelligence

Scassellati, B., Admoni, H., & Matarić, M. (2012). Robots for use in autism research. *Annual Review of Biomedical Engineering, 14*(1), 275–294. DOI: 10.1146/annurev-bioeng-071811-150036 PMID: 22577778

Scott, L. M., Wilder, T. L., Zaugg, T., & Romualdo, A. (2024). Enhancing Special Education Using AI. *Advances in Educational Technologies and Instructional Design Book Series*, 45–78. https://doi.org/ DOI: 10.4018/979-8-3693-5538-1.ch002

Şen, N., & Akbay, T. (2023). Artificial intelligence and innovative applications in special education. *Instructional Technology and Lifelong Learning, 4*(2), 176–199. DOI: 10.52911/itall.1297978

Shrestha, Y. R., Ben-Menahem, S. M., & Von Krogh, G. (2019). Organizational decision-making structures in the age of artificial intelligence. *California Management Review, 61*(4), 66–83. DOI: 10.1177/0008125619862257

Siegle, D. (2023). A role for ChatGPT and AI in gifted education. *Gifted Child Today, 46*(3), 211–219. DOI: 10.1177/10762175231168443

Slade, N., Eisenhower, A., Carter, A. S., & Blacher, J. (2018). Satisfaction with individualized education programs among parents of young children with ASD. *Exceptional Children, 84*(3), 242–260. DOI: 10.1177/0014402917742923

Smith, H. (2020). Algorithmic bias: Should students pay the price? *AI & Society, 35*(4), 1077–1078. DOI: 10.1007/s00146-020-01054-3 PMID: 32952313

Smith, T. E. (2015). *Serving students with special needs: A practical guide for administrators*. Routledge. DOI: 10.4324/9781315818634

Song, B., & Koo, A. (2022). Paradigm shift: Artificial intelligence, contemporary art, and implications for gifted arts education. *Journal of Gifted Education in Arts, 8*, 5–38.

Taneja, D., Prabagaren, H., & Thomas, M. R. (2025). AI in Academia: Balancing Integrity, Ethics, and Learning Amid Evolving Norms of Authorship and Scholarship. In *Pitfalls of AI Integration in Education: Skill Obsolescence, Misuse, and Bias*. IGI Global., DOI: 10.4018/979-8-3373-0122-8.ch014

Tsouktakou, A., Hamouroudis, A., & Horti, A. (2024). The use of artificial intelligence in the education of people with visual impairment. *World Journal of Advanced Engineering Technology and Sciences, 13*(1), 734–744. DOI: 10.30574/wjaets.2024.13.1.0481

Verma, S., Ernst, M., & Just, R. (2021). Removing biased data to improve fairness and accuracy. *arXiv*. https://arxiv.org/abs/2102.03054

Viswanathan, S., Ibrahim, S., Shankar, R., Binns, R., Van Kleek, M., & Slovák, P. (2024). *The Interaction Layer: An Exploration for Co-Designing User-LLM Interactions in Parental Wellbeing Support Systems*. https://doi.org//arxiv.2411.01228 DOI: 10.48550

Vuran, S. (Ed.). (2020). *Özel eğitim öğretmenleri için etik ilkeler kılavuzu*. Vize Akademik.

Wadhawan, A., & Kumar, P. (2021). Sign language recognition systems: A decade systematic literature review. *Archives of Computational Methods in Engineering*, *28*(3), 785–813. DOI: 10.1007/s11831-019-09384-2

Walugembe, T. A., Nakayenga, H. N., & Babirye, S. (2024). Artificial Intelligence-Driven Transformation in Special Education: Optimizing Software for Improved Learning Outcomes. *International Journal of Computer Applications Technology and Research*, *13*(8), 163–179. DOI: 10.7753/IJCATR1308.1015

Wang, Y. (2021). Artificial intelligence in educational leadership: A symbiotic role of human-artificial intelligence decision-making. *Journal of Educational Administration*, *59*(3), 256–270. DOI: 10.1108/JEA-10-2020-0216

Wang, Y., & Price, C. E. (2022). Accessible privacy. In Knijnenburg, B. P., Page, X., Wisniewski, P., Lipford, H. R., Proferes, N., & Romano, J. (Eds.), *Modern sociotechnical perspectives on privacy* (pp. 337–363). Springer. DOI: 10.1007/978-3-030-82786-1_13

Waters, A., & Miikkulainen, R. (2014). GRADE: Machine learning support for graduate admissions. *AI Magazine*, *35*(1), 64–75. DOI: 10.1609/aimag.v35i1.2504

WeWalk. (t.y.). *Product - WeWALK Smart Cane.* https://wewalk.io/tr/product/

Whittington, P., & Doğan, H. (2024). *Improving quality of life through the application of assistive technology.* Edward Elgar Publishing., DOI: 10.4337/9781800888647.00011

Wilson, J. D. (2017). Reimagining disability and inclusive education through universal design for learning. *Disability Studies Quarterly*, *37*(2). Advance online publication. DOI: 10.18061/dsq.v37i2.5417

Woolf, B. P. (2010). *Building intelligent interactive tutors: Student-centered strategies for revolutionizing e-learning.* Morgan Kaufmann.

Xiao, J., Bozkurt, A., Nichols, M., Pazurek, A., Stracke, C. M., Bai, J. Y. H., Farrow, R., Mulligan, D., Nerantzi, C., Sharma, R. C., Singh, L., Frumin, I., Swindell, A., Honeychurch, S., Bond, M., Dron, J., Moore, S., Leng, J., & Slagter van Tryon, P. J.. (2025). Venturing into the Unknown: Critical Insights into Grey Areas and Pioneering Future Directions in Educational Generative AI Research. *TechTrends*, ●●●, 1–16. DOI: 10.1007/s11528-025-01060-6

Yıldız, G. (2024a). Özel eğitimde yapay zekâ, dijital güvenlik ve etik konular. A. Kaya (Ed.) *Özel eğitim ve yapay zekâ* içinde (293-315). [Artificial intelligence, digital security and ethical issues in special education. In A. Kaya (Ed.), Special education and artificial intelligence]. Vize Akademik.

Yılmaz, Y., & Çolaklıoğlu, O. (2024). İşitme kayıplılar ve yapay zekâ. A. Kaya (Ed.) *Özel eğitim ve yapay zekâ* içinde (135-156). [Hearing loss and artificial intelligence. In A. Kaya (Ed.), Special education and artificial intelligence]. Vize Akademik.

Yuan, J., Holtz, C., Smith, T., & Luo, J. (2016). Autism spectrum disorder detection from semi-structured and unstructured medical data. *EURASIP Journal on Bioinformatics & Systems Biology*, *2017*(1), 3. Advance online publication. DOI: 10.1186/s13637-017-0057-1 PMID: 28203249

Zhumazhan, B., Zhumadilova, M., & Abdykerimova, E. (2024). The future of artificial intelligence in inclusive education. *Yessenov Science Journal*, *48*(3), 63–70. Advance online publication. DOI: 10.56525/AMWI6491

Zhuravleva, N. A., Cadge, K., Poliak, M., & Podhorska, I. (2019). Data privacy and security vulnerabilities of smart and sustainable urban space monitoring systems. *Contemporary Readings in Law and Social Justice*, *11*(2), 56–62. DOI: 10.22381/CRLSJ11220198

KEY TERMS AND DEFINITIONS

Artificial Intelligence (AI): AI refers to the ability of computer systems to perform tasks that typically require human intelligence, such as learning, reasoning, decision-making, and problem-solving.

Algorithmic Bias: Algorithmic bias occurs when AI systems produce unfair or discriminatory outcomes due to biases present in the training data or algorithm design.

Data Privacy and Security: Data privacy and security refer to the ethical and legal measures taken to protect sensitive student information collected by AI-driven educational tools.

Inclusive AI Design: Inclusive AI design involves creating AI systems that accommodate diverse learning needs, ensuring accessibility for students with disabilities. This includes adaptive learning technologies, speech-to-text tools, and AI-driven assistive devices tailored to different abilities.

Human Oversight in AI: Human oversight in AI refers to the role of educators, therapists, and caregivers in monitoring and guiding AI-assisted educational processes.

Personalized Learning: Personalized learning is an instructional approach that tailors educational content and teaching methods to students' individual needs, preferences, and progress. AI enhances personalized learning by analyzing student data and adjusting materials accordingly.

Chapter 12
Inclusive Transformation With Artificial Intelligence:
Ethical Aspects, Policies, and Strategic Approaches for Equitable Education

Ceren Ersoy
https://orcid.org/0000-0002-7168-744X
Gazi University, Turkey

ABSTRACT

In recent years, artificial intelligence (AI) has emerged as one of the most potent tools to promote digital transformation in education. The effective use of AI in education requires robust policy frameworks and ethical oversight mechanisms. Providing an overview of the transformative role of AI in education, this chapter discusses the prominent requirements for the ethical use of technology that supports inclusive and equitable education in education systems and offers policy recommendations that will maximize the potential of AI in creating equitable, fair, and inclusive educational environments. Special emphasis is placed on the role of interdisciplinary collaboration among stakeholders to ensure that AI systems are aligned with human-centered values and educational goals. The chapter aims to draw attention to the data-driven framework addressing the most debated issues of bias, data privacy, inclusion, risks, fair and equitable approach in education to establish an inclusive AI ecosystem in light of global standards, international policies, and evidence-based practices.

INTRODUCTION

With the advent of the Fourth Industrial Revolution, digital technologies, especially artificial intelligence (AI), have become transformative forces in shaping economic, social, and educational systems. While these advances promise innovation and efficiency, they have also exacerbated existing inequalities by disproportionately benefiting a small, highly skilled segment of society and marginalizing those with limited resources or educational opportunities. As social inequalities widen, barriers to educational ac-

DOI: 10.4018/979-8-3373-0122-8.ch012

cess and participation intensify, further deepening gaps in well-being and opportunity, especially among disadvantaged populations (Schwab, 2016).

In this context, the imperative to promote equity and inclusion in education is not just an economic concern, but a critical foundation for social stability, justice, and quality of life. Historically, educational systems have often excluded individuals who deviate from dominant normative standards. Policies and practices that promote discrimination are in sharp contrast to the fundamental principles of inclusive education, which emphasize equity, participation and respect for diversity in all educational settings (Mittler, 2008; UNESCO, 2005).

As a rapidly evolving technology, AI has the potential to either reinforce or help disassemble these exclusionary structures, depending on how it is developed, implemented, and governed. Therefore, examining the role of AI in inclusive education requires not only a technological lens, but also a critical ethical, social, and pedagogical perspective. This chapter explores the transformative possibilities and inherent risks of integrating AI into inclusive education, with the goal of contributing to a more equitable and human-centered digital future.

MAIN FOCUS OF THE CHAPTER

This chapter analyzes the ethical, social, pedagogical, and political risks of integrating AI into inclusive education. It provides a strategic framework for making this transformation more equitable, human-centered, and sustainable. Despite the growing interest in literature on the potential contributions of AI in education, there is a clear lack of comprehensive and critical analyses of how these technologies intersect with the principles of inclusion in education and how to respond to the risk of deepening inequalities. In the context of " Pitfalls of AI Integration in Education," this chapter systematically addresses risks such as algorithmic bias, privacy violations, impact on teacher roles, digitalization of social relations, obsolescence of professional skills, and deepening of the digital divide. The chapter also discusses the conditions under which AI's potential to support equity in education can be unleashed, what kind of risks it poses for which groups, the exclusionary effects of a lack of data diversity, and the socio-emotional effects of AI systems on human relationships. In this context, recommendations are provided on the development of AI applications based on a human-centered design approach, the structuring of inclusive ecosystems, and the delineation of the ethical boundaries of this transformation process. It presents not only a technological transformation, but also a normative inquiry into the social function of education. It argues that decisions about the use of artificial intelligence in education should be consistent with the principles of ethical responsibility, transparency, inclusion, and social justice. The proposed framework provides a roadmap for AI-powered systems to play a transformative and inclusive role, rather than reproducing inequalities in education.

THE TRANSFORMATIVE ROLE OF AI IN INCLUSIVE EDUCATION

Inclusive education is a philosophy that fosters collaboration among students, families, educators, and communities to build a sense of belonging (Salend, 2011). Every child is special, and each child has unique characteristics. This approach emphasizes the importance of children who exhibit individual differences in many ways to learn together in an inclusive educational environment. The inclusive education approach promotes educational environments with equal opportunities and fairer outcomes for all students (European Agency, 2012). In this philosophy, which strongly advocates the perspective of "education for all", education is seen as the most basic human right. Education systems that combine equity and quality will ensure the highest performance (OECD, 2012).

Societies that view education through the lens of inclusion will have the opportunity to create a self-reinforcing cycle of success in the system by ceasing to see the child as a problem and identifying the needs that exist in the education system, developing radical solutions that are appropriate for diversity (UNICEF, 2014). The main goal of inclusive education is not to ensure that the student adapts to the system, but that the system adapts to the student. It is essential to support all students, educators and the education system to meet all learning needs. Inclusive education requires a radical restructuring of the school in terms of curriculum, assessment and education. It emphasizes the need to overcome barriers within the system to enable all students to reach their potential. This requires first recognizing the existing barriers and taking the necessary measures.

Individual differences should not be seen as problems to be solved, but as opportunities for democratization and enrichment of learning. Flexibility is essential in the education system. Inclusive education emphasizes the importance of using strategies that promote all students' belonging to school and society, academic success, social emotional development, access and participation in education (Mezzanotte, 2022; UNESCO, 2020; UNICEF, 2014). In the long term, a quality inclusive education system not only enables children to be independent individuals of society but also gives them the chance to contribute to the economy as productive members of the community (Mezzanotte, 2022). Creating effective inclusive education system is a more cost-effective way to provide "education for all" (UNESCO, 2003).

When considering inclusive education, it is important to be aware that countries can exhibit examples of good practices, but no one has all the answers for inclusive education and all countries are still trying to move forward in this regard. It is known that this difference between countries is due to resource distribution and population density. While countries differ in their approaches and starting points, effective inclusive education demands equitable distribution of financial and human resources and sustainable partnerships. Targeted funding for disadvantaged groups and strong monitoring mechanisms enhance equity and participation (UNESCO, 2015).

Today, one of the most effective ways to support all students with an understanding of equal and quality education for all is to promote digital transformation in education. AI can support this transformation by enabling personalized learning paths based on students' pace, strengths, and needs (Luckin & Çukurova, 2019; Reich & Ito, 2017). AI helps teachers save time on routine tasks and supports assessment, differentiation, and enrichment processes. It can enhance student motivation, creativity, and higher-order thinking through adaptive content, while also facilitating individualized feedback, providing guidance in areas such as 3D modeling, VR, AR, coding, engineering, digital arts, music, videography and creative learning experiences (Chopra et al., 2024). It can also contribute to automating the process of early identification and placement of individuals in appropriate schools through AI-supported systems.

AI holds significant potential to identify individual talents, address needs tailored to personal differences, promote equal opportunities in education, and foster a deeper understanding of inclusion. When the power of technology is combined with ethical and equity principles, a brighter future can be built for students. However, despite these opportunities offered by AI, various problems are waiting to be solved, obstacles to be overcome and ethical, social and pedagogical risks to be considered to use it properly and effectively.

While research on the advantages and disadvantages of artificial intelligence as well as research focusing on its future shows that the success of industries and organizations in the world economy is based on the digital transformation they provide in their workflows, planning, production and evaluation processes under the pressure of technological developments, it is clear that a similar transformation process should be planned in education (Rowe, 2019). Therefore, while these issues generally reveal the urgency of an ethical debate on the role and limits of AI in education, they also highlight the importance of protecting human values and enhancing AI competencies in learning contexts. However, developing public policies that foster interpersonal relationships is crucial to prevent potential problems. Artificial intelligence should be designed with a human-centered approach, structured in a way that does not undermine human relationships but rather supports them as a complementary tool.

Dilemma in Education: Inclusion or Discrimination?

Artificial intelligence (AI) has the potential to revolutionize education systems, but it also raises serious ethical, social, and political issues. While AI can serve as a powerful tool to promote inclusion and equity in education, inadequate planning and implementation may result in discrimination, breaches of data privacy and security, and inequitable access to opportunities. For AI to be used responsibly in education, it is essential to carefully evaluate the current risks, opportunities and threats. Furthermore, strong policy frameworks and ethical oversight mechanisms must be established for its inclusive and effective use (Durovic & Watson, 2022). Determining the risks and possible precautions will only be possible with the increasing number of studies to be carried out in the field. In this context, when the discussions underlying the literature are examined, it is seen that there are arguments on a wide range of issues.

Ethics, Justice and Algorithmic Bias

Ethical Principles in AI Integration

In recent years, the ethical integration of AI in education has gained attention, emphasizing the need for responsible design, transparency, and inclusion. To ensure that AI is designed and used responsibly, it is recommended to set ethical principles for protecting people, managing the use of AI, and assessing the impact of AI on employment and jobs (Smith & Shum, 2021). There are six key principles for the responsible development and use of AI systems (Microsoft, n.d.). Fairness requires AI systems to treat all individuals fairly and be free from bias or discrimination. Reliability and Safety aims to ensure that AI systems perform reliably and consistently. Privacy and Security requires AI systems to respect and secure the privacy of users. Inclusiveness aims to ensure that AI systems are designed to benefit everyone and effectively involve the community. Transparency ensures that AI systems are understandable and interpretable and that users understand how they work. Finally, Accountability emphasizes that responsibility for the development and use of AI systems should always lie with people. These principles provide a critical framework to ensure that AI is developed in an ethical, trustworthy and human-centered way. The ethical use of AI requires that various risks are considered, and necessary precautions are taken.

Algorithmic Threats in AI Integration

AI systems risk reinforcing existing social inequalities due to biased data, lack of transparency and insufficient diversity in training data. Artificial intelligence (AI) can make decisions by identifying patterns in large data sets; however, when working on training data, there is a risk of inconsistent, faulty, and invalid results.

When training data is poorly structured, obtained from sources with insufficient reliability and validity, and often consists only of limited metrics such as students' grades (Lynch, 2018), it is unfortunately used to train AI models due to its ease of access and collectability, although it does not adequately represent the pedagogical context. This can lead to AI systems producing predictions based on a superficial and narrow data set rather than understanding the complex processes in education.

The errors in training AI-based systems arise not only from the weaknesses of the data structure, but also from the nature of the algorithms. The algorithms' data sources can be biased, make inferences incorrect, and fail to adapt to unexpected situations (Mittelstadt et al., 2016). Furthermore, both existing social biases in data and subconscious biases in human decision-making processes can deepen inequalities in AI outcomes (Crawford & Calo, 2016; Gallagher, 2019; Kahneman, 2011). The process of extracting and transforming data for algorithms also creates additional sources of bias and error. A lack of meaningful data can create an AI ecosystem that fails to represent the social contexts of certain groups and further excludes these groups. If this process is left unchecked, algorithms can further reinforce existing systemic inequalities (Rowe, 2019). For fair AI, creating multidisciplinary teams consisting of teachers, educational researchers, students, and technology developers will increase the likelihood that biases will be detected and corrected, providing data diversity across diverse student populations and contexts, enabling more accurate predictions. It is also clear that policies supporting the digital transformation of education should be focused on ensuring the participation of all stakeholders in this process. In summary, the importance of using and developing ethical AI applications that promote fair and equitable educational environment that prioritizes the needs of diverse student groups is emphasized. Furthermore, with a comprehensive collaboration involving all segments of society, it is possible to evaluate AI as an ethical tool in education (DiMatteo et al., 2022).

Another important issue to consider when discussing the ethical aspects of AI in education is algorithmic bias. With the increasing awareness of the societal risks of algorithmic bias and the advancement of automation, issues of fairness, accountability, and transparency in data-driven AI systems have become increasingly important (Holmes, Bialik et al., 2019; Holstein & Doroudi, 2022). The ethical use of AI in education requires creating a fair and inclusive learning environment that is free from bias. This goal can be achieved by increasing the diversity of data in AI systems and ensuring the transparency of algorithms. In this way, systematic errors based on gender, race, or socioeconomic status can be prevented (Shiohira & Holmes, 2023).

To ensure the safe and ethical use of AI technologies in education, data-driven systems must be developed following the principles of accountability and transparency. Educators and policymakers have a critical role in reducing bias and maintaining transparency in this process (Durovic & Watson, 2022). In addition, planning professional development programs to develop AI literacy allows all stakeholders, especially educators, who contribute to creating inclusive systems to use these technologies safely and effectively. It is recommended that schools and institutions responsible for teacher education continue their joint efforts to discover effective ways to turn individual differences into opportunities in classrooms and to develop suitable models for teacher training and vocational education (European Agency, 2011).

Threats for Equity

The use of AI as a potential tool for ensuring equal opportunities in education requires the development of models that offer more effective benefits, especially for students with low socio-economic backgrounds (Holmes & Porayska-Pomsta, 2022; UNESCO, 2019). Thus, AI contributes to actively transforming educational differences into an advantage to diversify learning and create effective inclusive environments. The use of AI in education brings with it both the potential to create equal opportunities and the risk of deepening inequalities. These risks become more apparent with the combination of algorithmic biases, data privacy issues, and inadequate ethical policies. Difficulties in affording and regularly accessing technology disproportionately affect specific segments of the global population. In addition to device and data costs, various factors, including low internet awareness, lack of education, inadequate digital skills, security concerns, and lack of infrastructure such as quality network access and electricity, are felt more intensely in disadvantaged groups. This situation also causes a lack of data from some regions or communities, limiting the creation of meaningful data to support machine learning. This lack of data can reinforce existing sociocultural barriers by making the needs and characteristics of disadvantaged groups invisible.

The lack of meaningful data on certain groups can create an AI ecosystem that excludes them by reducing their representation in the social context. In order to reduce these inequalities, more diverse and representative data sources should be used, and fair, inclusive AI systems that take into account the characteristics and needs of all groups should be developed. At the same time, technology should be considered not only as a facilitating tool but also as a sociocultural tool that affects social relations. Therefore, it should be known that AI is more than just a technological tool, it has the potential to reproduce or reduce social inequalities. The use of technology in education without considering its social and pedagogical effects can lead to superficial learning experiences that fail to meet deeper educational goals (Daniela, 2022). The future of education depends on our power to eliminate disadvantages resulting from the misuse of developments that can create advantages or limited access to technology. These changes are challenging to achieve in a system where educators lack the time and support to collect and analyze various data. Nevertheless, it is imperative to design algorithms that support inclusive and equitable education goals to prevent AI-powered learning processes from becoming confined to a narrow vision.

Human-Centered Desing in AI Systems

The design of educational systems based on artificial intelligence algorithms, on the other hand, poses various challenges and risks. One of the frequently emphasized issues is that machines cannot imitate the relationships, care, ethical and fair understanding that teachers establish during their teaching, and that the essence of the human-centered teaching approach is based on the nature of interactions between humans. Often, while people enthusiastically accept the radical changes created by technology, when it comes to their profession, they tend to find strong justifications to ensure that the changes experienced will not threaten their profession (Susskind & Susskind, 2015).

There are some human-specific abilities that are essential for meaningful interactions that are central to learning and teaching. Today, increasing the functional intelligence of an AI-based system is not enough to solve problems related to human values and relevance in the context of learning and teaching. However, it should be clear that the primary goal of AI research is not to attempt to accurately model all the components of human cognition that enable effective communication. The successful implementation of AI-based systems in education will not require consciousness, morality, or the ability to generalize across contexts (Frankish & Ramsey, 2017). The fact is that we are faced with a technology that can make meaningful inferences about the world, make accurate predictions, and, in some cases, produce results beyond human cognition, based solely on high computational power. In this context, predictions about what AI may offer in the future still fascinate us.

Teachers have expressed the view that intelligent algorithms and humanoid robots will not endanger the teaching profession because they cannot establish emotional bonds that will create a meaningful and socially constructed learning process (Yumrukaya & Ersoy, 2024). While AI is unlikely to replace teachers, automation may increasingly affect the profession as machines become more capable. Instead of fearing replacement, teachers may acknowledge that AI will gradually handle time-consuming tasks.

AI technologies allow teachers to reduce their workload by automating their routine tasks and making adaptations and enrichments to make lessons more engaging. It contributes to creating the best options to meet students' individual needs by creating personalized learning experiences in education. Moreover, for AI to perform routine tasks in education more effectively, it does not need to imitate the best qualities of teachers; it is sufficient to be more cost-effective than the average teacher (Brynjolfsson & McAfee, 2014). However, issues such as emotional support, mentoring, and creativity are areas that AI has not yet fully fulfilled. However, in the emerging digital age, the possibility that human relationships will diminish and interactions with machines will replace human relationships raises ethical and social concerns about technology and AI. While AI systems are trying to create more human experiences in human-machine interactions, it is known that users are not indifferent to this situation and that this may lead to a decrease in human-to-human interactions.

Technology attracts people by simulating human characteristics, making it easy for individuals to develop technology addiction and even deep emotional relationships (Zimmerman et al., 2024). People tend to perceive AI-based systems, such as Alexa or Siri, as conscious or human-like. This indicates the possibility that AI can create a false bond that can replace human relationships. As people begin to meet their social relationships and needs with these technologies, the habits that children who grow up exposed to this technology from a young age will bring about from their early experiences have the potential to make this situation more apparent in the future. This situation will be felt more clearly in children struggling with loneliness, the elderly, and individuals with special needs.

On the other hand, although artificial intelligence creates the impression that it establishes a real connection with people by simulating human emotions, such connections will be one-sided and misleading since it does not have human emotions. There are examples of individuals who think they have social relationships with artificial intelligence applications experiencing emotional trauma in the future (Zimmerman et al., 2024). From a social perspective, technology dependency in meeting socialization needs may lead to more significant social problems in the long term. Replacing human relationships with artificial intelligence can lead to increased loneliness in society and decreased empathy and social ties. The increase in such relationships will also reduce the motivation of individuals to contribute to society. Artificial intelligence systems will inevitably fit into the gaps left by traditional teaching practices. Their ability to efficiently perform routine tasks and pretend to care without having to imitate a fair and ethical pedagogy will facilitate the integration of artificial intelligence into education, as in other areas.

Machine learning-based systems do not need to make sense of the world, emotions, consciousness, or human relationships, because without these, they can perform tasks that are open to automation, such as preparing curriculum and syllabi, transcribing lecture notes, preparing and reviewing content, developing materials, and making adaptations, which take up a large portion of teachers' time. Algorithms are not conscious, they are not emotional, and yet the fact that they perform an increasing number of tasks better than humans is undeniable.

In the Shadow of Digital Transformation: Risks and Responsibilities

Using artificial intelligence systems in education is vital to promote high-quality digital education and training. These systems enable all learners and teachers to acquire and share the necessary digital skills and competencies, media literacy, and critical thinking. Artificial intelligence, which pioneers innovations in health, transportation, energy, and agriculture sectors, can also revolutionize educational technologies. While artificial intelligence offers significant transformation potential at both economic and societal levels, it is also essential to consider the risks it brings in detail. Discussions on various issues such as the protection of student and educator data and the risk of misuse of this data, lack of transparency and privacy in artificial intelligence systems, changing teacher roles and weakening professional competencies, loneliness and loss of empathy due to technologies that can replace human relationships, errors in artificial intelligence systems due to lack of data diversity based on gender, race or socioeconomic status, and the potential of algorithms to reinforce existing inequalities continue to be current. Key concerns include teacher role shifts, reduced human interaction, and tech-dominated pedagogy.

Skills Obsolescence

The use of AI technologies in education saves teachers' time and makes lessons more engaging by automating routine tasks, especially grading and content presentation, and allows teachers to focus on more complex skills, such as creative and critical thinking. However, using AI can lead some teachers to neglect their pedagogical responsibilities by over-relying on technology and to professional laziness. Furthermore, as AI takes over entry-level teaching tasks, educators just starting their careers may be deprived of gaining experience and developing expertise through "learning by doing". Young professionals should develop themselves by learning, observing, and imitating the daily working habits and methods of an experienced master. Experiencing tasks firsthand will facilitate the internalization of the process and provide professional experience, as well as transfer quality control mechanisms and critical thinking processes to work practice (Suskind & Suskind, 2022).

One of the concerns about teachers' professional skills is that the current methods and institutions used in the training of teachers are designed according to the needs of past centuries. However, in an age of rapid technological advancement, the development of countries is closely linked to their ability to keep pace with the requirements of the new century. Today, we are moving towards a future where online services have begun to dominate human services, and increasingly advanced artificial intelligence systems will take over some of the traditional roles of teachers. Another concern is that in addition to training teachers for roles that will no longer be necessary, policymakers cannot keep up with the speed of this transformation. Policymakers, who mostly come from previous generations, are resistant to radical changes and tend to maintain traditional models (Suskind & Suskind, 2022). As a result, education policies continue to focus on raising a generation that responds to the needs of the past rather than preparing the teachers of the future. Rights not secured through policies and regulations bring inequity of opportunity and means. This situation reveals the need to develop flexible and innovative policies that can respond to the changing needs of education. A strategic transformation is essential for teachers to embrace their new roles and adapt to the requirements of the digital age.

Shaping Future Professionals in the Era of Digital Transformation

The skills required for future professionals include problem-solving in a technology-driven world, effectively utilizing and managing machine-generated expertise, integrating human values and ethical principles into technological services, and managing complex professional environments based on human-machine collaboration (Gantalao et al., 2025). Although it is not possible to foresee all future tasks, these key areas demonstrate the importance of developing professional education models that are compatible with rapidly changing technological and societal dynamics (Ren et al., 2023; Van Laar et al., 2020). In this context, instead of repeating models from the past, education systems should focus on developing individuals with the skills and adaptability to succeed in a world dominated by automation, online services, and artificial intelligence-based processes. In addition, policymakers and educators should take steps to bridge the gaps between generations and ensure that forward-looking strategies are effectively implemented. This transformation will support the sustainable development of individuals and societal and professional structures.

With the age of artificial intelligence, digital transformations have also accelerated the increase of teacher competencies. Online courses, e-lessons, and virtual supervision are becoming integral to today's education system. E-learning tools are not limited to traditional education alone but are also widely applied in professional contexts. In addition, it is crucial to provide the opportunity to participate in learning opportunities in a global context, such as massive open online courses, outside of traditional structured learning systems, and to individualize the learning process with adaptable learning content (Bozkurt, 2016). These technologies provide the opportunity to be exposed to different scenarios, better understand practical challenges, and help individuals gain in-depth learning experience (Clark & Mayer, 2023). However, despite these advantages, some risks and pitfalls are also related to using e-learning technologies. Firstly, the inability of virtual environments to provide a one-to-one real-world experience can limit the learning process and lead to participants not being adequately prepared for the complex social and emotional interactions they will encounter in real life. Secondly, the intensive use of technology may cause individuals to become dependent on the solutions provided by the system rather than critical thinking and problem-solving skills. In addition, the accessibility and costs of these systems can increase inequalities in education by restricting access to these technologies for some groups. Finally, simulations or algorithms based on biased data sets can lead to inaccurate learning outcomes and misinformation. Therefore, to make the most of e-learning technologies, it is vital to balance pedagogical goals with ethical concerns in designing and implementing these tools. At the same time, continuous evaluation and improvement of these technologies will help minimize potential risks.

Navigating Challenges and Opportunities in Digital Transformation

The professional world created by the era necessitates rediscovering the skills required to adapt to rapid technological developments and social changes. In a technology-driven world, core competencies such as problem-solving, utilizing machine-generated expertise, integrating human values into services provided through technology, and working effectively in hybrid environments based on human-machine collaboration, creativity, critical thinking, and technical knowledge are vital for future professionals (Di-Matteo et al., 2022). These skills clearly demonstrate that education systems should shift from traditional paradigms to models that encourage adaptability, ethical reasoning, and digital literacy. However, the implementation of these models also brings some challenges.

The risk of dependence on technology in the skill acquisition process may increase existing injustices due to inequalities in digital literacy and access to technology. In addition, the automation of routine tasks may negatively affect the development of professional expertise by reducing experiential learning opportunities. Moreover, the ethical consequences of decisions made by machines increase the importance of human oversight and reveal the need to prevent possible biases. To overcome these challenges, policymakers and educators must adopt a holistic approach that ensures continuous education, equal access to resources, and the responsible use of technology in professional education. By embracing the role of technology as a complement to human values, the education system can prepare future professionals to succeed in a world dominated by digital transformation. This approach not only develops the digital skills of individuals but also encourages the creation of an education system that is in line with social responsibility and ethical values.

In this context, it is of great importance that all stakeholders know and adopt the conceptual framework for using artificial intelligence in education. The effective integration of artificial intelligence-based systems is only possible with a culture of collaboration that understands these technologies' potential benefits and limitations. This framework, developed to categorize concepts, theories, goals, applications, recommendations, and measures, will provide a mapping tool for researchers and practitioners.

Designing a Responsible and Equitable Ecosystem

One of the first steps in creating an artificial intelligence ecosystem in education is meeting stakeholder expectations (Jablonowska et al., 2018). Stakeholders have expectations for the components that make up the ecosystem, their responsibilities, the legal framework, the efforts required by the integration process, the challenges, possible risks, and measures to be created and understood collaboratively. In addition, it is evaluated that the European Union (EU) expectations regarding responsible artificial intelligence ecosystems have a layered structure. This framework includes a two-layered structure combining ethical trust-building and a normative European vision, forming the foundation of Europe's global leadership in responsible AI. It positions Europe as a central actor in responsible AI governance, reaches out to global networks, and offers solutions to the arguments generated in this context (European Commission, 2020). This "imaginary ecosystem" design is shaped by shared common beliefs and a desired normative orientation (Minkkinen et al., 2021).

Ethical challenges that stakeholders may face in creating an AI ecosystem include privacy violations, risks of AI-based decisions, and social inequalities created by systems that centralize power within large organizations but are not accessible (Chowdhury & Oredo, 2021). The first of these challenges is that AI systems carry risks such as privacy violations. In particular, AI applications based on large data sets can cause privacy violations by processing users' personal information. This situation raises significant concerns not only at the individual level but also at the societal level.

Moreover, the automation provided by AI and the lack of transparency in decision-making processes limit the capacity of individuals to defend their rights, while also causing a lack of trust in society. The concern that artificial intelligence may cause faulty, unfair, and prejudiced decisions if it becomes an independent decision-maker in decision-making processes is also frequently emphasized. Views that biased data sets may increase discrimination against certain groups underline the possibility of violating individuals' fundamental rights and negatively affecting social inequality. Therefore, it is essential to strengthen algorithmic decisions with human control. Instead of seeing algorithmic decisions as "right" or "wrong," educators should evaluate them critically, considering that there may be missing or incorrect information, and be aware that they must decide when to trust and ignore these outputs. However, research shows that individuals have difficulty objectively evaluating algorithms' decisions and often follow the instructions without questioning (Lyell & Coiera, 2017). This will tend to create an environment where systems narrow down information, limit the variety of activities, and limit access to different perspectives for teachers and students. However, research indicates that it is risky for these technologies to assume a central role in decision-making processes without understanding the effects of AI and developing appropriate accountability measures (Reisman et al., 2018).

It is also emphasized that AI-based decisions should be questionable and changeable by users in line with the principles of explainability and transparency (Brinkrolf & Hammer, 2018). On the other hand, based on the assumption that human evaluation is better and more ethical, other questions should be considered as an alternative. What if algorithmic evaluation is more accurate, consistent, and fair? What if algorithmic feedback and instructions increase students' intrinsic motivation? How can individuals' racial, gender, and socioeconomic biases be reduced? Can AI uncover biases and, more importantly, hold a magnifying glass to existing biases? Is AI an opportunity to address human biases as well? (Papaspyridis & La Greca, 2023). Essentially, purifying oneself from prejudices and investigating the advantages and disadvantages of technology in an unbiased manner will always yield better results.

When systems are not used correctly, instead of strengthening existing systems, an environment will emerge where teacher and student participation, creativity, and ideas are ignored, increasingly stereotyped judgments and a uniform understanding of education are exhibited, and systemic biases are reinforced. Artificial intelligence in education involves implicit ethical, social, political, and pedagogical choices. To minimize the risk of such undesirable outcomes, including students and teachers in this process and developing guiding principles and theoretical frameworks is critical. In addition, understanding AI's societal and educational impacts will make it possible to develop policies that support social inclusion and are based on a framework of responsibility.

Another critical issue is that artificial intelligence technologies are only accessible to large organizations and companies. Artificial intelligence systems, which require large amounts of data and high processing power, are generally developed by large international corporations due to their high cost and the fact that they include diverse areas of expertise. This results in a small number of organizations that control technology development gaining disproportionate power in using AI systems. This ecosystem, dominated by centralized structures, has a say in the access of small businesses, individuals, and, in fact, large segments of society to artificial intelligence technologies and to what extent they can benefit from them, and can deepen social inequalities by limiting their access. It is also stated that education technology companies primarily focus on efficiency in designing systems (Hendrick, 2018). This approach can lead to a narrower perspective of solutions. Processes need to be addressed not only based on efficiency but also based on social contexts, relationships, social risks, and cultural contexts. Designs and solutions should be based on a theoretical foundation. It should be emphasized that this will be possible with the active participation of teachers and education experts in the process and the collection of evidence supporting the acceptance or rejection of today's emerging assumptions. In order to understand the effects of artificial intelligence in research and to demonstrate an approach that will break prejudice, seek the answer to the question "Under which conditions and with which groups can this method be effective?" instead of "Which methods are effective?" will lead to more reasonable decisions.

These challenges make it clear that AI needs to be developed and used within an ethical framework. Protecting privacy, ensuring algorithmic transparency, and decentralizing power are critical to creating a more equitable and sustainable AI ecosystem. As the European Commission has stated, implementing regulations and oversight mechanisms that address such ethical issues is crucial for protecting individuals' rights and benefiting society as a whole.

AI-DRIVEN INCLUSION: POLICIES AND PATHWAYS

To create a structure that strengthens AI-supported inclusive education systems, it becomes crucial to build and sustain partnerships among key stakeholders such as researchers, local and national regional leaders, policymakers, and other educational stakeholders that constitute the school and local community (other schools in the region, universities, etc.) who will embrace and support the digital transformation process. (European Agency, 2016). Developing a common language and understanding of the principles of inclusion and equity regarding the use of AI in education, as well as developing an inclusive culture that reflects this consensus (Deppeler & Ainscow, 2016) will not only improve students' sense of belonging but also give them confidence that their needs will be met fairly.

Schools should lead inclusive initiatives to ensure sustainable and safe AI use in education, establish a strong team, and distribute tasks among stakeholders. AI-supported initiatives should be undertaken to determine evidence-based effective practices in both professional development and student education. Cooperation between AI developers, educators, and policymakers should be increased. Artificial intelligence-supported sharing platforms that are established for this purpose will enable teachers to establish a communication network with experts working in their fields worldwide. Continuity in professional development will be possible through quality sharing between teachers and stakeholders about what works and constructive feedback they provide to each other on the practices they implement. Processes that support collaboration between stakeholders should be supported (Ersoy, 2022). Necessary improvements should also be made at the policy level to eliminate the gap between theory and practice.

We must seek answers to what teacher competencies are required to create an inclusive society in 21st-century schools through inclusive artificial intelligence policies. It is imperative to focus on what achievements teachers graduate from higher education with that will support technology initiatives in education and to what extent they can reflect this in practice in their professional life in inclusive education initiatives. Teacher education programs for inclusive education should be planned to follow the principles of inclusiveness, not only based on knowledge and skill acquisition but also based on attitudes and values (World Health Organization, 2011).

Determining the possible answers to the questions "Do the policies support radical reforms in pre-service and in-service training to prepare teachers for an inclusive approach in education? Do they contribute to the perspective that inclusive education is an approach that includes all teachers responsible for education, regardless of their branch and level? Who should be responsible for the training of educators? Are the methods used in training old approaches that have become outdated, or are they up-to-date to meet the age requirements? Do the policies provide sufficient information about the different pedagogical needs and methods used in the education of children, youth, and adults?" is essential in forming and implementing teacher education policies (UNESCO, 2009).

Suppose the role of a teacher is to provide students with access to information and to develop student competencies within certain standards. In that case, artificial intelligence will inevitably replace teachers. However, suppose the teacher acts together with the student to support the student's cognitive, emotional, and social liberation to transform the world (Freire, 2005) and can make the progress required by the age by taking advantage of the advantages of artificial intelligence in this process. In that case, it can be said that artificial intelligence supports a creative, ethical, caring, and social justice-based system. As a result, the effective use of AI technologies in education can enrich teachers' pedagogical roles and contribute to students' cognitive, emotional, and social liberation. However, unconscious or excessive use of AI can lead to teachers neglecting their professional responsibilities and laziness. Therefore, it is unlikely that artificial intelligence will replace teachers, but teachers who use AI effectively may replace those who do not. The dominant discourse on AI in education is based on saving time, reducing costs, and increasing efficiency. Developing AI systems created with a human-centered design, with policies and regulations in which teachers are also decision-makers, will ensure that systems based on machine learning are integrated into education more inclusively and equitably. Any discussion on AI in education should emphasize that input should be obtained from all stakeholders, not just those with technological literacy (Jordan, 2018). The active participation of teachers and education experts in the design, implementation, and evaluation processes of AI-based systems will ensure that policies and regulations are shaped based on teachers' field experiences, allowing educational technologies to move away from the perception of fixing a broken system and to be developed within a context-focused framework that is appropriate for the real needs of educational environments. Educators are vital to ensuring that these technologies optimize processes and support the principles of equity, inclusion, and socially meaningful learning.

In summary, to create a self-empowering transformation in the education system, the top priorities should be to promote professional values and attitudes, increase teacher competencies, improve recruitment conditions to enhance the quality of education, improve the quality of teacher training, organize programs to promote professional development for all newly appointed teachers, establish a mentoring system to support professional development, improve the teacher training system to ensure continuity of professional development, support school leadership, and ensure the quality and competencies of those responsible for training of educators. Many countries have made initiatives towards inclusive education with varying success rates. However, some countries are still at the beginning of the road, where much work must be done to create equal opportunities. When it comes to the context of AI-supported inclusive education, it is clear that much more effort needs to be made to ensure that digital learning environments are inclusive for everyone and to eliminate existing barriers.

International Perspectives on AI and Inclusive Education

Today, it is seen that social, professional, ethical, and legal norms that will provide the most effective and inclusive use of AI in education have not yet been established, and the process towards this continues with the efforts of different organizations (Romero et. al., 2024). For AI to be used ethically and fairly in education, it is necessary to create standardized, solid policy frameworks and implementation guides in light of global cooperation, transparency, and accountability principles (Mello et al., 2023). In this context, countries can also organize or expand their own frameworks. International organizations such as UNESCO and OECD offer various policy recommendations for developing and implementing AI in education under inclusiveness, equity, and justice principles. In addition, some countries have established institutional mechanisms to implement inclusive AI policies and monitor the ethical use of AI in education. Case studies from these countries provide valuable information on how these frameworks can be adapted and scaled in different regions and socio-economic contexts. For example, the Equal Credit Opportunity Act ("ECOA"), Title VII of the Civil Rights Act of 1964, the Americans with Disabilities Act, the Age Discrimination in Employment Act, the Fair Housing Act, and the Genetic Information Nondiscrimination Act contain measures based on laws prohibiting discrimination based on protected characteristics such as race, color, sex or gender, religion, age, disability, national origin, marital status, and genetic information.

The OECD (2024a) recommends that student needs will be better met by providing individualized learning experiences, while also warning that attention should be paid to data privacy, ethical concerns, and accountability issues while using these tools. Since this action requires access to comprehensive data, it recommends developing policies to prevent data misuse. It has been stated that artificial intelligence can increase inclusiveness in the classroom through culturally sensitive content. However, it emphasizes the risk that algorithmic and linguistic biases will increase inequalities. In this context, it advocates the development of artificial intelligence tools adapted to consider local characteristics and support diversity. It states that artificial intelligence tools offer significant opportunities to increase accessibility for students with special educational needs. However, it criticizes the tendency of these tools to treat disability issues as a "problem" to be solved. Since it is advocated, that differences should not be seen as a problem in inclusive education but as an opportunity for enrichment and adaptation, the report emphasizes that AI tools should also be designed to reduce social barriers and should be carefully planned so that they do not negatively affect users' social-emotional skills and attitudes. It is suggested that teachers need continuous professional development programs to use AI tools effectively, and that virtual educators and AI-supported platforms can provide dynamic and interactive environments in teacher education. The report also points out the importance of ensuring data security and privacy. It emphasizes that the risk that increasing commercial effects may overshadow educational goals is created, and therefore, commercial and educational goals should be balanced. Therefore, it is stated that regulatory frameworks should be created to encourage the use of tools not only for profit but also for education-oriented purposes to ensure the security of educational data and personal data. Interdisciplinary research is needed to assess AI's impact on equity, bias, and learning outcomes.

The OECD (2024b) emphasizes that governments should support access to a trustworthy and inclusive digital AI ecosystem, including data, technologies, infrastructure, and knowledge-sharing mechanisms. In this context, it is recommended that data trusts be promoted to support security, fair, legal, and ethical data sharing. It emphasizes the need to enhance human capabilities and support the creative potential of AI to reduce economic, social, gender, and other potential inequalities by increasing the inclusion of underrepresented populations such as minorities and disadvantaged groups. It is recommended that social protection mechanisms be provided to mitigate the effects of AI on workforce transformation and that training programs be established in areas such as entrepreneurship, productivity, and vocational qualifications to increase the workforce. It is stated that artificial intelligence should be compatible with human rights and democratic values, artificial intelligence systems should be transparent enough to allow users to understand the logic of the processes, security measures should be taken, and precautions should be taken in order not to cause harm in unexpected situations. Approaches that will clarify the responsibilities of the mechanisms and actors responsible for artificial intelligence systems should be implemented. UNICEF, UNESCO, and the World Bank (2022) underline that all teachers and students should be prepared and supported to support their learning processes and include digital technologies in their teaching. In summary, it is recommended to create an artificial intelligence ecosystem that emphasizes inclusive growth, sustainable development and prosperity, accountability, transparency and explainability, robustness, safety and security, justice, the rule of law including privacy, and human rights and democratic values.

CONCLUSION

It is clear that education policies should be based on scientific data rather than assumptions. Therefore, any research conducted in light of current developments will provide evidence supporting this argument. For instance, Urmeneta and Romero (2024), in their book *Creative Applications of Artificial Intelligence in Education*, investigate the application of AI in various educational settings. It includes concrete examples of promising results on AI integration into education. The book *Artificial Intelligence and Inclusive Education: Speculative Futures and Emerging Practices*, written by Knox, Wang, & Gallagher (2019), provides a comprehensive framework on the role of artificial intelligence in inclusive education. Such research should be expanded to strengthen the field.

AI ethics committees and oversight mechanisms to be established in educational institutions can be critical in ensuring transparency, accountability, and inclusiveness in using AI tools and algorithms. These committees can contribute to policy development and implementation processes to promote fairness, data privacy, and inclusiveness. To this end, policymakers and educators will have to conduct comprehensive and challenging discussions to address the current situation in education. These discussions should cover the quality and diversity of data used in educational assessment, the effectiveness of teaching and learning processes, the reproducibility and generalizability issues of educational research, and the ethical, social, and pedagogical risks that may arise with the integration of AI into classrooms, such as algorithmic bias, the compromise of student privacy, and the undermining of trust in the education system. Addressing these issues will be a critical step in reshaping the education system with AI in a more inclusive, fair, and effective way.

Inclusive policy frameworks for using AI, built on global cooperation, accountability, and transparency, ensure that all student groups benefit equally from education. In this context, societies must develop solutions that support children in becoming independent members of society by adapting the education system to their needs rather than seeing them as "problems" (UNICEF, 2014). Equitable systems enhance teacher digital skills and address student diversity (DiMatteo et al., 2022).

At national and international levels, there is a need to increase interaction among stakeholders and strengthen cooperation mechanisms for inclusive education. The use of AI as a fair, inclusive, and ethical tool in education requires the participation of educators, students, parents, policymakers, and technology developers. The digital transformation process in education requires the development of technological infrastructure, ethical responsibility, and awareness. It is emphasized that the inclusion perspective should be prioritized to transform the education system into a structure that includes all students, supports them, and contributes to the welfare of society (Schwab, 2016; UNESCO, 2019). Accordingly, an assessment system that covers all students should be established in the education system, necessary steps should be taken for continuous professional development, processes that encourage knowledge and experience sharing and strengthen cooperation among stakeholders should be developed, and inconsistencies between policies and practices should be eliminated (Garcia et al., 2025). To create an inclusive society, it is necessary to improve the attitudes and values of educators, improve the quality of education, and reform teacher education (Ersoy, 2022; UNESCO, 2009).

In conclusion, AI can transform education, but only when guided by values like equity and transparency and social justice. Teachers and learners must be central to this process to ensure that algorithms transform education, not just facilitate it. Issues such as sociocultural bias, lack of transparency, and misuse can prevent AI from fulfilling its potential in educational and societal contexts. Therefore, research and policy must be built on an inclusive and ethical framework. Ensuring that AI technologies are accountable, explainable, and human-centered is critical to both building trust and preserving justice.

REFERENCES

Bozkurt, A. (2016). Learning analytics: E-learning, big data and personalized learning. *Journal of Open Education Applications and Research*, *2*(4), 55–81.

Brinkrolf, J., & Hammer, B. (2018). Interpretable machine learning with reject option. *Automatisierung-stechnik*, *66*(4), 283–290. DOI: 10.1515/auto-2017-0123

Brynjolfsson, E., & McAfee, A. (2014). *The second machine age: Work, progress, and prosperity in a time of brilliant technologies*. W. W. Norton & Company.

Chopra, A., Patel, H., Rajput, D. S., & Bansal, N. (2024). Empowering inclusive education: Leveraging AI-ML and innovative tech stacks to support students with learning disabilities in higher education. In *Applied assistive technologies and informatics for students with disabilities* (pp. 255–275). Springer Nature Singapore. DOI: 10.1007/978-981-97-0914-4_15

Chowdhury, T., & Oredo, J. (2021). Ethics in AI: A software developmental and philosophical perspective. In *Responsible AI and Analytics for an Ethical and Inclusive Digitized Society* (Vol. 20, pp. 233–241). Springer International Publishing. DOI: 10.1007/978-3-030-85447-8_21

Clark, R. C., & Mayer, R. E. (2023). *E-learning and the science of instruction: Proven guidelines for consumers and designers of multimedia learning* (5th ed.). John Wiley & Sons.

Crawford, K., & Calo, R. (2016). There is a blind spot in AI. *Nature*, *538*(7625), 311–313. DOI: 10.1038/538311a PMID: 27762391

Daniela, L. (Ed.). (2022). *Inclusive digital education*. Springer., DOI: 10.1007/978-3-031-14775-3

Deppeler, J., & Ainscow, M. (2016). Using inquiry-based approaches for equitable school improvement. *School Effectiveness and School Improvement*, *27*(1), 1–6. DOI: 10.1080/09243453.2015.1026671

DiMatteo, L. A., Poncibò, C., & Cannarsa, M. (Eds.). (2022). *The Cambridge handbook of artificial intelligence: Global perspectives on law and ethics*. Cambridge University Press. DOI: 10.1017/9781009072168

Durovic, M., & Watson, J. (2022). AI, consumer data protection and privacy. In Holmes, W., & Porayska-Pomsta, K. (Eds.), *The ethics of artificial intelligence in education: Practices, challenges, and debates* (pp. 173–192). Routledge.

Ersoy, C. (2022). Inclusive education and its components. In Sanır, H. (Ed.), *Supporting academic skills in inclusive educational environments* (pp. 1–32). Eğiten Kitap.

European Agency for Development in Special Needs Education. (2011). *Teacher education for inclusion across Europe – Challenges and opportunities*. https://www.european-agency.org/sites/default/files/te4i-synthesis-report-en.pdf

European Agency for Special Needs and Inclusive Education. (2012). *Raising achievement for all learners – Quality in inclusive education*. https://www.european-agency.org/sites/default/files/ra4al-synthesis-report_RA4AL-synthesis-report.pdf

European Agency for Special Needs and Inclusive Education. (2016). *Raising the achievement of all learners in inclusive education – Literature review*. https://www.european-agency.org/sites/default/files/Raising%20Achievement%20Literature%20Review.pdf

European Agency for Special Needs and Inclusive Education. (2018). *Key actions for raising achievement: Guidance for teachers and leaders*. https://www.european-agency.org/sites/default/files/Key%20Actions%20for%20Raising%20Achievement.pdf

European Commission. (2020). *White paper on artificial intelligence: A European approach to excellence and trust*. https://ec.europa.eu/commission/presscorner/detail/en/ip_20_273

Frankish, K., & Ramsay, W. M. (2017). *The Cambridge handbook of artificial intelligence*. Cambridge University Press.

Gallagher, M. (2019). Artificial intelligence and the mobilities of inclusion: The accumulated advantages of 5G networks and surfacing outliers. In *Artificial intelligence and inclusive education: Speculative futures and emerging practices* (pp. 179–194). Springer. DOI: 10.1007/978-981-13-8161-4_11

Gantalao, L. C., Calzada, J. G. D., Capuyan, D. L., Lumantas, B. C., Acut, D. P., & Garcia, M. B. (2025). Equipping the Next Generation of Technicians: Navigating School Infrastructure and Technical Knowledge in the Age of AI Integration. In *Pitfalls of AI Integration in Education: Skill Obsolescence, Misuse, and Bias*. IGI Global., DOI: 10.4018/979-8-3373-0122-8.ch009

Garcia, M. B., Rosak-Szyrocka, J., Yılmaz, R., Metwally, A. H. S., Acut, D. P., Ofosu-Ampong, K., Erdoğdu, F., Fung, C. Y., & Bozkurt, A. (2025). Rethinking Educational Assessment in the Age of Generative AI: Actionable Strategies to Mitigate Academic Dishonesty. In *Pitfalls of AI Integration in Education: Skill Obsolescence, Misuse, and Bias*. IGI Global., DOI: 10.4018/979-8-3373-0122-8.ch001

Hendrick, C. (2018). Challenging the 'education is broken' and Silicon Valley narratives. *ResearchED*. https://researched.org.uk/challenging-the-education-is-broken-and-silicon-valley-narratives/

Holmes, W., Bialik, M., & Fadel, C. (2019). *Artificial intelligence in education: Promises and implications for teaching and learning*. Center for Curriculum Redesign.

Holmes, W., & Porayska-Pomsta, K. (Eds.). (2023). *The ethics of artificial intelligence in education: Practices, challenges, and debates*. Routledge.

Holstein, K., & Doroudi, S. (2022). Equity and artificial intelligence in education. In Holmes, W., & Porayska-Pomsta, K. (Eds.), *The ethics of artificial intelligence in education* (pp. 151–173). Routledge. DOI: 10.4324/9780429329067-9

Jablonowska, A., Kuziemski, M., Nowak, A. M., Micklitz, H. W., Palka, P., & Sartor, G. (2018). *Consumer law and artificial intelligence: Challenges to the EU consumer law and policy stemming from the business' use of artificial intelligence (Final report of the ARTSY project)*. European University Institute. https://cadmus.eui.eu/handle/1814/60059

Jordan, M. (2018). Artificial intelligence—The revolution hasn't happened yet. *Medium*. https://medium.com/@mijordan3/artificial-intelligence-the-revolution-hasnt-happened-yet-5e1d5812e1e7

Kahneman, D. (2011). *Thinking, fast and slow*. Farrar, Straus and Giroux.

Knox, J., Wang, Y., & Gallagher, M. (2019). *Artificial intelligence and inclusive education.* Springer Singapore. DOI: 10.1007/978-981-13-8161-4

Luckin, R., & Cukurova, M. (2019). Designing educational technologies in the age of AI: A learning sciences-driven approach. *British Journal of Educational Technology, 50*(6), 2824–2838. DOI: 10.1111/bjet.12861

Lyell, D., & Coiera, E. (2017). Automation bias and verification complexity: A systematic review. *Journal of the American Medical Informatics Association : JAMIA, 24*(2), 423–431. DOI: 10.1093/jamia/ocw105 PMID: 27516495

Lynch, J. (2018). How AI will destroy education. *Medium.* https://buzzrobot.com/howai-will-destroy-education-20053b7b88a6

Mello, R. F., Freitas, E., Pereira, F. D., Cabral, L., Tedesco, P., & Ramalho, G. (2023). Education in the age of Generative AI: Context and recent developments. *arXiv.* https://arxiv.org/abs/2309.12332

Mezzanotte, C. (2022). The social and economic rationale of inclusive education: An overview of the outcomes in education for diverse groups of students. OECD. https://one.oecd.org/document/EDU/WKP(2022)1/en/pdf

Microsoft. (n.d.). Responsible AI resources for developers. *Azure Dev Community Blog.* https://techcommunity.microsoft.com/blog/azuredevcommunityblog/responsible-ai-resources-for-developers/4189381

Minkkinen, M., Zimmer, M. P., & Mäntymäki, M. (2021, August). Towards ecosystems for responsible AI: Expectations on sociotechnical systems, agendas, and networks in EU documents. In *Conference on e-Business, e-Services and e-Society* (pp. 220–232). Springer International Publishing. DOI: 10.1007/978-3-030-85447-8_20

Mittelstadt, B. D., Allo, P., Taddeo, M., Wachter, S., & Floridi, L. (2016). The ethics of algorithms: Mapping the debate. *Big Data & Society, 3*(2), 1–21. DOI: 10.1177/2053951716679679

Mittler, P. (2008). Planning for the 2040s: Everybody's business. *British Journal of Special Education, 35*(1), 3–10. DOI: 10.1111/j.1467-8578.2008.00363.x

OECD. (2012). *Equity and quality in education: Supporting disadvantaged students and schools.* OECD Publishing., DOI: 10.1787/9789264130852-

OECD. (2024a). *The potential impact of artificial intelligence on equity and inclusion in education* (OECD Artificial Intelligence Papers No. 23). https://www.oecd.org/publications/the-potential-impact-of-artificial-intelligence-on-equity-and-inclusion-in-education-0d7e9e00-en.htm

OECD. (2024b). *Revised recommendation of the Council on artificial intelligence* (C/MIN(2024)16/FINAL). OECD Publishing. https://one.oecd.org/document/C/MIN(2024)16/FINAL/en/pdf

Papaspyridis, A., & La Greca, J. (2023). AI and education: Will the promise be fulfilled? In *Augmented education in the global age* (pp. 119–136). Routledge.

Reich, J., & Ito, M. (2017). *From good intentions to real outcomes: Equity by design in learning technologies*. Digital Media and Learning Research Hub.

Reisman, D., Schultz, J., Crawford, K., & Whittaker, M. (2018). *Algorithmic impact assessments: A practical framework for public agency accountability*. AI Now Institute. https://ainowinstitute.org/aiareport2018.pdf

Ren, M., Chen, N., & Qiu, H. (2023). Human-machine collaborative decision-making: An evolutionary roadmap based on cognitive intelligence. *International Journal of Social Robotics, 15*(7), 1101–1114. DOI: 10.1007/s12369-023-01020-1

Romero, M., Galy, I., Camponovo, J., Tressols, F., & Urmeneta, A. (2024). International initiatives and regional ecosystems for supporting artificial intelligence acculturation. In *Creative applications of artificial intelligence in education* (pp. 75–88). Springer Nature Switzerland. DOI: 10.1007/978-3-031-55272-4_6

Rowe, M. (2019). Shaping our algorithms before they shape us. In *Artificial intelligence and inclusive education: Speculative futures and emerging practices* (pp. 151–163). Springer. DOI: 10.1007/978-981-13-8161-4_9

Salend, S. J. (2011). *Creating inclusive classrooms: Effective and reflective practices* (7th ed.). Pearson.

Schwab, K. (2016). *The fourth industrial revolution*. Crown Publishing Group.

Shiohira, K., & Holmes, W. (2023). Proceed with caution: The pitfalls and potential of AI and education. In Araya, D., & Marber, P. (Eds.), *Augmented education in the global age: Artificial intelligence and the future of learning and work* (pp. 137–156). Routledge.

Susskind, R., & Susskind, D. (2022). *The future of the professions: How technology will transform the work of human experts* (2nd ed.). Oxford University Press.

UNESCO. (2003). *Overcoming exclusion through inclusive approaches in education: A challenge and a vision*. UNESCO.

UNESCO. (2005). *Guidelines for inclusion: Ensuring access to education for all*. https://www.ibe.unesco.org/sites/default/files/Guidelines_for_Inclusion_UNESCO_2006.pdf

UNESCO. (2009). *Policy guidelines on inclusion in education*. https://unesdoc.unesco.org/ark:/48223/pf0000177849

UNESCO. (2015). *EFA global monitoring report, 2015: Education for all 2000–2015: Achievements and challenges*. UNESCO.

UNESCO. (2019). *Beijing consensus on artificial intelligence and education*. https://unesdoc.unesco.org/ark:/48223/pf0000368303

UNICEF. (2014). *Conceptualizing inclusive education and contextualizing it within the UNICEF mission*. https://www.unicef.org/eca/sites/unicef.org.eca/files/IE_Webinar_Booklet_1_0.pdf

UNICEF. (2020). *Inclusive education*. https://www.unicef.org/education/inclusive-education

UNICEF. UNESCO, & World Bank. (2022). *Where are we on education recovery?* https://unesdoc.unesco .org/ark:/48223/pf0000381091

Urmeneta, A., & Romero, M. (2024). *Creative applications of artificial intelligence in education.* Springer Nature. DOI: 10.1007/978-3-031-55272-4

Van Laar, E., Van Deursen, A. J. A. M., Van Dijk, J. A. G. M., & De Haan, J. (2020). Determinants of 21st-century skills and 21st-century digital skills for workers: A systematic literature review. *SAGE Open, 10*(1), 2158244019900176. DOI: 10.1177/2158244019900176

World Health Organization (WHO). (2011). *World report on disability.* https://www.who.int/publications/ i/item/9789241564182

Yumrukaya, R., & Ersoy, C. (2024). A phenomenon at the zenith of intelligence: Artificial intelligence in education from the perspective of BİLSEM teachers. In Bal Sezerel, B. (Ed.), *Proceedings of the IXth National Congress on Gifted Education* (pp. 297–299). Anadolu University MEMBER Publications., https://cdn.anadolu.edu.tr/files/anadolu-cms/06lOMZeW/uploads/uyek-2024-bildiri-kitabi -74dbbb813295d244.pdf

Zimmerman, A., Janhonen, J., & Beer, E. (2023). Human/AI relationships: Challenges, downsides, and impacts on human/human relationships. *AI and Ethics,* ●●●, 1–13. DOI: 10.1007/s43681-023-00268-5

ADDITIONAL READING

Gantalao, L. C., Calzada, J. G. D., Capuyan, D. L., Lumantas, B. C., Acut, D. P., & Garcia, M. B. (2025). Equipping the Next Generation of Technicians: Navigating School Infrastructure and Technical Knowledge in the Age of AI Integration. In *Pitfalls of AI Integration in Education: Skill Obsolescence, Misuse, and Bias.* IGI Global., DOI: 10.4018/979-8-3373-0122-8.ch009

KEY TERMS AND DEFINITIONS

Inclusive Education: An equitable and effective educational approach that embraces individual differences as a source of richness and ensures the equal participation of all students in learning processes, aiming to maximize their cognitive, emotional, and social potential.

Digital Divide: It refers to the disparities in access to technology, the internet, and digital literacy skills among individuals, groups, or societies. Differences in access to advanced digital technologies such as artificial intelligence undermine equal opportunities in education and represent one of the most significant barriers to creating inclusive learning environments.

Skills Obsolescence: A phenomenon that occurs when individuals are unable to utilize or develop certain skills as a result of specific tasks being automated by technologies such as artificial intelligence.

Human-Centered Design: A holistic design approach that aims to develop technological systems by placing users' needs, values, and experiences at the core, grounded in the principles of empathy, participation, and solution-oriented thinking.

Ecosystem: A dynamic and interaction-based integrated structure composed of stakeholders, technologies, policies, and practices that guide the digital transformation of education and contribute to the creation and sustainability of inclusive, ethical, and effective learning environments.

Data Privacy: The protection of individuals' personal information during its collection, storage, and sharing processes, ensuring security and preventing unauthorized use. It is particularly significant in the context of utilizing student data within artificial intelligence systems.

Algorithmic Bias: The unfair treatment of certain groups by AI systems caused by biased or unbalanced training data, often leading to inequality in education.

Chapter 13
Safeguarding Educational Innovations Amid AI Disruptions:
A Reassessment of Patenting for Sustained Intellectual Property Protection

Jivulter C. Mangubat
https://orcid.org/0000-0001-6596-1329
Cebu Technological University, Philippines

Milcah R. Mangubat
https://orcid.org/0009-0003-3239-4622
Cebu Technological University, Philippines

Timoteo Bernardo L. Uy
https://orcid.org/0000-0003-4368-3588
Cebu Technological University, Philippines

Dharel P. Acut
https://orcid.org/0000-0002-9608-1292
Cebu Technological University, Philippines

Manuel B. Garcia
https://orcid.org/0000-0003-2615-422X
FEU Institute of Technology, Philippines

ABSTRACT

In an era marked by rapid technological advancement, protecting the intellectual property (IP) of educational innovations has become more critical than ever. This chapter examines the intersection of educational innovation, artificial intelligence (AI), and IP protection. Patents, which safeguard the technical and functional aspects of inventions, are crucial for protecting these advancements amid rapid technological disruptions. As discussed in the chapter, several challenges are posed by AI in generating and managing IP, including the need to redefine inventorship, address skill obsolescence, and ensure

DOI: 10.4018/979-8-3373-0122-8.ch013

equitable IP frameworks. Despite the importance of addressing these issues to foster innovation, they remain underexplored in the existing literature. Therefore, this chapter calls for a reassessment of existing legal and procedural frameworks to adapt to the evolving IP landscape and sustain the integrity of educational innovations. Overall, this chapter aims to contribute to the development of robust strategies for safeguarding educational innovations in an AI-driven era.

INTRODUCTION

As a social institution, education champions innovation to address the demands of a rapidly changing globalized world (Segarra et al., 2024; Serdyukov, 2017). The need for quality improvement in the curriculum and the desire to produce students with 21st-century competency skills have made innovation the core emphasis in the educational context (Acut et al., 2025; Fuad et al., 2020). As posited by Garcia (2023), school cultures that cultivate innovation should be consequently developed and encouraged extensively. At its core, educational innovation thrives on the ability to formulate and integrate new ideas, tools, and methodologies into teaching and learning. For instance, the integration of technology in classrooms has spurred the development of interactive tools such as gamified learning platforms (Mustafa et al., 2022), personalized education systems (Mishra et al., 2024), serious games (Arif et al., 2025), virtual reality simulations (Petil et al., 2025), machine learning (Maaliw et al., 2023), knowledge-based system (Garcia et al., 2021), and even artificial intelligence (AI) technologies (Hasanah et al., 2025). Through such innovations, educational institutions create assets with significant societal and economic value. These educational assets are intellectual capital that embodies creativity, research, and innovation. They have the potential to reshape industries, create new revenue streams, and establish competitive advantages for institutions. Therefore, these educational innovations often qualify as intellectual property (IP), including patents for technological advancements, copyrights for curriculum designs, and trademarks for branded learning tools.

Protecting assets through IP frameworks is essential to ensure their creators—whether they are educators, researchers, or institutions—retain the rights and benefits derived from their use. Robust IP protection not only incentivizes innovation but also safeguards against unauthorized replication or misuse. However, the IP landscape is evolving with the rise of *artificial inventors*, with advanced AI systems no longer just tools to support human creativity (Garcia, 2024). These AI systems are increasingly capable of producing outputs that resemble those traditionally considered IP, such as algorithms, educational tools, and creative content. While debates are ongoing about whether such machine-generated creations meet the legal and conceptual criteria for IP, their potential to generate valuable innovations cannot be ignored. Some legal experts (e.g., Picht & Thouvenin, 2023) have even argued that the law should be amended to allow the designation of AI systems as inventors to provide clarity in ownership disputes. With the intensifying AI disruptions, a cautious reassessment of IP frameworks is crucial to ensuring fairness and protecting educational innovations.

MAIN FOCUS OF THE CHAPTER

The goal of this chapter is to examine the intersection of AI integration and patent registration for educational innovations. Among the various forms of intellectual property, patents stand out as a powerful tool for protecting innovations. Unlike copyrights, which safeguard creative expressions, or trademarks, which protect brand identity, patents specifically address the technical and functional aspects of new inventions. This specificity makes patents particularly suited for safeguarding educational technologies and methodologies that introduce novel processes, systems, or devices. It also aims to explore how AI technologies are reshaping the IP landscape in terms of opportunities and challenges in safeguarding the integrity of IP processes. Key concerns include skill obsolescence, where reliance on AI-driven tools may erode traditional expertise in patent law and technical assessments, and ethical issues related to recognizing AI-generated inventions as legitimate IP. The chapter seeks to provide a balanced analysis to protect inventors' rights while maintaining high standards in patent registration outcomes.

IMPACT OF AI INTEGRATION ON PATENT REGISTRATION

The integration of AI into the field of IP is significantly transforming how inventions and creative works are managed, protected, and commercialized (Cuntz et al., 2024). According to the World Intellectual Property Organization (WIPO, 2019), AI technologies are being utilized across various stages of the IP process, including automated patent searches, prior art analysis, and even drafting patent claims. The goal is to improve the speed and accuracy of patent examinations, reducing backlogs and enhancing the quality of granted patents (Setchi et al., 2021). For instance, AI tools can rapidly analyze extensive databases to identify prior art and suggest technical terms to structure patent applications (Elahi et al., 2023). These advancements represent a significant shift in how IP processes are conducted, highlighting the growing influence of AI in shaping modern IP frameworks. However, this transformation raises important considerations for the future of IP practices, particularly in ensuring that existing frameworks can accommodate the evolving role of AI in innovation and patent registration. Adapting to this new landscape is essential to maintain the integrity and fairness of IP systems as AI continues to redefine traditional approaches (Cuntz et al., 2024; Patel & Sahi, 2024; WIPO, 2024).

AI as a Catalyst of Innovation, Design, and Patent Processes

AI is significantly reshaping the landscape of innovation and design, providing new tools and methods to enhance creative processes (Sreenivasan & Suresh, 2024). AI systems have the capability to analyze vast amounts of data and generate novel solutions that would otherwise be beyond the scope of human designers or inventors. In industries such as pharmaceuticals, automotive, and electronics, AI has already been applied to create optimized designs and identify new technological solutions (Malik et al., 2024). This includes the use of AI for generative design, where algorithms autonomously generate design alternatives based on a set of constraints, or AI-based drug discovery, where AI models analyze molecular data to predict the efficacy of potential drugs. AI is not only aiding in creativity but also enabling the development of innovations at a faster pace (Füller et al., 2022). Beyond innovation, AI is also streamlining patent registration processes. Machine learning tools are now being utilized to automate various tasks traditionally handled by patent professionals, such as prior art searches and patent claims drafting

(Setchi et al., 2021). AI-based systems can rapidly search patent databases, identify similar existing patents, and even suggest modifications to claims to ensure that they meet patentability criteria. This efficiency reduces the time and cost associated with patent applications and accelerates the patent grant process. As AI continues to play an active role in the procedural aspects of patenting, the industry faces a significant transformation in how patents are filed, processed, and granted.

Challenges in Determining Inventorship and Ownership

A critical issue arising from the increasing involvement of AI in the innovation process is the challenge of determining inventorship and ownership. In traditional patent systems, the inventor is typically a human who has made a novel contribution to the creation of a product or process. However, as AI systems increasingly generate inventions, questions arise about who should be listed as the inventor in the patent application (Ozin et al., 2023). Can an AI system that generates an invention based on its algorithms be considered an inventor? Current patent laws typically require a human inventor, which means that AI-generated inventions pose a challenge to the existing legal frameworks governing IP. As AI technology becomes more advanced, it becomes increasingly difficult to assign human inventorship to creations that are produced by AI without direct human intervention (Rodrigues, 2020). The issue of ownership is equally complex. If an AI generates an invention, who owns the IP rights? Is it the developer of the AI system, the entity that owns the AI, or the user who provided the data to train the AI? These questions are complicated by the fact that AI-generated inventions often involve collaboration between human inventors and AI systems. Legal scholars and patent professionals are advocating for updates to patent laws to clarify these issues, suggesting that AI systems may need to be recognized as tools used by inventors rather than independent inventors themselves (Ouyang et al., 2022). Until legal frameworks are adjusted, patent offices will continue to grapple with cases where AI plays a central role in the inventive process, leading to potential disputes over patent rights.

AI-Enhanced Tools and Skill Obsolescence in Patent Professionals

The integration of AI into patent processes has the potential to cause skill obsolescence among patent professionals, including patent agents and examiners. AI-powered tools, such as those used for prior art searches, patent drafting, and examination, have automated many of the time-consuming and repetitive tasks traditionally performed by patent professionals (Coombs et al., 2020). These tools can quickly analyze vast databases, identify relevant patents, and even help draft patent applications by suggesting improvements to the claim language. As AI-driven systems become more advanced, there is a concern that patent professionals may no longer be required to perform these tasks manually, leading to a reduction in demand for specific skill sets. While AI enhances the efficiency and accuracy of patent work, it also poses a risk to the long-term viability of some patent professions. Patent agents and examiners who rely on manual research and drafting may find their roles diminished as AI tools take over these functions. To adapt, patent professionals will need to develop new skills that focus on the more complex and creative aspects of patent law, such as strategic patent portfolio management, legal interpretation, and AI ethics in patenting (Kim et al., 2022). This shift towards AI-enabled patenting processes will also require ongoing training and professional development to ensure that patent agents and examiners remain relevant in an increasingly automated environment. Consequently, education in IP law may need to evolve to incorporate AI knowledge and legal implications related to AI-driven innovation and automation in the patenting process (Poddar & Rao, 2024).

Role of AI in Identifying Patent Misuse and Fraudulent Applications

AI is playing an increasingly important role in detecting and preventing misuse in the patent system, including fraudulent patent applications and violations of prior art (WIPO, 2024). AI-enhanced tools can efficiently scan patent applications, compare them to vast databases of existing patents, and flag potential instances of plagiarism or infringement. One of the key benefits of AI in this area is its ability to quickly identify prior art. AI can assess large volumes of data from global patent filings, academic research papers, and other technical sources. It helps maintain the integrity of the patent system by ensuring patent applications are thoroughly vetted against existing inventions, preventing the approval of patents that are not genuinely novel. This process aids in upholding the quality and fairness of patents granted, ensuring that only genuine innovations are recognized and protected. AI can also assist in identifying fraudulent applications by analyzing patterns in patent filings. For instance, it can detect suspicious behavior, such as multiple applications filed by the same entity for similar inventions or the systematic use of certain claim types that are often associated with patent trolling (i.e., filing frivolous patents with the intent of exploiting the legal system for financial gain). The ability to detect fraudulent activity early in the patent process is crucial in preventing the abuse of the patent system, which could otherwise hinder innovation and economic growth (Ohlhausen, 2016). AI can also assist in enforcing patent rights by identifying infringements more quickly, allowing patent holders to protect their IPs and maintain the competitive advantages afforded by their patents (Cuntz et al., 2024). As the patent system continues to embrace AI, its role in safeguarding against misuse will likely become more central to maintaining fairness and integrity in patent law.

FUNDAMENTALS OF PATENT REGISTRATION

Overview of Patent Types

Patents are legal protections granted to inventors for their novel creations. It gives them exclusive rights to their inventions for a specified period (Krauß & Kuttenkeuler, 2021; Saha & Bhattacharya, 2011). For industrial designs, utility models, and inventions, obtaining a patent is essential for securing a competitive advantage and safeguarding the commercial value of new products and technologies (Ikeuchi & Motohashi, 2022; Tarasenko, 2023). Invention patents (often called utility patents) are the most common, which protect new and useful inventions, ranging from mechanical devices to software algorithms (Singh et al., 2009). To qualify for a utility patent, the invention must be novel, non-obvious, and useful. This category is crucial in fostering technological advancements and economic growth (Wandhe, 2024). Securing exclusive rights to an invention allows inventors to control its use and commercialization, providing them with a temporary monopoly in the market. Beyond invention patents, there are other IP protections suited for different types of innovation. Utility models (also known as innovation patents in some jurisdictions) are comparable to invention patents but have lower requirements for novelty and inventive steps. They typically protect incremental innovations and are granted a shorter term of protection, making them ideal for more straightforward or less radical innovations. On the other hand, industrial designs protect the aesthetic and ornamental aspects of a product (e.g., its shape, color, or surface decoration) but not its functionality. Its key goal is to encourage creators to invest in the visual appeal of their products (WIPO, 2022). Together, these various types of patent help safeguard a wide range of IP across industries.

Purpose of Patent Protection

The primary purpose of patent protection is to encourage and reward innovation. Patents grant inventors exclusive rights over their creations, serving as an incentive for developing new technologies and solutions while fostering creativity and driving progress (Caplanova, 2020). These rights allow inventors to prevent others from making, using, or selling their inventions without permission, ensuring they can profit from their efforts and investments. The ability to license or sell patent rights also opens avenues for collaboration, leading to the commercialization of inventions and the growth of industries. Another significant purpose of patent systems is to foster fair competition and maintain the balance between exclusivity and public knowledge. Requiring patents to disclose technical details about inventions ensures that knowledge becomes publicly available, enabling others to build upon existing ideas (de Rassenfosse et al., 2024). This transparency fosters further innovation and technological advancement by making foundational knowledge accessible to the public. Additionally, patents help maintain a competitive market by protecting original inventions, ensuring that companies are rewarded for their creativity rather than being undercut by unauthorized imitation (Cappelli et al., 2023). Ultimately, patents support the broader ecosystem of innovation by ensuring that creators and innovators can benefit from their contributions while also advancing the collective body of knowledge (OECD, 2015).

The Patent Registration Process

The process of patent registration involves several stages, each designed to assess the novelty and utility of an invention. It begins with the filing of a patent application, which includes a detailed description of the invention, supporting drawings, and claims that define its scope. A critical part of the application is conducting a thorough prior art search, which examines existing patents and publications to ensure the invention is novel. This step is crucial to avoid filing for an invention that has already been patented. Once the application is submitted, the patent office conducts an examination to determine if the invention meets the requirements of novelty, non-obviousness, and industrial applicability. This examination may involve additional back-and-forth between the applicant and the examiner (WIPO, 2022). If the invention is approved, the patent is granted, and the inventor is provided with exclusive rights for a specific period (usually 20 years for utility patents). After receiving the patent, inventors are responsible for enforcing their rights, meaning they must take action if others infringe upon their patent. In some cases, patents can be challenged by competitors or other stakeholders through opposition procedures. The process is complex and often requires the expertise of patent agents to navigate successfully to ensure that all legal requirements are met and the invention is adequately protected (Caplanova, 2020).

LEGAL AND ETHICAL CONSIDERATIONS

Issues of Originality, Inventor Recognition, and Copyright for AI-Generated Content

The integration of AI into the patent registration process raises fundamental legal questions, particularly regarding originality, inventor recognition, and copyright for AI-generated inventions (Al-Busaidi et al., 2024). In traditional patent systems, a human inventor is required to demonstrate original contributions to a novel invention, and this individual is typically credited as the inventor. However, with AI systems increasingly playing a dominant role in the generation of new ideas, the question arises: *who owns the rights to inventions created by AI?* Some argue that AI systems should be regarded as tools rather than inventors, with the credit for AI-generated inventions attributed to the human(s) responsible for programming or operating the AI. Others, however, argue that AI-generated inventions should be treated as distinct, with AI being given recognition as the inventor, which would require substantial changes to existing IP laws. In addition to inventorship, copyright issues emerge when considering the extent to which AI can claim authorship of original works (Guadamuz, 2017). Traditionally, copyright law protects the rights of creators of original works, such as literature, art, or inventions. However, as AI systems become capable of generating original content in various fields, such as writing, music composition, and visual arts, questions about ownership and copyright arise. If AI is solely responsible for generating an invention or piece of content, does the creator of the AI system or the user who inputted the data hold the copyright? Legal scholars and policymakers are grappling with these questions, and some jurisdictions have already begun to explore amendments to existing laws to account for AI-generated works. As AI becomes more sophisticated, the legal framework will need to evolve to reflect the role AI plays in creativity and innovation.

Bias in AI-Driven Patent Examinations

The use of AI in patent examinations presents the potential for bias in patent decision-making processes. AI algorithms are trained on historical data, which means they can inadvertently perpetuate existing biases that may have been present in earlier patent filings (Javed & Li, 2024). For instance, if an AI system is primarily trained on patents from specific industries, it may fail to recognize novel inventions that are outside of these established patterns. This could disproportionately disadvantage inventors from underrepresented fields or regions, as their inventions may not be properly assessed. Additionally, AI systems may struggle to understand the cultural context or societal impact of inventions, leading to the marginalization of certain types of innovations. For example, inventions that address specific needs in developing countries may be overlooked by AI-driven systems that are biased toward technologies more relevant to wealthy nations. Moreover, the lack of diverse data in the training sets used to develop patent examination algorithms may result in the automation of patenting processes that overlook certain types of inventions, such as those that involve unconventional or interdisciplinary approaches. Biases in AI algorithms can also affect the way patent claims are interpreted, leading to the rejection of legitimate patents or the approval of patents for inventions that are not genuinely novel (Ferrero Guillén & Breckwoldt Jurado, 2023). Therefore, it is essential to ensure that AI-driven patent examination systems are trained on a diverse, representative set of data to minimize biases and provide fair treatment to all inventors.

This also calls for transparent and explainable AI systems, where patent examiners can understand the rationale behind the AI's decisions, thereby mitigating the risk of biases influencing patent outcomes.

Ethical Dilemmas in Patent Registration

The introduction of AI into the patent registration process raises a host of ethical dilemmas that must be addressed to ensure fairness, accountability, and transparency. One of the key ethical concerns is the issue of fairness in the allocation of IP rights (Rodrigues, 2020). AI systems that generate inventions may not always consider the human impact of new technologies, potentially overlooking social, cultural, or environmental consequences. For instance, AI may prioritize efficiency or profitability over broader ethical concerns, such as equity or public health, in the patenting of specific technologies. This issue of fairness also extends to the dissemination of patent rights, as certain groups, such as small inventors or those from developing countries, may be disadvantaged by the rapid pace and complexity of AI-driven patent systems. Another critical ethical consideration is accountability in AI-driven patenting processes. If an AI system makes an error in the examination or approval of a patent, it is often unclear who is responsible for that mistake. In traditional patent systems, patent examiners are held accountable for their decisions, but with AI-assisted systems, accountability becomes more complex. Should the creators of the AI system be held responsible for errors in patenting decisions, or should the patent examiners who rely on AI take responsibility? Furthermore, the transparency of AI systems in patenting is a significant concern. Patent applicants and stakeholders need to understand how decisions are made, and the use of AI in patent examinations must be accompanied by clear guidelines on how AI algorithms are developed, trained, and evaluated. Ethical practices in patent registration require that AI systems be both transparent and accountable to ensure that innovation is safeguarded in a way that promotes just outcomes.

Regulatory Challenges in Adapting Patent Laws

As AI technologies continue to evolve, regulatory challenges in adapting patent laws to reflect AI-driven innovation become more pressing (Poddar & Rao, 2024). Current patent systems are primarily designed around human inventors, and many aspects of IP law do not yet account for the unique challenges presented by AI-generated inventions. The legal recognition of AI as an inventor or co-inventor is a contentious issue that requires careful legal analysis and potential changes to patent laws. Some jurisdictions have already begun to explore the possibility of recognizing AI as a tool in the invention process, but this raises further questions about who ultimately owns the patent rights for AI-generated inventions. Governments and regulatory bodies must grapple with the question of how to properly update existing laws to reflect the fact that AI systems are now capable of generating significant inventions, sometimes without direct human input. In addition to defining inventorship, patent laws will need to be revised to address the challenges of patent enforcement and disputes related to AI-generated patents (Ouyang et al., 2022). Given the complexity of AI technologies and the potential for AI systems to produce novel ideas across various industries, patent offices may need to develop specialized procedures for reviewing and granting patents that involve AI technologies. Additionally, the global nature of AI-driven innovation poses challenges for patent harmonization across different jurisdictions, as patent laws and standards vary significantly between countries. As a result, international cooperation and coordination will be necessary to create a unified regulatory framework that can effectively govern AI-driven patents (Cuntz et al., 2024). The regulatory changes needed to address AI's role in patenting must strike a balance between fostering innovation, protecting IP, and ensuring fairness across diverse stakeholders.

PITFALLS IN PATENT REGISTRATION AMID AI DISRUPTIONS

Risks of Skill Obsolescence

The integration of AI technologies into the patent registration process presents significant challenges, particularly in terms of skill obsolescence. As AI tools become more adept at automating tasks such as patent searches, prior art analysis, and the drafting of patent claims, there is a growing concern that specific traditional skills required by patent professionals could diminish or even become redundant. Patent agents, examiners, and attorneys who once relied on their expertise to assess the novelty and patentability of inventions may find their roles evolving or becoming obsolete. For instance, AI-driven systems can perform repetitive and time-consuming tasks at a much faster pace and with greater accuracy, thus reducing the need for manual intervention in routine processes. This shift toward automation could have implications for job opportunities within the patent industry. As more patent-related tasks are handled by AI, human workers may find fewer roles that require their expertise. In some cases, this could lead to job displacement, particularly for professionals who have specialized in areas that can now be automated. Additionally, the evolution of AI may necessitate a transformation in the skill sets required for patent professionals, requiring them to adapt and gain proficiency in working alongside AI systems or understanding the intricacies of AI-driven patent processes. The risk of skill obsolescence calls for continuous upskilling and reskilling efforts (Gantalao et al., 2025) to ensure that human expertise remains a valuable asset in the patent industry.

Misuse of AI in Patent Search and Examination Processes

One of the most significant risks associated with the increasing reliance on AI in patent registration is the potential misuse of AI in patent search and examination processes. While AI technologies can significantly enhance efficiency by automating patent searches and processing large volumes of data, they are not infallible. Automated search tools powered by AI may overlook critical prior art, misinterpret patent claims, or fail to recognize nuances in the technology being examined. AI systems, particularly those not trained on diverse datasets or those relying on outdated information, may generate incomplete or erroneous results, leading to the approval of patents that should not be granted or the rejection of valid applications. Moreover, AI-generated patent applications pose a risk in that they may lack the human insight that typically characterize innovative inventions. AI may be able to optimize existing ideas or combine existing technologies in novel ways, but it may struggle with genuinely novel inventions that require human intuition and creativity. Over-reliance on AI tools in the patent process could lead to an inaccurate reflection of true innovation, where inventions that rely too heavily on AI-generated suggestions could be approved, diminishing the human-driven essence of technological progress. Thus, AI should be used as an assistive tool, not a substitute for human judgment and expertise.

Impact of AI Bias on Patent Decision-Making

AI systems, while powerful, are not immune to inherent biases that can affect patent decision-making. As AI algorithms are trained on historical patent data, they may perpetuate biases present in the datasets, leading to unfair or discriminatory outcomes. For example, if the training data mainly consists of patents from specific industries, regions, or demographics, AI systems may unintentionally favor inventions from those groups and overlook contributions from others. In the context of patent examination, such biases could result in the unfair rejection of patent applications that originate from underrepresented or emerging fields or from inventors with less established reputations. The biases in AI algorithms could also manifest in the approval process, where certain types of inventions or specific technological approaches are given precedence over others, leading to skewed patent grants. Certain technologies related to AI, machine learning, or big data may be granted patents more easily than innovations in other fields simply because the AI algorithm has been trained to prioritize those domains. This issue stresses the importance of ensuring that AI systems used in patent examinations are trained on diverse, representative, and unbiased data. Patent offices must employ human oversight to mitigate the impact of AI bias and ensure that patent decisions are based on fairness and impartiality.

Infrastructural Limitations

The growing use of AI in patent registration also presents significant infrastructural challenges for patent offices worldwide. Many patent offices are still operating with legacy systems that were not designed to handle the complexities of AI-driven applications. As AI-generated inventions become more prevalent, patent offices may struggle to keep up with the increasing volume of submissions that require specialized tools and processes for review. The technical requirements for effectively implementing AI tools—such as powerful computing resources, specialized software, and trained personnel—may also be beyond the capacity of some patent offices, particularly in developing countries (Mesquita Machado & Winter, 2023). In addition to technological infrastructure, there are policy challenges in adapting the patent registration system to accommodate AI-driven innovations. Existing legal frameworks may not be sufficient to address the unique characteristics of AI-generated inventions, such as the question of who holds the rights to inventions produced by AI systems. To effectively handle AI-driven patent filings, patent offices will need to invest in updating their regulatory infrastructure, developing specialized procedures for handling AI-generated patents, and ensuring that their personnel are adequately trained in the complexities of AI technology. Without addressing these infrastructural limitations, the patent system may struggle to keep pace with AI-driven innovation, ultimately hindering the growth of AI technologies and the protection of IP rights.

STRATEGIES FOR SAFEGUARDING CREATIVITY AND IP

The rapid development of AI technologies has outpaced existing legal frameworks, which necessitates thoughtful reforms to address the unique dynamics of AI-driven innovations. Ensuring the protection of IP in this evolving landscape requires a multi-faceted approach, including policy reforms, proper attribution guidelines, professional upskilling, and inter-agency collaboration. By balancing the promotion of innovation with the prevention of system abuse, these strategies can safeguard creativity and IP in the

AI era while fostering an equitable and forward-looking patent ecosystem. Table 1 and the succeeding discussions outline key strategies and recommendations for navigating the intersection of AI and IP law.

Table 1. Strategies for safeguarding IP in the age of AI

Strategy	Description	Key Actions
Policy recommendations for AI and patent law reform	Reform patent laws to address AI-driven innovations, clarifying AI's role in inventorship and ensuring appropriate protection for AI-generated inventions while maintaining patent law principles.	• Clarify inventorship definitions for AI-generated inventions. • Establish international coordination for AI patent laws. • Develop rigorous examination standards for AI-generated patents.
Proper attribution for AI-assisted inventions	Develop guidelines for recognizing AI's role in invention processes, ensuring human inventors are credited while acknowledging AI's contributions. Joint inventorship arrangements may also be considered.	• Develop clear guidelines for AI's role in patent filings. • Recognize joint inventorship where both human and AI contributions are significant. • Introduce sections to patent filings acknowledging AI's involvement.
Upskilling and AI training in IP law education	Integrate AI-focused curricula in IP law education and provide continuous upskilling programs for professionals to understand the intersection of AI and patent law. Collaboration between academic institutions and industry is essential for practical training.	• Create AI and patent law-specific curricula for IP law students. • Develop professional development programs for current patent professionals. • Collaborate with industry leaders to create training modules.
Best practices for using AI tools in patent registration	Establish guidelines for responsibly using AI in patent searches, claim drafting, and prior art analysis. AI should assist, not replace human expertise, with transparency, accountability, and ethical use. Regular updates and diverse datasets are key to reducing biases.	• Set clear guidelines for AI tools in patent searches and drafting. • Ensure human oversight of AI-generated results. • Regularly update AI systems with diverse data sets to reduce bias.
Inter-agency collaboration	Foster collaboration between patent offices, regulatory bodies, academic institutions, and technology developers to integrate AI tools effectively, share best practices, and offer specialized training for patent professionals.	• Encourage partnerships between patent offices, academia, and tech developers. • Develop joint training programs for patent professionals. • Share best practices across jurisdictions.

Policy Recommendations for AI and Patent Law Reform

As AI continues to impact the patent landscape, it is essential for policymakers to reform existing patent laws to account for the unique challenges posed by AI-driven innovations (Poddar & Rao, 2024). Policy recommendations should focus on ensuring that AI-generated inventions are given appropriate protection while maintaining the core principles of patent law. One key reform could involve clarifying the role of

AI in patent creation, particularly in terms of inventorship. Current patent laws generally require human inventors, which may not align with the growing prevalence of AI systems contributing significantly to innovation. Legislative changes could involve adjusting the definitions of inventorship to recognize AI as a tool used by human creators, ensuring that the rights and protections afforded to inventions reflect the evolving nature of innovation. Furthermore, new guidelines could establish procedures for handling AI-generated patents, ensuring that the patent system is equipped to process applications from AI-driven technologies without stifling innovation or overcomplicating the process.

Alongside changes to the patent system, policies must address the balance between promoting innovation and preventing abuse of the system. Some AI tools may be used to generate inventions that are derivative or lack true novelty, which could result in a flood of low-quality patent applications. To safeguard the integrity of the system, regulatory reforms should include rigorous examination processes for AI-generated patents, ensuring that only genuinely innovative ideas are granted IP rights. Additionally, international coordination on AI patent laws could help create uniform standards across jurisdictions, ensuring that inventors and businesses can protect their innovations effectively in a global marketplace. By updating patent laws to reflect the realities of AI's role in innovation, policymakers can help ensure the continued evolution of patent law while safeguarding fairness and encouraging technological progress.

Proper Attribution for AI-Assisted Inventions

A significant challenge in AI-driven patent registration is the issue of proper attribution. As AI becomes increasingly capable of autonomously contributing to innovation, determining who should be credited for an AI-assisted invention becomes more complex. Patent law traditionally requires that the inventor be a human being, but AI systems, with their ability to generate novel solutions and assist in the development of inventions, challenge this framework. While the AI itself cannot be an inventor under current law, human creators who leverage AI tools must still be appropriately recognized for their contributions. A potential solution is to acknowledge the role of AI in the invention process while ensuring that the human contributors—whether they are the original developers of the AI, the individuals using the AI, or both—retain the rights to the invention. One approach to ensuring proper attribution would be to develop clear guidelines for recognizing AI's contribution without diminishing the role of human inventors. For instance, patent filings could include sections where inventors describe the role of AI in the creation of the invention, acknowledging the AI's assistance while also detailing the human contributions that led to the final product. Joint inventorship arrangements could also be considered, where both human and AI contributions are recognized, even if the AI is not formally named as an inventor. This model would preserve the integrity of the inventor recognition system while accounting for the evolving role of AI in technological innovation. These efforts would ensure that human creators are not overlooked while also fostering transparency and ethical practices in the patent process.

Upskilling and AI Training in IP Law Education

As AI continues to reshape the patent landscape, there is a pressing need for ongoing education and professional development in the field of IP law. Patent professionals, including patent agents, attorneys, and examiners, must acquire the necessary skills and knowledge to navigate the complexities introduced by AI-driven innovation. This aspect can be achieved through the integration of AI-focused curricula in IP law education, where students learn about the intersection of AI and patent law and gain an understanding of the technological advancements that are transforming the patent process. Furthermore, continuous upskilling programs should be developed for current professionals to ensure they remain up to date with AI tools and their implications for patent filing, examination, and enforcement. Training programs should focus on equipping patent professionals with both a technical understanding of AI technologies and the ability to apply legal frameworks to AI-generated inventions. These programs could include instruction on AI algorithms, machine learning, and the ethical and legal considerations of AI in patent law. Additionally, partnerships between academic institutions, patent offices, and industry leaders could foster a collaborative environment for developing training modules that are tailored to the needs of the patent industry. By ensuring that IP law professionals are proficient in AI technologies and aware of their legal implications, the patent system can continue to operate effectively while keeping pace with innovation.

Best Practices for Using AI Tools in Patent Registration

AI tools offer significant advantages for patent registration, particularly in the areas of patent searches, claim drafting, and prior art analysis. However, to ensure that these tools are used responsibly and effectively, best practices must be established. One essential guideline is that AI should be viewed as an assistive technology rather than a replacement for human expertise. AI tools should be used to enhance the efficiency and accuracy of patent searches, enabling patent professionals to quickly identify relevant prior art, but they should not be solely relied upon to make patentability decisions. Human oversight remains crucial in validating AI-generated results and ensuring that patent applications adhere to legal requirements. Best practices also include regularly updating AI systems with high-quality, diverse datasets to reduce biases and improve the accuracy of their output. Another critical practice involves ensuring that AI tools are used transparently and ethically. Patent offices and law firms must establish guidelines that promote fairness, accountability, and transparency in the use of AI during the patent registration process. This includes ensuring that the AI systems used in patent examinations are free from bias and that their decision-making processes can be explained and audited. AI tools should also be designed with built-in safeguards to prevent errors that could lead to unjust patent decisions. By following these best practices, the patent system can benefit from AI's capabilities while minimizing risks such as bias, errors, and over-reliance on automation.

Inter-Agency Collaboration

Given the evolving role of AI in patent registration, collaboration is essential for the successful integration of AI tools and processes (Broekhuizen et al., 2023). Patent offices, regulatory bodies, academic institutions, and technology developers must work together to ensure that AI technologies are effectively and ethically integrated into the patent system. By collaborating on the development of AI-driven tools for patent search, examination, and fraud detection, agencies can create standardized solutions that ensure consistency and fairness across jurisdictions. These partnerships could also promote the sharing of best practices and foster innovation in AI applications tailored to the needs of the patent system. Additionally, collaboration between patent offices and education providers is key to developing training programs for patent professionals. By combining the expertise of patent professionals with AI researchers and developers, educational institutions can offer specialized training that equips professionals with the necessary knowledge to work alongside AI tools effectively. This approach would help create a more dynamic, forward-thinking patent ecosystem capable of handling the complexities of AI-driven innovation while maintaining high standards of quality and fairness in patent registration. Inter-agency collaboration, therefore, is essential in preparing for the challenges and opportunities that AI integration brings to the patent system.

CASE STUDIES AND EXAMPLES

Notable Cases Involving AI-Generated Patents and Disputes

One of the landmark cases involving AI-generated patents is the 2019 dispute surrounding the Device for the Autonomous Bootstrapping of Unified Sentience (DABUS) system. DABUS, an AI developed by Dr. Stephen Thaler, created two inventions: (1) a beverage container and (2) a flashing light for emergency vehicles. Thaler filed patents for these inventions in multiple countries, naming DABUS as the inventor. However, patent offices in several jurisdictions, including the United States and the European Union, rejected these applications, stating that only a human inventor could be named in a patent application. The United States Patent and Trademark Office (USPTO) initially rejected Thaler's patent application, asserting that inventorship must be attributed to a natural person. However, Thaler appealed, and in 2021, a US district court ruled in his favor, stating that the patent law does not specify that the inventor must be a person. This case highlights the tension between existing patent law, which presumes human inventorship, and the reality of AI's role in creating new innovations (Thaler v. USPTO, 2021).

Another significant case occurred in the European Patent Office (EPO), where similar patent applications by DABUS were rejected on the grounds of not having a human inventor. The High Court of Justice in the UK ruled in 2020 that an AI system could not be named as the inventor, reaffirming the stance that patent law requires human inventors. However, the case sparked debates within the IP community, leading to calls for legal reforms to adapt to the role of AI in innovation. This situation also brought attention to the broader issue of ownership and attribution, particularly with AI systems capable of generating complex inventions that may otherwise be difficult to ascribe to a single human inventor. These cases demonstrate a significant challenge in patent law and underscore the need for more transparent policies surrounding AI-generated inventions and the concept of inventorship (European Patent Office, 2020).

Lessons Learned of AI's Role in Patent Registration

The ongoing legal battles over AI-generated patents have highlighted several critical lessons for patent law and the role of AI in the innovation process. A key takeaway is that existing patent laws are not equipped to handle the complexities of AI-driven inventions. The DABUS case particularly underscores the need for legal reform to accommodate AI's contributions to the innovation process. In these disputes, the central issue is not the novelty of the invention but the attribution of inventorship. As AI systems like DABUS become more advanced, the traditional notion of inventorship—which presumes human agency—faces increasing challenges. One solution that has been proposed is the creation of a new category of AI-assisted patents, which would clearly define how to handle the contribution of AI to inventions, ensuring that human inventors still receive proper recognition while acknowledging AI's role as a tool in the creative process.

Another lesson learned is the importance of international coordination in patent law (Tsay & Liu, 2020). The DABUS case was heard in multiple jurisdictions, with varying outcomes, illustrating the lack of uniformity in how patent offices approach AI-driven inventions (Schwartz & Rogers, 2022). This has led to calls for greater collaboration between national patent offices and international bodies such as the WIPO to create a cohesive legal framework that can accommodate the growing presence of AI in innovation. Establishing clear guidelines for AI involvement in invention would help patent systems globally keep pace with technological advancements while ensuring that patents are granted fairly and in line with the spirit of the law (WIPO, 2020). The case also underscores the importance of understanding the intersection of technology and law, as patent law must evolve to address the challenges AI brings to IP.

Case Studies Highlighting Skill Obsolescence and Legal Adaptation

The integration of AI tools into patent processes is driving significant changes in the way patent professionals work, with some experts predicting the obsolescence of specific skills. For example, AI-driven platforms like *PatentCloud* and *Derwent Innovation* use machine learning to assist patent professionals in performing complex tasks such as prior art searches, patentability assessments, and claim analysis. These tools have reduced the time and effort required for these tasks, enabling patent agents to focus on higher-level activities like legal strategy and client consultation. However, this shift has raised concerns about job displacement and the diminishing need for traditional patent examination skills. In response, many patent professionals are now focusing on upskilling by learning how to effectively use AI tools, and professional organizations like the American Intellectual Property Law Association (AIPLA) have begun offering training on AI's impact on patent law and practice. Moreover, the increasing reliance on AI has led to changes in how patent offices and legal firms operate. For instance, the USPTO has invested in AI and machine learning technologies to enhance the examination process. By automating routine tasks such as prior art searches, the USPTO has been able to improve the efficiency and accuracy of patent reviews, reducing backlogs and speeding up the granting process. This shift towards automation has sparked discussions within the legal community about the future role of human patent examiners and the potential for AI-driven patent examination to become the norm. As a result, patent professionals are being encouraged to embrace a new skill set that combines the technical knowledge of AI with traditional legal expertise. Patent education programs now include AI-related courses to prepare future professionals for the evolving landscape (USPTO, 2020). These developments point to a hybrid model in which AI complements rather than replaces human expertise, requiring patent professionals to acquire new technological competencies.

FUTURE DIRECTIONS AND PERSPECTIVES

Emerging Trends in AI and IP Protection

The integration of AI into IP protection is rapidly reshaping the landscape, creating new possibilities for patenting processes. One of the emerging trends is the increasing use of AI-driven patenting tools that automate various stages of the process, such as patent searches, prior art identification, and patent drafting. These tools help patent professionals speed up routine tasks while improving their accuracy and efficiency. As AI technology advances, we are likely to see more sophisticated algorithms that can predict patentability with greater precision, offering new opportunities for early-stage innovation assessment and global patent strategies. Another trend is AI-enhanced patent portfolio management, where companies are leveraging machine learning to monitor and evaluate their existing patents and identify gaps in their portfolios. This growing reliance on AI will enable businesses to optimize their IP protection strategies and maximize their competitive edge in fast-moving markets (Li et al., 2022). Looking ahead, AI is also expected to play a significant role in the protection of AI-generated inventions, with some experts suggesting that new patent laws may emerge to better account for AI's involvement in innovation. As the number of AI-created inventions continues to rise, there will be increased pressure to develop new frameworks that address the legal complexities of attributing inventorship to non-human entities. Moreover, the global harmonization of patent laws concerning AI will become a priority as patent offices around the world work toward creating consistent regulations for AI-generated inventions. These trends suggest that AI will not only enhance traditional patenting processes but also transform the way IP protection is viewed and applied in an era where machines contribute directly to creative processes (WIPO, 2023).

Role of AI in Patent Offices and Legal Frameworks

As AI becomes more integral to patent offices around the world, its impact on patenting procedures will continue to evolve. Patent examination is one area where AI has already begun to make a significant difference, with AI tools being used to conduct automated prior art searches and patentability assessments. These AI-assisted systems can analyze vast datasets and flag similar patents or innovations that might otherwise go unnoticed, improving the efficiency and thoroughness of the examination process. In the future, AI could play an even more active role in the entire patent lifecycle, from initial filing to post-grant reviews. By automating routine tasks and providing predictive analysis, AI has the potential to significantly reduce patent backlogs and shorten the time between filing and approval, benefiting both applicants and patent offices. However, the increasing reliance on AI raises important questions about the adequacy of current legal frameworks to manage these technological advancements. The current patent law system was designed with the assumption that human inventors would be the primary drivers of innovation. As AI-driven inventions become more common, legal frameworks will need to evolve to address issues such as inventorship, ownership, and the legal status of AI systems as inventors. This may involve redefining patent laws to ensure they remain relevant and fair in an environment where AI plays a more prominent role. Furthermore, there may be a need for international cooperation among patent offices to harmonize AI-related regulations, ensuring that patents are granted consistently across jurisdictions and that AI-generated inventions are protected globally.

New Challenges and Opportunities in Protecting Creativity

As AI continues to impact patent registration, new challenges and opportunities will emerge in protecting creativity and innovation. One of the key challenges is ensuring that the authenticity of AI-driven innovations is maintained. With AI playing an increasing role in generating ideas and designs, it is crucial to establish clear guidelines that prevent over-reliance on automation and ensure that human creativity is not overshadowed by machine-driven processes. Protecting the integrity of the patent system will require a balance between recognizing AI's contribution and safeguarding human inventorship.

Addressing the issue of AI-generated inventions and ownership rights will require the creation of legal frameworks that clarify how patents should be attributed when AI is involved, particularly when there is no clear human inventor. On the other hand, AI presents numerous opportunities to future-proof IP protection. One such opportunity is the development of AI-powered tools that can assist in the identification of emerging technologies and predict market trends, helping innovators stay ahead of the curve. Patent offices and companies can more effectively manage IP portfolios, spot potential infringements early, and align their patent strategies with technological advancements. Moreover, AI tools can help patent professionals navigate the increasingly complex global patent landscape, where patents for similar inventions are filed in multiple jurisdictions. As AI continues to evolve (Garcia et al., 2025), there will be a need for adaptive policy frameworks that embrace innovation while protecting the rights of inventors. This will involve a shift towards dynamic legal models that can accommodate the fast-paced nature of AI-driven technological change and ensure that patent law remains an effective tool for protecting creativity in the 21st century.

CONCLUSION

As the boundaries of human and AI-generated creations blur, the importance of robust IP protections becomes even more pronounced. Patents, with their focus on protecting technical and functional aspects, remain a vital mechanism for ensuring the exclusivity and value of educational advancements in a rapidly evolving technological landscape. This chapter has emphasized the critical need to reassess patent frameworks to address the disruptions brought by AI. While AI offers immense potential to streamline and enhance patent processes, it also challenges traditional notions of inventorship and ownership. This dual-edged transformation demands thoughtful legal and procedural adaptations to ensure fairness, accountability, and the integrity of intellectual property systems. In the field of education, where innovation directly impacts societal progress, maintaining a robust and equitable patent system is essential to incentivize creativity and ensure that groundbreaking ideas are not only recognized but also protected. As AI continues to shape the future of IP, collaboration among policymakers, educators, and legal experts will be essential to establish frameworks that balance innovation with fairness. By safeguarding educational innovations through patents and adapting to the disruptions brought by AI, we can ensure that the benefits of these advancements are preserved for future generations.

REFERENCES

Acut, D. P., Gamusa, E. V., Pernaa, J., Yuenyong, C., Pantaleon, A. T., Espina, R. C., Sim, M. J. C., & Garcia, M. B. (2025). AI Shaming Among Teacher Education Students: A Reflection on Acceptance and Identity in the Age of Generative Tools. In *Pitfalls of AI Integration in Education: Skill Obsolescence, Misuse, and Bias*. IGI Global., DOI: 10.4018/979-8-3373-0122-8.ch005

Al-Busaidi, A. S., Raman, R., Hughes, L., Albashrawi, M. A., Malik, T., Dwivedi, Y. K., Al- Alawi, T., AlRizeiqi, M., Davies, G., Fenwick, M., Gupta, P., Gurpur, S., Hooda, A., Jurcys, P., Lim, D., Lucchi, N., Misra, T., Raman, R., Shirish, A., & Walton, P. (2024). Redefining Boundaries in Innovation and Knowledge Domains: Investigating the Impact of Generative Artificial Intelligence on Copyright and Intellectual Property Rights. *Journal of Innovation & Knowledge*, 9(4), 1–28. DOI: 10.1016/j.jik.2024.100630

Arif, Y. M., Nugroho, F., Aini, Q., Fauzan, A. C., & Garcia, M. B. (2025). A Systematic Literature Review of Serious Games for Physical Education: Technologies, Implementations, and Evaluations. In *Global Innovations in Physical Education and Health*. IGI Global., DOI: 10.4018/979-8-3693-3952-7.ch001

Broekhuizen, T., Dekker, H., de Faria, P., Firk, S., Nguyen, D. K., & Sofka, W. (2023). AI for Managing Open Innovation: Opportunities, Challenges, and a Research Agenda. *Journal of Business Research*, 167, 1–14. DOI: 10.1016/j.jbusres.2023.114196

Caplanova, A. (2020). Intellectual Property. In Pacheco-Torgal, F., Rasmussen, E., Granqvist, C.-G., Ivanov, V., Kaklauskas, A., & Makonin, S. (Eds.), *Start-Up Creation* (2nd ed., pp. 81–105). Woodhead Publishing., DOI: 10.1016/B978-0-12-819946-6.00005-9

Cappelli, R., Corsino, M., Laursen, K., & Torrisi, S. (2023). Technological Competition and Patent Strategy: Protecting Innovation, Preempting Rivals and Defending the Freedom to Operate. *Research Policy*, 52(6), 1–14. DOI: 10.1016/j.respol.2023.104785

Coombs, C., Hislop, D., Taneva, S. K., & Barnard, S. (2020). The Strategic Impacts of Intelligent Automation for Knowledge and Service Work: An Interdisciplinary Review. *The Journal of Strategic Information Systems*, 29(4), 1–30. DOI: 10.1016/j.jsis.2020.101600

Cuntz, A., C., F., & H., S. (2024). *Artificial Intelligence and Intellectual Property: An Economic Perspective*. World Intellectual Property Organization. https://doi.org/https://www.wipo.int/edocs/pubdocs/en/wipo-pub-econstat-wp-77-en-artificial-intelligence-and-intellectual-property-an-economic-perspective.pdf

de Rassenfosse, G., Pellegrino, G., & Raiteri, E. (2024). Do Patents Enable Disclosure? Evidence From the Invention Secrecy Act. *International Journal of Industrial Organization*, 92, 1–16. DOI: 10.1016/j.ijindorg.2023.103044

Elahi, M., Afolaranmi, S. O., Martinez Lastra, J. L., & Perez Garcia, J. A. (2023). A Comprehensive Literature Review of the Applications of AI Techniques Through the Lifecycle of Industrial Equipment. *Discover Artificial Intelligence*, 3(1), 1–78. DOI: 10.1007/s44163-023-00089-x

Ferrero Guillén, R., & Breckwoldt Jurado, A. (2023). Vagueness in Artificial Intelligence: The 'Fuzzy Logic' of AI-Related Patent Claims. *Digital Society : Ethics, Socio-Legal and Governance of Digital Technology*, 2(1), 1–25. DOI: 10.1007/s44206-022-00032-0

Fuad, D. R. S. M., Musa, K., & Hashim, Z. (2020). Innovation Culture in Education: A Systematic Review of the Literature. *Management in Education*, *36*(3), 135–149. DOI: 10.1177/0892020620959760

Füller, J., Hutter, K., Wahl, J., Bilgram, V., & Tekic, Z. (2022). How AI Revolutionizes Innovation Management – Perceptions and Implementation Preferences of AI-Based Innovators. *Technological Forecasting and Social Change*, *178*, 1–22. DOI: 10.1016/j.techfore.2022.121598

Gantalao, L. C., Calzada, J. G. D., Capuyan, D. L., Lumantas, B. C., Acut, D. P., & Garcia, M. B. (2025). Equipping the Next Generation of Technicians: Navigating School Infrastructure and Technical Knowledge in the Age of AI Integration. In *Pitfalls of AI Integration in Education: Skill Obsolescence, Misuse, and Bias*. IGI Global., DOI: 10.4018/979-8-3373-0122-8.ch009

Garcia, M. B. (2023). Fostering an Innovation Culture in the Education Sector: A Scoping Review and Bibliometric Analysis of Hackathons. *Innovative Higher Education*, *48*(4), 739–762. DOI: 10.1007/s10755-023-09651-y PMID: 37361114

Garcia, M. B. (2024). The Paradox of Artificial Creativity: Challenges and Opportunities of Generative AI Artistry. *Creativity Research Journal*, ●●●, 1–14. DOI: 10.1080/10400419.2024.2354622

Garcia, M. B., Mangaba, J. B., & Tanchoco, C. C. (2021). Virtual Dietitian: A Nutrition Knowledge-Based System Using Forward Chaining Algorithm. *2021 International Conference on Innovation and Intelligence for Informatics, Computing, and Technologies (3ICT)*, 309-314. DOI: 10.1109/3ICT53449.2021.9581887

Garcia, M. B., Rosak-Szyrocka, J., Yılmaz, R., Metwally, A. H. S., Acut, D. P., Ofosu-Ampong, K., Erdoğdu, F., Fung, C. Y., & Bozkurt, A. (2025). Rethinking Educational Assessment in the Age of Generative AI: Actionable Strategies to Mitigate Academic Dishonesty. In *Pitfalls of AI Integration in Education: Skill Obsolescence, Misuse, and Bias*. IGI Global., DOI: 10.4018/979-8-3373-0122-8.ch001

Guadamuz, A. (2017). Artificial Intelligence and Copyright. *WIPO Magazine*. https://www.wipo.int/web/wipo-magazine/articles/artificial-intelligence-and-copyright-40141

Hasanah, N. A., Aziza, M. R., Junikhah, A., Arif, Y. M., & Garcia, M. B. (2025). Navigating the Use of AI in Engineering Education Through a Systematic Review of Technology, Regulations, and Challenges. In *Pitfalls of AI Integration in Education: Skill Obsolescence, Misuse, and Bias*. IGI Global., DOI: 10.4018/979-8-3373-0122-8.ch016

Ikeuchi, K., & Motohashi, K. (2022). Linkage of Patent and Design Right Data: Analysis of Industrial Design Activities in Companies at the Creator Level. *World Patent Information*, *70*, 1–6. DOI: 10.1016/j.wpi.2022.102114

Javed, K., & Li, J. (2024). Artificial Intelligence in Judicial Adjudication: Semantic Biasness Classification and Identification in Legal Judgement (SBCILJ). *Heliyon*, *10*(9), 1–17. DOI: 10.1016/j.heliyon.2024.e30184 PMID: 38737247

Kim, D., Alber, M., Kwok, M. W., Mitrović, J., Ramirez-Atencia, C., PÉrez, J. A. R., & Zille, H. (2022). Clarifying Assumptions About Artificial Intelligence Before Revolutionising Patent Law. *GRUR International*, *71*(4), 295-321. DOI: 10.1093/grurint/ikab174

Krauß, J., & Kuttenkeuler, D. (2021). When to File for a Patent? The Scientist's Perspective. *New Biotechnology, 60,* 124–129. DOI: 10.1016/j.nbt.2020.10.006 PMID: 33091617

Maaliw, R. R., Mabunga, Z. P., Veluz, M. R. D. D., Alon, A. S., Lagman, A. C., Garcia, M. B., Lacatan, L. L., & Dellosa, R. M. (2023). An Enhanced Segmentation and Deep Learning Architecture for Early Diabetic Retinopathy Detection. *2023 IEEE 13th Annual Computing and Communication Workshop and Conference (CCWC),* 0168-0175. DOI: 10.1109/CCWC57344.2023.10099069

Malik, S., Muhammad, K., & Waheed, Y. (2024). Artificial Intelligence and Industrial Applications-A Revolution in Modern Industries. *Ain Shams Engineering Journal, 15*(9), 1–11. DOI: 10.1016/j.asej.2024.102886

Mesquita Machado, T., & Winter, E. (2023). Artificial Intelligence and Patents in Brazil: Overview on Patentability and Comparative Study on Patent Filings. *World Patent Information, 72,* 1–11. DOI: 10.1016/j.wpi.2023.102177

Mishra, N., Garcia, P. S., Habal, B. G. M., & Garcia, M. B. (2024). Harnessing an AI-Driven Analytics Model to Optimize Training and Treatment in Physical Education for Sports Injury Prevention. *Proceedings of the 8th International Conference on Education and Multimedia Technology,* 309-315. DOI: 10.1145/3678726.3678740

Mustafa, A. S., Alkawsi, G. A., Ofosu-Ampong, K., Vanduhe, V. Z., Garcia, M. B., & Baashar, Y. (2022). Gamification of E-Learning in African Universities: Identifying Adoption Factors Through Task-Technology Fit and Technology Acceptance Model. In Portela, F., & Queirós, R. (Eds.), *Next-Generation Applications and Implementations of Gamification Systems* (pp. 73–96). IGI Global., DOI: 10.4018/978-1-7998-8089-9.ch005

OECD. (2015). *The Innovation Imperative: Contributing to Productivity, Growth and Well-Being.* OECD Publishing., DOI: 10.1787/9789264239814-

Ohlhausen, M. K. (2016). Patent Rights in a Climate of Intellectual Property Rights Skepticism. *Harvard Journal of Law & Technology, 30*(1), 103–124. https://jolt.law.harvard.edu/assets/articlePDFs/v30/30HarvJLTech103.pdf

Ouyang, X., Sun, Z., & Xu, X. (2022). Patent System in the Digital Era - Opportunities and New Challenges. *Journal of Digital Economy, 1*(3), 166–179. DOI: 10.1016/j.jdec.2022.12.003

Ozin, G. A., Qian, C., & MacIntosh, J. G. (2023). Can AI Be an Inventor in Materials Discovery? *Matter, 6*(10), 3117–3120. DOI: 10.1016/j.matt.2023.08.015

Patel, P. C., & Sahi, G. K. (2024). AI Patent Approvals in Service Firms, Patent Radicalness, and Stock Market Reaction. *Journal of Service Research, 10946705241230840.* Advance online publication. DOI: 10.1177/10946705241230840

Petil, E. D., Florece, M. E. A., Gomez, M. G. A., Villaruel, K. B., Fernandez, H. G. C. Q., Dela Cruz, C. M. B., & Ferrer-Rafols, R. B. (2025). Virtual Reality in Physical Education: An Innovative Approach to Optimize Physical and Mental Health. In *Global Innovations in Physical Education and Health.* IGI Global., DOI: 10.4018/979-8-3693-3952-7.ch005

Picht, P. G., & Thouvenin, F. (2023). AI and IP: Theory to Policy and Back Again – Policy and Research Recommendations at the Intersection of Artificial Intelligence and Intellectual Property. *IIC - International Review of Intellectual Property and Competition Law, 54*(6), 916-940. DOI: 10.1007/s40319-023-01344-5

Poddar, A., & Rao, S. R. (2024). Evolving Intellectual Property Landscape for AI-Driven Innovations in the Biomedical Sector: Opportunities in Stable IP Regime for Shared Success. *Frontiers in Artificial Intelligence, 7*, 1–15. DOI: 10.3389/frai.2024.1372161 PMID: 39355146

Rodrigues, R. (2020). Legal and Human Rights Issues of AI: Gaps, Challenges and Vulnerabilities. *Journal of Responsible Technology, 4*, 1–12. DOI: 10.1016/j.jrt.2020.100005

Saha, C. N., & Bhattacharya, S. (2011). Intellectual Property Rights: An Overview and Implications in Pharmaceutical Industry. *Journal of Advanced Pharmaceutical Technology & Research, 2*(2), 88–93. DOI: 10.4103/2231-4040.82952 PMID: 22171299

Schwartz, D. L., & Rogers, M. (2022). "Inventorless" Inventions? The Constitutional Conundrum of AI-Produced Inventions. *SSRN, 35*(2), 531–479. https://jolt.law.harvard.edu/assets/articlePDFs/v35/3. -Schwartz-Rogers-Inventorless-Inventions.pdf. DOI: 10.2139/ssrn.4025434

Segarra, J. R., Mengual-Andres, S., & Cortijo Ocaña, A. (Eds.). (2024). *Educational Innovation to Address Complex Societal Challenges.* IGI Global., DOI: 10.4018/979-8-3693-3073-9

Serdyukov, P. (2017). Innovation in Education: What Works, What Doesn't, and What to Do About it? *Journal of Research in Innovative Teaching & Learning, 10*(1), 4–33. DOI: 10.1108/JRIT-10-2016-0007

Setchi, R., Spasić, I., Morgan, J., Harrison, C., & Corken, R. (2021). Artificial Intelligence for Patent Prior Art Searching. *World Patent Information, 64*, 1–12. DOI: 10.1016/j.wpi.2021.102021

Singh, A., Hallihosur, S., & Rangan, L. (2009). Changing Landscape in Biotechnology Patenting. *World Patent Information, 31*(3), 219–225. DOI: 10.1016/j.wpi.2009.03.004

Sreenivasan, A., & Suresh, M. (2024). Design Thinking and Artificial Intelligence: A Systematic Literature Review Exploring Synergies. *International Journal of Innovation Studies, 8*(3), 297–312. DOI: 10.1016/j.ijis.2024.05.001

Tarasenko, L. (2023). Legislative Reforms on Patents, Utility Models and Industrial Designs in Ukraine. *Competition and Intellectual Property Law in Ukraine*, 373-414. DOI: 10.1007/978-3-662-66101-7_15

Tsay, M.-Y., & Liu, Z.-W. (2020). Analysis of the Patent Cooperation Network in Global Artificial Intelligence Technologies Based on the Assignees. *World Patent Information, 63*, 1–17. DOI: 10.1016/j.wpi.2020.102000

Wandhe, P. (2024). The Intellectual Property Landscape: Safeguarding Innovations Derived From Basic Science. In Trivedi, S., Grover, V., Balusamy, B., & Ganguly, A. (Eds.), *Unleashing the Power of Basic Science in Business* (pp. 285–310). IGI Global., DOI: 10.4018/979-8-3693-5503-9.ch015

WIPO. (2019). WIPO Technology Trends 2019 – Artificial Intelligence. *World Intellectual Property Organization.* DOI: 10.34667/tind.29084

WIPO. (2022). WIPO Guide to Using Patent Information. *World Intellectual Property Organization.* DOI: 10.34667/tind.46546

WIPO. (2024). Patent Landscape Report: Generative Artificial Intelligence. *World Intellectual Property Organization.* DOI: 10.34667/tind.49740

KEY TERMS AND DEFINITIONS

Artificial Intelligence: The simulation of human intelligence processes by machines, especially computer systems, to perform tasks such as learning, reasoning, and problem-solving.

Educational Innovation: The process of introducing new ideas, methods, or tools to improve teaching, learning, and educational outcomes.

Educational Patents: Patents that specifically protect inventions related to education, such as novel teaching methods, educational technologies, or tools designed to enhance learning.

Innovation Management: The systematic process of creating, organizing, and implementing new ideas and technologies within organizations to drive growth and improve efficiency.

Intellectual Property: Legal protections granted to creators and inventors to safeguard their creations, such as inventions, designs, literary works, and trademarks.

Inventorship: The legal recognition of individuals or entities who contribute to the creation of a patentable invention, typically requiring a direct contribution to the inventive concept.

Ownership: The legal right or title to a piece of property, including intellectual property, that grants control over its use, transfer, or commercialization.

Patent: A legal right granted by a government that provides an inventor exclusive rights to make, use, or sell an invention for a specific period in exchange for disclosing it to the public.

Chapter 14
AI in Academia:
Balancing Integrity, Ethics, and Learning Amid Evolving Norms of Authorship and Scholarship

Devanshi Taneja
https://orcid.org/0009-0004-1740-4391
Christ University, India

Harivarshini Prabagaren
https://orcid.org/0009-0007-4211-5518
Christ University, India

Mary Rani Thomas
https://orcid.org/0000-0003-1372-3032
Christ University, India

ABSTRACT

The integration of AI in academic and publication content generation is a recent development, significantly altering policies on citation and authorship, which were previously designed for human-generated work. While AI tools have eased administrative and academic workloads, their rapid adoption raises concerns about ethics and academic integrity. This chapter explores the role of AI as a transformative force in academia, highlighting both its benefits and potential downsides. A key concern is the potential erosion of critical thinking among researchers and scholars due to overreliance on AI, which could impact the quality of research. Despite being a game-changer for students, educators, and administrative staff, the academic community must address the ethical implications and develop new policies to ensure that AI enhances rather than undermines scholarly work. This chapter aims to foster dialogue on how academia can coexist with advancing AI innovations while maintaining research integrity and quality.

DOI: 10.4018/979-8-3373-0122-8.ch014

INTRODUCTION

Artificial Intelligence has traveled a rapid journey from being an academic phenomenon to becoming the main focus of technology's rites of passage. Early theories on the history of AI point to the mid-20th century, and it was during this period that the field was promoted by two great minds- Alan Turing and John McCarthy (Kuipers & Prasad, 2021). The early AI systems were rule-based, while very advanced machine learning and deep-learning methods have entered every corpus of business nowadays. These products include IBM's Watson, OpenAI's ChatGPT, and Google's DeepMind, representing distinct development models: automation, data analytics, and natural language processing. This has also proceeded to give a rational measure of the leverage of AI on labor productivity, user experience, and decision-making. AI has cast its net over the whole realm, providing healthcare, finance, education, and entertainment benefits with unbridled predictions, insight, and projections, ensuring work is completed promptly. Artificial intelligence has become one of the driving forces behind changing education by replacing outdated learning dynamics with methods by which students and teachers interact with the information.

Machine learning algorithms analyze student performance and customize lesson plans according to individual needs before allowing instant feedback and a more responsive and inclusive learning atmosphere (Owan et al., 2023). AI-powered search engine applications such as ChatGPT, Socratic by Google, and Coursera's AI recommendations shift education to a higher level of interaction and engagement, free from geographical and socio-economic barriers. It also helps teachers cut through mundane paperwork easily, allowing them to spend more time on teaching and mentoring. Still, with the immense promise that the use of artificial intelligence in education presents, worries about the increase are about data privacy, dependence on technology, and the digital divide. Meanwhile, the development of technology with the growing prevalence of AI in Education offers an opportunity and a challenge, where the balancing act between innovation and learner-centered approaches will demand precise and careful management.

MAIN FOCUS OF THE CHAPTER

This chapter describes the crucial challenges regarding the development of AI in the education system. This will center on issues regarding the obsolescence of skills, disinformation, moral dilemmas, and integrity in academia. While AI enhances the learning experience, its uncontrolled technology use is a concern for critical thinking, dependency, and plagiarism. In this research, we are led to the conflicts of the present time between technological advancement and traditional learning values and increasing demands on ethical principles. Identifying these pitfalls seals the gap between the promises of AI and its proper use by providing insights into sustainably successful AI adoption in education that does not compromise academic integrity or quality of learning.

LITERATURE REVIEW

AI is revolutionizing education through innovative learning-maximizing, administrating, and attendance-accessing solutions. AI-enabled tools allow educators to train their students as inclusively and creatively as possible. Some of the significant benefits AI is bringing to education are enormously changing commercial areas.

AI would reduce the time devoted to this tedious administration and training process. Assignment evaluation, lesson plan preparation, report writing, and feedback maintenance take up much of a teacher's time. AI tools would perform similar tasks quickly, allowing teachers to spend more time on personalized teaching and mentoring (Afonughe et al., 2021). Modern testing systems, whether MCQs or short-answer grading, will use NLP since they represent tedious endeavors even for teachers. AI implementation is to set up scheduling tools to ease the class agenda and offer resource allocation to ease academic interventions. One can now find additional time to engage students and implement curricula free of some tasks connected to the administration.

Every student learns differently at varying speeds and has different strengths and weaknesses. Such differences are rarely even afforded in a traditional educational environment, leaving lags in learning retainments. AI is informative personalized learning interfaces that use adaptive algorithms that can analyze students' learning patterns, thus recalibrating one or another aspect of the educational material. AI customization of lesson plans, recommending resources, and adjusting to every learner's rate by tools like Duolingo, Khan Academy, and Coursera. This personalization allows students to be supported with respect to their pace while grasping complex topics.

Hundreds of years ago, detecting gaps in learning and assessing progress afterward would have cost centuries of toil (Liu et al., 2022). Instant assessment, attendance, and engagement data are worked on by AI analytics to allow teachers to realize not just how their students are learning but how they are struggling (Mishra et al., 2024). The findings provided feedback for evidence-based decisions regarding potential curriculum, intervention, and individual support recommendations made by the teacher (Parab, 2020). AI will forecast student performance trends, allowing schools to intervene beforehand and thus enhancing the results.

AI also provides early notice of its data analysis, which is highly effective for on-time intervention for struggling learners. Language barriers among students from multilingual or global environments have long been a challenge for education. AI translators and speech recognizers remove barriers by offering aid at the optimal moment whenever needed. Google Translate and Microsoft Translator apps enable the students to gain an understanding of their study documents in their preferred language. It enables easier assimilation of the subject matter being presented. Furthermore, AI virtual assistants and chatbots can translate instructions and descriptions for non-native learners in real-time in their preferred language, enabling them to access the content AI will bring parity in quality education access to students from diverse language backgrounds by eliminating the language barrier (Wallace & Abel, 2024).

AI chatbots and tutors provide immediate explanations and adaptive quizzes that reinforce knowledge engagingly and amusingly. Such a shift would enable students to become capable problem solvers, imaginative, and knowledgeable about the topics at hand, despite any hurdles or blemishes that could have occurred in their selected learning paths vis a vis kinetics of assessments.

Gamification, artificial intelligence-enhanced VR, and AR technology make learning more personal. AI applications like Quizlet and Brainly make learning an adventure and trigger students' imagination. AI-powered chatbots and virtual teaching assistants provide student-centric academic assistance, where students can seek support at any given hour. Besides being interactive, incorporating AI makes learning engaging and fascinating, promoting greater student motivation and engagement (Bachiri et al., 2023). Such intelligent tutoring gives academic support to the student 24/7, allowing him to learn objects outside the classroom. These instructors simulate human interaction using AI when providing instructions, responding to questions, and guiding students to solve problems. With intelligent tutoring, platforms like ChatGPT, Squirrel AI, and Carnegie Learning's AI tutor provide students with the same service as their tutors, enabling them to attend to their queries unreasonably quickly. Such access is particularly convenient for self-directed students who cannot make it to their support staff out-of-class signal time.

AI-based learning programs enhance the efficiency of educational access. AI-enabled e-learning platforms endow students with free or low-cost course resources and thereby further make education available. Chatbots and automated customer services powered by AI would reduce administrative overheads for institutions since they allow them to answer queries more cost-effectively (Msekelwa, 2024). AI enables remote learning so learners off-campus or remotely and students from disadvantaged backgrounds can access quality education without any geographical limits. The reality of how work changes in the age of AI necessitates that they be groomed for the future workplace by integrating AI tools into learning. AI-powered career guidance systems give students suitable career choices according to interest, ability, and achievement. Through essential exposure to AI tools, students develop much-needed digital literacy, analytical skills, and problem-solving skills necessary for the technology of the modern age.

Opportunities from AI in Higher Education and Publications can be Efficiency Gain as AI-Assisted Tools Reduce Administrative Overhead (Lameras & Arnab, 2021), Allowing Faculty Time to Create and Examine. On a publication level, this is proofreading, plagiarism detection, citation formatting, etc. Apart from this, there is personalized learning, which shows that with AI, there will be adaptive learning platforms that address the diverse needs of learners and a customized curriculum that would enhance engagement and learning outcomes (Pratama et al., 2023). Sometimes, this is also called a last-minute push for help regarding a matter that had earlier been presented in class, ensuring touch upon areas of misunderstanding. Also, expanded research abilities are wherein the AI tool helps researchers analyze vast datasets and characterize the underlying patterns and essential points that would otherwise take them years to do (Chubb et al., 2021). Besides, literature reviews through AI applications manage to condense millions of articles into limited readable summaries and help speed up research. Greater Accessibility in the form of Translation/transcription tools makes academic resources available to the global audience sensitive barriers to linguistics and disability (Hadinezhad et al., 2024).

Table 1. Various AI tools used in creating academic content

AI Tools	Source	Year	Application	Usage	Payment	Stream
ChatGPT	(Adeshola & Adepoju, 2023)	2023	Generates human-like text and assists with assignments, research, and learning material creation.	Faculty and Students	Both are free with paid options	All
Grammarly	(Faisal & Carabella, 2023)	2023	Grammar and spelling check, writing improvement.	Faculty and Students	Free/Paid	All
Quizlet AI	(Luan et al., 2023)	2023	AI-generated study sets, personalized learning, and flashcards.	Faculty and Students	Free with basic features; Paid for advanced features.	All

continued on following page

Table 1. Continued

AI Tools	Source	Year	Application	Usage	Payment	Stream
Kahoot! AI	(Lopatynska et al., 2024)	2024	AI-driven quizzes, personalized learning, and formative assessments.	Faculty and Students	Free with basic features; Paid for advanced features	All
Coursera AI	(Zargoun, 2024)	2024	Personalized course recommendations AI-driven assessments.	Faculty and Students	Paid with some free courses.	All
DALL-E	Watermeyer et al., 2023	2023	Creation of images based on the prompts provided.	Students	It is free to generate a certain number of images, but unlimited images require a subscription	All
Quill Bot AI	Watermeyer et al., 2023	2023	Paraphrasing and Citation of articles	Faculty and Students	Free for a specific word limit, but for unlimited words, requires a subscription model	Research, General Writing
Jaser AI	Watermeyer et al., 2023	2023	Content Writing, SEO Optimisations, and creating original marketing copy.	Faculty	Subscription-based pricing model	Content and case-study writing

CHALLENGES

Misinformation

Educational AI software can provide tremendous information; unfortunately, this is also a source of significant risks, such as misinformation. Some possibilities are that AI models generate false or outdated information because their answers are extracted from the previous data. Students doing research and studies using AI-based platforms might unknowingly take in inaccurate or misleading information, which impacts their performance and critical thinking skills (Elsayed, 2024).

Another is bias in AI software. If AI software is built upon data that contains flaws, prejudices, or biases, it continues to perpetuate such flaws and does not correct them. They teach wrong facts and distort pupils' perception of significant issues. Through the AI-assisted assembly of the teaching material, history or social studies may be politically and ethnically biased and tend to bias learners into strange ways of thinking.

There is a significant issue with the misinformation. The constantly changing nature of technology also contributes to misinformation. Because AI models are not static, some have heightened response times than others to real-life changes. As such, today's correct answer from AI tools may not, in several months, receive knowledge on new findings or policy changes in the relevant sphere of expertise. Students may wrongly cite outdated information or unknowingly miss a significant new development in their practice area.

Another primary ignorance arises as an extension of how misinformation from AI tends to warp cognitive biases: either AI models developed with partial or unbalanced datasets or models presenting anything to back up one point of view while leaving opposing perspectives ignored or peripheral. This could lead students to ignorant understandings of specific historical events, social issues, or scientific debates without exposure to a more fully developed and neutral perspective (Pedro et al., 2019).

AI models cannot process text like humans do patterns rather than concepts in general. AI responses often contain the correct information, only conveyed or framed improperly or obscurely. For example, an AI may summarize a historical event while conveniently failing to mention facts that lead to an entirely different conclusion, thus leaving a one-sided, shallow understanding of the event.

Deepfake Uses and Human Simulation

AI technology used in deep fake enables it to spin stories. Artificial intelligence firmly implants this in speech, looks, and impersonating behavior bolder than humans. Deep Fakes threaten education by adding confusion to academic content, fraud personality interruptions, and other misinformation packaged in a box.

Deepfake technology and academic malpractice must be quite worrying. Students may, for any reason, through videos, audio, or practically AI-generated, submit fictitious assignments, presentations, or credentials. Such acts raise the question of integrity. AI detection mechanisms and verification checks for educational institutions will be crucial for thoroughly confirming the authenticity of digital content, presenting a challenge to deepfakes. Instructors should educate students on the ethics of generating AI media and engagement in acts of responsible digital citizenship of any learner. Proving identities by other due diligence, such as blockchain workings for credentialing and a distinct two-step authentication process, will almost eliminate academic fraud in an entirely safe learning environment.

As deepfake technology obliterates all distinctions between authentic and manipulated content, it unravels the basis for honesty in education. As AI-generated video and audio increasingly resemble reality, it challenges the distinction between accurate academic content and schlock. The stage can, therefore, accelerate the relentless spread of misinformation, making the two parties concerned vulnerable in such scenarios (Karnouskos, 2020). The fact that deepfake technology can replicate the image and voice of living persons aggravates the situation further; dubious educational content can, therefore, be held forward as credentials.

Another growing concern about deepfake technology is that students use it to cheat openly in their respective assignments. These students can prepare whole essays and PowerPoint presentations that look like they have delivered using deepfake technologies. Hence, regular assessments suffer, as the teachers cannot gauge students' performance in any subject. Further, deepfakes impersonate and result in cases of false negative accusations, generally muddled by the delicate nature of the educational setting. It's increasing fear that misuse abilities and possibilities are ever rising through the layers of education.

Confirmation Bias

The drift in AI may unintentionally reinforce confirmation bias by only validating certain viewpoints. People tend to look for information that supports and confirms their beliefs and ignores opposing perspectives. They might assume and interpret things that align with their views or remember things that support their belief. AI can reinforce this by showing students content that aligns with their existing opinions, limiting their exposure to diverse perspectives and critical thinking.

The training of AI models is on vast and diverse datasets, but these data might contain biases. If not managed, the biases may influence AI-generated content differently, leading to one-sided narratives in politics and history. This turns dreadfully damaging in subject areas such as history, politics, and social science, where only narratives must support certain ideologies while alternatives are silenced. This same reason strengthens previously stated views and makes it excruciatingly arduous for the learner to assess alternative views calmly.

Moreover, content recommendation algorithms focus on engagement rather than neutrality or accuracy. When a student interacts frequently with a particular theme and position, the AI feeds such ideas, deepening the confirmation bias. Combined with automated reinforcement of specific beliefs, this could generate prejudice as an opinion hardens into a mighty wall, blocking the way toward alternative views. In pedagogy, this might create a dead-end for reasoning. This bias does not exist in isolation, affecting other productive group deliberations and various environments. Classroom discussions, even, could tilt towards a viewpoint of the majority stemming from reliance upon biased AI-generated materials and hence lean back towards being biased again. A polarized environment could arise such that alternative views are never ventured into, examined, or discussed: a straightforward juncture in which they are dismissed or mocked up.

Thus, confirmation bias becomes a social problem. If AI-generated content repetitively is presented with bias in certain groups, cultures, or ideologies, students may develop subconscious prejudices. This can contribute to social divisions, decreased inclusivity, and a less welcoming learning environment (Ha & Kim, 2023).

Difficulty in Knowing the Actual Author

The major obstacle for AI-generated education content is tracing its original author or owner. This arises mainly because AI-generated tools produce new essays, summaries, or reports through various data collections from other sources, which might not have adequate attribution. This alone creates a big dilemma for students and teachers in assessing student works' credibility, raising essential concerns regarding academic integrity and intellectual property rights (Formosa et al., 2024). The hiding of attribution does not sincerely allow any distinction between a credible, peer-reviewed article on the one hand and, on the other, dubious or possibly misleading information.

In traditional settings, there is a transparent chain of ownership of materials treated credibly: textbooks, research papers, and journal articles all have identifiable authors who can lend their expertise, background, or knowledge in the field for evaluation purposes. The point here is that anything generated by AI does not foresee accountability. Furthermore, because the information is collected across various datasets from unverified sources across the web, there is no identifiable ever-existent author for the information used. As such, it is often difficult to know if the citation is peer-reviewed, up-to-date, or even, more importantly, fact-checked.

The submission of AI-generated material by students becomes another daunting issue. Given the uncredentialed authorship of works done, students may pass off AI-compiled works before which they did not know about plagiarism. This lends itself to an interesting gray area where any educator has to deal with novelty and artificial intelligence applications to assess further research and knowledge transformation by learners. Increased uncertainty surrounding authorship raises grave concerns among educationalists who devise their lessons and activities based on AI-generated materials. Suppose a teacher relies on AI to create lesson plans, quizzes, or study guides by scratching many sources without proper citations. In that case, he could unknowingly pass on inaccurate or prejudiced information.

In (Nguyen et al., 2024), it is mentioned that when AI and humans work together on a project, it is difficult to ascertain at the end of the project how much of the final product is to be credited to AI versus other sources. Giving due credit to the author becomes even more important when it affects the author's reputation and the effectiveness of the work. According to Jenkins & Lin (2023), materials that are readily available for public access and scrutiny, such as research papers, academic articles, or media articles, should start to give the due credit to Artificial Intelligence tools in generating the content as these influence the skill levels and expertise of the person in whose name the material would be put out for public usage and access. However, it has been mentioned that for creating content or material that is not used for publication but for personal usage on a day-to-day basis, the information generated by Artificial Intelligence tools could not be credited as the author's expertise may not be questioned based on it.

AI tools can provide similar work resembling human-written research, which could challenge the authenticity of the works and the value of the content done by humans (Elkhatat et al., 2023). AI generates information that could be vague, lacking deep understanding and critical thinking and solving logical problems to which humans can contribute. It can be challenging for researchers to compare their existing work with AI, making it less valuable and effortless.

Stringent Policies of Universities

The AI-enabled tools have given individuals in the field of research opportunities to assist them with writing essays and accessing various information (Chan, 2023). These include areas from literature, review, and draft of the papers for submission for publication. However, this could raise questions about the integrity and originality of the work. The university's primary concern is determining the originality check of the submissions. To rectify that, many universities have imposed strict rules prohibiting AI tools in the academic setting, penalizing the students if found in violation. It could be a significant disadvantage to students seeking help from AI tools.

The faculty members or research guides play a significant role in checking if the students adhere to the rules and regulations set by the universities. The additional challenge is ensuring originality in student submissions. With a high dependency on AI, they must verify unethical behavior and assist them academically. The guides are responsible for assessing and giving feedback to the students based on their research drafts (Dabis & Csáki, 2024).

As universities implement policies to ensure fairness and integrity, penalties are imposed on guides who encourage students to adopt AI content into their work. Some universities hold the guide accountable for the student's work and may face severe consequences ranging from a warning to termination. Hence, this could lead to limitations between the guides and the university's rules.

Universities across the globe are implementing different governance models to integrate and implement AI in Education. In the Indian context, pioneers of AI-based teaching for enhancing the learning process are institutions such as IIM Sambalpur. The program under it will personalize student learning using real-time data analysis while optimizing faculty productivity and maintaining student interactiveness (Pti, 2024). This model is one component of the more excellent Digital India program for education reform guided by the National Education Policy (NEP) 2020, which promotes the application of information and communication technology towards more extensive access and improved quality of learning. World universities are reorganizing governance frameworks to cope with AI-based education. Digital models of educational leadership are being adopted by most institutions, where university leaders will need to have technical proficiency in addition to conventional administrative skills. The test of governance is deciding on the use of ethical AI in balancing academic freedom and accountability. Universities are formulating a policy for AI-driven grading, plagiarism checking, and self-learning (Ullah et al., 2024). Other universities have even set up committees on AI ethics to discuss issues of concern regarding data privacy, algorithmic bias, and student surveillance. AI can be anticipated to bring in open governance frameworks to maintain educational equality while embracing the advantages of AI. Case studies from European and U.S. universities indicate that institutions embrace hybrid governance frameworks, usually integrating AI with human intervention. This is intended to ensure that AI-backed recommendations are aligned with the objectives of an institution and ethics.

Fabrication of Citations

As AI tools are increasingly used to generate content in the academic world (Acut et al., 2025), a serious issue has been seen at the forefront. It is related to fabricating citations, also known as hallucinated references. According to, when they checked the credibility of around 343 citations, 64% were fabricated, i.e., no source of them could be found on the open web (Da Silva et al., 2025). Researchers forget that the fundamental principles that AI tools work upon are pattern prediction and training of the data provided. They don't realize that AI cannot access databases or research journals. It is often seen that if any information is to be extracted from AI tools that it cannot provide, the information the tool would generate would be insufficient in this quality and will not be credible enough to be included in a research article. When an AI tool provides citations and sources, it is often untrustworthy (Bhattacharyya et al., 2023). This makes any bibliography generated by an AI tool invalid, which may even lead to action against the person whose name the content has been published for public scrutiny.

Demotivating Teachers

The tools formerly known as AI can provide or replicate ideas that teachers incorporate into their classes. The model of AI generates lessons, lecture notes, or lesson plans that almost match what a teacher could create on their own, leading to a sense of redundancy in some way (Chiu et al., 2023). During this overlap, the originality and worth of the teacher in the classroom become heavily undermined. This may fit within a sphere that diminishes the motivation of educators to carry out their lesson ideas upon realizing that AI can easily duplicate such materials.

A supply of pre-designed AI-generated lesson plans or exam preparation notes can discourage all teachers from playing into their inventive instincts. A long reliance on AI-installed teaching methods removes teachers' creativity and induces a more standardized and less creative experience for our youth. When AI can approach or even serve to replicate some aspects of an educator's work, such as assessment, production of instructional materials, and teaching, it can engender feelings of inadequacy and disenchantment-the effective loss of just those very qualities that mean value and prestige upon the profession. Teachers may then find their authority diminished, leading to dissatisfaction with their jobs (Almasri, 2024). These possibilities of AI creating high-quality learning materials put authors under pressure to frequently prove their usefulness and relevance in an AI-centric classroom. This leads to anxiety and stress, which is too bad for those teachers who are not very well-versed in technology or do not wish to incorporate AI within their teaching practices.

Hence, AI can generate similar content of ideas when compared with the teacher's idea, who is looking forward to presenting in the classroom to educate the students on various subjects. This could demotivate the teacher's creativity by giving the students similar notes and ideas while preparing for exams, discouraging traditional methods. The topic can be very similar to the teacher's strategy and processes, which could result in dissatisfaction with the job. This deteriorates the personal touch educators try to bring to their teaching methods (Holgado-Apaza et al., 2023).

Citations of Gray Literature

One issue that has often been noticed with the content generated through AI is that it gives equal importance to gray literature and peer-reviewed sources. Where peer-reviewed sources are credible, and the information is academically valid, gray literature is often sourced from blogs or podcasts, which may not have been verified rigorously as the peer-reviewed literature (Ashiq et al., 2021). Although gray literature does provide information that is easily accessible along the lines of blogs, podcasts, and YouTube videos, which have in the day and age become the go-to source for any new information, the unreviewed nature of these sources makes them uneasy to be considered for use in formal publications and academic work which would be out for the public scrutiny, Artificial Intelligence uses NLP(Natural Language Processing) technology to collect concise information from various sources across the internet. When gathering content and datasets, this technology is trained to collect it as fast as possible without caring for the quality or the credibility of the content presented to the user.

Gray literature is often associated with information driven by commercial or personal agendas. Hence, the validity of the information present in these sources is also essential. Gray literature can also not be defended academically because of its lack of depth in its content and its citation of sources. The array of gray literature available is massive, and it isn't easy to track it across the internet as it is very scattered. Hence, there comes an issue when AI tools need to cite the source of the gray literature in the content generated by it. This often leads to a problem that can be termed citation ambiguity, wherein the correct source of the information is not available.

The two most common types of citation ambiguities that appear in the case of gray literature usage are Dilution Of source Attribution and Unintentional Plagiarism. Dilution of source Attribution points out the lack of granularity in checking the source of a particular piece of content generated by Artificial Intelligence. If a piece of information is constructed based on two reports, one peer-reviewed and the other of a blog, it is basically out of gray literature. When AI creates content out of these, the final content does not reflect the part sourced from where. This dis-credits the peer-reviewed information and may give more importance to gray literature whose information may be vague. AI may cite the gray literature rather than the published source, which is more credible. This would reduce the quality of the report that would be produced.

AI-generated content can unintentionally promote plagiarism, even if users use it in good faith. Moreover, that happens when users copy AI-generated material without grasping the necessity to cite the sources it synthesized from or when they presume that the AI itself is the unique "author." It usually takes place when there is Unreferenced Paraphrasing AI, which can successfully paraphrase text to make it look essentially original by disguising the source text or between sequences. Opacity may also lead to Unintentional Plagiarism as most AI tools do not tell you what they are trained or generating. Users may not realize that citation is needed at all without clear signals. Unclear ownership may lead to the same if AI is involved at any stage of the process; users often assume that the resultant content is considered public domain and free for reproduction without attribution (Gilchrist & Perks, 2023).

Although gray literature may sometimes be more prosperous in its content quality than published sources, the problem of proper citation and attribution to the correct author has prevented it from being credited as a credible source till now. When the AI tool cannot achieve this distinction, it leads to ethical issues that may impact the scholarly discourse of researchers trying to publish their work.

SKILL OBSOLESCENCE OF FACULTY AND STUDENTS

Teachers and students face difficulties cultivating and implementing AI tools into their learning practices, where AI takes over traditional teaching methods due to technological advancements in all fields, often leading to Skill Obsolescence (Morandini et al., 2023). This segment examines the impact of faculties and students on the changing learning environment.

Faculty

Faculties used to traditional teaching practices find adapting to AI-enabled educational practices challenging to incorporate in their teaching methods and practices due to insufficient technical training or a reluctance to change.

The routine work of a teacher, like grading, feedback, etc., becomes unworthy, reducing the need for teachers to perform their teaching duties in the classrooms and their dependency on them. A recent study analyzed ChatGPT's capabilities in exploring the faculties and student's perceptions of completing undergraduate engineering coursework. The findings were that the faculties needed to adapt to the AI tools.

Student

AI-driven platforms are in high demand for students' activities like taking notes, doing assignments, solving problem sets, and preparing for exams. Dependence upon this technology can prevent students from honing the life skills they need to develop, namely critical thinking, problem-solving, and creativity. Writing assessments or solutions using AI tools like ChatGPT and Gemini offer instant satisfaction but deny students the opportunity to learn basic concepts.

AI tools help them do assessments and more activities, but if students use them too much, they might engage less in classroom participation or think outside the box.

Short-Term Progress, Long-Term Professional Setbacks

The use of AI tools in research-related processes has apparent short-term benefits because they can substantially increase the efficiency, speed, and accessibility of information (Owan et al., 2023). Automating repetitive activities, guiding data analysis, and even generating drafts buy more time for researchers to think critically and interpret, improving research quality. Such advantages enable the completion of research goals quicker, thus making deadlines easier to keep track of with greater productivity from researchers. The above are the immediate benefits. However, in the long run, overdependence on AI may tarnish a researcher's academic profile, raising ethical concerns and risk rendering the researcher less scholar's credibility in the land of academia and the value of their work comparatively diminished over time.

AI tools lend considerable short-term help in caring for different aspects of the research process. The most significant advantage is the possibility of processing vast amounts of data within a short time, which enables the analysis of complex datasets at higher speed and accuracy than would have been possible if done manually. AI tools can save considerable time when conducting literature reviews by checking research databases for relevant research and offering a summary of it. Besides that, the language component of the AI tools might help an author write sections of the paper so the researcher can organize their ideas and structure their findings. Such administrative benefits of efficiency and productivity are significant in situations where there is little time or tight deadlines in academia competing for funding for research.

AI technologies allow researchers to concentrate more on higher-order intellectual tasks, such as proposing hypotheses and interpreting results, rather than being bogged down by repeated or time-consuming tasks. For this reason, the advantages of AI in the short run result in speedier research completion and higher outputs, boosting the perception of researchers as highly productive and capable (Al-Zahrani, 2023).

While the benefits of AI in the short term are apparent, over the long term, researchers may face difficulties. More than anything else, the integrity of a researcher may be the foremost casualty in this whole AI exercise. Even though modern AI has advanced tremendously, it can still create issues arising from the underlying data on which they are trained and the algorithms that govern them. Such tools generate results based on existing patterns within the data, but they lack some critical analysis or originality to the same degree as human researchers. A fear could bring adverse effects to the researcher, a slowly declining ability to produce anything genuinely in the coming years, and much less to develop sufficiently innovative work (Khlaif et al., 2023).

Reliance on AI-generated content may influence one's career growth. Academic institutions, funding bodies, and publishing journals like Innovation, Critical Thinking, and Originality (Acut et al., 2025; Gantalao et al., 2025; Garcia et al., 2025). For such researchers, there is a great danger of being impelled to face irrelevant obstacles such as funding, promotion, and acceptance by an oversaturation of AI in place of original work (Checco et al., 2021).

Data Privacy

Despite these benefits- personalized learning, administrative efficiency, and maximum access- serious data privacy or confidentiality concerns exist. AI cannot develop without data. Thus, massive amounts of data are collected from each learner and analyzed through various means such as websites, blogs, etc. It may include personal information, academic performance statistics, behavioral trends, and, at times, such data sets may even incorporate biometric data. Although this data empowers the AI to function as intended, it puts everyone involved at risk of misuse or violation of personal privacy to ethical dilemmas.

Collecting personal information in varied forms is done through AI systems in educational institutes to create a personalized learning experience to obtain optimal educational results. This typically consists of personally identifiable information (PII), such as names, addresses, and contact details, made available with academic records, such as grades attended or assignments. It is viewed in behavioral data through engagement patterns, browsing history, and study habits typical for student populations. In more advanced systems, biometric data ranging from facial recognition to check attendance to typing patterns can be collected for authentication. Given the sheer volume and sensitivity of this information, they are highly prone to privacy violations that may encompass various ramifications (Wang & Zhu, 2024).

Serious privacy concerns arise relative to data assembled for educational purposes and other, often profit-generating purposes. AI systems are usually developed or operated by third-party vendors frequently motivated to arbitrage students' data for advertising. For example, suppose that an AI platform keeps a record of a student's internet use, and the company could sell this information to advertisers without either the student's or the institution's approval. Additionally, many AI tools provide little details on intended data use and often keep students and parents from adequately understanding the data collection process that has taken place. Informed consent is an issue with pretty small students, as they may not only be aged but may not fully comprehend the implications of giving out personal information (Kashik & Srinivas, 2023).

These AI tools aggravate the concerns of privacy, and these are evidenced by many states, which have resulted in uncontrolled breaches. Most educational AI systems monitor students' activities and engage in tracking to assess engagement, with a hidden agenda to improve student learning outcomes. This degree of supervision could often intrude upon students' privacy, leading to distrust. One such example is online surveillance techniques. Some of the proctoring tools use the webcam or microphones to prevent cheating, which subsequently has given rise to some very unflattering issues to the extent that many students claim they violate their rights concerning personal privacy. Such tools often gather sensitive personal data that might, in effect, be made accessible to hackers.

Other major security issues are armed at open AI algorithms and act in the shadows of the cybercriminal world. These vulnerabilities can be manipulated to manipulate AI algorithms' outputs and give rise to untrustworthy or dangerous effects. For example, the misuse of functions by an artificial intelligence recommendation engine may recommend inappropriate or misleading content for students if compromised by evil entities. Also, weak encryption protocols and insecure authentication in AI systems may offer a foothold for entry into the system and could lead to unauthorized access to data. These risks are further aggravated, as it has happened within the system, by human errors whereby the teachers or the administrative personnel entrusted with taking care of students could expose data inadvertently, owing to the weakness in cybersecurity practices, including the use of weak passwords or sharing of unencrypted records (Makarichev et al., 2022).

It is more suitable to reverse the question and consider continuous incidences to request a proactive measure to address those issues. A data privacy law must be enacted that broadly describes protocols for data collection, storage, and utilization. Such public laws should be scrutinized, and paradigms should be developed through transparent communications with all stakeholders, including students, parents, and educators. The cybersecurity countermeasures must be investigated to identify an appropriate blend of encryption, multi-factor authentication-protected access to systems, and the employment of timely updates. Through proper implementation of regular audits, such processes could also identify loopholes where AI system breaches could be exploited. Explicit permission must be sought from students or their guardians, with a reasonable explanation regarding the use of data whenever any other person or organization will collect data. Hence, data minimization should be part of the procedure, meaning that AI systems should collect only the information required for the activity, thereby easing the risks associated with large datasets. This means explaining the reason for their monitoring to the students or a guardian.

Hence, education and training play a huge role in reducing human error. Awareness and training given to administrative staff, teachers, and learners concerning data safety practices and cybersecurity protocols may significantly lessen the chances of breaches.

Accessibility and the Digital Divide in AI Use in Academics

The fundamental idea behind AI tools would be digital devices and non-stop internet access available to people who want to use AI tools and generate content with their help. The considerable challenge remains in accessing digital technologies and properly using AI in Education. While AI is changing grading, automated content generation, and personalized learning for many, it is still not an equal opportunity. For many students from poor and remote regions, such advances remain inaccessible, blocked from equipping themselves with a treatable share of education. It challenges the possibility of change altogether but still demonstrates that a digital divide must be bridged (Kitsara, 2022).

Most families and institutions find that the cost of AI tools and internet connections is out of their reach (Taylor, 2023). Students from less-privileged backgrounds lack devices or internet connectivity, leading to a disadvantage of AI. The various complexities include the fact that, while some groups are very marginalized, such as women and rural students, such individuals will have fewer and more limited growth prospects than others. Other complexities arise because of cultural and language issues, with some cultures opposing AI due to an irrational fear of their traditional ways and language exclusivity when using AI tools. In these negative situations, what is enforced are knowledge gaps and deficiencies in skills in being unprepared for the many challenges that exist in a global economy.

These can involve collaborative efforts by governments, corporations, and international bodies to address the digital divide in education. (Tripathi, 2024) Governments can subsidize AI tools, modernize infrastructure, and implement policies that foster technological equity. Corporate social responsibility initiatives include discounts, donations, and partnerships for underfunded schools. Successful examples such as India's Digital India initiative and the global One Laptop per Child program indicate the potential for targeted efforts to improve access. International cooperation, which organizations like UNESCO support, can further push forward the cause of digital equity. (RoX, 2024) It also suggests that Ngo and Governments can provide some devices and affordable internet access to make AI tools more accessible.

The long-term benefits of bridging this divide will include better employability, social inclusion, and global competitiveness. Sustainability and dependency issues are still valid concerns. Technological innovation, such as cost-effective AI systems and equitable infrastructure development, is crucial in attaining an inclusive future for education. Bridging this gap is not only an educational imperative but a societal responsibility that requires holistic approaches such as physical access, training, and content localization so that the benefits of AI are equitably distributed. (Kulal et al., 2024)

Impact on Critical Thinking and Learning Skills

The emerging trends in AI in the modern world can impact an individual's critical, learning, cognitive, and analytical skills due to personalized, instant answers, generating ideas, and automatic work, which save time and reduce effort, but students rely on it for all their academic work making it a disadvantage to the education system. (Darwin et al., 2023) The ability to assess matter critically, distill biases, and create solutions to problems creatively is known as critical thinking. It is one of the required abilities for undergraduate academic success.

Unfortunately, AI tools offer ready-made solutions to any problem, sparing students of all the required critical thinking processes, where they would have otherwise analyzed the problem from multiple perspectives before concluding reasoning (Msekelwa, 2024). Over-reliance on it may rob students of the ability to develop, cultivate, and exercise their critical and independent thought processes. Tools can accomplish these things in seconds, allowing students to skip the whole process because their work is now done for them. This removes the opportunities to experience and learn specific skills for gratifying academic and professional careers. The general understanding of concepts becomes slightly different rather than deep and significant. The process of attaining learning skills, such as problem-solving, time management, and the ability to transfer knowledge to other situations, is enhanced through active engagement with the educational narrative. AI tools are capable assistants but often put an end to active engagement.

One major criticism of AI in Education is that specific skills will become antiquated (Jarrahi, 2018). It is imperative to introduce AI ethics to institutional curricula to educate students and teachers about the responsible use of AI. Gaining such insight into the implications of AI will provide one with the necessary knowledge to make the right decision and do so ethically.

AI tools cultivate a passive amount of information instead of active participation in the learning process. Problem-solving is a skill requiring extensive practice and trial and error. AI tools allow learners to find an answer to any problem without attempting to solve it as an exercise; such behavior hampers the development of this skill. The student thus gets used to quick fixes that may leave one ill-equipped for real-life dilemmas that demand creative and independent thought. The ease of access to AI tools may create a dependency that affects one's personal growth. It will ultimately be a struggle for a student when manual effort or creativity is required since he has gotten comfortable with the AI doing all the hard work.

IMPLICATIONS

The development of legal frameworks surrounding AI-produced academic works-scripts granting rights of copyright and intellectual property to AI will set a precedent in determining whether AI can nominate for the title of "Author" under certain conditions (Hasanah et al., 2025; Mangubat et al., 2025). Academics are thus forging a new route for redefining "authorship" by positioning AI as an interactive research tool rather than a simple way of reporting. Across this policy or tool development, there is a demand for a cultural shift within academia itself. Researchers are to embrace transparency in the disclosure of ethical considerations and the disruptive influences of AI on the discipline.

Integrity and Ethics

AI has considerably changed learning, research, and management through automating processes. However, the increase in ethical accountability arising from AI brings several practical challenges, such as skills obsolescence and attacks on credibility in research. What the collateral output of integrity and ethics might surface could be another rippling effect that equally affiliates any technology all-a-user by making it counter to human welfare (Khatri & Karki, 2023).

Impact on Students, Researchers, and Institutions

Integrity is also paramount in the educational institution, which is catered to by artificial intelligence. No one from the student to the teacher to the researcher can escape the crosshairs of a fair deal:

For Students

The rising temptations for students, fed by mainstream AI-generated essay writers and problem solvers, lure the students into taking a shortcut in learning. Integrity signals the imposition of specific limits on the interrelationship between students and technological intervention (Sullivan et al., 2023). AI must, therefore, be treated as an assisting peripheral rather than the be-all of a student's academic endeavors. In the place of submitting AI-generated assignments, students must actively critique and edit the submissions they get to render a product that represents their viewpoints.

For the Researcher

For researchers, conforming requires originality and validity throughout the work. Therefore, over-reliance on AI, for instance, with data analysis or content creation, can easily transition you into the pitfalls of plagiarism with substandard findings. Integrity ensures that AI is involved in the assistance of research efficiency and does not diminish human thoughts or creativity (Farrokhnia et al., 2023).

For the Institutions

Educational institutions must equally manifest integrity by ensuring policies are in place to incorporate AI within the borders of ethical supervision (Farrokhnia et al., 2023). Accountability would develop into an ideal practice with policies stipulated therein that will classify the degrees to which one might rely on AI during assignments, research, and examinations.

SUGGESTIONS AND FURTHER SCOPE

Ethics provides guidelines for making the right decisions given reasonability and exculpating individual rights. However, AI brings out ethical educational dilemmas like data privacy and academic dishonesty. Within that, any framework of ethics may maintain the risk of mimicking the trust equity associated with AI systems (Krausman, 2023). Developers of AI tools in education should guarantee fairness, diversity, and confidentiality. The development of AI systems should be ensured through unbiased algorithms and adequate protection of students' data against misuse. AI in research sometimes leads to such situations when a researcher gets inculcated to the point of compromising ethics and cutting corners for fast desired outputs. Uncompromising ethical guidance with the support of intense mentorship can lead a researcher into such convoluted dilemmas.

The new significant journals, such as Nature and Science, suggest that authors disclose whether they have used AI tools during research or writing (Gaggioli, 2023). This move increases the transparency of the whole process, but there are no clear punishments and penalties for breaking the law yet. Developers are working on algorithms that can follow AI-authored content in academic submissions. Such tools are gaining acceptance in universities and journals in their quest to establish authenticity. The tools are not infallible since they have gone to lengths to differentiate highly paraphrased AI outputs from human writing.

Academic institutions are beginning to implement AI-usage training sessions that centre on properly acknowledging and applying AI tools (Georgia Tech, 2024). AI should be more assistive, not a substitute for retaining human creativity and critical thinking. The institutions must develop clear and strict policies to uphold academic integrity. As AI tends to change the structure of education dynamically, the ethical frameworks must evolve continuously. Beyond the calls to add the relevant AI tools as co-authors in publications due to their crucial role in content generation, serious questions abound concerning accountability, intellectual property, and how, in practice, such contributions will be credited (Hosseini et al., 2023).

CONCLUSION

AI should be incorporated into school curriculums as an overall positive facilitator, stressing the necessity of critical thought and active learning. For instance, instead of feeding students answers directly, assignments should provide and encourage the students to analyze and interpret the given task (Msekelwa, 2024). The assignments should allow students to collect and synthesize independently acquired knowledge. For these tasks, classes may include debates, studies with the aid of or referenced from case studies, and project-based learning, where AI functions more as an aid than a support crutch. AI tools should still be taught cautiously to instill a sense of the need to limit their use while providing intelligent contributions that will stay in their minds. Workshops or training activities on critical thinking and ethics should be implemented to allow such a balance to be obtained and sustained.

REFERENCES

Acut, D. P., Gamusa, E. V., Pernaa, J., Yuenyong, C., Pantaleon, A. T., Espina, R. C., Sim, M. J. C., & Garcia, M. B. (2025). AI Shaming Among Teacher Education Students: A Reflection on Acceptance and Identity in the Age of Generative Tools. In *Pitfalls of AI Integration in Education: Skill Obsolescence, Misuse, and Bias*. IGI Global., DOI: 10.4018/979-8-3373-0122-8.ch005

Acut, D. P., Malabago, N. K., Malicoban, E. V., Galamiton, N. S., & Garcia, M. B. (2025). "ChatGPT 4.0 Ghosted Us While Conducting Literature Search:" Modeling the Chatbot's Generated Non-Existent References Using Regression Analysis. *Internet Reference Services Quarterly*, *29*(1), 27–54. Advance online publication. DOI: 10.1080/10875301.2024.2426793

Afonughe, E., Onah, E. N., Uzoma, A. C., Andor, S. E., & Orisakwe, C. U. (2021). Integration of Artificial Intelligence Tool (AI-Chatbot) into Teaching and Learning: A Panacea for Improving Universities' Educational and Administrative Duties in South-South, Nigeria. *Journal of Computer Science and Systems Biology*, *14*(6), 1–6. DOI: 10.37421/0974-7230.2021.14.357

Al-Zahrani, A. M. (2023). The impact of generative AI tools on researchers and research: Implications for academia in higher education. *Innovations in Education and Teaching International*, *61*(5), 1029–1043. DOI: 10.1080/14703297.2023.2271445

Almasri, F. (2024). Exploring the Impact of Artificial intelligence in teaching and learning of Science: A Systematic Review of Empirical research. *Research in Science Education*, *54*(5), 977–997. DOI: 10.1007/s11165-024-10176-3

Ashiq, M., Akbar, A., Jabbar, A., & Saleem, Q. U. A. (2021). Gray Literature and Academic Libraries: How Do They Access, Use, Manage, and Cope with Gray Literature. *Serials Review*, *47*(3–4), 191–200. DOI: 10.1080/00987913.2021.2018224

Bachiri, Y., Mouncif, H., & Bouikhalene, B. (2023). Artificial intelligence empowers gamification: Optimizing student engagement and learning outcomes in e-learning and MOOCs. [iJEP]. *International Journal of Engineering Pedagogy*, *13*(8), 4–19. DOI: 10.3991/ijep.v13i8.40853

Bhattacharyya, M., Miller, V. M., Bhattacharyya, D., & Miller, L. E. (2023). High rates of fabricated and inaccurate references in ChatGPT-Generated medical content. *Cureus*. Advance online publication. DOI: 10.7759/cureus.39238 PMID: 37337480

Checco, A., Bracciale, L., Loreti, P., Pinfield, S., & Bianchi, G. (2021). AI-assisted peer review. *Humanities & Social Sciences Communications*, *8*(1), 25. Advance online publication. DOI: 10.1057/s41599-020-00703-8

Chiu, T. K., Moorhouse, B. L., Chai, C. S., & Ismailov, M. (2023). Teacher support and student motivation to learn with Artificial Intelligence (AI) based chatbot. *Interactive Learning Environments*, ●●●, 1–17. DOI: 10.1080/10494820.2023.2172044

Da Silva, J. T., Santos-d'Amorim, K., & Bornemann-Cimenti, H. (2025). The citation of retracted papers and impact on the integrity of the scientific biomedical literature. *Learned Publishing*, *38*(2), e1667. Advance online publication. DOI: 10.1002/leap.1667

Dabis, A., & Csáki, C. (2024). AI and ethics: Investigating the first policy responses of higher education institutions to the challenge of generative AI. *Humanities & Social Sciences Communications, 11*(1), 1006. Advance online publication. DOI: 10.1057/s41599-024-03526-z

Darwin, N., Rusdin, D., Mukminatien, N., Suryati, N., Laksmi, E. D., & Marzuki, N. (2023). Critical thinking in the AI era: An exploration of EFL students' perceptions, benefits, and limitations. *Cogent Education, 11*(1), 2290342. Advance online publication. DOI: 10.1080/2331186X.2023.2290342

Elkhatat, A. M., Elsaid, K., & Almeer, S. (2023). Evaluating the efficacy of AI content detection tools in differentiating between human and AI-generated text. *International Journal for Educational Integrity, 19*(1), 17. Advance online publication. DOI: 10.1007/s40979-023-00140-5

Elsayed, H. (2024). The impact of hallucinated information in large language models on student learning Outcomes: A Critical Examination of Misinformation Risks in AI-Assisted Education. https://northernreviews.com/index.php/NRATCC/article/view/2024-08-07

Formosa, P., Bankins, S., Matulionyte, R., & Ghasemi, O. (2024). Can ChatGPT be an author? Generative AI creative writing assistance and perceptions of authorship, creatorship, responsibility, and disclosure. *AI & Society*. Advance online publication. DOI: 10.1007/s00146-024-02081-0

Gaggioli, A. (2023). Ethics: Disclose use of AI in scientific manuscripts. *Nature, 614*(7948), 413. DOI: 10.1038/d41586-023-00381-x PMID: 36788370

Gantalao, L. C., Calzada, J. G. D., Capuyan, D. L., Lumantas, B. C., Acut, D. P., & Garcia, M. B. (2025). Equipping the Next Generation of Technicians: Navigating School Infrastructure and Technical Knowledge in the Age of AI Integration. In *Pitfalls of AI Integration in Education: Skill Obsolescence, Misuse, and Bias*. IGI Global., DOI: 10.4018/979-8-3373-0122-8.ch009

Garcia, M. B., Rosak-Szyrocka, J., Yılmaz, R., Metwally, A. H. S., Acut, D. P., Ofosu-Ampong, K., Erdoğdu, F., Fung, C. Y., & Bozkurt, A. (2025). Rethinking Educational Assessment in the Age of Generative AI: Actionable Strategies to Mitigate Academic Dishonesty. In *Pitfalls of AI Integration in Education: Skill Obsolescence, Misuse, and Bias*. IGI Global., DOI: 10.4018/979-8-3373-0122-8.ch001

Gilchrist, D., & Perks, B. (2023). Grey Lines in Grey Literature: Incorporating grey literature value into the research and evaluation of public policy and the social sciences. SSRN *Electronic Journal*. https://doi.org/DOI: 10.2139/ssrn.4630554

Ha, T., & Kim, S. (2023). Improving Trust in AI with Mitigating Confirmation Bias: Effects of Explanation Type and Debiasing Strategy for Decision-Making with Explainable AI. *International Journal of Human-Computer Interaction*, ●●●, 1–12. DOI: 10.1080/10447318.2023.2285640

Hasanah, N. A., Aziza, M. R., Junikhah, A., Arif, Y. M., & Garcia, M. B. (2025). Navigating the Use of AI in Engineering Education Through a Systematic Review of Technology, Regulations, and Challenges. In *Pitfalls of AI Integration in Education: Skill Obsolescence, Misuse, and Bias*. IGI Global., DOI: 10.4018/979-8-3373-0122-8.ch016

Holgado-Apaza, L. A., Carpio-Vargas, E. E., Calderon-Vilca, H. D., Maquera-Ramirez, J., Ulloa-Gallardo, N. J., Acosta-Navarrete, M. S., Barrón-Adame, J. M., Quispe-Layme, M., Hidalgo-Pozzi, R., & Valles-Coral, M. (2023). Modeling job satisfaction of Peruvian basic education teachers using machine learning techniques. *Applied Sciences (Basel, Switzerland)*, *13*(6), 3945. DOI: 10.3390/app13063945

Hosseini, M., Resnik, D. B., & Holmes, K. (2023). The ethics of disclosing the use of artificial intelligence tools in writing scholarly manuscripts. *Research Ethics*, *19*(4), 449–465. DOI: 10.1177/17470161231180449 PMID: 39749232

Jarrahi, M. H. (2018). Artificial intelligence and the future of work: Human-AI symbiosis in organizational decision making. *Business Horizons*, *61*(4), 577–586. DOI: 10.1016/j.bushor.2018.03.007

Karnouskos, S. (2020). Artificial intelligence in digital media: The era of Deepfakes. *IEEE Transactions on Technology and Society*, *1*(3), 138–147. Advance online publication. DOI: 10.1109/TTS.2020.3001312

Kashik, K., & Srinivas, V. IAS. (2023). *Navigating the Future: India's strategic approach to artificial intelligence regulations* (By National Centre for Good Governance (NCGG), Ministry of Personnel, Public Grievances & Pensions, & Government of India). https://ncgg.org.in/sites/default/files/lectures-document/Kshitija_Kashik__Research_Paper.pdf

Khlaif, Z. N., Mousa, A., Hattab, M. K., Itmazi, J., Hassan, A. A., Sanmugam, M., & Ayyoub, A. (2023). The potential and Concerns of using AI in Scientific Research: ChaTGPT Performance Evaluation. *JMIR Medical Education*, *9*, e47049. DOI: 10.2196/47049 PMID: 37707884

Kitsara, I. (2022). Artificial intelligence and the digital Divide: From an Innovation perspective. In *Progress in IS* (pp. 245–265). https://doi.org/DOI: 10.1007/978-3-030-90192-9_12

Krausman, P. R. (2023). Managing artificial intelligence. *The Journal of Wildlife Management*, *87*(8), e22492. Advance online publication. DOI: 10.1002/jwmg.22492

Kuipers, M., & Prasad, R. (2021). Journey of artificial intelligence. *Wireless Personal Communications*, *123*(4), 3275–3290. DOI: 10.1007/s11277-021-09288-0

Kulal, A., Dinesh, S., Abhishek, N., & Anchan, A. (2024). Digital access and learning outcomes: A study of equity and inclusivity in distance education. *International Journal of Educational Management*, *38*(5), 1391–1423. DOI: 10.1108/IJEM-03-2024-0166

Liu, Y., Chen, L., & Yao, Z. (2022). The application of artificial intelligence assistant to deep learning in teachers' teaching and students' learning processes. *Frontiers in Psychology*, *13*, 929175. Advance online publication. DOI: 10.3389/fpsyg.2022.929175 PMID: 36033031

Makarichev, V., Lukin, V., Illiashenko, O., & Kharchenko, V. (2022). Digital Image representation by atomic Functions: The compression and protection of data for edge computing in IoT systems. *Sensors (Basel)*, *22*(10), 3751. DOI: 10.3390/s22103751 PMID: 35632158

Mangubat, J. C., Mangubat, M. R., Uy, T. B. L., Acut, D. P., & Garcia, M. B. (2025). Safeguarding Educational Innovations Amid AI Disruptions: A Reassessment of Patenting for Sustained Intellectual Property Protection. In *Pitfalls of AI Integration in Education: Skill Obsolescence, Misuse, and Bias.* IGI Global., DOI: 10.4018/979-8-3373-0122-8.ch013

Mishra, N., Garcia, P. S., Habal, B. G. M., & Garcia, M. B. (2024). Harnessing an AI-Driven Analytics Model to Optimize Training and Treatment in Physical Education for Sports Injury Prevention. *Proceedings of the 8th International Conference on Education and Multimedia Technology*, 309-315. DOI: 10.1145/3678726.3678740

Morandini, S., Fraboni, F., De Angelis, M., Puzzo, G., Giusino, D., & Pietrantoni, L. (2023). The impact of artificial intelligence on workers' skills: upskilling and reskilling in organisations. *Informing Science the International Journal of an Emerging Transdiscipline, 26*, 039–068. https://doi.org/DOI: 10.28945/5078

Msekelwa, P. Z. (2024). Impact of AI on Education: Innovative tools and trends. *Deleted Journal, 5*(1), 227–236. DOI: 10.60087/jaigs.v5i1.198

Nguyen, A., Hong, Y., Dang, B., & Huang, X. (2024). Human-AI collaboration patterns in AI-assisted academic writing. *Studies in Higher Education, 49*(5), 847–864. DOI: 10.1080/03075079.2024.2323593

Owan, V. J., Abang, K. B., Idika, D. O., Etta, E. O., & Bassey, B. A. (2023). Exploring the potential of artificial intelligence tools in educational measurement and assessment. *Eurasia Journal of Mathematics, Science and Technology Education, 19*(8), em2307. Advance online publication. DOI: 10.29333/ejmste/13428

Parab, A. K. (2020). Artificial intelligence in Education: Teacher and teacher assistant improve learning process. *International Journal for Research in Applied Science and Engineering Technology, 8*(11), 608–612. DOI: 10.22214/ijraset.2020.32237

Pedro, F., Subosa, M., Rivas, A., & Valverde, P. (2019). *Artificial intelligence in education : challenges and opportunities for sustainable development*. https://repositorio.minedu.gob.pe/handle/20.500.12799/6533

PTI. (2024). IIM Sambalpur to introduce AI-enabled teaching. *The Economic Times*. https://m.economictimes.com/industry/services/education/iim-sambalpur-to-introduce-ai-enabled-teaching/articleshow/113625151.cms

RoX. (2024). Digital divide in AI education: Creating equal opportunities. *AI Proficiency Hub #AICompetence.org*. https://aicompetence.org/digital-divide-in-ai-education/?

Taylor, J. (2023). Digital tools, rhetoric, and meaning-making: A critical exploration of addressing the digital divide and accessibility to improve our digital landscape. https://doi.org/DOI: 10.31274/td-20240329-24

Tech, G. (2024). Office of Graduate Education, Graduate Student Government Association, Office of Research, Responsible Conduct of Research Office, & Directors of Graduate Programs. *Effective and Responsible use of AI in research: Guidance for performing graduate research and in writing dissertations, theses, and manuscripts for publications* (B. Ferri, Ed.). https://grad.gatech.edu/sites/default/files/documents/Guidance%20for%20Effective%20and%20Responsible%20Use%20of%20AI%20in%20Research.pdf

Tripathi, C. R. (2024). Awareness of Artificial Intelligence (AI) among Undergraduate Students. *NPRC Journal of Multidisciplinary Research., 1*(7), 126–142. DOI: 10.3126/nprcjmr.v1i7.72478

Ullah, M., Naeem, S. B., & Boulos, M. N. K. (2024). Assessing the guidelines on the use of generative artificial intelligence tools in universities: A survey of the world's top 50 universities. *Big Data and Cognitive Computing, 8*(12), 194. DOI: 10.3390/bdcc8120194

Wallace, B. C. S., & Abel, Y. (2024). Embracing artificial intelligence (AI) tools to enrich special education teacher preparation. In *Advances in educational technologies and instructional design book series* (pp. 325–354). https://doi.org/DOI: 10.4018/979-8-3693-5538-1.ch012

Wang, H., & Zhu, X. (2024). Challenges in education during digital transformation. In *Lecture notes in educational technology* (pp. 11–24). https://doi.org/DOI: 10.1007/978-981-97-0076-9_2

KEY TERMS AND DEFINITIONS

Academia: Refers to educational institutions and research environments—such as schools, universities, and laboratories—where AI technology is actively utilized for learning, experimentation, and the advancement of knowledge.

Integrity: Promotes ethical behavior and honesty in academic settings, ensuring that AI-generated content is used responsibly and does not contribute to plagiarism or academic dishonesty.

Ethics: Involves the responsible and moral use of AI, ensuring that it is applied fairly to support education, prevent misuse, and promote equal learning opportunities for all.

Learning: Represents the process of acquiring knowledge and skills, where AI acts as both a tool to enhance learning and a guide that can influence thinking and educational outcomes.

AI Tools: Refers to software and applications powered by artificial intelligence that assist with research, writing, testing, and automation, often available for academic and commercial use.

Bias: Focuses on addressing and reducing algorithmic discrimination and data-driven bias, recognizing that AI systems can unintentionally reinforce existing inequalities in academic environments.

Section 4
Systematic Reviews on AI Integration in Education

Chapter 15
A Systematic Review of Educators' Overreliance and Misuse of AI in Student Feedback:
Introducing the ETHICAL–FEED Framework

Asegul Hulus
https://orcid.org/0000-0001-8797-450X
University of Greenwich, Cyprus

ABSTRACT

The escalating adoption of AI in student feedback raises concerns about excessive reliance and misapplication, necessitating ethical scrutiny. This systematic review examines the patterns, consequences, and ethical implications of overdependence on AI in student feedback. Using PRISMA guidelines, 12 studies from 2020 to 2024 were analyzed with the MMAT tool and thematic analysis. Six themes emerged: "transparency and explainability," "human oversight," "fairness and bias mitigation," "data privacy," "personalization," and "continuous evaluation." These themes informed the ETHICAL-FEED framework, which integrates technofeminist perspectives to address power dynamics and gender biases in AI, fostering equity and inclusivity. The review highlights not only the pedagogical risks of unchecked AI use but also the urgent need for professional development to guide educators in ethical implementation. The framework promotes responsible AI use in education by emphasizing ethical practices, maintaining standards, and encouraging research on the intersection of technology, gender, and equity.

INTRODUCTION

The utilization of artificial intelligence (AI) in the field of education has experienced significant growth, particularly in the provision of student feedback (Naseer et al., 2024). The rapid adoption of this approach presents opportunities for improved efficiency and personalized feedback delivery (Ali et al., 2024; Gantalao et al., 2025; Hasanah et al., 2025). The role of effective feedback in student development and academic progress is of utmost importance (Flores et al., 2024). Nonetheless, the rapid

DOI: 10.4018/979-8-3373-0122-8.ch015

assimilation of AI in educational feedback has brought forth novel challenges, encompassing the possibility of excessive reliance on AI systems, the presence of algorithmic bias, apprehensions regarding data privacy, and the instructional implications of AI-generated feedback (Pang et al., 2024; Varsha, 2023). Examining how gendered power dynamics shape the challenges is imperative, particularly within AI design and implementation.

In spite of the increasing amount of literature on AI in education (Chiu et al., 2023; Fu & Weng, 2024; Kamalov et al., 2023), there continues to be a substantial knowledge gap concerning the precise patterns of excessive dependence and incorrect utilization of AI in student feedback procedures (Escalante et al., 2023). This chapter bridges the gap by offering a comprehensive analysis of the patterns, consequences, and ethical considerations arising from educators' excessive dependence and improper utilization of AI in providing student feedback. It concludes with the introduction of the ETHICAL-FEED framework: (E)ducators' (TH)oughtful (I)ntegration of (C)ollaborative (A)I in (L)earning (F)eedback for (E)thical (ED)ucation. The ETHICAL-FEED framework outlines a comprehensive and research-based approach for ethically deploying AI in educational feedback processes. Its objective is to provide guidance to educators and institutions on harnessing the advantages of AI, while also minimizing potential risks and ensuring conformity with fundamental educational principles and student requirements.

MAIN FOCUS OF THE CHAPTER

Education's adoption of AI has yielded both remarkable advancements and complex obstacles. Although AI-driven feedback mechanisms offer enhanced efficiency and personalization, they also necessitate a critical examination of potential skill obsolescence, misuse, and algorithmic bias. While AI-driven feedback is increasingly prevalent, a substantial research gap persists concerning the impact of over-reliance on AI on pedagogical approaches, the exacerbation of algorithmic biases, and the erosion of educators' autonomy in assessment (Al-Zahrani, 2024; Chiu et al., 2023; Garcia et al., 2025; Miranda et al., 2025). While the current body of literature highlights the benefits of AI, a systematic examination of its unintended consequences, particularly in ethical decision-making, fairness, and student learning, remains absent. This chapter endeavors to fill this research gap by offering a thorough examination of the patterns, ramifications, and ethical considerations of AI-generated student feedback. To be precise, this chapter aims to:

1. Examine the detrimental effects of excessive AI reliance in feedback mechanisms, focusing on the reduction of human oversight, the introduction of potential biases, and the weakening of students' critical thinking abilities.
2. Undertake a detailed examination of the ethical issues related to AI-based feedback, prioritizing fairness, transparency, and the autonomy of students.
3. Suggest the ETHICAL-FEED framework as a structured approach to address potential shortcomings and guarantee adherence to ethical, pedagogical, and policy guidelines in AI feedback tools.

Furthermore, this chapter's findings significantly advance the discourse concerning the misuse and inherent biases within AI's educational applications, providing both empirical data and a theoretical model to direct institutions toward ethical AI integration. Moreover, this chapter offers actionable strategies for educators and policymakers to mitigate the risk of AI compromising the pedagogical integrity of student assessment by highlighting the importance of transparency, human oversight, and equitable practices (Ali et al., 2024; Collin et al., 2024).

METHODOLOGY

To ensure transparency and reproducibility, this systematic review is conducted in accordance with the PRISMA guidelines (Sohrabi et al., 2021), encompassing the literature search, selection, and analysis phases (Bramer et al., 2018; Shaheen et al., 2023). The utilization of this guideline is illustrated in Figure 1 through a PRISMA flow diagram.

Figure 1. Visual representation of the PRIMSA flow diagram for this systematic review.

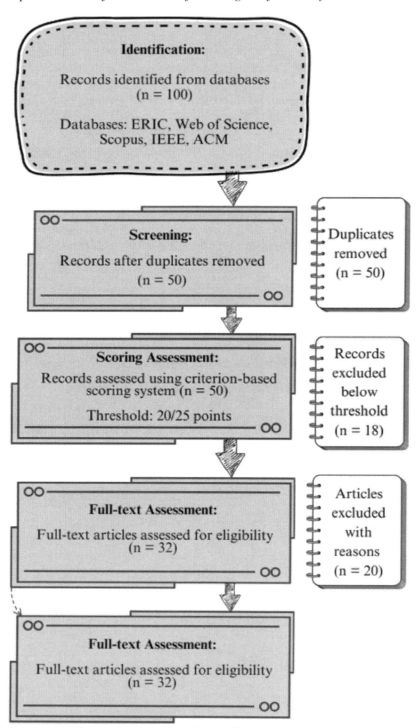

Note: The quantitative parameters illustrate the systematic, multi-stage filtering process used to select the final corpus of articles, which met all inclusion and quality criteria.

Search Strategy and Selection Criteria

A thorough search was conducted across several prominent databases, such as ERIC, Web of Science, Scopus, IEEE Xplore Digital Library, and ACM Digital Library, spanning the literature published between 2020 and 2024. The search strategy incorporated keywords associated with "*artificial intelligence,*" "*student feedback,*" and "*overreliance*" or "*misuse,*" alongside additional terms aimed at capturing specific facets of the research question (Ugwu & Opah, 2023). The inclusion criteria consisted of peer-reviewed journal articles, conference proceedings, and book chapters published from January 2020 to January 2024. These sources specifically explored the applications of AI in educational feedback and discussed the challenges of overreliance, misuse, and ethical concerns in higher education settings. Studies that did not meet these criteria were excluded, such as non-English language publications, those that solely focused on AI in education without referencing feedback processes, opinion pieces without original research, and studies primarily focused on technical aspects of AI without considering educational implications.

Study Selection and Data Extraction

Out of an initial sample of 100 studies, 50 distinct records were identified following the removal of duplicates. In order to ensure a systematic and objective selection process, a scoring system based on specific criteria was developed (Shaheen et al., 2023). The assessment of each study was conducted based on a 1 to 5 scale, considering 5 crucial criteria outlined in Table 1.

Table 1. Criterion-based scoring system for study selection

Criterion	Description	Score Range
Relevance to AI in student feedback	Extent to which the study focuses on AI applications in educational feedback processes	1-5
Focus on overreliance or misuse	Degree of attention given to issues of AI overreliance or misuse in educational contexts	1-5
Discussion of ethical implications	Depth and breadth of ethical considerations related to AI use in student feedback	1-5
Methodological rigor	Quality of research design, data collection, and analysis methods	1-5
Potential impact on understanding AI use in education	Significance of the study's findings for advancing knowledge in the field	1-5

For the purpose of attaining reliability and minimizing bias, each study was evaluated twice with a two-week interval between assessments (Ahmadi et al., 2022). Out of the fifty studies initially screened, thirty-two passed the scoring threshold (20 out of 25 points) and were subjected to full-text review. Following a thorough application of inclusion and exclusion criteria, a total of 12 studies were chosen for the final analysis.

Quality Assessment and Thematic Analysis

The use of the Mixed Methods Appraisal Tool (MMAT) was incorporated in this review to evaluate the quality of the studies, chosen for its proven validity in assessing diverse study designs (Hong et al., 2019). Each study underwent two separate evaluations, with a two-week gap between them, to improve intra-rater reliability (Ahmadi et al., 2022). Thorough documentation of the utilization of MMAT criteria was maintained to ensure the dependability of the evaluation. Subsequent to the quality assessment, the chosen studies underwent thematic analysis according to Braun and Clarke's (2006) six-step procedure. The selection of this approach was based on its adaptability in identifying, analyzing, and reporting data patterns. The procedure entailed becoming familiar with the data, creating initial codes, identifying themes, reviewing and refining themes, defining and labeling themes, and producing the report. Following this iterative process, six key themes were identified, establishing the basis of the ETHICAL-FEED framework. These include (1) transparency and explainability, (2) human oversight and intervention, (3) fairness and bias mitigation, (4) data privacy and security, (5) personalization and contextual understanding, and (6) continuous evaluation and improvement.

The utilization of a rigorous quality assessment and systematic thematic analysis in tandem ensured a comprehensive and reliable evaluation of the literature, establishing a solid foundation for the construction of the ETHICAL-FEED framework. The systematic approach was devised to guarantee that the selected studies yield comprehensive insights in addressing the main research question regarding patterns, consequences, and ethical implications of AI overreliance and misuse in student feedback.

Advanced Methodological Dimensions and Theoretical Integration

This review utilizes a methodological framework that surpasses conventional systematic review protocols by integrating advanced analytical techniques to examine the intricate socio-technical aspects of AI integration within educational settings. Integrating the PRISMA guidelines with thematic analysis, this novel methodology incorporates technofeminist perspectives (Wajcman, 2013) to analyze the influence of power dynamics and gender on technology integration in education, thus informing the development of the ETHICAL-FEED framework. This perspective recognizes that technological systems are not value-neutral but instead mirror the social and cultural environments of their creation, including gendered power structures that may affect their development and use in educational contexts.

Furthermore, this systematic review is enhanced by incorporating critical discourse analysis to investigate how technological narratives influence implementation in education. Examination of AI in education unveils intricate power structures, especially regarding knowledge generation and verification in digital learning contexts. This methodology employs intersectional analytical techniques to examine the interaction of structural inequalities within AI-mediated educational settings. This novel methodology provides a rigorous examination of how technological systems both reinforce and potentially alter existing social hierarchies in education, focusing on access, participation, and equity. In the following section, the results of this thematic analysis are presented, classifying the reviewed literature based on six themes and synthesizing the crucial findings that shape the ETHICAL-FEED framework.

RESULTS

This section provides an overview of the findings derived from the systematic review and thematic analysis performed on the 12 studies that were meticulously selected through a rigorous screening process. The findings are divided into two primary sections: (1) an evaluation of the methodological rigor of the studies utilizing the MMAT Tool and (2) the findings of the thematic analysis that underpin the ETHICAL-FEED framework.

Quality Assessment of Included Studies

To assess the quality of the studies included in this analysis, a two-step approach was followed. Initially, a screening process was implemented by applying specific criteria and subsequently followed by a comprehensive evaluation using the MMAT. The initial screening involved the application of five specific criteria, which encompassed the relevance of the research to AI in student feedback, the examination of overreliance or misuse, the exploration of ethical implications, the evaluation of methodological rigor, and the assessment of the potential impact on the understanding of AI usage in education. Each criterion was evaluated using a scale ranging from 1 to 5, with a maximum potential score of 25. The review included only studies that achieved a score of 20 or higher (Sohrabi et al., 2021). The selected studies then underwent evaluation using the MMAT, which was specifically chosen for its capability to assess a range of research methodologies. The MMAT assessment findings are summarized in Table 2.

Table 2. Summary of quality assessment using mixed methods appraisal tool

Study Type	Number of Studies	MMAT Score Range	Median MMAT Score	Mean MMAT Score
Qualitative	5	75% -100%	90%	88%
Quantitative Descriptive	3	80% - 100%	90%	90%
Mixed Methods	4	80% - 100%	90%	87.5%
Total	12	75% - 100%	90%	88.3%

Note: MMAT scores are depicted as percentages, indicating the fulfillment of all quality criteria.

The studies included were found to possess a high level of methodological quality. The establishment of a strong basis for the thematic analysis and subsequent development of the ETHICAL-FEED framework is supported by the median MMAT score of 90% and mean of 88.3% across all studies. The integration of this quality assessment, in conjunction with the initial screening criteria, guarantees that the conclusions are derived from a substantial and meticulous research body. With the inclusion of high-quality and relevant studies, this review can confidently proceed with a thematic analysis (Shaheen et al., 2023).

Thematic Analysis Findings: Emergent Themes from Literature

Through a thematic analysis of the 12 selected high-quality studies, six primary themes were identified, serving as the core pillars of the ETHICAL-FEED framework. The analysis yielded several themes, each of which contributes to the comprehension of the patterns, consequences, and ethical implications that are pivotal to the main research question. The themes depicted in Figure 2 encompass crucial aspects of ethical AI utilization for educational feedback. It highlights the interconnection of these themes, presenting a comprehensive approach to the ethical implementation of AI in student feedback processes.

Figure 2. Visual representation of the ETHICAL-FEED framework themes

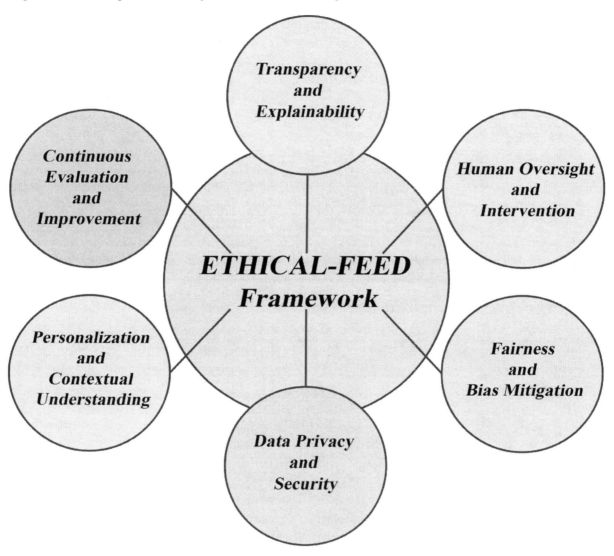

Transparency and Explainability

The principle of transparency and explainability has become a central concern when considering the ethical application of AI in providing feedback to students. Various studies consistently underscored the significance of transparent communication regarding the utilization of AI in feedback procedures and the requirement for explainable AI systems (e.g., Collin et al., 2024). Fu and Weng (2024) emphasized the necessity of transparency in AI-assisted feedback to foster trust between students and educational institutions. According to their study, students demonstrated a greater inclination to critically engage with the feedback they received when they were made aware of AI's role in generating it. In a similar vein, Chiu et al. (2023) contended that the utilization of explainable AI models within the educational context could yield benefits such as improved student understanding of feedback and enhanced learning outcomes. The ethical importance of transparency was further highlighted by Collin et al. (2024), who asserted that in educational settings, educators bear the responsibility of elucidating AI processes. According to their research findings, a lack of transparency may result in student skepticism and diminish the effectiveness of AI-generated feedback.

Human Oversight and Intervention

The requirement for human oversight and intervention in AI-assisted feedback processes emerged as a prominent theme. Academic research, such as the study conducted by Memarian and Doleck (2024), consistently cautions against excessive dependence on AI and highlights the pivotal role of human educators in the feedback loop.

Extensive empirical research has expanded the theoretical understanding of AI's role in educational feedback mechanisms, thereby providing fundamental analytical frameworks for human-AI interaction in pedagogical environments. Celik et al. (2022) offered a thorough theoretical framework for understanding AI's multifaceted educational implications, illuminating both its transformative potential and inherent challenges. Their findings demonstrate the considerable potential of AI-enhanced feedback systems for personalizing learning through adaptive assessment, while acknowledging the critical need to preserve pedagogical authenticity and ensure equitable access to technology in diverse educational environments. Moreover, Barrett and Pack's (2023) rigorous analysis of generative AI in composition significantly advances Celik et al.'s (2022) theoretical framework, providing nuanced insights into the interplay between technological affordances and pedagogical approaches, especially concerning AI-assisted feedback's impact on student revision and metacognition. Findings from this investigation show that AI feedback enhances analytical capabilities in student writing, while simultaneously demanding careful consideration for the preservation of student self-direction and authentic style.

Furthermore, Ivanov (2023) presented a critical viewpoint regarding the negative aspects of AI in higher education, emphasizing the possible drawbacks of over-automating feedback procedures. The study reveals that AI, despite its ability to enhance efficiency, frequently lacks the nuanced understanding of student context that is typically provided by human educators. Ivanov (2023) contended that a balanced approach is crucial, emphasizing the need for AI to augment, rather than substitute human judgment in educational feedback. Additionally, the perspective was reinforced by Memarian and Doleck (2024), who presented case studies illustrating that the AI-assisted feedback systems that yielded the best results were those that integrated consistent human evaluation and intervention. The findings of their research indicated that students placed importance on human involvement in feedback, even in cases where AI tools were utilized to augment the process.

Fairness and Bias Mitigation

The concept of fairness and bias mitigation has surfaced as a pivotal ethical aspect in AI-assisted feedback. Varsha (2023) conducted a study which demonstrated the potential of AI systems to perpetuate or exacerbate preexisting biases in educational assessment. The present findings are consistent with technofeminist critiques highlighting the link between bias in AI systems and the broader societal structures informing their development and deployment. Kamalov et al. (2023) recommended strategies aimed at reducing bias in AI-assisted feedback. These strategies encompass the utilization of diverse and representative datasets during AI training, as well as the integration of fairness-aware machine learning algorithms. The research findings highlighted the substantial impact of bias-mitigation strategies on enhancing the fairness of AI-generated feedback among diverse student populations.

Data Privacy and Security

The issue of data privacy and security has become a significant concern when implementing AI-assisted feedback systems. The importance of implementing strong data protection measures and transparent data handling practices was highlighted in studies such as Ali et al. (2024). In their study, Pang et al. (2024) performed a qualitative analysis on the utilization of AI in feedback. The results of their research indicated that students had significant concerns regarding the privacy and security of their data. The study suggested the adoption of stringent data protection policies that adhere to regulations such as the General Data Protection Regulation (GDPR), while also giving students autonomy over their data. The significance of data security in establishing trust in AI-assisted educational processes was further emphasized by Ali et al. (2024). A framework was proposed by their research for the secure and ethical management of data in AI-assisted feedback systems, with a focus on data minimization, encryption, and transparent consent procedures.

Personalization and Contextual Understanding

The recurring theme in the literature was the potential of AI to offer personalized feedback, while acknowledging its limitations in comprehending complex 'contextual' factors. Furthermore, Hooda et al. (2022) investigated the application of AI for personalized evaluation and feedback. Their findings demonstrated the effectiveness of AI systems in customizing feedback to cater to the unique requirements and learning preferences of individual students. Nevertheless, they also acknowledged the constraints on AI's capacity to grasp intricate elements of student work, especially in assignments that demand creativity or are highly contextual. The study conducted by Flores et al. (2024) focused on investigating the impact of AI-assisted feedback in online learning settings. The findings demonstrated that the provision of personalized AI feedback yielded significant improvements in both student engagement and learning outcomes. Nevertheless, their study highlighted the significance of integrating AI-generated feedback with human expertise to tackle intricate learning scenarios.

Continuous Evaluation and Improvement

The conclusive theme that materialized was the imperative for the "continuous evaluation and improvement" of AI-assisted feedback systems. Numerous studies have consistently highlighted the importance of continuous assessment and refinement for the ethical use of AI in education (e.g., Collin et al., 2024). The framework proposed by Ali et al. (2024) highlights the importance of incorporating both quantitative metrics and qualitative assessments to evaluate the efficacy of AI-generated feedback in terms of student satisfaction and learning outcomes. According to their research, regular evaluations can aid in identifying areas for improvement and ensuring that AI systems stay aligned with educational goals.

Collin et al. (2024) emphasized the significance of remaining knowledgeable regarding developments in AI technology and ethics. The study suggested the establishment of feedback mechanisms to facilitate the reporting of issues and the provision of suggestions by students and educators regarding AI-assisted feedback systems. To summarize, the thematic analysis of the chosen high-quality studies identified six interconnected themes that are vital for the ethical and efficient incorporation of AI in student feedback procedures. The themes, rigorously derived from a robust body of literature, form the foundational principles of the ETHICAL-FEED framework. A detailed discussion of this framework will be presented in the subsequent section.

DISCUSSION

The purpose of this discussion is to synthesize the findings from this systematic review, with a specific focus on addressing the main research question concerning the patterns, consequences, and ethical implications arising from educators' excessive reliance and improper utilization of AI when providing student feedback. Significant insights into the patterns, consequences, and ethical implications of educators' overreliance and misuse of AI in student feedback processes have been derived from a systematic review and thematic analysis. Through analyzing the interaction between AI capabilities and human expertise in educational feedback, the objective is to offer a comprehensive comprehension of the advantages and challenges of integrating AI in this vital area of education (Acut et al., 2025; Al-Zahrani, 2024; Escalante et al., 2023; Mangubat et al., 2025).

Synthesis of Included Studies: Answering the Main Research Question

Patterns and Theoretical Implications of AI Overreliance

Several key trends emerged, a notable one being the uncritical dependence on AI systems lacking adequate human oversight (Chiu et al., 2023). Moreover, the lack of transparency regarding AI's feedback generation remains a persistent concern (Fu & Weng, 2024). Furthermore, the deployment of AI systems without mitigating potential biases inherent in their training data or algorithms (Kamalov et al., 2023; Varsha, 2023) underscores systemic inequalities. The prevalent tendency to excessively utilize AI for personalized learning overlooks its inability to fully grasp the nuanced, context-specific details of student assignments. The observed patterns have produced a series of concerning results. A deficiency in nuanced, context-sensitive feedback, a pedagogical strength of human educators, is apparent. The opacity of the process has resulted in student confusion, mistrust, and disengagement from learning.

Moreover, the mismanagement of sensitive student data can result in privacy violations and a diminished level of trust in educational establishments (Ali et al., 2024; Pang et al., 2024).

Consequential Analysis and Empirical Evidence

Empirical studies have significantly advanced theoretical comprehension of AI-mediated feedback processes, especially concerning the intricate interplay between students and automated assessment tools. Er et al.'s (2024) rigorous study of diverse student reactions to feedback from instructors and AI offers significant insights into the pedagogical and psychological ramifications of automated assessment. Analysis indicates a significant correlation between students' epistemological beliefs and their acceptance of AI-generated feedback, particularly regarding the perceived validity and practicality of automated assessment.

The work of Guo et al. (2024) provides a thorough analysis of the application of AI to peer feedback in higher education, resulting in a significant theoretical advancement. Research indicates that technology may improve both the quality of feedback and student writing skills within current pedagogical frameworks. This research significantly contributes to the understanding of the synergistic potential inherent in human-AI collaborations within educational assessment, emphasizing the critical importance of robust pedagogical oversight. Nazaretsky et al. (2024) presented an innovative study of student perceptions of feedback within higher education, thereby enhancing the theoretical comprehension of student engagement with AI-generated feedback through an examination of its cognitive and affective aspects. This analysis unveils intricate patterns of student engagement with automated feedback systems, emphasizing the influence of technological integration on metacognitive growth and self-directed learning. The unchecked application of AI to educational assessment may amplify pre-existing biases, thereby potentially harming minority and underrepresented students (Kamalov et al., 2023). Mitigating these biases is crucial for achieving equity and inclusivity (Collin et al., 2024).

Synthesis of Ethical Implications

Algorithmic bias presents significant challenges to equitable education (Varsha, 2023), and concurrently jeopardizes student privacy and data security (Ali et al., 2024; Pang et al., 2024). A technofeminist perspective highlights the necessity of mitigating these biases, not merely within algorithms, but also by critically analyzing the societal and cultural frameworks shaping AI's development and deployment. Furthermore. the lack of transparency in educational practices could negatively impact student initiative and involvement (Chiu et al., 2023; Fu & Weng, 2024). Concerns have also been raised about the dehumanizing effects of overdependence on AI feedback within the educational system (Memarian & Doleck, 2024). These concerns necessitate a thorough ethical analysis of the optimal balance between AI efficacy and human judgment within feedback loops (Bozkurt et al., 2024). These findings demonstrate a crucial need for a robust framework, as exemplified by the ETHICAL-FEED framework, to oversee the ethical implementation of AI within student feedback procedures, further discussed in the section that follows. The ETHICAL-FEED framework is essential for optimizing the benefits, mitigating the risks, and upholding ethical considerations of AI in education.

ETHICAL-FEED Framework

The ETHICAL-FEED framework is constructed from six principles derived from the rigorous thematic analysis detailed in Section 4. This framework provides a comprehensive approach to ethically implementing AI in student feedback processes, effectively addressing the patterns, consequences, and ethical implications identified in the main research question. Current empirical investigations provide considerable reinforcement for the theoretical foundations of the ETHICAL-FEED framework, elucidating the multifaceted dimensions of AI's role in education. Ifelebuegu et al.'s (2023) systematic analysis of AI educational tools offers a refined analytical model for evaluating the transformative potential and inherent constraints of technological integration within pedagogical practices. Their investigation provides crucial insights into the dialectical interplay of technological progress and educational practice, highlighting the dual impact of AI feedback systems which simultaneously augment pedagogical effectiveness and introduce significant ethical challenges demanding rigorous theoretical analysis.

A more nuanced theoretical understanding is provided by Khlaif et al.'s (2024) robust investigation into university educators' perspectives regarding generative AI's role in assessment. Their analysis discloses intricate patterns of institutional adaptation and resistance, thereby elucidating the complex interplay between technological innovation and established pedagogical structures. Notably, their analysis highlights the impact of institutional frameworks and pedagogical approaches on AI-assisted assessment systems, offering key theoretical perspectives on the sociocultural aspects of technology integration within higher education. The combined results of these analyses offer a robust theoretical foundation for understanding the dynamic interaction of technological innovation and pedagogical practice, underscoring the ETHICAL-FEED framework's prioritization of systematic professional development and institutional support. In the sections that follow, the ETHICAL-FEED Framework's implementation is analyzed through overviews, practical applications, and ethical AI imperatives.

Overview of the ETHICAL-FEED Framework

The ETHICAL-FEED framework incorporates the six fundamental principles outlined in Section 4, which include transparency and explainability (Section 4.3), human oversight and intervention (Section 4.4), fairness and bias mitigation (Section 4.5), data privacy and security (Section 4.6), personalization and contextual understanding (Section 4.7), and continuous evaluation and improvement (Section 4.8). The integration of these principles creates an interconnected and comprehensive approach to the ethical implementation of AI in educational feedback, as highlighted by Fu and Weng (2024) in their research on responsible human-centered AI practices in the field of education. The interdependencies among these elements play a vital role in enhancing the framework's efficacy. As an example, the emphasis on transparency in Section 4.3 aligns with the fairness objectives stated in Section 4.5. This objective is accomplished by promoting the examination of AI processes, an approach strongly endorsed by Chiu et al. (2023) in their comprehensive analysis of AI's role in education. In a similar vein, the inclusion of human oversight as discussed in Section 4.5 ensures that the contextual appropriateness and pedagogical validity of the personalization initiatives outlined in Section 4.7 are maintained, aligning with Ivanov's (2023) warnings against excessive automation in higher education. The data privacy and security measures emphasized in Section 4.6 are crucial for upholding trust, which in turn facilitates the successful execution of all other elements of the framework. These findings align with the research conducted by

Pang et al. (2024), which emphasizes the significance of implementing comprehensive data protection policies. The focus of their qualitative analysis centers on the utilization of AI in feedback systems.

Practical Implications

From a practical standpoint, the ETHICAL-FEED framework holds considerable ramifications for educational institutions and professionals. It underscores the necessity for comprehensive professional development initiatives aimed at improving educators' proficiency in AI and their ability to make ethical decisions, as indicated in Sections 4.4 and 4.8, and corroborated by the proposals put forth by Memarian and Doleck (2024). The framework additionally emphasizes the significance of student engagement in the feedback process, fostering comprehension and critical involvement with AI-generated feedback, as elaborated in Sections 4.3 and 4.7. Integrating technofeminist perspectives into this process guarantees that feedback mechanisms do not reinforce existing inequalities, but rather actively work toward their eradication by prioritizing inclusivity in design and implementation. This is consistent with the research conducted by Flores et al. (2024) regarding the significance of feedback in online learning settings.

In terms of technology, the ETHICAL-FEED framework proposes that AI systems used for educational feedback should incorporate inherent characteristics of transparency, fairness, and data protection. This will address the concerns expressed in Sections 4.3, 4.5, and 4.6, and align with the suggestions made by Ali et al. (2024) regarding secure and ethical data management in AI-assisted feedback systems. Additionally, the framework places a strong focus on continuous evaluation and improvement, as described in Section 4.8. Consequently, routine audits and evaluations are imperative to guarantee continuous adherence to ethical standards and educational goals. The importance of this aspect lies in its ability to effectively address the ever-changing landscape of AI technology and its applications in education, as emphasized by Kamalov et al. (2023) in their comprehensive study on the multifaceted revolution of AI in education.

The Ethical Imperative in AI Implementation

The ETHICAL-FEED framework directly deals with the ethical considerations outlined in the review. The document suggests methods for addressing algorithmic bias by prioritizing fairness and ongoing assessment, as outlined in Sections 4.5 and 4.8, based on the research conducted by Varsha (2023) on managing bias in AI systems. The framework includes strong data protection measures to ensure student privacy, addressing the concerns raised in Section 4.6 and aligning with the recommendations of Ali et al. (2024). Importantly, it upholds the fundamental human aspect in education by highlighting the vital role of educator supervision, a prominent topic in Section 4.4 and a primary focus in Ivanov's (2023) examination of AI in higher education.

In summary, the ETHICAL-FEED framework, derived from the thematic analysis discussed in Section 4, presents a systematic and evidence-based strategy for managing the ethical intricacies of AI incorporation in educational feedback. By addressing concerns highlighted in the literature and offering practical guidelines, this initiative seeks to aid educators and institutions in harnessing the benefits of AI while upholding ethical standards and prioritizing student learning outcomes. The framework's comprehensive approach, which integrates all six principles identified in the review, offers a comprehensive roadmap for the responsible and effective implementation of AI in student feedback processes. This is in accordance with the suggestions put forth by multiple researchers in the respective field Fu and

Weng (2024). Subsequently, the subsequent sections will examine the six principles that were identified through thematic analysis in relation to the implementation processes and challenges associated with the ETHICAL-FEED framework.

ETHICAL-FEED Framework: Implementation Process and Challenges

A structured approach is required for the implementation of the ETHICAL-FEED framework in educational institutions, taking into consideration the complexities associated with integrating AI into current feedback systems. This section explores the manifestation of the six key principles of the framework throughout the implementation process, potential challenges, bias mitigation, and strategies for adaptation across various educational contexts.

Implementation Process

The implementation of the ETHICAL-FEED framework typically advances through multiple stages, with each stage highlighting different facets of the framework. In the beginning, institutions should carry out a comprehensive evaluation and planning stage, with a focus on transparency and explainability. The critical nature of aligning AI implementation with existing educational goals and ethical standards is emphasized by Fu and Weng (2024) in this preliminary stage. The subsequent pilot programs and testing phase enable institutions to enhance their approach to human oversight and intervention. Chiu et al. (2023) emphasize the significance of these small-scale implementations in identifying potential concerns pertaining to fairness and bias mitigation. When AI-assisted feedback systems are fully integrated throughout the institution during the deployment phase, ensuring data privacy and security becomes of utmost importance. Kamalov et al. (2023) highlighted the crucial role of a phased approach in this stage, aiming to facilitate a smooth transition, gain stakeholder acceptance, and uphold stringent data protection measures. The ultimate phase of monitoring and adjustment encompasses the principle of continuous evaluation and improvement. According to Collin et al. (2024), regular assessments and adaptations are crucial for ensuring the long-term success of AI in education, particularly in preserving personalization and contextual understanding.

Critical Analysis of Bias Mitigation Frameworks: A Technofeminist Perspective

A thorough theoretical exploration of bias mitigation in AI-mediated educational environments demands advanced analytical models which extend beyond purely practical technological implementations. Wajcman's (2013) technofeminist framework offers significant theoretical advancements in comprehending the influence of patriarchal power structures on gender-technology relations within educational settings. This theoretical lens reveals that algorithmic bias arises not simply from technical errors, but fundamentally from the social dynamics ingrained in the processes of technological design and implementation. This perspective is fundamental to the formulation of strategies mitigating the technical and societal dimensions of bias, consequently promoting fairer AI integration within education through the ETHICAL-FEED framework. Wajcman's (2013) analysis of the interplay between gender and technology provides valuable insights into mitigating bias in AI-driven education, particularly regarding power dynamics. A technofeminist perspective highlights the capacity of technological systems to simultaneously reinforce and potentially reshape existing social hierarchies within educational technology, thereby demanding rigorous theoretical consideration of bias mitigation strategies that address both technological and societal elements. This theoretical advancement posits that effective mitigation of bias necessitates acknowledging the material embedding of gender relations within the design, implementation, and evaluation of technology.

Integrating technofeminist perspectives into contemporary bias mitigation strategies necessitate transformative approaches that address inherent power imbalances in educational technology, exemplified by the ETHICAL-FEED framework. This theoretical framework highlights that bias mitigation in educational technology transcends mere algorithmic modification; it demands a comprehensive examination of design, implementation, and governance. This advanced theoretical model requires analysis of the interplay between gender, technology, and the conceptualization of bias and fairness in AI-integrated educational settings utilizing the ETHICAL-FEED framework.

Challenges in Implementation

The implementation of the ETHICAL-FEED framework may encounter various challenges, often related to multiple themes. Institutions often encounter technological obstacles when attempting to integrate AI systems with their current infrastructure, resulting in potential effects on transparency and explainability. Ali et al. (2024) suggested strategies to address these technical challenges, which involve establishing collaborative partnerships with EdTech providers to improve system transparency. The management of stakeholder expectations presents an additional and significant challenge, specifically with regards to human oversight and intervention. Ivanov (2023) advised against making exaggerated claims about AI capabilities and underscores the significance of transparently communicating AI's limitations to educators, students, and administrators. Furthermore, institutions are required to navigate the intricate equilibrium between harnessing the potential of AI for personalization and upholding ethical standards, especially in the aspect of fairness and bias mitigation. Varsha (2023) proposed the implementation of regular ethical audits to safeguard fairness and privacy, encompassing fairness and bias mitigation as well as the data privacy and security aspects outlined in the framework.

Case Studies

Real-world implementations offer valuable insights into the practical application of the ETHICAL-FEED framework across its various principles. The case study conducted by Memarian and Doleck (2024) examines the successful implementation of AI-assisted feedback in a prominent university's writing program. The study underscores the importance of human oversight and intervention facilitated by faculty training and student engagement. In contrast, Flores et al. (2024) examined an unsuccessful implementation at a community college, highlighting inadequate consideration for data privacy and security and a scarcity of human oversight and intervention as primary reasons for the project's termination. Hooda et al. (2022) demonstrate a successful implementation in a science, technology, engineering and mathematics (STEM) program, attributing its success to the robust features of personalization and contextual understanding, as well as the transparency and explainability regarding AI's role in feedback generation.

The ETHICAL-FEED framework should exhibit adaptability to encompass a range of educational environments while upholding its fundamental principles. Pang et al. (2024) investigated the necessary adaptations for the humanities and social sciences disciplines, where feedback often necessitates a more nuanced contextual comprehension. The study emphasizes the principles of personalization and contextual comprehension. Moreover, Al-Zahrani (2024) explored the adaptability of the framework for undergraduate and graduate education. They further emphasized the necessity of implementing more sophisticated AI systems and enhancing human supervision and intervention in providing feedback at the graduate level. This discussion pertains to the principles of human oversight and intervention, along with continuous evaluation and improvement.

Additionally, the significance of cultural sensitivity in AI-assisted feedback, especially in educational settings that are international or multicultural, is emphasized by Fu and Weng (2024). The findings of their study indicate that the ETHICAL-FEED framework may require modification to accommodate various cultural norms and expectations related to feedback and assessment. This highlights the interdependence between fairness and bias mitigation and personalization and contextual understanding. Educational institutions can enhance the integration of ethical AI-assisted feedback into their processes by examining the implementation stages, challenges, case studies, and contextual adaptations within the framework of the ETHICAL-FEED's six principles. The proposed approach emphasizes the preservation of the ethical principles that underlie the framework, all while permitting the necessary flexibility to cater to the specific demands of diverse educational contexts. According to Collin et al. (2024), the effective integration of ethical AI in education necessitates sustained dedication to all principles of the ETHICAL-FEED framework, encompassing transparency and explainability as well as continuous evaluation and improvement.

Implementation Framework: A Synthesis of Theoretical and Practical Dimensions

The systematic incorporation of AI within educational feedback mechanisms demands a methodologically sound approach that unites theoretical frameworks and practical implementation. Table 3 provides a thorough overview of the ETHICAL-FEED framework's implementation guidelines, creating a synthesis of theoretical underpinnings, implementation strategies, and assessment criteria to enhance scholarly comprehension of ethical AI integration within education. The following subsections offer a detailed exploration of this synthesis.

Table 3. Synthesis of ETHICAL-FEED framework implementation guidelines

Framework Principle	Theoretical Foundation	Implementation Mechanisms	Evaluation Metrics
Transparency and Explainability	Algorithmic Transparency Theory (Fu & Weng, 2024)	Documentation protocols for AI decision processes; Clear communication channels for feedback generation methodology	Stakeholder comprehension metrics; System transparency indices
Human Oversight and Intervention	Socio-technical Systems Theory (Ivanov, 2023)	Structured intervention protocols; Defined oversight responsibilities; Regular human review cycles	Intervention effectiveness rates; Quality assessment scores
Fairness and Bias Mitigation	Algorithmic Fairness Theory (Varsha, 2023)	Bias detection protocols; Diverse training data requirements; Regular fairness audits	Bias detection rates; Equity indices across student demographics

continued on following page

Table 3. Continued

Framework Principle	Theoretical Foundation	Implementation Mechanisms	Evaluation Metrics
Data Privacy and Security	Information Security Framework (Ali et al., 2024)	Encrypted data handling protocols; Consent management systems; Access control mechanisms	Security compliance metrics; Privacy breach prevention rates
Personalization and Contextual Understanding	Adaptive Learning Theory (Hooda et al., 2022)	Context-aware feedback algorithms; Individual learning profile management	Personalization effectiveness scores; Learning outcome improvements
Continuous Evaluation and Improvement	Quality Enhancement Framework (Collin et al., 2024)	Regular system audits; Feedback incorporation mechanisms; Performance monitoring protocols	System improvement metrics; Stakeholder satisfaction indices

Note. This table provides a structured summary of implementation guidelines informed by a systematic review, integrating theoretical principles with practical implementation approaches and their evaluation metrics.

Theoretical Integration and Implementation Mechanisms

A sophisticated theoretical foundation, integrating diverse epistemological viewpoints, underpins the implementation framework. Algorithmic transparency mandates the creation of thorough documentation outlining AI decision-making (Fu & Weng, 2024). The ETHICAL-FEED framework operates via formalized communication pathways that systematically clarify feedback generation processes, thus enabling stakeholders to understand the algorithmic basis of AI-generated feedback. Human oversight and intervention, based on socio-technical systems theory (Ivanov, 2023), constitutes a strong ETHICAL-FEED framework for effective human-AI partnerships in education. The ETHICAL-FEED framework provides a structured implementation, specifying intervention protocols and oversight, prioritizing human judgment in educational decisions and leveraging AI for improved efficiency and effectiveness.

Evaluation Metrics and Quality Assurance

The ETHICAL-FEED framework employs sophisticated evaluation metrics, integrating quantitative and qualitative assessments to rigorously measure implementation effectiveness. Each framework principle utilizes defined evaluation metrics to systematically assess implementation effectiveness. Metrics encompassing stakeholder comprehension indices (assessing transparency) and sophisticated bias detection rates (evaluating fairness) constitute a comprehensive ETHICAL-FEED framework for continuous quality improvement.

Integration with Educational Practice

Effective implementation of the ETHICAL-FEED framework requires careful consideration of the educational context. The implementation mechanisms outlined in Table 2 offer structured direction with flexibility to cater to institutional variations. This approach is exemplified by the integration of personalization mechanisms, based on adaptive learning theory (Hooda et al., 2022), resulting in context-aware feedback algorithms tailored to individual learning profiles while upholding theoretical integrity.

Improvement and Systemic Enhancement

The ETHICAL-FEED framework, grounded in quality enhancement theory (Collin et al., 2024), employs a systematic approach to continuous improvement through ongoing evaluation. Routine audits of the system, in conjunction with structured feedback mechanisms, ensure the implementation framework's responsiveness to emerging challenges and opportunities. This dynamic approach facilitates the maintenance of theoretical rigor within educational institutions while enabling adaptation to evolving technological and pedagogical needs.

Systemic Integration and Policy Implementation Framework

Effectively implementing the ETHICAL-FEED framework demands a thorough comprehension of the intricate interplay between educational policy development and its practical application. Figure 3 provides a systematic integration of the framework, illustrating the multifaceted nature of systemic integration, highlighting the dynamic interplay among institutional governance, pedagogical advancements, professional development, and technological infrastructure. The following subsections provide a detailed account of each integration within the framework, relative to the framework for AI educational policy.

Figure 3. The systematic integration of the ETHICAL-FEED framework for AI educational policy.

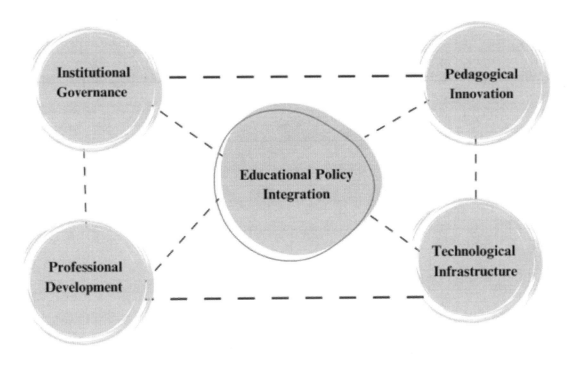

Note: This conceptual model depicts the dynamic interplay among institutional governance, pedagogical innovation, professional development frameworks, and technological infrastructure within the ETHICAL-FEED implementation model. Bidirectional pathways create recursive feedback loops, thus enabling continuous systemic improvement and policy refinement.

Institutional Governance Integration

The institutional principle of the systematic integration of the ETHICAL-FEED framework prioritizes the development of robust governance structures to ensure the ethical application of AI in educational feedback mechanisms. The governance framework integrates policy-making procedures consistent with national educational benchmarks and global ethical AI principles (Fu & Weng, 2024). When integrating institutional policies, it is crucial to consider local contextual factors while ensuring alignment with wider educational goals and ethical standards.

Pedagogical Innovation and Implementation

The pedagogical principle of the systematic integration of the ETHICAL-FEED framework emphasizes the transformation of teaching practices through theoretically grounded innovation. This transformation process integrates AI-assisted feedback mechanisms while preserving the essential human elements of education (Memarian & Doleck, 2024). The framework establishes structured approaches for curriculum development that incorporate AI literacy alongside traditional pedagogical objectives, ensuring that technological integration enhances rather than diminishes educational quality.

Professional Development Architecture

The systematic integration of the ETHICAL-FEED framework's professional development principle establishes sophisticated mechanisms for enhancing educator capacity in AI implementation. This includes comprehensive training programs addressing technical skills and ethical implications in AI-driven feedback mechanisms (Ivanov, 2023). Professional development is structured to promote continuous learning and adaptation, thereby enabling educators to maintain theoretical knowledge and acquire practical skills in implementation.

Technological Infrastructure Development

The technological principle of the ETHICAL-FEED framework's systematic integration addresses the intricate infrastructural demands of ethical AI implementation. This includes the technical specifications for AI systems and the creation of robust data protection mechanisms (Ali et al., 2024). This framework prioritizes scalable technological solutions ensuring ongoing regulatory compliance and alignment with pedagogical goals.

Cross-Dimensional Integration

Figure 3 illustrates how the effectiveness of the ETHICAL-FEED framework arises from the complex interaction of its constituent principles. The connections shown embody dynamic feedback loops, thereby enabling continuous improvement and adaptation. The interconnections between institutional governance and pedagogical innovation, as well as professional development and technological infrastructure, create avenues for systemic improvement in response to evolving circumstances. Subsequently, the ensuing section will address the limitations of the review.

LIMITATIONS OF THIS REVIEW

Despite its comprehensive approach, this systematic review encounters various limitations. The swift advancement of AI in education implies that the studies included might not comprehensively encompass the most recent advancements, thus requiring continuous reevaluation of ethical frameworks (Fu & Weng, 2024). The emphasis on higher education may restrict its relevance in other educational settings, while the prevalence of Western studies might introduce cultural bias. Methodological limitations encompass the possibility of publication bias (Hong et al., 2019), which is addressed by conducting MMAT quality assessment, as well as the interpretive nature of thematic analysis (Braun & Clarke, 2006). The lack of gender-specific (technofeminist) analysis in the reviewed studies limits a complete understanding of how AI systems interact with and potentially reinforce existing gender biases in educational feedback systems.

Furthermore, although the ETHICAL-FEED framework is pending extensive empirical testing in real-world settings (Chiu et al., 2023), this review has presented concrete instances and implementation procedures in Section 5.3, comprehensive practical recommendations in Section 5.4, and additional systemic ramifications and recommendations for educational policy and practice in Section 5.5. Collectively, these sections provide a comprehensive foundation for applying the framework in diverse educational settings, effectively connecting theoretical concepts, practical execution, and broader policy implications.

Despite these constraints, the evaluation and framework exhibit resilience through meticulous methodology, extensive thematic analysis, and adherence to established ethical principles in AI and education. The versatility of the framework makes it applicable to different educational settings and fills an important void in the literature on excessive dependence on AI for student feedback. The practical nature of this orientation provides educators and institutions with specific guidelines. The review's robust methodology, comprehensive analysis, and practical focus, along with the ETHICAL-FEED framework, establish a strong basis for tackling ethical dilemmas surrounding AI in educational feedback. This work can serve as a foundation for future research to enhance and validate the framework in a wide range of educational settings. These endeavors will contribute to the ongoing discussion surrounding the responsible application of AI in the field of education, as elaborated in the subsequent section.

FURTHER RECOMMENDATIONS FOR FUTURE RESEARCH

Expanding upon the ETHICAL-FEED framework and prior discussions, this section presents novel avenues for research on the ethical integration of AI in educational feedback. It is imperative to prioritize the implementation of extensive, longitudinal research studies that systematically assess the ETHICAL-FEED framework in various educational settings. Future research should examine how technofeminist perspectives can inform the design and evaluation of AI systems to mitigate gendered power dynamics and promote inclusiveness in educational feedback. A comprehensive assessment of the ETHICAL-FEED framework is required, encompassing its efficacy and its capacity for adaptation within varied cultural and educational contexts, in response to the limitations identified by Varsha (2023) and Al-Zahrani (2024). It is imperative to conduct innovative research on the design of AI systems that are purpose-built to align with the ETHICAL-FEED principles. This may entail collaborations among AI researchers, ethicists, and educators in order to develop feedback systems that inherently embody principles of transparency, fairness, and contextual understanding, as advocated by Fu and Weng (2024) and Chiu et al. (2023).

Additionally, a crucial aspect to consider is the examination of student agency within AI-assisted feedback systems. Further research should be conducted to explore methods of empowering students to actively engage in and influence their AI-mediated learning experiences, taking into consideration the research conducted by Flores et al. (2024) and addressing the concerns raised by Ivanov (2023) regarding potential dehumanization in AI-driven education. The convergence of AI feedback systems and emerging educational technologies, such as virtual and augmented reality, provides a promising field for further exploration. Potential research endeavors could explore the potential augmentation or complexity of ethical considerations as presented in the ETHICAL-FEED framework, thereby building upon the previous work of Kamalov et al. (2023) pertaining to the multifaceted influence of AI in the field of education.

Finally, an interdisciplinary research endeavor that incorporates cognitive science, ethics, and AI could delve into the lasting cognitive and psychological consequences of AI-assisted feedback on learners. The findings from this research endeavor have the capacity to yield significant insights into the influence of different AI feedback approaches on students' critical thinking, creativity, and metacognitive skills. Its purpose is to address the concerns expressed by Memarian and Doleck (2024) regarding the limitations of AI in comprehending the intricate aspects of student work. By leveraging the ETHICAL-FEED framework, the academic community can effectively address the emerging challenges of ethical AI usage in education

CONCLUSION

The present systematic review has undertaken a thorough examination of the excessive dependence on and improper utilization of AI in student feedback. The review has comprehensively examined 12 high-quality studies, resulting in the identification of crucial patterns, consequences, and ethical implications pertaining to the integration of AI in educational feedback processes. Grounded in these findings, the ETHICAL-FEED framework presents a comprehensive guide for responsibly implementing AI in student feedback. The six core principles, which encompass *"transparency and explainability," "human oversight and intervention," "fairness and bias mitigation," "data privacy and security," "personalization and contextual understanding,"* and *"continuous evaluation and improvement,"* effectively tackle the complex challenges identified in the literature. The ETHICAL-FEED framework achieves a harmonious equilibrium by harnessing the potential of AI for tailored and efficient feedback, while preserving the invaluable role of human educators. It underscores the necessity of transparent communication regarding the utilization of AI. Furthermore, the emphasis on regularly conducting audits is seen as a method to reduce bias in this framework. This framework emphasizes the importance of robust data protection measures and underscores the significance of continually adapting to evolving educational needs and technological advancements.

The ETHICAL-FEED framework offers solid groundwork for educators, institutions, and policymakers to effectively navigate the intricate realm of AI in education. Given the ongoing transformation of educational practices by AI, the implementation of this framework becomes imperative to ensure that technological advancements amplify rather than compromise the quality and equity of educational experiences. Integrating technofeminist perspectives reinforces this imperative by examining the complex interplay of technology, gender, and power, thereby promoting more equitable and inclusive pedagogical approaches. In summary, the ETHICAL-FEED framework represents a call to action for the educational community to actively shape the future of AI in education. The objective is to establish an environment in which technology enhances human capacity rather than displacing it. Through the adoption of this framework, educators and institutions can strive for an educational future that combines technological advancement with ethical principles, benefiting both learners and educators. To advance the field, it is crucial for educators, researchers, and policymakers to work together in refining and implementing ethical guidelines. By implementing this approach, it ensures that the integration of AI in education aligns with fundamental educational principles and places emphasis on the welfare and academic success of students.

REFERENCES

Acut, D. P., Gamusa, E. V., Pernaa, J., Yuenyong, C., Pantaleon, A. T., Espina, R. C., Sim, M. J. C., & Garcia, M. B. (2025). AI Shaming Among Teacher Education Students: A Reflection on Acceptance and Identity in the Age of Generative Tools. In *Pitfalls of AI Integration in Education: Skill Obsolescence, Misuse, and Bias*. IGI Global., DOI: 10.4018/979-8-3373-0122-8.ch005

Ahmadi, A., Yazdizadeh, B., Doshmangir, L., Majdzadeh, R., & Asghari, S. (2022). PROTOCOL: Systematic Review of Methods to Reduce Risk of Bias in Knowledge Translation Interventional Studies in Health-Related Issues. *Campbell Systematic Reviews*, *18*(2), e1236. Advance online publication. DOI: 10.1002/cl2.1236 PMID: 36911351

Al-Zahrani, A. M. (2024). Unveiling the Shadows: Beyond the Hype of AI in Education. *Heliyon*, *10*(9), e30696. DOI: 10.1016/j.heliyon.2024.e30696 PMID: 38737255

Ali, O., Murray, P. A., Momin, M., Dwivedi, Y. K., & Malik, T. (2024). The Effects of Artificial Intelligence Applications in Educational Settings: Challenges and Strategies. *Technological Forecasting and Social Change*, *199*, 123076. DOI: 10.1016/j.techfore.2023.123076

Barrett, A., & Pack, A. (2023). Not Quite Eye to A.I.: Student and Teacher Perspectives on the Use of Generative Artificial Intelligence in the Writing Process. *International Journal of Educational Technology in Higher Education*, *20*(1), 59. Advance online publication. DOI: 10.1186/s41239-023-00427-0

Bozkurt, A., Xiao, J., Farrow, R., Bai, J. Y. H., Nerantzi, C., Moore, S., Dron, J., Stracke, C. M., Singh, L., Crompton, H., Koutropoulos, A., Terentev, E., Pazurek, A., Nichols, M., Sidorkin, A. M., Costello, E., Watson, S., Mulligan, D., Honeychurch, S., & Asino, T. I. (2024). The Manifesto for Teaching and Learning in a Time of Generative AI: A Critical Collective Stance to Better Navigate the Future. *Open Praxis*, *16*(4), 487–513. DOI: 10.55982/openpraxis.16.4.777

Bramer, W. M., De Jonge, G. B., Rethlefsen, M. L., Mast, F., & Kleijnen, J. (2018). A Systematic Approach to Searching: An Efficient and Complete Method to Develop Literature Searches. *Journal of the Medical Library Association: JMLA*, *106*(4). Advance online publication. DOI: 10.5195/jmla.2018.283 PMID: 30271302

Braun, V., & Clarke, V. (2006). Using Thematic Analysis in Psychology. *Qualitative Research in Psychology*, *3*(2), 77–101. DOI: 10.1191/1478088706qp063oa

Celik, I., Dindar, M., Muukkonen, H., & Järvelä, S. (2022). The Promises and Challenges of Artificial Intelligence for Teachers: A Systematic Review of Research. *TechTrends*, *66*(4), 616–630. DOI: 10.1007/s11528-022-00715-y

Chiu, T. K. F., Xia, Q., Zhou, X., Chai, C. S., & Cheng, M. (2023). Systematic Literature Review on Opportunities, Challenges, and Future Research Recommendations of Artificial Intelligence in Education. *Computers and Education: Artificial Intelligence*, *4*, 100118. DOI: 10.1016/j.caeai.2022.100118

Collin, S., Lepage, A., & Nebel, L. (2024). Enjeux Éthiques Et Critiques De L'intelligence Artificielle En Éducation: Une Revue Systématique De La Littérature. *Canadian Journal of Learning and Technology*, *49*(4), 1–29. DOI: 10.21432/cjlt28448

Er, E., Akçapınar, G., Bayazıt, A., Noroozi, O., & Banihashem, S. K. (2024). Assessing Student Perceptions and Use of Instructor Versus AI-Generated Feedback. *British Journal of Educational Technology*. Advance online publication. DOI: 10.1111/bjet.13558

Escalante, J., Pack, A., & Barrett, A. (2023). AI-Generated Feedback on Writing: Insights into Efficacy and ENL Student Preference. *International Journal of Educational Technology in Higher Education*, *20*(1), 57. Advance online publication. DOI: 10.1186/s41239-023-00425-2

Flores, M. A., Veiga Simão, A. M., Ferreira, P. C., Pereira, D., Barros, A., Flores, P., Fernandes, E. L., & Costa, L. (2024). Online Learning, Perceived Difficulty and the Role of Feedback in COVID-19 Times. *Research in Post-Compulsory Education*, *29*(2), 324–344. DOI: 10.1080/13596748.2024.2330784

Fu, Y., & Weng, Z. (2024). Navigating the ethical terrain of AI in education: A systematic review on framing responsible human-centered AI practices. *Computers and Education: Artificial Intelligence*, *7*, 100306. DOI: 10.1016/j.caeai.2024.100306

Gantalao, L. C., Calzada, J. G. D., Capuyan, D. L., Lumantas, B. C., Acut, D. P., & Garcia, M. B. (2025). Equipping the Next Generation of Technicians: Navigating School Infrastructure and Technical Knowledge in the Age of AI Integration. In *Pitfalls of AI Integration in Education: Skill Obsolescence, Misuse, and Bias*. IGI Global., DOI: 10.4018/979-8-3373-0122-8.ch009

Garcia, M. B., Rosak-Szyrocka, J., Yılmaz, R., Metwally, A. H. S., Acut, D. P., Ofosu-Ampong, K., Erdoğdu, F., Fung, C. Y., & Bozkurt, A. (2025). Rethinking Educational Assessment in the Age of Generative AI: Actionable Strategies to Mitigate Academic Dishonesty. In *Pitfalls of AI Integration in Education: Skill Obsolescence, Misuse, and Bias*. IGI Global., DOI: 10.4018/979-8-3373-0122-8.ch001

Guo, K., Zhang, E. D., Li, D., & Yu, S. (2024). Using AI-Supported Peer Review to Enhance Feedback Literacy: An Investigation of Students' Revision of Feedback on Peers' Essays. *British Journal of Educational Technology*, bjet.13540. Advance online publication. DOI: 10.1111/bjet.13540

Hasanah, N. A., Aziza, M. R., Junikhah, A., Arif, Y. M., & Garcia, M. B. (2025). Navigating the Use of AI in Engineering Education Through a Systematic Review of Technology, Regulations, and Challenges. In *Pitfalls of AI Integration in Education: Skill Obsolescence, Misuse, and Bias*. IGI Global., DOI: 10.4018/979-8-3373-0122-8.ch016

Hong, Q. N., Pluye, P., Fàbregues, S., Bartlett, G., Boardman, F., Cargo, M., Dagenais, P., Gagnon, M.-P., Griffiths, F., Nicolau, B., O'Cathain, A., Rousseau, M.-C., & Vedel, I. (2019). Improving the Content Validity of the Mixed Methods Appraisal Tool: A Modified E-Delphi Study. *Journal of Clinical Epidemiology*, *111*, 49–59.e41. DOI: 10.1016/j.jclinepi.2019.03.008 PMID: 30905698

Hooda, M., Rana, C., Dahiya, O., Rizwan, A., & Hossain, M. S. (2022). Artificial Intelligence for Assessment and Feedback to Enhance Student Success in Higher Education. *Mathematical Problems in Engineering*, *2022*, 1–19. DOI: 10.1155/2022/5215722

Ifelebuegu, A. O., Kulume, P., & Cherukut, P. (2023). Chatbots and AI in Education (AIEd) Tools: The Good, the Bad, and the Ugly. *Journal of Applied Learning &amp. Teaching*, *6*(2). Advance online publication. DOI: 10.37074/jalt.2023.6.2.29

Ivanov, S. (2023). The Dark Side of Artificial Intelligence in Higher Education. *Service Industries Journal*, *43*(15-16), 1055–1082. DOI: 10.1080/02642069.2023.2258799

Kamalov, F., Santandreu Calonge, D., & Gurrib, I. (2023). New Era of Artificial Intelligence in Education: Towards a Sustainable Multifaceted Revolution. *Sustainability (Basel)*, *15*(16), 12451. DOI: 10.3390/su151612451

Khlaif, Z. N., Ayyoub, A., Hamamra, B., Bensalem, E., Mitwally, M. A. A., Ayyoub, A., Hattab, M. K., & Shadid, F. (2024). University Teachers' Views on the Adoption and Integration of Generative AI Tools for Student Assessment in Higher Education. *Education Sciences*, *14*(10), 1090. DOI: 10.3390/educsci14101090

Mangubat, J. C., Mangubat, M. R., Uy, T. B. L., Acut, D. P., & Garcia, M. B. (2025). Safeguarding Educational Innovations Amid AI Disruptions: A Reassessment of Patenting for Sustained Intellectual Property Protection. In *Pitfalls of AI Integration in Education: Skill Obsolescence, Misuse, and Bias*. IGI Global., DOI: 10.4018/979-8-3373-0122-8.ch013

Memarian, B., & Doleck, T. (2024). A Review of Assessment for Learning with Artificial Intelligence. *Computers in Human Behavior: Artificial Humans*, *2*(1), 100040. DOI: 10.1016/j.chbah.2023.100040

Miranda, J. P. P., Cruz, M. A. D., Fernandez, A. B., Balahadia, F. F., Aviles, J. S., Caro, C. A., Liwanag, I. G., & Gaña, E. P. (2025). Erosion of Critical Academic Skills Due to AI Dependency Among Tertiary Students: A Path Analysis. In *Pitfalls of AI Integration in Education: Skill Obsolescence, Misuse, and Bias*. IGI Global., DOI: 10.4018/979-8-3373-0122-8.ch002

Naseer, F., Khalid, M. U., Ayub, N., Rasool, A., Abbas, T., & Afzal, M. W. (2024). Automated Assessment and Feedback in Higher Education Using Generative AI. In *Advances in Educational Technologies and Instructional Design* (pp. 433-461). IGI Global. https://doi.org/DOI: 10.4018/979-8-3693-1351-0.ch021

Nazaretsky, T., Mejia-Domenzain, P., Swamy, V., Frej, J., & Käser, T. (2024). AI or Human? Evaluating Student Feedback Perceptions in Higher Education. *Lecture Notes in Computer Science*, *15159*, 284–298. DOI: 10.1007/978-3-031-72315-5_20

Pang, T. Y., Kootsookos, A., & Cheng, C.-T. (2024). Artificial Intelligence Use in Feedback: A Qualitative Analysis. *Journal of University Teaching & Learning Practice*, *21*(06). Advance online publication. DOI: 10.53761/40wmcj98

Shaheen, N., Shaheen, A., Ramadan, A., Hefnawy, M. T., Ramadan, A., Ibrahim, I. A., Hassanein, M. E., Ashour, M. E., & Flouty, O. (2023). Appraising Systematic Reviews: A Comprehensive Guide to Ensuring Validity and Reliability. *Frontiers in Research Metrics and Analytics*, *8*, 1268045. Advance online publication. DOI: 10.3389/frma.2023.1268045 PMID: 38179256

Sohrabi, C., Franchi, T., Mathew, G., Kerwan, A., Nicola, M., Griffin, M., Agha, M., & Agha, R. (2021). PRISMA 2020 Statement: What's New and the Importance of Reporting Guidelines. *International Journal of Surgery*, *88*, 105918. DOI: 10.1016/j.ijsu.2021.105918 PMID: 33789825

Ugwu, C. N., & Opah, A. C. (2023). Use of Boolean Search Strategy for Accessing the Databases of University of Technology Libraries by Postgraduate Students in South-East, Nigeria. *Journal of Library Services and Technologies*, *5*(2), 24–35. DOI: 10.47524/jlst.v5i2.25

Varsha, P. S. (2023). How Can We Manage Biases in Artificial Intelligence Systems – A Systematic Literature Review. *International Journal of Information Management Data Insights*, *3*(1), 100165. DOI: 10.1016/j.jjimei.2023.100165

Wajcman, J. (2013). *TechnoFeminism*. Polity Press. https://books.google.com.ph/books?id= c9TgUMIzhx8C

KEY TERMS AND DEFINITIONS

ETHICAL-FEED Framework: A thorough approach to ethically implement AI in student feedback processes, comprising six fundamental principles: transparency, human oversight, fairness, data privacy, personalization, and continuous evaluation.

AI-Assisted Feedback: The utilization of artificial intelligence technologies for generating, analyzing, or delivering feedback to students in educational environments, with the goal of enhancing learning outcomes and efficiency.

Algorithmic Bias: The systematic and repeatable errors found in AI systems result in unfair outcomes, wherein certain arbitrary user groups are favored at the expense of others. These biases often stem from societal prejudices embedded in the training data or algorithm design.

Transparency in AI: Ensuring comprehensibility and transparency in AI decision-making processes is of paramount importance in educational contexts, where students and educators rely on a thorough understanding of how feedback is generated.

Human Oversight: The practice of upholding human involvement and decision-making authority in AI-assisted processes, guaranteeing that AI functions as a tool to enhance rather than supplant human judgment in educational feedback.

Data Privacy in Educational: AI: Ensuring the protection of student information acquired, processed, and stored by AI feedback systems involve implementing data security measures, obtaining informed consent, and complying with relevant regulations.

Personalized Learning: An academic approach that utilizes AI to adapt instruction, feedback, and learning experiences to the specific needs, preferences, and progress of individual students.

Continuous Evaluation of AI Systems: The continuous evaluation and enhancement of AI feedback systems involve regular audits to address bias, effectiveness, and alignment with educational objectives and ethical principles.

AI Literacy in Education: The competencies necessary for educators and students to comprehend, analyze, and proficiently utilize AI-based educational tools, including those designed for feedback delivery.

Technofeminism: A theoretical and practical analysis of technology, gender, and power dynamics that critically examines the reciprocal relationship between technology and gender inequality, considering its potential to either perpetuate or challenge power dynamics and outlining strategies for achieving more equitable technological advancements.

Chapter 16
Navigating the Use of AI in Engineering Education Through a Systematic Review of Technology, Regulations, and Challenges

Novrindah Alvi Hasanah
https://orcid.org/0000-0001-9328-5065
Universitas Islam Negeri Maulana Malik Ibrahim Malang, Indonesia

Miladina Rizka Aziza
https://orcid.org/0000-0001-8832-7398
Universitas Islam Negeri Maulana Malik Ibrahim Malang, Indonesia

Allin Junikhah
https://orcid.org/0009-0001-5432-2457
Universitas Islam Negeri Maulana Malik Ibrahim Malang, Indonesia

Yunifa Miftachul Arif
https://orcid.org/0000-0002-2183-0762
Universitas Islam Negeri Maulana Malik Ibrahim Malang, Indonesia

Manuel B. Garcia
https://orcid.org/0000-0003-2615-422X
FEU Institute of Technology, Philippines

ABSTRACT

The integration of artificial intelligence (AI) into engineering education has emerged as a transformative force, offering innovative tools to enhance teaching, learning, and administrative processes. This study presents a systematic review of the current landscape, focusing on the AI technologies application, the regulatory frameworks, and the challenges encountered in engineering education. The findings reveal how AI can improve student learning outcomes, personalize educational experiences, and automate complex

DOI: 10.4018/979-8-3373-0122-8.ch016

processes. The review also addresses critical issues, such as ethical considerations and the imperative for regulatory compliance. Furthermore, it identifies key barriers to adoption, such as technological limitations and the preparedness of educators and students to embrace AI-powered solutions. This study provides a comprehensive understanding of the potential and limitations of AI in engineering education, offering actionable insights for educators, policymakers, and stakeholders aiming to foster effective and ethical AI integration in academic settings.

INTRODUCTION

Artificial intelligence (AI) has quickly become a transformative agent in education (Garcia, Arif, et al., 2024; Mangubat et al., 2025; Miller et al., 2025). In engineering education, educators can adopt advanced AI technologies to develop personalized, efficient, and engaging learning experiences (Gantalao et al., 2025; Ocak et al., 2023). For instance, generative AI (GenAI) systems (e.g., ChatGPT) offer personalized assistance that enables students to solve problems actively and foster a deeper understanding of engineering concepts (Qadir, 2023). The integration of AI with existing technologies, such as virtual reality (VR) and augmented reality (AR), allows learners to immerse themselves in simulated environments where they can engage with complex engineering topics more intuitively and experientially (Schleiss et al., 2022). The emergence of AI-driven tools—including machine learning (ML), natural language processing (NLP), and intelligent tutoring systems (ITS)—has opened new frontiers in engineering education. These tools, including AI-powered robots and tutors, enable learners to progress at their own pace and address areas of difficulty. Maximizing the usage of these pedagogical tools creates a more equitable and data-rich learning environment (Johri, 2020). Studies highlight the potential of these technologies to enhance student motivation and engagement by promoting interactive and accessible learning (Heck & Schouten, 2021). Collectively, these innovations help develop critical thinking skills and better prepare students for the complexities of the engineering profession.

However, with great power comes great responsibility—especially as we enter a realm where AI technologies require carefully crafted regulatory frameworks to ensure their ethical and responsible deployment. The thoughtful implementation of AI in education is critical, particularly given the sensitivity of student data and the potential for biases embedded in algorithms. Compliance with frameworks such as the General Data Protection Regulation (GDPR) is essential to safeguard student privacy and data security. Moreover, institutional policies must take a leading role in establishing transparency and accountability mechanisms that address algorithmic bias and promote the fair and equitable adoption of AI in educational contexts (Silva & Janes, 2023). Yet, translating these broad principles into practical guidelines remains a challenge as institutions struggle to balance innovation with regulatory compliance (Lu et al., 2022). In addition, the practical application of AI in engineering education is hindered by several barriers, including the high costs associated with acquiring and maintaining AI tools and a lack of technical expertise among educators. These efforts are further complicated by ethical concerns, particularly the persistence of biases within AI models (Heyn et al., 2021). The systemic nature of these challenges calls for a multifaceted approach—one that includes cost-effective solutions, professional development for educators, and strong institutional commitment.

MAIN FOCUS OF THE CHAPTER

This chapter explores the disruptive nature of AI in engineering education, including technological evolutions, regulatory considerations, and the challenges associated with implementing AI. Specifically, it focuses on how AI-based tools play a crucial role in enhancing learning outcomes, enabling seamless integration into engineering curricula, and addressing barriers to adoption. The chapter is guided by three overarching questions that contribute to a holistic understanding of how AI is becoming an integral part of engineering education:

1. **What AI technologies are currently used in engineering education?** This question examines the emerging tools and platforms being adopted, along with their usage levels and effectiveness in improving learning outcomes.
2. **What are the regulatory aspects to consider when applying AI in engineering education?** Analyzing regulatory frameworks offers insights into the mechanisms through which organizations can implement AI responsibly and ethically.
3. **What challenges are associated with implementing AI in engineering education?** Identifying tangible ethical and practical impediments enables the design of targeted solutions that support the smooth adoption of AI applications.

By addressing these questions, the study offers actionable insights for educators, policymakers, and technologists in harnessing the transformative potential of AI. Contributing to the literature on AI and education, this chapter underscores the importance of equipping future engineers with the skills necessary for a technology-driven era (Nti et al., 2021). Complementing the existing body of knowledge, this systematic study analyzes peer-reviewed literature, proceedings from major conferences, and up-to-date case studies to provide an in-depth overview of current AI practices in engineering education and the projected direction for future advancements. Adopting this lens allows readers to identify new trends, emerging technologies, and pragmatic approaches that can be leveraged to fulfill the promise of AI in education. The implications highlight the strategic significance of embracing AI to transform engineering education in ways that cultivate the competencies engineers need to succeed in increasingly complex, technology-driven environments. Moreover, the review identifies the synergistic relationship between AI technologies, ethical guidelines, and implementation strategies—essential frameworks for facilitating the ongoing discourse on the future of engineering education. This is a critical consideration in educational contexts, as it reinforces the need for a collective strategy toward AI integration that fosters innovation, equity, and ethical accountability.

BACKGROUND OF THE STUDY

AI in Education

More than 2,000 years ago, renowned ancient philosophers such as Socrates (469–399 BC), Plato (427–347 BC), and Aristotle (384–322 BC) explored theories concerning the emergence of new knowledge and its impact on human life—particularly on learning and teaching. The topics discussed by these philosophers remain relevant today, especially in relation to a transformative technology known as AI, which has introduced both benefits and challenges to the field of education (Ouyang & Jiao, 2021). AI refers to the capability of computer systems to perform tasks that typically require human intelligence. It has been developed to assist in various domains of life to enable individuals to complete tasks more efficiently, intelligently, and often in more engaging ways. This technology facilitates personalized learning and streamlines educational management, but it also raises important ethical and social concerns—particularly in terms of data privacy and the evolving relationship between humans and technology.

AI in education is instrumental in enhancing the learning process by making it more effective and efficient (Namatherdhala et al., 2022). It improves the educational experience through a range of innovations, such as automating time-consuming administrative tasks and developing modular prototypes for statistical reasoning, data visualization, and learning analytics (Alneyadi et al., 2023; Athilingam & He, 2024; Gupta et al., 2024; Lam et al., 2024; Shoaib et al., 2024). Leveraging data analysis, AI enables the creation of relevant and compelling learning experiences, supporting learners' development based on their individual capacities. Numerous studies have demonstrated the positive impact and significant benefits of AI in education. For instance, research has shown that AI is being successfully integrated into academic environments and student learning processes (Wang et al., 2023). Additionally, computer scientists have explored the theoretical and scientific foundations of AI in education and investigated the broader impact of AI technologies in educational contexts (Chen et al., 2020; Zawacki-Richter et al., 2019).

Engineering Education

AI is becoming an essential component of engineering education. It offers an engaging learning experience for students and enhances teaching effectiveness for educators. The integration of AI in engineering education opens up a wide range of applications, each offering its own benefits and challenges. For example, AI-powered chatbots provide more effective and practical learning experiences through personalized, interactive, and real-time support (Mthombeni et al., 2023). Additionally, combining project-based learning with Open Educational Resources (OERs) enables students to work on real-world problems, enhancing their intrinsic motivation and practical skills while shifting the lecturer's role toward that of a facilitator or guide (Schleiss et al., 2022). There is an urgent need to develop curricula that integrate AI with traditional engineering education. This integration is necessary to equip students with the skills to solve engineering problems using AI—such as in the development of self-driving vehicles, drone delivery systems, and the implementation of Artificial Narrow Intelligence (ANI) applications (Johri, 2020). It also enhances the learning experience in engineering design education by requiring continuous curriculum adaptation to new AI tools and ensuring that both teachers and students stay up to date with the latest AI applications and methodologies.

AI can also assist educators in efficiently performing routine tasks, such as assessments, thereby allowing them to focus on creating more interactive and personalized teaching strategies that improve the overall quality of education (Garcia et al., 2025; Johri, 2020). Furthermore, engineering programs have begun implementing web-based AI tools such as OpexAnalytics and CompareAssess, which are used to teach supply chain management and promote learning through evaluation. These tools have been shown to improve student perceptions and learning outcomes (Bosman et al., 2022). Moreover, Mthombeni et al. (2023) emphasized that AI chatbots enhance the learning experience in engineering design education by offering personalized, real-time support, reshaping both knowledge acquisition and skill development. Similarly, Xu and Ouyang (2022) highlighted the integration of robotics and AI in

STEM education, promoting hands-on learning while encouraging discussions about ethical considerations. These developments point to a future where AI not only augments engineering education but also redefines the roles of students and educators in shaping innovative, future-ready learning environments.

Gaps in Current Research on AI Integration in Engineering Education

Research on AI usability in engineering education has revealed several fascinating findings; however, there are still gaps that require further exploration. Santos et al. (2024) conducted a comprehensive literature review on the integration of Generative AI (GenAI) in teaching and learning processes. The study highlights the potential of GenAI technologies to enhance engineering educational practices. However, it focuses solely on information and communication technology (ICT) engineering education, leaving the broader applications of GenAI across other engineering disciplines unaddressed. Sah et al. (2024) also examined the integration of AI and large language models (LLMs) into software engineering education, offering a critical analysis of the literature, pedagogical frameworks, and persistent challenges. While the study emphasizes the ethical implications of using AI and LLMs, it does not propose comprehensive frameworks or educational strategies to integrate AI ethics deeply into the curriculum. Our research seeks to fill this gap by exploring AI ethics and the implementation of regulatory frameworks within engineering education. Al Husaeni et al. (2022) conducted a systematic review of the integration of chatbots as educational tools in science and engineering education. Although the research includes contributions from various countries, it does not examine how chatbots are utilized differently across educational contexts. There remains a need to investigate the effectiveness and challenges of AI technologies in diverse educational settings. Our research aims to bridge this gap by evaluating the use of AI across various engineering fields, as different disciplines may demand distinct pedagogical strategies or technologies.

METHODS

This study employed a systematic literature review (SLR) guided by the PRISMA (Preferred Reporting Items for Systematic Reviews and Meta-Analyses) framework to ensure a rigorous and transparent process in identifying, evaluating, and synthesizing relevant literature. The SLR approach was chosen for its suitability in exploring the integration of AI in engineering education, particularly in relation to technological applications, regulatory considerations, and implementation challenges (Arif et al., 2024; Arif et al., 2025; Lobo et al., 2025; Olugbade, 2025). Following the four principal phases of PRISMA—identification, screening, eligibility, and inclusion—the review process was conducted systematically to enhance the transparency, consistency, and accuracy of the findings. Relevant studies were retrieved from academic databases using predefined search terms, screened for relevance, assessed against inclusion and exclusion criteria, and included based on their alignment with the study's objectives.

Figure 1. Records selection process

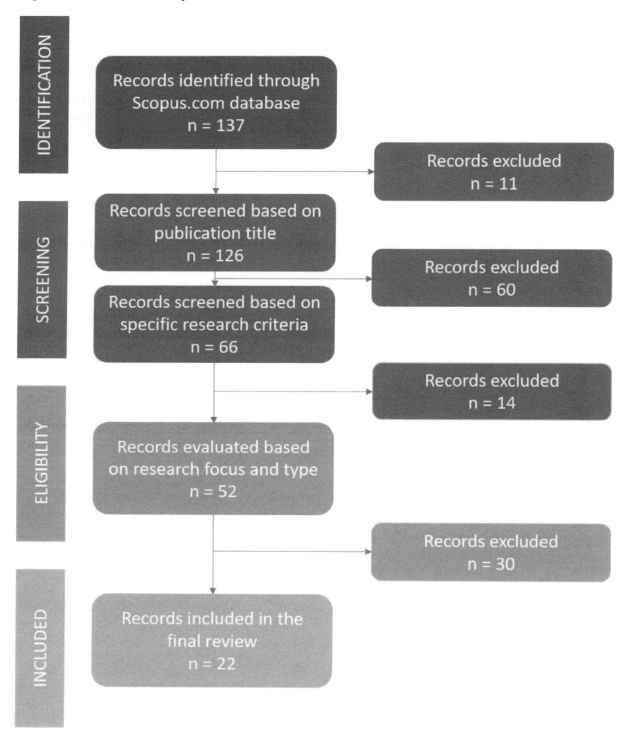

Selection Process and Inclusion Criteria

During the literature search process, the author utilized the Scopus database with a focus on the integration of AI in engineering education. The search was limited to publications from 2019 to 2024 to ensure the study reflected current trends in AI applications within this field. The keywords (*AI* OR "*Artificial Intelligence*") AND *Engineering* AND (*Education* OR *Learning*) were used, yielding an initial result of 137 articles, reflecting the global scope of AI applications in engineering education. The selection process began with the identification phase, during which 137 records were retrieved from the Scopus database. In the first screening phase, these records were assessed based on their titles, leading to the exclusion of 11 records due to duplication and irrelevance. The second screening phase applied more specific criteria related to engineering education, resulting in the exclusion of 60 additional records, leaving 66 articles for further analysis. In the eligibility phase, the remaining 66 articles were critically evaluated based on their research focus and type. This assessment led to the exclusion of 44 articles that did not meet the study's inclusion criteria—such as lacking a clear focus on AI implementation in engineering education or failing to address associated challenges and regulatory aspects. Finally, 22 publications were selected for inclusion, as they met all criteria and provided critical insights into AI technology applications, regulatory considerations, and implementation challenges in engineering education. Figure 1 presents the PRISMA flow diagram, which visually outlines the study selection process across the four phases: identification, screening, eligibility, and inclusion.

Presented in Table 1 is the reference list along with the diverse research areas in engineering education. These studies covered a wide range of topics, such as the development of AI technologies, the creation of teaching materials, and the integration of AI into curricula. The reviewed studies employed various research methodologies, including descriptive approaches, research and development (R&D) models, pedagogical utility exploration, quantitative analysis, and qualitative analysis. These research studies also encompassed a broad spectrum of learner populations, ranging from high school students to those in higher engineering education. Moreover, they addressed multiple engineering disciplines, including geotechnical engineering, software engineering, systems engineering, civil engineering, electrical engineering, network engineering, control engineering, and materials science and engineering.

Table 1. List of studies employing AI in engineering education

No.	References	Implementation Field	Study Design/Method	Target Population
1	Nikolic et al. (2024)	Implementation of various AI technologies	Descriptive	Engineering Teachers & Students
2	Bordel and Alcarria (2024)	Implementation of AI technologies	Experimental	Network Engineering Students
3	Baltaci et al. (2024)	Integration of AI technologies	Qualitative Analysis	Electrical & Computer Engineering Students
4	Osunbunmi et al. (2024)	Teaching & Learning Process	Qualitative Analysis	Engineering Teachers & Students
5	Martel et al. (2024)	Teaching & Learning Process	Pedagogical Utility Exploration	Higher Engineering Education
6	Oliveira and Vrančić (2024)	Integration of AI technologies	Experimental	Control Engineering

continued on following page

Table 1. Continued

No.	References	Implementation Field	Study Design/Method	Target Population
7	Modran et al. (2024)	Educational practices in engineering disciplines	Descriptive and Experimental	Higher Engineering Education
8	Rodríguez-Calderón and González-García (2024)	Educational technology in engineering education	Experimental and Descriptive analysis	Engineering Teachers & Students
9	Slomp et al. (2024)	Adaptive learning systems using AI technology	Qualitative analysis	Higher Engineering Education
10	Galos et al. (2024)	Integration of AI into curricula	Research and Development (R&D) Model	Materials Science and Engineering
11	Nikolic et al. (2023)	Engineering Education Assessment and Pedagogy	Descriptive	Higher Engineering Education
12	Asunda et al. (2023)	Integration of AI into K-12 education (STEM education)	Pedagogical Utility Exploration	High School Students
13	Ocak et al. (2023)	Integration of AI technologies	Descriptive	Civil Engineering
14	Johri (2020)	Integration of AI and ML in engineering education	Qualitative Analysis	Engineering Teachers & Students
15	Shvedchykova et al. (2023)	Development of new AI technologies	Research and Development (R&D) Model	Electrical Engineering Students
16	Yaghoubi et al. (2023)	Teaching & learning in engineering education	Experimental	Ph.D. and master's Program Teacher & Students
17	Memarian (2023)	The intersection of engineering education, cultural inclusivity, and AI-enhance pedagogy	Pedagogical Utility Exploration	Engineering Teachers
18	Moolman et al. (2023)	Virtual and remote learning environment	Research and Development (R&D) Model	Engineering Teachers
19	González et al. (2022)	AI Technology Development	Research and Development (R&D) Model	Software Engineering Students
20	Jaurez et al. (2022)	Integration of AI within the engineering lifecycle	Descriptive	Systems Engineering
21	Núñez and Lantada (2020)	Transformation of AI in engineering education	Descriptive	Engineering Teachers and Students
22	Lez'er et al. (2019)	Application of AI	Descriptive	Geotechnics and Engineering Students

The analysis of publication trends surrounding AI usability for engineering education is illustrated in Figure 2. The increasing number of research publications over the years indicates a growing research interest in this area. A notable peak in research activity was observed in 2024, with a maximum of 10 publications, followed by eight articles published in 2023. In both 2019 and 2020, there was a consistent output of one publication per year, whereas no publications were recorded in 2021. These findings suggest that AI usability in engineering education continues to be a significant focus within the academic community.

Figure 2. Number of annual publications

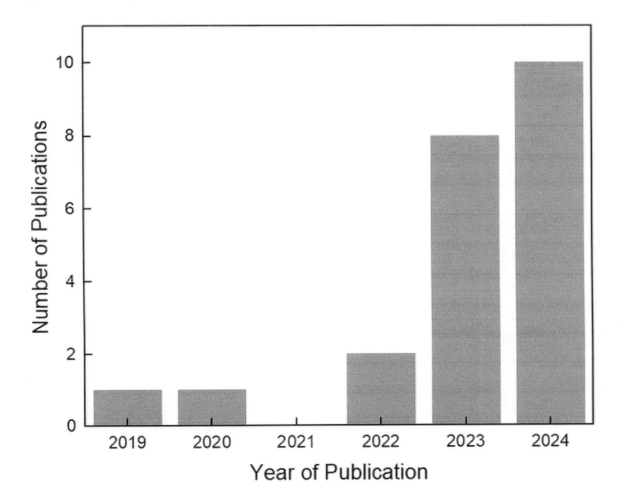

Figure 3 presents the distribution of publications across various publishers, highlighting the diverse contributions of different entities to the field. The American Society for Engineering Education (ASEE) leads with five publications, followed by the Institute of Electrical and Electronics Engineers Inc. (IEEE) and Springer, each contributing four publications. Taylor & Francis and the European Society of Engineering Education (ESEE) each published three papers, demonstrating their strong involvement in this research domain. Additionally, John Wiley and Sons Inc., Virginia Polytechnic Institute, Elsevier, Tempus Publications, and EDP Sciences each contributed one publication. This distribution reflects the broad engagement of publishers in advancing research on AI usability in engineering education.

Figure 3. Number of publications by publisher

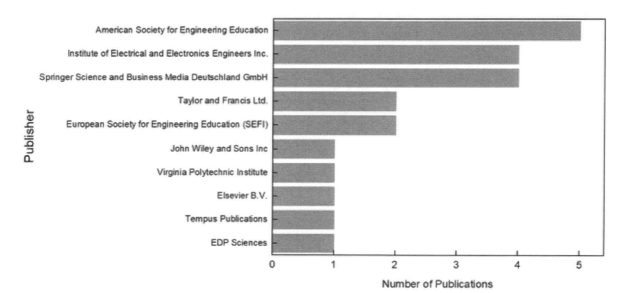

An analysis of publication types reveals that conference proceedings are the predominant medium for disseminating research on AI usability in engineering education. Of the 22 studies analyzed, 15 were published as conference proceedings, five as journal articles, and the remaining two as book chapters. This distribution highlights the preference for conference proceedings as the primary platform for sharing preliminary results and facilitating academic discourse.

Data Collection and Analysis Process

To synthesize data from the selected studies, we applied a systematic approach that began with thematic analysis to identify key concepts and patterns in AI usability within engineering education. Each publication was carefully coded to highlight themes related to AI technologies, educational regulations, and implementation challenges in the context of engineering education. This qualitative thematic synthesis enabled the development of a comprehensive narrative that captured the diverse dimensions of AI integration in this field. The selected studies were coded according to predefined themes—such as AI technology, regulation, and challenges—with the aim of organizing and categorizing information based on relevant topics. Subsequently, these codes were analyzed to identify patterns and relationships among themes. Based on this analysis, a thematic narrative was developed to reflect the main findings from the reviewed literature.

In addition to thematic analysis, bibliometric analysis was conducted to visualize the relationships between key terms, offering a macro-level view of the field without relying on statistical methods. This approach allowed for the identification of prevailing trends and central topics related to AI in engineering education. Figure 4 illustrates the word cloud visualization, providing insights into the keywords most frequently appearing in the selected dataset. The top three keywords identified in the publications were *artificial intelligence, engineering education*, and *ChatGPT. Artificial intelligence* emerged as the most dominant term, underscoring its central role in this study. *Engineering education* was the second most frequent term, reflecting a strong emphasis on AI integration in this domain. Meanwhile, *ChatGPT* highlights a focus on specific AI tools and their practical use in educational settings. The prominence of ChatGPT indicates a growing interest in leveraging AI technologies to support teaching and learning in engineering education, which supports recent literature review in other disciplines (e.g., Garcia, 2025). Keywords related to ethics, academic integrity, and personalization point to broader challenges and considerations surrounding the application of AI in academia (Garcia, Garcia, et al., 2024).

Figure 4. Distribution of keywords

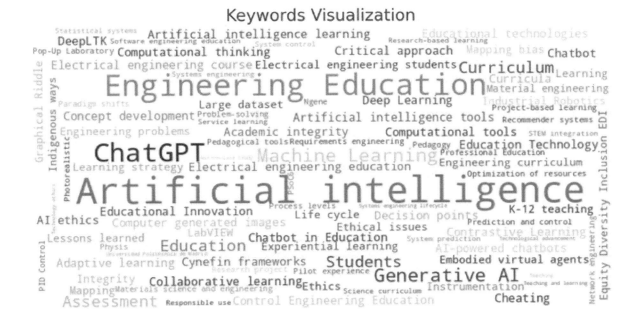

Figure 5 displays the frequency of the top 20 keywords found in the 22 selected papers. This visualization clearly highlights the prevalence and relationships among key terms such as *artificial intelligence, engineering education, ChatGPT, machine learning*, and others. These terms underscore their central role in shaping the current research landscape. Furthermore, the presence of terms like *generative AI, education, curriculum*, and *assessment* demonstrates a strong connection to engineering education and teaching methodologies. The inclusion of phrases such as *ChatGPT, chatbots in education*, and *AI-powered chatbots* also reflects a growing interest in the application of AI tools to enhance educational processes. This emphasizes researchers' focus on using these tools to improve the learning experience and outcomes for students. Notably, ethical considerations are also evident, as seen in the presence of terms like *AI ethics* and *academic integrity*, indicating attention to the ethical challenges associated with the use of AI in education.

Figure 5. Top 20 keywords in engineering education

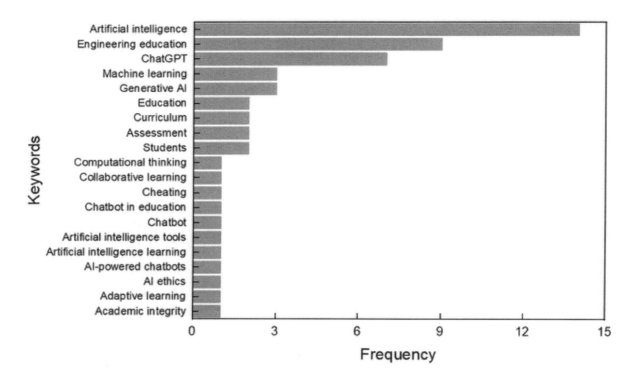

The distribution of research disciplines is illustrated in Figure 6. The selected studies were categorized into four areas according to the implementations listed in Table 1. The most common discipline in education is AI integration, which includes eight implementation fields. This category encompasses a wide range of AI applications and integration strategies in areas such as engineering education, K-12 STEM education, curriculum design, and the engineering systems lifecycle. Next, five implementation fields were classified under the development and implementation of AI technologies, focusing on the technical and practical aspects of AI, including the creation, deployment, and refinement of these tools. The teaching and learning processes discipline also includes five implementation fields, examining how AI can enhance pedagogical approaches and learning environments, such as through adaptive learning systems, innovative teaching methods, and virtual or remote learning platforms. Finally, four implementation fields were grouped under educational practices in engineering and assessment. This discipline focuses on improving educational quality and inclusivity within engineering, covering areas such as technology adoption, assessment methods, and culturally responsive practices.

Figure 6. Distribution of research disciplines

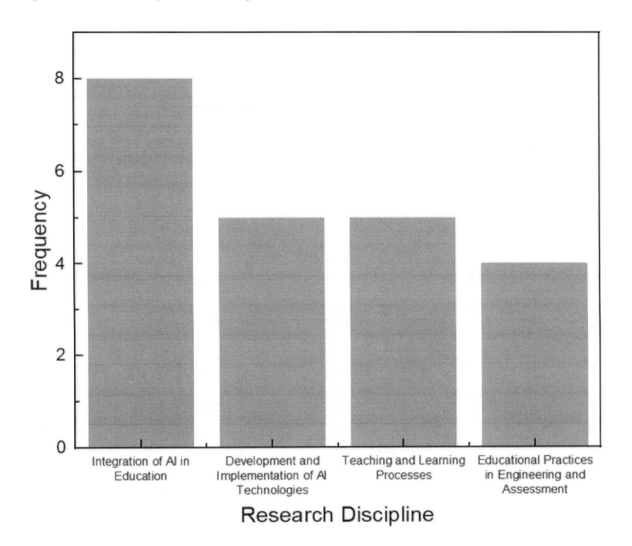

Following the selection of publications, each article was critically analyzed. This analysis involved examining the technologies used, the regulatory frameworks applied, and the challenges encountered in implementation. The objective was to gain a comprehensive understanding of the context, methodologies, findings, and overall contributions of each study.

RESULTS AND DISCUSSION

The Integration of AI Technology in Engineering Education

Previous studies have shown that supporting technologies are being applied to optimize the role of AI in different domains, particularly in engineering education. AI plays a vital role in helping humans complete a wide range of tasks more efficiently and engagingly. These supporting technologies are designed to enhance performance in assessment processes, enrich teaching methods, and support engineering-based learning environments (Nikolic et al., 2024).

The AI development roadmap for the period 2020–2030 is presented in Figure 8. This roadmap outlines scientific, technological, and educational goals aligned with the United Nations 2030 Agenda. It begins with an analysis of AI's emergence as a supportive tool in educational practices, particularly in teaching. The study ultimately proposes the concept of a "smart university," which leverages AI technologies to improve academic processes while also identifying key challenges in ensuring the sustainable use of AI in engineering education. One critical factor in the successful implementation of AI is the development of adequate capacity-building programs and training for educators, enabling them to effectively use AI to support teaching and prepare students for the future (Bozkurt et al., 2024; Núñez & Lantada, 2020).

Figure 8. AI in engineering education: Current situation and roadmap

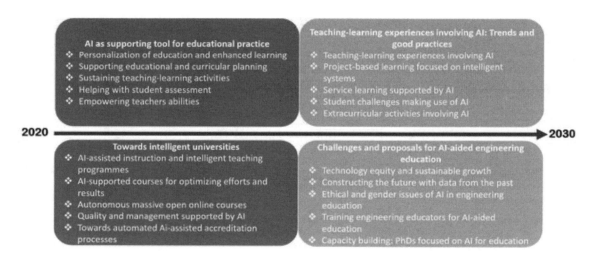

Traditional face-to-face and laboratory assessments remain effective methods for maintaining academic integrity. These approaches can be complemented by technologies such as ChatGPT to support student learning. For example, ChatGPT can provide high-quality annotations, allowing students to compare their solutions with AI-generated outputs and use these comparisons to deepen their understanding (Nikolic et al., 2023). However, as AI libraries rapidly evolve, the academic community must continually adapt assessment approaches to ensure both relevance and integrity. One promising strategy is the reverse assessment approach, where students are engaged in critical thinking tasks that require them to analyze and evaluate the output of technologies like ChatGPT. Research indicates that while AI technology offers numerous benefits, it must be implemented thoughtfully to mitigate potential negative impacts (Nikolic et al., 2024). Educators are significantly affected by the integration of AI in engineering education. AI simplifies the process of delivering instructional content by enabling real-time adaptation of materials based on student feedback and performance metrics. It also aids in laboratory preparation by predicting equipment needs, optimizing settings, and simulating potential outcomes—thereby enhancing hands-on lab experiences. Additionally, AI supports student learning by providing accessible explanations, visualizations, and simulations that help students grasp complex concepts quickly and effectively (Baltaci et al., 2024).

Despite its advantages, AI development in education—particularly in engineering—also presents challenges. Concerns related to ethics, data security, and overreliance on technology need to be addressed. Excessive dependence on AI can potentially diminish students' creativity (Garcia, 2024). To harness the full potential of AI, educators require adequate training on how to integrate these technologies effectively into the learning process. Therefore, further research is essential to develop strategies that address these challenges and ensure AI is used responsibly and productively. Looking ahead, AI is expected to become more integrated, intelligent, and accessible—supporting advancements across multiple disciplines, including engineering education. With its capacity to enhance accessibility, efficiency, and engagement, AI has the potential to revolutionize engineering education, making it more inclusive and responsive to diverse learner needs. Ultimately, AI can usher in a new era of engineering education that is more effective, affordable, and globally accessible (Núñez & Lantada, 2020). Analysis of AI integration in engineering education shows benefits such as customization of teaching and early detection of difficulties students face during teaching and learning activities (Slomp et al., 2024).

The Regulations for AI Utilization in Engineering Education

The role of AI technology in engineering education offers immense opportunities to revolutionize teaching and learning. However, alongside these benefits come challenges that necessitate well-defined regulations to ensure the ethical, safe, and effective use of AI. A key challenge, as identified in the study *Artificial Intelligence in Education: Challenges and Opportunities for Sustainable Development*, is the need for policy frameworks to guide the responsible use of AI in alignment with global goals, including the UN's 2030 Agenda for Sustainable Development. Similarly, *The Impact of Artificial Intelligence on Learning, Teaching and Education*, a report by the EU Commission, underscores the importance of regulating AI to harness its transformative potential while mitigating associated risks (Núñez & Lantada, 2020).

To leverage the capabilities of AI technologies and ensure a positive influence on teaching and learning, policymakers must design and implement regulations that benefit all stakeholders—educators, institutions, and especially engineering students. While engineering students must be adept in using advanced technologies, they also need strong critical thinking skills to verify and contextualize information. Overreliance on AI could hinder the development of foundational competencies such as problem-solving, analytical reasoning, and collaboration. Therefore, students should be encouraged to cross-reference AI-generated outputs with trusted academic sources, including textbooks, scholarly articles, and faculty guidance (Nikolic et al., 2024; Xiao et al., 2025). Policies must aim to strike a balance between technological application and the cultivation of human cognitive and creative skills—such as limiting AI use in certain hands-on or conceptual learning tasks. Importantly, AI should be viewed as a supplementary tool rather than a replacement for physical courses or laboratory experiences. Practical, hands-on learning remains a core component of engineering education, and designing real-world experiments in engineering disciplines can be challenging yet essential (Bordel & Alcarria, 2024; Modran et al., 2024).

Furthermore, regulations should require institutions to provide structured training programs for educators. These programs should cover the technical, pedagogical, and ethical dimensions of AI integration. Educators must be equipped not only to use AI tools but also to guide students in their ethical and effective application. Regulatory models like the *Academic Integrity Enforcement Pyramid* emphasize the importance of institutional commitment to responsible AI use (Nikolic et al., 2024). Governments and institutions should also fund and support research initiatives aimed at developing sustainable, AI-integrated educational models aligned with national education goals. Regular audits and internal reviews must also be mandated to ensure that AI is being used safely, ethically, and effectively in educational settings. A crucial component of AI regulation in engineering education is data protection and privacy. Since AI systems often rely on big data—including students' learning outcomes, preferences, and interactions—regulations must ensure that this data is processed securely. This includes enforcing encryption, access controls, and transparency regarding how student data is collected and used. Regulations must also align with local and international standards, such as GDPR, to ensure robust protection of learner data (Johri, 2020; Slomp et al., 2024). In addition, ethical regulation is essential to prevent algorithmic bias that could unfairly impact academic assessments or reinforce inequalities. Automated evaluation tools, for example, may inadvertently disadvantage certain groups. Broader ethical concerns include fairness, transparency, potential misuse, and the fear of AI displacing human educators. Regulations should require that AI systems be fair, inclusive, and transparent. Interdisciplinary expert panels can be instrumental in auditing algorithms and minimizing biases. With the rapid rise of generative AI, it is imperative to consider both its short-term implications and long-term effects on education (Acut et al., 2024).

When well-designed and properly enforced, AI regulations can minimize the risks of misuse, promote educational equity, and ensure that AI supports—not disrupts—core educational values. Such regulations will help educators deliver material in real time and assist students in understanding concepts more efficiently and deeply. Appropriate policy frameworks will not only support ethical AI integration but also enhance the inclusivity, personalization, and overall quality of engineering education. Looking ahead, further studies are needed to assess AI's strengths, limitations, and emerging opportunities in both engineering and pedagogical contexts (Osunbunmi et al., 2024). Ultimately, while AI has tremendous potential to advance engineering education, this potential can only be fully realized through thoughtful regulation, mature ethical considerations, and comprehensive training for educators (Slomp et al., 2024).

Recommendations for Addressing AI Challenges in Engineering Education

Among the 22 selected papers and the top 20 identified keywords, a clear emphasis is placed on the use of AI, particularly in the context of learning development. AI has a significant impact on engineering education, influencing teaching, learning, and assessment processes. For example, the integration of computational thinking (CT) into STEM education has been shown to develop critical and analytical thinking skills, including problem-solving capabilities. STEM learning environments help students acquire essential AI and ML competencies (Asunda et al., 2023). Additionally, AI-powered virtual assistants can support students in identifying similar problems related to their academic projects. Personalized AI assistants help reduce the time needed to solve complex challenges by offering relevant and timely solutions (González et al., 2022). Despite these benefits, AI also presents several challenges. One such challenge is academic integrity, particularly in relation to detecting plagiarism and misconduct during assessments. For instance, Nikolic et al. (2023) explored how ChatGPT performed across assessment prompts from ten subjects at seven Australian universities. The findings revealed that ChatGPT passed several assessments and excelled in some types, raising questions about the validity of traditional assessment formats in the presence of generative AI. Apart from that one example, integrating AI and engineering education has several challenges. The 22 selected papers address the following challenges in engineering education: academic integrity, pedagogical adaptation, discipline-specific implementation, curriculum integration and institutional, computational thinking, and interdisciplinary and ethical concerns. The following describes recommendations for the challenges that must be faced.

Ensuring Academic Integrity

Challenge: The emergence of generative AI tools like ChatGPT, GitHub Copilot, and Google Gemini has transformed how students approach assignments and assessments, posing risks to academic integrity. Nikolic et al. (2024) benchmarked ChatGPT's capabilities across institutions and found that its performance in academic settings complicates efforts to ensure fair evaluation. A key challenge lies in redesigning assessments that limit overreliance on AI tools while maintaining academic rigor. Educators must also teach students to use AI responsibly, leveraging its benefits without encouraging dishonesty. Further issues include AI-generated bias, inaccuracies, and over-dependence. Policies must clarify that ChatGPT and similar tools are intended as supplementary aids—not replacements for physical classes or laboratory experiences (Modran et al., 2024). Nikolic et al. (2024) recommend shifting towards open-book formats, oral examinations, and project-based assessments to counter AI misuse.

Recommendation: To safeguard academic integrity, institutions should implement comprehensive policies that combine open-book exams, oral assessments, and project-based evaluations. These formats can help reduce dependence on generative AI by assessing students' understanding through application and articulation. Additionally, the use of AI-detection tools should be mandated to identify possible misuse and ensure consistent enforcement. These strategies must be widely communicated across institutional levels and incorporated into standard academic policies to serve as benchmarks for responsible AI integration.

Reinforcing Pedagogical Practices

Challenge: AI introduces novel opportunities for teaching and learning, but its successful implementation requires a shift in pedagogical approaches—something many educators are not yet fully equipped to undertake (Acut et al., 2025). Núñez and Lantada (2020) identified a key challenge: striking a balance between harnessing AI's potential and preserving traditional engineering education's emphasis on critical thinking and problem-solving. Baltaci et al. (2024) found that integrating AI into electrical engineering requires educators to transition from instructor-centered models to more collaborative, AI-enhanced approaches. However, a significant barrier remains the lack of comprehensive faculty training programs. Rodríguez-Calderón and González-García (2024) also emphasized that current AI-enhanced models often fail to consider discipline-specific requirements and diverse learning styles. Bordel and Alcarria (2024) noted that while AI tools can boost engagement, they may not align well with all students' technological competencies. González et al. (2022) pointed out that virtual AI assistants can personalize learning, yet challenges persist in ensuring compatibility with existing pedagogical frameworks and promoting active student participation.

Recommendation: Faculty training programs should prioritize AI-enhanced pedagogical methods, focusing on active learning strategies, collaborative projects, and hybrid models that combine traditional and AI-driven instructional approaches. These programs must also address digital literacy and instructional design to ensure accessibility for both educators and students.

Overcoming Discipline-Specific Barriers

Challenge: Integrating AI into specialized engineering disciplines—such as civil, materials, or geotechnical engineering—requires domain-specific adaptations that are often resource-intensive and technologically complex. Ocak et al. (2023) emphasized the need for tailored AI training datasets and computational resources to enable meaningful integration in civil engineering. Galos et al. (2024) highlighted the difficulty of introducing AI to disciplines without a strong tradition in CT or computer programming. Lez'er et al. (2019) pointed out the steep learning curve and lack of tools tailored to geotechnics. Oliveira and Vrančić (2024) analyzed the use of Generative Pre-trained Transformers (GPTs) in control engineering and stressed the need for AI tools to provide technically accurate, context-specific outputs without oversimplifying complex concepts. Similarly, Yaghoubi et al. (2023) showcased innovative uses of AI in instrumentation engineering but also revealed challenges in applying AI creatively within technically demanding contexts. These studies collectively underscore the importance of discipline-specific AI solutions and cross-disciplinary collaboration.

Recommendation: Institutions should foster collaboration between AI specialists and engineering faculty to develop tailored AI applications for specific disciplines (Acut et al., 2025). Investments should be made in research, computing infrastructure, and simulation tools that allow students to apply AI to real-world engineering scenarios. Pilot programs, project-based learning, and case-based learning models can further facilitate this transition.

Redesigning Curricula for AI Integration

Challenge: Integrating AI into engineering curricula involves overcoming challenges related to resource constraints, faculty preparedness, and maintaining a balance between traditional engineering content and AI education. Shvedchykova et al. (2023) emphasized the paradigm shift needed to shift from theory-based curricula to practical, AI-driven learning. Memarian (2023) discussed the need to localize AI curricula to reflect cultural diversity and contextual relevance—an issue compounded by limited resources and expertise in many regions. Slomp et al. (2024) noted the difficulties of scaling AI-enhanced learning systems across institutions with varying levels of technological infrastructure. Jaurez et al. (2022), through the application of the Cynefin framework, highlighted the complexity of predicting and managing learning processes in AI-based systems, underscoring the need for innovative methodologies.

Recommendation: Universities should adopt a phased approach to curriculum redesign, beginning with AI-focused elective courses and interdisciplinary collaborations. AI should be embedded within traditional engineering problems to ensure relevance and contextual learning. Faculty development programs and institutional policies should support gradual integration, ensuring that all stakeholders are equipped to manage the evolving educational landscape.

Building Computational Literacy

Challenge: The integration of AI technologies often requires a foundational understanding of CT across disciplines, which presents an additional barrier in engineering education. Asunda et al. (2023) highlighted the difficulty of embedding CT into engineering curricula as a prerequisite for meaningful AI adoption. Many students and even educators lack the computational literacy necessary to fully leverage AI tools and techniques.

Recommendation: Engineering programs should introduce CT early in the curriculum by embedding AI literacy modules into foundational engineering courses. Moreover, interdisciplinary collaboration with computer science and data science departments should be encouraged to help students and faculty build essential computational skills and foster AI readiness.

Addressing Ethical Concerns and Accessibility

Challenge: The use of AI in education raises critical ethical concerns, especially related to fairness, transparency, accessibility, and the potential erosion of traditional educational models. Moolman et al. (2023) discussed the development of photorealistic AI-based virtual lecturers, revealing how such technologies challenge established norms of teacher authenticity and human interaction in the classroom. Similarly, Martel et al. (2024) explored the risks of bias embedded in AI algorithms and the diminishing human-centric nature of education. Osunbunmi et al. (2024), pointed out that generative AI tools may exacerbate inequalities, as underprivileged students often lack the resources to effectively access and utilize these technologies. These ethical and accessibility concerns require continuous attention and inclusive policy development.

Recommendation: Educational institutions should establish and enforce ethical guidelines for AI use in teaching and learning environments. These guidelines must ensure transparency, fairness, and accountability—particularly in AI-driven assessment systems (Garcia et al., 2025). Investments should be made in the development of accessible AI tools to ensure equitable learning opportunities for students across diverse socio-economic backgrounds.

CONCLUSION

AI is not only a new tool in learning but also part of a broader philosophical shift in how we understand teaching, learning, and knowledge creation. In the context of engineering education, AI offers transformative opportunities to enhance teaching practices, personalize learning, and modernize assessment methods. However, its integration also presents a range of challenges, including concerns about academic integrity, pedagogical adaptation, discipline-specific constraints, curriculum redesign, computational literacy, and ethical use. Addressing these challenges requires a strategic, multifaceted approach. Institutions must safeguard academic integrity through innovative assessment methods, train faculty in AI-supported pedagogies, invest in infrastructure for discipline-specific AI applications, and gradually integrate AI into existing curricula. Strengthening computational literacy by embedding foundational AI and data science concepts early in the program is equally crucial. Furthermore, ethical considerations must be central to policy development to ensure fair, transparent, and inclusive use of AI technologies. As AI becomes increasingly embedded in educational systems, future research should focus on scalable and equitable solutions tailored to the diverse needs of engineering education. With sustained investment in infrastructure, training, and ethical governance, AI has the potential to make engineering education more effective, engaging, and accessible—empowering future engineers to thrive in a rapidly evolving technological landscape.

REFERENCES

Acut, D. P., Gamusa, E. V., Pernaa, J., Yuenyong, C., Pantaleon, A. T., Espina, R. C., Sim, M. J. C., & Garcia, M. B. (2025). AI Shaming Among Teacher Education Students: A Reflection on Acceptance and Identity in the Age of Generative Tools. In *Pitfalls of AI Integration in Education: Skill Obsolescence, Misuse, and Bias*. IGI Global., DOI: 10.4018/979-8-3373-0122-8.ch005

Acut, D. P., Malabago, N. K., Malicoban, E. V., Galamiton, N. S., & Garcia, M. B. (2024). "ChatGPT 4.0 Ghosted Us While Conducting Literature Search:" Modeling the Chatbot's Generated Non-Existent References Using Regression Analysis. *Internet Reference Services Quarterly*, ●●●, 1–26. DOI: 10.1080/10875301.2024.2426793

Al Husaeni, D. F., Haristiani, N., Wahyudin, W., & Rasim, R. (2022). Chatbot Artificial Intelligence as Educational Tools in Science and Engineering Education: A Literature Review and Bibliometric Mapping Analysis with Its Advantages and Disadvantages. *ASEAN Journal of Science and Engineering*, 4(1), 93–118. DOI: 10.17509/ajse.v4i1.67429

Alneyadi, S., Wardat, Y., Alshannag, Q., & Abu-Al-Aish, A. (2023). The Effect of Using Smart E-Learning App on the Academic Achievement of Eighth-Grade Students. *Eurasia Journal of Mathematics, Science and Technology Education*, 19(4), 1–11. DOI: 10.29333/ejmste/13067

Arif, Y. M., Ayunda, N., Diah, N. M., & Garcia, M. B. (2024). A Systematic Review of Serious Games for Health Education: Technology, Challenges, and Future Directions. In *Transformative Approaches to Patient Literacy and Healthcare Innovation* (pp. 20–45). IGI Global., DOI: 10.4018/979-8-3693-3661-8.ch002

Arif, Y. M., Nugroho, F., Aini, Q., Fauzan, A. C., & Garcia, M. B. (2025). A Systematic Literature Review of Serious Games for Physical Education: Technologies, Implementations, and Evaluations. In *Global Innovations in Physical Education and Health*. IGI Global., DOI: 10.4018/979-8-3693-3952-7.ch001

Asunda, P., Faezipour, M., Tolemy, J., & Engel, M. (2023). Embracing Computational Thinking as an Impetus for Artificial Intelligence in Integrated STEM Disciplines through Engineering and Technology Education . *Journal of Technology Education*, 34(2), 43–63. DOI: 10.21061/jte.v34i2.a.3

Athilingam, P., & He, H.-G. (2024). ChatGPT in Nursing Education: Opportunities and Challenges. *Teaching and Learning in Nursing*, 19(1), 97–101. DOI: 10.1016/j.teln.2023.11.004

Baltaci, K., Herrmann, M., & Turkmen, A. (2024). Integrating Artificial Intelligence into Electrical Engineering Education: A Paradigm Shift in Teaching and Learning. *2024 ASEE Annual Conference & Exposition*. DOI: 10.18260/1-2--47644

Bordel, B., & Alcarria, R. (2024). Enhancing the Students' Motivation and Learning in Network Engineering Courses Through Artificial Intelligence Tools and Applications. *Lecture Notes in Educational Technology*, 21-31. DOI: 10.1007/978-981-97-2468-0_3

Bosman, L., Kotla, B., Madamanchi, A., Bartholomew, S., & Byrd, V. (2022). Preparing the Future Entrepreneurial Engineering Workforce Using Web-Based AI-Enabled Tools. *European Journal of Engineering Education*, 48(5), 972–989. DOI: 10.1080/03043797.2022.2119122

Bozkurt, A., Xiao, J., Farrow, R., Bai, J. Y. H., Nerantzi, C., Moore, S., Dron, J., Stracke, C. M., Singh, L., Crompton, H., Koutropoulos, A., Terentev, E., Pazurek, A., Nichols, M., Sidorkin, A. M., Costello, E., Watson, S., Mulligan, D., Honeychurch, S., & Asino, T. I. (2024). The Manifesto for Teaching and Learning in a Time of Generative AI: A Critical Collective Stance to Better Navigate the Future. *Open Praxis*, *16*(4), 487–513. DOI: 10.55982/openpraxis.16.4.777

Chen, X., Xie, H., Zou, D., & Hwang, G.-J. (2020). Application and Theory Gaps During the Rise of Artificial Intelligence in Education. *Computers and Education: Artificial Intelligence*, *1*, 1–20. DOI: 10.1016/j.caeai.2020.100002

Galos, J. L., Friedman, A. Z. C., Jamosmos, E., Allec, S. I., Blinzler, B., Grunenfelder, L., & Carberry, A. R. (2024). Teaching Artificial Intelligence and Machine Learning to Materials Engineering Students Through Plastic 3D Printing. *ASEE Annual Conference and Exposition, Conference Proceedings*. DOI: 10.18260/1-2--48057

Gantalao, L. C., Calzada, J. G. D., Capuyan, D. L., Lumantas, B. C., Acut, D. P., & Garcia, M. B. (2025). Equipping the Next Generation of Technicians: Navigating School Infrastructure and Technical Knowledge in the Age of AI Integration. In *Pitfalls of AI Integration in Education: Skill Obsolescence, Misuse, and Bias*. IGI Global., DOI: 10.4018/979-8-3373-0122-8.ch009

Garcia, M. B. (2024). The Paradox of Artificial Creativity: Challenges and Opportunities of Generative AI Artistry. *Creativity Research Journal*, ●●●, 1–14. DOI: 10.1080/10400419.2024.2354622

Garcia, M. B. (2025). Teaching and Learning Computer Programming Using ChatGPT: A Rapid Review of Literature Amid the Rise of Generative AI Technologies. *Education and Information Technologies*, ●●●, 1–25. DOI: 10.1007/s10639-025-13452-5

Garcia, M. B., Arif, Y. M., Khlaif, Z. N., Zhu, M., de Almeida, R. P. P., de Almeida, R. S., & Masters, K. (2024). Effective Integration of Artificial Intelligence in Medical Education: Practical Tips and Actionable Insights. In *Transformative Approaches to Patient Literacy and Healthcare Innovation* (pp. 1-19). IGI Global. DOI: 10.4018/979-8-3693-3661-8.ch001

Garcia, M. B., Garcia, P. S., Maaliw, R. R.III, Lagrazon, P. G. G., Arif, Y. M., Ofosu-Ampong, K., Yousef, A. M. F., & Vaithilingam, C. A. (2024). Technoethical Considerations for Advancing Health Literacy and Medical Practice: A Posthumanist Framework in the Age of Healthcare 5.0. In *Emerging Technologies for Health Literacy and Medical Practice*. IGI Global., DOI: 10.4018/979-8-3693-1214-8.ch001

Garcia, M. B., Rosak-Szyrocka, J., Yılmaz, R., Metwally, A. H. S., Acut, D. P., Ofosu-Ampong, K., Erdoğdu, F., Fung, C. Y., & Bozkurt, A. (2025). Rethinking Educational Assessment in the Age of Generative AI: Actionable Strategies to Mitigate Academic Dishonesty. In *Pitfalls of AI Integration in Education: Skill Obsolescence, Misuse, and Bias*. IGI Global., DOI: 10.4018/979-8-3373-0122-8.ch001

González, L. A., Neyem, A., Contreras-McKay, I., & Molina, D. (2022). Improving Learning Experiences in Software Engineering Capstone Courses Using Artificial Intelligence Virtual Assistants. *Computer Applications in Engineering Education*, *30*(5), 1370–1389. DOI: 10.1002/cae.22526

Gupta, P., Mahajan, R., Badhera, U., & Kushwaha, P. S. (2024). Integrating Generative AI in Management Education: A Mixed-Methods Study Using Social Construction of Technology Theory. *International Journal of Management Education, 22*(3), 1–19. DOI: 10.1016/j.ijme.2024.101017

Heck, P., & Schouten, G. (2021). Lessons Learned from Educating AI Engineers. *2021 IEEE/ACM 1st Workshop on AI Engineering - Software Engineering for AI (WAIN)*, 1-4. DOI: 10.1109/WAIN52551.2021.00013

Heyn, H.-M., Knauss, E., Muhammad, A. P., Eriksson, O., Linder, J., Subbiah, P., Pradhan, S. K., & Tungal, S. (2021). Requirement Engineering Challenges for AI-intense Systems Development. *2021 IEEE/ACM 1st Workshop on AI Engineering - Software Engineering for AI (WAIN)*, 89-96. DOI: 10.1109/WAIN52551.2021.00020

Jaurez, J., Radhakrishnan, B., & Altamirano, N. (2022). Application of Artificial Intelligence and the Cynefin Framework to establish a Statistical System Prediction and Control (SSPC) in Engineering Education. *2022 ASEE Annual Conference & Exposition.* DOI: 10.18260/1-2--41718

Johri, A. (2020). Artificial Intelligence and Engineering Education. *Journal of Engineering Education, 109*(3), 358–361. DOI: 10.1002/jee.20326

Lam, P. X., Mai, P. Q. H., Nguyen, Q. H., Pham, T., Nguyen, T. H. H., & Nguyen, T. H. (2024). Enhancing Educational Evaluation Through Predictive Student Assessment Modeling. *Computers and Education: Artificial Intelligence, 6*, 1–14. DOI: 10.1016/j.caeai.2024.100244

Lez'er, V., Semeryanova, N., Kopytova, A., & Kvach, I. (2019). Application of Artificial Intelligence in the Field of Geotechnics and Engineering Education. *E3S Web of Conferences, 110*, 1-8. DOI: 10.1051/e3sconf/201911002094

Lobo, M. D., Miravent, S., de Almeida, R. P. P., & Garcia, M. B. (2025). Advancing Precision in Physical Education and Sports Science: A Review of Medical Imaging Methods for Assessing Body Composition. In *Global Innovations in Physical Education and Health.* IGI Global., DOI: 10.4018/979-8-3693-3952-7.ch011

Lu, Q., Zhu, L., Xu, X., Whittle, J., & Xing, Z. (2022). Towards a Roadmap on Software Engineering for Responsible AI. *Proceedings of the 1st International Conference on AI Engineering: Software Engineering for AI*, 101-112. DOI: 10.1145/3522664.3528607

Mangubat, J. C., Mangubat, M. R., Uy, T. B. L., Acut, D. P., & Garcia, M. B. (2025). Safeguarding Educational Innovations Amid AI Disruptions: A Reassessment of Patenting for Sustained Intellectual Property Protection. In *Pitfalls of AI Integration in Education: Skill Obsolescence, Misuse, and Bias.* IGI Global., DOI: 10.4018/979-8-3373-0122-8.ch013

Martel, J.-L., Arsenault, R., & Brissette, F. (2024). Artificial Intelligence in Engineering Education: The Future Is Now. *Lecture Notes in Civil Engineering*, 103-117. DOI: 10.1007/978-3-031-60415-7_8

Memarian, B. (2023). Indigenizing the Artificial Intelligence (AI) Programmed Engineering Education Curriculum, Challenges and Future Potentials. *2023 ASEE Annual Conference & Exposition.* DOI: 10.18260/1-2--43678

Miller, J. C., Miranda, J. P. P., & Tolentino, J. C. G. (2025). Artificial Intelligence in Physical Education: A Review. In *Global Innovations in Physical Education and Health*. IGI Global., DOI: 10.4018/979-8-3693-3952-7.ch002

Modran, H. A., Chamunorwa, T., Ursu iu, D., & Samoilă, C. (2024). Integrating Artificial Intelligence and ChatGPT into Higher Engineering Education. *Lecture Notes in Networks and Systems*, 499-510. DOI: 10.1007/978-3-031-51979-6_52

Moolman, J. H., Boyle, F., & Walsh, J. (2023). Revolutionising Engineering Education: Creating Photorealistic Virtual Human Lecturers Using Artificial Intelligence And Computer Generated Images. *European Society for Engineering Education (SEFI)*. DOI: 10.21427/CDBM-4P41

Mthombeni, N. H., Maladzhi, R., Moloi, K., Mashifana, T., Tsoeu, M., & Nemavhola, F. (2023). AI ChatBots as Inherent Tools for Comprehensive Learning of Engineering Design: A Systematic review. *2023 World Engineering Education Forum - Global Engineering Deans Council (WEEF-GEDC)*, 1-6. DOI: 10.1109/WEEF-GEDC59520.2023.10343866

Nikolic, S., Daniel, S., Haque, R., Belkina, M., Hassan, G. M., Grundy, S., Lyden, S., Neal, P., & Sandison, C. (2023). ChatGPT Versus Engineering Education Assessment: A Multidisciplinary and Multi-Institutional Benchmarking and Analysis of This Generative Artificial Intelligence Tool to Investigate Assessment Integrity. *European Journal of Engineering Education*, 48(4), 559–614. DOI: 10.1080/03043797.2023.2213169

Nikolic, S., Sandison, C., Haque, R., Daniel, S., Grundy, S., Belkina, M., Lyden, S., Hassan, G. M., & Neal, P. (2024). ChatGPT, Copilot, Gemini, SciSpace and Wolfram Versus Higher Education Assessments: An Updated Multi-Institutional Study of the Academic Integrity Impacts of Generative Artificial Intelligence (GenAI) on Assessment, Teaching and Learning in Engineering. *Australasian Journal of Engineering Education*, 29(2), 126–153. DOI: 10.1080/22054952.2024.2372154

Nti, I. K., Adekoya, A. F., Weyori, B. A., & Nyarko-Boateng, O. (2021). Applications of Artificial Intelligence in Engineering and Manufacturing: A Systematic Review. *Journal of Intelligent Manufacturing*, 33(6), 1581–1601. DOI: 10.1007/s10845-021-01771-6

Núñez, J. L. M., & Lantada, A. D. (2020). Artificial Intelligence Aided Engineering Education: State of the Art, Potentials and Challenges. *International Journal of Engineering Education*, 36, 1740–1751. https://www.researchgate.net/publication/345141282

Ocak, A., Nigdeli, S. M., Bekdaş, G., & Işıkdağ, Ü. (2023). Artificial Intelligence and Deep Learning in Civil Engineering. *Studies in Systems, Decision and Control*, 265-288. DOI: 10.1007/978-3-031-34728-3_13

Oliveira, P. B. M., & Vrančić, D. (2024). Evaluation of GPTs for Control Engineering Education: Towards Artificial General Intelligence. *IFAC-PapersOnLine*, 58(7), 97–102. DOI: 10.1016/j.ifacol.2024.08.017

Olugbade, D. (2025). A Systematic Review of the Role of AI-Enabled Chatbots in Modern Education: Benefits, Risks, and Implementation Complexity. In *Pitfalls of AI Integration in Education: Skill Obsolescence, Misuse, and Bias*. IGI Global., DOI: 10.4018/979-8-3373-0122-8.ch018

Osunbunmi, I. S., Cutler, S., & Dansu, V. B., Y., Bamidele, B. R., Udosen, A. N., Arinze, L. C. O., A. V., Moyaki, D., Hicks, M. J., & Shih, B. P. (2024). Generative Artificial Intelligence (GAI)-Assisted Learning: Pushing the Boundaries of Engineering Education. *2024 ASEE Annual Conference & Exposition*. DOI: 10.18260/1-2--47041

Ouyang, F., & Jiao, P. (2021). Artificial Intelligence in Education: The Three Paradigms. *Computers and Education: Artificial Intelligence, 2*, 1–6. DOI: 10.1016/j.caeai.2021.100020

Qadir, J. (2023). Engineering Education in the Era of ChatGPT: Promise and Pitfalls of Generative AI for Education. *2023 IEEE Global Engineering Education Conference (EDUCON)*, 1-9. DOI: 10.1109/EDUCON54358.2023.10125121

Rodríguez-Calderón, R., & González-García, S. (2024). Learning Based on Artificial Intelligence for Engineering Courses. *2024 IEEE World Engineering Education Conference (EDUNINE)*, 1-5. DOI: 10.1109/EDUNINE60625.2024.10500547

Sah, C. K., Xiaoli, L., Islam, M. M., & Islam, M. K. (2024). Navigating the AI Frontier: A Critical Literature Review on Integrating Artificial Intelligence into Software Engineering Education. *2024 36th International Conference on Software Engineering Education and Training*, 1-5. DOI: 10.1109/CSEET62301.2024.10663054

Santos, P., Urgel, K., & Moreno, V. (2024). Generative Artificial Intelligence in Teaching and Learning of ICT Engineering Education: A Literature Review and Illustrative Scenarios. *2024 47th MIPRO ICT and Electronics Convention (MIPRO)*, 1338-1343. DOI: 10.1109/MIPRO60963.2024.10569779

Schleiss, J., Hense, J., Kist, A., Schlingensiepen, J., & Stober, S. (2022). Teaching AI Competencies in Engineering Using Projects and Open Educational Resources. *Towards a new future in engineering education, new scenarios that european alliances of tech universities open up*, 1592-1600. DOI: 10.5821/conference-9788412322262.1258

Shoaib, M., Sayed, N., Singh, J., Shafi, J., Khan, S., & Ali, F. (2024). AI Student Success Predictor: Enhancing Personalized Learning in Campus Management Systems. *Computers in Human Behavior, 158*, 108301. DOI: 10.1016/j.chb.2024.108301

Shvedchykova, I., Burger, W., & Soloshych, I. (2023). Research-Based Learning: Integration of Artificial Intelligence into the Curriculum of Electrical Engineering Students. *2023 IEEE 5th International Conference on Modern Electrical and Energy System (MEES)*, 1-5. DOI: 10.1109/MEES61502.2023.10402542

Silva, A. O., & Janes, D. S. (2023). Artificial Intelligence in Education: What are the Opportunities and Challenges? *Review of Artificial Intelligence in Education, 5*(00), e018. Advance online publication. DOI: 10.37497/rev.artif.intell.educ.v5i00.18

Slomp, E. M., Ropelato, D., Bonatti, C., & da Silva, M. D. (2024). Adaptive Learning in Engineering Courses: How Artificial Intelligence (AI) Can Improve Academic Outcomes. *2024 IEEE World Engineering Education Conference (EDUNINE)*, 1-6. DOI: 10.1109/EDUNINE60625.2024.10500580

Wang, T., Lund, B. D., Marengo, A., Pagano, A., Mannuru, N. R., Teel, Z. A., & Pange, J. (2023). Exploring the Potential Impact of Artificial Intelligence (AI) on International Students in Higher Education: Generative AI, Chatbots, Analytics, and International Student Success. *Applied Sciences (Basel, Switzerland)*, *13*(11), 1–15. DOI: 10.3390/app13116716

Xiao, J., Bozkurt, A., Nichols, M., Pazurek, A., Stracke, C. M., Bai, J. Y. H., Farrow, R., Mulligan, D., Nerantzi, C., Sharma, R. C., Singh, L., Frumin, I., Swindell, A., Honeychurch, S., Bond, M., Dron, J., Moore, S., Leng, J., & Slagter van Tryon, P. J.. (2025). Venturing into the Unknown: Critical Insights into Grey Areas and Pioneering Future Directions in Educational Generative AI Research. *TechTrends*, ●●●, 1–16. DOI: 10.1007/s11528-025-01060-6

Xu, W., & Ouyang, F. (2022). The Application of AI Technologies in STEM Education: A Systematic Review from 2011 to 2021. *International Journal of STEM Education*, *9*(1), 1–20. DOI: 10.1186/s40594-022-00377-5

Yaghoubi, A. A., Karimi, P., Moradi, E., & Gavagsaz-Ghoachani, R. (2023). Implementing Engineering Education Based on Posing a Riddle in Field of Instrumentation and Artificial Intelligence. *2023 9th International Conference on Control, Instrumentation and Automation (ICCIA)*, 1-5. DOI: 10.1109/ICCIA61416.2023.10506384

Zawacki-Richter, O., Marín, V. I., Bond, M., & Gouverneur, F. (2019). Systematic Review of Research on Artificial Intelligence Applications in Higher Education – Where Are the Educators? *International Journal of Educational Technology in Higher Education*, *16*(1), 1–27. DOI: 10.1186/s41239-019-0171-0

KEY TERMS AND DEFINITIONS

Artificial Intelligence (AI): A field of computer science focused on creating systems capable of performing tasks that typically require human intelligence, such as learning, reasoning, problem-solving, and language processing.

ChatGPT: An advanced language model developed by OpenAI that generates human-like responses in natural language, often used in educational settings for tutoring, answering questions, and interactive learning support.

Engineering Education: An academic discipline that prepares students for careers in engineering through a combination of theoretical instruction, applied learning, laboratory work, and project-based experiences.

Generative AI: A type of machine learning technology that produces new content—such as text, images, or audio—based on patterns in training data, often used to enhance creativity, automate writing tasks, or personalize educational content.

Open Educational Resources (OER): Freely available and openly licensed instructional materials that can be used, adapted, and shared to support learning, including textbooks, videos, assignments, and other teaching tools.

Systematic Literature Review: A structured research method used to collect, evaluate, and synthesize existing studies on a specific topic using predefined criteria and procedures. It aims to provide a comprehensive and unbiased summary of current knowledge, often following frameworks like PRISMA to ensure transparency and replicability.

Chapter 17
Challenges and Opportunities of Integrating Generative Artificial Intelligence in Higher Education:
A Systematic Review

Vanessa Izquierdo-Álvarez
https://orcid.org/0000-0002-0760-9017
University of Salamanca, Spain

Claudia Jimeno-Postigo
https://orcid.org/0009-0000-8671-3033
University of Salamanca, Spain

ABSTRACT

Generative artificial intelligence (GenAI) is an emerging technology that has significantly transformed the interaction between humans and machines. GenAI has the capacity to create content such as text, images, and videos, and it even uses human language. In the educational field, tools such as ChatGPT stand out for their ability to maintain coherent conversations, simulating human interactions. This study aims to offer a comprehensive and critical view of the convergence of GenAI and higher education. To this end, a systematic literature review has been carried out following the PRISMA protocol through the WoS and Dialnet databases. The analysis focuses on understanding the role of GenAI in this context, identifying both the opportunities and challenges associated with its implementation. The results of the study highlight key challenge areas, promising trends, and future prospects. Likewise, the effects of GenAI on students and teachers are analyzed, paying special attention to the ethical and social implications that accompany its integration into higher education.

DOI: 10.4018/979-8-3373-0122-8.ch017

INTRODUCTION

Generative Artificial Intelligence (GenAI) has become crucially important in the contemporary world, transforming key sectors such as education and learning by opening new and innovative opportunities for learning (Sánchez-Prieto et al., 2024). This growing impact is due to the role that companies and organizations have given in this technology to optimize their processes and services, making it a strategic tool with global reach. GenAI's ability to profoundly influence daily and professional life lies in its ability to perform human tasks more quickly and accurately, automating processes and increasing operational efficiency. This automation potential not only improves productivity but also redefines the way decision-making is carried out. Thanks to its learning capacity, accuracy and precision, GenAI is positioned as an invaluable resource in the management and analysis of large volumes of data. It can process complex information in real time, allowing it to identify patterns, generate relevant insights and optimize results. This level of analysis not only saves time but also promotes more informed and strategic decision-making. Ultimately, AI is not only transforming sectors such as education and learning, but it is redefining the very foundations of efficiency and innovation in multiple areas, consolidating itself as a driving force in the evolution of modern societies. In this sense, according to Kostopoulos and Kostopoulos (2021), GenAI has a key role to play in revolutionizing education by personalizing learning, providing educators with tools to improve teaching. However, it also poses ethical and practical challenges that need to be addressed (Bostrom & Yudkowsky, 2014). For Celik (2023), the use of technology in education over the past ten years has changed several aspects of learning. In this sense, making educational resources more easily accessible, expanding the reach of higher education outside of typical classroom settings, also creating new opportunities for both teachers and students. For example, by leveraging the potential of GenAI to improve teaching methods, the learning experience, or purely administrative tasks (Kshetri & Voas, 2024). Also, by providing personalized learning experiences for students or improving instructional processes for teachers (Sun & Zhou, 2024).

LITERATURE REVIEW

Origins of AI

The origins of AI date back to the mid-20th century, with pioneers such as Alan Turing who posed the question "Can machines think?" (Turing, 1950). Early research focused on creating machines capable of performing simple logic and calculation tasks. However, the computational limits of the time significantly restricted these advances. In the 1980s and 1990s, artificial neural networks experienced a resurgence. These networks, inspired by the functioning of the human brain, made it possible to tackle more complex problems such as pattern recognition and machine learning (LeCun et al., 2015). However, a lack of data and computational power limited its application on a large scale. Subsequently, with the increase in computational power and the availability of large data sets, deep learning became the driving force behind recent advances in AI. Deep, multi-layered neural networks have demonstrated an exceptional ability to learn complex representations of data, leading to significant advances in areas such as natural language processing, computer vision, and content generation (Goodfellow et al., 2016). Yet, despite impressive advances, AI still faces significant challenges, such as model interpretability, data privacy, and algorithmic bias. Future research is therefore geared towards developing more robust, explainable, and ethical models, as well as exploring new applications in fields such as medicine, science, or robotics (Russell & Norvig, 2021).

AI as a Concept

AI is a complex concept to define. For some authors, AI is a technical expression referring to "artefacts used to detect contexts or carry out actions in response to those contexts that have already been detected" (Bryson, 2018, pp. 127-159). The European Commission defines it as software systems (and possibly also hardware) designed by humans that, when faced with a complex objective, act in the physical or digital dimension, perceiving their environment and interpreting data (structured or unstructured) or processing the information derived from the data and deciding the best actions to achieve the previously stated objectives. According to the Recovery, Transformation and Resilience Plan of the Government of Spain, it can be defined as a field of computing that focuses on creating systems that can perform tasks that normally require human intelligence, such as learning, reasoning and perception (Government of Spain, 2021). For Hwang et al. (2020), is a machine-based technique with algorithmic power to make predictions, diagnoses, recommendations, and decisions, but other authors define it as *"the ability of a system to correctly interpret external data, learn from said data, and use that learning to achieve specific goals and tasks through flexible adaptation"* (Kaplan & Haenlein, 2019) or *"any technique that allows computers to imitate human behavior"* (Jiang et al., 2022). However, regardless of its conceptual diversity, the capacity to build such artifacts has increased and, with it, the impact they have on our society (Bryson, 2018).

In recent years, there have been great advances in the field of AI, giving rise to a new concept: GenAI. GenAI is a subfield of AI that focuses on the autonomous creation of data, images, text, and other content. Unlike conventional AI, which focuses on decision-making and data processing, GenAI focuses on the generation of content that can be indistinguishable from that created by humans (ISDI, 2023. Its potential extends beyond the creation and analysis of data, as it is also responsible for creating new content, simulating results, and streamlining processes, thus being more efficient (for example, creating new documents in record time) and more creative. When we talk about GenAI, we can differentiate between that which has only one type of input (unimodal) or that which allows us to use several inputs (multimodal). The most recent updates indicate that GenAI will be multimodal, that is, it will be able to listen, observe and interact with users (Du et al., 2023) and will access updated information from the Internet in real time.

ChatGPT: Background, Impact and Limitations

ChatGPT was launched in November 2022 (Sánchez, 2024), a chatbot developed by OpenAI to offer human-like responses (Eysenbach, 2023; Lo, 2023). For Kashyap (2023), ChatGPT is an AI language model that can provide conversations and answers to complex queries like those of a person. It can also be used to create individualized and engaging learning experiences, a capability that has significant implications for the educational field. Thanks to machine learning, large language models, such as ChatGPT, can carry out various tasks, such as summarizing, expanding information, translating texts, making predictions, creating scripts, writing code, and generating speeches with great accuracy (Brown et al., 2020). This is why ChatGPT can significantly improve learning based on the generation of personalized content, due to its feedback capacity, and its adaptation to the students' own requirements. Furthermore,

ChatGPT's automatic grading and feedback features can also reduce teachers' workload. In this way, it helps teachers focus on other types of tasks, such as leading discussions or offering specialized help. This is why the use of ChatGPT has seen a surge in popularity in recent months due to its ability to generate new content and answer questions naturally. However, as with any technology, it is important to point out its limitations and characteristics in the educational field (Celik et al., 2022) as it presents various challenges. For example, it is important to warn about privacy and security issues (Floridi & Taddeo, 2016), in addition to the lack of transparency in AI algorithms (Burrell, 2016). Specifically, one of the biggest limitations of ChatGPT is the lack of precision or consistency of the responses it generates, since many of them are unreliable or inappropriate (Sánchez-Prieto et al., 2024).

Another limitation of the GenAI tool is based on the bias of the training data, as it often lacks context or understanding in those topics that have to do with ethics and morals, as well as having linguistic restrictions since it was designed in English. In this sense, many of these limitations are generated by the prompts (Table 1), which are phrases or questions used to provide guidelines to a language model to produce a response (Radford et al., 2018). The quality of the prompts is one of the most important factors to achieve a successful conversation in ChatGPT (Sánchez-Prieto et al., 2024). On the other hand, poorly defined prompts can lead to unfocused and unproductive conversations, resulting in a less engaging and informative experience (Sun et al., 2019). Therefore, to interact appropriately with ChatGPT, it is necessary to provide a clear and precise context with very specific prompts so that it understands the task at hand (Sánchez-Prieto et al., 2024). In short, it is necessary to provide it with an adequate framework that allows it to understand the information provided to it.

Table 1. Classification of prompts

Types	Definition
Sequential	They seek to create a logical progression in the conversation by using a sequence of previous texts that allow obtaining a more elaborate and contextualized response.
Comparative	They intend for the AI to compare two or more things and/or situations to obtain more specific results.
Argumentative	They ensure that the AI generates a clear and coherent argument or position on a particular topic. In this type of prompts, direct requests are usually structured for the AI to argue for or against an idea, using information previously provided.
Professional Perspective	The AI is required to take on the role of a specific individual or role and describe a topic in each context.
Wishlist	Commonly used structure to get more specific and relevant responses from Chat GPT. By providing a list of specific requirements to be met, users can provide detailed information about their needs and preferences, allowing Chat GPT to provide a more precise and focused response.

Source: Adapted from Morales (2023)

In addition to the prompts mentioned above, new ways of using chatbot and ChatGPT technology in education are being investigated, such as the creation of personalized virtual tutors, gamification (Morales et al., 2016), and dialogue-based learning. These advances in educational technology aim to evolve the way students learn, and educators teach, offering more personalized and effective learning experiences.

Implementation of AI in Education and the Role of Teachers

With the arrival of GenAI in education, the responses to this innovation have been diverse over the last few years, ranging from enthusiastic adoption to absolute rejection. While it is true, the educational community does not remain on the sidelines of this opportunity for improvement. Since it is a simple and accessible tool that, with proper implementation, offers a great benefit in the teaching-learning process (Brown et al., 2021). Hence, since its implementation, it has been considered a technological benchmark and is used massively. Added to these characteristics is its wide availability from anywhere, just as it can enrich educational content by providing access to a wide range of resources and perspectives (Rosenberg, 2019). That is why, with the integration of this type of tool, teachers can dedicate more time to mentoring and individualized guidance (Dede, 2010). As González-González (2023) argues, GenAI has emerged as a disruptive technology in the field of higher education.

Although AI has been developing in the educational field internationally for decades, it has experienced a great advance in the last ten years driven by the development of machine learning techniques, natural language processing (NLP) and neural networks, among other techniques. All of them use a large corpus of data for their training (Chen et al., 2022; Prahani et al., 2022). Added to this is the capacity of educational systems powered by GenAI to analyze classroom dynamics and student engagement. This, in turn, helps to identify at-risk students in real time, thus allowing for timely intervention (Tsai et al., 2020). In addition, GenAI in education has also gained notable attention for its potential to achieve significant advances in instructional methods and administrative tasks within educational environments (Chiu et al., 2023). It is for all these reasons that educational technology plays a crucial role in reshaping the teaching and learning landscape (Valtonen et al., 2022). Furthermore, the implementation of these technologies can improve accessibility and inclusivity in education, providing educational resources tailored to diverse needs and learning styles. Williamson and Eynon (2020) adds that GenAI provides new solutions for creating and distributing educational materials and improving personalized learning experiences. Other authors complement and expand these ideas by stating that GenAI has opened the debate around the potential of tools such as ChatGPT in teaching, learning and assessment processes:

While their integration in this context offers numerous opportunities (e.g., instant feedback, generation of resources and teaching materials, adaptive learning, interactivity, etc.), it also poses significant challenges that raise ethical and academic integrity concerns, such as the reliability of information, transparency regarding the sources used, or data privacy and security. (Gallent-Torres et al., 2023, p.1).

Anderson and Dron (2011) state that teachers now act more as facilitators of learning rather than being the primary source of knowledge. It is thanks to these types of systems that teachers can guide students to explore and understand information on their own, encouraging a more student-centered approach. Authors such as Holmes et al. (2019) point out that GenAI in education is redefining the role of teachers, transforming them into mentors and designers of personalized learning experiences. This shift allows teachers to focus on developing critical skills in students, such as critical thinking and problem-solving, rather than simply transmitting information. The adoption of GenAI technologies in education also fosters innovation and creativity in teaching practices. Williamson and Eynon (2020) argue that these technologies allow teachers to experiment with new methodologies and pedagogical approaches, creating more dynamic and effective learning environments. This includes using ChatGPT to develop interactive and personalized activities that fit the individual needs and learning styles of students. Despite the benefits, GenAI integration presents significant challenges for teachers, who must adapt to new tools and pedagogical approaches. According to Forcier et al. (2016), ongoing training and professional development are essential for teachers to be able to effectively use GenAI technologies in their daily practices. This includes learning how to interpret and use the data generated by GenAI to inform and improve teaching and learning.

On the other hand, this technological artefact also transforms the way teachers assess and provide feedback to students. According to Davenport and Kirby (2016), GenAI tools allow for more accurate and timely assessments, offering students immediate feedback that can improve their understanding and academic performance. This not only saves teachers time, but also allows for more continuous and formative assessment, rather than relying solely on traditional summative exams. From a teacher perspective, there are a wealth of resources for the pedagogically correct use of GenAI tools, with collections of open access materials geared towards educational practice available online (Herft, 2023; Kasneci et al., 2023; Kukulska-Hulme et al., 2023; Mollick & Mollick, 2023; Nerantzi et al., 2023). Furthermore, it is evident that the maximum use of GenAI is achieved when a synergistic relationship is established with the teachers who carry out the management and supervision tasks. Working together improves productivity, since it frees up the time invested in repetitive tasks carried out in the traditional systematic methodology of searching and reviewing information (Carbajal-Degante et al., 2023). It also enhances creativity and exploration of new perspectives that complement its study to generate work in the scientific community.

Trends and Applications of AI in Education

The field of GenAI in education has demonstrated technological advancements, theoretical innovations, and successful pedagogical impact (Roll & Wylie, 2016), with diverse applications such as intelligent tutors for content delivery, feedback provision, and progress monitoring (Bayne, 2015). The possibilities of GenAI in education are widely recognized. GenAI can be used to provide specialized support and raise awareness of knowledge gaps, enabling instructors to teach effectively and efficiently through personalized and adaptive instruction (Guan et al., 2020). GenAI also provides algorithm-based decisions that enable effective real-time assessment of complex skills and knowledge (Chen et al., 2021). GenAI applications in education are based on a wide range of techniques, which in addition to those mentioned above, include educational data mining, learning analytics, multi-agent systems, fuzzy logic, and Bayesian systems, among others. First, learning data mining and data analytics techniques are used to analyze large amounts of student data to identify patterns and trends in student academic performance, behavior, and interaction (Mishra et al., 2024). This can help educators design personalized curricula and provide detailed feedback to students (Chan et al., 2022). In the case of multi-agent systems, they are used to create intelligent tutoring systems that can interact with students and provide real-time help based on their specific needs, providing a personalized and adaptive learning experience (Murtaza et al., 2022). On the other hand, neural networks are used for data classification and analysis, the identification of learning patterns and the creation of speech and text recognition systems. And finally, fuzzy logic is used for uncertainty modelling and for the creation of adaptive and personalised assessment systems. The same is true for Bayesian systems, which are used for decision making and uncertainty modelling in educational content recommendation systems and adaptive assessment systems and are even capable of automated grading.

Figure 1. Foundational techniques underpinning AI applications in education

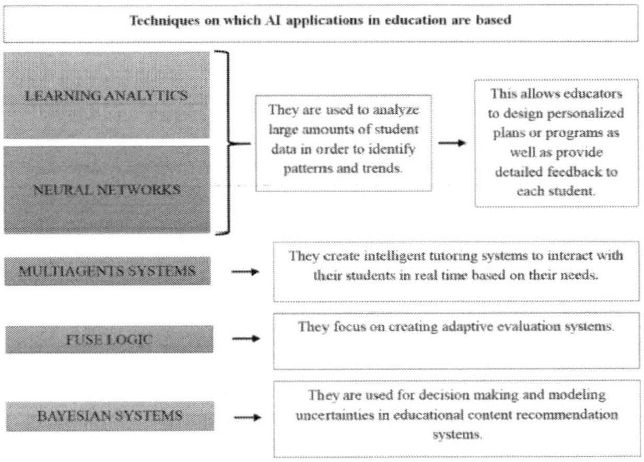

Gaps and Research Questions

The background present in the scientific literature are systematic literature reviews related to the study of ChatGPT aimed at exploring the concept, authors or areas of future research (Amarathunga, 2024). Amarathunga's study (2024) combined in its methodology the systematic literature review and bibliometric analysis, through articles from the Scopus database. For the quantitative and qualitative analysis, the Biblioshiny and VOSviewer software were used. Its main results revealed that the concept of ChatGPT in the educational sector is constantly evolving, especially the publications are concentrated in countries such as the United States, China or Indonesia. These publications have focused on topics such as educational systems, students, teaching, chatbots or technological acceptance. There are also reviews focused on the role of AI algorithms in relation to information systems (Bendig & Bräunche, 2024). The study developed by Bendig & Bräunche (2024) was developed under the systematic literature review model under the framework proposed by Templier and Paré (2015). The main results reveal a significant increase in publications related to AI algorithms and their use in the field of education. Other reviews are more focused on reviewing the security of chatbots (Yang et al., 2023). This work is developed under the PRISMA systematic review methodology. Its main conclusions reveal the security problems of chatbots and the relevance of ensuring both the trust and privacy of users. This work alerts to the need to incorporate user authentication systems to better control threats and user security.

Other approaches carried out study the role of AI and its potential for the automation of systematic reviews (Tomczyk et al., 2024). Specifically, Tomczyk et al. (2024) analyze studies from Scopus and Web of Science to examine the human-machine relationship, emphasizing the importance and key role of human supervision. Other studies have even been carried out related to higher education, focused on analyzing the impact and potential of GenAI and its capacity for transformation in the field of business education (Kumar et al., 2024). This study focuses on analyzing the role of ChatGPT, pointing out its role in pedagogical innovation or its significant role in the learning process. It also identifies challenges such as plagiarism or the negative impact on students' interpersonal skills. However, no literature reviews focused on the educational field in higher education have been found. Considering all the above, the interest of this work is to explore the opportunities and challenges that the use of generative AI generates in learning environments in higher education from an educational point of view. To do so, the following research questions are raised:

1. What opportunities does the use of GenAI in higher education generate?
2. What challenges does the use of GenAI in higher education generate?

MAIN FOCUS OF THE CHAPTER

This paper addresses the impact of AI in education, focusing specifically on higher education. An analysis of the existing literature is conducted to better understand the role AI plays in this context, as well as to identify opportunities and obstacles to its implementation. The results provide an overview of how AI is currently being used in higher education. AI-enabled tools and technologies are identified, as well as areas where obstacles are being encountered. Emerging trends are highlighted, and the future potential of AI in this field is discussed. The discussion focuses on findings in current educational practice. The implications of AI implementation on teaching and learning processes, as well as the effects on students and faculty, are highlighted. The ethical and social implications of the growing presence of AI in higher education are also discussed. Consequently, GenAI can be a useful strategy to overcome some of the challenges facing education, for example, by optimizing teaching and learning processes. Indeed, the sheer volume of data available to us, the ability of GenAI technologies to generate their own models, or the widespread adoption of learning analytics approaches force us to consider how to effectively use GenAI (Dogan et al., 2023). Thus, this systematic literature review (SLR) pursues several objectives:

- Analyze the opportunities offered by the GenAI tool, ChatGPT, in higher education based on a systematic review of literature.
- Identify the role of the teacher in the integration of GenAI in education.
- Understand the ways in which GenAI is transforming education.
- Describe the challenges that ChatGPT generates in higher education.
- Compare and synthesize the evidence found on the opportunities offered by ChatGPT from different authors.

METHOD

In recent decades, the number of scientific publications has increased significantly, which is why a new methodology is adopted that allows reducing or collecting information in such a way that it is more practical. In this case, the methodology to be used for the development of this study is based on the guidelines established by PRISMA (Preferred Reporting Items for Systematic Reviews and Meta-Analyses). The PRISMA methodology guarantees a transparent, reliable and reproducible approach in the performance of systematic and meta-analytical reviews. This allows obtaining conclusions supported by the best scientific evidence available (Moher et al., 2009; Liberati et al., 2009; Shamseer et al.,

2015). The PRISMA method is defined as a widely recognized and accepted guide in the academic field (Liberati et al. 2019; Moher et al. 2009; Shamseer et al., 2015).

Search Strategy

Based on the PRISMA guidelines, a complete and exhaustive search of data was carried out in different databases, in this case the Web of Science (WoS) and Dialnet databases were used. To carry out the search, the Boolean operators AND and OR were used. Boolean operators are logical links, used by most information retrieval systems to establish relationships between search terms (keywords or descriptors). With their help, different types of logical relationships between two or more sets are easily established: differentiating or discriminating concepts, grouping them, interrelating them, including or excluding them in certain sets, etc. (Mora, 2005). For this purpose, the following search string was used: *"Generative artificial intelligence"* AND (*challenge* OR *opportunity*) AND *higher education* AND *ChatGPT.*

Inclusion Criteria

To guide the article selection process, the following inclusion criteria were agreed upon by the two researchers:

CI1. The research papers have been published between 2023 and 2024.
CI2. The research papers are written in English or Spanish.
CI3. The papers are focused exclusively on higher education.
CI4. The included articles are accessible to researchers.
CI5. The included articles are based on empirical work.
CI6. The included articles belong to the area of research in education.

Review Process

The data were retrieved on November 15, 2024. The review process followed can be seen in Figure 2. A total of 66 documents were identified, 56 records were found in WoS and 10 in Dialnet. Subsequently, criteria CI1 and CI2 were applied to the databases themselves. For CI1, 0 records were eliminated, and for CI2, 2 were eliminated. The titles and abstracts of the publications were then examined to apply the remaining inclusion criteria. Thus, for CI3, 24 records were eliminated, for CI4, 17 records were eliminated, for CI5, 7 records were eliminated, and finally, for CI6, 3 records were eliminated from the databases. After applying the inclusion criteria, 13 records were obtained. Duplicate files were subsequently eliminated, specifically one article. Therefore, 53 works were excluded from the records examined. Finally, after analysis, 12 articles that met the established criteria were included in the review.

Figure 2. PRISMA flow chart

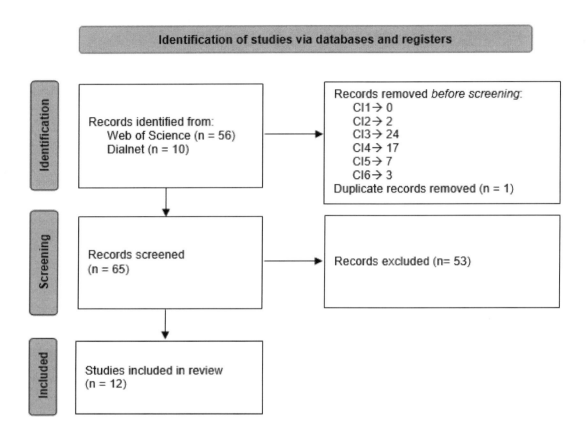

RESULTS

This section presents the results of the SLR carried out, considering the results from a quantitative or qualitative point of view.

Quantitative Results

In relation to the quantitative results of the study, the authorship and distribution of studies based on language are presented.

Authorship

Table 2 shows the authorship of the studies selected in the 12 articles subject to analysis.

Table 2. Authorship of studies

Authors	Qualification	Year
Nikolic, Sasha; Daniel, Scott; Haque, Rezwanul; Belkina, Marina; Hassan, Ghulam M. M.; Grundy, Sarah; Lyden, Sarah; Neal, Peter; Sandison, Caz	ChatGPT versus engineering education assessment: a multidisciplinary and multi-institutional benchmarking and analysis of this generative artificial intelligence tool to investigate assessment integrity	2023
Michel-Villarreal, Rosario; Vilalta-Perdomo, Eliseo; Salinas-Navarro, David Ernesto; Thierry-Aguilera, Ricardo; Gerardou, Flor Silvestre	Challenges and Opportunities of Generative AI for Higher Education as Explained by ChatGPT	2023
Farrelly, Tom; Baker, Nick	Generative Artificial Intelligence: Implications and Considerations for Higher Education Practice	2023
Gallent-Torres, Cinta; Zapata-Gonzalez, Alfredo; Ortego-Hernando, Jose Luis	The impact of Generative Artificial Intelligence in higher education: a focus on ethics and academic integrity	2023
Pelaez-Sanchez, Iris Cristina; Velarde-Camaqui, Davis; Glasserman-Morales, Leonardo David	The impact of large language models on higher education: exploring the connection between AI and Education 4.0	2024
He, Zhangying; Thomas Nguyen; Miari, Tahereh; Aliasgari, Mehrdad; Rafatirad, Setareh; Sayadi, Hossein	The AI Companion in Education: Analyzing the Pedagogical Potential of ChatGPT in Computer Science and Engineering	2024
Parra, Julia Lynn; Chatterjee, Suparna	Social Media and Artificial Intelligence: Critical Conversations and Where Do We Go from Here?	2024
Crawford, Joseph; Vallis, Carmen; Yang, Jianhua; Fitzgerald, Rachel; O'Dea, Christine	Editorial: Artificial Intelligence is Awesome, but Good Teaching Should Always Come First.	2023
Perkins, Mike; Roe, Jasper	Decoding Academic Integrity Policies: A Corpus Linguistics Investigation of AI and Other Technological Threats	2024
Essien, Aniekan; Bukoye, Oyegoke Teslim; O'Dea, Christine; Kremantzis, Marios	The influence of AI text generators on critical thinking skills in UK business schools	2024
Bozkurt, Aras	GenAI et al.: Cocreation, Authorship, Ownership, Academic Ethics and Integrity in a Time of Generative AI	2023
Linares, Luis Jiménez; Gómez, Julio Alberto López; Baos, José Ángel Martín; Chicharro, Francisco Romero; Guerrero, Jesús Serrano	ChatGPT: reflections on the emergence of generative artificial intelligence in university teaching	2023

Languages

The distribution of the articles according to the language of writing has been only in Spanish and English as indicated in the inclusion criteria. As shown in Figure 3, 92% of the articles are in English, which is equivalent to 11 of the 12 selected articles, while 8% of the total is equivalent to the only article we have in Spanish.

Figure 3. Distribution of articles depending on the language of writing

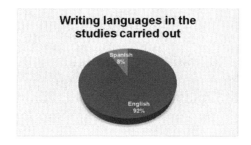

Qualitative Results

Regarding the qualitative results, the research questions posed in the study will be answered below. These questions will be addressed considering the 12 articles that met the quality criteria.

What Opportunities Does the Use of GenAI in Higher Education Generate? (RQ1)

In relation to opportunities, Bozkurt (2023) notes that the advent of GenAI in teaching and learning has brought great opportunities. Furthermore, in another study, Ipek et al. (2023) reaffirmed that the integration of GenAI in education is already underway, enabling advanced cognitive tasks using technology. One aspect to consider according to Bozkurt (2023) refers to promoting GenAI literacy to unlock future opportunities, and to this end, he highlights the need to improve our understanding of GenAI and the requirement to develop new literacies to effectively adopt these evolving technologies. It addresses the importance of GenAI literacy for educators and its relevance in the context of higher education, research and the need to prepare for the future adoption of GenAI.

For Michael-Villareal et al. (2023) ChatGPT presents several important benefits and opportunities for higher education. It offers 24/7 support and accessibility. This allows instant access to information and resources and can enhance the learning experience; it provides personalized learning and tutoring, so that students can receive personalized learning paths enhancing self-directed learning; it serves as a supplementary learning resource, as students can search for explanations or examples to explore topics in greater depth. This supports understanding, reinforces learning, and fosters autonomy for research in students; it fosters language learning and communication skills. These features offer opportunities to simulate conversational exchanges, provide language correction, and offer assistance with vocabulary and grammar; it offers support for instructors and teaching assistants. It therefore allows for routine queries, providing quick references, or offering guidance on frequently asked questions (Acut et al., 2024). This allows instructors to focus on higher-level tasks such as facilitating discussions, leading critical analysis, and providing personalized feedback to students; It facilitates innovative learning experiences, for example, through simulations or virtual characters powered by ChatGPT to engage students in role-playing scenarios, decision-making exercises, or historical reenactments. These immersive experiences can enhance students' motivation, critical thinking, and creativity; and lastly, it contributes to research and data analysis, assisting with literature reviews, data analysis, and hypothesis generation. ChatGPT can help uncover relevant sources, summarize findings, and even suggest possible research directions.

Nikolic et al. (2023) add other opportunities that GenAI offers, such as improving the quality of writing, summarising complex ideas, generating and structuring ideas and developing understanding. These views are countered by the assessment of Farrelly et al. (2023) who argue that while there are many in higher education who embrace and take advantage of the opportunities that GenAI presents, at the same time we are faced with warnings that academic integrity and contemporary understanding of disciplinary knowledge are under attack. This is complemented by Michael-Villareal et al. (2023) who point out that while the focus should be on taking advantage of the opportunities of GenAI, we must also manage the risks to essential aspects of scientific work: curiosity, imagination and discovery. The authors call for measures to ensure that creativity, originality, education, training and human interactions remain essential to conducting research.

To summarize, the study by Bozkurt (2023) points out that it is possible to say that GenAI will affect all our lives, but considering the rapid development of GenAI technology, it is difficult to predict to what extent it will do so. However, GenAI is here to stay and therefore GenAI technologies can be adopted and the opportunities they present can be taken advantage of. According to Crawforf et al. (2023) the focus is on the opportunities that GenAI now presents for higher education, as historically, these opportunities allow higher education to grow and progress. Finally, Bozkurt (2023) points out that the future of education does not lie in the dominance of GenAI but in the symbiotic relationship between humans and GenAI, forging an enriched, diversified and adaptable educational ecosystem that meets individual learning needs. This idea is also reinforced by Crawforf et al. (2023), remembering that processes occur in people, GenAI occurs around them and after human intelligence.

What Challenges Does the Use of GenAI in Higher Education Generate? (RQ 2)

Regarding the challenges, according to Gallent-Torres et al. (2023), while GenAI offers great opportunities, it also poses important ethical and pedagogical challenges for this group. This is because it calls into question ethics and academic integrity, undermining elements such as the reliability of information, transparency regarding the sources used, or the privacy and security of data. Bozkurt (2023) complements this by pointing out that GenAI also presents errors such as producing incorrect information and evading plagiarism controls. Therefore, it is crucial to quickly update assessment methods and policies in educational institutions (Garcia et al., 2025).

For Bozkurt (2023), the main challenges are those related to the lack of emotional intelligence, literacy, and problems in ensuring the accuracy and reliability of responses generated by GenAI, along with fears about replacing educators. In this regard, the author points out that while these technologies excel at processing information and generating responses, they often struggle to understand and respond to emotional cues and the nuanced needs of learners (Bozkurt et al., 2024). The absence of emotional intelligence in GenAI systems can hamper their ability to provide effective support and personalized guidance, which are crucial elements in the learning process. Regarding the lack of literacy, for Bozkurt (2023), just as people learn to read, write, and interpret language, they must also acquire competence to understand, interact with, and critically evaluate GenAI technologies. Therefore, developing generative literacy in AI is essential not only for the current digital age but also for shaping the future of education.

For Farrelly et al., (2023) another potential concern or challenge arises: equity. In this sense, the authors point out that there will always be a gap between the latest GenAI models, and any potential tool designed to detect their results, creating a self-reinforcing digital inequality. This challenge involves an imbalance between those who have access to the latest models and those who do not. Access to the latest models will inevitably have a cost, so only those who can afford that cost will be able to use them. To which Gallent-Torres et al. (2023) add that this technology could increase the digital divide among teachers, depending on their level of access, knowledge and competence in the use of GenAI. In this sense, ethical challenges arise related to security, data privacy, the ability to interact with these models or training; the latter being an essential aspect in this technological revolution. On the other hand, Crawforf, et al. (2023) also identified a number of practical and ethical challenges, including low technological readiness, lack of replicability and transparency, and insufficient privacy and beneficence considerations.

Finally, Michael-Villareal et al. (2023) point out other challenges complementary to those already mentioned, such as the lack of academic integrity, which means that there are risks to guarantee a fair evaluation and maintain academic standards; the lack of quality control in ChatGPT, since its responses are based on the data with which it has been trained and can generate incorrect information; that it does not respond to personalized learning, from the point of view that this system may not capture the specific needs of the student; that it lacks experience and authority understood as the inability to offer deep knowledge, critical analysis and guidance to specific fields; problems for communication and collaboration, since it does not have the fundamental elements for learning experiences in higher education, limiting the possibilities for human interaction or group work and collaborative activities; or ethical and privacy issues already mentioned such as data privacy or algorithmic biases, among others.

The challenges discussed here suggest that we are still a long way from a world where GenAI systems completely replace teaching staff (Michael-Villareal et al., 2023). Opinions of ChatGPT seem to suggest that it can serve as a tool, but it cannot completely replace the human element. Therefore, those wishing to incorporate it into education must provide teachers with the skills and training to effectively use the technology to minimize the challenges discussed here (Gantalao et al., 2025).

These challenges are not insurmountable and institutions can develop strategies to effectively address them (Michael-Villareal et al., 2023). With careful implementation and integration, ChatGPT can still offer significant benefits and opportunities for higher education. This is why this technological revolution will require the need to implement training, information and awareness-raising actions by and for the academic community in order to integrate GenAI, naturally and effectively, into teaching-learning processes; Likewise, it will require the establishment of clear guidelines that comply with the ethical codes and integrity policies of higher education institutions (Gallent Torres et al., 2023).

As a summary, Table 3 presents in a simpler and more schematic way the results obtained in the previously posed research questions.

Table 3. Opportunities and challenges of GenAI in higher education

Opportunities	Challenges
• Immediate 24/7 support, accessibility and feedback. • Personalized learning and mentoring. • Supplementary learning resource. • Language learning and communication skills. • Support for instructors and teaching assistants. • Innovative learning experiences. • Improving the quality of writing. • Ability to summarize complex ideas. • Willingness and ease when generating and structuring ideas as well as developing understanding. • Assistance in administrative tasks. • Innovation in educational methodology.	• Lack of emotional intelligence. • Lack of AI literacy. • Issues ensuring accuracy and reliability of AI-generated responses. • Fear about replacing educators. • Lack of equity. • Increase in the digital divide. • Ethical and privacy issues. • Lack of academic integrity. • Lack of quality control. • It does not respond to personalized learning. • It presents no experience or authority. • Communication and collaboration problems.

FUTURE RESEARCH DIRECTIONS

Despite the efforts made during this research, this study presents several limitations that should be considered. First, the sample used in this study was relatively small and focused on a limited number of articles focused on higher education, which could restrict the generalization of the results to a broader context.

Regarding research opportunities, we suggest replication of this study in other educational settings, which would allow for a broader understanding of the effects of GenAI in various educational contexts. Furthermore, we recommend the inclusion of additional databases to compare results and gain a broader view of emerging trends. Another interesting line of research is the implementation of mixed methods (quantitative and qualitative) in the analysis of the impact of GenAI in higher education. A combined approach would allow for capturing both student and faculty perceptions, facilitating a more complete understanding of how GenAI is perceived and used in educational practice. Furthermore, it would be advisable to explore the ethical and social dimensions of GenAI in higher education, not only from the student perspective, but also from the perspective of faculty and administrators, who play a crucial role in the adoption and regulation of these technologies.

Finally, expanding research in these fields will contribute to a real understanding of what is happening in classrooms and administrative settings, providing valuable data that can improve both teaching and educational management in the future.

CONCLUSION

GenAI, with models such as ChatGPT at the forefront, has emerged with great transformative force in society. The way we interact with technology and, above all, with each other has changed significantly. We now have automation of tasks that previously required significant human intervention. This not only increases efficiency but also opens up new opportunities for creativity and exploration in fields ranging from education to design. ChatGPT, as part of GenAI, represents one of the most recent developments in this field.

The integration of GenAI tools such as ChatGPT in higher education presents a number of significant opportunities for students, teachers and researchers. The availability of 24-hour support and access, personalisation of learning, enrichment of educational resources and innovation in learning experiences are just some of the advantages highlighted (Michael-Villareal, et al., 2023). In addition, improving the quality of writing, synthesising complex ideas and developing comprehension are also mentioned as additional opportunities (Nikolic et al., 2023). It is possible to adopt an attitude of resistance to change or to take advantage of the opportunities this technology offers for education. In either case, the first step would be to recognise that evolution is inherent to progress and that it benefits the individual but does not exempt him or her from critically evaluating its possible implications and consequences (Gallent-Torres et al., 2023). This is why this technological progress is not without significant challenges. The lack of emotional intelligence in GenAI tools, the need for literacy in the educational community, and ensuring the accuracy and reliability of responses are some of the ethical and pedagogical challenges identified (Bozkurt, 2023). In addition, concerns about fairness, academic integrity, data privacy, and community engagement have been identified (Bozkurt, 2023). Also, on effective communication identified as a major barrier to the implementation of these technologies (Farrellyet al., 2023; Gallent Torres et al., 2023).

Despite these challenges, it is crucial to recognise that the integration of GenAI in higher education is not an insurmountable process. With careful planning, appropriate training and attention to ethical and pedagogical considerations, these tools can offer significant benefits for learning and teaching in educational institutions (Michael-Villareal et al., 2023). It is essential that institutions adopt effective strategies to address these challenges and establish clear guidelines that promote the responsible and ethical use of GenAI in educational settings (Gallent Torres et al., 2023). It should also be noted that human-to-human collaboration and GenAI systems promise to enrich and diversify the educational ecosystem, offering innovative opportunities for learning and research in higher education (Bozkurt, 2023). By navigating these challenges and making the most of the opportunities offered by GenAI, institutions can move towards a more inclusive, adaptive and enriched educational future (Crawforf, et al., 2023). In conclusion, this paper recognises the disruptive potential of GenAI in higher education and calls for a balanced approach that addresses both the challenges and opportunities it presents. The importance of GenAI literacy and ethical considerations when adopting GenAI technologies should be emphasised to ensure equitable access and positive outcomes for all students (Farrelly, 2023). Broad reflection on what GenAI can do for education is also needed. This critical reflection must be developed by both faculty and students (Tlili et al., 2024).

AI, such as ChatGPT, has the potential to revolutionize education by providing broader access to knowledge and supporting more personalized learning experiences (Smith & Jones, 2020). ChatGPT can foster creativity by helping students generate new ideas and perspectives through dynamic and stimulating conversations among many other things (Brown et al., 2021). Still, according to LeCun (2018), continued advances in machine learning, especially in areas such as deep learning, are expected to drive the development of more sophisticated GenAI systems capable of performing increasingly complex tasks. For this reason, authors such as Goertzel and Pennachin (2007) claim that the development of GenAI seeks to replicate human cognitive versatility. In the words of Russell and Norvig (2021), GenAI is expected to improve collaboration between humans and computers, enabling more advanced assistance and decision-making systems in a variety of fields, from medicine to engineering, education and many others.

Throughout this chapter, the impact of artificial intelligence on higher education has been explored. Overall, it has been observed that the implementation of AI tools has proven promising in terms of personalizing learning, automating administrative processes, and enabling predictive analytics to improve decision-making. However, concerns have also arisen regarding ethical issues, the risk of algorithmic bias, and potential inequalities in access to the technology. Therefore, there are some viable strategies to realize the full potential of AI tools in education. For example, by promoting GenAI literacy among educators and students. Institutions can contribute to this task by promoting ongoing training programs focused not only on its use but also on understanding the ethical, social, and pedagogical implications. Another urgent task is to ensure the ethical and responsible use of GenAI. To this end, institutions must implement clear policies on its responsible use. For example, by ensuring data privacy, equitable access, and incorporating monitoring of the impact of this technology on users. Another advantage is the application of GenAI to personalize learning. This requires institutions to engage in the creation of specific platforms that incorporate AI. Finally, institutions and educators have an important role to play in ensuring a critical culture around GenAI. This reflection should focus on the role these technologies play in human-computer interaction and communication. Ultimately, the use of AI in education has the potential to transform the way educators interact with students by providing tools for more individualized and efficient learning. However, its implementation poses significant challenges that must be addressed to ensure that the benefits are equitable and sustainable in the long term.

REFERENCES

Acut, D. P., Malabago, N. K., Malicoban, E. V., Galamiton, N. S., & Garcia, M. B. (2024). "ChatGPT 4.0 Ghosted Us While Conducting Literature Search:" Modeling the Chatbot's Generated Non-Existent References Using Regression Analysis. *Internet Reference Services Quarterly*, ●●●, 1–26. DOI: 10.1080/10875301.2024.2426793

Amarathunga, B. (2024). ChatGPT in education: Unveiling frontiers and future directions through systematic literature review and bibliometric analysis. *Asian Education and Development Studies*, *13*(5), 412–431. DOI: 10.1108/AEDS-05-2024-0101

Anderson, T., & Dron, J. (2011). Tres generaciones de pedagogía de la educación a distancia. Revista internacional de investigación en aprendizaje abierto y distribuido, [Three Generations of Distance Education Pedagogy. International Journal of Research in Open and Distributed Learning], 12(3), 80-97.

Bayne, S. (2015). Teacherbot: Intervenciones en la enseñanza automatizada. *Docencia en Educación Superior*, [Teacherbot: Interventions in Automated Teaching. Teaching in Higher Education], *20*(4), 455–467. DOI: 10.1080/13562517.2015.1020783

Bendig, D., & Bräunche, A. (2024). *The role of artificial intelligence algorithms in information systems research: a conceptual overview and avenues for research.* Management Review Quartely., DOI: 10.1007/s11301-024-00451-y

Bostrom, N., & Yudkowsky, E. (2014). The Ethics of Artificial Intelligence. In Frankish, K., & Ramsey, W. M. (Eds.), *The Cambridge Handbook of Artificial Intelligence* (pp. 316–334). Cambridge University Press. DOI: 10.1017/CBO9781139046855.020

Bozkurt, A. (2023). Unleashing the potential of generative AI, conversational agents and chatbots in educational praxis: A systematic review and bibliometric analysis of GenAI in education. *Praxis Abierta*, *15*(4), 261–270. DOI: 10.55982/openpraxis.15.4.609

Bozkurt, A., Xiao, J., Farrow, R., Bai, J. Y. H., Nerantzi, C., Moore, S., Dron, J., Stracke, C. M., Singh, L., Crompton, H., Koutropoulos, A., Terentev, E., Pazurek, A., Nichols, M., Sidorkin, A. M., Costello, E., Watson, S., Mulligan, D., Honeychurch, S., & Asino, T. I. (2024). The Manifesto for Teaching and Learning in a Time of Generative AI: A Critical Collective Stance to Better Navigate the Future. *Open Praxis*, *16*(4), 487–513. DOI: 10.55982/openpraxis.16.4.777

Brown, A., Smith, J., Johnson, L., Lee, K., & Patel, R. (2021). The Creative Potential of AI: Exploring ChatGPT in Educational Contexts. *Journal of Educational Technology*, *35*(2), 105–120.

Brown, T. B., Mann, B., Ryder, N., Subbiah, M., Kaplan, J., Dhariwal, P., Neelakantan, A., Shyam, P., Sastry, G., Askell, A., Agarwal, S., Herbert-Voss, A., Krueger, G., Henighan, T., Child, R., Ramesh, A., Ziegler, D. M., Wu, J., Winter, C., . . . Amodei, D. (2020). Language models are few-shot learners. Computers Science. https://doi.org//arXiv.2005.14165DOI: 10.48550

Bryson, J. J. (2018). La última década y el futuro del impacto de la IA en la sociedad, Open Mind. Hacia una nueva Ilustración [The last decade and the future of AI's impact on society, Open Mind. Towards a new Enlightenment], 127-159. https://www.bbvaopenmind.com/articulos/la-ultima-decada-y-el-futuro-del-impacto-de-la-ia-en-la-sociedad/

Burrell, J. (2016). How the machine 'thinks': Understanding opacity in machine learning algorithms. *Big Data & Society*, *3*(1), 2053951715622512. DOI: 10.1177/2053951715622512

Carbajal-Degante, E., Hernández Gutiérrez, M., & Sánchez-Mendiola, M. (2023). Hacia revisiones de la literatura más eficientes potenciadas por inteligencia artificial. *Investigación en Educación Médica*, *12*(47), 111–119. DOI: 10.22201/fm.20075057e.2023.47.23526

Celik, I. (2023). Towards Intelligent-TPACK: An empirical study on teachers' professional knowledge to ethically integrate artificial intelligence (AI)-based tools into education. *Computers in Human Behavior*, *138*, 107468. DOI: 10.1016/j.chb.2022.107468

Celik, I., Dindar, M., Muukkonen, H., & Järvelä, S. (2022). The Promises and Challenges of Artificial Intelligence for Teachers: A Systematic Review of Research. *TechTrends*, *66*(66), 616–630. DOI: 10.1007/s11528-022-00715-y

Chan, L., Hogaboam, L., & Cao, R. (2022). Artificial intelligence in education. In *Applied Artificial Intelligence in Business: Concepts and Cases* (pp. 265–278). Springer International Publishing., DOI: 10.1007/978-3-031-05740-3_17

Chen, X., Zou, D., Xie, H., & Cheng, G. (2021). Veinte años de aprendizaje de idiomas personalizado: modelado de temas y mapeo de conocimientos. Tecnología educativa y sociedad, [Twenty Years of Personalized Language Learning: Topic Modeling and Knowledge Mapping. Educational Technology and Society], 24(1), 205–222.https://www.jstor.org/stable/10.2307/2697786

Chen, X., Zou, D., Xie, H., Cheng, G., & Liu, C. (2022). Two decades of artificial intelligence in education. *Journal of Educational Technology & Society*, *25*(1), 28–47.

Chiu, T. K., Xia, Q., Zhou, X., Chai, C. S., & Cheng, M. (2023). Systematic literature review on opportunities, challenges, and future research recommendations of artificial intelligence in education. *Computers and Education: Artificial Intelligence*, *4*, 100118. DOI: 10.1016/j.caeai.2022.100118

Crawford, J., Vallis, C., Yang, J., Fitzgerald, R., O'Dea, C., & Cowling, M. (2023). Editorial: Artificial Intelligence is awesome, but good teaching should always come first. Revista de práctica de enseñanza y aprendizaje universitario, 20(7). DOI: 10.53761/1.20.7.01

Davenport, T. H., & Kirby, J. (2016). *Only humans need apply: Winners and losers in the age of smart machines*. Harper Business.

Dogan, M. E., Goru Dogan, T., & Bozkurt, A. (2023). The use of artificial intelligence (AI) in online learning and distance education processes: A systematic review of empirical studies. *Applied Sciences (Basel, Switzerland)*, *13*(5), 3056. DOI: 10.3390/app13053056

Du, H., Liu, G., Niyato, D., Zhang, J., Kang, J., Xiong, Z., Ai, B., & Kim, D. I. (2023). Generative AI-aided joint training-free secure semantic communications via multi-modal prompts. Electrical Engineering and Systems Science.https://doi.org//arXiv.2309.02616DOI: 10.48550

Essien, A., Bukoye, O. T., O'Dea, X., & Kremantzis, M. (2024). The influence of AI text generators on critical thinking skills in UK business schools. *Studies in Higher Education*, *49*(5), 1–18. DOI: 10.1080/03075079.2024.2316881

Eysenbach, G. (2023). The role of ChatGPT, generative language models, and artificial intelligence in medical education: A conversation with ChatGPT and a call for papers. *JMIR Medical Education*, *9*(1), e46885. https://doi.org/e46885.10.2196/46885. DOI: 10.2196/46885 PMID: 36863937

Farrelly, T., & Baker, N. (2023). Generative Artificial Intelligence: Implications and Considerations for Higher Education Practice. *Education Sciences*, *13*(13), 11–19. DOI: 10.3390/educsci13111109

Gallent-Torres, C., Zapata-González, A., & Ortego-Hernando, J. L. (2023). El impacto de la inteligencia artificial generativa en educación superior: Una mirada desde la ética y la integridad académica. RELIEVE. *Revista Electrónica de Investigación y Evaluación Educativa*, *29*(2), 1–21. DOI: 10.30827/relieve.v29i2.29134

Gantalao, L. C., Calzada, J. G. D., Capuyan, D. L., Lumantas, B. C., Acut, D. P., & Garcia, M. B. (2025). Equipping the Next Generation of Technicians: Navigating School Infrastructure and Technical Knowledge in the Age of AI Integration. In *Pitfalls of AI Integration in Education: Skill Obsolescence, Misuse, and Bias*. IGI Global., DOI: 10.4018/979-8-3373-0122-8.ch009

Garcia, M. B., Rosak-Szyrocka, J., Yılmaz, R., Metwally, A. H. S., Acut, D. P., Ofosu-Ampong, K., Erdoğdu, F., Fung, C. Y., & Bozkurt, A. (2025). Rethinking Educational Assessment in the Age of Generative AI: Actionable Strategies to Mitigate Academic Dishonesty. In *Pitfalls of AI Integration in Education: Skill Obsolescence, Misuse, and Bias*. IGI Global., DOI: 10.4018/979-8-3373-0122-8.ch001

Goertzel, B., & Pennachin, C. (2007). *Artificial General Intelligence: A Gentle Introduction*. Springer Science& Business Media. DOI: 10.1007/978-3-540-68677-4

González-González, C. S. (2023). El impacto de la inteligencia artificial en la educación: Transformación de la forma de enseñar y de aprender. *Revista Qurriculum*, *36*(03), 51–60. Advance online publication. DOI: 10.25145/j.qurricul.2023.36.03

Goodfellow, I., Bengio, Y., & Courville, A. (2016). *Deep learning*. MIT press.

Guan, C., Mou, J., & Jiang, Z. (2020). Innovación en inteligencia artificial en la educación: Un análisis histórico de veinte años basado en datos. *Revista Internacional de Estudios de Innovación*, *4*(4), 134–147. DOI: 10.1016/j.ijis.2020.09.001

He, Z., Nguyen, T., Miari, T., Aliasgari, M., Rafatirad, S., & Sayadi, H. (2024, May). The AI Companion in Education: Analyzing the Pedagogical Potential of ChatGPT in Computer Science and Engineering. In *2024 IEEE Global Engineering Education Conference (EDUCON)* (pp. 1-10). IEEE. DOI: 10.1109/EDUCON60312.2024.10578820

Herft, A. (2023), A Teacher's Prompt Guide to ChatGPT Aligned with 'What Works Best', Retrieved 5 may 2024 https://usergeneratededucation.files.wordpress.com/2023/01/a-teachers-prompt-guide-to-chatgpt-aligned-with-what-worksbest.pdf

Holmes, W., Bialik, M., & Fadel, C. (2019). *Artificial intelligence in education: Promises and implications for teaching and learning.* Center for Curriculum Redesign.

Hwang, G. J., Xie, H., Wah, B. W., & Gašević, D. (2020). Computers and Education: Artificial Intelligence. *Computers and Education: Artificial Intelligence*, *1*, 100001. DOI: 10.1016/j.caeai.2020.100001

Ipek, Z. H., Gözüm, A. I. C., Papadakis, S., & Kallogiannakis, M. (2023). Educational Applications of the ChatGPT AI System: A Systematic Review Research. *International Journal Educational Process*, *12*(3). Advance online publication. DOI: 10.22521/edupij.2023.123.2

ISDI. (2023). Inteligencia artificial generativa: ¿Qué es y cómo funciona? [Generative Artificial Intelligence: What is it and how does it work?]. Digital Skills. https://www.isdi.education/es/blog/inteligencia-artificial-generativa-que-es

Jiang, Y., Xiang, L., Hao, L., Shen, Y., & Okyay, K. (2022). Quo Vadis Artificial Intelligence? *Discover Artificial Intelligence*, *2*(4), 4. Advance online publication. DOI: 10.1007/s44163-022-00022-8

Kaplan, A., & Haenlein, M. (2019). Siri, Siri, in my Hand: Who's the fairest in the land? On the interpretations, illustrations, and implications of artificial intelligence. *Business Horizons*, *62*(1), 15–25. DOI: 10.1016/j.bushor.2018.08.004

Kashyap, R., & OpenAI, C. (2023). A First Chat with ChatGPT: The First Step in the Road-Map for AI (Artificial Intelligence).

Kasneci, E., Sessler, K., Küchemann, S., Bannert, M., Dementieva, D., Fischer, F., Gasser, U., Groh, G., Günnemann, S., Hüllermeier, E., Krusche, S., Kutyniok, G., Michaeli, T., Nerdel, C., Pfeffer, J., Poquet, O., Sailer, M., Schmidt, A., Seidel, T., & Kasneci, G. (2023). ChatGPT for Good? On opportunities and challenges of large language models for education. *Learning and Individual Differences*, *103*, 102274. DOI: 10.1016/j.lindif.2023.102274

Kostopoulos, G., & Kostopoulos, I. (2021). Artificial Intelligence in Education: The Urgent Need for Critical Research. International Journal of Learning. *Teaching and Educational Research*, *20*(1), 127–140.

Kshetri, N., & Voas, J. (2024). Adapting to Generative Artificial Intelligence: Approaches in Higher Education Institutions. *Computer*, *57*(9), 128–133. DOI: 10.1109/MC.2024.3422589

Kukulska-Hulme, A., Bossu, C., Charitonos, K., Coughlan, T., Deacon, A., Deane, N., Ferguson, R., Herodotou, C., Huang, C.-W., Mayisela, T., Rets, I., Sargent, J., Scanlon, E., Small, J., Walji, S., Weller, M., & Whitelock, D. (2023). *Innovating Pedagogy 2023: Open University Innovation Report 11.* The Open University. Retrieved from., https://www.open.ac.uk/blogs/innovating/?p=784

Kumar, S., Rao, P., Singhania, S., Verma, S., & Kheterpal, M. (2024). Will artificial intelligence drive the advancements in higher education? A tri-phased exploration. *Technological Forecasting and Social Change*, *10*, 123258. DOI: 10.1016/j.techfore.2024.123258

LeCun, Y., Bengio, Y., & Hinton, G. (2015). Deep learning. *Nature*, *521*(7553), 436–444. DOI: 10.1038/nature14539 PMID: 26017442

Liberati, M., Tetzlaff, J., & Altman, D. G. (2009). Preferred Reporting items for systematic reviews and meta-analyses: THE PRISMA statement. *PLoS Medicine*, *6*(7), 1–6. DOI: 10.1371/journal.pmed.1000100 PMID: 19621070

Linares, L. J., Gómez, J. A. L., Baos, J. Á. M., Chicharro, F. P. R., & Guerrero, J. S. (2023). ChatGPT: reflexiones sobre la irrupción de la inteligencia artificial generativa en la docencia universitaria. Actas de las Jornadas sobre la Enseñanza Universitaria de la Informática [ChatGPT: Reflections on the emergence of generative artificial intelligence in university teaching. Proceedings of the Conference on University Teaching of Computer Science], (JENUI), 8, 113-120

Lo, C. K. (2023). What Is the Impact of ChatGPT on Education? A Rapid Review of the Literature. *Education Sciences*, *13*(4), 410. Advance online publication. DOI: 10.3390/educsci13040410

Michel-Villarreal, R., Vilalta Perdomo, E., Salinas-Navarro, D., Thierry-Aguilera, R., & Gerardou, F. S. (2023). Challenges and Opportunities of Generative AI for Higher Education as Explained by ChatGPT. *Education Sciences*, *13*(856), 856. Advance online publication. DOI: 10.3390/educsci13090856

Mishra, N., Garcia, P. S., Habal, B. G. M., & Garcia, M. B. (2024). Harnessing an AI-Driven Analytics Model to Optimize Training and Treatment in Physical Education for Sports Injury Prevention. *Proceedings of the 8th International Conference on Education and Multimedia Technology*, 309-315. DOI: 10.1145/3678726.3678740

Moher, D., Shamseer, L., Clarke, M., Ghersi, D., Liberati, A., Petticrew, M., Shekelle, P., & Stewart, L. A. (2015). Preferred reporting items for systematic review and meta-analysis protocols (PRISMA-P) statement. *Systematic Reviews*, *4*(1), 1–9. DOI: 10.1186/2046-4053-4-1 PMID: 25554246

Mollick, E. R., & Mollick, L. (2023). Using AI to Implement Effective Teaching Strategies in Classrooms: Five strategies, including prompts. Social Science Research Network Electronic Journal, 1-26. DOI: 10.2139/ssrn.4391243

Mora, A. G. (2005). Estrategia general de búsqueda de información. *Enfuro*, (93), 30–32.

Murtaza, M., Ahmed, Y., Shamsi, J. A., Sherwani, F., & Usman, M. (2022). AI-based personalized e-learning systems: Issues, challenges, and solutions. *IEEE Access: Practical Innovations, Open Solutions*, *10*, 81323–81342. DOI: 10.1109/ACCESS.2022.3193938

Nerantzi, C., Abegglen, S., Karatsiori, M., & Martínez-Arboleda, A. (2023). 101 creative ideas to use AI in education, A crowdsourced collection (2023 1.0) [Computer software]. *Zenodo*. DOI: 10.5281/zenodo.8072950

Nikolic, S., Daniel, S., Haque, R., Belkina, M., Hassan, G. M., Grundy, S., Lyden, S., Neal, P., & Sandison, C. (2023). ChatGPT versus engineering education assessment: A multidisciplinary and multi-institutional benchmarking and analysis of this generative artificial intelligence tool to investigate assessment integrity. *European Journal of Engineering Education*, *48*(4), 559–614. DOI: 10.1080/03043797.2023.2213169

Parra, J. L., & Chatterjee, S. (2024). Social Media and Artificial Intelligence: Critical Conversations and Where Do We Go from Here? Educativo. *Education Sciences*, *14*(68), 68. Advance online publication. DOI: 10.3390/educsci14010068

Peláez-Sánchez, I. C., Velarde-Camaqui, D., & Glasserman-Morales, L. D. (2024). The impact of large language models on higher education: Exploring the connection between AI and Education 4.0. *Frontiers in Education*, *9*, 1392091. Advance online publication. DOI: 10.3389/feduc.2024.1392091

Perkins, M., & Roe, J. (2024). Decoding academic integrity policies: A corpus linguistics investigation of AI and other technological threats. *Higher Education Policy*, *37*(3), 633–653. DOI: 10.1057/s41307-023-00323-2

Radford, A., Wu, J., Child, R., Luan, D., Amodei, D., & Sutskever, I. (2018). Language models are unsupervised multitask learners. OpenAI blog, 1(8).

Roll, I., & Wylie, R. (2016). Evolución y revolución de la inteligencia artificial en la educación. *Revista Internacional de Inteligencia Artificial en Educación*, *26*(2), 582–599. DOI: 10.1007/s40593-016-0110-3

Russell, S., & Norvig, P. (2021). *Artificial Intelligence: A Modern Approach*. Pearson.

Sánchez, M. M. (2024). La inteligencia artificial como recurso docente: Usos y posibilidades para el profesorado. *Educar*, *60*(1), 33–47. DOI: 10.5565/rev/educar.1810

Sánchez-Prieto, J. C., Izquierdo-Álvarez, V., del Moral-Marcos, M. T., & Martínez-Abad, F. (2024). Generative artificial intelligence for self-learning in higher education: Design and validation of an example machine. *RIED-Revista Iberoamericana de Educación a Distancia*, *28*(1). Advance online publication. DOI: 10.5944/ried.28.1.41548

Smith, J., & Jones, R. (2020). AI in Education: Promises and Pitfalls. *Educational Technology Research and Development*, *48*(2), 35–50.

Sun, L., & Zhou, L. (2024). Generative artificial intelligence attitude analysis of under graduate students and their precise improvement strategies: A differential analysis of multifactorial influences. *Education and Information Technologies*. Advance online publication. DOI: 10.1007/s10639-024-13236-3

Sun, S., Zhang, C., Huang, L., & Li, J. (2019). Context-aware response generation for multi-turn conversation with deep reinforcement learning. *IEEE Access : Practical Innovations, Open Solutions*, *7*, 49918–49927.

Templier, M., & Paré, G. (2015). A Framework for Guiding and Evaluating Literature Reviews. *Communications of the Association for Information Systems*, *37*. Advance online publication. DOI: 10.17705/1CAIS.03706

Tlili, A., Agyemang, M., Lo, C. K., Bozkurt, A., Burgos, D., Bonk, C. J., Costello, E., Mishra, S., Stracke, C. M., & Huang, R. (2024). Taming the Monster: How can Open Education Promote the Effective and Safe use of Generative AI in Education? *Journal of Learning for Development*, *11*(3), 398–413. DOI: 10.56059/jl4d.v11i3.1657

Tomczyk, P., Brüggemann, P., & Vrontis, D. (2024). AI meets academia: transforming systematic literature reviews. EuroMed Journal of Business, Vol. ahead-of-print No. ahead-of-print. DOI: 10.1108/EMJB-03-2024-0055

Turing, A. M. (1950). Computing machinery and intelligence. *Mind*, *59*(236), 433–460. DOI: 10.1093/mind/LIX.236.433

Valtonen, T., López-Pernas, S., Saqr, M., Vartiainen, H., Sointu, E., & Tedre, M. (2022). La naturaleza y componentes básicos de la investigación en tecnología educativa. Las computadoras en el comportamiento humano, 128, 107123. DOI: 10.1016/j.chb.2021.107123

Williamson, B., & Eynon, R. (2020). The automation of education: Artificial intelligence and the future of learning. *Learning, Media and Technology*, *45*(1), 1–9.

Yang, J., Chen, Y.-L., Por, L. Y., & Ku, C. S. (2023). A Systematic Literature Review of Information Security in Chatbots. *Applied Sciences (Basel, Switzerland)*, *13*(11), 6355. DOI: 10.3390/app13116355

KEY TERMS AND DEFINITIONS

Artificial Intelligence: The simulation of human intelligence processes by machines, especially computer systems. These processes include learning (the acquisition of information and rules for using the information), reasoning (the use of rules to reach approximate or definitive conclusions), and self-correction.

Higher Education: A formal educational level developed after secondary education that seeks to provide specialized training, whether for academic or professional purposes.

Educational Innovation: The introduction of significant changes and improvements in teaching and learning processes. It involves the implementation of new ideas, strategies, technologies, or approaches that seek to optimize the educational experience and improve student outcomes.

Methodology: A set of methods, techniques, and procedures that are used systematically to carry out research, a study, or any other activity that requires a structured approach in order to achieve a given objective.

Ethics: A set of moral principles and values that guide the design, development, and use of intelligent systems. This is a framework that seeks to ensure that AI is used responsibly and beneficially for society, avoiding potential negative consequences and minimising risks.

Skills Obsolescence: Loss of relevance or usefulness of the skills and knowledge that a person possesses due to rapid changes in the labour market, driven mainly by technology and globalisation.

Digital Divide: Inequality in access, use and exploitation of information and communication technologies (ICT) between different groups of people. The consequences of the digital divide are multiple and can limit the educational, employment and social opportunities of those who are at a disadvantage. To reduce this gap, it is necessary to increase access to the internet and devices, promote digital literacy and create accessible content for all.

Chapter 18
A Systematic Review of the Role of AI–Enabled Chatbots in Modern Education:
Benefits, Risks, and Implementation Complexity

Damola Olugbade

https://orcid.org/0000-0003-3938-6273

First Technical University, Nigeria

ABSTRACT

The growing adoption of AI-enabled chatbots in education stems from advances in artificial intelligence, offering both opportunities and challenges. This chapter reviews 41 high-impact studies published between 2017 and 2023, examining how chatbots are used in schools, as well as their impact, benefits, and associated challenges. Chatbots have shown potential to enhance personalized learning, improve student engagement, and support administrative tasks, though these benefits vary across subjects and strategies. Despite their promise, chatbots face challenges such as technical issues, ethical risks, and inconsistent effectiveness across educational contexts. The review underscores the need for further research, particularly longitudinal studies and evaluation frameworks, to better understand chatbot integration. This chapter contributes to the discussion on AI in education, highlighting both the advantages and the complexities of its implementation, with a focus on skill obsolescence, misuse, and bias in educational practices.

INTRODUCTION

The evolution of Artificial Intelligence (AI) technology is on the rise in many industries, and education is one of the most impacted (Bozkurt et al., 2024; Zawacki-Richter et al., 2019). Among the myriad AI-driven innovations, chatbots have emerged as a promising tool with the potential to revolutionize traditional educational paradigms (Okonkwo & Ade-Ibijola, 2021a; Olugbade, 2024; Wollny et al., 2021). These pedagogical AI-based conversational agents have gained a lot of popularity over the last several

DOI: 10.4018/979-8-3373-0122-8.ch018

years because of their ability to enhance individual learning, provide instant evaluations and be available for the learners all the time (Pérez et al., 2020; Smutny & Schreiberova, 2020).

As a type of educational technology, chatbots are effective educational resources which are computer programs designed to perform as interlocutors creating communication with the user via text and voice (Adamopoulou & Moussiades, 2020). Chatbots have also been used in educational settings for English as a second language, subject tutoring, student and administrative services and interactions (Fryer et al., 2020; Liu et al., 2019). The integration of chatbot technology in education aligns with the broader trend of digital transformation in learning environments, offering the potential to enhance accessibility, personalization, and efficiency in educational delivery (Adiguzel et al., 2023). The appeal of educational chatbots lies in their ability to offer immediate, personalized responses to student queries, provide adaptive learning pathways, and support administrative tasks, thereby freeing up educators' time for more critical teaching activities (Almada et al., 2022; Chang et al., 2021). Moreover, in an era where digital natives expect instant access to information and support, chatbots present an opportunity to meet these expectations within educational settings (Jeon, 2022; Olugbade & Ojo, 2024).

MAIN FOCUS OF THE CHAPTER

Although there are many encouraging prospects and motivations, the chatbot incorporation and integration into educational processes are still at the inception level with a lack of evidence-based guidelines and best ways of application (Hwang & Chang, 2021; Kuhail et al., 2022). While some studies have suggested improvement in educational outcomes and student willingness to participate in activities (Topal et al., 2021; Yin et al., 2020), other investigations have identified issues with ability to articulate encased information, great level of knowledge dependence, and issues of data protection and sensitiveness (Chocarro et al., 2021; Winkler & Soellner, 2018). This chapter differs from previous research by offering a comprehensive systematic literature review (SLR) of empirical studies on educational chatbots published between 2017 and 2023, addressing key gaps in existing knowledge. While prior studies have explored various aspects of chatbot integration in education, findings remain fragmented, with inconsistencies regarding their effectiveness, limitations, and best practices. By synthesizing empirical evidence, this chapter provides a clearer understanding of chatbot applications, their impact on student learning, and the challenges associated with their implementation. Furthermore, it presents practical implications for educators, researchers, and policymakers, offering a structured foundation for future research and informed decision-making in AI-driven education. Given the rapidly evolving landscape of AI in education and the mixed findings regarding the effectiveness of chatbots, there is a pressing need for a comprehensive synthesis of empirical evidence to guide future research and practice. This book chapter aims to shed light on the following gaps by synthesizing and critically analyzing the empirical research on educational chatbots published between 2017 and 2023:

1. What are the primary applications and roles of chatbots in educational settings?
2. How do educational chatbots impact student learning outcomes, motivation, and engagement?
3. What are the key factors influencing the effectiveness of educational chatbots?
4. What are the current limitations and challenges in implementing chatbots in education?

The chapter includes proper SLR with specific criteria to answer these questions. As mentioned by Aznoli and Navimipour (2017), systematic literature reviews SLRs, are of great use as they provide an overview concerning the available knowledge in a certain area and therefore, areas of a lack of knowledge and therefore areas of future research can be located (Gopalakrishnan & Ganeshkumar, 2013). In attempting to answer these questions, this chapter adds to the existing literature on AI in education and discusses practical implications for researchers, educators and policy makers on the promises and challenges that the chatbot technology holds for the teaching and learning practices.

OVERVIEW OF EDUCATIONAL CHATBOTS

This is owing to the fact that the incorporation of chatbots in teaching and learning processes is an entirely new trend in the use of artificial intelligence for sociocultural enhancement. This section provides a comprehensive overview of educational chatbots, exploring their evolution, applications, benefits, impact on learning outcomes, and the challenges associated with their implementation.

Evolution of Chatbots in Education

The trend of educational chatbots engagement can also be observed in the general change of the AI development. It has progressively moved from the basic rule-based systems to comprehensive systems that effectively communicate in natural (Adamopoulou & Moussiades, 2020). There were no expectations from the early educational chatbots since they were simply seeking for information or doing some administrative work and therefore too much interactivity or personal touch was not provided (Winkler & Soellner, 2018). Nevertheless, within the last few years, novel technologies have transitioned chatbots from simple Q&A type interfaces to more interactive functions such as using them for instructional purposes including personal tutoring, foreign language acquisition, and project-based learning (Fryer et al., 2020).

The trajectory of chatbot development in education has been influenced by several factors, including improvements in natural language processing, machine learning algorithms, and the increasing availability of large-scale educational datasets (Wang et al., 2021). These technological advancements have allowed for more nuanced and context-aware interactions, enabling chatbots to better understand and respond to student queries, provide personalized feedback, and adapt to individual learning styles (Mageira et al., 2022).

Applications and Benefits

Educational chatbots have proved and continue to prove their worth in contemporary educational institutions with regard to the students and teachers. One of the uses of a chatbot especially for learners is to learn a new language, an area that has shown great promise. Studies conducted by Fryer et al. (2017) and Belda-Medina and Calvo-Ferrer (2022) have provided compelling evidence on the effectiveness of chatbots for communicative practice in language education, since learners can engage in 'real' conversations, receive instant feedback on grammar or pronunciation or learn about culture. These studies emphasize the ability of chatbots to improve vocabulary acquisition, conversational skills, and cultural understanding among foreign language learners. Huang et al. (2022) further supported these findings, demonstrating that chatbots can play a crucial role in developing these essential language skills.

In addition to language learning, chatbots have been widely employed in subject-specific tutoring, particularly in fields like programming, mathematics, and science. Okonkwo and Ade-Ibijola (2021a) highlighted the effectiveness of chatbots in providing personalized tutoring and problem-solving assistance. For example, Python-Bot helps novice programmers grasp the basic syntactic structures and semantics of programming languages. This tailored approach to learning allows students to receive targeted assistance, thereby enhancing their understanding of complex subjects. Furthermore, chatbots have proved to be of great importance in assisting with administration within education. According to Yang and Evans (2019), chatbots take over routine queries and other general administrative work therefore educating professionals can concentrate more on teaching. This is particularly true of higher education, where there are course details, timetables and questions that can be handled by chatbots. As highlighted by Al-Abdullatif et al. (2023), chatbots perform this task efficiently which is very important due to the functioning of institutions of education.

Impact on Learning Outcomes

The impact of educational chatbots on learning outcomes has been a subject of considerable research, yielding mixed results. There are cases of more advancement academically and retention of knowledge due to the availability of chatbots as appendices in the learning process (Essel et al., 2022; Topal et al., 2021). In another study, Chang et al. (2021) observed that the mobile chatbot method employed in nursing training considerably improved students' learning achievement and self-efficacy. However, other research suggests that the effectiveness of chatbots may vary depending on factors such as the subject matter, the specific application of the chatbot, and the duration of implementation (Kuhail et al., 2022). (Hwang & Chang, 2021) noted that while chatbots show promise in enhancing certain aspects of learning, their impact may not be uniformly positive across all educational contexts.

The effectiveness of educational chatbots appears to be influenced by several factors, including the quality of the chatbot's design, its integration with existing pedagogical strategies, and students' perceptions and acceptance of the technology (Chocarro et al., 2021). Research has highlighted the importance of incorporating sound pedagogical principles into chatbot design to maximize their educational impact (Mendoza et al., 2022).

Challenges and Limitations

Although their potential advantages have been mentioned, the actual use of educational chatbots comes with certain obvious pitfalls (Hasanah et al., 2025; Izquierdo-Álvarez & Jimeno-Postigo, 2025). Chief among these shortcomings is the issue of the technology involved in the use of chatbots. As pointed out by Smutny and Schreiberova (2020), other issues such as natural language processing, situational understanding, and dialogue interaction nitty-gritties are some of the technological barriers. These and other technical shortcomings usually leave chat-bots unable to handle demanding and intricate questions and other approaches to interaction which reduce the value of using them in superior levels of educational settings. The present condition of chatbots should improve such that it fits into the complex nature of education setting to enhance it more.

Another critical challenge lies in user acceptance, which plays a crucial role in the effectiveness of chatbots in education. Chocarro et al. (2021) emphasize that factors such as the chatbot's design, the quality of interaction, and its perceived usefulness greatly influence how users accept and interact with these tools. However, research by Jeon (2022) indicates that some students remain hesitant to fully trust chatbots for important educational tasks. Many students prefer human interaction for certain aspects of their learning, especially in scenarios where they require personalized guidance or critical feedback. This hesitance can limit the extent to which chatbots are embraced and effectively utilized in educational environments. Additionally, integrating chatbots into existing curricula and pedagogical strategies presents a significant challenge. Wollny et al. (2021) highlighted that effective integration requires careful planning to ensure alignment with educational objectives. This process involves not only incorporating chatbots into the curriculum but also continuously assessing and refining their use to ensure they meet educational goals. Furthermore, Adiguzel et al. (2023) bring attention to the ethical considerations that arise from using AI and chatbots in education, particularly concerning data privacy, user consent, and potential biases in AI algorithms.

Addressing these ethical issues is essential for the responsible and sustainable deployment of chatbots. Moreover, Kuhail et al. (2022) pointed out the challenges related to scalability and maintenance, as developing and maintaining chatbots with extensive knowledge bases across various subjects can be resource intensive. Ensuring the long-term viability and scalability of these educational tools remains a significant concern for many institutions. While educational chatbots offer numerous benefits, their ethical implications, particularly concerning data privacy and algorithmic bias, require greater scrutiny. The collection and storage of student data raise concerns about security, consent, and potential misuse, necessitating strict data protection measures and regulatory compliance. Additionally, algorithmic bias in chatbots can lead to inequitable learning experiences, reinforcing stereotypes or disadvantaging certain student groups. Addressing these ethical challenges is crucial to ensuring that chatbot technology enhances education while safeguarding fairness, transparency, and student rights. Expanding on these aspects will provide a more comprehensive understanding of the ethical considerations in AI-driven education.

METHODOLOGY

This chapter involves a systematic review of existing literature on the use of chatbots systems in modern education. The study used the procedure guidelines for systematic reviews in software engineering, as described by Wohlin and Prikladnicki (2013), to synthesize and analyze the existing empirical research on educational chatbots. The planning, conducting, and reporting steps are divided into three steps in these standards. Every process is decomposed into many steps, with Figure 1 showing the process in its entirety. The recommendations listed below (Aznoli & Navimipour, 2017) are used to address the RQ1, RQ2, RQ3, and RQ4: 1) defining the context and scope of earlier research; 2) summarizing the study's conclusions and limitations; 3) identifying the most significant theoretical and practical implications; and 4) identifying emerging research gaps and possible future work areas.

Figure 1. Research processes

Planning

Over the last couple of years, the use of chatbot technology in the field of education has been on the increase with a number of studies presenting, championing and deploying chatbot systems in educational settings (Deng & Yu, 2023; Hwang & Chang, 2021; Pérez et al., 2020). Given this trend, it is essential to provide readers with a comprehensive understanding of the modern applications of chatbots in education. This includes exploring the current state of chatbot technology in the educational sector, examining the various domains where it has been applied, highlighting the advantages of using chatbots in educational settings, and addressing the challenges associated with implementing chatbot technology in education.

Inclusion and Exclusion Criteria

We conducted our search in line with Snyder (2019) that articles be chosen based on clear inclusion and exclusion requirements. For this study, below are the inclusion and exclusion criteria. Studies included in the review had to meet several criteria: they needed to be empirical, peer-reviewed, and written in English, to ensure the evidence was reliable and interpretable. Studies focusing on theoretical frameworks for chatbot implementation were also included. Studies were excluded for being duplicates, not addressing at least one research question, or lacking sufficient statistical data (such as effect sizes, significance tests, or complete demographic information).

Search Procedure

We conducted a comprehensive search of peer-reviewed articles published between January 2017 and December 2023. The selected period, from 2017 to 2023, is based on several key factors: 2017 saw significant advancements in chatbot technology, particularly in natural language processing, and the evolution of chatbots from simple rule-based systems to sophisticated AI-driven platforms. Additionally, this period spans the pre- and post-COVID-19 eras, which allows for a comparative analysis of chatbot adoption in both traditional and remote learning environments. Keyword combinations are found to be appropriate for the search based on prior studies that include such as "chatbot," "conversational agent," "education," "learning," and "teaching. Manual and automatic search approaches were applied. With manual approach, we search references of related papers and automatic search was used to search the digital libraries of the selected databases (IEEE, Scopus, Springer-Link, ScienceDirect, Taylor and Francis, ERIC and Web of Science) for all articles related to the topic under study. The review focused on seven primary databases: IEEE Digital Library, ScienceDirect, SpringerLink, Scopus, Taylor and

Francis, ERIC, and Web of Science. These were chosen for their comprehensive coverage of educational technology research, ensuring the capture of peer-reviewed studies relevant to the field while minimizing duplicate entries. Other databases like PubMed and Google Scholar were considered but excluded to maintain focus on educational technology.

Conducting the Review

Search Syntax

The search was based on the title, abstract, and keywords (TITLE-ABS-KEY). The defined search words were combined in various ways to search for the appropriate articles in the selected databases. The search follows the order of *AND* and *OR* operators' processes. In *AND* operator, all search syntax or keywords must be present while in the *OR* operator, either of the search syntax must be present. The review sought to locate all related papers, Journal articles, and Conference proceedings published in English between January 2017 and December 2023. The same search syntax was used to search all the databases, and these syntax or keywords are as follows. (*Chatbot** OR *Conversational Agent**) AND (*education** OR *teaching* OR *learning* OR *student** OR *school**) The sample of a search format in Scopus is displayed below. TITLE-ABS-KEY (chatbots AND in AND education) AND (LIMIT-TO (SUBJAREA," COMP") AND (LIMIT-TO (PUBYEAR, 2023) OR (LIMIT TO (PUBYEAR, 2022) OR LIMIT-TO (PUBYEAR, 2021) OR LIMIT-TO (PUBYEAR, 2020) OR LIMIT-TO (PUBYEAR, 2019) OR LIMIT-TO (PUBYEAR, 2018) OR LIMIT-TO (PUBYEAR, 2017). The search strategy involved the use of a broad search string that was adapted for each database. The template included keywords such as "*chatbot*," "*conversational agent*," and "*dialog system*," paired with educational terms like "*education*," "*teaching*," and "*learning*." The search specifically targeted studies published between 2017 and 2023.

Data Extraction

Using the inclusion, exclusion, and quality criterion, the extraction of quality data was performed. Figure 2 displays the data extraction processes. The Figure depicts the search approaches, which include the manual and automatic search processes, the selection process, and the final data set of selected articles. The extraction procedure began with the creation of search syntaxes. The syntaxes were used to search the specified databases for articles relevant to the study. The initial search yielded 1936 articles and 438 articles were downloaded. The number of articles was reduced to 108 using the inclusion/exclusion criteria. These articles were then subjected to quality control as described in the following section. Data extraction involved collecting details on study characteristics (research design, sample size, duration, and location), chatbot characteristics (technology platform, implementation approach, and features), and educational outcomes (learning performance, student engagement, and user satisfaction). These data were then synthesized using both thematic analysis and quantitative methods, where possible, to calculate effect sizes and aggregate outcomes.

Figure 2. Data extraction processes

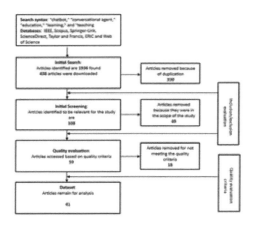

Quality Evaluation (QE)

It is critical to examine and evaluate the quality of the articles chosen for the final sample. In relation to the research objectives, the quality of all articles was evaluated with criteria presented in Table 1. The assessment was performed independently by the researchers using the QE criteria. All the QE questions are measured with a scale. Rating of 1–3 (1 - Not good, 2 - Good, and 3 - Very good). Two researchers conducted the evaluation. One researcher extracted the data, while the other double-checked it. Any conflicts of opinion were discussed and resolved. The authors achieved an agreement by consensus on the ultimate inclusion and exclusion of the articles. There was total agreement on the selected publications before they were included in the study. The minimum threshold value for inclusion is 7.5 (50% of the maximum). 41 well connected papers as shown in figure 3 were selected because they are ≥ 7.5. Table 2 shows the quality assessment results. Inter-rater reliability was checked using Cohen's Kappa coefficient, with disagreements resolved through consensus and a third reviewer whenever necessary. The review aimed to mitigate various biases. Publication bias was addressed by including both positive and negative findings and conducting funnel plot analyses. Selection bias was minimized by adhering to clear, pre-defined criteria and ensuring multiple reviewer screening. The review also acknowledged the limitation of only including English-language studies and documented the potential impact of this language bias on the findings.

Table 1. Quality evaluation (QE) criteria.

QE Questions	Criteria
QE1	Inclusion and Exclusion criteria – does the study meet these criteria?
QE2	Standard development platform – does the design follows a well-structured development concept?
QE3	Evaluation – does the paper presents a standard methodology?
QE4	Justifiable outcomes – does the study results compare well with the aim?
QE5	Credibility – does the paper published in a recognized source?

Ethical considerations were also integrated into the review process, with a focus on data privacy, AI-related biases, and accessibility. The review assessed the privacy protection measures of studies, examined the ethical approval documentation and consent procedures, and considered algorithmic bias and cultural sensitivity in the use of chatbots in education. Finally, the review recognized its limitations, including database restrictions, language constraints, and potential publication biases. A clear depiction of the research process and data extraction flow, aligned with PRISMA guidelines, is provided in the figures to clarify the methodology used in the review.

Figure 3. Connected papers

Table 2. Quality evaluation results

S/N	Title (T)	Authors (Year)	Type	QE1	QE2	QE3	QE4	QE5	Score
1.	Rediscovering the Use of Chatbots in Education: A Systematic Literature Review	Pérez et al. (2020)	Journal	3	3	3	3	3	15
2.	Are We There Yet? - A Systematic Literature Review on Chatbots in Education	Wollny et al. (2021)	Journal	3	3	3	3	3	15
3.	Chatbots Applications in Education: A Systematic Review	Okonkwo and Ade-Ibijola (2021a)	Journal	3	3	3	3	3	15
4.	A Review of Opportunities and Challenges of Chatbots in Education	Hwang and Chang (2021)	Journal	3	3	3	3	1	13
5.	Educational AI Chatbots for Content and Language Integrated Learning	Mageira et al. (2022)	Journal	3	3	3	3	3	15
6.	Chatbots for Learning: A Review of Educational Chatbots for the Facebook Messenger	Smutny and Schreiberova (2020)	Journal	3	3	3	3	1	13
7.	Interacting with Educational Chatbots: A Systematic Review	Kuhail et al. (2022)	Journal	3	3	1	3	1	11

continued on following page

Table 2. Continued

S/N	Title (T)	Authors (Year)	Type	QE1	QE2	QE3	QE4	QE5	Score
8.	Directions of the 100 most cited chatbot-related human behavior research: A review of academic publications	Wang et al. (2021)	Journal	3	3	3	3	3	15
9.	Chatbots for Language Learning—Are They Really Useful? A Systematic Review of Chatbot-Supported Language Learning	Huang et al. (2022)	Journal	3	3	3	3	3	15
10.	Opportunities and Challenges in Using AI Chatbots in Higher Education	Yang and Evans (2019)	Conference	3	3	3	3	1	13
11.	Educational Chatbots for Project-Based Learning: Investigating Learning Outcomes for a Team-Based Design Course	Kumar (2021)	Journal	3	3	3	3	1	13
12.	Chatbots: History, Technology, and Applications	Adamopoulou and Moussiades (2020)	Journal	3	3	3	3	3	15
13.	Promoting Students' Learning Achievement and Self-Efficacy: A Mobile Chatbot Approach for Nursing Training	Chang et al. (2021)	Journal	3	3	3	3	3	15
14.	A ChatBot for Learning Chinese: Learning Achievement and Technology Acceptance	Chen et al. (2020)	Journal	3	3	3	3	3	15
15.	Conversation Technology with Micro-Learning: The Impact of Chatbot-Based Learning on Students' Learning Motivation and Performance	Yin et al. (2020)	Journal	3	3	3	3	3	15
16.	How to Design and Deliver Courses for Higher Education in the AI Era: Insights from Exam Data Analysis	Wazan et al. (2023)	Preprint	1	3	3	3	1	11
17.	Python-Bot: A Chatbot for Teaching Python Programming	Okonkwo and Ade-Ibijola (2021b)	Journal	3	3	3	3	3	15
18.	The impact of a virtual teaching assistant (chatbot) on students' learning in Ghanaian higher education	Essel et al. (2022)	Journal	3	3	3	3	2	14
19.	Revolutionizing Education with AI: Exploring the Transformative Potential of ChatGPT	Adiguzel et al. (2023)	Journal	3	3	3	3	3	15
20.	Proactive Chatbot Framework Based on the PS2CLH Model: An AI-Deep Learning Chatbot Assistant for Students	Almada et al. (2022)	Journal	3	3	3	3	3	15
21.	Chatbot Learning Partners: Connecting Learning Experiences, Interest and Competence	Fryer et al. (2019)	Conference	3	3	3	3	3	15
22.	Bots for Language Learning Now: Current and Future Directions	Fryer et al. (2020)	Journal	3	3	3	3	1	13

continued on following page

Table 2. Continued

S/N	Title (T)	Authors (Year)	Type	QE1	QE2	QE3	QE4	QE5	Score
23.	An Overview of Chatbot Technology	Adamopoulou and Moussiades (2020)	Conference	1	3	1	3	3	11
24.	Chatbot Application in a 5th Grade Science Course	Topal et al. (2021)	Journal	3	3	3	3	3	15
25.	Implementing the Bashayer Chatbot in Saudi Higher Education: Measuring the Influence on Students' Motivation and Learning Strategies	Al-Abdullatif et al. (2023)	Journal	3	3	3	3	1	13
26.	Using Chatbots as AI Conversational Partners in Language Learning	Belda-Medina and Calvo-Ferrer (2022)	Journal	3	3	3	3	3	15
27.	Chatbot to improve learning punctuation in Spanish and to enhance open and flexible learning environments	Vázquez-Cano et al. (2021)	Journal	3	3	3	1	3	13
28.	Exploring AI chatbot affordances in the EFL classroom: young learners' experiences and perspectives	Jeon (2022)	Journal	3	3	3	3	3	15
29.	The Making and Development of Baxter the Empowered Chatbot Impered with Machine Intelligence	Jagadesan et al. (2021)	Journal	3	3	3	3	3	15
30.	Use of Chatbots in E-Learning Context: A Systematic Review	Riza et al. (2023)	Conference	3	3	1	3	3	13
31.	Usability Evaluation on Educational Chatbot Using the System Usability Scale (SUS)	Hidayat et al. (2022)	Conference	3	3	3	3	1	13
32.	Teachers' Attitudes Towards Chatbots in Education: A Technology Acceptance Model Approach Considering the Effect of Social Language, Bot Proactiveness, and Users' Characteristics	Chocarro et al. (2021)	Journal	3	3	3	3	3	15
33.	Supporting the Instructional Videos with Chatbot and Peer Feedback Mechanisms in Online Learning: The Effects on Learning Performance and Intrinsic Motivation	Fidan and Gencel (2022)	Journal	3	3	3	1	2	12
34.	Proposing a Task-Oriented Chatbot System for EFL Learners Speaking Practice	Hsu et al. (2021)	Journal	3	3	3	3	3	15
35.	Unleashing the Potential of Chatbots in Education: A State-Of-The-Art Analysis	Winkler and Soellner (2018)	Conference	1	2	1	3	3	10
36.	CBET: Design and Evaluation of a Domain-Specific Chatbot for Mobile Learning	Liu et al. (2019)	Journal	3	3	3	3	3	15

continued on following page

Table 2. Continued

S/N	Title (T)	Authors (Year)	Type	QE1	QE2	QE3	QE4	QE5	Score
37.	ChatGPT for Language Teaching and Learning	Kohnke et al. (2023)	Journal	3	3	3	1	3	13
38.	A Model to Develop Chatbots for Assisting the Teaching and Learning Process	Mendoza et al. (2022)	Journal	3	3	3	3	3	15
39.	Stimulating and Sustaining Interest in a Language Course: An Experimental Comparison of Chatbot and Human Task Partners	Fryer et al. (2017)	Journal	3	3	3	3	3	15
40.	Artificial Intelligence (AI) Chatbot as Language Learning Medium: An inquiry	Haristiani (2019)	Conference	3	3	2	3	1	12
41.	Chatbot: An Education Support System for Student	Clarizia et al. (2018)	Conference	3	3	3	1	2	12

Reporting the Review

This section presents the findings from our systematic literature review on the role of chatbots in modern education. Following a rigorous search process across multiple recognized academic databases, we carefully selected and evaluated the most relevant articles (Figure 3). After applying quality evaluation criteria, a final dataset of 41 articles was compiled for this research. The results are presented in relation to our four primary research questions.

What are the Primary Applications and Roles of Chatbots in Educational Settings?

This chapter reveals that educational chatbots serve a diverse range of applications and roles, primarily focused on enhancing the learning experience and supporting administrative functions. Language learning has perhaps, been the most valuable application. The ability of language learners to engage conversation practice has been provided by chatbots for detailed language learning, enlisting prompt response and tailoring to the learners' needs. Fryer et al. (2017) and Belda-Medina and Calvo-Ferrer (2022) have also supported the importance of chatbots for language learning in their respective studies. For instance, Huang et al. (2022) undertook a critical assessment of literature on language learning through chatbots enhancing self-efficacy; particularly, how chatbots elevate the nine constructs in a self-efficacy approach, lexical skill, articulation and language. Such research confirms how chatbots can be integrated into the teaching-learning process for languages as they enhance the practice of language learning by learners through providing them with simple and effective ways of practicing the language.

In the realm of subject-specific learning, chatbots have been employed across various disciplines to enhance student engagement and learning outcomes. Okonkwo and Ade-Ibijola (2020) developed "Python-Bot," a chatbot designed to teach Python programming, which demonstrated the potential of chatbots in computer science education. Their work highlights how chatbots can provide tailored assistance in complex subjects like programming (Garcia, 2025), making them more accessible to learners. Similarly, Topal et al. (2021) implemented a chatbot in a 5th-grade science course, showing its effectiveness in improving student engagement and academic performance. These examples illustrate the versatility of chatbots in supporting subject-specific learning across different educational levels and disciplines.

Personalized learning is another critical area where chatbots have shown significant promise. Almada et al. (2022) proposed a proactive chatbot framework based on the PS2CLH model, aimed at providing personalized assistance to students. This approach aligns with the findings of Chang et al. (2021), who reported that mobile chatbots could enhance students' learning achievement and self-efficacy, particularly in nursing training. In addition to these instructional roles, chatbots also offer substantial benefits in administrative support. Yang and Evans (2019) highlighted the potential of chatbots in higher education to handle routine queries and administrative tasks, thus freeing up educators' time for more critical teaching activities. Furthermore, chatbots have been used to support project-based learning and collaborative activities. Kumar (2021) examined the educational chatbots within the parameters of a team-based design course, while analyzing the impact of the given technological support on the local learning outcomes, thus proving the broader scale of application of educational chatbots within other educational settings.

How do Educational Chatbots Impact Student Learning Outcomes, Motivation, and Engagement?

The impact of educational chatbots on student learning outcomes, motivation, and engagement is a central focus of many studies in our review, and the overall findings suggest a generally positive influence. However, the extent and nature of this impact can vary based on specific contexts and implementation strategies. With respect to learning outcomes, there seems to be a consensus in a number of studies that students' academic performance improves with the inclusion of chatbots in the learning process. For instance, Chen et al. (2020) state that students' learning achievement improved greatly through the use of chatbots in the teaching of the Chinese language. Similarly, Yin et al. (2020) showed that learning through chatbots enhanced the learning performances of the students especially in micro-learning contexts. However, not all studies have been able to demonstrate such upgrades, which is the case part of the investigation. The systematic assessment of the studies conducted by Wollny et al. (2021) also produced inconclusive results that hinted at the relevance of the context in which the chatbots are used.

In terms of motivation and engagement, the outcomes reported by literature can be regarded with a degree of consistency in their positivity. Fryer et al. (2017) compared the performance of chatbots and humans in a task and found that chatbots are capable of inducing and retaining a desire to learn a language. This is supported by Al-Abdullatif et al. (2023), who reported that the implementation of a chatbot in Saudi higher education positively influenced students' motivation and learning strategies. Furthermore, Jeon (2022) explored the use of AI chatbots in EFL (English as a Foreign Language) classrooms, noting that young learners found the experience both engaging and motivating. These findings align with those of Essel et al. (2022), who observed positive impacts on student engagement when a virtual teaching assistant (chatbot) was introduced in Ghanaian higher education settings. The review by Hwang and Chang (2021) synthesized these findings and highlighted the opportunities that chatbots present in enhancing student engagement and motivation. They noted that the interactive and immediate nature of chatbot responses contributes significantly to maintaining student interest and participation. Being able to sufficiently engage the students using chatbots is made possible by the instant feedback that is available with the use of the electronic apparatus as well as the creation of active learning using the program.

What are the Key Factors Influencing the Effectiveness of Educational Chatbots?

This chapter identified several key factors that influence the effectiveness of educational chatbots, which can be broadly categorized into technological aspects, pedagogical considerations, and user-related factors. From a technological standpoint, the quality of natural language processing and understanding is critical. Adamopoulou and Moussiades (2020) emphasized that advanced AI techniques play a crucial role in enhancing chatbot performance. Active respondents identified the context understanding, query complexity management, and accuracy of answers as the most important parameters for chatbots' effectiveness. These aspects will reflect the extent to which the educational goals of the chatbots can be met and the quality of interactions they can enable with the users.

Pedagogical design is another vital factor in determining the effectiveness of educational chatbots. Mendoza et al. (2022) proposed a model for developing chatbots that assist in the teaching and learning process, stressing the importance of aligning chatbot functionalities with specific pedagogical goals. Hsu et al. (2021) also highlighted the need for task-oriented design, particularly in chatbots designed for language learning. Furthermore, personalization has been identified as a key component of effective chatbot design. Almada et al. (2022) proposed a proactive chatbot framework that adapts to individual student needs, which was found to significantly enhance the learning experience by tailoring interactions and content to each learner's specific requirements.

Users' acceptance and perception are no less important with regard to achieving these results in the educational context. Chocarro et al. (2021) investigated the attitude towards chatbots among teachers through the lens of the technology acceptance model, concluding that network structure, chatbot proactivity and individual factors determine acceptance level. This acceptance, in turn, impacts the overall effectiveness of the chatbot in achieving educational outcomes. Additionally, the integration of chatbots with other educational technologies and existing curricula is essential for maximizing their effectiveness. Fidan and Gencel (2022) studied how the combination of chatbots with instructional videos and peer feedback mechanisms positively affected learning performance and intrinsic motivation. Finally, the specific application context is another significant factor, as highlighted by Kohnke et al. (2023), who discussed the potential of ChatGPT in language teaching and learning. Their findings indicate that the effectiveness of advanced AI models like ChatGPT can vary depending on the particular language learning tasks and objectives, underscoring the importance of context in the successful deployment of chatbots in education.

What are the Current Limitations and Challenges in Implementing Chatbots in Education?

Despite the potential benefits, several limitations and challenges in implementing chatbots in educational settings have been identified. One of the most significant challenges is technical limitations. Adamopoulou and Moussiades (2020) highlighted the issues related to limited natural language understanding and the necessity for extensive knowledge bases. One of the observations made by these authors is that chatbots tend to work poorly with complicated queries and retention of context when the dialog extends into longer timeframes. It is these limitations that will prevent using them effectively in creating an integrated education of the learners especially in situations that require full comprehension and context. Ethical concerns and data privacy issues also present substantial challenges in the implementation of chatbots in education. Winkler and Soellner (2018) emphasized the importance of addressing ethical considerations, particularly regarding data protection and user privacy. The rapid advancements in AI, including the emergence of sophisticated models like ChatGPT, have heightened these concerns, as noted by Adiguzel et al. (2023). Ensuring that chatbot technology complies with ethical standards and protects user data is critical for building trust and ensuring the responsible use of AI in educational settings.

Integration with existing educational systems and curricula poses another significant challenge. Vázquez-Cano et al. (2021) discussed the difficulties in seamlessly incorporating chatbots into established educational practices and technologies. This process often requires considerable time, resources, and potential adjustments to current pedagogical approaches. Additionally, user acceptance can be a barrier, particularly among educators. Chocarro et al. (2021) found that teachers' attitudes towards chatbots vary, with factors such as perceived usefulness and ease of use influencing their acceptance. Overcoming resistance and providing proper training for both educators and students are essential for successful implementation. Furthermore, the development of high-quality, domain-specific content for chatbots requires significant effort, as highlighted by Liu et al. (2019). Lastly, concerns about overreliance on chatbots and the impact on critical thinking skills have been raised by Kohnke et al. (2023), who stressed the need for balancing the use of AI-powered tools with traditional learning methods to ensure the development of independent thinking and problem-solving skills. In order to accomplish these, future studies will aim at resolving these issues so as to promote the integration of the use of chatbots in the education sector while enhancing the delivery of education.

DISCUSSION

This chapter presents a systematic review of 41 high-impact studies published between 2017 and 2023, revealing the growing body of evidence supporting the transformative potential of chatbots in education. The findings highlight both the promising applications, and the challenges associated with the implementation of chatbot technology across various educational contexts.

RQ1: Primary Applications and Roles of Chatbots in Education

The first research question explored the primary applications and roles of chatbots in educational settings. A thorough examination of the 41 studies revealed that language learning is one of the most advanced areas where chatbot technology has been successfully deployed. Studies by Fryer et al. (2020) and Huang et al. (2022) highlighted how chatbots, especially in platforms like Facebook Messenger, facilitate foreign language learning by offering immediate feedback, conversational engagement, and personalized learning opportunities. The use of chatbots for language learning aligns with findings from Smutny and Schreiberova (2020), who also observed the dominance of such chatbots in educational applications.

Beyond language learning, chatbots are being increasingly utilized for administrative assistance, subject area instruction, and fostering student interactions across different disciplines (Pérez et al., 2020). For instance, Okonkwo and Ade-Ibijola (2021b) employed a Python-based chatbot to introduce programming concepts, demonstrating its potential for STEM education. These applications extend chatbots' role from merely serving as language-learning tools to becoming versatile educational assistants.

RQ2: Impact of Chatbots on Learning Outcomes, Motivation, and Engagement

The second research question investigated the impact of AI-enabled chatbots on learning outcomes, motivation, and engagement. Overall, the reviewed studies presented a positive impact of chatbots on educational outcomes, including enhanced learning performance, increased motivation, and greater engagement. For example, Chang et al. (2021) found that a mobile chatbot in nursing training not only improved learning achievement but also increased students' self-efficacy. This aligns with Yin et al. (2020), who found similar positive shifts in student engagement and motivation after chatbot implementation.

However, the effectiveness of chatbots in these areas is not uniform across disciplines or educational contexts. Kumar (2021) identified mixed results in project-based learning, emphasizing the importance of context in determining the success of chatbot applications. Chatbot effectiveness can vary significantly depending on the subject area (e.g., language learning vs. STEM subjects), student levels (e.g., beginner vs. advanced learners), and the educational setting (e.g., self-paced vs. instructor-led environments). For example, in STEM education, chatbots may face challenges in complex problem-solving contexts where human instructors can provide more nuanced guidance. In contrast, in language learning, the rapid feedback and conversational elements provided by chatbots may lead to more consistent improvements.

RQ3: Key Factors Influencing Chatbot Effectiveness

The third research question focused on the factors influencing chatbot effectiveness. Key findings emphasize the importance of personalization and adaptivity in chatbot design. Studies like Hsu et al. (2021) highlighted the value of task-oriented chatbots that adapt to individual learner needs. Additionally, the quality of natural language processing (NLP) and the underlying knowledge base are critical factors for effective chatbot operation (Adamopoulou & Moussiades, 2020). However, while NLP has made significant strides, technical limitations remain, particularly when it comes to understanding context and maintaining appropriate conversations. These limitations can lead to misunderstandings in educational contexts, frustrating users and potentially hindering learning outcomes.

Furthermore, user acceptance and perception play a crucial role in determining the success of chatbots. Chocarro et al. (2021) found that teachers' perceptions of chatbots significantly influenced their willingness to integrate these technologies into their classrooms. Similarly, Jeon (2022) explored young learners' attitudes toward AI chatbots in language education, emphasizing the importance of addressing social factors such as language, proactivity, and user traits in chatbot design.

RQ4: Limitations and Challenges in Chatbot Implementation

The fourth research question explored the limitations and challenges in chatbot implementation. Despite the promising results, several challenges persist. Technical limitations, particularly in NLP and maintaining contextual relevance in conversations, remain significant barriers. When these limitations are not adequately addressed, chatbots can lead to confusion or disengagement, which diminishes their potential effectiveness in education. For example, in scenarios where the chatbot fails to understand or respond appropriately to a student's query, the user experience can be severely impacted, leading to frustration.

Ethical challenges are also becoming more prominent. Data privacy concerns regarding the handling of student information are an ongoing issue, with several studies highlighting the importance of secure data practices (Adiguzel et al., 2023). Moreover, the risk of algorithmic bias in AI systems, which may affect learning outcomes, is an area requiring further attention. For example, biased chatbot responses could perpetuate stereotypes or provide unequal learning experiences for different student groups. Kohnke et al. (2023) raised concerns about ethical issues in the use of chatbots like ChatGPT, particularly related to language education and the implications for fairness in AI-driven interactions.

Integration with existing curricula and pedagogical approaches is another challenge. As Hwang and Chang (2021) noted, successful integration requires careful consideration of how chatbots fit within traditional teaching methods. Educators must thoughtfully design curricula that accommodate the limitations of chatbot technology, particularly in areas like natural language understanding. Strategies for integrating chatbots with instructor-led teaching methods and knowing when to use chatbots versus other instructional methods, are critical to maximize their effectiveness. For example, chatbots may be better suited for repetitive tasks like vocabulary practice in language learning, while more complex learning activities may require human intervention. This systematic review reveals that while chatbots hold significant promise for enhancing education across various disciplines, their implementation requires careful consideration of both technical and pedagogical factors. To fully realize the potential of chatbots in education, further research is needed, particularly in addressing the challenges of technical limitations, ethical issues, and effective integration into diverse educational settings. Collaboration among educators, technologists, and policymakers will be essential in shaping the future of chatbot-enhanced education.

IMPLICATIONS

The findings of this systematic review have significant implications for educational practice, policy, and future research. In terms of educational practice, the positive impact of chatbots on student engagement, motivation, and learning outcomes suggests that educators should consider integrating these AI-powered tools into their teaching strategies (Chang et al., 2021; Yin et al., 2020). Particularly in language learning and subject-specific tutoring, chatbots offer opportunities for personalized, interactive learning experiences that can complement traditional instruction methods (Fryer et al., 2020; Okonkwo & Ade-Ibijola, 2021a). However, educators must carefully consider the design and implementation of chatbots, ensuring they align with pedagogical goals and are seamlessly integrated into existing curricula (Acut et al., 2025; Hsu et al., 2021; Mendoza et al., 2022).

From a policy perspective, the growing adoption of chatbots in education necessitates the development of comprehensive guidelines and standards (Gantalao et al., 2025). Educational institutions and policymakers should focus on establishing ethical frameworks for the use of AI in education, addressing concerns related to data privacy, AI bias, and responsible AI usage (Adiguzel et al., 2023; Kohnke et al., 2023). Additionally, policies should be developed to support the professional development of educators in effectively utilizing chatbot technologies and integrating them into their teaching practices (Chocarro et al., 2021; Görgülü et al., 2025; Srinivasan et al., 2025). Furthermore, funding initiatives may be necessary to support the development and implementation of high-quality, domain-specific chatbots across various educational contexts (Liu et al., 2019). Finally, as the field of AI continues to advance rapidly, ongoing research is crucial to exploring the potential of more sophisticated AI models, like ChatGPT, in educational settings, while also addressing the ethical and practical challenges they may present (Adiguzel et al., 2023; Kohnke et al., 2023).

CONCLUSION

A systematic evaluation of evidence-based adaptive learning using educational chatbots points to favorable results when used in varying learning environments. The results confirm that learning outcomes, user (student) engagement, and motivation, especially in a language learning context and using some adaptivity features of the chatbots, can be enhanced by implementing chatbots. Many researchers have recognized the usefulness of chatbots in the context of education, whereby improvement of learning performance and self-efficacy is reported. However, the impact varies depending on factors such as subject area, design features, and implementation duration, underscoring the need for context-specific approaches in chatbot integration. The potential of chatbots to support personalized learning and provide immediate feedback aligns with contemporary educational goals of creating more interactive and engaging learning environments. There are some limitations and difficult circumstances that have been reported in the research on educational chatbots. However technical barriers in natural language understanding and pragmatics still represent serious issues. If not properly addressed, these deficiencies might cause dissatisfaction and drop out. Ethical issues surrounding chatbot technology have recently emerged and gained more relevance, especially with the increasing utilization of such technology within educational settings. The integration of chatbots with existing curricula and pedagogical approaches presents another challenge, requiring careful consideration to maximize their benefits while maintaining educational integrity.

Further work can concentrate on refining these limitations, while also advancing the scope of educational chatbots. In order to represent the effectiveness of the chatbot at various educational domains, there is a need to design multi-dimensional evaluation frameworks that enable the assessment of effectiveness with regards to engagement, learning, and satisfaction. Designing clear ethical policy for medicine delivery without any data privacy breach while not violating user consent and the principle of this AI is the only way that practice will be implemented in an ethical and transparent manner. It will also contribute to the understanding of how effective these technologies are as they will be used in different educational levels from primary education to tertiary education and across different socioeconomic disparities. Expanding studies that will ensure that it will be possible to study the resulting post-interventions or the ongoing changes with respect to cognitive engagement, quantitative measurable learning or retention of learners will provide crucial information that helps understand efficiency in the given post-intervention education environment. Finally, investigating the integration of chatbots with other educational technologies, such as learning management systems, virtual reality, and augmented reality, holds promise for creating more holistic and immersive learning experiences.

REFERENCES

Acut, D. P., Gamusa, E. V., Pernaa, J., Yuenyong, C., Pantaleon, A. T., Espina, R. C., Sim, M. J. C., & Garcia, M. B. (2025). AI Shaming Among Teacher Education Students: A Reflection on Acceptance and Identity in the Age of Generative Tools. In *Pitfalls of AI Integration in Education: Skill Obsolescence, Misuse, and Bias*. IGI Global., DOI: 10.4018/979-8-3373-0122-8.ch005

Adamopoulou, E., & Moussiades, L. (2020). Chatbots: History, Technology, and Applications. *Machine Learning with Applications*, 2, 100006. DOI: 10.1016/j.mlwa.2020.100006

Adiguzel, T., Kaya, M. H., & Cansu, F. K. (2023). Revolutionizing Education with AI: Exploring the Transformative Potential of ChatGPT. *Contemporary Educational Technology*, 15(3), ep429. DOI: 10.30935/cedtech/13152

Al-Abdullatif, A. M., Al-Dokhny, A. A., & Drwish, A. M. (2023). Implementing the Bashayer Chatbot in Saudi Higher Education: Measuring the Influence on Students' Motivation and Learning Strategies. *Frontiers in Psychology*, 14, 1129070. Advance online publication. DOI: 10.3389/fpsyg.2023.1129070 PMID: 37255522

Almada, A., Yu, Q., & Patel, P. (2022). Proactive Chatbot Framework Based on the PS2CLH Model: An AI-Deep Learning Chatbot Assistant for Students. *Lecture Notes in Networks and Systems*, 751-770. https://doi.org/DOI: 10.1007/978-3-031-16072-1_54

Aznoli, F., & Navimipour, N. J. (2017). Cloud Services Recommendation: Reviewing the Recent Advances and Suggesting the Future Research Directions. *Journal of Network and Computer Applications*, 77, 73–86. DOI: 10.1016/j.jnca.2016.10.009

Belda-Medina, J., & Calvo-Ferrer, J. R. (2022). Using Chatbots as AI Conversational Partners in Language Learning. *Applied Sciences (Basel, Switzerland)*, 12(17), 8427. DOI: 10.3390/app12178427

Bozkurt, A., Xiao, J., Farrow, R., Bai, J. Y. H., Nerantzi, C., Moore, S., Dron, J., Stracke, C. M., Singh, L., Crompton, H., Koutropoulos, A., Terentev, E., Pazurek, A., Nichols, M., Sidorkin, A. M., Costello, E., Watson, S., Mulligan, D., Honeychurch, S., & Asino, T. I. (2024). The Manifesto for Teaching and Learning in a Time of Generative AI: A Critical Collective Stance to Better Navigate the Future. *Open Praxis*, 16(4), 487–513. DOI: 10.55982/openpraxis.16.4.777

Chang, C. Y., Hwang, G. J., & Gau, M. L. (2021). Promoting Students' Learning Achievement and Self-Efficacy: A Mobile Chatbot Approach for Nursing Training. *British Journal of Educational Technology*, 53(1), 171–188. DOI: 10.1111/bjet.13158

Chen, H.-L., Vicki Widarso, G., & Sutrisno, H. (2020). A ChatBot for Learning Chinese: Learning Achievement and Technology Acceptance. *Journal of Educational Computing Research*, 58(6), 1161–1189. DOI: 10.1177/0735633120929622

Chocarro, R., Cortiñas, M., & Marcos-Matás, G. (2021). Teachers' Attitudes Towards Chatbots in Education: A Technology Acceptance Model Approach Considering the Effect of Social Language, Bot Proactiveness, and Users' Characteristics. *Educational Studies*, 49(2), 295–313. DOI: 10.1080/03055698.2020.1850426

Clarizia, F., Colace, F., Lombardi, M., Pascale, F., & Santaniello, D. (2018). Chatbot: An Education Support System for Student. *Lecture Notes in Computer Science*, *11161*, 291–302. DOI: 10.1007/978-3-030-01689-0_23

Deng, X., & Yu, Z. (2023). A Meta-Analysis and Systematic Review of the Effect of Chatbot Technology Use in Sustainable Education. *Sustainability (Basel)*, *15*(4), 2940. DOI: 10.3390/su15042940

Essel, H. B., Vlachopoulos, D., Tachie-Menson, A., Johnson, E. E., & Baah, P. K. (2022). The Impact of a Virtual Teaching Assistant (Chatbot) on Students' Learning in Ghanaian Higher Education. *International Journal of Educational Technology in Higher Education*, *19*(1), 57. Advance online publication. DOI: 10.1186/s41239-022-00362-6

Fidan, M., & Gencel, N. (2022). Supporting the Instructional Videos With Chatbot and Peer Feedback Mechanisms in Online Learning: The Effects on Learning Performance and Intrinsic Motivation. *Journal of Educational Computing Research*, *60*(7), 1716–1741. DOI: 10.1177/07356331221077901

Fryer, L., Coniam, D., Carpenter, R., & Lăpu neanu, D. (2020). Bots for Language Learning Now: Current and Future Directions. *Language Learning & Technology*, *24*(2), 8–22. https://www.lltjournal.org/item/10125-44719/

Fryer, L. K., Ainley, M., Thompson, A., Gibson, A., & Sherlock, Z. (2017). Stimulating and Sustaining Interest in a Language Course: An Experimental Comparison of Chatbot and Human Task Partners. *Computers in Human Behavior*, *75*, 461–468. DOI: 10.1016/j.chb.2017.05.045

Fryer, L. K., Nakao, K., & Thompson, A. (2019). Chatbot Learning Partners: Connecting Learning Experiences, Interest and Competence. *Computers in Human Behavior*, *93*, 279–289. DOI: 10.1016/j.chb.2018.12.023

Gantalao, L. C., Calzada, J. G. D., Capuyan, D. L., Lumantas, B. C., Acut, D. P., & Garcia, M. B. (2025). Equipping the Next Generation of Technicians: Navigating School Infrastructure and Technical Knowledge in the Age of AI Integration. In *Pitfalls of AI Integration in Education: Skill Obsolescence, Misuse, and Bias*. IGI Global., DOI: 10.4018/979-8-3373-0122-8.ch009

Garcia, M. B. (2025). Teaching and Learning Computer Programming Using ChatGPT: A Rapid Review of Literature Amid the Rise of Generative AI Technologies. *Education and Information Technologies*, ●●●, 1–25. DOI: 10.1007/s10639-025-13452-5

Görgülü, D., Sipahioğlu, M., & Brazzolotto, M. (2025). Investigation of the Opinions of Classroom Teachers Working in Science and Art Centers on the Pitfalls of Artificial Intelligence in Education. In *Pitfalls of AI Integration in Education: Skill Obsolescence, Misuse, and Bias*. IGI Global., DOI: 10.4018/979-8-3373-0122-8.ch006

Haristiani, N. (2019). Artificial Intelligence (AI) Chatbot as Language Learning Medium: An inquiry. *Journal of Physics: Conference Series*, *1387*(1), 012020. DOI: 10.1088/1742-6596/1387/1/012020

Hasanah, N. A., Aziza, M. R., Junikhah, A., Arif, Y. M., & Garcia, M. B. (2025). Navigating the Use of AI in Engineering Education Through a Systematic Review of Technology, Regulations, and Challenges. In *Pitfalls of AI Integration in Education: Skill Obsolescence, Misuse, and Bias*. IGI Global., DOI: 10.4018/979-8-3373-0122-8.ch016

Hidayat, A., Nugroho, A., & Nurfaizin, S. (2022). Usability Evaluation on Educational Chatbot Using the System Usability Scale (SUS). *2022 Seventh International Conference on Informatics and Computing (ICIC)*, 01-05. https://doi.org/DOI: 10.1109/ICIC56845.2022.10006991

Hsu, M.-H., Chen, P.-S., & Yu, C.-S. (2021). Proposing a Task-Oriented Chatbot System for EFL Learners Speaking Practice. *Interactive Learning Environments*, *31*(7), 4297–4308. DOI: 10.1080/10494820.2021.1960864

Huang, W., Hew, K. F., & Fryer, L. K. (2022). Chatbots for Language Learning—Are They Really Useful? A Systematic Review of Chatbot-Supported Language Learning. *Journal of Computer Assisted Learning*, *38*(1), 237–257. DOI: 10.1111/jcal.12610

Hwang, G.-J., & Chang, C.-Y. (2021). A Review of Opportunities and Challenges of Chatbots in Education. *Interactive Learning Environments*, *31*(7), 4099–4112. DOI: 10.1080/10494820.2021.1952615

Izquierdo-Álvarez, V., & Jimeno-Postigo, C. (2025). Challenges and Opportunities of Integrating Generative Artificial Intelligence in Higher Education: A Systematic Review. In *Pitfalls of AI Integration in Education: Skill Obsolescence, Misuse, and Bias*. IGI Global., DOI: 10.4018/979-8-3373-0122-8.ch017

Jagadesan, S., Girish, P., & Kurane, A. R. (2021). The Making and Development of Baxter the Empowered Chatbot Impered with Machine Intelligence. *Trends in Computer Science and Information Technology*, 036-041. https://doi.org/DOI: 10.17352/tcsit.000037

Jeon, J. (2022). Exploring AI chatbot affordances in the EFL classroom: Young learners' experiences and perspectives. *Computer Assisted Language Learning*, *37*(1-2), 1–26. DOI: 10.1080/09588221.2021.2021241

Kohnke, L., Moorhouse, B. L., & Zou, D. (2023). ChatGPT for Language Teaching and Learning. *RELC Journal*, *54*(2), 537–550. DOI: 10.1177/00336882231162868

Kuhail, M. A., Alturki, N., Alramlawi, S., & Alhejori, K. (2022). Interacting with Educational Chatbots: A Systematic Review. *Education and Information Technologies*, *28*(1), 973–1018. DOI: 10.1007/s10639-022-11177-3

Kumar, J. A. (2021). Educational Chatbots for Project-Based Learning: Investigating Learning Outcomes for a Team-Based Design Course. *International Journal of Educational Technology in Higher Education*, *18*(1), 65. Advance online publication. DOI: 10.1186/s41239-021-00302-w PMID: 34926790

Liu, Q., Huang, J., Wu, L., Zhu, K., & Ba, S. (2019). CBET: Design and Evaluation of a Domain-Specific Chatbot for Mobile Learning. *Universal Access in the Information Society*, *19*(3), 655–673. DOI: 10.1007/s10209-019-00666-x

Mageira, K., Pittou, D., Papasalouros, A., Kotis, K., Zangogianni, P., & Daradoumis, A. (2022). Educational AI Chatbots for Content and Language Integrated Learning. *Applied Sciences (Basel, Switzerland)*, *12*(7), 3239. DOI: 10.3390/app12073239

Mendoza, S., Sánchez-Adame, L. M., Urquiza-Yllescas, J. F., González-Beltrán, B. A., & Decouchant, D. (2022). A Model to Develop Chatbots for Assisting the Teaching and Learning Process. *Sensors (Basel)*, *22*(15), 5532. DOI: 10.3390/s22155532 PMID: 35898035

Okonkwo, C. W., & Ade-Ibijola, A. (2021a). Chatbots Applications in Education: A Systematic Review. *Computers and Education: Artificial Intelligence*, *2*, 100033. DOI: 10.1016/j.caeai.2021.100033

Okonkwo, C. W., & Ade-Ibijola, A. (2021b). Python-Bot: A Chatbot for Teaching Python Programming. *Engineering Letters*, *29*, 25–34.

Olugbade, D. (2024). Democratizing Education in Rural Nigeria Through AI and Mobile Technologies as a Transformative Pathway to Inclusive Learning. In *Advances in Educational Technologies and Instructional Design* (pp. 233-250). IGI Global. https://doi.org/DOI: 10.4018/979-8-3693-7255-5.ch010

Olugbade, D., & Ojo, O. A. (2024). Immersion Technologies: Going Beyond Textbooks to Improve Learning in Developing Nations. *Lecture Notes in Educational Technology*, 297-316. https://doi.org/ DOI: 10.1007/978-981-97-8752-4_16

Pérez, J. Q., Daradoumis, T., & Puig, J. M. M. (2020). Rediscovering the Use of Chatbots in Education: A Systematic Literature Review. *Computer Applications in Engineering Education*, *28*(6), 1549–1565. DOI: 10.1002/cae.22326

Riza, A. N. I., Hidayah, I., & Santosa, P. I. (2023). Use of Chatbots in E-Learning Context: A Systematic Review. *2023 IEEE World AI IoT Congress (AIIoT)*, 0819-0824. https://doi.org/DOI: 10.1109/ AIIoT58121.2023.10174319

Smutny, P., & Schreiberova, P. (2020). Chatbots for Learning: A Review of Educational Chatbots for the Facebook Messenger. *Computers & Education*, *151*, 103862. DOI: 10.1016/j.compedu.2020.103862

Snyder, H. (2019). Literature Review as a Research Methodology: An Overview and Guidelines. *Journal of Business Research*, *104*, 333–339. DOI: 10.1016/j.jbusres.2019.07.039

Srinivasan, K. R., Rahman, N. H. A., & Ravana, S. D. (2025). Reskilling and Upskilling Future Educators for the Demands of Artificial Intelligence in the Modern Era of Education. In *Pitfalls of AI Integration in Education: Skill Obsolescence, Misuse, and Bias*. IGI Global., DOI: 10.4018/979-8-3373-0122-8.ch008

Topal, A. D., Dilek Eren, C., & Kolburan Geçer, A. (2021). Chatbot Application in a 5th Grade Science Course. *Education and Information Technologies*, *26*(5), 6241–6265. DOI: 10.1007/s10639-021-10627-8 PMID: 34177344

Vázquez-Cano, E., Mengual-Andrés, S., & López-Meneses, E. (2021). Chatbot to improve learning punctuation in Spanish and to enhance open and flexible learning environments. *International Journal of Educational Technology in Higher Education*, *18*(1), 33. Advance online publication. DOI: 10.1186/ s41239-021-00269-8

Wang, J., Hwang, G.-H., & Chang, C.-Y. (2021). Directions of the 100 Most Cited Chatbot-Related Human Behavior Research: A Review of Academic Publications. *Computers and Education: Artificial Intelligence*, *2*, 100023. DOI: 10.1016/j.caeai.2021.100023

Wazan, A., Taj, I., Shoufan, A., Laborde, R., & Venant, R. (2023). How to Design and Deliver Courses for Higher Education in the AI Era: Insights from Exam Data Analysis. *ArXiv*. https://doi.org//arXiv .2308.02441DOI: 10.48550

Winkler, R., & Soellner, M. (2018). Unleashing the Potential of Chatbots in Education: A State-Of-The-Art Analysis. *Proceedings - Academy of Management, 2018*(1), 15903. DOI: 10.5465/AMBPP.2018.15903abstract

Wohlin, C., & Prikladnicki, R. (2013). Systematic Literature Reviews in Software Engineering. *Information and Software Technology, 55*(6), 919–920. DOI: 10.1016/j.infsof.2013.02.002

Wollny, S., Schneider, J., Di Mitri, D., Weidlich, J., Rittberger, M., & Drachsler, H. (2021). Are We There Yet? - A Systematic Literature Review on Chatbots in Education. *Frontiers in Artificial Intelligence, 4*, 654924. Advance online publication. DOI: 10.3389/frai.2021.654924 PMID: 34337392

Yang, S., & Evans, C. (2019). Opportunities and Challenges in Using AI Chatbots in Higher Education. *Proceedings of the 2019 3rd International Conference on Education and E-Learning.* https://doi.org/ DOI: 10.1145/3371647.3371659

Yin, J., Goh, T.-T., Yang, B., & Xiaobin, Y. (2020). Conversation Technology With Micro-Learning: The Impact of Chatbot-Based Learning on Students' Learning Motivation and Performance. *Journal of Educational Computing Research, 59*(1), 154–177. DOI: 10.1177/0735633120952067

Zawacki-Richter, O., Marín, V. I., Bond, M., & Gouverneur, F. (2019). Systematic Review of Research on Artificial Intelligence Applications in Higher Education – Where Are the Educators? *International Journal of Educational Technology in Higher Education, 16*(1), 39. Advance online publication. DOI: 10.1186/s41239-019-0171-0

KEY TERMS AND DEFINITIONS

Artificial Intelligence (AI): A branch of computer science focused on developing systems capable of performing tasks that typically require human intelligence, including learning, problem-solving, and pattern recognition in educational contexts.

Chatbots: Computer programs designed to engage in text or voice-based conversations with users, specifically engineered to provide educational support, answer queries, and facilitate learning through automated interactions.

Digital Transformation: The systematic integration of digital technologies into educational processes and practices, fundamentally changing how education is delivered and how learning occurs.

Educational Technology: Tools, systems, and resources that leverage technology to enhance teaching and learning processes, improve educational outcomes, and facilitate administrative tasks in educational settings.

Pedagogical AI-Based Conversational Agents: Advanced artificial intelligence systems specifically designed to support teaching and learning through interactive dialogue, providing personalized educational experiences and immediate feedback to learners.

Systematic Literature Review: A comprehensive research methodology that systematically identifies, evaluates, and synthesizes all relevant research on a specific topic, following predetermined criteria to minimize bias and ensure thoroughness.

Digital Natives: Individuals who have grown up in the digital age and are inherently familiar with digital technologies, characterized by their expectation for immediate access to information and technological integration in learning processes.

Adaptive Learning Pathways: Personalized learning sequences that automatically adjust to individual student needs, progress, and performance levels, facilitated by AI-powered educational tools like chatbots.

Compilation of References

Abbasi, B. N., Wu, Y., & Luo, Z. (2024). Exploring the impact of artificial intelligence on curriculum development in global higher education institutions. *Education and Information Technologies*. Advance online publication. DOI: 10.1007/s10639-024-13113-z

Abbas, N., Ali, I., Manzoor, R., Hussain, T., & Hussain, M. H. A. L. i. (2023). Role of Artificial Intelligence Tools in Enhancing Students' Educational Performance at Higher Levels. *Journal of Artificial Intelligence. Machine Learning and Neural Network*, (35), 36–49. DOI: 10.55529/jaimlnn.35.36.49

Abides, R. J. P. (2024). Bridging the Skills Gap: Examining the Electronics Technology Students' Competence and Industry Demands. *Journal of Interdisciplinary Perspectives*, 2(10), 1–1. DOI: 10.69569/jip.2024.0407

Abimbola, C., Eden, C., Chisom, O., & Adeniyi, I. (2024). Integrating AI in education: Opportunities, challenges, and ethical considerations. *Magna Scientia Advanced Research and Reviews, 10*(02), 006–013. https://doi.org/.DOI: 10.30574/msarr.2024.10.2.0039

Acut, D. (2022). Developing SIPCaR projects utilizing modern technologies: Its impact to students' engagement, R&D skills, and learning outcomes. *LUMAT: International Journal on Math. Science and Technology Education*, 10(1), 294–318. DOI: 10.31129/LUMAT.10.1.1667

Acut, D. P. (2024). From Classroom Learning to Real-World Skills: An Autoethnographic Account of School Field Trips and STEM Work Immersion Program Management. *Disciplinary and Interdisciplinary Science Education Research*, 6(1), 1–13. DOI: 10.1186/s43031-024-00111-x

Acut, D. P., Gamusa, E. V., Pernaa, J., Yuenyong, C., Pantaleon, A. T., Espina, R. C., Sim, M. J. C., & Garcia, M. B. (2025). AI Shaming Among Teacher Education Students: A Reflection on Acceptance and Identity in the Age of Generative Tools. In *Pitfalls of AI Integration in Education: Skill Obsolescence, Misuse, and Bias*. IGI Global., DOI: 10.4018/979-8-3373-0122-8.ch005

Acut, D. P., Lobo, J. T., & Garcia, M. B. (2025). Determinants of Teachers' Intentions to Integrate Education for Sustainable Development (ESD) Into Physical Education and Health Curricula. In Garcia, M. B. (Ed.), *Global Innovations in Physical Education and Health* (pp. 439–472). IGI Global., DOI: 10.4018/979-8-3693-3952-7.ch016

Acut, D. P., Malabago, N. K., Malicoban, E. V., Galamiton, N. S., & Garcia, M. B. (2024). "ChatGPT 4.0 Ghosted Us While Conducting Literature Search:" Modeling the Chatbot's Generated Non-Existent References Using Regression Analysis. *Internet Reference Services Quarterly*, ●●●, 1–26. DOI: 10.1080/10875301.2024.2426793

Adamopoulou, E., & Moussiades, L. (2020). Chatbots: History, Technology, and Applications. *Machine Learning with Applications*, *2*, 100006. DOI: 10.1016/j.mlwa.2020.100006

Adams, C., Pente, P., Lemermeyer, G., Turville, J., & Rockwell, G. (2022). Artificial Intelligence and Teachers' New Ethical Obligations. *International Journal of Information Ethics*, *31*(1). Advance online publication. DOI: 10.29173/irie483

Adams, R. (2021). Can Artificial Intelligence be Decolonized? *Interdisciplinary Science Reviews*, *46*(1-2), 176–197. DOI: 10.1080/03080188.2020.1840225

Adel, A., Ahsan, A., & Davison, C. (2024). ChatGPT Promises and Challenges in Education: Computational and Ethical Perspectives. *Education Sciences*, *14*(8), 1–27. DOI: 10.3390/educsci14080814

Adelana, O., Ayanwale, M., & Sanusi, I. (2024). Exploring pre-service biology teachers intention to teach genetics using an AI intelligent tutoring—Based system. *Cogent Education*, *11*(1), 1–25. DOI: 10.1080/2331186X.2024.2310976

Adeshola, I., & Adepoju, A. P. (2024). The opportunities and challenges of ChatGPT in education. *Interactive Learning Environments*, *32*(10), 6159–6172. DOI: 10.1080/10494820.2023.2253858

Adetayo, A. J. (2024). Reimagining Learning Through AI Art: The Promise of DALL-E and MidJourney for Education and Libraries. *Library Hi Tech News*. Advance online publication. DOI: 10.1108/LHTN-01-2024-0005

Adiguzel, T., Kaya, M., & Cansu, F. (2023). Revolutionizing education with AI: Exploring the transformative potential of ChatGPT. *Contemporary Educational Technology*, *15*(3), ep429. Advance online publication. DOI: 10.30935/cedtech/13152

Afonughe, E., Onah, E. N., Uzoma, A. C., Andor, S. E., & Orisakwe, C. U. (2021). Integration of Artificial Intelligence Tool (AI-Chatbot) into Teaching and Learning: A Panacea for Improving Universities' Educational and Administrative Duties in South-South, Nigeria. *Journal of Computer Science and Systems Biology*, *14*(6), 1–6. DOI: 10.37421/0974-7230.2021.14.357

Afrin, M. F. N., Hoque, K. E., & Chaiti, R. D. (2024). *Emotion Recognition of Autistic Children from Facial Images Using Hybrid Model*. 1–6. https://doi.org/DOI: 10.1109/ICCCNT61001.2024.10724499

Aghaziarati, A., Nejatifar, S., & Abedi, A. (2023). Artificial Intelligence in Education: Investigating Teacher Attitudes. *AI and Tech in Behavioral and Social Sciences*, *1*(1), 35–42. DOI: 10.61838/kman.aitech.1.1.6

Agyei, E. A., Annim, S. K., Acquah, B. Y. S., Sebu, J., & Agyei, S. K. (2024). Education Infrastructure Inequality and Academic Performance in Ghana. *Heliyon*, *10*(14), 1–25. DOI: 10.1016/j.heliyon.2024.e34041 PMID: 39108894

Ahmad, W., Raj, R., & Shokeen, R. (2024). Reshaping special education. *Advances in Educational Technologies and Instructional Design Book Series*, 1–44. https://doi.org/DOI: 10.4018/979-8-3693-5538-1.ch001

Ahmadi, A., Yazdizadeh, B., Doshmangir, L., Majdzadeh, R., & Asghari, S. (2022). PROTOCOL: Systematic Review of Methods to Reduce Risk of Bias in Knowledge Translation Interventional Studies in Health-Related Issues. *Campbell Systematic Reviews*, *18*(2), e1236. Advance online publication. DOI: 10.1002/cl2.1236 PMID: 36911351

Ahmad, S. F., Han, H., Alam, M. M., Rehmat, M. K., Irshad, M., Arraño-Muñoz, M., & Ariza-Montes, A. (2023). Impact of Artificial Intelligence on Human Loss in Decision Making, Laziness and Safety in Education. *Humanities & Social Sciences Communications*, *10*(1), 1–14. DOI: 10.1057/s41599-023-01787-8 PMID: 37325188

Ahmed, F. F. (2017). Subh-e-Azadi. Penguin Random House. India. https://www.penguin.co.in/subh-e-azadi-an-anguished-evocation-of-the-pain-of-partition/

Ahmed, F., Fattani, M. T., Ali, S. R., & Enam, R. N. (2022). Strengthening the Bridge Between Academic and the Industry Through the Academia-Industry Collaboration Plan Design Model. *Frontiers in Psychology*, *13*, 1–11. DOI: 10.3389/fpsyg.2022.875940 PMID: 35734456

Ahmed, M. A., Zaidan, B. B., Zaidan, A. A., Salih, M. M., & Lakulu, M. M. B. (2018). A review on systems-based sensory gloves for sign language recognition state of the art between 2007 and 2017. *Sensors (Basel)*, *18*(7), 2208. DOI: 10.3390/s18072208 PMID: 29987266

AI at Stanford Advisory Committee. (2025). Report of the AI at Stanford Advisory Committee. Stanford University. https://provost.stanford.edu/2025/01/09/report-of-the-ai-at-stanford-advisory-committee/

Ajjawi, R., Tai, J., Dollinger, M., Dawson, P., Boud, D., & Bearman, M. (2023). From Authentic Assessment to Authenticity in Assessment: Broadening Perspectives. *Assessment &amp. Assessment & Evaluation in Higher Education*, *49*(4), 499–510. DOI: 10.1080/02602938.2023.2271193

Akgun, S., & Greenhow, C. (2021). Artificial Intelligence in Education: Addressing Ethical Challenges in K-12 Settings. *AI and Ethics*, *2*(3), 431–440. DOI: 10.1007/s43681-021-00096-7 PMID: 34790956

Akhtar, P., Moazzam, M., Ashraf, A., & Khan, M. N. (2024). The Interdisciplinary Curriculum Alignment to Enhance Graduates' Employability and Universities' Sustainability. *International Journal of Management Education*, *22*(3), 1–17. DOI: 10.1016/j.ijme.2024.101037

Akkaş, Ö. M., Tosun, C., & Gökçearslan, Ş. (2024). Artificial Intelligence (AI) and Cheating. In *Advances in educational technologies and instructional design book series* (pp. 182–199). DOI: 10.4018/979-8-3693-1351-0.ch009

Akram, H., Abdelrady, A. H., Al-Adwan, A. S., & Ramzan, M. (2022). Teachers' Perceptions of Technology Integration in Teaching-Learning Practices: A Systematic Review. *Frontiers in Psychology*, *13*, 1–9. DOI: 10.3389/fpsyg.2022.920317 PMID: 35734463

Akter, S., Dwivedi, Y. K., Sajib, S., Biswas, K., Bandara, R. J., & Michael, K. (2022). Algorithmic bias in machine learning-based marketing models. *Journal of Business Research*, *144*, 201–216. DOI: 10.1016/j.jbusres.2022.01.083

Al Darayseh, A. (2023). Acceptance of Artificial Intelligence in Teaching Science: Science Teachers' Perspective. *Computers and Education: Artificial Intelligence*, *4*, 1–9. DOI: 10.1016/j.caeai.2023.100132

Al Husaeni, D. F., Haristiani, N., Wahyudin, W., & Rasim, R. (2022). Chatbot Artificial Intelligence as Educational Tools in Science and Engineering Education: A Literature Review and Bibliometric Mapping Analysis with Its Advantages and Disadvantages. *ASEAN Journal of Science and Engineering*, *4*(1), 93–118. DOI: 10.17509/ajse.v4i1.67429

Al-Abdullatif, A. M., Al-Dokhny, A. A., & Drwish, A. M. (2023). Implementing the Bashayer Chatbot in Saudi Higher Education: Measuring the Influence on Students' Motivation and Learning Strategies. *Frontiers in Psychology*, *14*, 1129070. Advance online publication. DOI: 10.3389/fpsyg.2023.1129070 PMID: 37255522

Aladini, A., Bayat, S., & Abdellatif, M. S. (2024). Performance-Based Assessment in Virtual Versus Non-Virtual Classes: Impacts on Academic Resilience, Motivation, Teacher Support, and Personal Best Goals. *Asian-Pacific Journal of Second and Foreign Language Education*, *9*(1), 1–27. DOI: 10.1186/s40862-023-00230-4

Al-Adwan, A. S., Li, N., Al-Adwan, A., Abbasi, G. A., Albelbisi, N. A., & Habibi, A. (2023). Extending the Technology Acceptance Model (TAM) to Predict University Students' Intentions to Use Metaverse-Based Learning Platforms. *Education and Information Technologies*, *28*(11), 15381–15413. DOI: 10.1007/s10639-023-11816-3 PMID: 37361794

Alasgarova, R., & Rzayev, J. (2024). The Role of Artificial Intelligence in Shaping High School Students' Motivation. *International Journal of Technology in Education and Science*, *8*(2), 311–324. DOI: 10.46328/ijtes.553

Al-Busaidi, A. S., Raman, R., Hughes, L., Albashrawi, M. A., Malik, T., Dwivedi, Y. K., Al- Alawi, T., AlRizeiqi, M., Davies, G., Fenwick, M., Gupta, P., Gurpur, S., Hooda, A., Jurcys, P., Lim, D., Lucchi, N., Misra, T., Raman, R., Shirish, A., & Walton, P. (2024). Redefining Boundaries in Innovation and Knowledge Domains: Investigating the Impact of Generative Artificial Intelligence on Copyright and Intellectual Property Rights. *Journal of Innovation & Knowledge*, *9*(4), 1–28. DOI: 10.1016/j.jik.2024.100630

Alenizi, M., Mohamed, A., & Shaaban, T. (2023). Revolutionizing EFL Special Education: How ChatGPT is Transforming the Way Teachers Approach Language Learning. *Innoeduca-International Journal Of Technology And Educational Innovation*, *9*(2), 5–23. DOI: 10.24310/innoeduca.2023.v9i2.16774

Alfredo, R., Echeverria, V., Jin, Y., Yan, L., Swiecki, Z., Gašević, D., & Martinez-Maldonado, R. (2024). Human-Centred Learning Analytics and AI in Education: A Systematic Literature Review. *Computers and Education: Artificial Intelligence*, *6*, 100215. DOI: 10.1016/j.caeai.2024.100215

Ali, M. S., Suchiang, T., Saikia, T. P., & Gulzar, D. D. (2024). Perceived benefits and concerns of Ai integration in higher education: Insights from India. *Educational Administration Theory and Practices*, *30*, 656–668. DOI: 10.53555/kuey.v30i5.5122

Ali, O., Murray, P. A., Momin, M., Dwivedi, Y. K., & Malik, T. (2024). The effects of artificial intelligence applications in educational settings: Challenges and strategies. *Technological Forecasting and Social Change*, *199*, 123076. DOI: 10.1016/j.techfore.2023.123076

Aliu, T. V. (2024). Artificial Intelligence in Special Education: A Literature Review. *International Journal of Advanced Networking and Applications*, *16*(2), 6360–6367. DOI: 10.35444/IJANA.2024.16208

Aljemely, Y. (2024). Challenges and best practices in training teachers to utilize artificial intelligence: A systematic review. *Frontiers in Education, 9*, 1–10. DOI: 10.3389/feduc.2024.1470853

Alkan, A. (2024). Yapay zekâ: Eğitimdeki rolü ve potansiyeli. *İnsan ve Toplum Bilimleri Araştırma Dergisi [Artificial intelligence: Its role and potential in education. Journal of Human and Social Sciences Research], 13*(1), 483-497.

Alkeraida, A. (2024). Teachers' Competencies in Implementing Technologies and Artificial Intelligence Applications to Teach Students with Disabilities in Inclusive Classrooms in Saudi Arabia. *Eurasıan Journal of Educatıonal Research, 112*, 177–195. DOI: 10.14689/ejer.2024.112.10

Al-kfairy, M., Mustafa, D., Kshetri, N., Insiew, M., & Alfandi, O. (2024). Ethical Challenges and Solutions of Generative AI: An Interdisciplinary Perspective. *Informatics (MDPI), 11*(3), 58. DOI: 10.3390/informatics11030058

Almada, A., Yu, Q., & Patel, P. (2022). Proactive Chatbot Framework Based on the PS2CLH Model: An AI-Deep Learning Chatbot Assistant for Students. *Lecture Notes in Networks and Systems*, 751-770. https://doi.org/DOI: 10.1007/978-3-031-16072-1_54

Almasri, F. (2024). Exploring the Impact of Artificial intelligence in teaching and learning of Science: A Systematic Review of Empirical research. *Research in Science Education, 54*(5), 977–997. DOI: 10.1007/s11165-024-10176-3

Alneyadi, S., Wardat, Y., Alshannag, Q., & Abu-Al-Aish, A. (2023). The Effect of Using Smart E-Learning App on the Academic Achievement of Eighth-Grade Students. *Eurasia Journal of Mathematics, Science and Technology Education, 19*(4), 1–11. DOI: 10.29333/ejmste/13067

Alotaibi, N. S. (2024). The impact of AI and LMS integration on the future of higher Education: Opportunities, challenges, and strategies for transformation. *Sustainability (Basel), 16*(23), 10357. DOI: 10.3390/su162310357

Alshahrani, K., & Qureshi, R. J. (2024). Review the Prospects and Obstacles of AI-Enhanced Learning Environments: The Role of ChatGPT in Education. *I.J.Modern Education And Computer Science, 16*(4), 71–86. DOI: 10.5815/ijmecs.2024.04.06

Alshater, M. (2022). M. Exploring the role of artificial intelligence in enhancing academic performance: A case study of ChatGPT. Available at *SSRN*. https://doi.org/DOI: 10.2139/ssrn.4312358

Alshehri, B. (2023). Pedagogical Paradigms in the AI Era: Insights from Saudi Educators on the Long-term Implications of AI Integration in Classroom Teaching. *International Journal of Educational Sciences and Arts, 2*(8), 159–180. DOI: 10.59992/IJESA.2023.v2n8p7

Altun, T., & Vural, S. (2012). Evaluation of the Views of Teachers and Administrators of a Science and Art Center (SAC) About Professional Development and School Improvement. *Electronic Journal of Social Sciences, 11*(42), 152-177. https://dergipark.org.tr/tr/download/article-file/70406

Altun, S., Alkan, A., & Altun, H. (2021). The investigation of WISC-R profiles in children with border intelligence and intellectual disability with machine learning algorithms. *Pamukkale University Journal of Engineering Sciences, 27*(5), 589–596. DOI: 10.5505/pajes.2020.53077

Âlvarez-Guerrero, G., Fry, D., Lu, M., & Gaitis, K. K. (2024). Online child sexual exploitation and abuse of children and adolescents with disabilities: A systematic review. *Disabilities*, *4*(2), 264–276. DOI: 10.3390/disabilities4020017

Al-Zahrani, A. M. (2024). The impact of generative AI tools on researchers and research: Implications for academia in higher education. *Innovations in Education and Teaching International*, *61*(5), 1029–1043. DOI: 10.1080/14703297.2023.2271445

Al-Zahrani, A. M. (2024). Unveiling the shadows: Beyond the hype of AI in education. *Heliyon*, *10*(9), e30696. DOI: 10.1016/j.heliyon.2024.e30696 PMID: 38737255

Amarathunga, B. (2024). ChatGPT in education: Unveiling frontiers and future directions through systematic literature review and bibliometric analysis. *Asian Education and Development Studies*, *13*(5), 412–431. DOI: 10.1108/AEDS-05-2024-0101

Anderson, A., & Johnston, B. (2016). Student Learning and Information Literacy. In A. Anderson & B. Johnston (Eds.), *From Information Literacy to Social Epistemology* (pp. 67-79). Chandos Publishing. DOI: 10.1016/B978-0-08-100545-3.00005-3

Anderson, T., & Dron, J. (2011). Tres generaciones de pedagogía de la educación a distancia. Revista internacional de investigación en aprendizaje abierto y distribuido, [Three Generations of Distance Education Pedagogy. International Journal of Research in Open and Distributed Learning], 12(3), 80-97.

Andriichuk, N. (2017). Special Education vs Inclusive Education in the Synergy of Educational Environments. *Multidisciplinary Journal of School Education, 6*(2 (12). https://doi.org/DOI: 10.35765/mjse.2017.0612.04

Anjum, T., Farrukh, M., Heidler, P., & Tautiva, J. A. D. (2021). Entrepreneurial intention: Creativity, entrepreneurship, and university support. *Journal of Open Innovation, 7*(1), 11. DOI: 10.3390/joitmc7010011

Arent, K., Brown, D. J., Kruk-Lasocka, J., Niemiec, T. L., Pasieczna, A. H., Standen, P. J., & Szczepanowski, R. (2022). The use of social robots in the diagnosis of autism in preschool children. *Applied Sciences (Basel, Switzerland)*, *12*(17), 8399. DOI: 10.3390/app12178399

Arif, Y. M., Ayunda, N., Diah, N. M., & Garcia, M. B. (2024). A Systematic Review of Serious Games for Health Education: Technology, Challenges, and Future Directions. In *Transformative Approaches to Patient Literacy and Healthcare Innovation* (pp. 20–45). IGI Global., DOI: 10.4018/979-8-3693-3661-8.ch002

Armitage, K. L., & Gilbert, S. J. (2024). The nature and development of cognitive offloading in children. *Child Development Perspectives, n/a*(n/a). DOI: 10.1111/cdep.12532

Arthur-Kelly, M., & Foreman, P. (2020). *Inclusive and Special Education in Australia*. Acrefore., DOI: 10.1093/acrefore/9780190264093.013.1198

ARxVision. (t.y.). *ARxVision*. https://arx.vision

Ashiq, M., Akbar, A., Jabbar, A., & Saleem, Q. U. A. (2021). Gray Literature and Academic Libraries: How Do They Access, Use, Manage, and Cope with Gray Literature. *Serials Review*, *47*(3–4), 191–200. DOI: 10.1080/00987913.2021.2018224

Asian Development Bank. (2021). *Technical and Vocational Education and Training in the Philippines in the Age of Industry 4.0*. DOI: 10.22617/TCS210084

Askarova, S., Madiyeva, G., Mirqosimova, M., Boqiyeva, R., Nazarov, A., & Baratova, D. (2024, May). A well-designed personalized and optimized model system implementation for specific education system. *In 2024 4th International Conference on Advance Computing and Innovative Technologies in Engineering (ICACITE)* (pp. 607–611). IEEE.

Asunda, P., Faezipour, M., Tolemy, J., & Engel, M. (2023). Embracing Computational Thinking as an Impetus for Artificial Intelligence in Integrated STEM Disciplines through Engineering and Technology Education . *Journal of Technology Education*, *34*(2), 43–63. DOI: 10.21061/jte.v34i2.a.3

Ateeq, A., Alzoraiki, M., Milhem, M., & Ateeq, R. A. (2024). Artificial intelligence in education: Implications for academic integrity and the shift toward holistic assessment. *Frontiers in Education*, *9*, 1470979. https://www.frontiersin.org/journals/education/articles/10.3389/feduc.2024.1470979. DOI: 10.3389/feduc.2024.1470979

Athilingam, P., & He, H.-G. (2024). ChatGPT in Nursing Education: Opportunities and Challenges. *Teaching and Learning in Nursing*, *19*(1), 97–101. DOI: 10.1016/j.teln.2023.11.004

Atlas, S. (2023). *ChatGPT for Higher Education and Professional Development: A guide to Conversational AI*. DigitalCommons@URI. https://digitalcommons.uri.edu/cba_facpubs/548

Autor, D. H. (2015). Why Are There Still So Many Jobs? The History and Future of Workplace Automation. *The Journal of Economic Perspectives*, *29*(3), 3–30. DOI: 10.1257/jep.29.3.3

Avellan, T., Sharma, S., & Turunen, M. (2020). "AI for All: Defining the What, Why, and How of Inclusive AI." *Proceedings of the 23rd International Conference on Academic Mindtrek*, 142–144. https://doi.org/DOI: 10.1145/3377290.3377317

Ayanwale, M., Adelana, O., Molefi, R., Adeeko, O., & Ishola, A. (2024). Examining artificial intelligence literacy among pre-service teachers for future classrooms. *Computers and Education Open*, *6*, 1–15. DOI: 10.1016/j.caeo.2024.100179

Aydın, M., & Yurdugül, H. (2024). Developing a Curriculum Framework of Artificial Intelligence Teaching for Gifted Students. *Kastamonu Education Journal*, *32*(1), 14–37. DOI: 10.24106/kefdergi.1426429

Azaria, A., Azoulay, R., & Reches, S. (2024). ChatGPT is a remarkable tool—For experts. *Data Intelligence*, *6*(1), 240–296. DOI: 10.1162/dint_a_00235

Azevedo, A., & Azevedo, J. (Eds.). (2019). *Handbook of Research on E-Assessment in Higher Education*. IGI Global., DOI: 10.4018/978-1-5225-5936-8

Aznoli, F., & Navimipour, N. J. (2017). Cloud Services Recommendation: Reviewing the Recent Advances and Suggesting the Future Research Directions. *Journal of Network and Computer Applications*, *77*, 73–86. DOI: 10.1016/j.jnca.2016.10.009

Baber, H., (2021). Social Interaction and Effectiveness of the Online Learning - A Moderating Role of Maintaining Social Distance During the Pandemic COVID-19. DOI: 10.1108/AEDS-09-2020-0209

Bachiri, Y., Mouncif, H., & Bouikhalene, B. (2023). Artificial intelligence empowers gamification: Optimizing student engagement and learning outcomes in e-learning and MOOCs. [iJEP]. *International Journal of Engineering Pedagogy, 13*(8), 4–19. DOI: 10.3991/ijep.v13i8.40853

Backfisch, I., Lachner, A., Stürmer, K., & Scheiter, K. (2021). Variability of Teachers' Technology Integration in the Classroom: A Matter of Utility! *Computers & Education, 166*, 1–21. DOI: 10.1016/j.compedu.2021.104159

Badir, A., O'Neill, R., Kinzli, K.-D., Komisar, S., & Kim, J.-Y. (2023). Fostering Project-Based Learning through Industry Engagement in Capstone Design Projects. *Education Sciences, 13*(4), 1–14. DOI: 10.3390/educsci13040361

Bae, M., Wang, J., Xue, H., Chong, S. M., Kwon, O., & Ki, C. W. (2024). Does ChatGPT help or hinder education? Exploring its benefits, challenges, student guilt, and the need for educator training. *International Journal of Fashion Design, Technology and Education*, ●●●, 1–16. DOI: 10.1080/17543266.2024.2430585

Bai, L., Liu, X., & Su, J. (2023). ChatGPT: The cognitive effects on learning and memory. *Brain-X, 1*(3), e30. DOI: 10.1002/brx2.30

Baker, R. S., & Hawn, A. (2022). Algorithmic bias in education. *International Journal of Artificial Intelligence in Education, 41*(1), 1052–1092. DOI: 10.1007/s40593-021-00285-9

Balachandran, M., & Rabbiraj, C. (2025). Artificial intelligence: A support system in inclusive education. *International Journal of Knowledge and Learning, 18*(1), 52–64. Advance online publication. DOI: 10.1504/IJKL.2025.143069

Balakrishnan, S., & Vidya, B. (2024). Unveiling the role of ChatGPT in higher education: A qualitative inquiry into its implementation among teaching faculties in Chennai, India. *Multidisciplinary Science Journal, 7*(4), 2025167. DOI: 10.31893/multiscience.2025167

Baltaci, A. (2019). Qualitative Research Process: How to Conduct Qualitative Research? *Ahi Evran University Journal of Social Sciences Institute, 5*(2), 368–388. DOI: 10.31592/aeusbed.598299

Baltaci, K., Herrmann, M., & Turkmen, A. (2024). Integrating Artificial Intelligence into Electrical Engineering Education: A Paradigm Shift in Teaching and Learning. *2024 ASEE Annual Conference & Exposition.* DOI: 10.18260/1-2--47644

Bandara, L. K., Nawodya, A., Amandi, K., Vihangana, K., Pandithage, D., & Gamage, N. (2024). Innovative system for early detection and intervention in developmental disorders: A multi-sensory, child-centric approach. *16th IEEE International Conference on Computational Intelligence and Communication Networks, 10*(10), 6–12. https://doi.org/DOI: 10.1109/CICN63059.2024.10847351

Bandhu, D., Mohan, M. M., Nittala, N. A. P., Jadhav, P., Bhadauria, A., & Saxena, K. K. (2024). Theories of motivation: A comprehensive analysis of human behavior drivers. *Acta Psychologica, 244*, 104177. https://doi.org/https://doi.org/10.1016/j.actpsy.2024.104177. DOI: 10.1016/j.actpsy.2024.104177 PMID: 38354564

Bandura, A. (1997). *Self-Efficacy: The Exercise of Control.* https://psycnet.apa.org/record/1997-08589-000

Banerjee, S., & Banerjee, B. (2023). College Teachers' Anxiety Towards Artificial Intelligence: A Comparative Study. *RESEARCH REVIEW International Journal of Multidisciplinary, 8*(5), 36–43. DOI: 10.31305/rrijm.2023.v08.n05.005

Banse, G., & Grunwald, A. (2009). *Coherence and Diversity in the Engineering Sciences.* Elsevier., DOI: 10.1016/B978-0-444-51667-1.50010-0

Barrett, A., & Pack, A. (2023). Not Quite Eye to A.I.: Student and Teacher Perspectives on the Use of Generative Artificial Intelligence in the Writing Process. *International Journal of Educational Technology in Higher Education, 20*(1), 59. Advance online publication. DOI: 10.1186/s41239-023-00427-0

Barrett, P., Treves, A., Shmis, T., Ambasz, D., & Ustinova, M. (2018). *The Impact of School Infrastructure on Learning: A Synthesis of the Evidence.* World Bank., DOI: 10.1596/978-1-4648-1378-8

Bartlett, R., Morse, A., Stanton, R., & Wallace, N. (2022). Consumer-lending discrimination in the FinTech era. *Journal of Financial Economics, 143*(1), 30–56. DOI: 10.1016/j.jfineco.2021.05.047

Barua, P. D., Vicnesh, J., Gururajan, R., Oh, S. L., Palmer, E., Azizan, M. M., Kadri, N. A., & Acharya, U. R. (2022). Artificial intelligence enabled personalised assistive tools to enhance education of children with neurodevelopmental disorders—A review. *International Journal of Environmental Research and Public Health, 19*(3), 1–26. DOI: 10.3390/ijerph19031192 PMID: 35162220

Basha, J. Y. (2024). The Negative Impacts of AI Tools on Students in Academic and Real-Life Performance. *International Journal of Social Sciences and Commerce, 1*(3), 1–16. DOI: 10.51470/IJSSC.2024.01.03.01

Bayne, S. (2015). Teacherbot: Intervenciones en la enseñanza automatizada. *Docencia en Educación Superior*, [Teacherbot: Interventions in Automated Teaching. Teaching in Higher Education], *20*(4), 455–467. DOI: 10.1080/13562517.2015.1020783

Beege, M., Hug, C., & Nerb, J. (2024). AI in STEM education: The relationship between teacher perceptions and ChatGPT use. *Computers in Human Behavior Reports, 16*, 1–9. DOI: 10.1016/j.chbr.2024.100494

Bekdemir, Y. (2024). The Urgency of AI integration in Teacher Training: Shaping the Future of Education. *Journal of Research in Didactical Sciences., 3*(1), 3. DOI: 10.51853/jorids/15485

Belda-Medina, J., & Calvo-Ferrer, J. R. (2022). Using Chatbots as AI Conversational Partners in Language Learning. *Applied Sciences (Basel, Switzerland), 12*(17), 8427. DOI: 10.3390/app12178427

Belitski, M., & Desai, S. (2016). Creativity, entrepreneurship and economic development: City-level evidence on creativity spillover of entrepreneurship. *The Journal of Technology Transfer, 41*(6), 1354–1376. DOI: 10.1007/s10961-015-9446-3

Bender, E. M., Gebru, T., McMillan-Major, A., & Shmit, S. (2021). On the Dangers of Stochastic Parrots: Can Language Models Be Too Big? *Proceedings of the 2021 ACM Conference on Fairness, Accountability, and Transparency* (pp. 610-623). DOI: 10.1145/3442188.3445922

Bendig, D., & Bräunche, A. (2024). *The role of artificial intelligence algorithms in information systems research: a conceptual overview and avenues for research.* Management Review Quartely., DOI: 10.1007/s11301-024-00451-y

Benke, E., & Szoke, A. (2024). Academic Integrity in the Time of Artificial Intelligence: Exploring Student Attitudes. *Italian Journal of Sociology of Education, 16*(2), 91–108. DOI: 10.14658/PUPJ-IJSE-2024-2-5

Bernhard, J. (2018). What Matters for Students' Learning in the Laboratory? Do Not Neglect the Role of Experimental Equipment! *Instructional Science, 46*(6), 819–846. DOI: 10.1007/s11251-018-9469-x

Bernius, J. P., Krusche, S., & Bruegge, B. (2022). Machine learning based feedback on textual student answers in large courses. *Computers and Education: Artificial Intelligence, 3*, 100081. Advance online publication. DOI: 10.1016/j.caeai.2022.100081

Bettayeb, A. M., Abu Talib, M., Sobhe Altayasinah, A. Z., & Dakalbab, F. (2024). Exploring the impact of ChatGPT: Conversational AI in education. *Frontiers in Education, 9*, 1379796. Advance online publication. DOI: 10.3389/feduc.2024.1379796

Bezzina, S., & Dingli, A. (2024). The Transformative Potential of Artificial Intelligence for Education. *Proceedings of the International Conference on Networked Learning, 14*. https://doi.org/DOI: 10.54337/nlc.v14i1.8077

Bhattacharya, P., Prasad, V. K., Verma, A., Gupta, D., Sapsomboon, A., Viriyasitavat, W., & Dhiman, G. (2024). Demystifying ChatGPT: An In-depth Survey of OpenAI's Robust Large Language Models. *Archives of Computational Methods in Engineering, 31*(8), 4557–4600. Advance online publication. DOI: 10.1007/s11831-024-10115-5

Bhattacharyya, M., Miller, V. M., Bhattacharyya, D., & Miller, L. E. (2023). High rates of fabricated and inaccurate references in ChatGPT-Generated medical content. *Cureus*. Advance online publication. DOI: 10.7759/cureus.39238 PMID: 37337480

Bhushan, S., Arunkumar, S., Eisa, T. A. E., Nasser, M., Singh, A. K., & Kumar, P. (2024). AI-Enhanced Dyscalculia Screening: A Survey of Methods and Applications for Children. *Diagnostics (Basel), 14*(13), 1441. DOI: 10.3390/diagnostics14131441 PMID: 39001330

Bigman, Y. E., Yam, K. C., Marciano, D., Reynolds, S. J., & Gray, K. (2021). Threat of racial and economic inequality increases preference for algorithm decision-making. *Computers in Human Behavior, 122*, 106859. DOI: 10.1016/j.chb.2021.106859

Bilgen, Ö. B., & Doğan, N. (2017). The Comparison of Interrater Reliability Estimating Techniques [Puanlayıcılar Arası Güvenirlik Belirleme Tekniklerinin Karşılaştırılması]. *Journal of Measurement and Evaluation in Education and Psychology, 8*(1), 63–78. DOI: 10.21031/epod.294847

Bin-Nashwan, S. A., Sadallah, M., & Bouteraa, M. (2023). Use of ChatGPT in academia: Academic integrity hangs in the balance. *Technology in Society, 75*, 102370. https://doi.org/https://doi.org/10.1016/j.techsoc.2023.102370. DOI: 10.1016/j.techsoc.2023.102370

Binns, R., & Kirkham, R. (2021). How could equality and data protection law shape AI fairness for people with disabilities? [TACCESS]. *ACM Transactions on Accessible Computing, 14*(3), 1–32. DOI: 10.1145/3473673

Birks, D., & Clare, J. (2023). Linking artificial intelligence facilitated academic misconduct to existing prevention frameworks. *International Journal for Educational Integrity*, *19*(1), 20. DOI: 10.1007/s40979-023-00142-3

Bisht, P., & Pujari, J. P. (2024). Past Meets the Future—ChatGPT Integrated Pedagogy to Teach the 1947 Partition in Secondary Classes. In Lahby, M., Bucchiarone, Y. M. A., & Schaeffer, S. E. (Eds.), *General Aspects of Applying Generative AI in Higher Education Opportunities and Challenges* (pp. 55–68)., DOI: 10.1007/978-3-031-65691-0_4

Bobitan, N., Dumitrescu, D., Popa, A. F., Sahlian, D. N., & Turlea, I. C. (2024). Shaping Tomorrow: Anticipating Skills Requirements Based on the Integration of Artificial Intelligence in Business Organizations—A Foresight Analysis Using the Scenario Method. *Electronics (Basel)*, *13*(11), 1–17. DOI: 10.3390/electronics13112198

Bolat, H. (2020). The Metaphorical Perceptions of the Gifted and Talented Students towards Social Studies Lesson in the Science and Art Centre and in Their School. *Anemon Muş Alparslan Üniversitesi Sosyal Bilimler Dergisi*, *8*(4), 1135–1144. DOI: 10.18506/anemon.647705

Bordel, B., & Alcarria, R. (2024). Enhancing the Students' Motivation and Learning in Network Engineering Courses Through Artificial Intelligence Tools and Applications. *Lecture Notes in Educational Technology*, 21-31. DOI: 10.1007/978-981-97-2468-0_3

Bornsztejn, H. (2022). Do academic integrity policies within foundation studies programmes adopt an educative perspective for supporting students? *Journal of Higher Education Policy and Management*, *44*(5), 428–442. DOI: 10.1080/1360080X.2022.2112272

Bosman, L., Kotla, B., Madamanchi, A., Bartholomew, S., & Byrd, V. (2022). Preparing the Future Entrepreneurial Engineering Workforce Using Web-Based AI-Enabled Tools. *European Journal of Engineering Education*, *48*(5), 972–989. DOI: 10.1080/03043797.2022.2119122

Bostrom, N., & Yudkowsky, E. (2014). The Ethics of Artificial Intelligence. In Frankish, K., & Ramsey, W. M. (Eds.), *The Cambridge Handbook of Artificial Intelligence* (pp. 316–334). Cambridge University Press. DOI: 10.1017/CBO9781139046855.020

Bowers, W. J. (1964). *Student dishonesty and its control in college*. Bureau of Applied Social Research, Columbia University.

Bozkurt, A. (2016). Learning analytics: E-learning, big data and personalized learning. *Journal of Open Education Applications and Research*, *2*(4), 55–81.

Bozkurt, A. (2023). ChatGPT, Generative AI and Algorithmic Paradigm Shift. *Alanyazın*, *4*(1), 63–72. DOI: 10.59320/alanyazin.1283282

Bozkurt, A. (2023). Unleashing the potential of generative AI, conversational agents and chatbots in educational praxis: A systematic review and bibliometric analysis of GenAI in education. *Praxis Abierta*, *15*(4), 261–270. DOI: 10.55982/openpraxis.15.4.609

Bozkurt, A., Xiao, J., Farrow, R., Bai, J. Y. H., Nerantzi, C., Moore, S., Dron, J., Stracke, C. M., Singh, L., Crompton, H., Koutropoulos, A., Terentev, E., Pazurek, A., Nichols, M., Sidorkin, A. M., Costello, E., Watson, S., Mulligan, D., Honeychurch, S., & Asino, T. I. (2024). The Manifesto for Teaching and Learning in a Time of Generative AI: A Critical Collective Stance to Better Navigate the Future. *Open Praxis*, *16*(4), 487–513. DOI: 10.55982/openpraxis.16.4.777

Bramer, W. M., De Jonge, G. B., Rethlefsen, M. L., Mast, F., & Kleijnen, J. (2018). A Systematic Approach to Searching: An Efficient and Complete Method to Develop Literature Searches. *Journal of the Medical Library Association: JMLA*, *106*(4). Advance online publication. DOI: 10.5195/jmla.2018.283 PMID: 30271302

Brandão, A., Pedro, L., & Zagalo, N. (2024). Teacher Professional Development for a Future with Generative Artificial Intelligence – An Integrative Literature Review. *Digital Education Review*, (45), 151–157. DOI: 10.1344/der.2024.45.151-157

Braun, V., & Clarke, V. (2006). Using Thematic Analysis in Psychology. *Qualitative Research in Psychology*, *3*(2), 77–101. DOI: 10.1191/1478088706qp063oa

Braun, V., & Clarke, V. (2021). To saturate or not to saturate? Questioning data saturation as a useful concept for thematic analysis and sample-size rationales. *Qualitative Research in Sport, Exercise and Health*, *13*(2), 201–216. DOI: 10.1080/2159676X.2019.1704846

Bridges, K. M. (2017). *The poverty of privacy rights*. Stanford University Press. DOI: 10.1515/9781503602304

Brinkrolf, J., & Hammer, B. (2018). Interpretable machine learning with reject option. *Automatisierungstechnik*, *66*(4), 283–290. DOI: 10.1515/auto-2017-0123

Broekhuizen, T., Dekker, H., de Faria, P., Firk, S., Nguyen, D. K., & Sofka, W. (2023). AI for Managing Open Innovation: Opportunities, Challenges, and a Research Agenda. *Journal of Business Research*, *167*, 1–14. DOI: 10.1016/j.jbusres.2023.114196

Brown, A., Smith, J., Johnson, L., Lee, K., & Patel, R. (2021). The Creative Potential of AI: Exploring ChatGPT in Educational Contexts. *Journal of Educational Technology*, *35*(2), 105–120.

Brown, S., Davidovic, J., & Hasan, A. (2021). The algorithm audit: Scoring the algorithms that score us. *Big Data & Society*, *8*(1), 1–8. DOI: 10.1177/2053951720983865

Brynjolfsson, E., & McAfee, A. (2014). *The second machine age: Work, progress, and prosperity in a time of brilliant technologies*. W. W. Norton & Company.

Bryson, J. J. (2018). La última década y el futuro del impacto de la IA en la sociedad, Open Mind. Hacia una nueva Ilustración [The last decade and the future of AI's impact on society, Open Mind. Towards a new Enlightenment], 127-159. https://www.bbvaopenmind.com/articulos/la-ultima-decada-y-el-futuro -del-impacto-de-la-ia-en-la-sociedad/

Bulathwela, S., Pérez-Ortiz, M., Holloway, C., Cukurova, M., & Shawe-Taylor, J. (2024). Artificial Intelligence Alone Will Not Democratise Education: On Educational Inequality, Techno-Solutionism and Inclusive Tools. *Sustainability (Basel)*, *16*(2), 1–20. DOI: 10.3390/su16020781

Burrell, J. (2016). How the machine "thinks2: Understanding opacity in machine learning algorithms. *Big Data & Society*, *3*(1), 1–12. DOI: 10.1177/2053951715622512

Bustillo, E., & Aguilos, M. (2022). The challenges of modular learning in the wake of covid-19: A digital divide in the Philippine countryside revealed. *Education Sciences*, *12*(7), 449. DOI: 10.3390/educsci12070449

Butakor, P. K. (2023). Exploring Pre-Service Teachers' Beliefs About the Role of Artificial Intelligence in Higher Education in Ghana. *International Journal of Innovative Technologies in Social Science*, (3(39)). Advance online publication. DOI: 10.31435/rsglobal_ijitss/30092023/8057

Cacho, R. (2024). Integrating Generative AI in University Teaching and Learning: A Model for Balanced Guidelines. *Online Learning : the Official Journal of the Online Learning Consortium*, *28*(3), 1–28. DOI: 10.24059/olj.v28i3.4508

Cai, J., & Kosaka, M. (2024). Conceptualizing Technical and Vocational Education and Training as a Service Through Service-Dominant Logic. *SAGE Open*, *14*(2), 1–16. DOI: 10.1177/21582440241240847

Caldwell, B., Cooper, M., Reid, L. G., Vanderheiden, G., Chisholm, W., Slatin, J., & White, J. (2008). Web content accessibility guidelines (WCAG) 2.0. *WWW Consortium (W3C)*, *290*(1-34), 5-12.

Calzada, I. (2024). Artificial intelligence for social innovation: Beyond the noise of algorithms and datafication. *Sustainability (Basel)*, *16*(19), 8638. DOI: 10.3390/su16198638

Caplanova, A. (2020). Intellectual Property. In Pacheco-Torgal, F., Rasmussen, E., Granqvist, C.-G., Ivanov, V., Kaklauskas, A., & Makonin, S. (Eds.), *Start-Up Creation* (2nd ed., pp. 81–105). Woodhead Publishing., DOI: 10.1016/B978-0-12-819946-6.00005-9

Cappelli, R., Corsino, M., Laursen, K., & Torrisi, S. (2023). Technological Competition and Patent Strategy: Protecting Innovation, Preempting Rivals and Defending the Freedom to Operate. *Research Policy*, *52*(6), 1–14. DOI: 10.1016/j.respol.2023.104785

Carbajal-Degante, E., Hernández Gutiérrez, M., & Sánchez-Mendiola, M. (2023). Hacia revisiones de la literatura más eficientes potenciadas por inteligencia artificial. *Investigación en Educación Médica*, *12*(47), 111–119. DOI: 10.22201/fm.20075057e.2023.47.23526

Carr, N. (2020). *The shallows: What the Internet is doing to our brains*. WW Norton & Company.

Çela, E., Fonkam, M. M., & Potluri, R. M. (2024). Risks of AI-Assisted Learning on Student Critical Thinking: A Case Study of Albania. *International Journal of Risk and Contingency Management*, *12*(1), 1–19. DOI: 10.4018/IJRCM.350185

Celdran, C. (2024). Establishing the Philippine AI Research Center: Pioneering AI Adoption in a Filipino Context. *CoinGeek*. https://coingeek.com/establishing-the-philippine-ai-research-center-pioneering-ai-adoption-in-a-filipino-context/

Celik, I. (2023). Towards Intelligent-TPACK: An empirical study on teachers professional knowledge to ethically integrate artificial intelligence (AI)-based tools into education. *Computers in Human Behavior*, *138*, 107468. Advance online publication. DOI: 10.1016/j.chb.2022.107468

Celik, I., Dindar, M., Muukkonen, H., & Järvelä, S. (2022). The Promises and Challenges of Artificial Intelligence for Teachers: A Systematic Review of Research. *TechTrends*, *66*(4), 616–630. DOI: 10.1007/s11528-022-00715-y

Chadwick, D. D. (2019). Online risk for peoplewith intellectual disabilities. *Tizard Learning Disability Review*, *24*(4), 180–187. DOI: 10.1108/TLDR-03-2019-0008

Chan, C. K. Y. (2023). A comprehensive AI policy education framework for university teaching and learning. *International Journal of Educational Technology in Higher Education*, *20*(38), 38. Advance online publication. DOI: 10.1186/s41239-023-00408-3

Chan, C. K. Y., & Hu, W. (2023). Students' Voices on Generative AI: Perceptions, Benefits, and Challenges in Higher Education. *International Journal of Educational Technology in Higher Education*, *20*(1), 1–18. DOI: 10.1186/s41239-023-00411-8

Chan, C. K. Y., & Lee, K. K. W. (2023). The AI Generation Gap: Are Gen Z Students More Interested in Adopting Generative AI Such as ChatGPT in Teaching and Learning Than Their Gen X and Millennial Generation Teachers? *Smart Learning Environments*, *10*(1), 1–23. DOI: 10.1186/s40561-023-00269-3

Chang, C. Y., Hwang, G. J., & Gau, M. L. (2021). Promoting Students' Learning Achievement and Self-Efficacy: A Mobile Chatbot Approach for Nursing Training. *British Journal of Educational Technology*, *53*(1), 171–188. DOI: 10.1111/bjet.13158

Chang, H. (2016). *Autoethnography as Method*. Routledge., DOI: 10.4324/9781315433370

Chan, L., Hogaboam, L., & Cao, R. (2022). Artificial intelligence in education. In *Applied Artificial Intelligence in Business: Concepts and Cases* (pp. 265–278). Springer International Publishing., DOI: 10.1007/978-3-031-05740-3_17

Chanturia, N., & Chakhvadze, L. (2023). Generative Artificial Intelligence and Holocaust Education. *Baskent International Conference on Multidisciplinary Studies*. https://www.researchgate.net/publication/377078571

ChatGPT. (2024). *ChatGPT: 4o free version*. chatgpt.com. Retrieved January 1, 2025, from https://chatgpt.com/

Checco, A., Bracciale, L., Loreti, P., Pinfield, S., & Bianchi, G. (2021). AI-assisted peer review. *Humanities & Social Sciences Communications*, *8*(1), 25. Advance online publication. DOI: 10.1057/s41599-020-00703-8

Chen, H. (2024). The ethical challenges of educational artificial intelligence and coping measures: A discussion in the context of the 2024 World Digital Education Conference. *Science Insights Education Frontiers, 20*(2), 3263-3281. https://doi.org/DOI: 10.15354/sief.24.re339

Chen, H. (2024). Using AI in education: Cheating or a balanced view? Preface. LinkedIn. https://www.linkedin.com/pulse/using-ai-education-cheating-balanced-view-preface

Chen, X., Zou, D., Xie, H., & Cheng, G. (2021). Veinte años de aprendizaje de idiomas personalizado: modelado de temas y mapeo de conocimientos. Tecnología educativa y sociedad, [Twenty Years of Personalized Language Learning: Topic Modeling and Knowledge Mapping. Educational Technology and Society], 24(1), 205–222.https://www.jstor.org/stable/10.2307/2697786

Chen, C. C., & Unal, A. F. (2023). Individualism-Collectivism: A Review of Conceptualization and Measurement. In *Oxford Research Encyclopedia of Business and Management*. Oxford University Press., DOI: 10.1093/acrefore/9780190224851.013.350

Cheng, L. T. W., Armatas, C. A., & Wang, J. W. (2019). The Impact of Diversity, Prior Academic Achievement and Goal Orientation on Learning Performance in Group Capstone Projects. *Higher Education Research & Development*, 39(5), 913–925. DOI: 10.1080/07294360.2019.1699028

Cheng, M., Adekola, O., Albia, J., & Cai, S. (2021). Employability in Higher Education: A Review of Key Stakeholders' Perspectives. *Higher Education Evaluation and Development*, 16(1), 16–31. DOI: 10.1108/HEED-03-2021-0025

Chen, H.-L., Vicki Widarso, G., & Sutrisno, H. (2020). A ChatBot for Learning Chinese: Learning Achievement and Technology Acceptance. *Journal of Educational Computing Research*, 58(6), 1161–1189. DOI: 10.1177/0735633120929622

Chen, J. J., & Lin, J. C. (2024). Artificial intelligence as a double-edged sword: Wielding the POWER principles to maximize its positive effects and minimize its negative effects. *Contemporary Issues in Early Childhood*, 25(1), 146–153. DOI: 10.1177/14639491231169813

Chen, J., Lai, P., Chan, A., Man, V., & Chan, C.-H. (2022). AI-Assisted Enhancement of Student Presentation Skills: Challenges and Opportunities. *Sustainability (Basel)*, 15(1), 1–19. DOI: 10.3390/su15010196

Chen, K., Tallant, A. C., & Selig, I. (2025). Exploring generative AI literacy in higher education: Student adoption, interaction, evaluation and ethical perceptions. *Information and Learning Science*, 126(1/2), 132–148. DOI: 10.1108/ILS-10-2023-0160

Chen, L., Chen, P., & Lin, Z. (2020). Artificial intelligence in education: A review. *IEEE Access : Practical Innovations, Open Solutions*, 8, 198250–198265. DOI: 10.1109/ACCESS.2020.2988510

Chen, X. (2022). AI literacy in education: A framework for teachers and students. *Journal of Educational Technology & Innovation*, 10(3), 45–67. DOI: 10.3102/jeti.2022.34

Chen, X., Xie, H., Zou, D., & Hwang, G.-J. (2020). Application and Theory Gaps During the Rise of Artificial Intelligence in Education. *Computers and Education: Artificial Intelligence*, 1, 1–20. DOI: 10.1016/j.caeai.2020.100002

Chen, X., Zou, D., Xie, H., Cheng, G., & Liu, C. (2022). Two decades of artificial intelligence in education. *Journal of Educational Technology & Society*, 25(1), 28–47.

Chen, Y., Jensen, S., Albert, L. J., Gupta, S., & Lee, T. (2022). Artificial Intelligence (AI) Student Assistants in the Classroom: Designing Chatbots to Support Student Success. *Information Systems Frontiers*, 25(1), 161–182. DOI: 10.1007/s10796-022-10291-4

Chen, Z. (2023). Ethics and Discrimination in Artificial Intelligence-Enabled Recruitment Practices. *Humanities & Social Sciences Communications*, *10*(1), 1–12. DOI: 10.1057/s41599-023-02079-x

Chiu, T. K. F. (2024). A classification tool to foster self-regulated learning with generative artificial intelligence by applying self-determination theory: A case of ChatGPT. *Educational Technology Research and Development*, *72*(4), 2401–2416. DOI: 10.1007/s11423-024-10366-w

Chiu, T. K. F., Xia, Q., Zhou, X., Chai, C. S., & Cheng, M. (2023). Systematic Literature Review on Opportunities, Challenges, and Future Research Recommendations of Artificial Intelligence in Education. *Computers and Education: Artificial Intelligence*, *4*, 100118. DOI: 10.1016/j.caeai.2022.100118

Chiu, T., Moorhouse, B., Chai, C., & Ismailov, M. (2024). Teacher support and student motivation to learn with Artificial Intelligence (AI) based chatbot. *Interactive Learning Environments*, *32*(7), 3240–3256. DOI: 10.1080/10494820.2023.2172044

Chocarro, R., Cortiñas, M., & Marcos-Matás, G. (2021). Teachers' Attitudes Towards Chatbots in Education: A Technology Acceptance Model Approach Considering the Effect of Social Language, Bot Proactiveness, and Users' Characteristics. *Educational Studies*, *49*(2), 295–313. DOI: 10.1080/03055698.2020.1850426

Chopra, A., Patel, H., Rajput, D. S., & Bansal, N. (2024). Empowering inclusive education: Leveraging AI-ML and innovative tech stacks to support students with learning disabilities in higher education. In *Applied assistive technologies and informatics for students with disabilities* (pp. 255–275). Springer Nature Singapore. DOI: 10.1007/978-981-97-0914-4_15

Chounta, I., Bardone, E., Raudsep, A., & Pedaste, M. (2022). Exploring Teachers Perceptions of Artificial Intelligence as a Tool to Support their Practice in Estonian K-12 Education. *International Journal of Artificial Intelligence in Education*, *32*(3), 725–755. DOI: 10.1007/s40593-021-00243-5

Chowdhury, T., & Oredo, J. (2021). Ethics in AI: A software developmental and philosophical perspective. In *Responsible AI and Analytics for an Ethical and Inclusive Digitized Society* (Vol. 20, pp. 233–241). Springer International Publishing. DOI: 10.1007/978-3-030-85447-8_21

Christie, S. T., Jarratt, D. C., Olson, L. A., & Taijala, T. T. (2019). Machine-learned school dropout early warning at scale. In *Proceedings of the 12th International Conference on Educational Data Mining* (pp. 726–731). EDM., https://files.eric.ed.gov/fulltext/ED599217.pdf

Ciavaldini-Cartaut, S., Métral, J.-F., Olry, P., Guidoni-Stoltz, D., & Gagneur, C.-A. (2024). Artificial Intelligence in Professional and Vocational Training. In *Palgrave Studies in Creativity and Culture* (pp. 145–155). Springer Nature Switzerland.

Clarizia, F., Colace, F., Lombardi, M., Pascale, F., & Santaniello, D. (2018). Chatbot: An Education Support System for Student. *Lecture Notes in Computer Science*, *11161*, 291–302. DOI: 10.1007/978-3-030-01689-0_23

Clarke, L., & McFlynn, P. (2019). All Animals Learn, but Only Humans Teach: The Professional Place of Teacher Educators. *Education Sciences*, *9*(3), 192. Advance online publication. DOI: 10.3390/educsci9030192

Clark, R. C., & Mayer, R. E. (2023). *E-learning and the science of instruction: Proven guidelines for consumers and designers of multimedia learning* (5th ed.). John Wiley & Sons.

Coghlan, S., Miller, T., & Paterson, J. (2021). Good Proctor or "Big Brother"? Ethics of Online Exam Supervision Technologies. *Philosophy & Technology, 34*(4), 1581–1606. DOI: 10.1007/s13347-021-00476-1 PMID: 34485025

Cohen, R., Katz, I., Aelterman, N., & Vansteenkiste, M. (2022). Understanding shifts in students' academic motivation across a school year: the role of teachers' motivating styles and need-based experiences. In *European Journal of Psychology of Education* (pp. 1–26). DOI: 10.1007/s10212-022-00635-8

Cojocariu, V. M., & Mareş, G. (2022). Academic Integrity in the Technology-Driven Education Era. In: Mâ ă, L. (eds) *Ethical Use of Information Technology in Higher Education*. EAI/Springer Innovations in Communication and Computing. Springer. https://doi.org/DOI: 10.1007/978-981-16-1951-9_1

Coleman, F. (2020). *A human algorithm: How Artificial Intelligence is redefining who we are*. Catapult.

Collin, S., Lepage, A., & Nebel, L. (2024). Enjeux Éthiques Et Critiques De L'intelligence Artificielle En Éducation: Une Revue Systématique De La Littérature. *Canadian Journal of Learning and Technology, 49*(4), 1–29. DOI: 10.21432/cjlt28448

Coman, A. W., & Cardon, P. (2024). Perceptions of Professionalism and Authenticity in AI-Assisted Writing. *Business and Professional Communication Quarterly*, 23294906241233224. Advance online publication. DOI: 10.1177/23294906241233224

Coombs, C., Hislop, D., Taneva, S. K., & Barnard, S. (2020). The Strategic Impacts of Intelligent Automation for Knowledge and Service Work: An Interdisciplinary Review. *The Journal of Strategic Information Systems, 29*(4), 1–30. DOI: 10.1016/j.jsis.2020.101600

Coots, M., Linn, K. A., Goel, S., Navathe, A. S., & Parikh, R. B. (2025). Racial bias in clinical and population health algorithms: A critical review of current debates. *Annual Review of Public Health, 46*(1), 507–523. Advance online publication. DOI: 10.1146/annurev-publhealth-071823-112058 PMID: 39626231

Cope, B., Kalantzis, M., & Searsmith, D. (2020). Artificial intelligence for education: Knowledge and its assessment in AI-enabled learning ecologies. *Educational Philosophy and Theory, 53*(12), 1229–1245. DOI: 10.1080/00131857.2020.1728732

Costa, K., Ntsobi, P. M., & Mfolo, L. (2024). Challenges, benefits and recommendations for using generative artificial intelligence in academic writing - A case of ChatGPT. *Medicon Engineering Themes, 7*(4), 03-38. https://themedicon.com/pdf/engineeringthemes/MCET-07-236.pdf

Cotton, D. R., Cotton, P. A., & Shipway, J. R. (2024). Chatting and cheating: Ensuring academic integrity in the era of ChatGPT. *Innovations in Education and Teaching International, 61*(2), 228–239. DOI: 10.1080/14703297.2023.2190148

Council for Exceptional Children [CEC]. (2023). *Special education professional ethical principles.* https://exceptionalchildren.org/standards/ethical-principles-and-practice-standards

Crawford, J., Cowling, M., & Allen, K. A. (2023). Leadership is needed for ethical ChatGPT: Character, assessment, and learning using artificial intelligence (AI). *Journal of University Teaching & Learning Practice, 20*(3), 02. . DOI: 10.53761/1.20.3.02

Crawford, J., Vallis, C., Yang, J., Fitzgerald, R., O'Dea, C., & Cowling, M. (2023). Editorial: Artificial Intelligence is awesome, but good teaching should always come first. Revista de práctica de enseñanza y aprendizaje universitario, 20(7). DOI: 10.53761/1.20.7.01

Crawford, K., & Calo, R. (2016). There is a blind spot in AI research. *Nature, 538*(7625), 311–313. DOI: 10.1038/538311a PMID: 27762391

Cukurova, M., Kralj, L., Hertz, B., & Saltidou, E. (2024). *Professional Development for Teachers in the Age of AI.* European Schoolnet Academy Thematic Seminar Report. Retrieved November 20, 2024 from: http://www.eun.org/documents/411753/11183389/EUNA-Thematic-Seminar-Report-V5.pdf/b16bf795 -b147-43ac-9f58-4dd1249b5e48

Çukurova, M., Kent, C., & Luckin, R. (2019). Artificial intelligence and multimodal data in the service of human decision-making: A case study in debate tutoring. *British Journal of Educational Technology, 50*(6), 3032–3046. DOI: 10.1111/bjet.12829

Cuntz, A., C., F., & H., S. (2024). *Artificial Intelligence and Intellectual Property: An Economic Perspective.* World Intellectual Property Organization. https://doi.org/https://www.wipo.int/edocs/pubdocs/en/wipo -pub-econstat-wp-77-en-artificial-intelligence-and-intellectual-property-an-economic-perspective.pdf

Cypress, B. S. (2021). *Fundamentals of qualitative phenomenological nursing research.* John Wiley & Sons.

da Silva, G. S., & Ulbricht, V. R. (2024). Learning with Conversational AI: ChatGPT and Bard/Gemini in Education. *Cognition and Exploratory Learning in the Digital Age,* 101-117. DOI: 10.1007/978-3-031-66462-5_6

Da Silva, J. T., Santos-d'Amorim, K., & Bornemann-Cimenti, H. (2025). The citation of retracted papers and impact on the integrity of the scientific biomedical literature. *Learned Publishing, 38*(2), e1667. Advance online publication. DOI: 10.1002/leap.1667

Dabis, A., & Csáki, C. (2024). AI and ethics: Investigating the first policy responses of higher education institutions to the challenge of generative AI. *Humanities & Social Sciences Communications, 11*(1), 1006. Advance online publication. DOI: 10.1057/s41599-024-03526-z

Daft, R. L., & Lengel, R. H. (1986). Organizational Information Requirements, Media Richness and Structural Design. *Management Science, 32*(5), 554–571. DOI: 10.1287/mnsc.32.5.554

Dainys, A. (2024). Human Creativity Versus Machine Creativity: Will Humans Be Surpassed by AI? In *IntechOpen eBooks.* DOI: 10.5772/intechopen.1007369

Dang, J., & Liu, L. (2022). A Growth Mindset About Human Minds Promotes Positive Responses to Intelligent Technology. *Cognition, 220,* 1–14. DOI: 10.1016/j.cognition.2021.104985 PMID: 34920301

Daniela, L. (Ed.). (2022). *Inclusive digital education.* Springer., DOI: 10.1007/978-3-031-14775-3

Dan, S. (2022). Teacher Intelligence Training Based on Big Data and Artificial Intelligence. *International Journal of e-Collaboration, 18*(3), 1–11. DOI: 10.4018/IJeC.307137

Darling-Hammond, L., Flook, L., Cook-Harvey, C., Barron, B., & Osher, D. (2019). Implications for Educational Practice of the Science of Learning and Development. *Applied Developmental Science, 24*(2), 97–140. DOI: 10.1080/10888691.2018.1537791

Darwin, N., Rusdin, D., Mukminatien, N., Suryati, N., Laksmi, E. D., & Marzuki, N. (2023). Critical thinking in the AI era: An exploration of EFL students' perceptions, benefits, and limitations. *Cogent Education, 11*(1), 2290342. Advance online publication. DOI: 10.1080/2331186X.2023.2290342

Davenport, T. H., & Kirby, J. (2016). *Only humans need apply: Winners and losers in the age of smart machines.* Harper Business.

Davis, A. (2023). Academic integrity in the time of contradictions. *Cogent Education, 10*(2), 2289307. Advance online publication. DOI: 10.1080/2331186X.2023.2289307

Davis, R. A. (2001). A cognitive-behavioral model of pathological Internet use. *Computers in Human Behavior, 17*(2), 187–195. DOI: 10.1016/S0747-5632(00)00041-8

Dawson, P. (2021). *Defending assessment security in a digital world: Preventing e-cheating and supporting academic integrity in higher education.* Routledge.

Dawson, P., & Sutherland-Smith, W. (2023). AI-assisted writing: Opportunities, challenges, and ethical considerations. *Journal of Academic Ethics, 21*(1), 1–18.

Dayal, D. (2023). Cyber Risks in the Education Sector: Why Cybersecurity Needs to Be Top of the Class. *Digital First Magazine.* https://www.digitalfirstmagazine.com/cyber-risks-in-the-education-sector-why -cybersecurity-needs-to-be-top-of-the-class/

de Rassenfosse, G., Pellegrino, G., & Raiteri, E. (2024). Do Patents Enable Disclosure? Evidence From the Invention Secrecy Act. *International Journal of Industrial Organization, 92*, 1–16. DOI: 10.1016/j. ijindorg.2023.103044

Delcker, J., Heil, J., & Ifenthaler, D. (2024). Evidence-based development of an instrument for the assessment of teachers self-perceptions of their artificial intelligence competence. *ETR&D-Educational Technology Research And Development, 1-19.* DOI: 10.1007/s11423-024-10418-1

Delcker, J., & Ifenthaler, D. (2022). Digital Distance Learning and the Transformation of Vocational Schools From a Qualitative Perspective. *Frontiers in Education, 7*, 1–15. DOI: 10.3389/feduc.2022.908046

Delello, J. A., Sung, W., Mokhtari, K., Hebert, J., Bronson, A., & De Giuseppe, T. (2025). AI in the Classroom: Insights from Educators on Usage, Challenges, and Mental Health. *Education Sciences, 15*(2), 1–27. DOI: 10.3390/educsci15020113

Dempere, J., Modugu, K., Hesham, A., & Ramasamy, L. K. (2023). The impact of ChatGPT on higher education. *Frontiers in Education, 8*, 1206936. DOI: 10.3389/feduc.2023.1206936

Deng, X., & Yu, Z. (2023). A Meta-Analysis and Systematic Review of the Effect of Chatbot Technology Use in Sustainable Education. *Sustainability (Basel), 15*(4), 2940. DOI: 10.3390/su15042940

Deppeler, J., & Ainscow, M. (2016). Using inquiry-based approaches for equitable school improvement. *School Effectiveness and School Improvement*, *27*(1), 1–6. DOI: 10.1080/09243453.2015.1026671

Dergaa, I., Ben Saad, H., Glenn, J. M., Amamou, B., Ben Aissa, M., Guelmami, N., Fekih-Romdhane, F., & Chamari, K. (2024). From tools to threats: A reflection on the impact of artificial-intelligence chatbots on cognitive health. *Frontiers in Psychology*, *15*, 15. DOI: 10.3389/fpsyg.2024.1259845 PMID: 38629037

Diederich, S., Brendel, A. B., Morana, S., & Kolbe, L. (2022). On the design of and interaction with conversational agents: An organizing and assessing review of human-computer interaction research. *Journal of the Association for Information Systems*, *23*(1), 96–138. DOI: 10.17705/1jais.00724

DiMatteo, L. A., Poncibò, C., & Cannarsa, M. (Eds.). (2022). *The Cambridge handbook of artificial intelligence: Global perspectives on law and ethics.* Cambridge University Press. DOI: 10.1017/9781009072168

Ding, A.-C. E., Shi, L., Yang, H., & Choi, I. (2024). Enhancing Teacher AI Literacy and Integration Through Different Types of Cases in Teacher Professional Development. *Computers and Education Open*, *6*, 1–13. DOI: 10.1016/j.caeo.2024.100178

Diniz, E. H., Sanches, B. H., Pozzebon, M., & Luvizan, S. (2024). Do black fintechs matter? The long and winding road to develop inclusive algorithms for social justice. *Management Information Systems Quarterly*, *48*(4), 1721–1744. DOI: 10.25300/MISQ/2024/18288

Djajasoepena, R., Setiawan, I., Bhakti, M. A. C., Purnomo, A. T., Ayu, M. A., Alibasa, M. J., & Wandy, W. (2024). Utilization of Artificial Intelligence to Support the Development of Teaching and Project Modules. *Journal of Community Services: Sustainability and Empowerment*, *4*(01), 7–11. DOI: 10.35806/jcsse.v4i1.440

Dogan, M. E., Goru Dogan, T., & Bozkurt, A. (2023). The use of artificial intelligence (AI) in online learning and distance education processes: A systematic review of empirical studies. *Applied Sciences (Basel, Switzerland)*, *13*(5), 3056. DOI: 10.3390/app13053056

Doğan, Y., Yıldırım, N. T., & Batdı, V. (2024). Effectiveness of Portfolio Assessment in Primary Education: A Multi-Complementary Research Approach. *Evaluation and Program Planning*, *106*, 1–12. DOI: 10.1016/j.evalprogplan.2024.102461 PMID: 38925046

Doğuş, M. (2024a). Görme yetersizliği ve yapay zekâ. A. Kaya (Ed.) *Özel eğitim ve yapay zekâ* içinde (155-186). Vize Akademik.

Doğuş, M. (2024b, Eylül). Visual Impairment and Artificial Intelligence: Where We Are and What Awaits Us in the. Future? *BILTEVT2024 International Barrier-Free Information Techonogy Congress*, Manisa, Türkiye.

Drigas, A., & Ioannidou, R. (2012). Artificial intelligence in special education: A decade review. *International Journal of Engineering Education*, *28*, 1366–1372.

du Boulay, B. (2022). Artificial intelligence in education and ethics. In *Handbook of open, distance and digital education* (pp. 1–16). Springer Nature. DOI: 10.1007/978-981-19-0351-9_6-2

Duarte, R. Sara (2023). Oportunidades y desafíos del uso de Chat GPT en educación superior. *Aula Magna 2.0* [Blog]. https://cuedespyd.hypotheses.org/14349

Duhaylungsod, A. V., & Chavez, J. V. (2023). ChatGPT and other AI users: Innovative and creative utilitarian value and mindset shift. *Journal of Namibian Studies: History Politics Culture*, *33*, 4367–4378.

Duque, R. C. S., Silva, J. S., Loureiro, V. J. S., Darcanchy, M., Eccard, A. F. C., Durigon, S., Placido, I. T. M., Sousa, T. S. R., Xavier, R. M. L., & Oliveira, E. A. R. (2024). Tecnologias Digitais Associadas a Ia Na Formação Docente. *Caderno Pedagógico*, *21*(4), e3651. DOI: 10.54033/cadpedv21n4-053

Durovic, M., & Watson, J. (2022). AI, consumer data protection and privacy. In Holmes, W., & Porayska-Pomsta, K. (Eds.), *The ethics of artificial intelligence in education: Practices, challenges, and debates* (pp. 173–192). Routledge.

Dwivedi, Y. K., Hughes, L., Ismagilova, E., Aarts, G., Coombs, C., Crick, T., Duan, Y., Dwivedi, R., Edwards, J., Eirug, A., Galanos, V., Ilavarasan, P. V., Janssen, M., Jones, P., Kar, A. K., Kizgin, H., Kronemann, B., Lal, B., Lucini, B., & Williams, M. D. (2021). Artificial Intelligence (AI): Multidisciplinary perspectives on emerging challenges, opportunities, and agenda for research, practice and policy. *International Journal of Information Management*, *57*, 101994. DOI: 10.1016/j.ijinfomgt.2019.08.002

Dwivedi, Y. K., Sharma, A., Rana, N. P., Giannakis, M., Goel, P., & Dutot, V. (2023). Evolution of artificial intelligence research in Technological Forecasting and Social Change: Research topics, trends, and future directions. *Technological Forecasting and Social Change*, *192*, 122579. DOI: 10.1016/j.techfore.2023.122579

Edwards, C., Edwards, A., Spence, P., & Lin, X. (2018). I, teacher: Using artificial intelligence (AI) and social robots in communication and instruction. *Communication Education*, *67*(4), 473–480. DOI: 10.1080/03634523.2018.1502459

Edwards, J., Nguyen, K., & Lämsä, J. (2025). Socially shared regulation of learning in AI-enhanced collaborative education: An empirical study. *British Journal of Educational Technology*, *56*(1), 78–98. DOI: 10.1111/bjet.13534

Elahi, M., Afolaranmi, S. O., Martinez Lastra, J. L., & Perez Garcia, J. A. (2023). A Comprehensive Literature Review of the Applications of AI Techniques Through the Lifecycle of Industrial Equipment. *Discover Artificial Intelligence*, *3*(1), 1–78. DOI: 10.1007/s44163-023-00089-x

Elkhatat, A. M., Elsaid, K., & Almeer, S. (2023). Evaluating the efficacy of AI content detection tools in differentiating between human and AI-generated text. *International Journal for Educational Integrity*, *19*(1), 17. Advance online publication. DOI: 10.1007/s40979-023-00140-5

Elsayed, H. (2024). The impact of hallucinated information in large language models on student learning Outcomes: A Critical Examination of Misinformation Risks in AI-Assisted Education. https://northernreviews.com/index.php/NRATCC/article/view/2024-08-07

Elsen-Rooney, M. (2023, Jan, 4). NYC education department blocks ChatGPT on school devices, networks. Chalkbeat New York. https:// ny.chalk beat.org/2023/1/3/23537 987/nyc- schools- ban- chatgpt-writing- artificial- intelligence.

Er, E., Akçapınar, G., Bayazıt, A., Noroozi, O., & Banihashem, S. K. (2024). Assessing Student Perceptions and Use of Instructor Versus AI-Generated Feedback. *British Journal of Educational Technology*. Advance online publication. DOI: 10.1111/bjet.13558

Ersoy, C. (2022). Inclusive education and its components. In Sanır, H. (Ed.), *Supporting academic skills in inclusive educational environments* (pp. 1–32). Eğiten Kitap.

Escalante, J., Pack, A., & Barrett, A. (2023). AI-Generated Feedback on Writing: Insights into Efficacy and ENL Student Preference. *International Journal of Educational Technology in Higher Education*, *20*(1), 57. Advance online publication. DOI: 10.1186/s41239-023-00425-2

Espinoza, O. (2007). Solving the equity–equality conceptual dilemma: A new model for analysis of the educational process. *Educational Research*, *49*(4), 343–363. DOI: 10.1080/00131880701717198

Essel, H. B., Vlachopoulos, D., Tachie-Menson, A., Johnson, E. E., & Baah, P. K. (2022). The Impact of a Virtual Teaching Assistant (Chatbot) on Students' Learning in Ghanaian Higher Education. *International Journal of Educational Technology in Higher Education*, *19*(1), 57. Advance online publication. DOI: 10.1186/s41239-022-00362-6

Essien, A., Bukoye, O. T., O'Dea, X., & Kremantzis, M. (2024). The influence of AI text generators on critical thinking skills in UK business schools. *Studies in Higher Education*, *49*(5), 1–18. DOI: 10.1080/03075079.2024.2316881

European Agency for Development in Special Needs Education. (2011). *Teacher education for inclusion across Europe – Challenges and opportunities*. https://www.european-agency.org/sites/default/files/te4i-synthesis-report-en.pdf

European Agency for Special Needs and Inclusive Education. (2012). *Raising achievement for all learners – Quality in inclusive education*. https://www.european-agency.org/sites/default/files/ra4al-synthesis-report_RA4AL-synthesis-report.pdf

European Agency for Special Needs and Inclusive Education. (2016). *Raising the achievement of all learners in inclusive education – Literature review*. https://www.european-agency.org/sites/default/files/Raising%20Achievement%20Literature%20Review.pdf

European Agency for Special Needs and Inclusive Education. (2018). *Key actions for raising achievement: Guidance for teachers and leaders*. https://www.european-agency.org/sites/default/files/Key%20Actions%20for%20Raising%20Achievement.pdf

European Commission. (2020). *Digital Education Action Plan (2021-2027)*. Retrieved November 25, 2024 from https://ec.europa.eu/education/education-in-the-eu/digital-education-action-plan_en

European Commission. (2020). *White paper on artificial intelligence: A European approach to excellence and trust*. https://ec.europa.eu/commission/presscorner/detail/en/ip_20_273

European Commission. (2024). *Educational support and guidance*.https://eurydice.eacea.ec.europa.eu/national-education-systems/germany/educational-support-and-guidance

European Commission. (2024). Scenarios for the future of school education in the EU: A Foresight Study. Brussels: Publications Office of the European Union. Retrieved November 25, 2024 from https://www.vleva.eu/storage/1016/scenarios-for-the-future-of-school-education-in-the-NC0523475ENN.pdf

European Commission. Directorate-General for Education, Youth, Sport and Culture (2022). Ethical guidelines on the use of artificial intelligence (AI) and data in teaching and learning for educators. Publications Office of the European Union. https://data.europa.eu/doi/10.2766/153756

European Parliament. (2023). *Ley de IA de la UE: primera normativa sobre inteligencia artificial.* Temas. Retrieved November 25, 2024 from https://www.europarl.europa.eu/topics/es/article/20230601STO93804/ley-de-ia-de-la-ue-primera-normativa-sobre-inteligencia-artificial

Eysenbach, G. (2023). The role of ChatGPT, generative language models, and artificial intelligence in medical education: A conversation with ChatGPT and a call for papers. *JMIR Medical Education, 9*(1), e46885. https://doi.org/e46885.10.2196/46885. DOI: 10.2196/46885 PMID: 36863937

Fahimirad, M., & Kotamjani, S. S. (2018). A review on application of artificial intelligence in teaching and learning in educational contexts. *International Journal of Learning and Development, 8*(4), 106–118. DOI: 10.5296/ijld.v8i4.14057

FakhrHosseini, S., Chan, K., Lee, C., Jeon, M., Son, H., Rudnik, J., & Coughlin, J.FakhrHosseini. (2022). User Adoption of Intelligent Environments: A review of technology adoption models, challenges, and prospects. *International Journal of Human-Computer Interaction, 40*(4), 986–998. DOI: 10.1080/10447318.2022.2118851

Falebita, O. S. (2024). Assessing the Relationship Between Anxiety and the Adoption of Artificial Intelligence Tools Among Mathematics Preservice Teachers. *Interdisciplinary Journal of Education Research, 6*, 1–13. DOI: 10.38140/ijer-2024.vol6.20

Fan, Y., Tang, L., Le, H., Shen, K., Tan, S., Zhao, Y., Shen, Y., Li, X., & Gašević, D. (2024). Beware of metacognitive laziness: Effects of generative artificial intelligence on learning motivation, processes, and performance. *British Journal of Educational Technology, n/a*(n/a). https://doi.org/https://doi.org/10.1111/bjet.13544

Fang, X., Che, S., Mao, M., Zhang, H., Zhao, M., & Zhao, X. (2023). Bias of AI-Generated Content: An examination of news produced by large language models. SSRN *Electronic Journal.* https://doi.org/ DOI: 10.2139/ssrn.4574226

Farrelly, T., & Baker, N. (2023). Generative Artificial Intelligence: Implications and Considerations for Higher Education Practice. *Education Sciences, 13*(11), 1109. DOI: 10.3390/educsci13111109

Ferikoğlu, D., & Akgün, E. (2022). An Investigation of Teachers' Artificial Intelligence Awareness: A Scale Development Study. *Malaysian Online Journal of Educational Technology, 10*(3), 215–231. DOI: 10.52380/mojet.2022.10.3.407

Ferrara, E. (2023). Fairness and Bias in Artificial Intelligence: A Brief Survey of Sources, Impacts, and Mitigation Strategies. *Sci, 6*(1), 1–15. DOI: 10.3390/sci6010003

Ferrero Guillén, R., & Breckwoldt Jurado, A. (2023). Vagueness in Artificial Intelligence: The 'Fuzzy Logic' of AI-Related Patent Claims. *Digital Society : Ethics, Socio-Legal and Governance of Digital Technology, 2*(1), 1–25. DOI: 10.1007/s44206-022-00032-0

Fidan, M., & Gencel, N. (2022). Supporting the Instructional Videos With Chatbot and Peer Feedback Mechanisms in Online Learning: The Effects on Learning Performance and Intrinsic Motivation. *Journal of Educational Computing Research*, 60(7), 1716–1741. DOI: 10.1177/07356331221077901

Fiialka, S., Kornieva, Z., & Honchar, T. (2023). ChatGPT in Ukrainian Education: Problems and Prospects. *International Journal of Emerging Technologies in Learning*, 18(17), 236–250. Advance online publication. DOI: 10.3991/ijet.v18i17.42215

Filippi, E., Bannò, M., & Trento, S. (2023). Automation Technologies and Their Impact on Employment: A Review, Synthesis and Future Research Agenda. *Technological Forecasting and Social Change*, 191, 1–21. DOI: 10.1016/j.techfore.2023.122448

Fillis, I. A. N., & Rentschler, R. (2010). The role of creativity in entrepreneurship. *Journal of Enterprising Culture*, 18(1), 49–81. DOI: 10.1142/S0218495810000501

Firth, J., Torous, J., Stubbs, B., Firth, J. A., Steiner, G. Z., Smith, L., Alvarez-Jimenez, M., Gleeson, J., Vancampfort, D., Armitage, C. J., & Sarris, J. (2019). The "online brain": How the Internet may be changing our cognition. *World Psychiatry; Official Journal of the World Psychiatric Association (WPA)*, 18(2), 119–129. https://doi.org/https://doi.org/10.1002/wps.20617. DOI: 10.1002/wps.20617 PMID: 31059635

Fissore, C., Floris, F., Conte, M. M., & Sacchet, M. (2024). Teacher Training on Artificial Intelligence in Education. *Cognition and Exploratory Learning in the Digital Age*, 227-244. https://doi.org/DOI: 10.1007/978-3-031-54207-7_13

Flores, M. A., Veiga Simão, A. M., Ferreira, P. C., Pereira, D., Barros, A., Flores, P., Fernandes, E. L., & Costa, L. (2024). Online Learning, Perceived Difficulty and the Role of Feedback in COVID-19 Times. *Research in Post-Compulsory Education*, 29(2), 324–344. DOI: 10.1080/13596748.2024.2330784

Floridi, L. (2021). Establishing the Rules for Building Trustworthy AI. In Floridi, L. (Ed.), Philosophical Studies Series: Vol. 144. *Ethics, Governance, and Policies in Artificial Intelligence*. Springer., DOI: 10.1007/978-3-030-81907-1_4

Floridi, L., & Cowls, J. (2019). AI ethics: Mapping ethical issues in AI applications in education. *Journal of Information Ethics*, 28(4), 345–362.

Floridi, L., Cowls, J., Beltrametti, M., Chatila, R., Chazerand, P., Dignum, V., Luetge, C., Madelin, R., Pagallo, U., Rossi, F., Schafer, B., Valcke, P., & Vayena, E. (2018). AI4People—An ethical framework for a good AI society: Opportunities, risks, principles, and recommendations. *Minds and Machines*, 28(4), 689–707. DOI: 10.1007/s11023-018-9482-5 PMID: 30930541

Formosa, P., Bankins, S., Matulionyte, R., & Ghasemi, O. (2024). Can ChatGPT be an author? Generative AI creative writing assistance and perceptions of authorship, creatorship, responsibility, and disclosure. *AI & Society*. Advance online publication. DOI: 10.1007/s00146-024-02081-0

Fragiadakis, G., Diou, C., & Kousiouris, G. (2024). Evaluating human-AI collaboration: A review and methodological framework. *arXiv Preprint*, 1-25. https://doi.org//arXiv.2407.19098DOI: 10.48550

Franganillo, J., Lopezosa, C., & Salse, M. (2023). *La inteligencia artificial generativa en la docencia universitaria.* Col·lecció del CRICC. Universitat de Barcelona. http://hdl.handle.net/2445/202932

Frankish, K., & Ramsay, W. M. (2017). *The Cambridge handbook of artificial intelligence.* Cambridge University Press.

Fryer, L. K., Ainley, M., Thompson, A., Gibson, A., & Sherlock, Z. (2017). Stimulating and Sustaining Interest in a Language Course: An Experimental Comparison of Chatbot and Human Task Partners. *Computers in Human Behavior, 75*, 461–468. DOI: 10.1016/j.chb.2017.05.045

Fryer, L. K., Nakao, K., & Thompson, A. (2019). Chatbot Learning Partners: Connecting Learning Experiences, Interest and Competence. *Computers in Human Behavior, 93*, 279–289. DOI: 10.1016/j.chb.2018.12.023

Fryer, L., Coniam, D., Carpenter, R., & Lăpu neanu, D. (2020). Bots for Language Learning Now: Current and Future Directions. *Language Learning & Technology, 24*(2), 8–22. https://www.lltjournal.org/item/10125-44719/

Fuad, D. R. S. M., Musa, K., & Hashim, Z. (2020). Innovation Culture in Education: A Systematic Review of the Literature. *Management in Education, 36*(3), 135–149. DOI: 10.1177/0892020620959760

Füller, J., Hutter, K., Wahl, J., Bilgram, V., & Tekic, Z. (2022). How AI Revolutionizes Innovation Management – Perceptions and Implementation Preferences of AI-Based Innovators. *Technological Forecasting and Social Change, 178*, 1–22. DOI: 10.1016/j.techfore.2022.121598

Funa, A. A., & Gabay, R. A. E. (2025). Policy Guidelines and Recommendations on AI Use in Teaching and Learning: A Meta-Synthesis Study. *Social Sciences & Humanities Open, 11*, 1–13. DOI: 10.1016/j.ssaho.2024.101221

Fu, Y., & Weng, Z. (2024). Navigating the ethical terrain of AI in education: A systematic review on framing responsible human-centered AI practices. *Computers and Education: Artificial Intelligence, 7*, 100306. DOI: 10.1016/j.caeai.2024.100306

Gaggioli, A. (2023). Ethics: Disclose use of AI in scientific manuscripts. *Nature, 614*(7948), 413. DOI: 10.1038/d41586-023-00381-x PMID: 36788370

Gallagher, K. (2024). Siemens NX CAM Integrates AI-Powered CAM Assist. *Siemens.* https://blogs.sw.siemens.com/nx-manufacturing/the-future-of-ai-cnc-programming-siemens-nx-cam-integrates-ai-powered-cam-assist/

Gallagher, M. (2019). Artificial intelligence and the mobilities of inclusion: The accumulated advantages of 5G networks and surfacing outliers. In *Artificial intelligence and inclusive education: Speculative futures and emerging practices* (pp. 179–194). Springer. DOI: 10.1007/978-981-13-8161-4_11

Gallent-Torres, C., Zapata-González, A., & Ortego-Hernando, J. L. (2023). El impacto de la inteligencia artificial generativa en educación superior: Una mirada desde la ética y la integridad académica. RELIEVE. *Revista Electrónica de Investigación y Evaluación Educativa, 29*(2), 1–21. DOI: 10.30827/relieve.v29i2.29134

Galos, J. L., Friedman, A. Z. C., Jamosmos, E., Allec, S. I., Blinzler, B., Grunenfelder, L., & Carberry, A. R. (2024). Teaching Artificial Intelligence and Machine Learning to Materials Engineering Students Through Plastic 3D Printing. *ASEE Annual Conference and Exposition, Conference Proceedings*. DOI: 10.18260/1-2--48057

Gao, J., 2021. Exploring the feedback quality of an automated writing evaluation system Pigai. *Int. J. Emerg. Technol. Learn. 16* (11), 322. https://doi.org/. v16i11.19657.DOI: 10.3991/ijet

Gao, C. A., Howard, F. M., Markov, N. S., Dyer, E. C., Ramesh, S., Luo, Y., & Pearson, A. T. (2022). Comparing scientific abstracts generated by ChatGPT to original abstracts using an artificial intelligence output detector, plagiarism detector, and blinded human reviewers. npj. *Digital Medicine*, 6, 75. DOI: 10.1038/s41746-023-00819-6 PMID: 37100871

Garcia, M. B., Arif, Y. M., Khlaif, Z. N., Zhu, M., de Almeida, R. P. P., de Almeida, R. S., & Masters, K. (2024). Effective Integration of Artificial Intelligence in Medical Education: Practical Tips and Actionable Insights. In *Transformative Approaches to Patient Literacy and Healthcare Innovation* (pp. 1-19). IGI Global. DOI: 10.4018/979-8-3693-3661-8.ch001

Garcia, M. B., Goi, C.-L., Shively, K., Maher, D., Rosak-Szyrocka, J., Happonen, A., Bozkurt, A., & Damaševičius, R. (2025). Understanding Student Engagement in AI-Powered Online Learning Platforms: A Narrative Review of Key Theories and Models. In *Cases on Enhancing P-16 Student Engagement With Digital Technologies* (pp. 1-30). IGI Global. DOI: 10.2139/ssrn.5074608

Garcia, M. B. (2022). Hackathons as Extracurricular Activities: Unraveling the Motivational Orientation Behind Student Participation. *Computer Applications in Engineering Education*, *30*(6), 1903–1918. DOI: 10.1002/cae.22564

Garcia, M. B. (2023). Facilitating Group Learning Using an Apprenticeship Model: Which Master is More Effective in Programming Instruction? *Journal of Educational Computing Research*, *61*(6), 1207–1231. DOI: 10.1177/07356331231170382

Garcia, M. B. (2023). Fostering an Innovation Culture in the Education Sector: A Scoping Review and Bibliometric Analysis of Hackathons. *Innovative Higher Education*, *48*(4), 739–762. DOI: 10.1007/s10755-023-09651-y PMID: 37361114

Garcia, M. B. (2024a). Addressing the Mental Health Implications of ChatGPT Dependency: The Need for Comprehensive Policy Development. *Asian Journal of Psychiatry*, *98*, 104140. Advance online publication. DOI: 10.1016/j.ajp.2024.104140 PMID: 38943840

Garcia, M. B. (2024b). The Paradox of Artificial Creativity: Challenges and Opportunities of Generative AI Artistry. *Creativity Research Journal*, ●●●, 1–14. DOI: 10.1080/10400419.2024.2354622

Garcia, M. B. (2025). Teaching and Learning Computer Programming Using ChatGPT: A Rapid Review of Literature Amid the Rise of Generative AI Technologies. *Education and Information Technologies*, ●●●, 1–25. DOI: 10.1007/s10639-025-13452-5

Garcia, M. B., Goi, C. L., Shively, K., Maher, D., Rosak-Szyrocka, J., Happonen, A., Bozkurt, A., & Damaševičius, R. (2025). Understanding Student Engagement in AI-Powered Online Learning Platforms: A Narrative Review of Key Theories and Models. In Gierhart, A. R. (Ed.), *Cases on Enhancing P-16 Student Engagement With Digital Technologies* (pp. 1–30). IGI Global., DOI: 10.4018/979-8-3693-5633-3.ch001

Garcia, M. B., Mangaba, J. B., & Tanchoco, C. C. (2021). Virtual Dietitian: A Nutrition Knowledge-Based System Using Forward Chaining Algorithm. *2021 International Conference on Innovation and Intelligence for Informatics, Computing, and Technologies (3ICT)*, 309-314. DOI: 10.1109/3ICT53449.2021.9581887

Garcia, M. B., Yousef, A. M. F., de Almeida, R. P. P., Arif, Y. M., Happonen, A., & Barber, W. (2023). Teaching physical fitness and exercise using computer-assisted instruction: A School-based public health intervention. In *Handbook of research on instructional technologies in health education and allied disciplines* (pp. 177–195). IGI Global. DOI: 10.4018/978-1-6684-7164-7.ch008

García-Martínez, I., Fernández-Batanero, J. M., Fernández-Cerero, J., & León, S. P. (2023). Analysing the impact of artificial intelligence and computational sciences on student performance: Systematic review and meta-analysis. *Journal of New Approaches in Educational Research*, *12*(1), 171–197. DOI: 10.7821/naer.2023.1.1240

Gee, J. P. (2000). Identity as an Analytic Lens for Research in Education. *Review of Research in Education*, *25*, 99–125. DOI: 10.2307/1167322

Gentile, M., Città, G., Perna, S., & Allegra, M. (2023). Do we still need teachers? Navigating the paradigm shift of the teacher's role in the AI era. *Frontiers in Education*, *8*, 1161777. Advance online publication. DOI: 10.3389/feduc.2023.1161777

George, A. S., Baskar, T., & Srikaanth, P. B. (2024). The Erosion of Cognitive Skills in the Technological Age: How Reliance on Technology Impacts Critical Thinking, Problem-Solving, and Creativity. *Partners Universal Innovative Research Publication, 2*(3 SE-Articles), 147–163. DOI: 10.5281/zenodo.11671150

Gerlich, M. (2025). AI Tools in Society: Impacts on Cognitive Offloading and the Future of Critical Thinking. In *Societies* (Vol. 15, Issue 1). DOI: 10.3390/soc15010006

Ghimire, A., & Edwards, J. (2024). From Guidelines to Governance: A Study of AI Policies in Education. In *Communications in computer and information science* (pp. 299–307). https://doi.org/DOI: 10.1007/978-3-031-64312-5_36

Ghimire, S. N., Bhattarai, U., & Baral, R. K. (2024). Implications of ChatGPT for higher education institutions: Exploring Nepali university students' perspectives. *Higher Education Research & Development*, *43*(8), 1–15. DOI: 10.1080/07294360.2024.2366323

Ghosh, S. S. (2025). Ghosts of the border: Trauma, identity, and the fragmented self in partition-era narratives of Punjab through the DSM-5 framework. *Sikh Formations*, ●●●, 1–17. DOI: 10.1080/17448727.2025.2454070

Ghotbi, N. (2024). Ethics of Artificial Intelligence in Academic Research and Education. *Springer International Handbooks of Education*, 1355-1366. https://doi.org/DOI: 10.1007/978-3-031-54144-5_143

Giannakos, M., Azevedo, R., Brusilovsky, P., Cukurova, M., Dimitriadis, Y., Hernandez-Leo, D., Järvelä, S., Mavrikis, M., & Rienties, B. (2024). The Promise and Challenges of Generative AI in Education. *Behaviour & Information Technology*, ●●●, 1–27. DOI: 10.1080/0144929X.2024.2394886

Gibson, B., & Green, C. N. (2025). Teaching Literature in the Age of AI. In *Advances in library and information science (ALIS) book series* (pp. 179–210). DOI: 10.4018/979-8-3693-3053-1.ch009

Gikandi, J. W., Morrow, D., & Davis, N. E. (2011). Online Formative Assessment in Higher Education: A Review of the Literature. *Computers & Education*, *57*(4), 2333–2351. DOI: 10.1016/j.compedu.2011.06.004

Gilchrist, D., & Perks, B. (2023). Grey Lines in Grey Literature: Incorporating grey literature value into the research and evaluation of public policy and the social sciences. SSRN *Electronic Journal*. https://doi.org/DOI: 10.2139/ssrn.4630554

Gillespie, T. (2024). *Doing literary criticism: The Cultivation of Thinkers in the Classroom*. Taylor & Francis. DOI: 10.4324/9781003579083

Giray, L. (2024). AI Shaming: The Silent Stigma among Academic Writers and Researchers. *Annals of Biomedical Engineering*, *52*(9), 2319–2324. DOI: 10.1007/s10439-024-03582-1 PMID: 38977530

Gligorea, I., Cioca, M., Oancea, R., Gorski, A., Gorski, H., & Tudorache, P. (2023). Adaptive Learning Using Artificial Intelligence in e-Learning: A Literature review. *Education Sciences*, *13*(12), 1216. DOI: 10.3390/educsci13121216

Glover, E. (2024, December 11). What is ChatGPT? Built In. https://builtin.com/artificial-intelligence/what-is-chatgpt

Gocen, A., & Aydemir, F. (2020). Artificial intelligence in education and schools. *Research on Education and Media*, *12*(1), 13–21. DOI: 10.2478/rem-2020-0003

Goertzel, B., & Pennachin, C. (2007). *Artificial General Intelligence: A Gentle Introduction*. Springer Science& Business Media. DOI: 10.1007/978-3-540-68677-4

Goffman, E. (1963). *Stigma: Notes on the Management of Spoiled Identity*. Touchstone. https://books.google.com.ph/books?id=7CNUUMKTbIoC

Goksu, D. Y., & Yalcin, S. (2023). Effectiveness Evaluation of the Trainer Training Project Program Applied to BİLSEM Teachers Working with Specially Gifted Students. *National Education Journal*, *52*(240), 2863–2886. DOI: 10.37669/milliegitim.1184848

Goldman, S. R., Taylor, J., Carreon, A., & Smith, S. J. (2024). Using AI to support special education teacher workload. *Journal of Special Education Technology*, *39*(3), 434–447. DOI: 10.1177/01626434241257240

Gold, N. E. (2021). Virginia Dignum: Responsible Artificial Intelligence: How to Develop and Use AI in a Responsible Way. *Genetic Programming and Evolvable Machines*. *22*(1), 137–139. DOI: 10.1007/s10710-020-09394-1

Gomez-del Rio, T., & Rodriguez, J. (2022). Design and Assessment of a Project-Based Learning in a Laboratory for Integrating Knowledge and Improving Engineering Design Skills. *Education for Chemical Engineers*, *40*, 17–28. DOI: 10.1016/j.ece.2022.04.002

Gong, C., & Yang, Y. (2024). Google effects on memory: A meta-analytical review of the media effects of intensive Internet search behavior. *Frontiers in Public Health*, *12*, 12. DOI: 10.3389/fpubh.2024.1332030 PMID: 38304178

Gonsalves, C. (2024). Generative AI's Impact on Critical Thinking: Revisiting Bloom's Taxonomy. *Journal of Marketing Education*, *02734753241305980*, 02734753241305980. Advance online publication. DOI: 10.1177/02734753241305980

González-González, C. S. (2023). El impacto de la inteligencia artificial en la educación: Transformación de la forma de enseñar y de aprender. *Revista Qurriculum*, *36*(03), 51–60. Advance online publication. DOI: 10.25145/j.qurricul.2023.36.03

González, L. A., Neyem, A., Contreras-McKay, I., & Molina, D. (2022). Improving Learning Experiences in Software Engineering Capstone Courses Using Artificial Intelligence Virtual Assistants. *Computer Applications in Engineering Education*, *30*(5), 1370–1389. DOI: 10.1002/cae.22526

Goodfellow, I., Bengio, Y., & Courville, A. (2016). *Deep learning*. MIT press.

Grapin, S. E. (2023). Assessment of English Learners and Their Peers in the Content Areas: Expanding What "Counts" as Evidence of Content Learning. *Language Assessment Quarterly*, *20*(2), 215–234. DOI: 10.1080/15434303.2022.2147072

Grassini, S. (2023). Shaping the Future of Education: Exploring the Potential and Consequences of AI and ChatGPT in Educational Settings. *Education Sciences*, *13*(7), 692. DOI: 10.3390/educsci13070692

Gray, S. L. (2020). Artificial Intelligence in Schools: Towards a Democratic Future. *London Review of Education*, *18*(2). Advance online publication. DOI: 10.14324/LRE.18.2.02

Grebenshchikova, E. (2016). NBIC-Convergence and Technoethics: Common Ethical Perspective. [IJT]. *International Journal of Technoethics*, *7*(1), 77–84. DOI: 10.4018/IJT.2016010106

Grinschgl, S., & Neubauer, A. C. (2022). Supporting Cognition With Modern Technology: Distributed Cognition Today and in an AI-Enhanced Future. *Frontiers in Artificial Intelligence*, *5*, 5. DOI: 10.3389/frai.2022.908261 PMID: 35910191

Gruenhagen, J. H., Sinclair, P. M., Carroll, J.-A., Baker, P. R. A., Wilson, A., & Demant, D. (2024). The rapid rise of generative AI and its implications for academic integrity: Students' perceptions and use of chatbots for assistance with assessments. *Computers and Education: Artificial Intelligence*, *7*, 100273. https://doi.org/https://doi.org/10.1016/j.caeai.2024.100273

Gruenhagen, J. H., Sinclair, P. M., Carroll, J.-A., Baker, P. R. A., Wilson, A., & Demant, D. (2024). The Rapid Rise of Generative AI and Its Implications for Academic Integrity: Students' Perceptions and Use of Chatbots for Assistance With Assessments. *Computers and Education: Artificial Intelligence*, *7*, 1–10. DOI: 10.1016/j.caeai.2024.100273

Guadamuz, A. (2017). Artificial Intelligence and Copyright. *WIPO Magazine*. https://www.wipo.int/web/wipo-magazine/articles/artificial-intelligence-and-copyright-40141

Guan, H. (2023). Advantages and challenges of using artificial intelligence in primary and secondary school education. *Educational Technology and Psychological Sciences, 22*. https://doi.org/. v22i. 12469DOI: 10.54097/ehss

Guan, C., Mou, J., & Jiang, Z. (2020). Innovación en inteligencia artificial en la educación: Un análisis histórico de veinte años basado en datos. *Revista Internacional de Estudios de Innovación, 4*(4), 134–147. DOI: 10.1016/j.ijis.2020.09.001

Guhan, M., & Chandramohan, S. (2023). A Study on Analyzing the Role of ChatGPT in English Acquisition Among ESL Learners During English Language. *ResearchGate*. DOI: 10.13140/RG.2.2.28252.56961

Güneyli, A., Burgul, N. S., Dericioğlu, S., Cenkova, N., Becan, S., Şimşek, Ş. E., & Güneralp, H. (2024). Exploring Teacher Awareness of Artificial Intelligence in Education: A Case Study from Northern Cyprus. *European Journal of Investigation in Health, Psychology and Education, 14*(8), 2358–2376. DOI: 10.3390/ejihpe14080156 PMID: 39194950

Guo, K., Zhang, E. D., Li, D., & Yu, S. (2024). Using AI-Supported Peer Review to Enhance Feedback Literacy: An Investigation of Students' Revision of Feedback on Peers' Essays. *British Journal of Educational Technology*, bjet.13540. Advance online publication. DOI: 10.1111/bjet.13540

Gupta, P., Mahajan, R., Badhera, U., & Kushwaha, P. S. (2024). Integrating Generative AI in Management Education: A Mixed-Methods Study Using Social Construction of Technology Theory. *International Journal of Management Education, 22*(3), 1–19. DOI: 10.1016/j.ijme.2024.101017

Gustilo, L., Ong, E., & Lapinid, M. R. (2024). Algorithmically-driven writing and academic integrity: Exploring educators' practices, perceptions, and policies in AI era. *International Journal for Educational Integrity, 20*(1), 3. DOI: 10.1007/s40979-024-00153-8

Guz, E., Niderla, K., & Kata, G. (2024). Advancing autism therapy: Emotion analysis using rehabilitation robots and AI for children with ASD. *Journal of Modern Science, 57*(3), 340–355. DOI: 10.13166/jms/191144

Gyonyoru, K. I. K. (2024). The Role of AI-Based Adaptive Learning Systems in Digital Education. *Journal of Applied Technical and Educational Sciences, 14*(2), 1–12. DOI: 10.24368/jates380

Hadi Mogavi, R., Deng, C., Juho Kim, J., Zhou, P., & Kwon, D. Y., Hosny Saleh Metwally, A., Tlili, A., Bassanelli, S., Bucchiarone, A., Gujar, S., Nacke, L. E., & Hui, P. (2024). ChatGPT in education: A blessing or a curse? A qualitative study exploring early adopters' utilization and perceptions. *Computers in Human Behavior: Artificial Humans, 2*(1), 100027. https://doi.org/https://doi.org/10.1016/j.chbah.2023.100027

Halamka, J. D. (2017). Privacy and Security. In Sheikh, A., Cresswell, K. M., Wright, A., & Bates, D. W. (Eds.), *Key advances in clinical informatics: Transforming health care through health information technology* (pp. 79–86). Academic., DOI: 10.1016/B978-0-12-809523-2.00006-6

Haleem, A., Javaid, M., Qadri, M. A., & Suman, R. (2022). Understanding the Role of Digital Technologies in Education: A Review. *Sustainable Operations and Computers*, *3*, 275–285. DOI: 10.1016/j.susoc.2022.05.004

Hamdani, A., Aulia, E., Listiana, Y., & Herlambang, Y. (2024). Moralitas di Era Digital: Tinjauan Filsafat tentang Technoethics. *Indo-MathEdu Intellectuals Journal*, *5*(1), 767–777. DOI: 10.54373/imeij.v5i1.648

Hamutoglu, N. B., Işbulan, O., & Kiyici, M. (2022). Major tendencies in special education within the framework of educational technology between 1960-2019. *Ankara Üniversitesi Eğitim Bilimleri Fakültesi Özel Eğitim Dergisi*, *23*(4), 751–773. DOI: 10.21565/ozelegitimdergisi.835696

Hanaysha, J. R., Shriedeh, F. B., & In'airat, M. (2023). Impact of Classroom Environment, Teacher Competency, Information and Communication Technology Resources, and University Facilities on Student Engagement and Academic Performance. *International Journal of Information Management Data Insights*, *3*(2), 1–12. DOI: 10.1016/j.jjimei.2023.100188

Haque, S. A. (2021). *Dialogue on partition: Literature Knows No Borders*. Rowman & Littlefield. DOI: 10.5771/9781793636256

Haristiani, N. (2019). Artificial Intelligence (AI) Chatbot as Language Learning Medium: An inquiry. *Journal of Physics: Conference Series*, *1387*(1), 012020. DOI: 10.1088/1742-6596/1387/1/012020

Harry, A., & Sayudin, S. (2023). Role of AI in Education. [INJURITY]. *Interdiciplinary Journal and Hummanity*, *2*(3), 260–268. DOI: 10.58631/injurity.v2i3.52

Harvard Office of Academic Integrity and Scholarly Conduct. (2025.). Academic integrity and teaching without AI. Harvard University. https://oaisc.fas.harvard.edu/academic-integrity-and-teaching-without-ai/

Hasanein, A. M., & Sobaih, A. E. E. (2023). Drivers and consequences of ChatGPT use in higher education: Key stakeholder perspectives. *European Journal of Investigation in Health, Psychology and Education*, *13*(11), 2599–2614. DOI: 10.3390/ejihpe13110181 PMID: 37998071

Ha, T., & Kim, S. (2023). Improving Trust in AI with Mitigating Confirmation Bias: Effects of Explanation Type and Debiasing Strategy for Decision-Making with Explainable AI. *International Journal of Human-Computer Interaction*, •••, 1–12. DOI: 10.1080/10447318.2023.2285640

Hazari, S. (2024). *Justification and Roadmap for Artificial intelligence (AI) literacy courses in Higher education*. ScholarWorks. https://scholarworks.waldenu.edu/jerap/vol14/iss1/7/

Heck, P., & Schouten, G. (2021). Lessons Learned from Educating AI Engineers. *2021 IEEE/ACM 1st Workshop on AI Engineering - Software Engineering for AI (WAIN)*, 1-4. DOI: 10.1109/WAIN52551.2021.00013

Heffernan, N. T., & Heffernan, C. L. (2014). The Assessment's Ecosystem: Building a Platform that Brings Scientists and Teachers Together for Minimally Invasive Research on Human Learning and Teaching. *International Journal of Artificial Intelligence in Education*, *24*(4), 470–497. DOI: 10.1007/s40593-014-0024-x

Heidari, H., Loi, M., Gummadi, K. P., & Krause, A. (2019). A moral framework for understanding fairness in machine learning. *Communications of the ACM*, *64*(8), 64–71. DOI: 10.1145/3419764

Heil, J., & Ifenthaler, D. (2023). Online Assessment in Higher Education: A Systematic Review. *Online Learning : the Official Journal of the Online Learning Consortium, 27*(1), 187–218. DOI: 10.24059/olj.v27i1.3398

Hendrick, C. (2018). Challenging the 'education is broken' and Silicon Valley narratives. *ResearchED.* https://researched.org.uk/challenging-the-education-is-broken-and-silicon-valley-narratives/

Hennessy, S., D'Angelo, S., McIntyre, N., Koomar, S., Kreimeia, A., Cao, L., Brugha, M., & Zubairi, A. (2022). Technology Use for Teacher Professional Development in Low- and Middle-Income Countries: A systematic review. *Computers and Education Open, 3*, 1–32. DOI: 10.1016/j.caeo.2022.100080

Herft, A. (2023), A Teacher's Prompt Guide to ChatGPT Aligned with 'What Works Best', Retrieved 5 may 2024 https://usergeneratededucation.files.wordpress.com/2023/01/a-teachers-prompt-guide-to-chatgpt-aligned-with-what-worksbest.pdf

Heward, W. L., Alber-Morgan, S. R., & Konrad, M. (2017). *Exceptional Children: An Introduction to Special Education.* Pearson.

Heyn, H.-M., Knauss, E., Muhammad, A. P., Eriksson, O., Linder, J., Subbiah, P., Pradhan, S. K., & Tungal, S. (2021). Requirement Engineering Challenges for AI-intense Systems Development. *2021 IEEE/ACM 1st Workshop on AI Engineering - Software Engineering for AI (WAIN)*, 89-96. DOI: 10.1109/WAIN52551.2021.00020

He, Z., Nguyen, T., Miari, T., Aliasgari, M., Rafatirad, S., & Sayadi, H. (2024, May). The AI Companion in Education: Analyzing the Pedagogical Potential of ChatGPT in Computer Science and Engineering. In *2024 IEEE Global Engineering Education Conference (EDUCON)* (pp. 1-10). IEEE. DOI: 10.1109/EDUCON60312.2024.10578820

Hidayat, A., Nugroho, A., & Nurfaizin, S. (2022). Usability Evaluation on Educational Chatbot Using the System Usability Scale (SUS). *2022 Seventh International Conference on Informatics and Computing (ICIC)*, 01-05. https://doi.org/DOI: 10.1109/ICIC56845.2022.10006991

Hmelo-Silver, C. E., Duncan, R. G., & Chinn, C. A. (2007). Scaffolding and achievement in problem-based and inquiry learning: A response to Kirschner, Sweller, and Clark. *Educational Psychologist, 42*(2), 99–107. DOI: 10.1080/00461520701263368

Hmoud, M., Swaity, H., Hamad, N., Karram, O., & Daher, W. (2024). Higher Education Students' Task Motivation in the Artificial Intelligence Context: The Case of ChatGPT. *Information (Basel), 2024*(15), 33. DOI: 10.3390/info15010033

Hodges, C. B., & Kirschner, P. A. (2024). Innovation of instructional design and assessment in the age of generative artificial intelligence. *TechTrends, 68*(1), 195–199. DOI: 10.1007/s11528-023-00926-x

Holgado-Apaza, L. A., Carpio-Vargas, E. E., Calderon-Vilca, H. D., Maquera-Ramirez, J., Ulloa-Gallardo, N. J., Acosta-Navarrete, M. S., Barrón-Adame, J. M., Quispe-Layme, M., Hidalgo-Pozzi, R., & Valles-Coral, M. (2023). Modeling job satisfaction of Peruvian basic education teachers using machine learning techniques. *Applied Sciences (Basel, Switzerland), 13*(6), 3945. DOI: 10.3390/app13063945

Holman, K., Marino, M. T., Vasquez, E., Taub, M., Hunt, J. H., & Tazi, Y. (2024). Navigating ai-powered personalized learning in special education: A guide for preservice teacher faculty. *Journal of Special Education Preparation*, *4*(2), 90–95. DOI: 10.33043/5b2xqcb3

Holmes, W., Bialik, M., & Fadel, C. (2023). Artificial intelligence in education: Promises and implications for teaching and learning.

Holmes, W., Bialik, M., & Fadel, C. (2019). *Artificial Intelligence in Education. Promise and Implications for Teaching and Learning.* Center for Curriculum Redesign.

Holmes, W., Bialik, M., & Fadel, C. (2019). *Artificial intelligence in education: Promises and implications for teaching and learning.* Center for Curriculum Redesign.

Holmes, W., Porayska-Pomsta, K., Holstein, K., Sutherland, E., Baker, T., Shum, S., Santos, O., Rodrigo, M., Cukurova, M., Bittencourt, I., & Koedinger, K. (2021). Ethics of AI in Education: Towards a Community-Wide Framework. *International Journal of Artificial Intelligence in Education*, *32*(3), 504–526. DOI: 10.1007/s40593-021-00239-1

Holstein, K., & Doroudi, S. (2022). Equity and artificial intelligence in education. In Holmes, W., & Porayska-Pomsta, K. (Eds.), *The ethics of artificial intelligence in education* (pp. 151–173). Routledge. DOI: 10.4324/9780429329067-9

Hong, Q. N., Pluye, P., Fàbregues, S., Bartlett, G., Boardman, F., Cargo, M., Dagenais, P., Gagnon, M.-P., Griffiths, F., Nicolau, B., O'Cathain, A., Rousseau, M.-C., & Vedel, I. (2019). Improving the Content Validity of the Mixed Methods Appraisal Tool: A Modified E-Delphi Study. *Journal of Clinical Epidemiology*, *111*, 49–59.e41. DOI: 10.1016/j.jclinepi.2019.03.008 PMID: 30905698

Hooda, M., Rana, C., Dahiya, O., Rizwan, A., & Hossain, M. S. (2022). Artificial Intelligence for Assessment and Feedback to Enhance Student Success in Higher Education. *Mathematical Problems in Engineering*, *2022*, 1–19. DOI: 10.1155/2022/5215722

Hosseini, M., Resnik, D. B., & Holmes, K. (2023). The ethics of disclosing the use of artificial intelligence tools in writing scholarly manuscripts. *Research Ethics*, *19*(4), 449–465. DOI: 10.1177/17470161231180449 PMID: 39749232

Howorth, S. K., Marino, M. T., Flanagan, S., Cuba, M. J., & Lemke, C. (2024). Integrating emerging technologies to enhance special education teacher preparation. *Journal of Research in Innovative Teaching & Learning*, (ahead-of-print). https://doi.org/DOI: 10.1108/JRIT-08-2024-0208

Hsu, M.-H., Chen, P.-S., & Yu, C.-S. (2021). Proposing a Task-Oriented Chatbot System for EFL Learners Speaking Practice. *Interactive Learning Environments*, *31*(7), 4297–4308. DOI: 10.1080/10494820.2021.1960864

Hsu, T.-C., Hsu, T.-P., & Lin, Y.-T. (2023). The Artificial Intelligence Learning Anxiety and Self-Efficacy of In-Service Teachers Taking AI Training Courses. *2023 International Conference on Artificial Intelligence and Education (ICAIE)*, 97-101. https://doi.org/DOI: 10.1109/ICAIE56796.2023.00034

Hu, Y. (2023). Literature in the age of artificial intelligence. In *Advances in Social Science, Education and Humanities Research/Advances in social science, education and humanities research* (pp. 1781–1787). DOI: 10.2991/978-2-38476-092-3_228

Hua, J. H. (2023). Beyond exams: Investigating AI tool impact on student attitudes, ethical awareness, and academic dishonesty in online college assessments. *International Journal of Educational Management and Development Studies*, *4*(4), 160–185. https://doi.org/https://doi.org/10.53378/353030. DOI: 10.53378/353030

Huang, A. Y., Lu, O. H., & Yang, S. J. (2023). Effects of artificial Intelligence-Enabled personalized recommendations on learners' learning engagement, motivation, and outcomes in a flipped classroom. *Computers & Education*, *194*, 104684. DOI: 10.1016/j.compedu.2022.104684

Huang, J., Saleh, S., & Liu, Y. (2021). A review on artificial intelligence in education. *Academic Journal of Interdisciplinary Studies*, *10*(3), 206–217. DOI: 10.36941/ajis-2021-0077

Huang, J., Shi, Y., Chen, Y., Tang, L., & Zhang, Z. (2024). How social support influences learned helplessness in lung cancer patients: The chain mediation role of individual resilience and self-efficacy. *Frontiers in Psychology*, *15*, 1436495. DOI: 10.3389/fpsyg.2024.1436495 PMID: 39300997

Huang, K.-L., Liu, Y., & Dong, M.-Q. (2024). Incorporating AIGC Into Design Ideation: A Study on Self-Efficacy and Learning Experience Acceptance Under Higher-Order Thinking. *Thinking Skills and Creativity*, *52*, 1–16. DOI: 10.1016/j.tsc.2024.101508

Huang, L. (2023). Ethics of artificial intelligence in education: Student privacy and data protection. *Science Insights Education Frontiers*, *16*(2), 2577–2587. DOI: 10.15354/sief.23.re202

Huang, S., Lai, X., Ke, L., Li, Y., Wang, H., Zhao, X., Dai, X., & Wang, Y. (2024). AI Technology panic-is AI Dependence Bad for Mental Health? A Cross-Lagged Panel Model and the Mediating Roles of Motivations for AI Use Among Adolescents. *Psychology Research and Behavior Management*, *17*, 1087–1102. DOI: 10.2147/PRBM.S440889 PMID: 38495087

Huang, W., Hew, K. F., & Fryer, L. K. (2022). Chatbots for Language Learning—Are They Really Useful? A Systematic Review of Chatbot-Supported Language Learning. *Journal of Computer Assisted Learning*, *38*(1), 237–257. DOI: 10.1111/jcal.12610

Hurajová, L. (2021). can close cooperation between ESP/CLIL experts and disciplinary teachers in higher education lead to fostering english education environment. *Journal Of Teaching English For Specific And Academic Purposes*, *9*(1), 129–136. DOI: 10.22190/JTESAP2101129H

Hurwitz, S., Perry, B., Cohen, E. D., & Skiba, R. (2020). Special education and individualized academic growth: A longitudinal assessment of outcomes for students with disabilities. *American Educational Research Journal*, *57*(2), 576–611. DOI: 10.3102/0002831219857054

Hutson, J., & Plate, T. (2023). Evaluating AI-driven inquiry-based learning: Challenges and best practices. *International Journal of Artificial Intelligence in Education*, *33*(2), 289–310. DOI: 10.1007/s40593-023-00312-8

Hwang, G. J., Xie, H., Wah, B. W., & Gašević, D. (2020). Computers and Education: Artificial Intelligence. *Computers and Education: Artificial Intelligence*, *1*, 100001. DOI: 10.1016/j.caeai.2020.100001

Hwang, G.-J., & Chang, C.-Y. (2021). A Review of Opportunities and Challenges of Chatbots in Education. *Interactive Learning Environments*, *31*(7), 4099–4112. DOI: 10.1080/10494820.2021.1952615

Ifelebuegu, A. O., Kulume, P., & Cherukut, P. (2023). Chatbots and AI in Education (AIEd) tools: The good, the bad, and the ugly. *Journal of Applied Learning and Teaching*, *6*(2). Advance online publication. DOI: 10.37074/jalt.2023.6.2.29

Ikermane, M., & El Mouatasim, A. (2023). Digital handwriting characteristics for dysgraphia detection using artificial neural network. *Bulletin of Electrical Engineering and Informatics*, *12*(3), 1693–1699. DOI: 10.11591/eei.v12i3.4571

Ikeuchi, K., & Motohashi, K. (2022). Linkage of Patent and Design Right Data: Analysis of Industrial Design Activities in Companies at the Creator Level. *World Patent Information*, *70*, 1–6. DOI: 10.1016/j.wpi.2022.102114

Ilchenko, O. (2024). Academic integrity as a factor of ensuring quality training of specialists in institutions of Higher Education. *The Sources of Pedagogical Skills*, (33), 100–103. DOI: 10.33989/2075-146x.2024.33.310004

Inci, G., & Köse, H. (2024). The landscape of technology research in special education: A bibliometric analysis. *Journal of Special Education Technology*, *39*(1), 94–107. DOI: 10.1177/01626434231180582

International Center for Academic Integrity. (2024). The fundamental values of academic integrity. Retrieved February 19, 2025 from: https://academicintegrity.org/aws/ICAI/asset_manager/get_file/911282?ver=1

Ipek, Z. H., Gözüm, A. I. C., Papadakis, S., & Kallogiannakis, M. (2023). Educational Applications of the ChatGPT AI System: A Systematic Review Research. *International Journal Educational Process*, *12*(3). Advance online publication. DOI: 10.22521/edupij.2023.123.2

Irfan, M., Aldulaylan, F., & Alqahtani, Y. (2023). Ethics and privacy in Irish higher education: A comprehensive study of Artificial Intelligence (AI) tools implementation at University of Limerick. *Global Social Sci Rev*, *8*(2), 201–210. DOI: 10.31703/gssr.2023(VIII-II).19

ISDI. (2023). Inteligencia artificial generativa: ¿Qué es y cómo funciona? [Generative Artificial Intelligence: What is it and how does it work?]. Digital Skills. https://www.isdi.education/es/blog/inteligencia-artificial-generativa-que-es

Israni, R. K. (2024). The Potential Future with ChatGPT Technology and AI Tools. In *Advances in computational intelligence and robotics book series* (pp. 226–256). DOI: 10.4018/979-8-3693-6824-4.ch013

Isro'iyah, N. L., & Herminingsih, N. D. I. (2023). Teaching Culture of Others through English Literature. *International Journal of Language and Literary Studies*, *5*(2), 136–146. DOI: 10.36892/ijlls.v5i2.1248

Ivanov, S. (2023). The Dark Side of Artificial Intelligence in Higher Education. *Service Industries Journal*, *43*(15-16), 1055–1082. DOI: 10.1080/02642069.2023.2258799

Ivanov, S., Soliman, M., Tuomi, A., Alkathiri, N. A., & Al-Alawi, A. N. (2024). Drivers of generative AI adoption in higher education through the lens of the Theory of Planned Behaviour. *Technology in Society*, *77*, 102521. https://doi.org/https://doi.org/10.1016/j.techsoc.2024.102521. DOI: 10.1016/j.techsoc.2024.102521

Jablonowska, A., Kuziemski, M., Nowak, A. M., Micklitz, H. W., Palka, P., & Sartor, G. (2018). *Consumer law and artificial intelligence: Challenges to the EU consumer law and policy stemming from the business' use of artificial intelligence (Final report of the ARTSY project)*. European University Institute. https://cadmus.eui.eu/handle/1814/60059

Jackson, M. C. (2021). Artificial intelligence & algorithmic bias: The issues with technology reflecting history & humans. *Journal of Business & Technology Law.*, *16*, 299–316.

Jadán-Guerrero, J., Tamayo-Narvaez, K., Méndez, E., & Valenzuela, M. (2024). *Adaptive Learning Environments: Integrating Artificial Intelligence for Special Education Advances*. https://doi.org/DOI: 10.1007/978-3-031-61953-3_10

Jagadesan, S., Girish, P., & Kurane, A. R. (2021). The Making and Development of Baxter the Empowered Chatbot Impered with Machine Intelligence. *Trends in Computer Science and Information Technology*, 036-041. https://doi.org/DOI: 10.17352/tcsit.000037

Jain, S., Basu, S., Ray, A., & Das, R. (2023). Impact of irritation and negative emotions on the performance of voice assistants: Netting dissatisfied customers' perspectives. *International Journal of Information Management*, *72*, 102662. DOI: 10.1016/j.ijinfomgt.2023.102662

Jarrahi, M. H. (2018). Artificial intelligence and the future of work: Human-AI symbiosis in organizational decision making. *Business Horizons*, *61*(4), 577–586. DOI: 10.1016/j.bushor.2018.03.007

Jaurez, J., Radhakrishnan, B., & Altamirano, N. (2022). Application of Artificial Intelligence and the Cynefin Framework to establish a Statistical System Prediction and Control (SSPC) in Engineering Education. *2022 ASEE Annual Conference & Exposition*. DOI: 10.18260/1-2--41718

Javed, K., & Li, J. (2024). Artificial Intelligence in Judicial Adjudication: Semantic Biasness Classification and Identification in Legal Judgement (SBCILJ). *Heliyon*, *10*(9), 1–17. DOI: 10.1016/j.heliyon.2024.e30184 PMID: 38737247

Jenkins, B. D., Golding, J. M., Le Grand, A. M., Levi, M. M., & Pals, A. M. (2023). When opportunity knocks: College students' cheating amid the COVID-19 pandemic. *Teaching of Psychology*, *50*(4), 407–419. DOI: 10.1177/00986283211059067

Jeon, J. (2022). Exploring AI chatbot affordances in the EFL classroom: Young learners' experiences and perspectives. *Computer Assisted Language Learning*, *37*(1-2), 1–26. DOI: 10.1080/09588221.2021.2021241

Jerrin, N. B., & Bhuvaneswari G, . (2024). Comprehending AI's Role in Literature and Arts from a Transhumanist Perspective. *International Research Journal of Multidisciplinary Scope*, *05*(02), 846–859. DOI: 10.47857/irjms.2024.v05i02.0670

Jiang, Y., Xiang, L., Hao, L., Shen, Y., & Okyay, K. (2022). Quo Vadis Artificial Intelligence? *Discover Artificial Intelligence*, *2*(4), 4. Advance online publication. DOI: 10.1007/s44163-022-00022-8

Ji, H., Han, I., & Ko, Y. (2023). A systematic review of conversational AI in language education: Focusing on the collaboration with human teachers. *Journal of Research on Technology in Education*, *55*(1), 48–63. DOI: 10.1080/15391523.2022.2142873

Jin, S.-H., Im, K., Yoo, M., Roll, I., & Seo, K. (2023). Supporting students' self-regulated learning in online learning using artificial intelligence applications. *International Journal of Educational Technology in Higher Education*, *20*(1), 37. DOI: 10.1186/s41239-023-00406-5

Johri, A. (2020). Artificial Intelligence and Engineering Education. *Journal of Engineering Education*, *109*(3), 358–361. DOI: 10.1002/jee.20326

Jordan, M. (2018). Artificial intelligence—The revolution hasn't happened yet. *Medium*. https://medium.com/@mijordan3/artificial-intelligence-the-revolution-hasnt-happened-yet-5e1d5812e1e7

Kabudi, T., Pappas, I., & Olsen, D. H. (2021). Ai-Enabled Adaptive Learning Systems: A Systematic Mapping of the Literature. *Computers and Education: Artificial Intelligence*, *2*, 1–12. DOI: 10.1016/j.caeai.2021.100017

Kadiresan, A., Baweja, Y., & Ogbanufe, O. (2022). Bias in AI-based decision-making. In *Bridging Human Intelligence and Artificial Intelligence* (pp. 275–285). Springer International Publishing. DOI: 10.1007/978-3-030-84729-6_19

Kahneman, D. (2011). *Thinking, fast and slow*. Farrar, Straus and Giroux.

Kamalov, F., Santandreu Calonge, D., & Gurrib, I. (2023). New Era of Artificial Intelligence in Education: Towards a Sustainable Multifaceted Revolution. In *Sustainability* (Vol. 15, Issue 16). DOI: 10.3390/su151612451

Kaplan, A., & Haenlein, M. (2019). Siri, Siri, in my Hand: Who's the fairest in the land? On the interpretations, illustrations, and implications of artificial intelligence. *Business Horizons*, *62*(1), 15–25. DOI: 10.1016/j.bushor.2018.08.004

Karami, B., Koushki, R., Arabgol, F., Rahmani, M., & Vahabie, A. H. (2021). Effectiveness of Virtual/Augmented Reality-Based Therapeutic Interventions on Individuals With Autism Spectrum Disorder: A Comprehensive Meta-Analysis. *Frontiers in Psychiatry*, *12*, 665326. DOI: 10.3389/fpsyt.2021.665326 PMID: 34248702

Karataş, F., Abedi, F. Y., Ozek Gunyel, F., Karadeniz, D., & Kuzgun, Y. (2024). Incorporating AI in foreign language education: An investigation into ChatGPT's effect on foreign language learners. *Education and Information Technologies*, *29*(15), 19343–19366. DOI: 10.1007/s10639-024-12574-6

Karnouskos, S. (2020). Artificial intelligence in digital media: The era of Deepfakes. *IEEE Transactions on Technology and Society*, *1*(3), 138–147. Advance online publication. DOI: 10.1109/TTS.2020.3001312

Karsenti, T. (2019). Acting as ethical and responsible digital citizens: The teacher's key role. *Formation et profession, 27*(1), 112-116. https://dx.doi.org/DOI: 10.18162/fp.2019.a167

Kartal, G. (2024). The influence of ChatGPT on thinking skills and creativity of EFL student teachers: A narrative inquiry. *Journal of Education for Teaching*, *50*(4), 1–16. DOI: 10.1080/02607476.2024.2326502

Kashik, K., & Srinivas, V. IAS. (2023). *Navigating the Future: India's strategic approach to artificial intelligence regulations* (By National Centre for Good Governance (NCGG), Ministry of Personnel, Public Grievances & Pensions, & Government of India). https://ncgg.org.in/sites/default/files/lectures -document/Kshitija_Kashik__Research_Paper.pdf

Kashyap, R., & OpenAI, C. (2023). A First Chat with ChatGPT: The First Step in the Road-Map for AI (Artificial Intelligence).

Kasneci, E., Sessler, K., Küchemann, S., Bannert, M., Dementieva, D., Fischer, F., Gasser, U., Groh, G., Günnemann, S., Hüllermeier, E., Krusche, S., Kutyniok, G., Michaeli, T., Nerdel, C., Pfeffer, J., Poquet, O., Sailer, M., Schmidt, A., Seidel, T., & Kasneci, G. (2023). ChatGPT for Good? On opportunities and challenges of large language models for education. *Learning and Individual Differences*, *103*, 102274. DOI: 10.1016/j.lindif.2023.102274

Kasy, M. (2024). Algorithmic bias and racial inequality: A critical review. *Oxford Review of Economic Policy*, *40*(3), 530–546. DOI: 10.1093/oxrep/grae031

Kauffman, J., & Hornby, G. (2020). Inclusive Vision Versus Special Education Reality. *Education Sciences*, *10*(9), 258. DOI: 10.3390/educsci10090258

Kaya, A. (Ed.). (2024). *Özel eğitim ve yapay zeka [Special education and artificial intelligence]*. Vize Akademik.

Kaya, F., Aydin, F., Schepman, A., Rodway, P., Yetişensoy, O., & Demir Kaya, M. (2022). The Roles of Personality Traits, AI Anxiety, and Demographic Factors in Attitudes toward Artificial Intelligence. *International Journal of Human-Computer Interaction*, *40*(2), 497–514. DOI: 10.1080/10447318.2022.2151730

Kelly, R. (2024). [% of Students Already Use AI in Their Studies. Campus Technology.]. *Survey (London, England)*, ●●●, 86.

Khalil, M., & Er, E. (2023, June). Will ChatGPT Get You Caught? Rethinking of Plagiarism Detection. In: *International Conference on Human-Computer Interaction* (pp. 475-487). Cham: Springer Nature Switzerland. DOI: 10.1007/978-3-031-34411-4_32

Khan, S. (2025). ChatGPT for Writing Literature and Songs: End of the Road for Poets and Songwriters? In *Lecture notes in electrical engineering* (pp. 405–414). https://doi.org/DOI: 10.1007/978-981-97-4780-1_30

Khan, I., Ahmad, A. R., Jabeur, N., & Mahdi, M. N. (2021). An Artificial Intelligence Approach to Monitor Student Performance and Devise Preventive Measures. *Smart Learning Environments*, *8*(1), 1–18. DOI: 10.1186/s40561-021-00161-y

Kharbat, F. F., Alshawabkeh, A., & Woolsey, M. L. (2021). Identifying gaps in using artificial intelligence to support students with intellectual disabilities from education and health perspectives. *Aslib Journal of Information Management*, *73*(1), 101–128. DOI: 10.1108/AJIM-02-2020-0054

Khlaif, Z. N., Ayyoub, A., Hamamra, B., Bensalem, E., Mitwally, M. A. A., Ayyoub, A., Hattab, M. K., & Shadid, F. (2024). University Teachers' Views on the Adoption and Integration of Generative AI Tools for Student Assessment in Higher Education. *Education Sciences, 14*(10), 1090. DOI: 10.3390/educsci14101090

Khlaif, Z. N., Mousa, A., Hattab, M. K., Itmazi, J., Hassan, A. A., Sanmugam, M., & Ayyoub, A. (2023). The potential and Concerns of using AI in Scientific Research: ChaTGPT Performance Evaluation. *JMIR Medical Education, 9*, e47049. DOI: 10.2196/47049 PMID: 37707884

Khlaif, Z. N., Sanmugam, M., Joma, A. I., Odeh, A., & Barham, K. (2022). Factors Influencing Teacher's Technostress Experienced in Using Emerging Technology: A Qualitative Study. *Technology. Knowledge and Learning, 28*(2), 865–899. DOI: 10.1007/s10758-022-09607-9

Khosravi, H., Buckingham Shum, S., Chen, G., Conati, C., Tsai, Y.-S., Kay, J., & Knight, S. (2022). Explainable artificial intelligence in education. *Computers and Education: Artificial Intelligence, 3*, 100074. DOI: 10.1016/j.caeai.2022.100074

Kilic, S., & Ozkan, T. K. (2022). A Study on the Self-Efficacy of BİLSEM Teachers in Educational Technology. *International Journal of Education Science and Technology, 8*(3), 165–190. DOI: 10.47714/uebt.1173885

Kim, D., Alber, M., Kwok, M. W., Mitrović, J., Ramirez-Atencia, C., PÉrez, J. A. R., & Zille, H. (2022). Clarifying Assumptions About Artificial Intelligence Before Revolutionising Patent Law. *GRUR International, 71*(4), 295-321. DOI: 10.1093/grurint/ikab174

Kim, Y., Lee, M., Kim, D., & Lee, S. J. (2023). Towards explainable ai writing assistants for non-native english speakers. *arXiv preprint arXiv:2304.02625*.

Kim, J. (2024). Leading teachers perspective on teacher-AI collaboration in education. *Education and Information Technologies, 29*(7), 8693–8724. DOI: 10.1007/s10639-023-12109-5

Kim, J., Kelly, S., Colón, A. X., Spence, P. R., & Lin, X. (2024). Toward thoughtful integration of AI in education: Mitigating uncritical positivity and dependence on ChatGPT via classroom discussions. *Communication Education, 73*(4), 388–404. DOI: 10.1080/03634523.2024.2399216

Kim, J., Lee, H., & Cho, Y. H. (2022). Learning design to support student-AI collaboration: Perspectives of leading teachers for AI in education. *Education and Information Technologies, 27*(5), 6069–6104. DOI: 10.1007/s10639-021-10831-6

Kim, J., Yu, S., Detrick, R., & Li, N. (2024). Exploring students' perspectives on Generative AI-assisted academic writing. *Education and Information Technologies*. Advance online publication. DOI: 10.1007/s10639-024-12878-7

Kim, K., & Kwon, K. (2023). Exploring the AI Competencies of Elementary School Teachers in South Korea. *Computers and Education: Artificial Intelligence, 4*, 100137. DOI: 10.1016/j.caeai.2023.100137

Kim, K., & Kwon, K. (2024). Designing an Inclusive Artificial Intelligence (AI) Curriculum for Elementary Students to Address Gender Differences With Collaborative and Tangible Approaches. *Journal of Educational Computing Research, 62*(7), 1837–1864. DOI: 10.1177/07356331241271059

Kim, S. C., Covington, B., Benavente, V., & Willson, P. (2019). Capstone Projects As Experiential Evidence-Based Practice Education. *The Journal for Nurse Practitioners*, *15*(3), 51–56. DOI: 10.1016/j. nurpra.2018.12.011

King, S., Boyer, J., Bell, T., & Estapa, A. (2022). An Automated Virtual Reality Training System for Teacher-Student Interaction: A Randomized Controlled Trial. *JMIR Serious Games*, *10*(4), e41097. Advance online publication. DOI: 10.2196/41097 PMID: 36480248

Kiritchenko, S., Nejadgholi, I., & Fraser, K. C. (2021). Confronting Abusive Language Online: A Survey from the Ethical and Human Rights Perspective. *Journal of Artificial Intelligence Research*, *71*, 431–478. DOI: 10.1613/jair.1.12590

Kiroglu, E. S., & Trust, H. (2024). Investigation of Bilsem Teachers' Views on Web 2.0 Tools. *Bayburt Faculty of Education Journal*, *19*(41), 1803–1826. DOI: 10.35675/befdergi.1239568

Kitcharoen, P., Howimanporn, S., & Chookaew, S. (2024). Enhancing Teachers' AI Competencies through Artificial Intelligence of Things Professional Development Training. [iJIM]. *International Journal of Interactive Mobile Technologies*, *18*(02), 4–15. DOI: 10.3991/ijim.v18i02.46613

Kitsara, I. (2022). Artificial intelligence and the digital Divide: From an Innovation perspective. In *Progress in IS* (pp. 245–265). https://doi.org/DOI: 10.1007/978-3-030-90192-9_12

Kivunja, C. (2015). Teaching Students to Learn and to Work Well with 21st Century Skills: Unpacking the Career and Life Skills Domain of the New Learning Paradigm. *International Journal of Higher Education*, *4*(1), 1–11. DOI: 10.5430/ijhe.v4n1p1

Klimova, B., & de Campos, V. P. L. (2024). University undergraduates' perceptions on the use of ChatGPT for academic purposes: Evidence from a university in Czech Republic. *Cogent Education*, *11*(1), 2373512. DOI: 10.1080/2331186X.2024.2373512

Klimova, B., & Pikhart, M. (2025). Exploring the effects of artificial intelligence on student and academic well-being in higher education: A mini-review. *Frontiers in Psychology*, *16*, 16. DOI: 10.3389/fpsyg.2025.1498132 PMID: 39963679

Knox, J., Wang, Y., & Gallagher, M. (2019). *Artificial intelligence and inclusive education*. Springer Singapore. DOI: 10.1007/978-981-13-8161-4

Kohnke, L., & Moor Di, P. (2023). Language teachers' readiness for generative AI in the classroom. *Language Education Review*, *14*(2), 101–119.

Kohnke, L., Moorhouse, B. L., & Zou, D. (2023). ChatGPT for Language Teaching and Learning. *RELC Journal*, *54*(2), 537–550. DOI: 10.1177/00336882231162868

Kong, S. C., & Yang, Y. (2024). A human-centred learning and teaching framework using generative artificial intelligence for self-regulated learning development through domain knowledge learning. *IEEE Transactions on Learning Technologies*, *17*(1), 110–125. DOI: 10.1109/TLT.2024.10507034

Kong, Z. Y., Omar, A. A., Lau, S. L., & Sunarso, J. (2024). Introducing Process Simulation as an Alternative to Laboratory Session in Undergraduate Chemical Engineering Thermodynamics Course: A Case Study From Sunway University Malaysia. *Digital Chemical Engineering, 12*, 1–10. DOI: 10.1016/j.dche.2024.100167

Kooli, C. (2023). Chatbots in Education and Research: A Critical Examination of Ethical Implications and Solutions. *Sustainability (Basel), 15*(7), 1–15. DOI: 10.3390/su15075614

Koraishi, O., & Karatepe, Ç. (2025). Minds vs machines: A comparative study of AI and teacher-generated summaries in ELT. *Technology in Language Teaching & Learning, 7*(1), 1796. DOI: 10.29140/tltl.v7n1.1796

Kordzadeh, N., & Ghasemaghaei, M. (2022). Algorithmic bias: Review, synthesis, and future research directions. *European Journal of Information Systems, 31*(3), 388–409. DOI: 10.1080/0960085X.2021.1927212

Korucu-Kis, S. (2024). Zone of proximal creativity: An empirical study on EFL teachers use of ChatGPT for enhanced practice. *Thinking Skills and Creativity, 54*, 101639. Advance online publication. DOI: 10.1016/j.tsc.2024.101639

Kosmicki, J. A., Sochat, V., Duda, M., & Wall, D. P. (2015). Searching for a minimal set of behaviors for autism detection through feature selection-based machine learning. *Translational Psychiatry, 5*(2), e514–e514. DOI: 10.1038/tp.2015.7 PMID: 25710120

Kostopoulos, G., & Kostopoulos, I. (2021). Artificial Intelligence in Education: The Urgent Need for Critical Research. International Journal of Learning. *Teaching and Educational Research, 20*(1), 127–140.

Kovaleva, Y., Happonen, A., Garcia, M. B., & Kasurinen, J. (2024). Female-Inclusive Practices for Software Engineering and Computer Science Higher Education: A Literature Review. *Proceedings of the Annual Doctoral Symposium of Computer Science 2024.* https://doi.org/https://ceur-ws.org/Vol-3776/paper08.pdf

Kraemer, F., Van Overveld, K., & Peterson, M. (2011). Is there an ethics of algorithms? *Ethics and Information Technology, 13*(3), 251–260. DOI: 10.1007/s10676-010-9233-7

Krausman, P. R. (2023). Managing artificial intelligence. *The Journal of Wildlife Management, 87*(8), e22492. Advance online publication. DOI: 10.1002/jwmg.22492

Krauß, J., & Kuttenkeuler, D. (2021). When to File for a Patent? The Scientist's Perspective. *New Biotechnology, 60*, 124–129. DOI: 10.1016/j.nbt.2020.10.006 PMID: 33091617

Kshetri, N., & Voas, J. (2024). Adapting to Generative Artificial Intelligence: Approaches in Higher Education Institutions. *Computer, 57*(9), 128–133. DOI: 10.1109/MC.2024.3422589

Kuhail, M. A., Alturki, N., Alramlawi, S., & Alhejori, K. (2022). Interacting with Educational Chatbots: A Systematic Review. *Education and Information Technologies, 28*(1), 973–1018. DOI: 10.1007/s10639-022-11177-3

Kuipers, M., & Prasad, R. (2021). Journey of artificial intelligence. *Wireless Personal Communications, 123*(4), 3275–3290. DOI: 10.1007/s11277-021-09288-0

Kukulska-Hulme, A., Bossu, C., Charitonos, K., Coughlan, T., Deacon, A., Deane, N., Ferguson, R., Herodotou, C., Huang, C.-W., Mayisela, T., Rets, I., Sargent, J., Scanlon, E., Small, J., Walji, S., Weller, M., & Whitelock, D. (2023). *Innovating Pedagogy 2023: Open University Innovation Report 11*. The Open University. Retrived from., https://www.open.ac.uk/blogs/innovating/?p=784

Kulal, A., Dinesh, S., Abhishek, N., & Anchan, A. (2024). Digital access and learning outcomes: A study of equity and inclusivity in distance education. *International Journal of Educational Management*, *38*(5), 1391–1423. DOI: 10.1108/IJEM-03-2024-0166

Kumar, J. A. (2021). Educational Chatbots for Project-Based Learning: Investigating Learning Outcomes for a Team-Based Design Course. *International Journal of Educational Technology in Higher Education*, *18*(1), 65. Advance online publication. DOI: 10.1186/s41239-021-00302-w PMID: 34926790

Kumar, M. (2023). Technology Acceptance Model: A Review. *Journal of Advanced Research in Information Technology. Systems and Management*, *7*(1), 4–7.

Kumar, R. (2023). Faculty Members' Use of Artificial Intelligence to Grade Student Papers: A Case of Implications. *International Journal for Educational Integrity*, *19*(1), 1–10. DOI: 10.1007/s40979-023-00130-7

Kumar, S., Rao, P., Singhania, S., Verma, S., & Kheterpal, M. (2024). Will artificial intelligence drive the advancements in higher education? A tri-phased exploration. *Technological Forecasting and Social Change*, *10*, 123258. DOI: 10.1016/j.techfore.2024.123258

Kuprenko, V. (2020). Artificial intelligence in education: Benefits, challenges, and use cases. https://pub.towardsai.net/artificial-intelligence-in-education-benefits-challenges-and-use-cases-db52d8921f7a

Kurtz, G., Amzalag, M., Shaked, N., Zaguri, Y., Kohen-Vacs, D., Gal, E., Zailer, G., & Barak-Medina, E. (2024). Strategies for Integrating Generative AI into Higher Education: Navigating Challenges and Leveraging Opportunities. In *Education Sciences* (Vol. 14, Issue 5). DOI: 10.3390/educsci14050503

Laakso, A. (2023). *Ethical challenges of large language models - a systematic literature review* (pp. 1–67) [Thesis, Helsinki University Library]. https://helda.helsinki.fi/server/api/core/bitstreams/e507d025-8c84-4789-a043-f185fa51eb0a/content

Lakhani, K. (2023, September 28). *How Can We Counteract Generative AI's Hallucinations?* Digital Data Design Institute at Harvard. https://d3.harvard.edu/how-can-we-counteract-generative-ais-hallucinations/

Lambert, J., & Stevens, M. (2023). ChatGPT and Generative AI Technology: A Mixed Bag of Concerns and New Opportunities. *Computers in the Schools*, *41*(4), 559–583. DOI: 10.1080/07380569.2023.2256710

Lameras, P., & Arnab, S. (2021). Power to the Teachers: An Exploratory Review on Artificial Intelligence in Education. *Information (Basel)*, *13*(1), 1–38. DOI: 10.3390/info13010014

Lam, P. X., Mai, P. Q. H., Nguyen, Q. H., Pham, T., Nguyen, T. H. H., & Nguyen, T. H. (2024). Enhancing Educational Evaluation Through Predictive Student Assessment Modeling. *Computers and Education: Artificial Intelligence*, *6*, 1–14. DOI: 10.1016/j.caeai.2024.100244

Landfried, M., Chen, E., Savelli, L. B., Cooper, M., Price, B. N., & Emmerling, D. (2023). MPH Capstone experiences: Promising practices and lessons learned. *Frontiers in Public Health, 11*, 1–11. DOI: 10.3389/fpubh.2023.1129330 PMID: 37250082

Lashley, C. (2007). Principal leadership for special education: An ethical framework. *Exceptionality, 15*(3), 177–187. DOI: 10.1080/09362830701503511

Latham, A., & Goltz, S. (2019). A Survey of the General Public's Views on the Ethics of Using AI in Education. In *Artificial Intelligence in Education:20th International Conference, AIED 2019,Chicago, IL, USA,June 25-29, 2019, Proceedings, Part I 20* (pp. 194-206). Springer International Publishing. https://doi.org/DOI: 10.1007/978-3-030-23204-7_17

Latip, M. S. A., Latip, S. N. N. A., Tamrin, M., & Rahim, F. A. (2024). Modelling Physical Ergonomics And student Performance in Higher Education: The Mediating Effect Of student Motivation. *Journal of Applied Research in Higher Education*. Advance online publication. DOI: 10.1108/JARHE-01-2024-0052

Lazar, J., Wentz, B., & Winckler, M. (2017). Information privacy and security as a human right for people with disabilities. *Disability, Human Rights, and Information Technology*, 199-211. https://doi.org/DOI: 10.9783/9780812294095-014

Lazăr, A. M., Repanovici, A., Popa, D., Ionas, D. G., & Dobrescu, A. I. (2024). Ethical principles in AI use for education. *Education Sciences, 14*(11), 1239. DOI: 10.3390/educsci14111239

Leaning, J., & Bhadada, S. (2022). *The 1947 partition of British India: Forced Migration and Its Reverberations*. SAGE Publishing India. DOI: 10.4135/9789354793127

LeCun, Y., Bengio, Y., & Hinton, G. (2015). Deep learning. *Nature, 521*(7553), 436–444. DOI: 10.1038/nature14539 PMID: 26017442

Lee, D., Arnold, M., Srivastava, A., Plastow, K., Strelan, P., Ploeckl, F., Lekkas, D., & Palmer, E. (2024). The Impact of Generative AI on Higher Education Learning and Teaching: A Study of Educators' Perspectives. *Computers and Education: Artificial Intelligence, 6*, 1–10. DOI: 10.1016/j.caeai.2024.100221

Lee, K., & Leonard, R. (2023). High-speed internet access and diffusion of new technologies in nonmetro areas. *Telecommunications Policy, 47*(9), 102620. DOI: 10.1016/j.telpol.2023.102620

Lee, V. R., Pope, D., Miles, S., & Zárate, R. C. (2024). Cheating in the Age of Generative AI: A High School Survey Study of Cheating Behaviors Before and After the Release of ChatGPT. *Computers and Education: Artificial Intelligence, 7*, 1–10. DOI: 10.1016/j.caeai.2024.100253

Lee, Y.-J., Davis, R. O., & Lee, S. O. (2024). University Students' Perceptions of Artificial Intelligence-Based Tools for English Writing Courses. *Online Journal of Communication and Media Technologies, 14*(1), 1–11. DOI: 10.30935/ojcmt/14195

Lez'er, V., Semeryanova, N., Kopytova, A., & Kvach, I. (2019). Application of Artificial Intelligence in the Field of Geotechnics and Engineering Education. *E3S Web of Conferences, 110*, 1-8. DOI: 10.1051/e3sconf/201911002094

Li, Z., Dhruv, A., & Jain, V. (2024). Ethical Considerations in the Use of AI for Higher Education: A Comprehensive Guide. *2024 IEEE 18th International Conference on Semantic Computing (ICSC)*, 218-223. https://doi.org/DOI: 10.1109/ICSC59802.2024.00041

Liberati, M., Tetzlaff, J., & Altman, D. G. (2009). Preferred Reporting items for systematic reviews and meta-analyses: THE PRISMA statement. *PLoS Medicine*, *6*(7), 1–6. DOI: 10.1371/journal.pmed.1000100 PMID: 19621070

Lid, I. M. (2014). Universal design and disability: An interdisciplinary perspective. *Disability and Rehabilitation*, *36*(16), 1344–1349. DOI: 10.3109/09638288.2014.931472 PMID: 24954388

Li, M. (2024). Integrating Artificial Intelligence in Primary Mathematics Education: Investigating Internal and External Influences on Teacher Adoption. *International Journal of Science and Mathematics Education*. Advance online publication. DOI: 10.1007/s10763-024-10515-w

Lim, E. (2023). The effects of pre-service early childhood teachers digital literacy and self-efficacy on their perception of AI education for young children. *Education and Information Technologies*, *28*(10), 12969–12995. DOI: 10.1007/s10639-023-11724-6

Linares, L. J., Gómez, J. A. L., Baos, J. Á. M., Chicharro, F. P. R., & Guerrero, J. S. (2023). ChatGPT: reflexiones sobre la irrupción de la inteligencia artificial generativa en la docencia universitaria. Actas de las Jornadas sobre la Enseñanza Universitaria de la Informática [ChatGPT: Reflections on the emergence of generative artificial intelligence in university teaching. Proceedings of the Conference on University Teaching of Computer Science], (JENUI), 8, 113-120

Lin, D. (2023). AI's Role in Enhancing the Construction of Regional Primary and Secondary School Teachers. *Science Insights Education Frontiers*, *15*(S1), 7. DOI: 10.15354/sief.23.s1.ab007

Lin, H., & Chen, Q. (2024). Artificial intelligence (AI) -integrated educational applications and college students' creativity and academic emotions: Students and teachers perceptions and attitudes. *BMC Psychology*, *12*(1), 487. Advance online publication. DOI: 10.1186/s40359-024-01979-0 PMID: 39285268

Lin, X. (2024). Exploring the role of ChatGPT as a facilitator for motivating self-directed learning among adult learners. *Adult Learning*, *35*(3), 156–166. DOI: 10.1177/10451595231184928

Liu, J., Li, S., & Dong, Q. (2024). Collaboration with generative artificial intelligence: An exploratory study based on learning analytics. *Journal of Educational Computing Research*, *62*(5), 1234–1266. DOI: 10.1177/07356331241242441

Liu, M., Ren, Y., Nyagoga, L. M., Stonier, F., Wu, Z., & Yu, L. (2023). Future of education in the era of generative artificial intelligence: Consensus among Chinese scholars on applications of ChatGPT in schools. *Future Educ. Res.*, *1*(1), 72–101. DOI: 10.1002/fer3.10

Liu, Q., Huang, J., Wu, L., Zhu, K., & Ba, S. (2019). CBET: Design and Evaluation of a Domain-Specific Chatbot for Mobile Learning. *Universal Access in the Information Society*, *19*(3), 655–673. DOI: 10.1007/s10209-019-00666-x

Liu, Y., Chen, L., & Yao, Z. (2022). The application of artificial intelligence assistant to deep learning in teachers' teaching and students' learning processes. *Frontiers in Psychology*, *13*, 929175. Advance online publication. DOI: 10.3389/fpsyg.2022.929175 PMID: 36033031

Liu, Y., Saleh, S., Huang, J., & Syed Mohamad, S. A. (2020). Review of the application of artificial intelligence in education. *International Journal of Innovation. Creativity and Change*, *12*(8), 548–562. DOI: 10.53333/IJICC2013/12850

Lo, C. K. (2023). What is the impact of ChatGPT on education? A rapid review of the literature. *Education Sciences*, *13*(4), 410. DOI: 10.3390/educsci13040410

Löfström, E., Trotman, T., Furnari, M., & Shephard, K. (2015). ¿Quién enseña integridad académica y cómo la enseña? *Educación Superior*, *69*, 435–448. DOI: 10.1007/s10734-014-9784-3

Lo, K. W. K., Ngai, G., Chan, S. C. F., & Kwan, K. (2022). How Students' Motivation and Learning Experience Affect Their Service-Learning Outcomes: A Structural Equation Modeling Analysis. *Frontiers in Psychology*, *13*, 13. DOI: 10.3389/fpsyg.2022.825902 PMID: 35519642

Long, D., & Magerko, B. (2020). What is AI Literacy? Competencies and Design Considerations. *Proceedings of the 2020 CHI Conference on Human Factors in Computing Systems*, Honolulu, HI, USA. https://doi.org/DOI: 10.1145/3313831.3376727

Lopez, R. M., & Tadros, E. (2023). Motivational Factors for Undergraduate Students During COVID-19 Remote Learning. In *Family Journal (Alexandria, Va.)*. DOI: 10.1177/10664807231163245

Lorenzo, G., & Lorenzo-Lledó, A. (2024). The use of artificial intelligence for detecting the duration of autistic students' emotions in social interaction with the NAO robot: A case study. *International Journal of Information Technology : an Official Journal of Bharati Vidyapeeth's Institute of Computer Applications and Management*, *16*(2), 1–7. DOI: 10.1007/s41870-023-01682-0

Lowther, D. L., Inan, F. A., Strahl, J. D., & Ross, S. M. (2012). Do One-to-One Initiatives Bridge the Way to 21st Century Knowledge and Skills? *Journal of Educational Computing Research*, *46*(1), 1–30. DOI: 10.2190/EC.46.1.a

Lozano, A., & Fontao, C. (2023). Is the Education System Prepared for the Irruption of Artificial Intelligence? A Study on the Perceptions of Students of Primary Education Degree from a Dual Perspective: Current Pupils and Future Teachers. *Education Sciences*, *13*(7), 733. Advance online publication. DOI: 10.3390/educsci13070733

Luckin, R., & Cukurova, M. (2019). Designing educational technologies in the age of AI: A learning sciences-driven approach. *British Journal of Educational Technology*, *50*(6), 2824–2838. DOI: 10.1111/bjet.12861

Luckin, R., Cukurova, M., Kent, C., & du Boulay, B. (2022). Empowering Educators to Be AI-Ready. *Computers and Education: Artificial Intelligence*, *3*, 1–11. DOI: 10.1016/j.caeai.2022.100076

Luppicini, R., & Adell, R. (Eds.). (2008). *Handbook of research on technoethics*. IGI Global., DOI: 10.4018/978-1-60566-022-6

Lu, Q., Zhu, L., Xu, X., Whittle, J., & Xing, Z. (2022). Towards a Roadmap on Software Engineering for Responsible AI. *Proceedings of the 1st International Conference on AI Engineering: Software Engineering for AI*, 101-112. DOI: 10.1145/3522664.3528607

Lyell, D., & Coiera, E. (2017). Automation bias and verification complexity: A systematic review. *Journal of the American Medical Informatics Association : JAMIA*, 24(2), 423–431. DOI: 10.1093/jamia/ocw105 PMID: 27516495

Lynch, J. (2018). How AI will destroy education. *Medium*. https://buzzrobot.com/howai-will-destroy-education-20053b7b88a6

Maaliw, R. R., Mabunga, Z. P., Veluz, M. R. D. D., Alon, A. S., Lagman, A. C., Garcia, M. B., Lacatan, L. L., & Dellosa, R. M. (2023). An Enhanced Segmentation and Deep Learning Architecture for Early Diabetic Retinopathy Detection. *2023 IEEE 13th Annual Computing and Communication Workshop and Conference (CCWC)*, 0168-0175. DOI: 10.1109/CCWC57344.2023.10099069

Maanu, V., Boateng, F. O., & Larbi, E. (2025). AI-assisted instructions in collaborative learning in mathematics education: A aualitative approach. *American Journal of STEM Education*, 7, 11–36. DOI: 10.32674/68zzkz60

MacLeod, K., Causton, J. N., Radel, M., & Radel, P. (2017). Rethinking the individualized education plan process: Voices from the other side of the table. *Disability & Society*, 32(3), 381–400. DOI: 10.1080/09687599.2017.1294048

Madden, M., Gilman, M., Levy, K., & Marwick, A. (2017). Privacy, poverty, and big data: A matrix of vulnerabilities for poor Americans. *Washington University Law Review*, 95(1), 53–125.

Mageira, K., Pittou, D., Papasalouros, A., Kotis, K., Zangogianni, P., & Daradoumis, A. (2022). Educational AI Chatbots for Content and Language Integrated Learning. *Applied Sciences (Basel, Switzerland)*, 12(7), 3239. DOI: 10.3390/app12073239

Mahapatra, S. (2024). Impact of ChatGPT on ESL students' academic writing skills: A mixed methods intervention study. *Smart Learning Environments*, 11(1), 9. Advance online publication. DOI: 10.1186/s40561-024-00295-9

Maheswary, B. G. U., & Lourdusamy, A. (2023). An Evaluation of the Partition Narratives: A Special Focus on Psychological Trauma. *International Journal of Philosophy and Languages (IJPL)*, 18–26. DOI: 10.47992/IJPL.2583.9934.0010

Mahmoudi-Dehaki, M., & Nasr-Esfahani, N. (2025). Artificial intelligence (AI) in special education: AI therapeutic pedagogy for language disorders. In *Transforming special education through artificial intelligence* (pp. 193–222). IGI Global.

Makarichev, V., Lukin, V., Illiashenko, O., & Kharchenko, V. (2022). Digital Image representation by atomic Functions: The compression and protection of data for edge computing in IoT systems. *Sensors (Basel)*, 22(10), 3751. DOI: 10.3390/s22103751 PMID: 35632158

Malik, A. R., Pratiwi, Y., Andajani, K., Numertayasa, I. W., Suharti, S., Darwis, A., & Marzuki, . (2023). Exploring Artificial Intelligence in Academic Essay: Higher Education Student's Perspective. *International Journal of Educational Research Open*, *5*, 1–11. DOI: 10.1016/j.ijedro.2023.100296

Malik, S., Muhammad, K., & Waheed, Y. (2024). Artificial Intelligence and Industrial Applications- A Revolution in Modern Industries. *Ain Shams Engineering Journal*, *15*(9), 1–11. DOI: 10.1016/j.asej.2024.102886

Mallinger, K., Corpaci, L., Neubauer, T., Tikász, I. E., Goldenits, G., & Banhazi, T. M. (2024). Breaking the barriers of technology adoption: Explainable AI for requirement analysis and technology design in smart farming. *Smart Agricultural Technology*, *9*, 100658. DOI: 10.1016/j.atech.2024.100658

Manninen, M., Dishman, R., Hwang, Y., Magrum, E., Deng, Y., & Yli-Piipari, S. (2022). Self-determination theory based instructional interventions and motivational regulations in organized physical activity: A systematic review and multivariate meta-analysis. *Psychology of Sport and Exercise*, *62*, 102248. https://doi.org/https://doi.org/10.1016/j.psychsport.2022.102248. DOI: 10.1016/j.psychsport.2022.102248

Manto, S. H. (1955). *Toba Tek Singh*. www.sacw.net. http://www.sacw.net/partition/tobateksingh.html

Manu, A. (2024). *Transcending imagination: Artificial Intelligence and the Future of Creativity*. CRC Press. DOI: 10.1201/9781003450139

Marino, M. T., Vasquez, E., Dieker, L., Basham, J., & Blackorby, J. (2023). The future of artificial intelligence in special education technology. *Journal of Special Education Technology*, *38*(3), 404–416. DOI: 10.1177/01626434231165977

Martel, J.-L., Arsenault, R., & Brissette, F. (2024). Artificial Intelligence in Engineering Education: The Future Is Now. *Lecture Notes in Civil Engineering*, 103-117. DOI: 10.1007/978-3-031-60415-7_8

Martineau, K. (2023, January 25). What is generative AI? IBM Research. https://research.ibm.com/blog/what-is-generative-AI

Marzuki, W., Widiati, U., Rusdin, D., Darwin, , & Indrawati, I. (2023). The impact of AI writing tools on the content and organization of students' writing: EFL teachers' perspective. *Cogent Education*, *10*(2), 2236469. DOI: 10.1080/2331186X.2023.2236469

Maslikova, I. (2021). *The ways of developing a culture of education quality and academic integrity in the contemporary University*. Ukranian Cultural Studies., DOI: 10.17721/UCS.2021.2(9).12

Matthews, J. T., Beach, S. R., Downs, J., de Bruin, W. B., Mecca, L. P., & Schulz, . (2010). Preferences and concerns for quality of life technology among older adults and persons with disabilities: National survey results. *Technology and Disability*, *22*(1-2), 5–15. DOI: 10.3233/TAD-2010-0279

Mazumder, M. (2024, August). Significance of artificial intelligence in the realm of special education. *Artificial Intelligence in Education* (pp. 242-249). Red Unicorn.

McDonald, N., & Forte, A. (2022). Privacy and vulnerable populations. In Knijnenburg, B. P., Page, X., Wisniewski, P., Lipford, H. R., Proferes, N., & Romano, J. (Eds.), *Modern sociotechnical perspectives on privacy* (pp. 337–363). Springer. DOI: 10.1007/978-3-030-82786-1_15

McGrath, S., & Yamada, S. (2023). Skills for Development and Vocational Education and Training: Current and Emergent Trends. *International Journal of Educational Development*, *102*, 1–9. DOI: 10.1016/j.ijedudev.2023.102853

McPeck, J. E. (2016). *Critical thinking and education*. Routledge. DOI: 10.4324/9781315463698

Mello, R. F., Freitas, E., Pereira, F. D., Cabral, L., Tedesco, P., & Ramalho, G. (2023). Education in the age of Generative AI: Context and recent developments. *arXiv*. https://arxiv.org/abs/2309.12332

Memarian, B. (2023). Indigenizing the Artificial Intelligence (AI) Programmed Engineering Education Curriculum, Challenges and Future Potentials. *2023 ASEE Annual Conference & Exposition*. DOI: 10.18260/1-2--43678

Memarian, B., & Doleck, T. (2024). A Review of Assessment for Learning with Artificial Intelligence. *Computers in Human Behavior: Artificial Humans*, *2*(1), 100040. DOI: 10.1016/j.chbah.2023.100040

Mendoza, S., Sánchez-Adame, L. M., Urquiza-Yllescas, J. F., González-Beltrán, B. A., & Decouchant, D. (2022). A Model to Develop Chatbots for Assisting the Teaching and Learning Process. *Sensors (Basel)*, *22*(15), 5532. DOI: 10.3390/s22155532 PMID: 35898035

Meng, J., & Dai, Y. (2021). Emotional support from AI chatbots: Should a supportive partner self-disclose or not? *Journal of Computer-Mediated Communication*, *26*(4), 207–222. DOI: 10.1093/jcmc/zmab005

Mesquita Machado, T., & Winter, E. (2023). Artificial Intelligence and Patents in Brazil: Overview on Patentability and Comparative Study on Patent Filings. *World Patent Information*, *72*, 1–11. DOI: 10.1016/j.wpi.2023.102177

Mezzanotte, C. (2022). The social and economic rationale of inclusive education: An overview of the outcomes in education for diverse groups of students. OECD. https://one.oecd.org/document/EDU/WKP(2022)1/en/pdf

Mhlanga, D. (2023). Open AI in Education, The responsible and ethical use of ChaTGPT towards lifelong Learning. In *Sustainable development goals series* (pp. 387–409). https://doi.org/DOI: 10.1007/978-3-031-37776-1_17

Mhlongo, S., Mbatha, K., Ramatsetse, B., & Dlamini, R. (2023). Challenges, Opportunities, and Prospects of Adopting and Using Smart Digital Technologies in Learning Environments: An Iterative Review. *Heliyon*, *9*(6), 1–20. DOI: 10.1016/j.heliyon.2023.e16348 PMID: 37274691

Michel-Villarreal, R., Vilalta Perdomo, E., Salinas-Navarro, D., Thierry-Aguilera, R., & Gerardou, F. S. (2023). Challenges and Opportunities of Generative AI for Higher Education as Explained by ChatGPT. *Education Sciences*, *13*(856), 856. Advance online publication. DOI: 10.3390/educsci13090856

Microsoft. (n.d.). Responsible AI resources for developers. *Azure Dev Community Blog*. https://techcommunity.microsoft.com/blog/azuredevcommunityblog/responsible-ai-resources-for-developers/4189381

Mıjwıl, M. M., Sadıkoğlu, E., Cengiz, E., & Candan, H. (2022). Siber güvenlikte yapay zekânın rolü ve önemi: Bir derleme. *Veri Bilimi*, *5*(2), 97–105.

Milic, S., & Simeunovic, V. (2022). Teachers' roles in online learning communities: A case study from the digitally underdeveloped country. *Interactive Learning Environments*, *32*(1), 144–155. DOI: 10.1080/10494820.2022.2081210

Miller, J. C., Fernando, E. Q., Miranda, J. P. P., Bansil, J. A., Hernandez, H. E., & Regala, A. R. (2024). Extended Reality Technologies in Physical Fitness for Health Promotion: Insights from Bibliometric Research. In *Emerging Technologies for Health Literacy and Medical Practice*. IGI Global., DOI: 10.4018/979-8-3693-1214-8.ch005

Milliron, M. D., Malcolm, L., & Kil, D. (2014). Insight and action analytics: Three case studies to consider. *Research & Practice in Assessment*, 9, 70–89. https://files.eric.ed.gov/fulltext/EJ1062814.pdf

Ministry of Education and Vocation Training. (2021). *Plan de Digitalización y Competencias Digitales del Sistema Educativo*. Spanish Government. Retrieved November 19, 2024 from https://www.educacionyfp.gob.es

Minkkinen, M., Zimmer, M. P., & Mäntymäki, M. (2021, August). Towards ecosystems for responsible AI: Expectations on sociotechnical systems, agendas, and networks in EU documents. In *Conference on e-Business, e-Services and e-Society* (pp. 220–232). Springer International Publishing. DOI: 10.1007/978-3-030-85447-8_20

Mishra, N., Garcia, P. S., Habal, B. G. M., & Garcia, M. B. (2024). Harnessing an AI-Driven Analytics Model to Optimize Training and Treatment in Physical Education for Sports Injury Prevention. *Proceedings of the 8th International Conference on Education and Multimedia Technology*, 309-315. DOI: 10.1145/3678726.3678740

Mittelstadt, B. D., Allo, P., Taddeo, M., Wachter, S., & Floridi, L. (2016). The ethics of algorithms: Mapping the debate. *Big Data & Society*, *3*(2), 1–21. DOI: 10.1177/2053951716679679

Mittler, P. (2008). Planning for the 2040s: Everybody's business. *British Journal of Special Education*, *35*(1), 3–10. DOI: 10.1111/j.1467-8578.2008.00363.x

Modran, H. A., Chamunorwa, T., Ursu iu, D., & Samoilă, C. (2024). Integrating Artificial Intelligence and ChatGPT into Higher Engineering Education. *Lecture Notes in Networks and Systems*, 499-510. DOI: 10.1007/978-3-031-51979-6_52

Mohamed, Y. A., Mohamed, A. H. H. M., Khanan, A., Bashir, M., Adiel, M. E., & Elsadig, M. A. (2024). Navigating the Ethical Terrain of AI-Generated Text Tools: A Review. *IEEE Access : Practical Innovations, Open Solutions*, ●●●, 12.

Moher, D., Shamseer, L., Clarke, M., Ghersi, D., Liberati, A., Petticrew, M., Shekelle, P., & Stewart, L. A. (2015). Preferred reporting items for systematic review and meta-analysis protocols (PRISMA-P) statement. *Systematic Reviews*, *4*(1), 1–9. DOI: 10.1186/2046-4053-4-1 PMID: 25554246

Molenaar, I. (2022). Hybrid intelligence in education: Augmenting teachers with AI. *European Journal of Education*, *57*(4), 614–631. DOI: 10.1111/ejed.12527

Mollick, E. R., & Mollick, L. (2023). Using AI to Implement Effective Teaching Strategies in Classrooms: Five strategies, including prompts. *Social Science Research Network Electronic Journal*, 1-26. DOI: 10.2139/ssrn.4391243

Montenegro-Rueda, M., Fernández-Cerero, J., Fernández-Batanero, J. M., & López-Meneses, E. (2023). Impact of the implementation of ChatGPT in education: A systematic review. *Computers*, *12*(8), 153. DOI: 10.3390/computers12080153

Montenegro-Rueda, M., Luque-de la Rosa, A., Sarasola Sánchez-Serrano, J. L., & Fernández-Cerero, J. (2021). Assessment in Higher Education during the COVID-19 Pandemic: A Systematic Review. *Sustainability (Basel)*, *13*(19), 1–13. DOI: 10.3390/su131910509

Montero Guerra, J. M., Danvila-del-Valle, I., & Méndez-Suárez, M. (2023). The Impact of Digital Transformation on Talent Management. *Technological Forecasting and Social Change*, *188*, 1–10. DOI: 10.1016/j.techfore.2022.122291

Moolman, J. H., Boyle, F., & Walsh, J. (2023). Revolutionising Engineering Education: Creating Photorealistic Virtual Human Lecturers Using Artificial Intelligence And Computer Generated Images. *European Society for Engineering Education (SEFI)*. DOI: 10.21427/CDBM-4P41

Mora, A. G. (2005). Estrategia general de búsqueda de información. *Enfuro*, (93), 30–32.

Moraitis, V. (2025). Why the Guidelines for AI in Finland's Education System Could Redefine Learning Globally. *The AI Track*. https://theaitrack.com/ai-in-finland-education-global-model/

Morales-García, W. C., Sairitupa-Sanchez, L. Z., Morales-García, S. B., & Morales-García, M. (2024). Development and validation of a scale for dependence on artificial intelligence in university students. *Frontiers in Education*, *9*, 1323898. Advance online publication. DOI: 10.3389/feduc.2024.1323898

Morandini, S., Fraboni, F., De Angelis, M., Puzzo, G., Giusino, D., & Pietrantoni, L. (2023). The impact of artificial intelligence on workers' skills: upskilling and reskilling in organisations. *Informing Science the International Journal of an Emerging Transdiscipline*, *26*, 039–068. https://doi.org/DOI: 10.28945/5078

Msekelwa, P. Z. (2024). Impact of AI on Education: Innovative tools and trends. *Deleted Journal*, *5*(1), 227–236. DOI: 10.60087/jaigs.v5i1.198

Mthombeni, N. H., Maladzhi, R., Moloi, K., Mashifana, T., Tsoeu, M., & Nemavhola, F. (2023). AI ChatBots as Inherent Tools for Comprehensive Learning of Engineering Design: A Systematic review. *2023 World Engineering Education Forum - Global Engineering Deans Council (WEEF-GEDC)*, 1-6. DOI: 10.1109/WEEF-GEDC59520.2023.10343866

Muñoz-Cantero, J., Crego, M., & Espiñeira-Bellón, E. (2024). Desarrollo de la integridad académica como oportunidad de justicia. *Revista Electrónica Interuniversitaria de Formación del Profesorado*, *27*(3), 153–169. DOI: 10.6018/reifop.615081

Mupaikwa, E. (2023). The Use of Artificial Intelligence in Education. In *Advances in Library and Information Science* (pp. 26-50). IGI Global. https://doi.org/DOI: 10.4018/978-1-6684-8671-9.ch002

Murphy, R. F. (2019). *Artificial intelligence applications to support K–12 teachers and teaching*. RAND Corporation, PE-315-RC. https://doi.org/DOI: 10.7249/PE315

Murtaza, M., Ahmed, Y., Shamsi, J. A., Sherwani, F., & Usman, M. (2022). AI-based personalized e-learning systems: Issues, challenges, and solutions. *IEEE Access : Practical Innovations, Open Solutions*, *10*, 81323–81342. DOI: 10.1109/ACCESS.2022.3193938

Mustafa, A. S., Alkawsi, G. A., Ofosu-Ampong, K., Vanduhe, V. Z., Garcia, M. B., & Baashar, Y. (2022). Gamification of E-Learning in African Universities: Identifying Adoption Factors Through Task-Technology Fit and Technology Acceptance Model. In Portela, F., & Queirós, R. (Eds.), *Next-Generation Applications and Implementations of Gamification Systems* (pp. 73–96). IGI Global., DOI: 10.4018/978-1-7998-8089-9.ch005

Mustofa, R. H., Kuncoro, T. G., Atmono, D., & Hermawan, H. D. (2025). Extending the Technology Acceptance Model: The Role of Subjective Norms, Ethics, and Trust in AI Tool Adoption Among Students. Computers and Education: Artificial Intelligence, 100379.

Muttaqin, I. (2022). Necessary to Increase Teacher Competency in Facing the Artificial Intelligence Era. *Al-Hayat: Journal of Islamic Education*, *6*(2), 549. DOI: 10.35723/ajie.v6i2.460

Nacaroglu, O., & Mutlu, F. (2020). Examination of Science and Art Center Students' Metaphorical Perceptions About the Concept of Project. *Abant İzzet Baysal University Journal of Education Faculty*, *20*(2), 992–1007. DOI: 10.17240/aibuefd.2020.-587573

Najjar, M., Courtemanche, F., Hamam, H., & Mayers, A. (2010). Deepkover-An adaptive artful intelligent assistance system for cognitively impaired people. *Applied Artificial Intelligence*, *24*(5), 381–413. DOI: 10.1080/08839514.2010.481486

Nasar, I., Uzer, Y., Aisyah, , Ridayani, , & Purwanto, M. B. (2023). Artificial Intelligence in Smart Classrooms. [AJAE]. *Asian Journal of Applied Education*, *2*(4), 547–556. DOI: 10.55927/ajae.v2i4.6038

Naseer, F., Khalid, M. U., Ayub, N., Rasool, A., Abbas, T., & Afzal, M. W. (2024). Automated Assessment and Feedback in Higher Education Using Generative AI. In *Advances in educational technologies and instructional design book series* (pp. 433–461). DOI: 10.4018/979-8-3693-1351-0.ch021

Natividad Escalona-Márquez, L., Johanna Cedeño-Tapia, S., Alberto Camputaro, L., & Oscar Orlando Aparicio-Escalante, C. (2024). *Teachers in the Age of Artificial Intelligence: Preparation and Response to Challenges*. IntechOpen., DOI: 10.5772/intechopen.1005172

Nazaretsky, T., Ariely, M., Cukurova, M., & Alexandron, G. (2022). Teachers' Trust in AI-Powered Educational Technology and a Professional Development Program to Improve It. *British Journal of Educational Technology*, *53*(4), 914–931. DOI: 10.1111/bjet.13232

Nazaretsky, T., Mejia-Domenzain, P., Swamy, V., Frej, J., & Käser, T. (2024). AI or Human? Evaluating Student Feedback Perceptions in Higher Education. *Lecture Notes in Computer Science*, *15159*, 284–298. DOI: 10.1007/978-3-031-72315-5_20

Nerantzi, C., Abegglen, S., Karatsiori, M., & Martínez-Arboleda, A. (2023). 101 creative ideas to use AI in education, A crowdsourced collection (2023 1.0) [Computer software]. *Zenodo*. DOI: 10.5281/zenodo.8072950

Ng, D. T. K., Leung, J. K. L., Chu, S. K. W., & Qiao, M. S. (2021). Conceptualizing AI literacy: An exploratory review. *Computers and Education: Artificial Intelligence*, *2*, 100041. DOI: 10.1016/j.caeai.2021.100041

Ng, D. T. K., Leung, J. K. L., Su, J., Ng, R. C. W., & Chu, S. K. W. (2023). Teachers' AI Digital Competencies and Twenty-First Century Skills in the Post-Pandemic World. *Educational Technology Research and Development*, *71*(1), 137–161. DOI: 10.1007/s11423-023-10203-6 PMID: 36844361

Ng, D. T. K., Tan, C. W., & Leung, J. K. L. (2024). Empowering student self-regulated learning and science education through ChatGPT: A pioneering pilot study. *British Journal of Educational Technology*, *55*(4), 1328–1353. DOI: 10.1111/bjet.13454

Nguyen, A., Hong, Y., Dang, B., & Huang, X. (2024). Human-AI collaboration patterns in AI-assisted academic writing. *Studies in Higher Education*, *49*(5), 847–864. DOI: 10.1080/03075079.2024.2323593

Nguyen, A., Kremantzis, M., Essien, A., Petrounias, I., & Hosseini, S. (2024). Enhancing student engagement through artificial intelligence (AI): Understanding the basics, opportunities, and challenges. *Journal of University Teaching & Learning Practice*, *21*(6), 1–13. DOI: 10.53761/caraaq92

Nguyen, A., Ngo, H. N., Hong, Y., Dang, B., & Nguyen, B.-P. T. (2022). Ethical Principles for Artificial Intelligence in Education. *Education and Information Technologies*, *28*(4), 4221–4241. DOI: 10.1007/s10639-022-11316-w PMID: 36254344

Nguyen, T. N. T., Van Lai, N., & Nguyen, Q. T. (2024). Artificial Intelligence (AI) in Education: A Case Study on ChatGPT's Influence on Student Learning Behaviors. *Educational Process*, *13*(2), 105–121. DOI: 10.22521/edupij.2024.132.7

Nikitina, I., & Ishchenko, T. (2024). The impact of AI on teachers: Support or replacement? *Scientific Journal of Polonia University*, *65*(4), 93–99. DOI: 10.23856/6511

Nikolic, S., Daniel, S., Haque, R., Belkina, M., Hassan, G. M., Grundy, S., Lyden, S., Neal, P., & Sandison, C. (2023). ChatGPT Versus Engineering Education Assessment: A Multidisciplinary and Multi-Institutional Benchmarking and Analysis of This Generative Artificial Intelligence Tool to Investigate Assessment Integrity. *European Journal of Engineering Education*, *48*(4), 559–614. DOI: 10.1080/03043797.2023.2213169

Nikolic, S., Sandison, C., Haque, R., Daniel, S., Grundy, S., Belkina, M., Lyden, S., Hassan, G. M., & Neal, P. (2024). ChatGPT, Copilot, Gemini, SciSpace and Wolfram Versus Higher Education Assessments: An Updated Multi-Institutional Study of the Academic Integrity Impacts of Generative Artificial Intelligence (GenAI) on Assessment, Teaching and Learning in Engineering. *Australasian Journal of Engineering Education*, *29*(2), 126–153. DOI: 10.1080/22054952.2024.2372154

Nikou, S., De Reuver, M., & Mahboob Kanafi, M. (2022). Workplace literacy skills—How information and digital literacy affect adoption of digital technology. *The Journal of Documentation*, *78*(7), 371–391. DOI: 10.1108/JD-12-2021-0241

Nissenbaum, H., & Walker, D. (1998). Will computers dehumanize education? A grounded approach to values at risk. *Technology in Society*, *20*(3), 237–273. DOI: 10.1016/S0160-791X(98)00011-6

Nja, C. O., Idiege, K. J., Uwe, U. E., Meremikwu, A. N., Ekon, E. E., Erim, C. M., Ukah, J. U., Eyo, E. O., Anari, M. I., & Cornelius-Ukpepi, B. U. (2023). Adoption of Artificial Intelligence in Science Teaching: From the Vantage Point of the African Science Teachers. *Smart Learning Environments*, *10*(1), 42. Advance online publication. DOI: 10.1186/s40561-023-00261-x

Novopashina, L., Grigorieva, E., Ilyina, N., & Bidus, I. (2024). Readiness of future teachers to work at school: review of theoretical and empirical research. *Obrazovanie i nauka-. Education in Science*, *26*(2), 60–96. DOI: 10.17853/1994-5639-2024-2-60-96

Nti, I. K., Adekoya, A. F., Weyori, B. A., & Nyarko-Boateng, O. (2021). Applications of Artificial Intelligence in Engineering and Manufacturing: A Systematic Review. *Journal of Intelligent Manufacturing*, *33*(6), 1581–1601. DOI: 10.1007/s10845-021-01771-6

Ntoutsi, E., Fafalios, P., Gadiraju, U., Iosifidis, V., Nejdl, W., Vidal, M., Ruggieri, S., Turini, F., Papadopoulos, S., Krasanakis, E., Kompatsiaris, I., Kinder-Kurlanda, K., Wagner, C., Karimi, F., Fernández, M., Alani, H., Berendt, B., Kruegel, T., Heinze, C., & Staab, S. (2020). Bias in data-driven artificial intelligence systems—An introductory survey. *Wiley Interdisciplinary Reviews. Data Mining and Knowledge Discovery*, *10*(3), e1356. DOI: 10.1002/widm.1356

Núñez, J. L. M., & Lantada, A. D. (2020). Artificial Intelligence Aided Engineering Education: State of the Art, Potentials and Challenges. *International Journal of Engineering Education*, *36*, 1740–1751. https://www.researchgate.net/publication/345141282

Nurjanah, A., Salsabila, I. N., Azzahra, A., Rahayu, R., & Marlina, N. (2024). Artificial Intelligence (AI) Usage In Today's Teaching And Learning Process: A Review. *Syntax Idea*, *6*(3), 1517–1523. DOI: 10.46799/syntax-idea.v6i3.3126

Nyaaba, M., & Zhaı, X. (2024). Generative AI Professional Development Needs for Teacher Educators. *Journal of AI*, *8*(1), 1–13. DOI: 10.61969/jai.1385915

Obaid, O. I., Ali, A. H., & Yaseen, M. G. (2023). Impact of Chat GPT on Scientific Research: Opportunities, Risks, Limitations, and Ethical Issues. *Iraqi J. Comput. Sci. Math*, *4*, 13–17. DOI: 10.52866/ijcsm.2023.04.04.002

Ocak, A., Nigdeli, S. M., Bekdaş, G., & Işıkdağ, Ü. (2023). Artificial Intelligence and Deep Learning in Civil Engineering. *Studies in Systems, Decision and Control*, 265-288. DOI: 10.1007/978-3-031-34728-3_13

Ocaña-Fernández, Y., Valenzuela-Fernández, L. A., & Garro-Aburto, L. L. (2019). Artificial Intelligence and Its Implications in Higher Education. *Journal of Educational Psychology-Propositos y Representaciones*, *7*(2), 553–568.

OECD. (2012). *Equity and quality in education: Supporting disadvantaged students and schools*. OECD Publishing., DOI: 10.1787/9789264130852-

OECD. (2015). *The Innovation Imperative: Contributing to Productivity, Growth and Well-Being*. OECD Publishing., DOI: 10.1787/9789264239814-

OECD. (2024a). *The potential impact of artificial intelligence on equity and inclusion in education* (OECD Artificial Intelligence Papers No. 23). https://www.oecd.org/publications/the-potential-impact-of-artificial-intelligence-on-equity-and-inclusion-in-education-0d7e9e00-en.htm

OECD. (2024b). *Revised recommendation of the Council on artificial intelligence* (C/MIN(2024)16/FINAL). OECD Publishing. https://one.oecd.org/document/C/MIN(2024)16/FINAL/en/pdf

Ofosu-Ampong, K., Agyekum, M. W., & Garcia, M. B. (2024). Long-Term Pandemic Management and the Need to Invest in Digital Transformation: A Resilience Theory Perspective. In *Transformative Approaches to Patient Literacy and Healthcare Innovation* (pp. 242-260). IGI Global. DOI: 10.4018/979-8-3693-3661-8.ch012

Ofosu-Ampong, K., Acheampong, B., Kevor, M., & Amankwah-Sarfo, F. (2023). Acceptance of Artificial Intelligence (ChatGPT) in Education: Trust, Innovativeness and Psychological Need of Students. *Information and Knowledge Management*, *13*(4), 37–47. DOI: 10.7176/IKM/13-4-03

Ohlhausen, M. K. (2016). Patent Rights in a Climate of Intellectual Property Rights Skepticism. *Harvard Journal of Law & Technology*, *30*(1), 103–124. https://jolt.law.harvard.edu/assets/articlePDFs/v30/30HarvJLTech103.pdf

Okonkwo, C. W., & Ade-Ibijola, A. (2021a). Chatbots Applications in Education: A Systematic Review. *Computers and Education: Artificial Intelligence*, *2*, 100033. DOI: 10.1016/j.caeai.2021.100033

Okonkwo, C. W., & Ade-Ibijola, A. (2021b). Python-Bot: A Chatbot for Teaching Python Programming. *Engineering Letters*, *29*, 25–34.

Oliveira, P. B. M., & Vrančić, D. (2024). Evaluation of GPTs for Control Engineering Education: Towards Artificial General Intelligence. *IFAC-PapersOnLine*, *58*(7), 97–102. DOI: 10.1016/j.ifacol.2024.08.017

Olmos-Vega, F. M., Stalmeijer, R. E., Varpio, L., & Kahlke, R. (2022). A Practical Guide to Reflexivity in Qualitative Research: AMEE Guide No. 149. *Medical Teacher*, *45*(3), 241–251. DOI: 10.1080/0142159X.2022.2057287 PMID: 35389310

Olugbade, D. (2024). Democratizing Education in Rural Nigeria Through AI and Mobile Technologies as a Transformative Pathway to Inclusive Learning. In *Advances in Educational Technologies and Instructional Design* (pp. 233-250). IGI Global. https://doi.org/DOI: 10.4018/979-8-3693-7255-5.ch010

Olugbade, D., & Ojo, O. A. (2024). Immersion Technologies: Going Beyond Textbooks to Improve Learning in Developing Nations. *Lecture Notes in Educational Technology*, 297-316. https://doi.org/DOI: 10.1007/978-981-97-8752-4_16

Open, A. I. (2024, May 13). *Be My Eyes Accessibility with GPT-4o* [Video]. YouTube. https://www.youtube.com/watch?v=Kw- NUJ69RbwY

Orru, G., Piarulli, A., Conversano, C., & Gemignani, A. (2023). Human-like problem-solving abilities in large language models using ChatGPT. *Frontiers in Artificial Intelligence*, *6*, 1199350. DOI: 10.3389/frai.2023.1199350 PMID: 37293238

Osunbunmi, I. S., Cutler, S., & Dansu, V. B., Y., Bamidele, B. R., Udosen, A. N., Arinze, L. C. O., A. V., Moyaki, D., Hicks, M. J., & Shih, B. P. (2024). Generative Artificial Intelligence (GAI)-Assisted Learning: Pushing the Boundaries of Engineering Education. *2024 ASEE Annual Conference & Exposition*. DOI: 10.18260/1-2--47041

Ouyang, F., & Jiao, P. (2021). Artificial Intelligence in Education: The Three Paradigms. *Computers and Education: Artificial Intelligence*, 2, 1–6. DOI: 10.1016/j.caeai.2021.100020

Ouyang, X., Sun, Z., & Xu, X. (2022). Patent System in the Digital Era - Opportunities and New Challenges. *Journal of Digital Economy*, 1(3), 166–179. DOI: 10.1016/j.jdec.2022.12.003

Owan, V. J., Abang, K. B., Idika, D. O., Etta, E. O., & Bassey, B. A. (2023). Exploring the potential of artificial intelligence tools in educational measurement and assessment. *Eurasia Journal of Mathematics, Science and Technology Education*, 19(8), em2307. Advance online publication. DOI: 10.29333/ejmste/13428

Oyedokun, G. E. (2025). AI and Ethics, Academic Integrity and the Future of Quality Assurance in Higher Education. *ResearchGate*. https://www.researchgate.net/publication/387999374_AI_and_Ethics_Academic_Integrity_and_the_Future_of_Quality_Assurance_in_Higher_Education

Özbek Güven, G., Yilmaz, Ş., & Inceoğlu, F. (2024). Determining Medical Students' Anxiety and Readiness Levels About Artificial Intelligence. *Heliyon*, 10(4), e25894. DOI: 10.1016/j.heliyon.2024. e25894 PMID: 38384508

Özer, M. (2021). Science and Art Centers in Support of Talent Development for Gifted and Talented Students: Current Situation and Areas for Improvement. *International Journal of Society Researchers*, 17(33), 727–749. DOI: 10.26466/opus.810856

Ozer, Z., & Demirbatir, R. E. (2023). Determining the Views of BİLSEM Art Field Teachers on STEAM Education. *Afyon Kocatepe University Journal of Social Sciences*, 25(4), 1349–1364. DOI: 10.32709/akusosbil.1116157

Ozin, G. A., Qian, C., & MacIntosh, J. G. (2023). Can AI Be an Inventor in Materials Discovery? *Matter*, 6(10), 3117–3120. DOI: 10.1016/j.matt.2023.08.015

Ozkazanc-Pan, B. (2021). Diversity and future of work: Inequality abound or opportunities for all? *Management Decision*, 59(11), 2645–2659. DOI: 10.1108/MD-02-2019-0244

Padovano, A., & Cardamone, L. (2024). Artificial intelligence in education: A roadmap for ethical and effective implementation. *Computers & Education: Artificial Intelligence*, 5, 100076. DOI: 10.1016/j.caeai.2024.100076

Pagliara, S., Bonavolontà, G., Pia, M., Falchi, S., Zurru, A., Fenu, G., & Mura, A. (2024). The Integration of Artificial Intelligence in Inclusive Education: A Scoping Review. *Information (Basel)*, 15(12), 774. Advance online publication. DOI: 10.3390/info15120774

Palen, L., & Dourish, P. (2003). Unpacking "privacy" for a networked world. In *Proceedings of the SIGCHI Conference on Human Factors in Computing Systems*, 129–136. SIGCHI.

Pandey, A., & Caliskan, A. (2021). Disparate impact of artificial intelligence bias in ridehailing economy's price discrimination algorithms. In *Proceedings of the 2021 AAAI/ACM Conference on AI, Ethics, and Society* (pp. 822-833). DOI: 10.1145/3461702.3462561

Pandita, A., & Kiran, R. (2023). The Technology Interface and Student Engagement Are Significant Stimuli in Sustainable Student Satisfaction. *Sustainability (Basel), 15*(10), 1–21. DOI: 10.3390/su15107923

Pandya, K. T. (2024). The Role of Artificial Intelligence in Education 5.0: Opportunities and Challenges. *SDGs Studies Review, 5*, e011. DOI: 10.37497/sdgs.v5igoals.11

Pane, J. F., Griffin, B. A., McCaffrey, D. F., & Karam, R. (2014). Effectiveness of cognitive tutor algebra I at scale. *Educational Evaluation and Policy Analysis, 36*(2), 127–144. DOI: 10.3102/0162373713507480

Pang, T. Y., Kootsookos, A., & Cheng, C.-T. (2024). Artificial Intelligence Use in Feedback: A Qualitative Analysis. *Journal of University Teaching & Learning Practice, 21*(06). Advance online publication. DOI: 10.53761/40wmcj98

Panjwani-Charania, S., & Zhai, X. (2024). AI for Students with Learning Disabilities: A Systematic Review. In X. Zhai & J. Krajcik (Eds.), *Uses of Artificial Intelligence in STEM Education* (p. 0). Oxford University Press. https://doi.org/DOI: 10.1093/oso/9780198882077.003.0021

Papaspyridis, A., & La Greca, J. (2023). AI and education: Will the promise be fulfilled? In *Augmented education in the global age* (pp. 119–136). Routledge.

Parab, A. K. (2020). Artificial intelligence in Education: Teacher and teacher assistant improve learning process. *International Journal for Research in Applied Science and Engineering Technology, 8*(11), 608–612. DOI: 10.22214/ijraset.2020.32237

Parente, A., & Roecklein-Canfield, J. (2020). Strategies for fostering academic integrity in the classroom. *The FASEB Journal, 34*(S1), 1–1. DOI: 10.1096/fasebj.2020.34.s1.07239

Park, W., & Kwon, H. (2023). Implementing Artificial Intelligence Education for Middle School Technology Education in Republic of Korea. *International Journal of Technology and Design Education, 34*(1), 109–135. DOI: 10.1007/s10798-023-09812-2 PMID: 36844448

Parra, J. L., & Chatterjee, S. (2024). Social Media and Artificial Intelligence: Critical Conversations and Where Do We Go from Here? Educativo. *Education Sciences, 14*(68), 68. Advance online publication. DOI: 10.3390/educsci14010068

Pasupuleti, R. S., & Thiyyagura, D. (2024). An empirical evidence on the continuance and recommendation intention of ChatGPT among higher education students in India: An extended technology continuance theory. *Education and Information Technologies, 29*(14), 17965–17985. DOI: 10.1007/s10639-024-12573-7

Patel, P. C., & Sahi, G. K. (2024). AI Patent Approvals in Service Firms, Patent Radicalness, and Stock Market Reaction. *Journal of Service Research, 10946705241230840*. Advance online publication. DOI: 10.1177/10946705241230840

Pattier, D., & Redondo-Duarte, S. (2025). La vida online, la inteligencia artificial y su lectura pedagógica. *Márgenes. Revista de Educación de la Universidad de Málaga*, 6(1), 28–45. DOI: 10.24310/mar.6.1.2025.20784

Paulus, J. K., & Kent, D. M. (2020). Predictably unequal: Understanding and addressing concerns that algorithmic clinical prediction may increase health disparities. *NPJ Digital Medicine*, 3(1), 1–8. DOI: 10.1038/s41746-020-0304-9 PMID: 32821854

Pavlik, J. V. (2023). Collaborating with ChatGPT: Considering the implications of generative artificial intelligence for journalism and media education. *Journalism & mass communication educator*, 78(1), 84-93. DOI: 10.1177/10776958221149577

PBSP. (2022). Digital and IT equipment for Last Mile Schools. https://www.pbsp.org.ph/news/digital-and-it-equipment-for-last-mile-schools

Pedro, F., Subosa, M., Rivas, A., & Valverde, P. (2019). *Artificial intelligence in education : challenges and opportunities for sustainable development.* https://repositorio.minedu.gob.pe/handle/20.500.12799/6533

Pegoraro, A., Kumari, K., Fereidooni, H., & Sadeghi, A. R. (2023). To ChatGPT, or not to ChatGPT: That is the question! *arXiv preprint arXiv:2304.01487.* . 2304. 01487DOI: 10. 48550/ arXiv

Peláez-Sánchez, I. C., Velarde-Camaqui, D., & Glasserman-Morales, L. D. (2024). The impact of large language models on higher education: Exploring the connection between AI and Education 4.0. *Frontiers in Education*, 9, 1392091. Advance online publication. DOI: 10.3389/feduc.2024.1392091

Peng, H., Ma, S., & Spector, J. M. (2019). Personalized adaptive learning: An emerging pedagogical approach enabled by a smart learning environment. *Smart Learning Environments*, 6(1), 1–14. DOI: 10.1186/s40561-019-0089-y

Pentina, I., Hancock, T., & Xie, T. (2023). Exploring relationship development with social chatbots: A mixed-method study of replika. *Computers in Human Behavior*, 140, 107600. DOI: 10.1016/j.chb.2022.107600

Peres, R., Schreier, M., Schweidel, D., & Sorescu, A. (2023). On ChatGPT and beyond: How generative artificial intelligence may affect research, teaching, and practice. *International Journal of Research in Marketing*, 40(2), 269–275. DOI: 10.1016/j.ijresmar.2023.03.001

Pérez, J. Q., Daradoumis, T., & Puig, J. M. M. (2020). Rediscovering the Use of Chatbots in Education: A Systematic Literature Review. *Computer Applications in Engineering Education*, 28(6), 1549–1565. DOI: 10.1002/cae.22326

Perkins, M. (2023). Academic Integrity considerations of AI Large Language Models in the post-pandemic era: ChatGPT and beyond. *Journal of University Teaching & Learning Practice*, 20(2), 6–24. DOI: 10.53761/1.20.02.07

Perkins, M., & Roe, J. (2024). Decoding academic integrity policies: A corpus linguistics investigation of AI and other technological threats. *Higher Education Policy*, 37(3), 633–653. DOI: 10.1057/s41307-023-00323-2

Perkins, M., Roe, J., Postma, D., McGaughran, J., & Hickerson, D. (2024). Detection of GPT-4 generated text in higher education: Combining academic judgement and software to identify generative AI tool misuse. *Journal of Academic Ethics*, *22*(1), 89–113. DOI: 10.1007/s10805-023-09492-6

Peters, U. (2022). Algorithmic political bias in artificial intelligence systems. *Philosophy & Technology*, *35*(2), 1–25. DOI: 10.1007/s13347-022-00512-8 PMID: 35378902

Piascik, P., & Brazeau, G. (2010). Promoting a Culture of Academic Integrity. *American Journal of Pharmaceutical Education*, *74*(6), 1–2. DOI: 10.5688/aj7406113 PMID: 21045955

Picht, P. G., & Thouvenin, F. (2023). AI and IP: Theory to Policy and Back Again – Policy and Research Recommendations at the Intersection of Artificial Intelligence and Intellectual Property. *IIC - International Review of Intellectual Property and Competition Law*, *54*(6), 916-940. DOI: 10.1007/s40319-023-01344-5

Placed, J. A., Strader, J., Carrillo, H., Atanasov, N., Indelman, V., Carlone, L., & Castellanos, J. A. (2023). A survey on active simultaneous localization and mapping: State of the art and new frontiers. *IEEE Transactions on Robotics*, *39*(3), 1686–1705. DOI: 10.1109/TRO.2023.3248510

Plackett, B. (2022). The rural areas missing out on AI opportunities. *Nature*, *610*(7931), S17. DOI: 10.1038/d41586-022-03212-7

Poddar, A., & Rao, S. R. (2024). Evolving Intellectual Property Landscape for AI-Driven Innovations in the Biomedical Sector: Opportunities in Stable IP Regime for Shared Success. *Frontiers in Artificial Intelligence*, *7*, 1–15. DOI: 10.3389/frai.2024.1372161 PMID: 39355146

Poláková, M., Suleimanová, J. H., Madzík, P., Copuš, L., Molnárová, I., & Polednová, J. (2023). Soft Skills and Their Importance in the Labour Market Under the Conditions of Industry 5.0. *Heliyon*, *9*(8), 1–20. DOI: 10.1016/j.heliyon.2023.e18670 PMID: 37593611

Ponce, P., Anthony, B., Bradley, R., Maldonado-Romo, J., Méndez, J. I., Montesinos, L., & Molina, A. (2024). Developing a Virtual Reality and Ai-Based Framework for Advanced Digital Manufacturing and Nearshoring Opportunities in Mexico. *Scientific Reports*, *14*(1), 1–24. DOI: 10.1038/s41598-024-61514-4 PMID: 38755242

Praveena, K. R., & Sasikumar, S. (2021). Application of Colaizzi's method of data analysis in phenomenological research. *Medico-Legal Update*, *21*(2), 914–918. DOI: 10.37506/mlu.v21i2.2800

Preiksaitis, C., & Rose, C. (2023). Opportunities, Challenges, and Future Directions of Generative Artificial Intelligence in Medical Education: Scoping Review. *JMIR Medical Education*, *9*, 1–13. DOI: 10.2196/48785 PMID: 37862079

PTI. (2024). IIM Sambalpur to introduce AI-enabled teaching. *The Economic Times*. https://m.economictimes.com/industry/services/education/iim-sambalpur-to-introduce-ai-enabled-teaching/articleshow/113625151.cms

Puerta-Beldarrain, M., & Gómez-Carmona, D. (2025). Student engagement with AI-supported learning environments: A comparative analysis. *IEEE Transactions on Education*, *68*(1), 35–51. DOI: 10.1109/TE.2025.10857320

Putra, F. W., Rangka, I. B., Aminah, S., & Aditama, M. H. (2023). ChatGPT in the higher education environment: Perspectives from the theory of high order thinking skills. *Journal of Public Health (Oxford, England)*, *45*(4), e840–e841. DOI: 10.1093/pubmed/fdad120 PMID: 37455540

Qadir, J. (2023). Engineering Education in the Era of ChatGPT: Promise and Pitfalls of Generative AI for Education. *2023 IEEE Global Engineering Education Conference (EDUCON)*, 1-9. DOI: 10.1109/EDUCON54358.2023.10125121

Qualys. (2025, February 7). *AI and Data Privacy: Mitigating Risks and Ensuring Protection | Qualys Security Blog*. Qualys Security Blog. https://blog.qualys.com/misc/2025/02/07/ai-and-data-privacy-mitigating-risks-in-the-age-of-generative-ai-tools

Radford, A., Wu, J., Child, R., Luan, D., Amodei, D., & Sutskever, I. (2018). Language models are unsupervised multitask learners. OpenAI blog, 1(8).

Rafiq, S., Iqbal, S., & Afzal, A. (2024). The impact of digital tools and online learning platforms on higher education learning outcomes. *Al-Mahdi Research Journal*, *5*(4), 359–367.

Rahman, M. M., & Watanobe, Y. (2023). ChatGPT for education and research: Opportunities, threats, and strategies. *Applied Sciences (Basel, Switzerland)*, *13*(9), 5783. DOI: 10.3390/app13095783

Rakap, S. (2024). Navigating the role of artificial intelligence in special education: Advantages, disadvantages, and ethical considerations. *Practice*, *6*(2-3), 1–6. DOI: 10.1080/25783858.2024.2411948

Ram, B., & Verma, P. (2023). Artificial intelligence AI-based Chatbot study of ChatGPT, Google AI Bard and Baidu AI. *World Journal of Advanced Engineering Technology and Sciences*, *8*(01), 258–261. DOI: 10.30574/wjaets.2023.8.1.0045

Ramineni, C., & Williamson, D. M. (2013). Automated essay scoring: Psychometric guidelines and practices. *Assessing Writing*, *18*(1), 25–39. DOI: 10.1016/j.asw.2012.10.004

Rane, N. L. (2024). Artificial Intelligence and Industry in Society 5.0. In *Artificial Intelligence and Industry in Society 5.0*. https://doi.org/DOI: 10.70593/978-81-981271-1-2

Rane, N., Shirke, S., Choudhary, S. P., & Rane, J. (2024). Artificial Intelligence in Education: A SWOT Analysis of ChatGPT and Its Impact on Academic Integrity and Research. *Journal of ELT Studies*, *1*(1), 16–35. DOI: 10.48185/jes.v1i1.1315

Rani, P. S., Rani, K. R., Daram, S. B., & Angadi, R. V. (2023). Is it feasible to reduce academic stress in Net-Zero Energy buildings? Reaction from ChatGPT. *Annals of Biomedical Engineering*, *51*(12), 2654–2656. DOI: 10.1007/s10439-023-03286-y PMID: 37332007

Rapanta, C., Botturi, L., Goodyear, P., Guàrdia, L., & Koole, M. (2020). Online university teaching during and after the covid-19 crisis: Refocusing teacher presence and learning activity. *Postdigital Science and Education*, *2*(3), 923–945. DOI: 10.1007/s42438-020-00155-y

Rasul, T., Nair, S., Kalendra, D., Balaji, M. S., Santini, F. de O., Ladeira, W. J., Rather, R. A., Yasin, N., Rodriguez, R. V., Kokkalis, P., Murad, M. W., & Hossain, M. U. (2024). Enhancing academic integrity among students in GenAI Era: A holistic framework. *International Journal of Management Education*, *22*(3), 101041. https://doi.org/https://doi.org/10.1016/j.ijme.2024.101041. DOI: 10.1016/j.ijme.2024.101041

Ray, P. P. (2023). ChatGPT: A comprehensive review on background, applications, key challenges, bias, ethics, limitations and future scope. *Internet of Things and Cyber-Physical Systems*, *3*, 121–154. https://doi.org/https://doi.org/10.1016/j.iotcps.2023.04.003. DOI: 10.1016/j.iotcps.2023.04.003

Redondo-Duarte, S., Martínez-Requejo, S., Jiménez-García, E., & Ruiz-Lázaro, J. (2024). The potential of educational chatbots for the support and formative assessment of students. In Ibrahim, M., Aydoğmuş, M., & Tükel, Y. (Eds.), *New trends and promising directions in modern education* (pp. 113–148). Palet Yayinlari.

Redondo-Duarte, S., Ruiz-Lázaro, J., Jiménez-García, E., & Requejo, S. M. (2024). Didactic Strategies for the Use of AI in the Classroom in Higher Education. In *Integration Strategies of Generative AI in Higher Education* (pp. 23–50). IGI Global., DOI: 10.4018/979-8-3693-5518-3.ch002

Reich, J., & Ito, M. (2017). *From good intentions to real outcomes: Equity by design in learning technologies*. Digital Media and Learning Research Hub.

Reichwein, F. (2023). *Ethical and societal implications of Generative AI-Models*.

Reisman, D., Schultz, J., Crawford, K., & Whittaker, M. (2018). *Algorithmic impact assessments: A practical framework for public agency accountability*. AI Now Institute. https://ainowinstitute.org/aiareport2018.pdf

Rejan, A. (2024). Close Reading for the Twenty-First Century: Rehumanizing Literary Reading. *English Journal*, *114*(2), 59–67. DOI: 10.58680/ej2024114259

Rekhta. (n.d.). https://www.rekhta.org/nazms/subh-e-aazaadii-august-47-ye-daag-daag-ujaalaa-ye-shab-gaziida-sahar-faiz-ahmad-faiz-nazms?lang=ur

Ren, M., Chen, N., & Qiu, H. (2023). Human-machine collaborative decision-making: An evolutionary roadmap based on cognitive intelligence. *International Journal of Social Robotics*, *15*(7), 1101–1114. DOI: 10.1007/s12369-023-01020-1

Revano, T. F., & Garcia, M. B. (2020). Manufacturing Design Thinkers in Higher Education Institutions: The Use of Design Thinking Curriculum in the Education Landscape. *2020 IEEE 12th International Conference on Humanoid, Nanotechnology, Information Technology, Communication and Control, Environment, and Management (HNICEM)*, 1-5. DOI: 10.1109/HNICEM51456.2020.9400034

Revano, T. F., & Garcia, M. B. (2021). Designing Human-Centered Learning Analytics Dashboard for Higher Education Using a Participatory Design Approach. *2021 IEEE 13th International Conference on Humanoid, Nanotechnology, Information Technology, Communication and Control, Environment, and Management (HNICEM)*, 1-5. DOI: 10.1109/HNICEM54116.2021.9731917

Riebe, L., Girardi, A., & Whitsed, C. (2016). A Systematic Literature Review of Teamwork Pedagogy in Higher Education. *Small Group Research*, *47*(6), 619–664. DOI: 10.1177/1046496416665221

Riera-Negre, L., Hidalgo-Andrade, P., Rosselló, M., & Verger, S. (2024). Exploring support strategies and training needs for teachers in navigating illness, bereavement, and death-related challenges in the classroom: A scoping review supporting teachers in classroom grief and loss. *Frontiers in Education*, *9*, 1328247. Advance online publication. DOI: 10.3389/feduc.2024.1328247

Rintala, H., & Nokelainen, P. (2019). Vocational Education and Learners' Experienced Workplace Curriculum. *Vocations and Learning*, *13*(1), 113–130. DOI: 10.1007/s12186-019-09229-w

Risko, E. F., & Gilbert, S. J. (2016). Cognitive Offloading. *Trends in Cognitive Sciences*, *20*(9), 679–688. DOI: 10.1016/j.tics.2016.07.002 PMID: 27542527

Ritter, S., Yudelson, M., Fancsali, S. E., & Berman, S. R. (2016). How mastery learning works at scale. In *Proceedings of the Third (2016) ACM Conference on Learning @ Scale* (pp. 71–79). ACM. https://doi.org/DOI: 10.1145/2876034.2876039

Riza, A. N. I., Hidayah, I., & Santosa, P. I. (2023). Use of Chatbots in E-Learning Context: A Systematic Review. *2023 IEEE World AI IoT Congress (AIIoT)*, 0819-0824. https://doi.org/DOI: 10.1109/AIIoT58121.2023.10174319

Rocheleau, J. N., Chalghoumi, H., Jutai, J., Farrell, S., Lachapelle, Y., & Cobigo, V. (2021). Caregivers' role in cybersecurity for aging information technology users with intellectual disabilities. *Cyberpsychology, Behavior, and Social Networking*, *24*(9), 624–629. DOI: 10.1089/cyber.2020.0572 PMID: 34182769

Rodrigues, M., Silva, R., Borges, A. P., Franco, M., & Oliveira, C. (2024). Artificial intelligence: threat or asset to academic integrity? A bibliometric analysis. *Kybernetes, ahead-of-p*(ahead-of-print). DOI: 10.1108/K-09-2023-1666

Rodrigues, R. (2020). Legal and Human Rights Issues of AI: Gaps, Challenges and Vulnerabilities. *Journal of Responsible Technology*, *4*, 1–12. DOI: 10.1016/j.jrt.2020.100005

Rodríguez-Calderón, R., & González-García, S. (2024). Learning Based on Artificial Intelligence for Engineering Courses. *2024 IEEE World Engineering Education Conference (EDUNINE)*, 1-5. DOI: 10.1109/EDUNINE60625.2024.10500547

Roll, I., & Wylie, R. (2016). Evolución y revolución de la inteligencia artificial en la educación. *Revista Internacional de Inteligencia Artificial en Educación*, *26*(2), 582–599. DOI: 10.1007/s40593-016-0110-3

Romero, M., Galy, I., Camponovo, J., Tressols, F., & Urmeneta, A. (2024). International initiatives and regional ecosystems for supporting artificial intelligence acculturation. In *Creative applications of artificial intelligence in education* (pp. 75–88). Springer Nature Switzerland. DOI: 10.1007/978-3-031-55272-4_6

Rott, K. J., Lao, L., Petridou, E., & Schmidt-Hertha, B. (2022). Needs and Requirements for an Additional AI Qualification During Dual Vocational Training: Results from Studies of Apprentices and Teachers. *Computers and Education: Artificial Intelligence*, *3*, 1–10. DOI: 10.1016/j.caeai.2022.100102

RoX. (2024). Digital divide in AI education: Creating equal opportunities. *AI Proficiency Hub #AICompetence.org*. https://aicompetence.org/digital-divide-in-ai-education/?

Roy, A. D., Das, D., & Mondal, H. (2024). Efficacy of ChatGPT in solving attitude, ethics, and communication case scenario used for competency-based medical education in India: A case study. *Journal of Education and Health Promotion*, *13*(1). Advance online publication. DOI: 10.4103/jehp.jehp_625_23 PMID: 38545309

Roy, D., & Putatunda, T. (2023). From Textbooks to Chatbots: Integrating AI in English literature classrooms of India. *Journal of e-Learning and Knowledge Society - SIe-L - the Italian e-Learning Association.* DOI: 10.20368/1971-8829/1135860

Rozado, D. (2020). Wide range screening of algorithmic bias in word embedding models using large sentiment lexicons reveals underreported bias types. *PLoS One, 15*(4), e0231189. DOI: 10.1371/journal.pone.0231189 PMID: 32315320

Rožman, M., Oreški, D., & Tominc, P. (2023). Artificial-Intelligence-Supported Reduction of Employees' Workload to Increase the Company's Performance in Today's VUCA Environment. *Sustainability (Basel), 15*(6), 1–21. DOI: 10.3390/su15065019

Rudin, C. (2019). Stop explaining black box machine learning models for high stakes decisions and use interpretable models instead. *Nature Machine Intelligence, 1*(5), 206–215. DOI: 10.1038/s42256-019-0048-x PMID: 35603010

Rusandi, M. A., Ahman, , Saripah, I., Khairun, D. Y., & Mutmainnah, . (2023). No worries with ChatGPT: Building bridges between artificial intelligence and education with critical thinking soft skills. *Journal of Public Health (Oxford, England), 45*(3), e602–e603. DOI: 10.1093/pubmed/fdad049 PMID: 37099761

Russell, S., & Norvig, P. (2021). *Artificial Intelligence: A Modern Approach.* Pearson.

Rütti-Joy, O., Winder, G., & Biedermann, H. (2023). Building AI Literacy for Sustainable Teacher Education. *Zeitschrift für Hochschulentwicklung, 18*(4), 175–189. DOI: 10.21240/zfhe/18-04/10

Ryan, M. (2011). Evaluating Portfolio Use as a Tool for Assessment and Professional Development in Graduate Nursing Education. *Journal of Professional Nursing, 27*(2), 84–91. DOI: 10.1016/j.profnurs.2010.09.008 PMID: 21420040

Saeed, S., Rana, O., & Dhanaraj, R. K. (2024). *Higher education and quality assurance practices.* IGI Global. DOI: 10.4018/979-8-3693-6765-0

Sağdıç, Z. A., & Sani-Bozkurt, S. (2020). Otizm spektrum bozukluğu ve yapay zekâ uygulamaları. *Açıköğretim Uygulamaları ve Araştırmaları Dergisi, 6*(3), 92–111.

Sah, C. K., Xiaoli, L., Islam, M. M., & Islam, M. K. (2024). Navigating the AI Frontier: A Critical Literature Review on Integrating Artificial Intelligence into Software Engineering Education. *2024 36th International Conference on Software Engineering Education and Training*, 1-5. DOI: 10.1109/CSEET62301.2024.10663054

Saha, C. N., & Bhattacharya, S. (2011). Intellectual Property Rights: An Overview and Implications in Pharmaceutical Industry. *Journal of Advanced Pharmaceutical Technology & Research, 2*(2), 88–93. DOI: 10.4103/2231-4040.82952 PMID: 22171299

Salas-Pilco, S., Xiao, K., & Hu, X. (2022). Artificial Intelligence and Learning Analytics in Teacher Education: A Systematic Review. *Education Sciences, 12*(8), 1–18. DOI: 10.3390/educsci12080569

Salazar, L. R., Peeples, S. F., & Brooks, M. E. (2024). Generative AI Ethical Considerations and Discriminatory Biases on Diverse Students Within the Classroom. In *Advances in Educational Technologies and Instructional Design* (pp. 191-213). IGI Global. DOI: 10.4018/979-8-3693-0831-8.ch010

Salend, S. J. (2011). *Creating inclusive classrooms: Effective and reflective practices* (7th ed.). Pearson.

Salinas-Navarro, D. E., Vilalta-Perdomo, E., Michel-Villarreal, R., & Montesinos, L. (2024). Using Generative Artificial Intelligence Tools to Explain and Enhance Experiential Learning for Authentic Assessment. *Education Sciences, 14*(1), 1–24. DOI: 10.3390/educsci14010083

Sallam, M. (2023). ChatGPT utility in healthcare education, research, and practice: Systematic review on the promising perspectives and valid concerns. *Health Care, 11*(6), 887. DOI: 10.3390/healthcare11060887 PMID: 36981544

Sánchez, M. M. (2024). La inteligencia artificial como recurso docente: Usos y posibilidades para el profesorado. *Educar, 60*(1), 33–47. DOI: 10.5565/rev/educar.1810

Sánchez-Prieto, J. C., Izquierdo-Álvarez, V., del Moral-Marcos, M. T., & Martínez-Abad, F. (2024). Generative artificial intelligence for self-learning in higher education: Design and validation of an example machine. *RIED-Revista Iberoamericana de Educación a Distancia, 28*(1). Advance online publication. DOI: 10.5944/ried.28.1.41548

Sanfo, J.-B. M. B. (2023). Factors Explaining Rural-Urban Learning Achievement Inequalities in Primary Education in Benin, Burkina Faso, Togo, and Cameroon. *International Journal of Educational Research Open, 4*, 1–11. DOI: 10.1016/j.ijedro.2023.100234

Santiago, C. S., Jr., Embang, S. I., Conlu, M. T. N., Acanto, R. B., Lausa, S. M., Ambojia, K. W. P., Laput, E. Y., Aperocho, M. D. B.,Malabag, B. A., & Balilo, B. B., Jr. (2023). Utilization of writing assistance tools in research in selected higher learning institutions in the philippines: A text mining analysis. International Journal of Learning, Teaching and Educational Research, 22(11), 259–284. . 22. 11. 14DOI: 10.26803/ijlter

Santos, P., Urgel, K., & Moreno, V. (2024). Generative Artificial Intelligence in Teaching and Learning of ICT Engineering Education: A Literature Review and Illustrative Scenarios. *2024 47th MIPRO ICT and Electronics Convention (MIPRO)*, 1338-1343. DOI: 10.1109/MIPRO60963.2024.10569779

Santra, P., & Majhi, D. (2023). Scholarly Communication and Machine-Generated Text: Is it Finally AI vs AI in Plagiarism Detection. *Journal of Information and Knowledge, 60*(3), 175–183. DOI: 10.17821/srels/2023/v60i3/171028

Sanusi, I., Ayanwale, M., & Chiu, T. (2024). Investigating the moderating effects of social good and confidence on teachers intention to prepare school students for artificial intelligence education. *Education and Information Technologies, 29*(1), 273–295. DOI: 10.1007/s10639-023-12250-1

Sapienza, M., Nurchis, M. C., Riccardi, M. T., Bouland, C., Jevtić, M., & Damiani, G. (2022). The adoption of digital technologies and artificial intelligence in urban health: A scoping review. *Sustainability (Basel), 14*(12), 7480. DOI: 10.3390/su14127480

Sardi, J., Candra, O., Yuliana, D. F., Yanto, D. T. P., & Eliza, F. (2025). How Generative AI Influences Students' Self-Regulated Learning and Critical Thinking Skills? A Systematic Review. *International Journal of Engineering Pedagogy, 15*(1).

Sari, H., Tumanggor, B., & Efron, D. (2024). Improving Educational Outcomes Through Adaptive Learning Systems using AI. *International Transactions on Artificial Intelligence*, *3*(1), 21–31. DOI: 10.33050/italic.v3i1.647

Saroğlu, Ö. C. (2024). Players Retell This Story. In *Advances in human and social aspects of technology book series* (pp. 133–158). DOI: 10.4018/979-8-3693-7235-7.ch006

Sartor, G., & Lagioia, F. (2020). *The Impact of the General Data Protection Regulation (GDPR) on Artificial Intelligence*. European Parliamentary Research Service., DOI: 10.2861/293

Saxena, P., Saxena, V., Pandey, A., Flato, U., & Shukla, K. (2023). *Multiple aspects of artificial intelligence*. Book Saga Publications. DOI: 10.60148/muasartificialintelligence

Saylam, S., Duman, N., Yildirim, Y., & Satsevich, K. (2023). Empowering education with AI: Addressing ethical concerns. *London Journal of Social Sciences*, (6), 39–48. DOI: 10.31039/ljss.2023.6.103

Scassellati, B., Admoni, H., & Matarić, M. (2012). Robots for use in autism research. *Annual Review of Biomedical Engineering*, *14*(1), 275–294. DOI: 10.1146/annurev-bioeng-071811-150036 PMID: 22577778

Schechner, S. (2023). ChatGPT Ban Lifted in Italy After Data-Privacy Concessions. Wall Street J. https://www.wsj.com/articles/chatgpt-ban-lifted-in-italy-after-data-privacy-concessions-d03d53e7

Schleiss, J., Hense, J., Kist, A., Schlingensiepen, J., & Stober, S. (2022). Teaching AI Competencies in Engineering Using Projects and Open Educational Resources. *Towards a new future in engineering education, new scenarios that european alliances of tech universities open up*, 1592-1600. DOI: 10.5821/conference-9788412322262.1258

Schwab, K. (2016). *The fourth industrial revolution*. Crown Publishing Group.

Schwartz, D. L., & Rogers, M. (2022). "Inventorless" Inventions? The Constitutional Conundrum of AI-Produced Inventions. *SSRN*, *35*(2), 531–479. https://jolt.law.harvard.edu/assets/articlePDFs/v35/3.-Schwartz-Rogers-Inventorless-Inventions.pdf. DOI: 10.2139/ssrn.4025434

Scott, L. M., Wilder, T. L., Zaugg, T., & Romualdo, A. (2024). Enhancing Special Education Using AI. *Advances in Educational Technologies and Instructional Design Book Series*, 45–78. https://doi.org/ DOI: 10.4018/979-8-3693-5538-1.ch002

See, B. H., Gorard, S., Lu, B., Dong, L., & Siddiqui, N. (2022). Is Technology Always Helpful?: A Critical Review of the Impact on Learning Outcomes of Education Technology in Supporting Formative Assessment in Schools. *Research Papers in Education*, *37*(6), 1064–1096. DOI: 10.1080/02671522.2021.1907778

Segarra, J. R., Mengual-Andres, S., & Cortijo Ocaña, A. (Eds.). (2024). *Educational Innovation to Address Complex Societal Challenges*. IGI Global., DOI: 10.4018/979-8-3693-3073-9

Selwyn, N. (2019). *Should robots replace teachers?: AI and the future of education*. John Wiley & Sons.

Semrl, N., Feigl, S., Taumberger, N., Bracic, T., Fluhr, H., Blockeel, C., & Kollmann, M. (2023). AI language models in human reproduction research: Exploring ChatGPT's potential to assist academic writing. *Human Reproduction (Oxford, England)*, *38*(12), 2281–2288. DOI: 10.1093/humrep/dead207 PMID: 37833847

Şen, N., & Akbay, T. (2023). Artificial intelligence and innovative applications in special education. *Instructional Technology and Lifelong Learning*, *4*(2), 176–199. DOI: 10.52911/itall.1297978

Seo, K., Tang, J., Roll, I., Fels, S., & Yoon, D. (2021). The impact of artificial intelligence on learner–instructor interaction in online learning. *International Journal of Educational Technology in Higher Education*, *18*(1), 54. DOI: 10.1186/s41239-021-00292-9 PMID: 34778540

Serdyukov, P. (2017). Innovation in Education: What Works, What Doesn't, and What to Do About it? *Journal of Research in Innovative Teaching & Learning*, *10*(1), 4–33. DOI: 10.1108/JRIT-10-2016-0007

Setchi, R., Spasić, I., Morgan, J., Harrison, C., & Corken, R. (2021). Artificial Intelligence for Patent Prior Art Searching. *World Patent Information*, *64*, 1–12. DOI: 10.1016/j.wpi.2021.102021

Seth. (2024, June 17). Run AI models offline: No internet required. NoCode MBA. https://www.nocode.mba/articles/ai-mac

Shah, V. M., & Shah, D. (2023). Impact of Digitalisation in Education-a Literature Review Analysis. *Towards Excellence*, 333-343. https://doi.org/DOI: 10.37867/TE150234

Shaheen, N., Shaheen, A., Ramadan, A., Hefnawy, M. T., Ramadan, A., Ibrahim, I. A., Hassanein, M. E., Ashour, M. E., & Flouty, O. (2023). Appraising Systematic Reviews: A Comprehensive Guide to Ensuring Validity and Reliability. *Frontiers in Research Metrics and Analytics*, *8*, 1268045. Advance online publication. DOI: 10.3389/frma.2023.1268045 PMID: 38179256

Shahzad, M. F., Xu, S., Lim, W. M., Yang, X., & Khan, Q. R. (2024). Artificial intelligence and social media on academic performance and mental well-being: Student perceptions of positive impact in the age of smart learning. *Heliyon*, *10*(8), e29523. DOI: 10.1016/j.heliyon.2024.e29523 PMID: 38665566

Shahzalal, M., & Adnan, H. M. (2022). Attitude, Self-Control, and Prosocial Norm to Predict Intention to Use Social Media Responsibly: From Scale to Model Fit towards a Modified Theory of Planned Behavior. *Sustainability (Basel)*, *14*(16), 1–38. DOI: 10.3390/su14169822

Shanmugasundaram, M., & Tamilarasu, A. (2023). The impact of digital technology, social media, and artificial intelligence on cognitive functions: A review. *Frontiers in Cognition*, *2*, 1203077. DOI: 10.3389/fcogn.2023.1203077

Shead, S. (2020). How a Computer Algorithm Caused a Grading Crisis in British Schools. *CNBC*. https://www.cnbc.com/2020/08/21/computer-algorithm-caused-a-grading-crisis-in-british-schools.html

Shengelia, R., Gabisonia, L., Tsiklauri-Shengelia, Z., & Shengelia, N. (2024). Assessing AI Dependency: A Multifactorial Analysis and AIDI Index. *Proceedings of Azerbaijan High Technical Educational Institutions Journal*.

Shih, P., Lin, C., Wu, L., & Yu, C. (2021). Learning Ethics in AI—Teaching Non-Engineering Undergraduates through Situated Learning. *Sustainability (Basel)*, *13*(7), 3718. DOI: 10.3390/su13073718

Shiohira, K. (n.d.). *Understanding the Impact of artificial intelligence on skills Development. Education 2030.* https://eric.ed.gov/?id=ED612439

Shiohira, K., & Holmes, W. (2023). Proceed with caution: The pitfalls and potential of AI and education. In Araya, D., & Marber, P. (Eds.), *Augmented education in the global age: Artificial intelligence and the future of learning and work* (pp. 137–156). Routledge.

Shiri, R., El-Metwally, A., Sallinen, M., Pöyry, M., Härmä, M., & Toppinen-Tanner, S. (2023). The Role of Continuing Professional Training or Development in Maintaining Current Employment: A Systematic Review. *Health Care*, *11*(21), 1–17. DOI: 10.3390/healthcare11212900 PMID: 37958044

Shoaib, M., Sayed, N., Singh, J., Shafi, J., Khan, S., & Ali, F. (2024). AI Student Success Predictor: Enhancing Personalized Learning in Campus Management Systems. *Computers in Human Behavior*, *158*, 108301. DOI: 10.1016/j.chb.2024.108301

Shobha, J. M., & T.Anbu. (2023). *Global Trends in teaching English Language and Literature*. Alborear (OPC) Pvt. Ltd.

Shrestha, Y. R., Ben-Menahem, S. M., & Von Krogh, G. (2019). Organizational decision-making structures in the age of artificial intelligence. *California Management Review*, *61*(4), 66–83. DOI: 10.1177/0008125619862257

Shvedchykova, I., Burger, W., & Soloshych, I. (2023). Research-Based Learning: Integration of Artificial Intelligence into the Curriculum of Electrical Engineering Students. *2023 IEEE 5th International Conference on Modern Electrical and Energy System (MEES)*, 1-5. DOI: 10.1109/MEES61502.2023.10402542

Sidorkin, A. M. (2024). *Embracing chatbots in higher education: The Use of Artificial Intelligence in Teaching, Administration, and Scholarship*. Taylor & Francis. DOI: 10.4324/9781032686028

Siegel, H. (1987). Critical thinking as an intellectual right. *Analytic Teaching*, *8*(1), 19–24.

Siegle, D. (2023). A role for ChatGPT and AI in gifted education. *Gifted Child Today*, *46*(3), 211–219. DOI: 10.1177/10762175231168443

Silva, A. O., & Janes, D. S. (2023). Artificial Intelligence in Education: What are the Opportunities and Challenges? *Review of Artificial Intelligence in Education*, *5*(00), e018. Advance online publication. DOI: 10.37497/rev.artif.intell.educ.v5i00.18

Singer, N. (2018, July 26). Amazon's facial recognition wrongly identifies 28 lawmakers, ACLU says. *The New York Times*. Retrieved February 7, 2024 from https://www.nytimes.com/2018/07/26/technology/amazon-aclu-facial-recognition-congress.html

Singh, A., Lakhera, G., Ojha, M., Mishra, A. K., & Nain, A. (2024). Balancing Innovation with Responsibility. In *Advances in human and social aspects of technology book series* (pp. 467–500). DOI: 10.4018/979-8-3693-4147-6.ch020

Singh, T. M., Reddy, C. K. K., Murthy, B. V. R., Nag, A., & Doss, S. (2025). AI and Education: Bridging the Gap to Personalized, Efficient, and Accessible Learning. In *Advances in Educational Technologies and Instructional Design* (pp. 131-160). IGI Global. DOI: 10.4018/979-8-3693-8151-9.ch005

Singh, A., Hallihosur, S., & Rangan, L. (2009). Changing Landscape in Biotechnology Patenting. *World Patent Information*, *31*(3), 219–225. DOI: 10.1016/j.wpi.2009.03.004

Singh, S. V., & Hiran, K. K. (2022). The impact of AI on teaching and learning in higher education technology. *Journal of Higher Education Theory and Practice*, *22*(13), 135–148. DOI: 10.33423/jhetp. v22i13.5514

Sirghi, N., Voicu, M., Noja, G. G., & Gurita, O. S. (2024). Challenges of artificial intelligence on the learning process in higher education. *Amfiteatru Economic*, *26*, 53–70. DOI: 10.24818/EA/2024/65/53

Slack, H. R., & Priestley, M. (2023). Online Learning and Assessment During the COVID-19 Pandemic: Exploring the Impact on Undergraduate Student Well-Being. *Assessment & Evaluation in Higher Education*, *48*(3), 333–349. DOI: 10.1080/02602938.2022.2076804

Slade, N., Eisenhower, A., Carter, A. S., & Blacher, J. (2018). Satisfaction with individualized education programs among parents of young children with ASD. *Exceptional Children*, *84*(3), 242–260. DOI: 10.1177/0014402917742923

Slavinska, A., Palkova, K., Grigoroviča, E., Edelmers, E., & Pētersons, A. (2024). Narrative Review of Legal Aspects in the Integration of Simulation-Based Education into Medical and Healthcare Curricula. *Laws*, *13*(2), 1–20. DOI: 10.3390/laws13020015

Slomp, E. M., Ropelato, D., Bonatti, C., & da Silva, M. D. (2024). Adaptive Learning in Engineering Courses: How Artificial Intelligence (AI) Can Improve Academic Outcomes. *2024 IEEE World Engineering Education Conference (EDUNINE)*, 1-6. DOI: 10.1109/EDUNINE60625.2024.10500580

Smith, H. (2020). Algorithmic bias: Should students pay the price? *AI & Society*, *35*(4), 1077–1078. DOI: 10.1007/s00146-020-01054-3 PMID: 32952313

Smith, J., & Jones, R. (2020). AI in Education: Promises and Pitfalls. *Educational Technology Research and Development*, *48*(2), 35–50.

Smith, T. E. (2015). *Serving students with special needs: A practical guide for administrators*. Routledge. DOI: 10.4324/9781315818634

Smutny, P., & Schreiberova, P. (2020). Chatbots for Learning: A Review of Educational Chatbots for the Facebook Messenger. *Computers & Education*, *151*, 103862. DOI: 10.1016/j.compedu.2020.103862

Snyder, H. (2019). Literature Review as a Research Methodology: An Overview and Guidelines. *Journal of Business Research*, *104*, 333–339. DOI: 10.1016/j.jbusres.2019.07.039

Sohrabi, C., Franchi, T., Mathew, G., Kerwan, A., Nicola, M., Griffin, M., Agha, M., & Agha, R. (2021). PRISMA 2020 Statement: What's New and the Importance of Reporting Guidelines. *International Journal of Surgery*, *88*, 105918. DOI: 10.1016/j.ijsu.2021.105918 PMID: 33789825

Song, B., & Koo, A. (2022). Paradigm shift: Artificial intelligence, contemporary art, and implications for gifted arts education. *Journal of Gifted Education in Arts*, *8*, 5–38.

Soomro, S. A., Casakin, H., Nanjappan, V., & Georgiev, G. V. (2023). Makerspaces Fostering Creativity: A Systematic Literature Review. *Journal of Science Education and Technology*, *32*(4), 530–548. DOI: 10.1007/s10956-023-10041-4

Soori, M., Jough, F. K. G., Dastres, R., & Arezoo, B. (2024). Robotical Automation in CNC Machine Tools: A Review. *Acta Mechanica et Automatica*, *18*(3), 434–450. DOI: 10.2478/ama-2024-0048

Southworth, J., Migliaccio, K., Glover, J., Glover, J. N., Reed, D., McCarty, C., Brendemuhl, J., & Thomas, A. (2023). Developing a Model for AI Across the Curriculum: Transforming the Higher Education Landscape via Innovation in AI Literacy. *Computers and Education: Artificial Intelligence*, *4*, 1–10. DOI: 10.1016/j.caeai.2023.100127

Sparrow, B., Liu, J., & Wegner, D. M. (2011). Google Effects on Memory: Cognitive Consequences of Having Information at Our Fingertips. *Science*, *333*(6043), 776–778. DOI: 10.1126/science.1207745 PMID: 21764755

Sperling, K., Stenberg, C.-J., McGrath, C., Åkerfeldt, A., Heintz, F., & Stenliden, L. (2024). In Search of Artificial Intelligence (AI) Literacy in Teacher Education: A Scoping Review. *Computers and Education Open*, *6*, 1–13. DOI: 10.1016/j.caeo.2024.100169

Spiro, R., Coulson, R., Feltovich, P., & Anderson, D. (1988). Cognitive flexibility theory: Advanced knowledge acquisition in ill-structured domains. In V. Patel (Ed.), Tenth annual conference of the cognitive science society (pp. 375–383). Hillsdale, NJ: Erlbaum.

Sreenivasan, A., & Suresh, M. (2024). Design Thinking and Artificial Intelligence: A Systematic Literature Review Exploring Synergies. *International Journal of Innovation Studies*, *8*(3), 297–312. DOI: 10.1016/j.ijis.2024.05.001

Sridhar, V. (2024). *ChatGPT and artificial Intelligence*. Academic Guru Publishing House.

Stanford Teaching Commons. (2024). Integrating AI Into Assignments. *Stanford University*. https://teachingcommons.stanford.edu/teaching-guides/artificial-intelligence-teaching-guide/integrating-ai-assignments

Stephenson, S., Rogers, O., Ivy, C., Barron, R., & Burke, J. (2020). Designing Effective Capstone Experiences and Projects for Entry-Level Doctoral Students in Occupational Therapy: One Program's Approaches and Lessons Learned. *The Open Journal of Occupational Therapy*, *8*(3), 1–12. DOI: 10.15453/2168-6408.1727 PMID: 33552752

Stiles, B. L., Wong, N. C. W., & LaBeff, E. E. (2018). College cheating thirty years later: The role of academic entitlement. *Deviant Behavior*, *39*(7), 823–834. DOI: 10.1080/01639625.2017.1335520

Stivers, S. (2018). AI and Bias in University Admissions. *ISM Insights*. https://www.ism.edu/ism-insights/ai-and-bias-in-university-admissions-3.html

Stojanov, A. (2023). Learning with ChatGPT 3.5 as a more knowledgeable other: An autoethnographic study. *International Journal of Educational Technology in Higher Education*, *20*(1), 35. DOI: 10.1186/s41239-023-00404-7

Stolpe, K., & Hallström, J. (2024). Artificial Intelligence Literacy for Technology Education. *Computers and Education Open*, *6*, 1–8. DOI: 10.1016/j.caeo.2024.100159

Su, J., & Yang, W. (2023). A systematic review of integrating computational thinking in early childhood education. *Computers and Education Open*, *4*, 100122. DOI: 10.1016/j.caeo.2023.100122

Summak, M. S., & Çelik-Şahin, Ç. (2014). Examining the Opinions About Determining Standards at Science and Arts Centers. *Asian Journal of Instruction*, *2*(1), 1–15. https://dergipark.org.tr/tr/download/article-file/17637

Sun, L., & Zhou, L. (2024). Generative artificial intelligence attitude analysis of under graduate students and their precise improvement strategies: A differential analysis of multifactorial influences. *Education and Information Technologies*. Advance online publication. DOI: 10.1007/s10639-024-13236-3

Sun, S., Zhang, C., Huang, L., & Li, J. (2019). Context-aware response generation for multi-turn conversation with deep reinforcement learning. *IEEE Access : Practical Innovations, Open Solutions*, *7*, 49918–49927.

Susskind, R., & Susskind, D. (2022). *The future of the professions: How technology will transform the work of human experts* (2nd ed.). Oxford University Press.

Swiecki, Z., Khosravi, H., Chen, G., Martinez-Maldonado, R., Lodge, J. M., Milligan, S., Selwyn, N., & Gašević, D. (2022). Assessment in the Age of Artificial Intelligence. *Computers and Education: Artificial Intelligence*, *3*, 1–10. DOI: 10.1016/j.caeai.2022.100075

Tabier, E., & Bakanay, Ç. D. (2023). Museum Education Environments and Artificial Intelligence Applications in Preschool Education. *Journal Of Social Humanities and Administrative Sciences*, *65*(65), 3082–3088. DOI: 10.29228/JOSHAS.70500

Tamrin, S. I., Omar, N. F., Kamaruzaman, K. N., Zaghlol, A. K., & Aziz, M. R. A. (2024). Evaluating the Impact of AI Dependency on Cognitive Ability among Generation Z in Higher Educational Institutions: A Conceptual Framework. *Information Management and Business Review*, *16*(3), 1027–1033. DOI: 10.22610/imbr.v16i3S(I)a.4191

Tang, C., Mao, S., Naumann, S. E., & Xing, Z. (2022). Improving student creativity through digital technology products: A literature review. *Thinking Skills and Creativity*, *44*, 101032. DOI: 10.1016/j.tsc.2022.101032

Tang, L., & Su, Y.-S. (2024). Ethical Implications and Principles of Using Artificial Intelligence Models in the Classroom: A Systematic Literature Review. *International Journal of Interactive Multimedia and Artificial Intelligence*, *8*(5), 25–36. DOI: 10.9781/ijimai.2024.02.010

Tarafdar, S., Afroz, S., & Ashrafuzzaman, M. (2025). Artificial Intelligence and the Future of Education in Bangladesh. In *Advances in Educational Technologies and Instructional Design* (pp. 287-320). IGI Global. DOI: 10.4018/979-8-3693-7949-3.ch011

Tarasenko, L. (2023). Legislative Reforms on Patents, Utility Models and Industrial Designs in Ukraine. *Competition and Intellectual Property Law in Ukraine*, 373-414. DOI: 10.1007/978-3-662-66101-7_15

Tatar, C., Jiang, S., Rosé, C., & Chao, J. (2024). Exploring Teachers Views and Confidence in the Integration of an Artificial Intelligence Curriculum into Their Classrooms: A Case Study of Curricular Co-Design Program. *International Journal of Artificial Intelligence in Education*. Advance online publication. DOI: 10.1007/s40593-024-00404-2

Taylor, J. (2023). Digital tools, rhetoric, and meaning-making: A critical exploration of addressing the digital divide and accessibility to improve our digital landscape. https://doi.org/DOI: 10.31274/td-20240329-24

Taylor, W., Benson, G. M., & Hendon, M. (2025). An Examination of Phenomenological Research Design for Doctoral Students. In *Qualitative Research Methods for Dissertation Research* (pp. 279-316). IGI Global Scientific Publishing.

Tech, G. (2024). Office of Graduate Education, Graduate Student Government Association, Office of Research, Responsible Conduct of Research Office, & Directors of Graduate Programs. *Effective and Responsible use of AI in research: Guidance for performing graduate research and in writing dissertations, theses, and manuscripts for publications* (B. Ferri, Ed.). https://grad.gatech.edu/sites/default/files/documents/Guidance%20for%20Effective%20and%20Responsible%20Use%20of%20AI%20in%20Research.pdf

Templier, M., & Paré, G. (2015). A Framework for Guiding and Evaluating Literature Reviews. *Communications of the Association for Information Systems, 37.* Advance online publication. DOI: 10.17705/1CAIS.03706

Tenhunen, S., Männistö, T., Luukkainen, M., & Ihantola, P. (2023). A Systematic Literature Review of Capstone Courses in Software Engineering. *Information and Software Technology, 159,* 1–21. DOI: 10.1016/j.infsof.2023.107191

TESDA. (2010). The Dual Training System in the Philippines. https://tesda.gov.ph/about/tesda/91

Thomas, T. (2024). The Role of Artificial Intelligence in Formal and Informal Education for Students. *International Journal for Research in Applied Science and Engineering Technology, 12*(3), 69–71. DOI: 10.22214/ijraset.2024.58738

Thorp, H. H. (2023). ChatGPT is Fun, But not an Author. *Science, 379*(6630), 313. DOI: 10.1126/science.adg7879 PMID: 36701446

Tias, I. W. U., Izzatika, A., & Perdana, R. (2022). Empowerment of Critical and Creative Thinking (CCT) Skills Through Student Worksheets Based on Inquiry Social Complexity (ISC). *WSEAS Transactions on Environment and Development, 18,* 865–872. DOI: 10.37394/232015.2022.18.81

Tlili, A., Agyemang, M., Lo, C. K., Bozkurt, A., Burgos, D., Bonk, C. J., Costello, E., Mishra, S., Stracke, C. M., & Huang, R. (2024). Taming the Monster: How can Open Education Promote the Effective and Safe use of Generative AI in Education? *Journal of Learning for Development, 11*(3), 398–413. DOI: 10.56059/jl4d.v11i3.1657

Tomczyk, P., Brüggemann, P., & Vrontis, D. (2024). AI meets academia: transforming systematic literature reviews. EuroMed Journal of Business, Vol. ahead-of-print No. ahead-of-print. DOI: 10.1108/EMJB-03-2024-0055

Tooliqa. (2023, March 27). The Ethical Dilemma of Generative AI. Tooliqa Insights. Retrieved from https://www.tooli.qa/insights/the-ethical-dilemma-of-generative-ai

Topal, A. D., Dilek Eren, C., & Kolburan Geçer, A. (2021). Chatbot Application in a 5th Grade Science Course. *Education and Information Technologies*, *26*(5), 6241–6265. DOI: 10.1007/s10639-021-10627-8 PMID: 34177344

Topping, K. J., Gehringer, E., Khosravi, H., Gudipati, S., Jadhav, K., & Susarla, S. (2025). Enhancing Peer Assessment with Artificial Intelligence. *International Journal of Educational Technology in Higher Education*, *22*(1), 1–33. DOI: 10.1186/s41239-024-00501-1

Treceñe, J. K. D. (2022). COVID-19 and remote learning in the Philippine basic education system: Experiences of teachers, parents, and students. In *Socioeconomic Inclusion During an Era of Online Education* (pp. 92-110). IGI Global.

Treceñe, J. K. D. (2021). The digital transformation strategies of the Philippines from 1992 to 2022: A review. *Eng. Technol. Rev*, *2*(1), 8–13. DOI: 10.47285/etr.v2i1.66

Treceñe, J. K. D., Batan, M. B., & Abines, A. L. (2023). Development of a digital snake and ladder game as a strategic intervention material for basic education. *Journal of Engineering Science and Technology*, *18*, 48–58.

Trevisan, O., Christensen, R., Drossel, K., Friesen, S., Forkosh-Baruch, A., & Phillips, M. (2024). Drivers of Digital Realities for Ongoing Teacher Professional Learning. *Technology Knowledge And Learning*, *29*(4), 1851–1868. DOI: 10.1007/s10758-024-09771-0

Triansyah, F. A., Muhammad, I., Rabuandika, A., Siregar, K. D. P., Teapon, N., & Assabana, M. S. (2023). Bibliometric Analysis: Artificial Intelligence (AI) in High School Education. *Jurnal Imiah Pendidikan dan Pembelajaran, 7*(1), 112-123. https://doi.org/DOI: 10.23887/jipp.v7i1.59718

Tripathi, C. R. (2024). Awareness of Artificial Intelligence (AI) among Undergraduate Students. *NPRC Journal of Multidisciplinary Research., 1*(7), 126–142. DOI: 10.3126/nprcjmr.v1i7.72478

Triplett, W. J. (2023). Impact of Technology Integration in STEM Education. *Cybersecurity and Innovative Technology Journal, 1*(1), 16–22. DOI: 10.53889/citj.v1i1.295

Tsay, M.-Y., & Liu, Z.-W. (2020). Analysis of the Patent Cooperation Network in Global Artificial Intelligence Technologies Based on the Assignees. *World Patent Information, 63*, 1–17. DOI: 10.1016/j.wpi.2020.102000

Tsouktakou, A., Hamouroudis, A., & Horti, A. (2024). The use of artificial intelligence in the education of people with visual impairment. *World Journal of Advanced Engineering Technology and Sciences, 13*(1), 734–744. DOI: 10.30574/wjaets.2024.13.1.0481

Tubella, A. A., Mora-Cantallops, M., & Nieves, J. C. (2023). How to teach responsible AI in Higher Education: Challenges and opportunities. *Ethics and Information Technology, 26*(1), 3. Advance online publication. DOI: 10.1007/s10676-023-09733-7

Turing, A. M. (1950). Computing machinery and intelligence. *Mind, 59*(236), 433–460. DOI: 10.1093/mind/LIX.236.433

Ugwu, C. N., & Opah, A. C. (2023). Use of Boolean Search Strategy for Accessing the Databases of University of Technology Libraries by Postgraduate Students in South-East, Nigeria. *Journal of Library Services and Technologies*, 5(2), 24–35. DOI: 10.47524/jlst.v5i2.25

Ullah, M., Naeem, S. B., & Boulos, M. N. K. (2024). Assessing the guidelines on the use of generative artificial intelligence tools in universities: A survey of the world's top 50 universities. *Big Data and Cognitive Computing*, 8(12), 194. DOI: 10.3390/bdcc8120194

UNESCO (2023). *AI and education: Guidance for policy makers*. https://doi.org/DOI: 10.54675/PCSP7350

UNESCO (Ed.). (2023b). *Technology in Education: A Case Study on Singapore.*, DOI: 10.54676/HOOV5879

UNESCO. (2003). *Overcoming exclusion through inclusive approaches in education: A challenge and a vision*. UNESCO.

UNESCO. (2005). *Guidelines for inclusion: Ensuring access to education for all*. https://www.ibe.unesco.org/sites/default/files/Guidelines_for_Inclusion_UNESCO_2006.pdf

UNESCO. (2009). *Policy guidelines on inclusion in education*. https://unesdoc.unesco.org/ark:/48223/pf0000177849

UNESCO. (2015). *EFA global monitoring report, 2015: Education for all 2000–2015: Achievements and challenges*. UNESCO.

UNESCO. (2019). *Beijing consensus on artificial intelligence and education*. https://unesdoc.unesco.org/ark:/48223/pf0000368303

UNESCO. (2023). Guidance for Generative AI in Education and Research https://www.unesco.org/en/articles/guidance-generative-ai-education-and-research

UNESCO. (2023a). CENTURY, An AI-Powered Teaching and Learning Platform. https://www.unesco.org/en/articles/century-ai-powered-teaching-and-learning-platform

UNESCO. (2024). How Generative AI is Reshaping Education in Asia-Pacific. https://www.unesco.org/en/articles/how-generative-ai-reshaping-education-asia-pacific

UNICEF. (2014). *Conceptualizing inclusive education and contextualizing it within the UNICEF mission*. https://www.unicef.org/eca/sites/unicef.org.eca/files/IE_Webinar_Booklet_1_0.pdf

UNICEF. (2020). *Inclusive education*. https://www.unicef.org/education/inclusive-education

UNICEF. UNESCO, & World Bank. (2022). *Where are we on education recovery?* https://unesdoc.unesco.org/ark:/48223/pf0000381091

Universidad Europea de Madrid. (2024, July 7). Transformando la evaluación con IA. De la teoría a la práctica. Guía para el profesorado. [Unit for Innovation in Academic Programs and Learning Assessment. Vice Rectorate for Faculty and Research]. Retrieved November 29, 2024 from https://es.slideshare.net/slideshow/transformando-la-evaluacion-con-inteligencia-artificial-ccesa007-pdf/270101605

University of Arizona. (2025). Transforming Teaching with AI: Integrating GPT and LLMs. https://libcal.library.arizona.edu/event/14136655

Uygun, D. (2024). Teachers' Perspectives on Artificial Intelligence in Education. *Advances in Mobile Learning Educational Research*, *4*(1), 931–939. DOI: 10.25082/AMLER.2024.01.005

Uymaz, M. (2024). Present and Future of Artificial Intelligence: A Case Study on Prospective Teachers. *Sakarya University Journal of Education*, *14*(Special Issue-AI in Education), 194-212. https://doi.org/ DOI: 10.19126/suje.1466052

Vaidya, B. (2024). Harnessing AI for STEM Education in South Asia: Impact, Opportunities, and Challenges. *Journal of Development Innovations.*, *8*(2), 1–29. DOI: 10.69727/jdi.v8i2.113

Valderama, A. M., Tuazon, J. B., & Garcia, M. B. (2022). Promoting Student Thinking and Engagement Through Question-Based and Gamified Learning. *2022 IEEE 14th International Conference on Humanoid, Nanotechnology, Information Technology, Communication and Control, Environment and Management (HNICEM).* DOI: 10.1109/HNICEM57413.2022.10109470

Valtonen, T., López-Pernas, S., Saqr, M., Vartiainen, H., Sointu, E., & Tedre, M. (2022). La naturaleza y componentes básicos de la investigación en tecnología educativa. Las computadoras en el comportamiento humano, 128, 107123. DOI: 10.1016/j.chb.2021.107123

van den Berg, G., & du Plessis, E. (2023). ChatGPT and Generative AI: Possibilities for Its Contribution to Lesson Planning, Critical Thinking and Openness in Teacher Education. *Education Sciences*, *13*(10), 1–12. DOI: 10.3390/educsci13100998

Van Laar, E., Van Deursen, A. J. A. M., Van Dijk, J. A. G. M., & De Haan, J. (2020). Determinants of 21st-century skills and 21st-century digital skills for workers: A systematic literature review. *SAGE Open*, *10*(1), 2158244019900176. DOI: 10.1177/2158244019900176

Van Oijen, V. (2023). AI-generated text detectors: Do they work? SURF Communities. https:// communities. surf. nl/ en/ ai- in- educa tion/ artic le/ ai- gener ated- text- detec tors- do- they- work.

Van Rensburg, J. J. (2024). Artificial human thinking: ChatGPT's capacity to be a model for critical thinking when prompted with problem-based writing activities. *Discover Education*, *3*(1), 42. Advance online publication. DOI: 10.1007/s44217-024-00113-x

Varsha, P. S. (2023). How Can We Manage Biases in Artificial Intelligence Systems – A Systematic Literature Review. *International Journal of Information Management Data Insights*, *3*(1), 100165. DOI: 10.1016/j.jjimei.2023.100165

Varsik, S., & Vosberg, L. (2024). *The Potential Impact of Artificial Intelligence on Equity and Inclusion in Education.* OECD Artificial Intelligence Papers., DOI: 10.1787/15df715b-

Vázquez-Cano, E., Mengual-Andrés, S., & López-Meneses, E. (2021). Chatbot to improve learning punctuation in Spanish and to enhance open and flexible learning environments. *International Journal of Educational Technology in Higher Education*, *18*(1), 33. Advance online publication. DOI: 10.1186/s41239-021-00269-8

Ventayen, R. J. M. (2023). ChatGPT by OpenAI: Students' viewpoint on cheating using artificial intelligence-based application. *Available atSSRN* 4361548. DOI: 10.2139/ssrn.4361548

Verma, S., Ernst, M., & Just, R. (2021). Removing biased data to improve fairness and accuracy. *arXiv*. https://arxiv.org/abs/2102.03054

Viberg, O., Cukurova, M., Feldman-Maggor, Y., Alexandron, G., Shirai, S., Kanemune, S., Wasson, B., Tomte, C., Spikol, D., Milrad, M., Coelho, R., & Kizilcec, R. (2024). What Explains Teachers Trust in AI in Education Across Six Countries? *International Journal of Artificial Intelligence in Education*. Advance online publication. DOI: 10.1007/s40593-024-00433-x

Vickroy, L. (2015). Reading Trauma Narratives: The Contemporary Novel and the Psychology of Oppression. http://muse.jhu.edu/chapter/1635214

Villarino, R. T. (2024). Rural Philippine College Students' Perspectives and Experiences on AI Tools in Education: a mixed-method research. *Artificial Intelligence (AI) Integration in Rural Philippine Higher Education: Perspectives, Challenges, and Ethical Considerations*. https://doi.org/DOI: 10.31219/osf.io/ehcb9

von Garrel, J., & Mayer, J. (2024). Which features of AI-based tools are important for students? A choice-based conjoint analysis. *Computers and Education: Artificial Intelligence, 7*, 100311. https://doi.org/https://doi.org/10.1016/j.caeai.2024.100311

Vuran, S. (Ed.). (2020). *Özel eğitim öğretmenleri için etik ilkeler kılavuzu*. Vize Akademik.

Wadhawan, A., & Kumar, P. (2021). Sign language recognition systems: A decade systematic literature review. *Archives of Computational Methods in Engineering, 28*(3), 785–813. DOI: 10.1007/s11831-019-09384-2

Wajcman, J. (2013). *TechnoFeminism*. Polity Press. https://books.google.com.ph/books?id=c9TgUMIzhx8C

Wallace, B. C. S., & Abel, Y. (2024). Embracing artificial intelligence (AI) tools to enrich special education teacher preparation. In *Advances in educational technologies and instructional design book series* (pp. 325–354). https://doi.org/DOI: 10.4018/979-8-3693-5538-1.ch012

Walsh, B., Dalton, B., Forsyth, S., & Yeh, T. (2023). Literacy and STEM Teachers Adapt AI Ethics Curriculum. *Proceedings of the AAAI Conference on Artificial Intelligence, 37*(13), 16048–16055. DOI: 10.1609/aaai.v37i13.26906

Walter, Y. (2024). Embracing the Future of Artificial Intelligence in the Classroom: The Relevance of Ai Literacy, Prompt Engineering, and Critical Thinking in Modern Education. *International Journal of Educational Technology in Higher Education, 21*(1), 1–29. DOI: 10.1186/s41239-024-00448-3

Walugembe, T. A., Nakayenga, H. N., & Babirye, S. (2024). Artificial Intelligence-Driven Transformation in Special Education: Optimizing Software for Improved Learning Outcomes. *International Journal of Computer Applications Technology and Research, 13*(8), 163–179. DOI: 10.7753/IJCATR1308.1015

Wandhe, P. (2024). The Intellectual Property Landscape: Safeguarding Innovations Derived From Basic Science. In Trivedi, S., Grover, V., Balusamy, B., & Ganguly, A. (Eds.), *Unleashing the Power of Basic Science in Business* (pp. 285–310). IGI Global., DOI: 10.4018/979-8-3693-5503-9.ch015

Wang, H., & Zhu, X. (2024). Challenges in education during digital transformation. In *Lecture notes in educational technology* (pp. 11–24). https://doi.org/DOI: 10.1007/978-981-97-0076-9_2

Wang, C. (2024). *Exploring Students' Generative AI-Assisted Writing Processes: Perceptions and Experiences from Native and Nonnative English Speakers.* Technology, Knowledge and Learning., DOI: 10.1007/s10758-024-09744-3

Wang, J., Hwang, G.-H., & Chang, C.-Y. (2021). Directions of the 100 Most Cited Chatbot-Related Human Behavior Research: A Review of Academic Publications. *Computers and Education: Artificial Intelligence, 2,* 100023. DOI: 10.1016/j.caeai.2021.100023

Wang, J., & Li, J. (2024). Artificial intelligence empowering public health education: Prospects and challenges. *Frontiers in Public Health, 12,* 1389026. DOI: 10.3389/fpubh.2024.1389026 PMID: 39022411

Wang, S., Wang, F., Zhu, Z., Wang, J., Tran, T., & Du, Z. (2024). Artificial Intelligence in Education: A Systematic Literature Review. *Expert Systems with Applications, 252,* 1–19. DOI: 10.1016/j.eswa.2024.124167

Wang, T., Lund, B. D., Marengo, A., Pagano, A., Mannuru, N. R., Teel, Z. A., & Pange, J. (2023). Exploring the Potential Impact of Artificial Intelligence (AI) on International Students in Higher Education: Generative AI, Chatbots, Analytics, and International Student Success. *Applied Sciences (Basel, Switzerland), 13*(11), 1–15. DOI: 10.3390/app13116716

Wang, X., Dai, M., & Short, K. M. (2024). One size doesn't fit all: How different types of learning motivations influence engineering undergraduate students' success outcomes. *International Journal of STEM Education, 11*(1), 41. DOI: 10.1186/s40594-024-00502-6

Wang, X., Gao, Q., Lu, J., Shang, J., & Zhou, Y. (2021). The construction and practical cases of human-machine collaboration teaching mode in the era of artificial intelligence. *Journal of Distance Education, 39*(04), 24–33.

Wang, Y. (2021). Artificial intelligence in educational leadership: A symbiotic role of human-artificial intelligence decision-making. *Journal of Educational Administration, 59*(3), 256–270. DOI: 10.1108/JEA-10-2020-0216

Wang, Y., & Wang, X. (2024). Artificial intelligence in physical education: Comprehensive review and future teacher training strategies. *Frontiers in Public Health, 12,* 1484848. Advance online publication. DOI: 10.3389/fpubh.2024.1484848 PMID: 39583072

Waters, A., & Miikkulainen, R. (2014). GRADE: Machine learning support for graduate admissions. *AI Magazine, 35*(1), 64–75. DOI: 10.1609/aimag.v35i1.2504

Weber-Wulff, D., Anohina-Naumeca, A., Bjelobaba, S., Foltýnek, T., Guerrero-Dib, J., Popoola, O., Šigut, P., & Waddington, L. (2023). Testing of detection tools for AI-generated text. *International Journal for Educational Integrity, 19*(1), 1–39. DOI: 10.1007/s40979-023-00146-z

Wei, L. (2023). Artificial intelligence in language instruction: Impact on English learning achievement, L2 motivation, and self-regulated learning. *Frontiers in Psychology*, *14*, 14. DOI: 10.3389/fpsyg.2023.1261955 PMID: 38023040

Weld Australia. (2025). Soldamatic Augmented Reality Welding Simulators. *Weld Australia*. https://weldaustralia.com.au/welding-technology/soldamatic-augmented-reality-welding-simulators/

Wetzel, J., Burkhardt, H., Cheema, S., Kang, S., Pead, D., Schoenfeld, A., & VanLehn, K. (2018). A Preliminary Evaluation of the Usability of an AI-Infused Orchestration System. *Lecture Notes in Computer Science*, *379-383*, 379–383. Advance online publication. DOI: 10.1007/978-3-319-93846-2_71

WeWalk. (t.y.). *Product - WeWALK Smart Cane*. https://wewalk.io/tr/product/

Whittington, P., & Doğan, H. (2024). *Improving quality of life through the application of assistive technology*. Edward Elgar Publishing., DOI: 10.4337/9781800888647.00011

Williamson, B., & Eynon, R. (2020). The automation of education: Artificial intelligence and the future of learning. *Learning, Media and Technology*, *45*(1), 1–9.

Williamson, S. M., & Prybutok, V. (2024). The Era of Artificial Intelligence Deception: Unraveling the Complexities of False Realities and Emerging Threats of Misinformation. *Information (Basel)*, *15*(6), 299. DOI: 10.3390/info15060299

Wilson, J. D. (2017). Reimagining disability and inclusive education through universal design for learning. *Disability Studies Quarterly*, *37*(2). Advance online publication. DOI: 10.18061/dsq.v37i2.5417

Windelband, L. (2023). *Artificial Intelligence and Assistance Systems for Technical Vocational Education and Training – Opportunities and Risks*. Springer International Publishing., DOI: 10.1007/978-3-031-26490-0_12

Winkler, R., & Soellner, M. (2018). Unleashing the Potential of Chatbots in Education: A State-Of-The-Art Analysis. *Proceedings - Academy of Management*, *2018*(1), 15903. DOI: 10.5465/AMBPP.2018.15903abstract

WIPO. (2019). WIPO Technology Trends 2019 – Artificial Intelligence. *World Intellectual Property Organization*. DOI: 10.34667/tind.29084

WIPO. (2022). WIPO Guide to Using Patent Information. *World Intellectual Property Organization*. DOI: 10.34667/tind.46546

WIPO. (2024). Patent Landscape Report: Generative Artificial Intelligence. *World Intellectual Property Organization*. DOI: 10.34667/tind.49740

Wiredu, J. K., Seidu Abuba, N., & Zakaria, H. (2024). Impact of generative AI in academic integrity and learning outcomes: A case study in the upper east region. *Asian Journal of Research in Computer Science*, *17*(8), 10–9734. DOI: 10.9734/ajrcos/2024/v17i7491

Wogu, I. A. P., Misra, S., Olu-Owolabi, E. F., Assibong, P. A., Udoh, O. D., Ogiri, S. O., & Damasevicius, R. (2018). Artificial intelligence, artificial teachers and the fate of learners in the 21st century education sector: Implications for theory and practice. *International Journal of Pure and Applied Mathematics*, *119*(16), 2245–2259. https://acadpubl.eu/hub/2018-119-16/2/232.pdf

Wohlin, C., & Prikladnicki, R. (2013). Systematic Literature Reviews in Software Engineering. *Information and Software Technology*, *55*(6), 919–920. DOI: 10.1016/j.infsof.2013.02.002

Wollny, S., Schneider, J., Di Mitri, D., Weidlich, J., Rittberger, M., & Drachsler, H. (2021). Are We There Yet? - A Systematic Literature Review on Chatbots in Education. *Frontiers in Artificial Intelligence*, *4*, 654924. Advance online publication. DOI: 10.3389/frai.2021.654924 PMID: 34337392

Wood, D., & Moss, S. H. (2024). Evaluating the impact of students' generative AI use in educational contexts. *Journal of Research in Innovative Teaching & Learning*, *17*(2), 152–167. DOI: 10.1108/JRIT-06-2024-0151

Woolf, B. P. (2010). *Building intelligent interactive tutors: Student-centered strategies for revolutionizing e-learning*. Morgan Kaufmann.

World Health Organization (WHO). (2011). *World report on disability*. https://www.who.int/publications/i/item/9789241564182

Writer, S. C., & Erkoc, M. (2023). Analysis of Science Group Teachers' Use of Artificial Intelligence in the Distance Education Process. *Dokuz Eylül University Buca Faculty of Education Journal*, (58), 2682–2704. DOI: 10.53444/deubefd.1316144

Wu, D., Zhang, S., Ma, Z., Yue, X. G., & Dong, R. K. (2024). Unlocking potential: Key factors shaping undergraduate self-directed learning in ai-enhanced educational environments. *Systems*, *12*(9), 332. DOI: 10.3390/systems12090332

Wu, D., Zhang, X., Wang, K., Wu, L., & Yang, W. (2024). *A multi-level factors model affecting teachers behavioral intention in AI-enabled education ecosystem*. ETR&D-Educational Technology Research And Development., DOI: 10.1007/s11423-024-10419-0

Wu, W., Zhang, B., Li, S., & Liu, H. (2022). Exploring Factors of the Willingness to Accept AI-Assisted Learning Environments: An Empirical Investigation Based on the UTAUT Model and Perceived Risk Theory. *Frontiers in Psychology*, *13*, 1–10. DOI: 10.3389/fpsyg.2022.870777 PMID: 35814061

Wu, Y. (2023). Integrating generative AI in education: How ChatGPT brings challenges for future learning and teaching. *Journal of Advanced Research in Education*, *2*(4), 6–10. DOI: 10.56397/JARE.2023.07.02

Xiao, J., Bozkurt, A., Nichols, M., Pazurek, A., Stracke, C. M., Bai, J. Y. H., Farrow, R., Mulligan, D., Nerantzi, C., Sharma, R. C., Singh, L., Frumin, I., Swindell, A., Honeychurch, S., Bond, M., Dron, J., Moore, S., Leng, J., & Slagter van Tryon, P. J.. (2025). Venturing into the Unknown: Critical Insights into Grey Areas and Pioneering Future Directions in Educational Generative AI Research. *TechTrends*, •••, 1–16. DOI: 10.1007/s11528-025-01060-6

Xu, W., & Ouyang, F. (2022). The Application of AI Technologies in STEM Education: A Systematic Review from 2011 to 2021. *International Journal of STEM Education*, *9*(1), 1–20. DOI: 10.1186/s40594-022-00377-5

Yaghoubi, A. A., Karimi, P., Moradi, E., & Gavagsaz-Ghoachani, R. (2023). Implementing Engineering Education Based on Posing a Riddle in Field of Instrumentation and Artificial Intelligence. *2023 9th International Conference on Control, Instrumentation and Automation (ICCIA)*, 1-5. DOI: 10.1109/ICCIA61416.2023.10506384

Yangambi, M. (2023). Impact of School Infrastructures on Students Learning and Performance: Case of Three Public Schools in a Developing Country. *Creative Education*, *14*(04), 788–809. DOI: 10.4236/ce.2023.144052

Yang, J., Chen, Y.-L., Por, L. Y., & Ku, C. S. (2023). A Systematic Literature Review of Information Security in Chatbots. *Applied Sciences (Basel, Switzerland)*, *13*(11), 6355. DOI: 10.3390/app13116355

Yang, S., & Evans, C. (2019). Opportunities and Challenges in Using AI Chatbots in Higher Education. *Proceedings of the 2019 3rd International Conference on Education and E-Learning*. https://doi.org/ DOI: 10.1145/3371647.3371659

Yang, Y., Sun, W., Sun, D., & Salas-Pilco, S. Z. (2024). Navigating the AI-Enhanced STEM education landscape: A decade of insights, trends, and opportunities. *Research in Science & Technological Education*, ●●●, 1–25. DOI: 10.1080/02635143.2024.2370764

Yan, Y., & Liu, H. (2024). Ethical framework for AI education based on large language models. *Education and Information Technologies*. Advance online publication. DOI: 10.1007/s10639-024-13241-6

Yıldız, G. (2024a). Özel eğitimde yapay zekâ, dijital güvenlik ve etik konular. A. Kaya (Ed.) *Özel eğitim ve yapay zekâ* içinde (293-315). [Artificial intelligence, digital security and ethical issues in special education. In A. Kaya (Ed.), Special education and artificial intelligence]. Vize Akademik.

Yılmaz, Y., & Çolaklıoğlu, O. (2024). İşitme kayıplılar ve yapay zekâ. A. Kaya (Ed.) *Özel eğitim ve yapay zekâ* içinde (135-156). [Hearing loss and artificial intelligence. In A. Kaya (Ed.), Special education and artificial intelligence]. Vize Akademik.

Yilmaz, R., & Karaoglan Yilmaz, F. G. (2023). The Effect of Generative Artificial Intelligence (AI)-Based Tool Use on Students' Computational Thinking Skills, Programming Self-Efficacy and Motivation. *Computers and Education: Artificial Intelligence*, *4*, 1–14. DOI: 10.1016/j.caeai.2023.100147

Yilmaz, R., & Yilmaz, F. G. K. (2023). Augmented intelligence in programming learning: Examining student views on the use of ChatGPT for programming learning. *Computers in Human Behavior: Artificial Humans*, *1*(2), 100005. DOI: 10.1016/j.chbah.2023.100005

Yin, J., Goh, T.-T., Yang, B., & Xiaobin, Y. (2020). Conversation Technology With Micro-Learning: The Impact of Chatbot-Based Learning on Students' Learning Motivation and Performance. *Journal of Educational Computing Research*, *59*(1), 154–177. DOI: 10.1177/0735633120952067

Yin, W. J. (2024). *Will Our Educational System Keep Pace with AI? A Student's Perspective on AI and Learning*. Educause.

Younis, B. (2024). Effectiveness of a Professional Development Program Based on the Instructional Design Framework for AI Literacy in Developing AI Literacy Skills Among Pre-Service Teachers. *Journal of Digital Learning in Teacher Education*, *40*(3), 142–158. DOI: 10.1080/21532974.2024.2365663

Yuan, J., Holtz, C., Smith, T., & Luo, J. (2016). Autism spectrum disorder detection from semi-structured and unstructured medical data. *EURASIP Journal on Bioinformatics & Systems Biology*, *2017*(1), 3. Advance online publication. DOI: 10.1186/s13637-017-0057-1 PMID: 28203249

Yue, M., Jong, M. S.-Y., & Ng, D. T. K. (2024). Understanding K–12 teachers' technological pedagogical content knowledge readiness and attitudes toward artificial intelligence education. *Education and Information Technologies*, *29*(15), 19505–19536. DOI: 10.1007/s10639-024-12621-2

Yu, H. (2023). Reflection on Whether Chat GPT Should Be Banned by Academia from the Perspective of Education and Teaching. *Frontiers in Psychology*, *14*, 1181712. DOI: 10.3389/fpsyg.2023.1181712 PMID: 37325766

Yu, H. (2024). The application and challenges of ChatGPT in educational transformation: New demands for teachers roles. *Heliyon*, *10*(2), e24289. Advance online publication. DOI: 10.1016/j.heliyon.2024.e24289 PMID: 38298626

Yumrukaya, R., & Ersoy, C. (2024). A phenomenon at the zenith of intelligence: Artificial intelligence in education from the perspective of BİLSEM teachers. In Bal Sezerel, B. (Ed.), *Proceedings of the IXth National Congress on Gifted Education* (pp. 297–299). Anadolu University MEMBER Publications., https://cdn.anadolu.edu.tr/files/anadolu-cms/06lOMZeW/uploads/uyek-2024-bildiri-kitabi-74dbbb813295d244.pdf

Yun, H., Lee, J., & Park, S. (2023). Exploring the impact of generative AI on student creativity and learning. *Journal of Educational Innovation Studies*, *18*(4), 55–72.

Yu, R., Li, Q., Fischer, C., Doroudi, S., & Xu, D. (2020). Towards Accurate and Fair Prediction of College Success: Evaluating Different Sources of Student Data. *Proceedings of The 13th International Conference on Educational Data Mining (EDM 2020)*, 292–301

Yusof, R., Harith, N. H. M., Lokman, A., Abdul, M. F., Zain, B. M., & Rahmat, N. H. (2023). A Study of Perception on Students' Motivation, Burnout and Reasons for Dropout. *International Journal of Academic Research in Business & Social Sciences*, *13*(7), 392–420. https://doi.org/http://dx.doi.org/10.6007/IJARBSS/v13-i7/17187. DOI: 10.6007/IJARBSS/v13-i7/17187

Yusuf, A., Pervin, N., & Román-González, M. (2024). Generative AI and the future of higher education: A threat to academic integrity or reformation? Evidence from multicultural perspectives. *International Journal of Educational Technology in Higher Education*, *21*(1), 21. DOI: 10.1186/s41239-024-00453-6

Zawacki-Richter, O., Marín, V. I., Bond, M., & Gouverneur, F. (2019). Systematic review of research on artificial intelligence applications in higher education. *International Journal of Educational Technology in Higher Education*, *16*(1), 1–27. DOI: 10.1186/s41239-019-0171-0

Zhai, C., Wibowo, S., & Li, L. D. (2024). The effects of over-reliance on AI dialogue systems on students' cognitive abilities: A systematic review. *Smart Learning Environments*, *11*(1), 28. DOI: 10.1186/s40561-024-00316-7

Zhang, H., Lee, I., & Moore, K. (2024). An Effectiveness Study of Teacher-Led AI Literacy Curriculum in K-12 Classrooms. *Proceedings of the AAAI Conference on Artificial Intelligence*, *38*(21), 23318–23325. DOI: 10.1609/aaai.v38i21.30380

Zhang, J., & Zhang, Z. (2024). AI in teacher education: Unlocking new dimensions in teaching support, inclusive learning, and digital literacy. *Journal of Computer Assisted Learning*, *40*(4), 1871–1885. DOI: 10.1111/jcal.12988

Zhang, S., Zhao, X., Zhou, T., & Kim, J. H. (2024). Do you have AI dependency? The roles of academic self-efficacy, academic stress, and performance expectations on problematic AI usage behavior. *International Journal of Educational Technology in Higher Education*, *21*(1), 34. DOI: 10.1186/s41239-024-00467-0

Zhang, Y., Wu, J., Yu, F., & Xu, L. (2023). Moral Judgments of Human vs. AI Agents in Moral Dilemmas. *Behavioral Sciences (Basel, Switzerland)*, *13*(2), 1–14. DOI: 10.3390/bs13020181 PMID: 36829410

Zhao, C., & Yu, J. (2024). Relationship between teacher's ability model and students' behavior based on emotion-behavior relevance theory and artificial intelligence technology under the background of curriculum ideological and political education. *Learning and Motivation*, *88*, 102040. Advance online publication. DOI: 10.1016/j.lmot.2024.102040

Zhao, Y., & Frank, K. A. (2003). Factors Affecting Technology Uses in Schools: An Ecological Perspective. *American Educational Research Journal*, *40*(4), 807–840. DOI: 10.3102/00028312040004807

Zhongtuo, (2020). Artificial intelligence techniques for stability analysis and control in smart grids: Methodologies, applications, challenges and future directions https://doi.org/DOI: 10.1016/j.apenergy.2020.115733

Zhong, W., Luo, J., & Lyu, Y. (2024). How Do Personal Attributes Shape AI Dependency in Chinese Higher Education Context? Insights from Needs Frustration Perspective. *PLoS One*, *19*(11), e0313314. https://doi.org/https://doi.org/10.1371/journal.pone.0313314. DOI: 10.1371/journal.pone.0313314 PMID: 39485818

Zhou, J., Shen, L., & Chen, W. (2024). How ChatGPT transformed teachers: The role of basic psychological needs in enhancing digital competence. *Frontiers in Psychology*, *15*, 1–9. DOI: 10.3389/fpsyg.2024.1458551 PMID: 39421844

Zhu, C., Sun, M., Luo, J., Li, T., & Wang, M. (2023). How to Harness the Potential of ChatGPT in Education? *Knowledge Management & E-Learning*, *15*(2), 133–152. DOI: 10.34105/j.kmel.2023.15.008

Zhumazhan, B., Zhumadilova, M., & Abdykerimova, E. (2024). The future of artificial intelligence in inclusive education. *Yessenov Science Journal*, *48*(3), 63–70. Advance online publication. DOI: 10.56525/AMWI6491

Zhuravleva, N. A., Cadge, K., Poliak, M., & Podhorska, I. (2019). Data privacy and security vulnerabilities of smart and sustainable urban space monitoring systems. *Contemporary Readings in Law and Social Justice*, *11*(2), 56–62. DOI: 10.22381/CRLSJ11220198

Zimmerman, A., Janhonen, J., & Beer, E. (2023). Human/AI relationships: Challenges, downsides, and impacts on human/human relationships. *AI and Ethics*, ●●●, 1–13. DOI: 10.1007/s43681-023-00268-5

Zimmerman, B. J. (2002). Becoming a self-regulated learner: An overview. *Theory into Practice*, *41*(2), 64–70. DOI: 10.1207/s15430421tip4102_2

Zirar, A., Ali, S. I., & Islam, N. (2023). Worker and Workplace Artificial Intelligence (AI) Coexistence: Emerging Themes and Research Agenda. *Technovation*, *124*, 1–17. DOI: 10.1016/j.technovation.2023.102747

Zulkarnain, N. S., & Yunus, M. M. (2023). Primary Teachers' Perspectives on Using Artificial Intelligence Technology in English as a Second Language Teaching and Learning: A Systematic Review. *International Journal of Academic Research in Progressive Education and Development*, *12*(2), 861–875.

About the Contributors

Manuel B. Garcia is a professor of information technology and the founding director of the Educational Innovation and Technology Hub (EdITH) at FEU Institute of Technology, Manila, Philippines. He holds a Doctor of Information Technology degree from the University of the East and is currently pursuing a Doctor of Philosophy in Education at the University of the Philippines. His interdisciplinary research interests include topics that, individually or collectively, span the disciplines of education and information technology. He is a licensed professional teacher and a proud member of the National Research Council of the Philippines – an attached agency to the country's Department of Science and Technology (DOST-NRCP). Dr. Garcia is the first-ever recipient of the Ramon Dimacali Award for Information Technology, conferred by the Philippine Association for the Advancement of Science and Technology, and has been recognized as one of the World's Top 2% Scientists for 2023 and 2024 by Elsevier.

Joanna Rosak-Szyrocka is an Assistant Professor and Erasmus+ Coordinator at the Faculty of Management, Czestochowa University of Technology, Poland. She specializes in digitalization, Industry 5.0, Quality 4.0, education, IoT, AI, and quality management. She completed research internships at the University of Žilina, Slovakia, and the Silesian University of Technology, Poland. She has participated in multiple Erasmus+ teacher mobility programs in Italy, the UK, Slovenia, Hungary, the Czech Republic, Slovakia, and France. She has also delivered a series of lectures on Quality Management at universities in countries such as Great Britain, the Czech Republic, Slovakia, Slovenia, France, Hungary, and Italy. She collaborates with numerous universities both domestically (University of Szczecin, Rzeszów University of Technology, and Silesian University of Technology) and internationally, including the University of Tabuk (Saudi Arabia), Széchenyi István University (Hungary), the University of Faisalabad (Pakistan), the University of Humanities (China), the University of Technology Sydney (Australia), the Bucharest University of Economic Studies (Romania), and the Federal University Dutse (Nigeria). She is also a member of the editorial boards of PLOS ONE, PeerJ, and the International Journal for Quality Research (IJQR).

Aras Bozkurt is a researcher and faculty member at Anadolu University, Türkiye. Holding MA and PhD degrees in distance education, Dr. Bozkurt focuses on empirical studies in areas such as distance education, online learning, networked learning, and educational technology. He applies critical theories such as connectivism, rhizomatic learning, and heutagogy to his research. Dr. Bozkurt is also interested in emerging research paradigms, including social network analysis, sentiment analysis, and data mining. His work further explores the integration of artificial intelligence technologies into educational processes, particularly in the context of human-machine interaction. His dedication to advancing the field is reflected in his editorial roles as Editor-in-Chief of Open Praxis and the Asian Journal of Distance Education, as well as his positions as an associate editor for prestigious journals such as Higher Education Research and Development, Online Learning, eLearn Magazine, and Computer Applications in Engineering Education.

***

Dharel P. Acut is a licensed professional teacher and a Science Education instructor at Cebu Technological University in Cebu City, Philippines. He holds a bachelor's degree in Secondary Education with a major in General Science from MSU-Iligan Institute of Technology. Currently, he is completing his master's degree in Science Education at Cebu Normal University. As an Associate Member of the National Research Council of the Philippines (DOST-NRCP), his research interests focus on science education, STEM education, systematic literature reviews, education for sustainable development, science instrumentation, and educational technology.

Yunifa Miftachul Arif is an Associate Professor at the Departments of Informatics Engineering and Electrical Engineering at Universitas Islam Negeri Maulana Malik Ibrahim Malang, Indonesia. His research interests encompass game technology, artificial intelligence, recommender systems, blockchain, and the Internet of Things (IoT), with a focus on advancing interdisciplinary solutions in computing and intelligent systems.

Joey S. Aviles brings a wealth of academic expertise and leadership experience to the field of Information Technology and Computer Science. His extensive teaching background, combined with a commitment to research and continuous learning, reflects his dedication to excellence in education. He is currently serving as a faculty member and Service Unit Coordinator of the College of Computer Studies, as well as the Program Chair of the IT Education Programs at the Graduate School of Angeles University Foundation. He has previously worked with Panpacific University and Al Farabi Colleges in Saudi Arabia. Furthermore, he is an active officer of the Philippine Society of IT Educators in the Ilocos Region and the Council of IT Education Deans and Heads, and a former RQAT member. He is an enthusiastic researcher with Scopus-indexed publications in IEEE and ACM, and holds certifications from various bodies in Computer Science and Information Technology, including Microsoft and Adobe.

Miladina Rizka Aziza is a lecturer and researcher specializing in renewable energy, electronic materials, and the Internet of Things (IoT). She earned her Bachelor's degree in Electrical Engineering from Brawijaya University with a focus on renewable energy and semiconductor devices. She later completed her Master's degree at National Cheng Kung University in Taiwan under the International Curriculum for Advanced Materials Program, where her research emphasized hydrogen generation. Currently a lecturer at the Department of Electrical Engineering, UIN Maulana Malik Ibrahim Malang, her work centers on developing sustainable energy systems and exploring advanced materials for next-generation technologies. Committed to both research and education, she actively mentors students and contributes to the advancement of energy-efficient and smart electronic systems.

Francis F. Balahadia, a distinguished scholar in the field of Information Technology Education (ITE), holds a Doctor of Information Technology degree from University of the East-Manila. Currently, Dr. Balahadia hold the academic rank of Professor 1 and serves as Dean of the College of Computer Studies, Laguna State Polytechnic University last January 2024. In addition to his academic roles, Dr.

Balahadia is an ICT Cluster Representative of LSPU in STAARRDEC, and Focal Person of DOST SEI Scholarship of LSPU. He is also former Program Coordinator for BS Information Technology, Masters of Information Technology, and Chairperson of the Innovation Technology Service Office (ITSO). Dr. Balahadia also gained certifications, including TESDA NC 2 and 3 certifications, PD 977-Scientific and Technological Specialist, and ISO certification for Train the Trainer and other IT-related certificates. Moreover, Dr. Balahadia's commitment to knowledge dissemination he received invitations as Resource Speaker in various training, seminars, workshop and research conferences. Furthermore, he served as a diligent research paper reviewer for both national and international conferences and journals. .His prolific research output includes more or less 60 published research papers, with almost 30 refereed journals, 31 Scopus Indexed and one ISI Index paper among them. Notably, his work has been cited by numerous authors, with 376 citations under Google Scholar. Lastly, Dr. Balahadia serves as a valuable member of the editorial board for prestigious journals, including the International Journal of Computing Science Research and the Asia Pacific Journal for Multidisciplinary Research. His unwavering commitment to advancing ITE, research and extension involvement continues to make a profound impact on the academic community. He also the Chairman of Committee for the Formulation of the LSPU Publication Office and Journal entitled "Journal of Interdisciplinary Science and Innovation Research (JISIR)".

Priyanka Bisht is a doctoral candidate in the Department of English and Cultural Studies at Christ University, Delhi NCR, specializing in Partition Literature and Migration Studies. Her research interests extend beyond traditional literary analysis to include emerging fields such as Artificial Intelligence (AI) and Virtual Reality (VR), with a particular focus on their intersection with literature, history, and pedagogy. Bisht's scholarly contributions are reflected in her recent Scopus-indexed publications. Her chapter "Past Meets the Future—ChatGPT Integrated Pedagogy to Teach the 1947 Partition in Secondary Classes," published by Springer Nature, innovatively explores the use of AI tools like ChatGPT in secondary school history education. Another chapter, "Pedagogy: The 1947 Partition Archive—A Contemporary Pedagogical Resource to Teach the Rival History of the Partition of India," published by Routledge, demonstrates her expertise in leveraging historical archives for educational purposes.

Martina Brazzolotto completed her Ph.D. in Pedagogical Sciences, specializing in Special Pedagogy, at the University of Bologna in November 2020, with a dissertation focused on Teaching for PlusDotation and Talent Development. In September 2021, she completed a Post-Doctoral Fellowship at the Great Plains Center for Gifted Studies at Emporia State University in Kansas, U.S.A. She has served as a member of the Technical Table on PlusDotation established by the Italian Ministry of Education (MIUR). Since 2019, she has been a member and the official delegate for Italy of the World Council for Gifted and Talented Children (WCGTC), a global nonprofit organization supporting children with high abilities. Additionally, she is a member of the European Council for High Ability (ECHA) and the Italian Society for Educational and Training Research (SIREF).

Dennis L. Capuyan is a Professor of Civil Technology and Technical Education at the College of Technology, Cebu Technological University, Cebu City, Philippines. He holds a Doctor of Philosophy in Technology Management from the same institution. Dr. Capuyan is actively involved in the Center for Scholarly Researchers of Educators in the Philippines and the Philippine Institute of 21st Century Educators. His research encompasses civil technology, technical education, technology education, and the strategic management of technology in both educational and industrial sectors.

Maria Anna D. Cruz is an assistant professor and the concurrent Director of the Don Honorio Ventura State University - City of San Fernando Campus. Her research interests mostly pertain to tourism, hospitality, business management and tertiary education. With the advent of technology, particularly AI, her interests have delved into how technology and creativity can further enhance business and education.

Jeffrey G. Dela Calzada is an Assistant Professor of Automotive Technology and Technical Education at the College of Technology, Cebu Technological University, Cebu City, Philippines. He holds a Master's degree in Technician Education and is currently pursuing a Doctor of Philosophy in Technology Management at the same university. His research interests focus on autotronics, automotive technology, and the management of technology in educational and industrial contexts.

Mustafa Doğuş received his bachelor's degree in Special Education from Gazi University in 2009. He completed his Master's and Ph.D. degrees in Special Education at the Institute of Educational Sciences, Gazi University, in 2016 and 2022, respectively. He began his career as a teacher at the Afyonkarahisar Guidance and Research Center (2009–2013) before joining Anadolu University's Faculty of Education, Department of Special Education, as a Research Assistant in 2013. In 2022, he was appointed as an Assistant Professor and currently serves as Head of the Division of Education for the Visually Impaired. His research interests include assistive technologies for individuals with visual impairments, accessibility in information technologies, exam accessibility, Braille literacy, and artificial intelligence. Dr. Doğuş has authored numerous articles and book chapters published in national and international peer-reviewed journals and books.

Mustafa Çakmak earned his bachelor's degree in Teaching Individuals with Intellectual Disabilities from Anadolu University in 2011. He worked as a special education teacher for four years before completing his Master's degree in the same field in 2017. In 2025, he completed his Ph.D. in Special Education Teaching. He is currently employed as a Research Assistant.

Fatih Erdoğdu is an Associate Professor of Computer Technologies at Zonguldak Bülent Ecevit University, Türkiye. He earned his bachelor's degree from the Middle East Technical University and completed his master's degree in Computer Education and Instructional Technology at Gazi University in 2015. He obtained his Ph.D. in Computer Education and Instructional Technology from Karadeniz Technical University. His academic interests include instructional technology, distance learning, teacher training, and humorous learning. He has conducted over 30 scientific studies and currently serves as the Head of the Department of Computer Technologies at Zonguldak Bülent Ecevit University.

Ceren Ersoy is a researcher and academician at Gazi University, Gazi Faculty of Education, Department of Special Education, where she has served since 2013. Since 2022, she has also been affiliated with the Gazi University Educational Policy Research Center. She completed her undergraduate studies in English Language Teaching at Dokuz Eylül University and pursued graduate studies in the field of giftedness and special education. She earned her first master's degree in Gifted Education from Anadolu University and successfully completed all coursework in the Education of the Mentally Handicapped program at Gazi University. She later obtained her Ph.D. from Gazi University's Institute of Educational Sciences, with a specialization in the identification of gifted students. Throughout her academic career, Dr. Ersoy has actively contributed to various national and international projects focused on inclusive education, special education, gifted education, and digital learning. Her areas of expertise include the identification and assessment of giftedness, cognitive and metacognitive skills, acceleration and enrichment strategies, technology-assisted learning, curriculum development, teacher competencies and professional development, as well as educational gamification, artificial intelligence in education, virtual reality, creativity, and education policy. She continues to make significant scholarly contributions through numerous conference presentations, published book chapters, and collaborative research projects.

Raymond C. Espina currently serves as the Officer-in-Charge (OIC) Dean of the College of Education at Cebu Technological University. He completed the "Train the Trainer" program for welding at Metaphil, an Aboitiz company, and was a KorPhil scholar and a recipient of the Japan International Cooperation Agency (JICA) grant, through which he participated in Japan's Country Focused Training Program for Senior High Schools. His research interests include teacher training in technology education, curriculum development, educational assessment, and the enhancement of technical education standards.

Antonia B. Fernandez is an associate professor at Don Honorio Ventura State University - Main Campus. She is a part of the faculty roster in the College of Education handling professional language subjects and other general education subjects in English.

Chorng Yuan Fung is a multidisciplinary academic and researcher. He is a professional accountant and holds a Ph.D. in educational psychology and a Master of Science in human resource development. His research interests span behavioral accounting, human resource development, educational psychology, technology, and pedagogy. He regularly publishes in reputable indexed journals and frequently speaks at seminars, forums, and workshops organized by corporations, universities, and professional accounting bodies on topics related to his research interests.

Larry C. Gantalao is an Associate Professor V of Automotive Technology and Technical Education at the College of Technology, Cebu Technological University, Cebu City, Philippines. He earned his Doctor of Philosophy in Technology Management from the same institution. Dr. Gantalao is an active member of the Philippine Association of Colleges and Universities in Industrial Technology. His research interests include autotronics, automotive technology, technical education, and technology management in both academic and industrial environments.

Deniz Görgülü is an independent researcher and classroom teacher specializing in educational administration and the integration of technology in education. He earned his doctorate in Educational Administration from Hacettepe University. Currently, he serves as a classroom teacher at Selçuklu BİLSEM (Science and Art Center) in Konya, Türkiye. His research interests include educational leadership, primary education, and the application of technology in educational settings.

İlyas Gürses graduated from the Undergraduate Program in Education of Individuals with Intellectual Disabilities at Marmara University in 2016 and completed his Master's degree in Autism Spectrum Disorder Education at Hacettepe University in 2023. He is currently pursuing his Ph.D. in Education of Individuals with Intellectual Disabilities at Anadolu University and serves as a Research Assistant in the Department of Autism Spectrum Disorder Education.

Novrindah Alvi Hasanah is a dedicated researcher and lecturer with a Bachelor's and Master's degree in Informatics Engineering, specializing in Artificial Intelligence (AI), Internet of Things (IoT), Deep Learning, and Data Mining. As a faculty member in the Department of Electrical Engineering at UIN Maulana Malik Ibrahim Malang, she is passionate about integrating AI and IoT to develop smart and adaptive systems. Her research primarily focuses on deep learning algorithms and data mining techniques to extract meaningful insights from large datasets. She has actively contributed to various projects in machine learning, predictive analytics, and real-time data processing, continually exploring innovative methodologies to enhance automation, decision-making, and intelligent computing.

Asegul Hulus holds the position of Assistant Professor and Lecturer in the field of computing and is also recognized as a Fellow of the Higher Education Academy (FHEA). She is a distinguished researcher and published author with expertise in S.T.E.A.M., encompassing areas such as Artificial Intelligence (AI), Human-Computer Interaction (HCI), User Experience (UX) and Interaction Design, and Web 3 (Metaverse, Blockchain, Digital Assets). She is a member of prestigious organizations such as the Association for Computing Machinery (ACM) and the Institute of Electrical and Electronics Engineers (IEEE), among others. In addition, her skill set includes graphic design, video editing, audio production, and video game proficiency. Dr. Hulus actively serves as a chair, chief editor, and peer reviewer for a diverse array of journals, conferences, and publication houses. She also holds a prominent position as one of the founding authorities in her field. Additionally, she mentors for the Women4Cyber Foundation and holds several leadership positions within professional computing committees. Among these is the Council on Women in Computing (ACM-W) of the Association for Computing Machinery, where she serves as an investigative journalist and is one of the four main committee members of the Professional Chapters Committee of ACM-W. In recognition of her significant contributions to the field of AI, Dr. Hulus has been granted honorary membership on the Technical Advisory Board of the AI Foundation Trust. She is the inaugural female member of the board, specializing in both AI technology and the encouragement of women in the field. Her commitment to S.T.E.A.M. education and diversity initiatives, along with her other affiliations, has earned her recognition. She is celebrated for her prolific writing and public speaking on the intersection of these areas, with a particular focus on advocating for gender diversity and addressing systemic challenges within the computing sector.

Vanessa Izquierdo-Álvarez is a professor in the Department of Didactics, Organization, and Research Methods at the University of Salamanca. She holds a Ph.D., a degree in Pedagogy, and a Master's degree in Advanced Studies in Learning Difficulties, all from the University of Salamanca. She has served as a specialist in the Digital Learning Unit of the Digital Production and Innovation Service at the same university. Prior to her academic role, she worked as a training manager and project manager in several education-sector companies. Dr. Izquierdo-Álvarez has led numerous initiatives related to content virtualization and open knowledge, including MOOCs. Her research and publications focus on information and communication technologies, instructional design, MOOCs, content virtualization, and virtual teaching and learning.

Eva Jiménez-García holds a Ph.D. in Educational Sciences from Universidad Complutense de Madrid (2016), graduating Sobresaliente Cum Laude and receiving the Extraordinary Doctorate Award. She is accredited as a tenured professor by ANECA in Research Methods and Educational Diagnosis (MIDE) and holds an active six-year research period (sexenio). She has received numerous prestigious grants, including those from the Ministry of Education and Science and the Universidad Complutense de Madrid, with a funded research stay abroad. She currently serves as Director of Research at the Faculty of Legal, Educational, and Human Sciences at Universidad Europea and as Director of the Chair in Talent Measurement and Evaluation in collaboration with People Experts. Her research focuses on educational evaluation, analysis, and measurement, as well as teaching innovation and its impact on education. She is a member of the Measurement and Evaluation of Educational Systems Research Group at Universidad Complutense (evaluated by AEI with a score of 86) and the Educational Innovation Research Group at Universidad Europea de Madrid. Dr. Jiménez-García also serves on the editorial boards of leading journals, including Revista de Educación (Ministry of Education, Culture, and Sport, JCR), Bordón (Scopus), Educación XXI (JCR and Scopus), and Revista Complutense de Educación (Scopus), as well as on the Advisory Board of Tendencias Pedagógicas.

Claudia Jimeno-Postigo holds a degree in Pedagogy and is currently pursuing a Master's Degree in Teaching for Compulsory Secondary Education, Vocational Training, and Language Teaching at the University of Salamanca, with a specialization in Educational Guidance.

Allin Junikhah is an academic and technology practitioner specializing in digital media technology and game development. She holds a Master of Engineering from the Bandung Institute of Technology and a Bachelor of Applied Science in Informatics Engineering from the Electronic Engineering Polytechnic Institute of Surabaya. Currently a lecturer at UIN Maulana Malik Ibrahim Malang, she engages in teaching, research, and community service. Her academic interests include software engineering, AI, machine learning, game technology, wireless sensor networks, IoT, and digital media, with numerous publications in national and international journals and conferences, including IEEE, IC2SE, and ICED-QA. She is Cisco CCNA certified and a graduate of Harvard's CS50x course. A recipient of scholarships from the Ministry of Education and Culture and the Ministry of Religious Affairs in Indonesia, she remains committed to driving innovation in IT education and digital literacy.

Elif Karamuk is a Ph.D. candidate in Educational Administration at Marmara University and a Research Assistant at Istanbul Galata University. She holds a bachelor's degree in Foreign Language Education from Boğaziçi University. After graduation, she taught English to various age groups before pursuing a master's degree in Educational Administration and Planning. Her research interests include educational administration, higher education studies, artificial intelligence in education, and emerging technologies in learning environments. She has published in international academic journals and actively participates in EU youth training programs. With a strong interdisciplinary approach, she focuses on integrating technological innovations and pedagogical advancements to enhance higher education practices.

Bernabe C. Lumantas is an Associate Professor of Civil Technology and Technical Education at the College of Technology, Cebu Technological University, Cebu City, Philippines. He earned his Doctor of Philosophy in Technology Management from the same institution. Dr. Lumantas is an active member of the Center for Scholarly Researchers of Educators in the Philippines and the Philippine Institute of 21st Century Educators. His research interests include civil technology, technical education, and the advancement of technology management in educational and industrial settings.

Jivulter C. Mangubat is an Associate Professor V at the College of Technology, Cebu Technological University, Cebu City, Philippines. He holds a Doctor of Philosophy in Technology Management from the same institution. Dr. Mangubat has co-authored several books on technical drawing and holds multiple registrations for utility models, industrial designs, and copyrights. He is an active member of the DOST-National Research Council of the Philippines and the Mechatronics and Robotics Society of the Philippines. His research interests include drafting technology, technology education, intellectual property (IP) education, and technology management.

Milcah R. Mangubat is an Associate Professor III at the College of Technology, Cebu Technological University, Cebu City, Philippines. She is currently pursuing a doctoral degree in Technology Management at the same university. Prof. Mangubat has co-authored several books on technical drawing and holds multiple registrations for utility models, industrial designs, and copyrights. Her research interests focus on technology management, drafting technology, technology education, and intellectual property (IP) education.

Sonia Martínez-Requejo holds a European Doctorate Cum Laude in Education from the European University of Madrid, with a strong background in pedagogy and educational technology. With over 16 years of teaching experience, she has taught both undergraduate and postgraduate courses and has supervised doctoral theses focused on educational innovation and emerging technologies. She has contributed to numerous research projects and authored publications in international journals and conferences. Previously, she served as Director of the Steelcase Chair of Research in Educational Spaces and Equipment. Currently, she leads the Educational Innovation Research Group at the European University of Madrid. Her research interests include teaching innovation, methodology, evaluation, learning space design, and the integration of emerging technologies—particularly artificial intelligence.

Ahmed Hosny Saleh Metwally is an Assistant Professor in the Department of Educational Technology at Helwan University and a Visiting Researcher at the HCI Games Group, University of Waterloo. He obtained his Ph.D. from Northeast Normal University. His research focuses on gamification, gamified learning assignments, learning analytics, human-computer interaction, instructional design, artificial intelligence, the metaverse, and digital learning resources. Additionally, he serves as an Academic Editor for PLOS ONE and as an Editorial Board Member for the Educational Technology & Society journal. He is also a reviewer for numerous international SSCI journals, including Educational Technology & Society (ET&S), Computers & Education, The International Review of Research in Open and Distance Learning (IRRODL), and IEEE Access.

John Paul P. Miranda is an associate professor V at Don Honorio Ventura State University. He is currently the international linkages and partnerships project head for the office for the international partnerships and programs of his university.

Kingsley Ofosu-Ampong is a Lecturer of Information Systems at Heritage Christian University College, Ghana. He earned his Ph.D. in Information Systems from the University of Ghana. His research focuses on behavioral science and theories, artificial intelligence, technology-enhanced learning, and psychological needs in computing. Dr. Ofosu-Ampong's research has been published in outlets such as the Journal of Information Systems Education, Education and Information Technologies, Digital

Business, and Digital Transformation and Society. He currently serves as the President of the Association for Information Systems Special Interest Group in Game Design and Research (AIS SIGGAME).

Damola Olugbade is a Research Fellow at Abiola Ajimobi Technical University (formerly First Technical University), Ibadan, Nigeria. He holds a Ph.D. in Educational Technology from Obafemi Awolowo University and specializes in innovative learning solutions and the integration of emerging technologies in education. His research focuses on leveraging artificial intelligence, virtual reality, and other advanced technologies to enhance learning outcomes, with a strong emphasis on sustainability and inclusivity in education. Dr. Olugbade has published extensively in high-impact academic journals and serves as a peer reviewer for several prestigious publications, including Education and Information Technologies. He is actively engaged in international academic collaborations and has made significant contributions to the advancement of educational technology in West Africa.

Halil Öztürk graduated from Ankara University's Faculty of Educational Sciences, Department of Teaching Individuals with Intellectual Disabilities, in 2011. He worked at a special education and rehabilitation center for one and a half years, gaining experience with various disability groups. In 2013, he transitioned to academia as a Research Assistant at Muğla Sıtkı Koçman University. He completed his Master's degree in Special Education at Dokuz Eylül University in 2016 and earned his Ph.D. in Special Education at Anadolu University in 2024. His research focuses on learning disabilities, autism, stakeholder collaboration, counseling, and the integration of technology in special education. He currently continues his academic work in the Department of Special Education at Muğla Sıtkı Koçman University.

Anabelle T. Pantaleon is a passionate advocate for research, nationally recognized for her contributions, including receiving the Best Research in Women and Technology award at the Research Congress. She has published and presented her work on various local and international platforms. Her leadership transcends academia—serving as Area Coordinator for Production, Chair for Extension and Business Resource Generation, and a dedicated participant in barangay and provincial outreach initiatives in Cebu, reflecting her deep belief in education as a catalyst for societal transformation. She currently serves as the University Director for Instructional Monitoring at Cebu Technological University, where she oversees the quality assurance of 252 academic programs. Guided by her mantra, "Education is the bridge between vision and impact," Dr. Pantaleon continues to champion inclusive growth and research-driven solutions, making a lasting impact on Philippine education and beyond.

Harivarshini Prabagaren is a Master of Commerce student at CHRIST (Deemed to be University), Bengaluru, India. Passionate about research, her key areas of interest include behavioral finance, strategic management, and marketing. She has actively participated in various academic activities and university fests, demonstrating her commitment to innovative learning and strong organizational skills.

Jyoti Prakash Pujari is an Assistant Professor in the Department of English and Cultural Studies at Christ University, Delhi NCR Campus, India. His research interests include intellectual history, postcolonial studies, and the lives of unconventional women during the British Raj. His doctoral research focused on the colonial encounters of English memsahibs in India and their role in establishing a distinct literary canon. A former Jawaharlal Nehru Memorial Fund (JNMF) scholar, he currently teaches American and World Literature.

Nur Hairani Abd Rahman is a Senior Lecturer in Public Policy and Administration at Universiti Malaya. She holds a Ph.D. in Public Policy from Universiti Sains Malaysia, a Master of Public Administration from Universiti Malaya, and a Bachelor of Social Science (Honours) from Universiti Kebangsaan Malaysia. Her research focuses on social policy, including social care, governance, social inclusion and exclusion, inequality, and well-being. Dr. Rahman has served as a Visiting Scholar at the University of Messina in Italy and was awarded a Fulbright Scholarship in 2023 to join the University of California, Berkeley. She also serves as an Associate Editor for the Journal of Public Administration and Governance and is on the editorial board of the Malaysian Journal of Social Sciences and Humanities.

Sri Devi Ravana is an Associate Professor at the Department of Information Systems, Faculty of Computer Science and Information Technology, Universiti Malaya. She earned her Ph.D. in Computer Science and Software Engineering from the University of Melbourne, Australia. Her research interests include information retrieval evaluation, text retrieval, data science, data mining, and machine learning. Dr. Ravana has collaborated with various international institutions and has published extensively in high-impact journals.

Sara Redondo Duarte is an Assistant Professor at the Faculty of Education (Department of Educational Studies) at Universidad Complutense de Madrid, Spain. She holds a Ph.D. in Education, a Master's degree in Educational Technology, and a Master's in Business Administration and Management. From 2005 to 2008, she was a research fellow at the Educational Research and Documentation Center of the Spanish Ministry of Education. Her professional focus has been on faculty development and managing educational innovation projects. She is a member of the consolidated research group Technological Development, Socio-cultural Exclusion, and Education at Universidad Complutense. Her research centers on faculty development, educational project management, and the didactic use of technologies. She has held university leadership positions, including Director of Educational Innovation and Faculty Development and Director of Student Experience at Universidad Europea. She has co-authored several publications under the Eurydice Network (European Commission), the Spanish Ministry of Education, and academic journals, and has been recognized for excellence in university leadership by Universitat Politècnica de Catalunya (2021) and the Management Excellence Club (2019). She was also honored at the International e-Learning Awards in 2018, 2019, and 2022.

Judit Ruiz-Lázaro earned her Ph.D. in Education from the Complutense University of Madrid (2021), graduating as an "International Doctor" with the distinction Sobresaliente Cum Laude and receiving the Extraordinary Doctorate Award. She was accredited as a Tenured University Professor by ANECA in 2024 and holds an active six-year research period (sexenio). Currently, she serves as an Assistant Professor at the National University of Distance Education (UNED), in the Department of Didactics, School Organization, and Specific Didactics. Her most recent research and publications address university admission assessment in Spain, teacher training analysis, and the role of artificial intelligence in education. She is a member of the consolidated research group Measurement, Evaluation, and Educational Systems (MESE) at UCM and Innedu-UEM at Universidad Europea de Madrid.

Volkan Şahin graduated from the Department of Special Education in 2008, specializing in Teaching Individuals with Intellectual Disabilities. He worked as a special education teacher for ten years across various educational levels. He obtained his Master's degree in 2014 and completed his Ph.D. in 2024 in the Department of Special Education, specializing in Education of the Mentally Handicapped at Anadolu University. Since 2018, he has been affiliated with the Faculty of Education, Department of Special Education at Anadolu University and currently works in the Department of Autism Spectrum Disorder Education. His research interests include applied behavior analysis, evidence-based practices for individuals with ASD, family education, teacher training, and the use of technology in special education.

Mete Sipahioğlu is an Associate Professor and the Coordinator of European Mobilities at Samsun University, Türkiye. He holds a BA in English Language Teaching (ELT), as well as an MA and PhD in Educational Sciences with a specialization in Educational Administration, Leadership, and Policy Studies. He was also an exchange PhD student at the Institute of Education, University College London. His primary research interests include Teacher Education, Educational Leadership, and the Internationalization of Higher Education Institutions.

Karthik Raja Srinivasan is affiliated with the Department of Political Science, Public Administration, and Development Studies at Universiti Malaya, Malaysia. While detailed public information about his academic background and research interests is limited, his association with the department suggests involvement in areas related to political science and public administration.

Devanshi Taneja is currently pursuing her Master of Commerce at CHRIST (Deemed to be University), Bengaluru, India. She recently completed an internship with KPMG India, where she gained experience in the field of taxation. Her research interests include artificial intelligence, startups, taxation, and business management.

Mary Rani Thomas has been serving as an Assistant Professor at CHRIST (Deemed to be University), Bengaluru, India, since 2010. She holds both an MPhil and PhD from the same university. Her academic expertise spans Marketing, Management, Human Resource Management, and Organizational Behavior. Dr. Thomas's research focuses on consumer behavior and organizational behavior, with her work published in reputable UGC-listed and Scopus-indexed journals.

Timoteo Bernardo L. Uy is an Associate Professor V at the College of Technology, Cebu Technological University, Cebu City, Philippines. He holds a Doctor of Philosophy in Technology Management and is a licensed architect and master plumber. Prof. Uy is an active member of the United Architects of the Philippines and the National Master Plumbers' Association of the Philippines. His research interests encompass technical education, architectural and structural drafting, and technology management.

Ramazan Yılmaz is an Associate Professor in the Department of Computer Education and Instructional Technology (CEIT) at Bartın University, Türkiye. He earned his B.S. degree from Hacettepe University, Faculty of Education, Department of CEIT in 2007. He completed his M.A. in CEIT at Gazi University in 2010 and obtained his Ph.D. in CEIT from Ankara University in 2014. His research interests include educational technology, human-computer interaction, smart learning environments, learning analytics, educational data mining, eye tracking, multimedia design, adaptive learning, and augmented and virtual reality (AR and VR).

Index

P

Partition Literature 49, 50, 51, 52, 53, 55, 56, 57, 59, 60, 65, 66, 67, 72

Patent 275, 276, 277, 278, 279, 280, 281, 282, 283, 284, 285, 286, 287, 288, 289, 290, 291, 292, 293, 294

Personalized Learning 75, 76, 103, 113, 116, 124, 128, 130, 133, 152, 153, 154, 155, 160, 164, 165, 166, 177, 182, 183, 184, 191, 227, 228, 229, 234, 235, 242, 249, 253, 257, 267, 297, 298, 299, 306, 308, 329, 345, 350, 371, 376, 379, 386, 388, 389, 390, 399, 411, 413, 416, 422

Policy and Regulation 216, 218

Policy Frameworks 14, 219, 251, 254, 263, 265, 289, 361, 362

Professional Development 3, 21, 68, 73, 83, 85, 86, 87, 88, 89, 90, 92, 94, 96, 97, 102, 104, 111, 116, 119, 120, 121, 122, 151, 152, 153, 154, 160, 161, 163, 164, 165, 167, 170, 174, 188, 191, 192, 217, 220, 255, 262, 263, 264, 265, 276, 283, 284, 319, 331, 332, 337, 338, 348, 379, 415

R

Readiness for Learning 117

Reliability 12, 15, 33, 36, 39, 65, 106, 114, 120, 160, 161, 204, 209, 211, 226, 254, 255, 323, 324, 344, 379, 387, 389, 390, 406

Reskilling and Upskilling 123, 148, 149, 151, 152, 153, 156, 162, 163, 166, 420

S

Scholarship 3, 16, 22, 41, 65, 71, 225, 247, 295

School Infrastructure 18, 43, 93, 121, 142, 172, 177, 178, 179, 180, 181, 184, 186, 187, 191, 192, 194, 200, 268, 271, 291, 313, 343, 368, 394, 418

Science and Art Centre 101, 120

Self-Regulated Learning 14, 27, 29, 31, 32, 43, 45, 46, 47, 130, 138, 144, 150

Skill Obsolescence 17, 18, 19, 20, 21, 22, 43, 44, 45, 75, 93, 94, 119, 121, 123, 142, 143, 148, 149, 172, 173, 178, 184, 187, 190, 193, 195, 196, 221, 222, 223, 224, 225, 242, 245, 247, 268, 271, 273, 275, 276, 281, 287, 290, 291, 305, 312, 313, 314, 320, 342, 343, 344, 367, 368, 369, 370, 394, 399, 417, 418, 419, 420

Special Education 154, 171, 224, 227, 228, 229, 239, 241, 242, 243, 244, 245, 246, 247, 248, 269, 316

Student Engagement 4, 9, 15, 19, 52, 84, 93, 96, 101, 111, 117, 124, 133, 134, 135, 136, 145, 146, 159, 179, 188, 195, 196, 197, 312, 328, 330, 332, 334, 379, 399, 405, 410, 411, 414, 415

Systematic Review 19, 20, 21, 44, 45, 46, 47, 94, 95, 96, 124, 143, 144, 145, 148, 149, 151, 154, 156, 171, 172, 175, 193, 196, 198, 222, 224, 239, 240, 246, 269, 291, 312, 313, 319, 321, 324, 325, 329, 336, 339, 340, 342, 343, 347, 351, 367, 370, 372, 375, 381, 382, 392, 393, 395, 396, 399, 403, 407, 408, 409, 413, 415, 418, 419, 420, 421

T

Teacher Competency Development 151, 152, 153, 156, 161, 167, 175

Teacher Education 17, 73, 74, 75, 76, 77, 78, 79, 80, 83, 87, 88, 89, 95, 96, 97, 119, 123, 152, 153, 156, 173, 174, 193, 217, 255, 262, 264, 266, 267, 290, 312, 342, 367, 417

Teacher Training 86, 103, 121, 135, 153, 154, 155, 156, 163, 164, 166, 170, 174, 186, 188, 190, 191, 216, 217, 219, 229, 255, 263

Technical Education 177, 178, 179, 180, 181, 182, 183, 184, 187, 189, 191, 192, 199, 200

Technical Knowledge 18, 43, 93, 121, 142, 172, 177, 178, 180, 181, 182, 184, 190, 192, 200, 259, 268, 271, 287, 291, 313, 343, 368, 394, 418

Technoethics 20, 173, 203, 204, 205, 206, 210, 222, 223, 226, 245

Technofeminism 345

Technology 1, 2, 9, 16, 17, 19, 21, 22, 23, 31, 39, 42, 43, 44, 45, 47, 69, 70, 71, 73, 74, 75, 76, 81, 82, 83, 84, 87, 88, 89, 92, 94, 95, 96, 102, 103, 106, 109, 111, 112, 115, 116, 117, 120, 121, 122, 123, 124, 127, 129, 131, 132, 134, 135, 139, 140, 141, 142, 144, 145, 147, 148, 149, 152, 155, 156, 157, 158, 159, 160, 161, 162, 163, 167, 168, 169, 170, 171, 172, 173, 174, 175, 177, 178, 179, 181, 182, 185, 186, 188, 189, 190, 191, 193, 194, 195, 196, 197, 198, 199, 200, 204, 205, 206, 207, 208, 210, 212, 213, 214, 216, 219, 220, 222, 223, 225, 226, 228, 232, 233, 235, 238, 242, 243, 244, 245, 246, 247, 248, 251, 252, 253, 255, 256, 257, 258, 259, 260, 261, 262, 265, 269, 270, 271, 273, 274, 276, 281, 282, 283, 285, 287, 288, 290, 291, 292, 293, 296, 297, 298, 299, 300, 302, 304, 305, 309, 313, 314, 315, 316, 319, 324, 327, 329, 330, 331, 332, 333, 334, 340, 341, 342, 343, 344, 345, 347, 349, 350, 351, 353, 354, 356, 358, 360, 361, 367, 369, 372, 375, 376, 378, 379, 386, 387, 388, 389, 390, 391, 392, 393, 396, 397, 398, 399, 400, 401, 402, 403, 404, 405, 408, 409, 412, 413, 415, 416, 417,

Printed in the United States
by Baker & Taylor Publisher Services